Advances in Inorganic and Bioinorganic Mechanisms

Volume 1

Advances in Inorganic and Bioinorganic Mechanisms

Volume 1

edited by
A. G. Sykes

**Department of Inorganic Chemistry
The University, Newcastle upon Tyne, England**

1982

Academic Press

A subsidiary of Harcourt Brace Jovanovich, Publishers

London   New York
Paris   San Diego   San Francisco
San Paulo   Sydney   Tokyo   Toronto

ACADEMIC PRESS INC. (LONDON) LTD.
24/28 Oval Road,
London NW1

United States Edition published by
ACADEMIC PRESS INC.
111 Fifth Avenue
New York, New York 10003

British Library Cataloguing in Publication Data

Sykes, A. G.
Advances in inorganic and bioinorganic
mechanisms. Vol. 1
1. Chemistry, Inorganic
2. Biological chemistry
546'.05   QD146
ISBN 0-12-023801-2

Printed in Great Britain by
Page Bros (Norwich) Ltd

Contributors

Fraser Armstrong
Department of Inorganic Chemistry
South Parks Road
Oxford
UK

Edward Deutsch
Department of Chemistry
University of Cincinnati
Cincinnati
Ohio 45221
USA

James H. Espenson
Ames Laboratory and Department of Chemistry
Iowa State University of Science and Technology
Ames
Iowa 50011
USA

D. Geselowitz
Department of Chemistry
Stanford University
Stanford
CA 94305
USA

J. C. Lockhart
Department of Inorganic Chemistry
The University
Newcastle upon Tyne NE1 7RU
UK

D. L. Nosco
Department of Chemistry
University of Cincinnati
Cincinnati
Ohio 45221
USA

Michael J. Root
Department of Chemistry
University of Cincinnati
Cincinnati
Ohio 45221
USA

Kazuo Saito
Department of Chemistry
Tohoku University
Aoba
Aramaki
Sendai 980
JAPAN

Yiochi Sasaki
Department of Chemistry
Tohoku University
Aoba
Aramaki
Sendai 980
JAPAN

A. G. Sykes
Department of Inorganic Chemistry
The University
Newcastle upon Tyne NE1 7RU
UK

H. Taube
Department of Chemistry
Stanford University
Stanford
CA 94305
USA

Preface

The aims of this series are firstly to provide a long overdue forum for critical and authoritative reviews in the area of inorganic mechanisms, and secondly to cover the new and rapidly expanding area of bioinorganic mechanisms. The interest which many have in both areas, and the overlap of established techniques and approaches of inorganic mechanisms into the bioinorganic area, has made it desirable to develop further the dialogue between the two. The intention is that the reviews be written by leading researchers who are able to highlight significant advances without necessarily providing a comprehensive catalogue of each and every event (which chemical abstracting services do very well anyway).

The subject matter will undoubtedly be largely (though not entirely) confined to a consideration of metal ions, where research activity in the transition metal and metalloprotein areas is particularly extensive at this time. Categories of inorganic reaction which are relevant include not only substitution and electron transfer, but ligand addition (oxidative and non-oxidative) as well as elimination, insertion and acid-base processes. Organo-metallic reactions and reactions of vitamin B_{12} (which can be regarded as a naturally occurring organometallic compound) are of course relevant under these various headings. The effects of different solvents and influence of the second coordination sphere (about which still relatively little is known) are also of interest. On the theoretical side the Marcus-Hush treatment of electron transfer is relevant not only to small inorganic complexes but to the reactions of metalloproteins. While the influence of physical parameters such as ionic strength on the reactivity of small charged reactants is well understood this is not so for larger metalloproteins and developments here are awaited with interest. Due attention will also be paid to techniques. It is hoped that the reviews will prove useful in the context of lecture course work as well as to those directly involved in research.

With regard to units and nomenclature author preferences will be retained as much as possible. While S.I. recommendations and suggestions are welcome it is clear that these are not always acceptable, often due to respect for conventions established and used extensively in the earlier literature. It is intended in all such cases that conversion factors should be given.

Comments and suggestions with regard to any aspect of these volumes will be welcome at all times.

Finally it is for me to emphasize that the authors themselves are responsible for the high standard of articles in this volume. My thanks go to them for all their efforts and enthusiastic collaboration.

Newcastle   A. G. Sykes
February 1982

Contents

Reactions and Reaction Mechanisms of Organochromium(III) Complexes

James H. Espenson

*Ames Laboratory and Department of Chemistry,
Iowa State University*

I. INTRODUCTION

This chapter concerns the kinetics and mechanisms of reactions involving the complexes (H$_2$O)$_5$CrR^{2+}—where R is an alkyl group or similar organic group sigma bonded through carbon to the metal—and numerous closely related species. Among the reactions studied are those in which the Cr–C bond is formed and in which it is cleaved in unimolecular or solvolytic processes, as well as reactions with other substances which often but not invariably result in cleavage of the chromium–carbon bond.

A. Organochromium compounds and complexes

Numerous reports have appeared describing syntheses of isolable organo-chromium complexes, often accompanied by structural characterization. These include such substances as (C$_6$H$_5$)$_3$Cr(THF)$_3$,[1] Li$_3$Cr(CH$_3$)$_8$,[2] Cr(CH$_2$SiMe$_3$)$_4$,[3] and [Li(THF)$_4$]Cr$_2$(CH$_3$)$_8$.[4] Compounds or complexes containing but a single organic group have also been prepared and char-acterized over roughly the same period—1957 to the present—starting with the dipositive benzyl(pentaaquo)chromium(III) ion, (H$_2$O)$_5$Cr-CH$_2$Ph^{2+}.[5,6] A large number of complexes which are members of the family (H$_2$O)$_5$CrR^{2+} are now known.

Species such as (H$_2$O)$_5$CrR^{2+} offer some advantages in mechanistic work over those containing several organic groups bound to the metal, in that it is possible to focus on single chemical processes free of the complications expected if several groups, each likely to undergo concurrent or sequential reaction, are present. Although substances such as RCrCl$_2$(THF)$_3$ are more readily isolable in solid form,[7] the cationic species (H$_2$O)$_5$CrR^{2+} (and related L$_5$Cr^{III}R complexes) are particularly well suited for work in aqueous and semi-aqueous media. Substances such as $RCrCl_2(THF)_3$, on the other hand, usually suffer ligand (Cl^- and THF) substitution reactions when dissolved in coordinating solvents.

A great many $(H_2O)_5CrR^{2+}$ complexes—often CrR^{2+} for short—can be separated using ion-exchange chromatography. The lifetimes of these complexes vary greatly from one member to the next (Sections III and IV), and may also depend on what other substances are present. Dissolved oxygen, for example, reacts with some but not others (Section VIII.A). On the other hand, to some extent every one of the $(H_2O)_5CrR^{2+}$ complexes is subject to one or more decomposition processes, the rate and circumstances of which affect the isolation and purification procedures. In a few cases the lifetime of the complex is so short that separation is not feasible, in which case the complex, its identity inferred from the reactions used for its preparation, must be studied directly in the synthetic medium. In no case has a pure salt of any $(H_2O)_5CrR^{2+}$ complex been obtained, although materials which are unstable but seemingly pure,[8] as well as impure materials,[9] have been reported. This is not unique to the organometallic complexes, however; complexes $(H_2O)_5CrX^{2+}$ with other ligands X (halide, pseudohalide, carboxylate, etc.) are notoriously difficult to precipitate. The problem is to some extent alleviated by the use of other ligands. Organochromium cations containing the macrocyclic ligand 1,4,8,12-tetraazacyclopentadecane (or [15]aneN$_4$) are easily isolable; thus several alkylchromium complexes $[RCr([15]aneN_4)OH_2][B(C_6H_5)_4]_2$ have been prepared.[10]

It has been characteristic of progress in this chemistry that synthesis and mechanism have developed concurrently. Indeed, the particular reactions which might occur, and the circumstances under which they occur efficiently, have become known only as the understanding of synthetic possibilities and reaction mechanisms has deepened. The mechanistic postulates have often suggested the need for certain new complexes to test a particular postulate, and have quite often suggested routes to them as well. Over the same period the central role of free radicals in many reactions of transition metal compounds has come to be appreciated.[11,12] Many reactions of the organochromium complexes considered here have been shown to involve free-radical intermediates, although by no means do they all do so.

B. Properties and characterization of $L_5Cr^{III}R^{2+}$ complexes

Complexes having the formulas $(H_2O)_5CrR^{2+}$ and $[RCr([15]-aneN_4)OH_2]^{2+}$, where R is an alkyl, substituted alkyl, or aralkyl group, can be shown to have 2+ ionic charges based on their elution patterns from ion-exchange resins.[6,10,13–15] They elute immediately behind the corresponding dipositive inorganic complexes $(H_2O)_5CrX^{2+}$, but usually separated from them, yet well ahead of the 3+ ion $Cr(H_2O)_6^{3+}$. The ionic charge will, of course, not be 2+ if the R group itself contains a basic site which is protonated (or alkylated) in acidic solution, such as the 2-,3- and 4-pyridinomethylchromium cations $(H_2O)_5CrCH_2C_5H_4NH^{3+}$ and $(H_2O)_5CrCH_2C_5H_4NCH_3^{3+}$.[16,17]

The organochromium cations referred to are typical of aquochromium(III) complexes in general, in that they can be obtained and handled only in rather acidic solutions, 10^{-4} to $1 M H^+$ being the usual acidity range employed. Pathways for base hydrolysis are evidently so prevalent that even momentary exposure to a low $[H^+]$ promotes very rapid decomposition.

Solutions containing any of the $(H_2O)_5CrR^{2+}$ complexes are yellow, orange, or red depending on the particular species and its concentration. They appear distinctly different from the typical blue, violet, or green inorganic species $(H_2O)_5CrX^{2+}$. Most of the methods used to detect CrR^{2+} and to follow its reactions are based on UV–visible spectrophotometry. It has played a much more prominent role in the experimental studies than in many organometallic systems owing to the paramagnetism of these complexes which have three unpaired electrons and are thus not amenable to study by nmr techniques.

TABLE 1
Visible–ultraviolet spectra of a representative group of organochromium complexes

$(H_2O)_5Cr–R^{2+}$	$\lambda/nm(\varepsilon/M^{-1}cm^{-1})$			Ref.
R =				
—CH$_2$Cl	517(23)	391(224)	265(3620)	[13, 18, 28]
—CH$_3$	530(16)	392(240)	258(2520)	[14, 19]
—CH(CH$_3$)$_2$	560(10)	400(488)	290(2330)	[26]
—CH(CH$_3$)OC$_2$H$_5$	561(23)	390(468)	290(2270)	[20, 21, 25]
—CF$_3$	500(40)	380(67)		[22]
—CH$_2$CH$_2$CN	524(16)	396(320)	264(3530)	[23]
—CH$_2$C$_6$H$_5$	356(2220)	295(6970)	273(7670)	[6, 24]

The absorption spectra of typical organochromium cations[6,13,14,18–28] are presented in Table 1. As a general rule, except for the benzylchromium ion which has a spectrum dominated by intense charge-transfer transitions, the aliphatic complexes feature a weak absorption band between 500 and 560 nm having a molar absorptivity typical of the d–d transitions found in

$(H_2O)_5CrX^{2+}$ complexes, except that the maximum is shifted to higher energies by the high ligand field strength of the (formal) carbanion $R:^-$ when coordinated to $Cr(H_2O)_5^{3+}$. The second band, the one that is quite typical of organochromium cations and most useful for their detection and determination is that found usually at 385–400 nm, typically having ε of several hundred. Although this band is probably largely a d–d transition, its intensity suggests[25] that there is an interaction between the d–d transition and the charge-transfer state. The dominant UV band, whose position is strongly affected by the group R, arises from a charge-transfer transition. In complexes such as $CrCH_2X^{2+}$ both electron-donating ($X = CH_3$) and electron-attracting groups ($X = Cl, Br$) shift the band to lower energies than the parent $CrCH_3^{2+}$ ($X = H$). Thus λ_{max} increases along the series $R = $ —CH_3 ($\lambda_{max} = 258$ nm), —CH_2Cl (265), —$CHCl_2$ (266), —CH_2CN, (268), —CH_2CH_3 (275), —$CH(CH_3)_2$ (290), —CH_2I (296), —$C(CH_3)_2OH$ (311), and —CHI_2 (324). It has been pointed out[25] that all the aliphatic CH_2X groups would be expected to have lower optical electronegativities[27] than CH_3, and that the optical electronegativities for benzyl ($\lambda = 356$) and pyridinomethyl ($CH_2C_5H_4NH^+$, $\lambda \sim 320$) would be lower still.

The oxidation state assignments implied in the preceding discussion regard the species $(H_2O)_5CrR^{2+}$ as consisting of a carbanion $R:^-$ coordinated to $Cr(H_2O)_5^{3+}$, or at least designate them in that manner for purposes of nomenclature. This usage is consistent with the usual assignments in organometallic compounds. The basicity of the carbanion is so great as to preclude its existence as such in solution, and CrR^{2+} complexes have never been observed to dissociate according to the equilibrium $CrR^{2+} \rightleftharpoons Cr^{3+} + R^-$. In this respect they appear to differ from CrX^{2+} complexes for which the corresponding slowly-established dissociation equilibrium is well known. (This point will be pursued further in Sections III and IV.) On the other hand, there is considerable evidence for the occurrence of a reversible homolytic dissociation, $CrR^{2+} \rightleftharpoons Cr^{2+} + R \cdot$ (Section III). The reverse of this reaction, combination of chromium(II) ion with an organic radical, is the primary method of synthesis (Section II). The reactions themselves, of course, have little to say in a direct manner about the ground-state composition of CrR^{2+} complexes. The question should not be whether these "are" Cr(III)–carbanion or Cr(II)–radical complexes, but rather the relative importance of these as the limiting canonical forms. Many of the common characteristics of these species—including their absorption spectra, the relative kinetic inertness of the four *cis* waters and even the *trans* water,[28] the oxygen stability of many, and the failure of any to react directly (but not indirectly via prior homolytic dissociation) with $Co(NH_3)_5Cl^{2+}$—makes it convenient to retain the chief descriptive terminology in which these are regarded as Cr(III) complexes, albeit a group of them having rather distinctive characteristics and reactions.

The absorption spectra characteristic of the CrR^{2+} complexes generally provide the most useful tool for analysis and kinetic determinations. The purity and identity of a given complex must usually be established on the basis of the chemical reactions that occur and the products, both organic and inorganic, of controlled decomposition and other reactions. Specific instances are to be found in later sections and in the references cited.

II. SYNTHESIS OF $L_5Cr^{III}R$ COMPLEXES

By far the most common route to these complexes is the reaction of an appropriate chromium(II) complex, $Cr(H_2O)_6^{2+}$ or others, with the desired carbon-centred radical: $Cr^{2+} + R\cdot \rightarrow [Cr^{III}R]^{2+}$. This reaction itself will be considered first, followed by an account of some of the reactions—often of considerable interest in their own right—used to generate $R\cdot$.

A. Reactions of free radicals and chromium(II)

The pulse radiolysis technique has been used to generate a variety of aliphatic radicals in solutions containing $Cr(H_2O)_6^{2+}$.[25,29] The radicals which have been examined in this fashion are those derived from such organic solutes as alcohols, amides, ethers, and carboxylic acids having at least modest solubility ($\geqslant \sim 0.1$ M) in dilute aqueous perchloric acid. Generation of $R\cdot$ occurs via hydrogen atom abstraction from the substrate upon reaction with hydroxyl radicals in acidic solutions. The solutes used give rise to particular carbon-centred free radicals which are well known independently.[30-33] (It would distract us from the chemistry at hand to dwell on the results, largely from radiation chemical studies, of the modes of generation of free radicals from organic precursors; readers interested in this point should consult the references indicated.)

In these cases, as in several others where carbon-centred radicals are generated in the presence of metal ions or complexes, the predominant reaction, which occurs quantitatively under the conditions employed, is formation of the metal–carbon bond. As it turns out, many of the organochromium complexes are quite long-lived species several of which were previously (or subsequently) prepared using conventional chemical methods for radical generation. The rates of formation of the organo-chromium ions, although generally quite rapid, could be determined using the pulse radiolysis technique. The equation for the chemical reaction occurring and for its reaction rate are:

$$R\cdot + Cr(H_2O)_6^{2+} \rightarrow (H_2O)_5CrR^{2+} + H_2O \tag{1}$$

$$d[(H_2O)_5CrR^{2+}]/dt = k_1[R\cdot]\,[Cr(H_2O)_6^{2+}] \tag{2}$$

The values of k[10,25,36,37] are independent of $[H_3O^+]$, 0·1–1 M, and are summarized in Table 2. The reaction represents, in at least a formal sense,

TABLE 2

Rate constants[a] for formation of $(H_2O)_5CrR^{2+}$ complexes according to Equations (1)–(2)

R	$10^{-7}k_1$ $(M^{-1}\,s^{-1})$	R	$10^{-7}k_1$ $(M^{-1}\,s^{-1})$
$\cdot CH_2OH$	16	$\cdot CH_2COOH$	25
$\cdot CH(CH_3)OH$	7·9	$\cdot CH(CH_3)COOH$	11
$\cdot C(CH_3)_2OH$	5·1	$\cdot CH_2C(CH_3)_2COOH$	11
$\cdot CH(COOH)OH$	14	$\cdot CH(COOH)_2$	6·0
$\cdot C(CH_3)(COOH)OH$	9·2		
$\cdot CH_2C(CH_3)_2OH$	10	$\cdot CH_2CHO$	35
$\cdot CH(OH)CH_2OH$	15	$4\text{-}CH_2C_5H_4NH^+$	$\sim 0\cdot 1^b$
$\cdot CH(CH_3)OC_2H_5$	3·4	$\cdot CH_2(CH_2)_3CH{=}CH_2$	4^c
		$\cdot CH_2(CH_2)_3CH{=}CH_2$	$\sim 0\cdot 9 \pm 0\cdot 2^d$
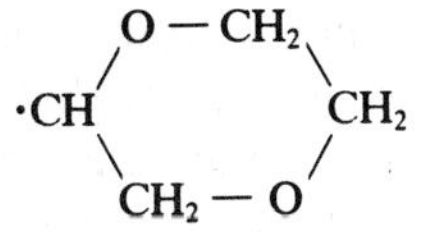 $\cdot CH \begin{smallmatrix} O-CH_2 \\ \\ CH_2-O \end{smallmatrix} CH_2$	10		

[a] Rate constants from Ref. [25] at $22 \pm 2°C$ in argon-saturated aqueous solutions containing 0·15–1 M organic solutes, $1\text{–}15 \times 10^{-4}$ M Cr^{2+}, and 0·1–1 M perchloric acid.
[b] Rough estimate[36].
[c] Ref. [37]; the Cr(II) complex is $Cr(en)_2^{2+}$ in aq dmf.
[d] Ref. [10]; the Cr(II) complex is $[(H_2O)_2Cr([15]aneN_4)]^{2+}$ in 1:1 water–t-butanol at pH 3–4.

an oxidation–reduction process in which the radical has been reduced by Cr^{2+}. The radical is captured within the coordination sphere of the kinetically inert product, however, so that one is not dealing with a system in which a free carbanion is produced by reduction of $R\cdot$. (In view of that, the polarographic half-wave potentials[34] may not be applicable; they may, in addition, reflect large overpotentials.[25]) Although radicals such as $\cdot CH_2OH$, $\cdot C(CH_3)_2OH$, etc., are noted for their strong reducing character, their ability to oxidize Cr^{2+} illustrates the dual nature of their chemistry, as shown by the half-reactions

$$\cdot CH_2OH + e^- + H^+ = CH_3OH \qquad E^0 = 1\cdot 29 \text{ V}$$

$$HCHO + e^- + H^+ = \cdot CH_2OH \qquad E^0 = -0.92 \text{ V}$$

The oxidation of Cr^{2+} by these aliphatic radicals resembles its reaction with hydrogen atoms,[35]

$$Cr(H_2O)_6^{2+} + H\cdot \rightarrow (H_2O)_5CrH^{2+} \tag{3}$$

with a rate constant $1\cdot 5 \times 10^9 \text{ M}^{-1} \text{s}^{-1}$. In fact one might adopt the view that the hydrido complex is the simplest member of the series of alkyl-chromium cations.

The rates of reaction between $Cr(H_2O)_6^{2+}$ and $R\cdot$, although high, are well below the diffusion-controlled limit. Also, the reactions are evidently not seriously limited by the rate of solvent exchange of Cr^{2+}, $7 \times 10^9 \text{ s}^{-1}$.[38] The data (Table 2) suggest steric effects are not a dominant factor. There is a suggestion in the results that electron-donating groups (e.g. CH_3) on the α-carbon lower the rate constant, and electron-attracting groups (e.g. CH_2OR) increase it.[25] These trends parallel the extent to which spin density is removed from or located on the reacting carbon atom.[39,40] These conclusions must be tempered by the realization that the reaction of Equation (1) is just the reverse of the bond homolysis process to be considered subsequently (Section III), wherein *for this same group of complexes* there are rate constant differences over many orders of magnitude along the series of compounds in a fashion which suggest that, within a homologous series, steric effects play a very substantial role. In the context of those changes the rate constants for all the reactions given in Table 2 seem nearly invariant.

The involvement of free radicals has been demonstrated in the reactions of two Cr(II) complexes—$Cr(en)_2^{2+}$ in aq. dmf[37] and $(H_2O)_2Cr([15]aneN_4)^{2+}$ in water/*tert*-butanol[10]—with alkyl halides. These experiments employed 6-bromo-1-hexene, which gives rise to a radical $\cdot CH_2(CH_2)_3CH{=}CH_2$, whose rate of cyclization to the methylcyclopentyl radical, $\sim 10^5 \text{ s}^{-1}$,[41] is competitive with the capture of the original radical by the Cr(II) complex. The products obtained verify the intermediacy of the radical and permit an estimate of its new rate constants with $Cr(en)_2^{2+}$ ($k = 4 \times 10^7 \text{ M}^{-1} \text{s}^{-1}$) and with $(H_2O)_2Cr([15]aneN_4)^{2+}$ ($0\cdot 9 \pm 0\cdot 2 \times 10^7 \text{ M}^{-1} \text{s}^{-1}$). There is more than a passing resemblance between the chemistry embodied in Equation (1) and reactions in which Cr^{2+} is oxidized by a one-electron inorganic radical, in the course of which the latter is caught within the primary coordination sphere of the newly formed chromium(III). Examples include $HO\cdot$, $Cl\cdot$, $Br\cdot$, and $I\cdot$.[42,43]

B. Reactions of chromium(II) and organic halides

Aqueous solutions of chromium(II) perchlorate have sufficient reducing strength to react with only the most "activated" of organic halides, such as benzyl halides, polyhaloalkanes, and polyhalocarboxylic acids. The reaction is considerably more general, however, and the more strongly reducing Cr(II) complexes such as may exist in aqueous dimethylformamide, in solutions containing nitrogen ligands such as ethylenediamine, and discrete complexes such as $[(H_2O)_2Cr([15]aneN_4)]^{2+}$, convert even alkyl chlorides to alkanes. These reactions occur via organometallic complexes such as $[RCr([15]aneN_4)OH_2]^{2+}$, many of which are stable for substantial periods of time in solution.

The general scheme by which these reactions occur has been commented on extensively by other authors.[12,44] The overall reaction proceeds by a sequence of two reactions—halogen atom abstraction and free radical capture—the former invariably rate-limiting. The net process consumes two Cr^{II} per RX, and equimolar quantities of alkyl and halo products are formed:

$$Cr(II) + RX \underset{-4}{\overset{4}{\rightleftarrows}} Cr^{III}X + R\cdot \tag{4}$$

$$Cr(II) + R\cdot \overset{5}{\rightarrow} Cr^{III}R \tag{5}$$

Net: $2Cr(II) + RX = Cr^{III}X + Cr^{III}R$ (6)

The general rate expression for this scheme, with the steady-state approximation made for $[R\cdot]$, its reaction with Cr(II) presumed to dominate over any other pathway for its loss (including self-reaction) is:

$$\frac{-d[RX]}{dt} = \frac{-d[Cr(II)]}{2dt} = \frac{k_4 k_5 [RX][Cr(II)]^2}{k_{-4}[Cr^{III}X] + k_5[Cr(II)]} \tag{7}$$

There appears to be no instance known where the reverse of the first step competes with the second, so the rate expression invariably found is the limiting form where $k_{-4}[Cr^{III}X] \ll k_5[Cr(II)]$, or

$$\frac{-d[RX]}{dt} = \frac{-d[Cr(II)]}{2dt} = k_4[RX][Cr(II)] \tag{8}$$

Determinations have been made for an extensive series of organic halides. Values of k_4 are summarized in Table 3 for a selected group of the reactions of $Cr^{II}(en)_2^{2+}$ [6,37] (the solutions may contain other species in labile equilibrium with free ethylenediamine and with dimethylformamide; the values given refer to solutions of constant composition). Values are also given for

TABLE 3

Rate constants k_4 (M^{-1} s^{-1}) for halogen atom abstraction reactions between organic halides and M(II) complexes according to Equations (4)–(8)

Organic halide	M(II) reagent					
	"$Cr^{II}(en)_2^{2+}$" [a]			$(H_2O)_2Cr([15]aneN_4)^{2+}$ [b]		$Co^{II}(CN)_5^{3-}$ [c]
	RCl	RBr	RI	RBr	RI	RI
(a) Primary alkyls						
Methyl					0·046	9.5×10^{-3}
Ethyl					0·413	5.9×10^{-2}
n-Propyl	1.5×10^{-3}	0·22	18	0·164		4.3×10^{-2}
n-Butyl	1.7×10^{-3}	0·23	17	0·169		
i-Butyl	1.2×10^{-3}	0·17	13	0·138		
(b) Secondary alkyls						
i-Propyl	1.1×10^{-2}	1·8	105	1·91	4·93	1·20
s-Butyl		2·3	180			
(c) Tertiary alkyls						
t-Butyl	4.8×10^{-2}	10		6·3		9·1
1-Adamantyl				19·4		
(d) Benzyl halides						
$C_6H_5CH_2Cl$		3.2×10^{-3}			3.23×10^{2}	4.9×10^{-4}
$C_6H_5CH_2Br$		4.1×10^{-1}			1.91×10^{4}	2·33
$C_6H_5CH_2I$		1·8				3.8×10^{3}

[a] From Ref. [37] at 25°C in 83% dmf–water with [en]/[Cr(II)] = 3, except for the data[6] for the benzyl halides where the reagent is $Cr(H_2O)_6^{2+}$ in 71.5% ethanol–water at 27.5°C.

[b] From Ref. [10] in 50% t-butanol/water at 25·0°C.

[c] From Ref. [45] in 80% methanol–water at 25·0°C.

$[(H_2O)_2Cr([15]aneN_4)]^{2+}$,[10] and the cobalt(II) complex $Co(CN)_5^{3-}$ [45] which is one of several other reduced metal complexes believed to follow the same mechanism.

The following trends in reactivity should be noted: (a) for a given halide, the rate constants follow the trend tertiary > secondary > primary, falling roughly one power of ten between each; (b) for a given alkyl group, the rate constants decline in the order iodide > bromide > chloride. These trends, together with evidence based on the stoichiometry of the reaction and the trapping of the carbon-centred free-radical, constitute evidence in support of the mechanism assigned.

For this to be a successful route to the alkyl metal, (1) the parent metal complex must be a sufficiently strong and reactive reducing agent that the first step, Equation (4), is feasible, and (2) the coordination sphere of the metal complex must be sufficiently labile as to permit capture of R·. All of the Cr(II) complexes satisfy the second requirement, although V(II) complexes do not and would thus not be expected to react by this mechanism.[46,47] The first criterion, as mentioned before, poses a limitation such that many of the simpler halides do not react with $Cr(H_2O)_6^{2+}$ or with bis(dimethylglyoximato)cobalt(II), a still milder reducing agent.

It was recognized at the outset[6] that these reactions, referred to as halogen atom abstraction processes, bear a strong resemblance to inner-sphere or atom transfer reactions between $Cr(H_2O)_6^{2+}$ and halopenta-ammine–cobalt(III) ions,

$$Cr^{2+} + Co(NH_3)_5X^{2+} \rightarrow Cr^{III}X^{2+} + \text{``}Co^{II}(NH_3)_5\text{''} \tag{9}$$

except that the reduced metal product is not subject to further oxidation–reduction reactions, only to aquation to $Co(H_2O)_6^{2+}$.

Another analogy should be drawn between the reactions of the chromium(II) (and cobalt(II)) complexes with organic halides and the reactions of the same metal complexes with halogens, hydrogen peroxide, hydroxyl-amine, and other reagents of this X–Y character. A scheme analogous to Equations (4–5) may be written to account for the observations in these systems as well. Even O_2 might be considered in this fashion except here the single O–O bond remaining in the first intermediate ($Cr^{2+} + O_2 \rightarrow$ Cr—O—O^{2+}) gives rise to other chemistry, including capture of this "metalloperoxy radical" by Cr(II) ($Cr^{2+} + Cr$—$OO^{2+} \rightarrow CrOOCr^{4+}$). These reactions may provide a pathway to the dinuclear chromium(III) products ultimately formed in the reaction with O_2.[48,49]

Reactions of $Cr(en)_2^{2+}$ with methyl halides in aqueous dmf were studied to determine the relative rate constants for $^{12}CH_3X$ versus $^{13}CH_3X$ using high precision isotope-ratio mass spectrometry and ^{13}C at natural abundance.[50] Converted to rate constant ratios, the values of k_{12}/k_{13} are

$1 \cdot 0625 \pm 0 \cdot 0021$ (X = Cl), $1 \cdot 0514 \pm 0 \cdot 0012$ (Br), $1 \cdot 0433 \pm 0 \cdot 0009$ (I) at 0°C. Since these values are larger than the equilibrium isotope effect for $CH_3X \rightleftarrows \cdot CH_3 + X \cdot$ ($1 \cdot 027$ for I, $1 \cdot 035$ for Cl), the results obtained suggest extensive carbon–halogen bond breaking in the transition state.[50]

There are numerous examples of reactions between chromium(II) and organic halides where the organochromium complex, if it is detected at all, has a short life-time. Thus polyhalomethanes produce short-lived compounds (e.g., $CrCCl_3^{2+}$ from Cr^{2+} and CCl_4 or $BrCCl_3$).[51,52] In many cases, only the ultimate organic products are observed; but even in cases where CrR^{2+} was not detected the reactions were most easily explained by considering an organometallic intermediate. Electronegative substituents (halogen, OH, NH_2, etc.) on the beta carbon atom of an organochromium cation are usually subject to rapid decomposition via acid-catalyzed attack at that substituent (Section VIII.D). Thus organochromium complexes are, at best, transient species when produced from vicinal dihalides[53,54] or from radicals such as $\cdot CH_2CH_2OH$[55] or $\cdot CH_2C(CH_3)_2OH$.[25]

C. Reactions of chromium(II) and organic peroxides

Formation of $(H_2O)_5CrR^{2+}$ has been noted during the reactions of chromium(II) salts with hydroperoxides $RC(CH_3)_2OOH$.[14,20,56,57] The detection of CrR^{2+}, at first limited to $CrCH_2Ph^{2+}$ [56] and then to $CrCH_3^{2+}$,[14,20] has since been extended to encompass a considerable range of complexes.[57] The idealized stoichiometry given by Equation (10) is often far from realized with the quantity of CrR^{2+} produced usually well below the theoretical.

$$2Cr^{2+} + RC(CH_3)_2OOH + H^+ = Cr^{3+} + CrR^{2+} + (CH_3)_2CO \qquad (10)$$

The mechanism of the reaction, borne out by product and kinetic studies, as well as by tests for the reaction intermediates, is believed to be:

$$Cr^{2+} + RC(CH_3)_2OOH \longrightarrow CrOH^{2+} + RC(CH_3)_2O \cdot \qquad (11)$$

$$RC(CH_3)_2O \cdot \longrightarrow (CH_3)_2CO + R \cdot \qquad (12)$$

$$Cr^{2+} + R \cdot \longrightarrow CrR^{2+} \qquad (13)$$

Consistent with this proposal, in which the first step is rate-limiting, the rate of reaction is given by

$$\frac{-d[ROOH]}{dt} = \frac{-d[Cr^{2+}]}{2dt} = k_{11}[Cr^{2+}][RC(CH_2)_2OOH] \qquad (14)$$

Values of k_{11} for a series of such hydroperoxides lie within a narrow range,

TABLE 4

Rate constants[a] for the reaction of $Cr(H_2O)_6^{2+}$ with organic peroxides according to Equations (11)–(14)

Peroxide	CrR^{2+} formed[b]	k_{11} (M^{-1} s^{-1})
(a) Hydroperoxides		
t-BuOOH	$CrCH_3^{2+}$	$(1.65 \pm 0.11) \times 10^4$
$C_2H_5C(CH_3)_2OOH$	$CrCH_2CH_3^{2+}$	$(1.60 \pm 0.11) \times 10^4$
$PhC(CH_3)_2OOH$	$CrCH_3^{2+}$	$(0.99 \pm 0.06) \times 10^4$
$PhCH_2C(CH_3)_2OOH$	$CrCH_2Ph^{2+}$	$(2.13 \pm 0.18) \times 10^4$
s-BuOOH	$CrCH_2CH_3^{2+}$	$(3.63 \pm 0.61) \times 10^4$
n-BuOOH	$CrCH_2(CH_2)_2CH_2OH^{2+}(?)$	$(5.77 \pm 0.43) \times 10^4$
(b) Alkyl peroxides		
$t\text{-}BuOOC_2H_5$	$CrCH_3^{2+}$	2.35 ± 0.25
$t\text{-}BuOOCH(CH_3)_2$	$CrCH_3^{2+}$	$(4.19 \pm 0.40) \times 10^{-2}$
t-BuOO-t-BU	—	$<8 \times 10^{-6}$
(c) Acyl peroxides		
$PhC(O)OOC(O)Ph$	—	$(5.2 \pm 0.2) \times 10^1$
$CH_3(CH_2)_3C(O)OOC(O)(CH_2)_3CH_3$	$Cr\text{-}n\text{-}Bu^{2+}(?)^{c,d}$	2.6^c
$PhCH_2C(O)OOC(O)CH_2Ph$	$CrCH_2Ph^{2+}$ ^{c}	—
(d) Peroxy esters		
t-BuOOC(O)Ph	$CrCH_3^{2+}$	$(1.18 \pm 0.09) \times 10^4$
$t\text{-}BuOOC(O)\text{-}p\text{-}ClC_6H_4$	$CrCH_3^{2+}$	$(8.9 \pm 101) \times 10^3$
$t\text{-}BuOOC(O)\text{-}m\text{-}ClC_6H_4$	$CrCH_3^{2+}$	$(1.02 \pm 0.13) \times 10^4$
$t\text{-}BuOOC(O)\text{-}p\text{-}CH_3OC_6H_4$	$CrCH_3^{2+}$	$(1.50 \pm 0.12) \times 10^4$
$t\text{-}BuOOC(O)\text{-}m\text{-}CH_3C_6H_4$	$CrCH_3^{2+}$	$(1.23 \pm 0.04) \times 10^4$
$t\text{-}BuOOC(O)\text{-}p\text{-}NCC_6H_4$	$CrCH_3^{2+}$	$(8.2 \pm 0.1) \times 10^3$
(e) Peroxy acids		
PhC(O)OOH	$CrC_6H_5^{2+}(??)^e$	$(3.3 \pm 0.5) \times 10^6$

[a] Ref. [57]; at 25.0°C, $\mu = 1.00\,\text{M}$, in 1:1 $CH_3OH:H_2O$.

[b] CrR^{2+} in aqueous solution; $CrCH_2OH^{2+}$ is often (but not invariably) formed in aqueous methanol, depending on the competitive rates involved.

[c] Ref. [56].

[d] CrR^{2+} product inferred from the isolation of n-butane.

[e] Identification tenuous.

$(1\text{–}6) \times 10^4 \, M^{-1} \, s^{-1}$ at 25°C (Table 4). That is not surprising, considering the changes along the series are being made at a long distance from the OH group which is the site of Cr^{2+} attack in the reaction. On the other hand, considering a series of $(CH_3)_3COOR$ molecules, with Cr^{2+} attack at the oxygen atom of OR, profound changes are seen along the series in which R is changed from H to primary, secondary, tertiary alkyl: R = H ($k_{11} = 1\text{·}65 \times 10^4 \, M^{-1} s^{-1}$), Et (2·35), i-Pr ($4\text{·}19 \times 10^{-2}$), and t-Bu ($<8 \times 10^{-6}$).

It is not necessary to review here all of the complicating features,[56,57] including side reactions that lower the yield of R· (and thus of CrR^{2+}). It is useful to note that a key step in the overall process is the β-scission reaction of the intermediate alkyloxy radical in Equation (12). The timing of that cleavage[58] is a critical feature in comparison with reduction of the alkyloxy radical to alcohol by Cr^{2+} or its reaction with another molecule in the system such as an organic cosolvent, usually by hydrogen atom abstraction from a C–H bond.

D. Chromium(II) and hydrogen peroxide ("modified Fenton's reagent" method)

The reaction between $Cr(H_2O)_6^{2+}$ and H_2O_2, conducted in the presence of a suitably chosen organic solute, constitutes a powerful and versatile route to $(H_2O)_5CrR^{2+}$ complexes. The first application yielded several complexes containing R groups derived from alcohols and diethyl ether.[20] The principle behind the method is to use the hydroxyl radical generated in the first step of the reaction between Cr^{2+} and H_2O_2 to abstract a hydrogen atom from a C–H bond of the substrate. (The latter is the same reaction as used in the pulse radiolysis method, Section II.A). The reactions are then the following:

$$Cr^{2+} + H_2O_2 \rightarrow CrOH^{2+} + HO\cdot \tag{15}$$

$$HO\cdot + RH \rightarrow H_2O + R\cdot \tag{16}$$

$$Cr^{2+} + R\cdot \rightarrow CrR^{2+} \tag{17}$$

The same problems of selectivity may arise as in the pulse radiolysis experiments. The reaction of ethanol with hydroxyl radical yields two carbon-centred radicals, $CH_3\overset{\cdot}{C}HOH$ (84·3%) and $\cdot CH_2CH_2OH$ (13·2%) together with a minor amount of $CH_3CH_2O\cdot$ (2·5%).[59] The first gives the only organochromium cation observed under these conditions, however, since $CrCH_2CH_2OH^{2+}$ decomposes very rapidly in acidic solution by β-elimination[25,55] (Section VIII.D). In other cases the radical formed may produce mixtures of complexes, and so some caution is called for in applying the method.[60] It has also proved successful with organic nitriles,[23] and in preparing complexes such as [Cr^{III}(edta)CH_2OH] starting with the Cr^{II}–edta complex.[61]

Owing to solubility characteristics and the regioselectivity problem alluded to in the preceding paragraph, only a few CrR^{2+} complexes in which R is a hydrocarbon radical have been prepared in this manner. One successful preparation is the cyclopentyl(pentaaquo)chromium(III) ion, [$(H_2O)_5Cr$—c-C_5H_9]$^{2+}$ whose preparation proceeds cleanly[62] because cyclopentane is reasonably water-soluble ($\sim 10^{-2}$ M) and reacts with HO· to produce but a single free-radical species.

Another alkylchromium cation realized by this route is $(H_2O)_5CrCH_3^{2+}$ through the reaction of Cr^{2+}, H_2O_2, and $(CH_3)_2SO$.[47] The key reaction is the production of methyl radicals by reaction of dimethyl sulphoxide with hydroxyl radical:

$$HO\cdot + (CH_3)_2SO \rightarrow CH_3S(O)OH + \cdot CH_3 \qquad (18)$$

This could develop into a general and convenient route for those alkyl-chromium cations for which dialkyl sulphoxides are readily prepared.

E. Other routes to organochromium(III) complexes

In this section other synthetic methods will be dealt with in less detail, focusing especially on those where some mechanistic information is available.

1. Transalkylation reactions

Chromium(II) ions react with other alkyl-metals, notably with alkylcob-alt(chelate) complexes, quantitatively transferring the group R to Cr^{2+}:

$$Cr_{aq}^{2+} + RCo(chelate) \rightarrow (H_2O)_5CrR^{2+} + Co^{II}(chelate) \qquad (19)$$

where the indicated chelate groups are bis(dimethylglyoximato) (or Co(dmgH)$_2$, cobaloximes)[19] or corrin (Vitamin B$_{12}$ or cobalamins),[63] although it is highly likely other chelate groups work as well.[64]

The mechanism of this transformation and other similar reactions will be dealt with subsequently (Section VII.B), but it is mentioned here not so much because it has great synthetic value—the free radical routes mentioned previously usually give higher concentrations of more easily purified product—but because of a stereochemical possibility, unfortunately unrealized as yet. No organochromium complex $(H_2O)_5CrR^{2+}$ containing a chiral carbon bound to chromium has been prepared, which is not suprising since all the synthetic routes involve free radicals. Since chiral

organocobaloximes such as sec-butyl and 2-methylheptyl are easily prepared, the reaction of Equation (19) should afford a chiral group R bound
to chromium(III) assuming direct transfer occurs. (Transfer with inversion
of configuration at carbon seems probable.) Unfortunately the slowness
of the transfer reaction for the more highly substituted R groups, together
with their relatively high rates of decomposition have, as yet, prevented
the realization of that goal. This leaves unexplored the major questions of
proof of stereochemistry in the reactions of CrR^{2+} subsequently considered
(such as Equation (20), Section VI), and the best one can do at present

$$CrR^{2+} + E^+ = Cr^{3+} + ER \qquad (E^+ = \text{electrophile}) \tag{20}$$

is assign a likely stereochemcial course based on kinetic data and presumed
analogies.

2. Photochemical production of CrR^{2+}

Methods which photochemically generate carbon-centred radicals $R \cdot$ in
solutions containing Cr^{2+} produce the complex CrR^{2+}. The method can be
used for otherwise accessible species such as $CrC(CH_3)_2OH^{2+}$ [60] starting
with the UV photolysis of acetone,[65–68] preferably in the presence of 2-
propanol, via the reactions

$$(CH_3)_2CO + (CH_3)_2CHOH \xrightarrow{h\nu} 2 \cdot C(CH_3)_2OH \tag{21}$$

$$Cr^{2+} + \cdot C(CH_3)_2OH \longrightarrow CrC(CH_3)_2OH^{2+} \tag{22}$$

The most useful application, however, is to the preparation of complexes
which are so short-lived that conventional or even stopped-flow techniques
are not suitable. Thus UV photolysis of Cr^{2+} in solutions saturated with
N_2O and C_2H_4 is used to prepare[55] β-hydroxyethyl(pentaaquo)chromium
ions via the reactions

$$Cr^{2+} \xrightarrow{h\nu} Cr^{3+} + e^-_{aq} \tag{23}$$

$$e^-_{aq} + N_2O \xrightarrow{H_3O^+} N_2 + H_2O + HO \cdot \tag{24}$$

$$HO \cdot + C_2H_4 \longrightarrow \cdot CH_2CH_2OH \tag{25}$$

$$Cr^{2+} + \cdot CH_2CH_2OH \longrightarrow CrCH_2CH_2OH^{2+} \tag{26}$$

3. Addition of Cr^{2+} to alkene double bonds

The general reaction—although it is successful only for selected olefinic double bonds—proceeds in two steps according to the equation[8] (see also [69], [70]):

$$2Cr^{2+} + CHR{=}CHR + H^+ = Cr^{3+} + Cr{-}CHR{-}CH_2R^{2+}$$

The structures of the organometallic complex (or complexes, there being two species obtained with some reagents, for example, fumaric acid) have been assigned[8] to the 3+ and 2+ products separated chromatographically:

$$
\left[
\begin{array}{c}
\text{O} \\
\backslash\!\!\backslash \\
\text{C} - \text{OCr}^{\text{III}} \\
| \\
\text{HC} - \text{Cr}^{\text{III}} \\
| \quad\quad | \\
\text{H}_2\text{C} \quad \text{O} \\
\backslash \quad / \\
\text{C} \\
\| \\
\text{O}
\end{array}
\right]^{3+}
\quad
\left[
\begin{array}{c}
\text{O} \diagdown \quad \diagup \text{OCr}^{\text{III}} \\
\text{C} \\
| \quad\quad\quad\quad \text{O} \\
\quad\quad\quad\quad \diagup\!\!\diagup \\
\text{HC} - \text{Cr}^{\text{III}}\text{OCCH} = \text{CHCOOH} \\
| \quad\quad | \\
\text{H}_2\text{C} \quad \text{O} \\
\backslash \quad / \\
\text{C} \\
\| \\
\text{O}
\end{array}
\right]^{2+}
$$

Cr^{2+} does not react with ordinary alkenes. Although it does reduce acetylenes to *trans*-alkenes,[71] the data do not suggest that the reaction proceeds via a σ-bonded organochromium complex.

4. Use of Grignard reagents

The interaction of a Grignard reagent and $CrCl_3(THF)_3$ leads to $R_3Cr(THF)_3$. Its reaction with further $CrCl_3(THF)_3$ in the correct ratio yields $RCrCl_2(THF)_3$ compounds which, although thermally unstable, are isolable as crystalline materials:[72,73]

$$CrCl_3(THF)_3 \xrightarrow[\text{THF}]{\text{3RMgX}} R_3Cr(THF)_3 \tag{27}$$

$$R_3Cr(THF)_3 + 2CrCl_3(THF)_3 \longrightarrow 3RCrCl_2(THF)_3 \tag{28}$$

The instability of the organochromium complexes requires a judicious choice of solvent and temperature. The stability of the product is improved if THF is displaced by pyridine or bipyridine, yielding, for example, $C_6H_5CH_2CrCl_2(py)_3$.[73]

Similar results can be obtained with aluminium or lithium alkyls or aryls although the mono-substituted product is often obtained directly:[7,74]

$$CrCl_3(THF)_3 + R_3Al \xrightarrow{\text{THF}} R_2AlCl + RCrCl_2(THF)_3 \tag{29}$$

$(R = Ph, CH_3, C_2H_5, n\text{-}C_3H_7, i\text{-}C_3H_7, i\text{-}C_4H_9)$

Solvolysis of $PhCH_2CrCl_2(THF)_3$ in water at 0°C gives the familiar benzyl(pentaaquo)chromium(III) cation;[74,75] one can only presume this would happen also with other alkyls although this route does not appear to have been examined.

5. Oxidation of organochromium(II) compounds

Oxidation of the chromium(II) bis(aryl) complexes $[(C_6H_5)_2Cr(LL)_2]$ (where LL = 2,2'-bipyridine or 1,10-phenanthroline) by O_2 produces *cis*[bis(aryl)chromium(III)] complexes which can be isolated as the iodide salts:[76,77]

$$[(C_6H_5)_2Cr(LL)_2] \xrightarrow[KI]{O_2/H_2O} [cis\text{-}(C_6H_5)_2Cr(LL)_2]^+I^- \qquad (30)$$

This method has now been extended to several other bis(organo)chromium(III) products, which are also stable to oxygen and water.[78,79] These compounds have been characterized by single-crystal x-ray determinations[80] (see also Section V.C). The versatility of the method was improved once it was realized that the unstable chromium(II) complex did not need to be isolated prior to its oxidation.[81]

An extensive summary of these methods and their products is given by Sneeden.[32]

One method offering some potential has, as yet, received only limited attention. Reaction of organic hydrazines with Schiff-base chelate complexes (in acetonitrile, and subsequent oxidation with oxygen and water) afforded products such as $RCr(sal_2en)H_2O$ for R = CH_3 and C_6H_5.[83] This method is reminiscent of that applied to iron and cobalt complexes.[84]

III. UNIMOLECULAR HOMOLYSIS OF Cr–C BONDS

A. Unimolecular pathways for decomposition of organochromium(III) complexes

All of the complexes $L_5Cr^{III}R$ decompose in aqueous or semi-aqueous solution resulting in cleavage of the chromium–carbon bond. The rate at which a given complex decomposes varies widely with the particular R group. A considerable body of results now points to two different mechanisms for decomposition taking place independently and concurrently. These processes correspond to homolytic ($CrR^{2+} \rightleftarrows Cr^{2+} + R\cdot$) and heterolytic ($CrR^{2+} \rightarrow Cr^{3+} + R^-$) cleavage reactions. The relative importance of each pathway and the rate of reaction along either depend not only on the identity of R but also (because the homolytic process is reversible) on other chemical reagents in solution. As will be shown shortly, the relative proportions of each reaction are subject to control and adjustment by variation of the reaction conditions.

The heterolytic process—usually referred to as protonolysis or more generally as acidolysis—will be dealt with in the following section. It is helpful to recognize at this point, however, that the representation given above for heterolytic cleavage, which suggests formation of $Cr(H_2O)_6^{3+}$ and the carbanion R^-, does not really represent the situation accurately. Since the acidity of $Cr(H_2O)_6^{3+}$ is much greater than that of the aliphatic compound RH, it is surely the case that the immediate products of the reaction are instead $(H_2O)_5CrOH^{2+}$ and RH.

The homolytic pathway for decomposition of CrR^{2+} is, in every case encountered to date, a thermodynamically unfavourable reaction. The reverse of homolysis is the reaction between Cr^{2+} and $R\cdot$, which as earlier demonstrated (Section II.A) is the most widely used reaction for formation of CrR^{2+} complexes. A more complete representation of the reaction also serves as a reminder that somewhere along this reaction coordinate an additional solvent molecule is involved:

$$(H_2O)_5CrR^{2+} + H_2O \rightleftarrows Cr(H_2O)_6^{2+} + R\cdot \tag{31}$$

B. Energetics and kinetics of the homolytic cleavage of an inorganic analogue

It is helpful to consider the chemistry of the organochromium(III) complexes in the light of similar reactions of inorganic analogues. The iodo(pentaaquo)chromium(III) ion provides a useful comparison. The homolytic reaction

$$(H_2O)_5CrI^{2+} + H_2O \rightleftarrows Cr(H_2O)_6^{2+} + I_{aq}\cdot \tag{32}$$

has not been studied directly, but from the thermodynamic data available the equilibrium constant for Equation (32) can be calculated. The conventional stability constant is known: $Cr^{3+} + I^- = CrI^{2+}$, $K = 7.0 \times 10^{-5} M^{-1}$,[85] as are the standard reduction potentials of Cr^{3+} and $I\cdot$, respectively, -0.41 and ~ 1.42 V.[86] These values combine to give $K_{32} \simeq 10^{-27} M$. The value of k_{-32} is necessarily $< 10^{10} M^{-1} s^{-1}$, although it is likely to be near the diffusion-controlled limit since Cr^{2+} and I_2^- react with $k = 1.5 \times 10^9 M^{-1} s^{-1}$.[43] The forward rate constant is thus $k_{32} = k_{-32}K_{32} \leqslant 10^{-17} s^{-1}$.

It should be evident from this analysis that iodochromium(III) ion would not be expected to decompose according to Equation (32), and that another mechanism involving heterolytic dissociation would dominate. Experiments designed to detect directly any homolytic dissociation of CrI^{2+} were unable to do so;[90] the analysis given above indicates why that was to be expected.

C. Evidence for the homolysis of $(H_2O)_5CrR^{2+}$ complexes

The reversibility of the homolytic decomposition reaction of Equation (31) provides the major key to controlling the channelling of reaction *via* acidolysis or homolysis;[24,60] other variables ([H^+], ionic strength, H/D ratio, etc.) play less decisive roles. When the decomposition reaction is studied in solutions containing excess Cr^{2+}, the homolytic decomposition process is reversed and acidolysis provides the only measured pathway. We designate the [H^+]-dependent rate constant so obtained as k_A (Section IV). On the other hand, consider the situation when there is added to the system a substance which reacts very efficiently with *either* Cr^{2+} or R. In that case the thermodynamically unfavourable homolysis reaction of Equa-

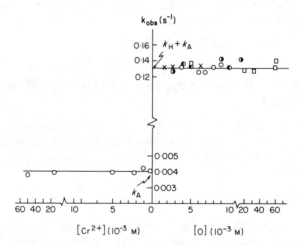

Fig. 1. Kinetic data (at 25°C, 1·0 M ionic strength, 1·0 M 2-propanol in water) for the decomposition of $(H_2O)_5CrC(CH_3)_2OH^{2+}$ were obtained under different reaction conditions:

Left: k_{obs} in solutions containing various [Cr^{2+}] at 0·100 M H^+. The value corresponds to acidolysis, k_A.

Right: k_{obs} in solutions containing varying concentrations of oxidizing scavengers for Cr^{2+} and R·. The points shown represent data at 0·01–1·00 M H^+ for the following reagents: $Co(NH_3)_5F^{2+}$ (◐), $Co(NH_3)_5Cl^{2+}$ (○), $Co(NH_3)_5Br^{2+}$ (◑), VO^{2+} (□), and H_2O_2 (×). The rate constant obtained under these conditions corresponds to $k_{obs} = k_H + k_A$. (The latter constant is [H^+] dependent (Table 7), but the changes are almost imperceptible on this scale.)

tion (31) is drawn to completion and the observed rate constant is the *sum* of the two contributions, $k_H + k_A$. The value of k_H can be obtained by difference using the value of k_A appropriate to the given $[H^+]$.

A wide variety of compatible reagents meet the requirements that they react rapily with Cr^{2+} or $R\cdot$, but do not react directly with the parent CrR^{2+} complex. The most useful are the family of $Co(NH_3)_5X^{2+}$ complexes $(X = F, Cl, Br)$ which react rapidly with Cr^{2+} and also with many of the free radicals—$\cdot C(CH_3)_2OH$, $\cdot CH(CH_3)_2$, etc., react;[87] $\cdot CH_2Ph$ does not.[24] Other reagents, including VO^{2+}, Cu^{2+}, Fe^{3+}, H_2O_2, and O_2 have proved useful in many cases (but not in all since each reacts directly with certainly CrR^{2+} complexes; Sections VIII.A, B).

A graphic illustration of the effect of experiments with $CrC(CH_3)_2OH^{2+}$ under two conditions is shown in Fig. 1. Runs conducted with added Cr^{2+} give the value $k_{obs} = k_A = 4\cdot0 \times 10^{-3}\,s^{-1}$ (at 25°C, 0·1 M H^+, 1·00 M ionic strength). Runs with any of several added oxidizing agents give a much higher value, $\sim 0\cdot132\,s^{-1}$ but increasing slightly with $[H^+]$, corresponding to $k_H + k_A$. After allowance for k_A and its dependence on $[H^+]$, the result is the $[H^+]$-independent quantity $k_H = 0\cdot127 \pm 0\cdot003\,s^{-1}$ (25·0°C, 1·00 M ionic strength).

Evidence that the greatly enhanced reaction rate in the presence of added oxidant does, in fact, correspond to homolytic cleavage is the following: (a) the rate constant is independent of oxidant concentration, consistent with its involvement in much faster reactions following the rate-limiting step; (b) the oxidizing agents, listed above, span a wide variety of chemical species, making it most unlikely that the concentration independence could arise from some sort of pre-equilibrium; (c) the oxidizing agents which are successful are those which can be shown independently to react with Cr^{2+} or with $R\cdot$; unsuccessful oxidants (e.g., $Co(en)_3^{3+}$ for $CrCH_2Ph^{2+}$ homolysis) correspond to species which do not react rapidly with either homolytic fragment; (d) the inorganic products are those kinetically derived species (not the preferred thermodynamic product, $Cr(H_2O)_6^{3+}$), which can be recognized as uniquely arising from reactions of Cr^{2+}, such as CrF^{2+} from $Co(NH_3)_5F^{2+}$, etc.; (e) the organic products are similarly compatible with those expected from free-radical oxidation, such as the quantitative yield of $(CH_3)_2CO$ from $\cdot C(CH_3)_2OH$,[60] the change from $PhCH_2OH$ to $PhCHO$ to $PhCH_2CH_2Ph$ as Fe^{3+} (or Cu^{2+}) is replaced by O_2 or by $Co(NH_3)_5Cl^{2+}$ when $PhCH_2$ is involved;[24] (f) the initiation of polymerization of acrylonitrile if present during homolysis of $CrCH_2Ph^{2+}$.[24]

As general as the kinetic method is in most cases, it fails when homolysis is very much slower than acidolysis. In such instances the difference between k_{obs} $(=k_H + k_A)$ and k_A is too small to permit calculation of an accurate

TABLE 5

Rate constants[a] at 25°C for the unimolecular homolytic cleavage reaction for $(H_2O)_5CrR^{2+}$ complexes according to Equations (31) and (33)

R	k_H (s^{-1})	$\Delta H^{\ddagger}$ (kJ mol^{-1})	$\Delta S^{\ddagger}$ (J mol^{-1} K^{-1})	Ref.
(a) Alkyls				
—CH(CH$_3$)$_2$	$(1.78 \pm 0.11) \times 10^{-4}$			[26]
—c-C$_5$H$_9$	$(1.10 \pm 0.26) \times 10^{-4}$	126 ± 3	102 ± 9	[62]
(b) α-Hydroxyalkyls				
—CH$_2$OH	$(3.7 \pm 0.2) \times 10^{-5}$	125	92	[60]
—CH(CH$_3$)OH	$(8.5 \pm 0.3) \times 10^{-4}$			[60]
—CH(C$_2$H$_5$)OH	$(1.01 \pm 0.04) \times 10^{-3}$	136	155	[60]
—C(CH$_3$)$_2$OH	$(1.27 \pm 0.03) \times 10^{-1}$	114 ± 1	120 ± 2	[60]
—C(CH$_3$)(C$_2$H$_5$)OH	$(9.2 \pm 0.3) \times 10^{-1}$	108.2 ± 2	117 ± 7	[60]
—C(C$_2$H$_5$)$_2$OH	$(8.39 \pm 0.09) \times 10^{0}$	97.1 ± 2.1	98.7 ± 6.7	[60]
—C(CH$_3$)(i-C$_3$H$_7$)OH	$(2.16 \pm 0.01) \times 10^{1}$	90.3 ± 1.7	84.1 ± 5.0	[60]
—C(CH$_3$)(t-C$_4$H$_9$)OH	$\sim3 \times 10^{2}$	92	113	[60]
—CH(CF$_3$)OH	$<3 \times 10^{-5}$			[60]
(c) α-Alkoxyalkyls				
—CH$_2$OCH$_3$	$<10^{-6}$			[60]
—CH(CH$_3$)OC$_2$H$_5$	$(2.04 \pm 0.02) \times 10^{-3}$	125.9 ± 0.4	126.3 ± 1.3	[60]
—C(CH$_3$)$_2$O—i-C$_3$H$_7$	$(5.77 \pm 0.15) \times 10^{0}$	100.0 ± 2.9	105.4 ± 9.2	[60]

(d) Aralkyls

—$CH_2C_6H_5$	$(2\cdot63 \pm 0\cdot21) \times 10^{-3}$	133 ± 3	153 ± 11	[24]
—$CH_2C_6H_4$-p-CH_3	$(3\cdot74 \pm 0\cdot04) \times 10^{-3}$			[24]
—$CH_2C_6H_4$-p-C_6H_5	$(3\cdot22 \pm 0\cdot05) \times 10^{-3}$			[88]
—$CH_2C_6H_4$-p-CH_2OH	$(1\cdot66 \pm 0\cdot02) \times 10^{-3}$			[88]
—$CH_2C_6H_4$-p-Br	$(1\cdot56 \pm 0\cdot07) \times 10^{-3}$			[24]
—$CH_2C_6H_4$-m-CH_2Br	$(1\cdot23 \pm 0\cdot02) \times 10^{-3}$			[88]
—$CH_2C_6H_4$-p-CF_3	$(7\cdot28 \pm 0\cdot08) \times 10^{-4}$			[24]
—$CH_2C_6H_4$-p-CN	$(5\cdot56 \pm 0\cdot34) \times 10^{-4}$			[24]
—$CH_2C_6H_4$-m-$OC_6H_4CH_2Cr^{2+}$	$(8\cdot3 \pm 0\cdot04) \times 10^{-3}$			[89]
—$CH_2C_6H_4$-p-$C_6H_4CH_2Cr^{2+}$	$(2\cdot51 \pm 0\cdot04) \times 10^{-3}$			[88]
—$CH_2C_6H_4$-m-$C_6H_4CH_2Cr^{2+}$	$(2\cdot11 \pm 0\cdot05) \times 10^{-3}$			[88]
—$CH_2C_6H_4$-(CH_2)-p-$C_6H_4CH_2CH_2Cr^{2+}$	$(2\cdot65 \pm 0\cdot05) \times 10^{-3}$			[88]
—$CH_2C_6H_4CH_2CH_2$-p-$C_6H_4CH_2CH_2Cr^{2+}$	$(3\cdot14 \pm 0\cdot04) \times 10^{-3}$			[88]
—2-$CH_2C_5H_4NH^+$	$(1\cdot44 \times 10^{-5})^b$			[17]
—2-$CH_2C_5H_4NCH_3^+$	$(3\cdot41 \times 10^{-5})^b$			[17]
—3-$CH_2C_5H_4NH^+$	$(4\cdot33 \times 10^{-4})^b$			[17]
—4-$CH_2C_5N_4NH^+$	$(5\cdot17 \times 10^{-5})^b$	$122\cdot1 \pm 3\cdot5$	$44\cdot6 \pm 11\cdot0$	[17, 90]

^{a} In water (or 0·1–1 M aqueous alcohol or ether in water) at 1·00 M ionic strength.
^{b} 55°C.

value for k_H. Such is the situation for $CrCH_2OH^{2+}$, requiring a different approach. The small yield of HCHO obtained when $CrCH_2OH^{2+}$ was allowed to decompose in solutions containing $Co(NH_3)_5Br^{2+}$ was determined. Its value, together with k_{obs}, afforded the desired rate constant k_H, given by $k_H = k_{obs}[HCHO]_\infty/[CrCH_2OH^{2+}]_0$.

D. Kinetic data for the homolysis of $(H_2O)_5CrR^{2+}$ complexes

The rate law for the unimolecular homolysis reaction is

$$\frac{-d[(H_2O)_5CrR^{2+}]}{dt} = k_H[(H_2O)_5CrR^{2+}] \tag{33}$$

Table 5 summarizes the rate constants for all the complexes studied[24,60,62,88–90] and also gives values of $\Delta H^\ddagger$ and $\Delta S^\ddagger$ calculated from the temperature dependence of k_H.

A change in the reaction conditions, other than temperature variation, causes little variation of k_H. The value for $CrC(CH_3)_2OH^{2+}$, for example, is independent of $[H^+]$ (0·01–1·00 M) and of ionic strength (0·1–1·0 M). It is essentially the same in deuterated water: $(D_2O)_5CrC(CH_3)_2OD^{2+}$ has $k_H = 0·130\ s^{-1}$ in D_2O at 25·0°C.[91]

Homolysis seems to provide an important reaction pathway mainly for those CrR^{2+} complexes having a benzyl group or an aliphatic group with a substituted alpha carbon atom. The possibility of homolysis was specifically examined for the following complexes and no evidence for it being a major reaction was obtained: $CrCH_2CN^{2+}$,[23] $CrCH_2CH_2CN^{2+}$,[23] $CrCH_2CH(CH_3)CN^{2+}$,[23] $CrCH_2OCH_3^{2+}$,[60] $CrCH_2COOH^{2+}$,[92] and $CrCH_2CH_3^{2+}$. Its failure to compete with acidolysis in cases such as this reflects, among other things, the lower stability of the radicals which would be produced.

E. Mechanism of the homolysis reaction

The activation parameters are consistent with the assignment that homolysis proceeds by the S_H1 mechanism. The substantial activation enthalpies, 90–133 kJ mol^{-1}, are consistent with dissociation of the Cr–C bond largely uncompensated for by other bond-making processes. The large positive values of $\Delta S^\ddagger$ are very characteristic of the homolysis reaction. The range of values, some 84–155 J mol^{-1} K^{-1}, suggests that the cleavage of the chromium–carbon bond has proceeded to a substantial extent at the transition state. The values are so large, in fact, that it appears there is an additional contribution. It may arise from disruption of the solvent as the organic radical is released into it.

Owing to the reversibility of the homolysis equilibrium (Equation (31)), it is possible to calculate K_H from the rate constants for the forward and reverse reactions for four of the complexes, and to estimate it for others.

$$(H_2O)_5CrR^{2+} + H_2O \underset{k_{-1}}{\overset{k_H}{\rightleftharpoons}} Cr(H_2O)_6^{2+} + R\cdot \tag{31}$$

$$K_{eq} = K_H = k_H/k_{-1} \tag{34}$$

The resulting equilibrium constants are given in Table 6.[60] They all correspond to the case in which equilibrium in Equation (31) lies far to the

TABLE 6
Calculated equilibrium constants[a] for the homolysis reaction according to Equations (31) and (34)

R	$10^{-7}k_{-1}$ (M^{-1} s^{-1})	$-\log_{10}K_H$ (M)	$\Delta G_{H,298}$ (kJ mol^{-1})
—CH$_2$OH	16	12·64	72·1
—CH(CH$_3$)OH	7·9	10·96	62·6
—CH(C$_2$H$_5$)OH	(8)	10·9	62
—C(CH$_3$)$_2$OH	5·1	8·6	49·1
—C(CH$_3$)(C$_2$H$_5$)OH	(5)	7·7	44
—C(C$_2$H$_5$)$_2$OH	($\leq$5)	6·8	39
—C(CH$_3$)(i-C$_3$H$_7$)OH	($\leq$5)	6·4	36
—C(CH$_3$)(t-C$_4$H$_9$)OH	($\leq$5)	5·2	30
—CH$_2$OCH$_3$	(7)	>13·8	>79
—CH(CH$_3$)OC$_2$H$_5$	3·4	10·22	58·3
—C(CH$_3$)$_2$O—i-C$_3$H$_7$	($\leq$3)	6·7	38

[a] K_H calculated as k_H/k_{-1}, with k_H from Table 5 and k_{-1} from Table 2. Estimated values in parentheses. Data from Refs. [25, 60].

left, K_H lying in the range 10^{-14}–10^{-6} M. A plot of log k_H versus log K_H, given in Fig. 2, is linear with a slope of 0·93; this is consistent with a highly endothermic reaction in which the transition state closely resembles the products.

The analysis of these values may be extended further.[60] With certain assumptions the values of $\Delta H^{\ddagger}$ (Table 5) may be taken as an approximation of the chromium–carbon bond enthalpy. It can be seen that the bond strength declines regularly with the degree of substitution on the alpha carbon atom.

Steric and electronic factors both contribute to the values of k_H. Substitution with electron-attracting groups (F, Br, CF$_3$, etc.) greatly retards homolysis. Within a series of similarly constituted complexes, on the other

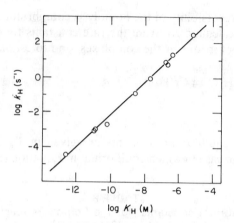

Fig. 2. The log–log plot showing the measured rate constant for homolytic dissociation of $(H_2O)_5CrR^{2+}$ plotted against the calculated equilibrium constant. The line drawn has slope 0·93.

hand, where electronic effects might be more constant, the steric effect will play a determining role. To assess that, consider the correlation of log k_H (or $\Delta G_H^{\ddagger}$) with $\Delta G_{C-C}^{\ddagger}$ for the homolytic dissociation of similarly constituted ethanes:[93]

$$\begin{array}{ccc} R^1 & R^1 & R^1 \\ | & | & | \\ R^2\!-\!C\!-\!C\!-\!R^2 \xrightarrow[\Delta G_{C-C}^{\ddagger}]{k_{C-C}} 2 & C\cdot \\ | & | & \diagup \quad \diagdown \\ R^3 & R^3 & R^2 \qquad R^3 \end{array} \qquad (35)$$

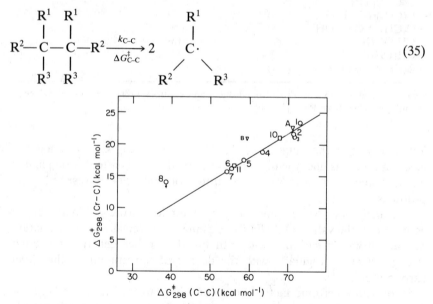

Fig. 3. An attempted LFER correlation showing $\Delta G_{Cr-C}^{\ddagger}$ for homolysis of CrR^{2+} complexes versus $\Delta G_{C-C}^{\ddagger}$ for homolysis of substituted ethanes.

This approach[60] suggests that a linear free-energy correlation, $\Delta G_H^{\ddagger}$ versus $\Delta G_{C-C}^{\ddagger}$, might be successful. Considering that the organochromium cations are substituted on one side only and the ethanes on both, a successful correlation would be expected to have a slope of $\sim 1/2$ if bond-breaking were equally important in both. The correlation is adequate (Fig. 3), and suggests a slope of 0·36, although the neglect of the variation of electronic effects along the series limits it to a semi-quantitative concept.

IV. ACIDOLYSIS OF ORGANOCHROMIUM(III) COMPLEXES

A. Acidolysis reactions and reaction products

The main pathway for decompositon of $(H_2O)_5CrR^{2+}$ complexes in the absence of added oxidizing agents (often in the presence of excess Cr^{2+}) is a heterolytic reaction:

$$(H_2O)_5CrR^{2+} + H_3O^+ = Cr(H_2O)_6^{3+} + RH \tag{36}$$

This class of reactions is referred to by many authors by the generic term "acidolysis" (or, more specifically for H_3O^+, "protonolysis"); other authors prefer the term "aquation". The latter term suggests—perhaps correctly, perhaps not—that the process is analogous to the heterolytic pathways for ligand substitution reactions of the inorganic coordination complexes.

The acidolysis reaction has been studied for most of the CrR^{2+} complexes which have been prepared. Where products have been identified, RH is the major or sole organic product. That is to say, $CrCH_3^{2+}$ produces methane, or CH_3D in D_2O,[20] $CrCH(CH_3)_2^{2+}$ propane,[26] $CrCH_2COOH^{2+}$ acetic acid,[92] and $CrCH_2OH^{2+}$ methanol,[20] or CH_2DOD in D_2O.[94]

These are the products expected from the heterolytic cleavage reaction in which H_3O^+ is viewed as an attacking electrophile. As mentioned earlier, the high basicity precludes any mechanism involving release of free R^-, although an acid-independent pathway is important for most comlexes.

B. Kinetic data for the acidolysis of $(H_2O)_5CrR^{2+}$ complexes

As a general result the rate of decomposition of CrR^{2+} by the acidolysis pathway is described by a rate law having two terms. These represent parallel paths, each having a first-order dependence on $[CrR^{2+}]$, but with zero-order and first-order dependences on $[H_3O^+]$. The rate law is

$$\frac{-d[(H_2O)_5CrR^{2+}]}{dt} = (k_{1A} + k_{2A}[H_3O^+])[(H_2O)_5CrR^{2+}] \tag{37}$$

TABLE 7

Rate constants[a] for the acidolysis of organochromium(III) complexes according to Equations (36) and (37)

R	k_{1A} (s^{-1})	k_{2A} (M^{-1} s^{-1})	Ref.
(a) Alkyls			
—H	~0	$(1.0 \pm 0.1) \times 10^4$	[95]
—CH$_3$	<10^{-4}	4.94×10^{-3}	[14, 20, 57, 96]
—CH$_2$CH$_3$	2.2×10^{-4}	1.15×10^{-4}	[57]
—CH$_2$C$_2$H$_5$	3.0×10^{-4}	6.5×10^{-5}	[57]
—CH(CH$_3$)$_2$	1.05×10^{-4}	~0	[26]
—c-C$_5$H$_9$	4.82×10^{-4}	~0	[62]
(b) α-Hydroxyalkyls			
—CH$_2$OH	6.6×10^{-4}	4.65×10^{-4}	[20, 57]
—CH(CH$_3$)OH	1.90×10^{-3}	1.22×10^{-3}	[20]
—CH(CF$_3$)OH	<10^{-6}	<10^{-6}	[60]
—CH(C$_2$H$_5$)OH	3.17×10^{-3}	2.14×10^{-3}	[20, 60]
—C(CH$_3$)$_2$OH	3.31×10^{-3}	4.91×10^{-3}	[20, 60]
—C(CH$_3$)(C$_2$H$_5$)OH	8×10^{-3}	4.69×10^{-1}	[60]
—C(C$_2$H$_5$)$_2$OH	3×10^{-2}	8.58×10^{-1}	[60]
—C(CH$_3$)(i-C$_3$H$_7$)OH	3.5×10^{-2}	3.0×10^{-1}	[60]
—CH(OH)COOH	1.0	≤0.1	[25]
—CCH$_3$(OH)COOH	4.7×10^2	2.8×10^2	[25]

(c) α-Alkoxyalkyls

—CH$_2$OCH$_3$	<10^{-6}	<10^{-6}	[60]
—CH(CH$_3$)OC$_2$H$_5$	≤5 × 10^{-7}	3·1 × 10^{-5}	[20, 94]
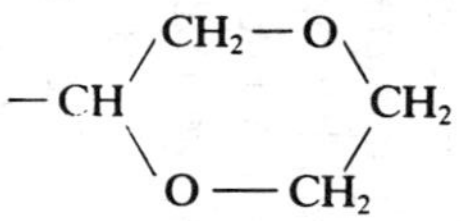 (cyclic: —CH, CH$_2$—O, O—CH$_2$, CH$_2$)	≤2 × 10^{-2}	4·8 × 10^{-1}	[20]

(d) α-Carboxyalkyls

—CH$_2$COOH	5·2 × 10^{-6}	~0	[92]
—CH(OH)COOH	1·0	≤0.1	[25]
—CCH$_3$(OH)COOH	4·7 × 10^{2}	2·8 × 10^{2}	[25]
—CH(COOH)$_2$	1·8 × 10^{-4}	5·3 × 10^{-4}	[25]
—CH(CH$_3$)COOH	2·0 × 10^{-3}	≤3 × 10^{-4}	[25]
—CH(Cl)COOH	1·66 × 10^{-5} ^{c}		[97]

(e) Halo-substituted complexes

—CH$_2$Cl	5·6 × 10^{-7}	~0	[98]
—CH$_2$Br	2·4 × 10^{-6}	~0	[98]
—CH$_2$I	4·5 × 10^{-6}	~0	[98]
—CHCl$_2$	4·0 × 10^{-6}	~0	[99]
—CHBr$_2$	1·4 × 10^{-6}	~0	[99]
—CHI$_2$	8·5 × 10^{-8}	~0^b	[99]
—CF$_3$	3·3 × 10^{-8}		[22]
—CCl$_3$	8·6 × 10^{-4} ^{c}	8·6 × 10^{-8}	[52]

^{a} In water (or water containing 0·1–1·0 M organic solute) at 25°C, μ = 1·0 M (except data from Ref. [25], 22 ± 2°C, 0·1–1·0 M HClO$_4$).
^{b} CrCHI$_2^{2+}$ has an additional term, k'[CrCHI$_2^{2+}$][H$^+$]$^{-1}$ with k' = 2·0 × 10^{-9} M s^{-1}.
^{c} Value in 1 M HClO$_4$.

This relation is useful for representing the behaviour of all complexes by a single equation, although for any particular complex one rate constant or the other may make an inappreciable contribution. Data for two typical complexes, $CrCH_3^{2+}$ and $CrC(CH_3)_2OH^{2+}$, are shown in Fig. 4, which depicts the linear dependence of the observed rate constant on $[H_3O^+]$. The rate constants for the reactions which have been studied[14,20,22,26,52,57,60,62,92,95–99] are given in Table 7.

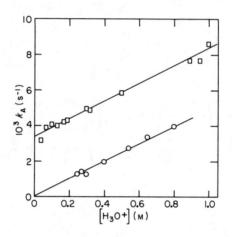

Fig. 4. The pseudo-first-order rate constant for acidolysis is a linear function of $[H_3O^+]$. Data are shown for $CrCH_3^{2+}$ (circles) and $CrC(CH_3)_2OH^{2+}$ (squares) at 25·0°C and 1·00 M ionic strength.

The rate constants for acidolysis, unlike those for homolysis, *do* vary appreciably with solvent composition. Thus protonolysis of $(D_2O)_5CrD^{2+}$ in D_2O shows an appreciable kinetic isotope effect ($k_H/k_D = 4·8$) as does the protonolysis of $CrCH_3^{2+}$ in the same two solvents ($k_H/k_D = 6·3$).[95] Similarly, $CrCH_2OH^{2+}$ shows $k_{1A}(H)/k_{1A}(D) = 8·4$ and $k_{2A}(H)/k_{2A}(D) \sim 6$,[94] and $CrC(CH_3)_2OH^{2+}$ has $k_{1A}(H)/k_{1A}(D) = 6·4$.[91]

The values of k_1 and k_2 have been determined for several of these complexes as a function of temperature. Activation parameters are listed in Table 8 for a representative sample of complexes. It is interesting to compare the parameters associated with the acid-independent terms for homolysis (k_H) and acidolysis (k_{1A}). The former shows, generally speaking, a greater temperature dependence: $\Delta H_H^\ddagger > \Delta H_{1A}^\ddagger$. But what is most striking is the very substantial change from the large positive values of $\Delta S_H^\ddagger$ to the (usually) negative values of $\Delta S_{1A}^\ddagger$. This illustrates the substantial difference between the two modes of unassisted dissociation for any given complex.

TABLE 8

Activation parameters for acidolysis reactions of selected $(H_2O)_5CrR^{2+}$ complexes (Equations (36) and (37))

R	k_{1A} term		k_{2A} term		Ref.
	$\Delta H^{\ddagger}$ (kJ mol⁻¹)	$\Delta S^{\ddagger}$ (J mol⁻¹ K⁻¹)	$\Delta H^{\ddagger}$ (kJ mol⁻¹)	$\Delta S^{\ddagger}$ (J mol⁻¹ K⁻¹)	
—H	73·5 ± 2·4	−61·5 ± 7·9	26·4 ± 0·9	−79·9 ± 29	[95]
—c-C₅H₉	71·5 ± 2·9	−46·0 ± 8·4			[62]
—C(CH₃)₂OH			81·1 ± 3·3	−21 ± 8	[60]
—C(C₂H₅)₂OH			50·6 ± 0·4	−76·6 ± 2·1	[60]
—CH₂COOH	96·1	−23·7			[92]
—CH₂Cl	109·9 ± 0·8	3·7 ± 2·3ᵃ			[98]
—CF₃	104 ± 8	−38 ± 25	96 ± 16	−59 ± 33	[22]
—CH₂OHᵇ	74·2 ± 6·8	−65 ± 22	98·6 ± 0·8	132 ± 3	[61]
—CH(CH₃)OHᵇ	81·9 ± 2·0	−25 ± 7	81·8 ± 5·5	65 ± 18	[61]
—C(CH₃)₂OHᵇ	80·9 ± 4·2	−10 ± 14	72·9 ± 7·7	43 ± 10	[61]

ᵃ Recalculated from the data in Ref. [98].
ᵇ For the complex $[RCr(edta)]^{2-}$.[61]

C. Mechanism of the acidolysis reaction

It is reasonable to interpret the acid-dependent rate term (k_2) as arising from attack of the external electrophile H_3O^+ on the α-carbon of the organochromium complex. The fact that H_3O^+ is a relatively unreactive electrophile compared to Hg^{2+} or Br_2 should be noted; for these three reagents reacting with (for example) $CrCH_3^{2+}$, the rate constants are H_3O^+, $4\cdot94 \times 10^{-3} M^{-1} s^{-1}$;[20,57] Br_2, $2\cdot1 \times 10^6$;[100] and Hg^{2+}, $1\cdot0 \times 10^7$.[15]

Nonetheless, the kinetic data can be interpreted in terms of a transition state involving H_3O^+ attack on the alpha carbon atom. To avoid formation of a free carbanion, C–H bond making must be fairly advanced in the transition state; that is to say, $H^+ \cdots OH_2$ bond breaking is an appreciable part of the activation process, consistent with the large solvent isotope effect. Note, however, that after allowance for the solvent effect, CrH^{2+} and CrD^{2+} do not show an appreciable effect, suggesting Cr–H or C–C bond breaking is a less critical feature. We venture to suggest, in view of the changes in k_{2A} among the alkyl complexes† (Table 7), that the pathway may involve attack of H_3O^+ on the opposite side of the alpha carbon atom to which the $Cr(OH_2)_5$ entity is bound (see also Section VI.E). These ideas are incorporated into the following activated complex:

$$\left[(H_2O)_5Cr^{2+} \text{----} \underset{\underset{R^2}{\diagup} \overset{\overset{R^1}{|}}{\underset{R^3}{\diagdown}}}{C} \text{----} H^+ \text{----} O \overset{\diagup H}{\underset{\diagdown H}{}} \right]^{\ddagger}$$

The acid-independent pathway (k_{1A} term) can be regarded as proceeding by a similar mechanism, with H_2O the attacking electrophile rather than H_3O^+. It remains to be demonstrated whether that water molecule is coordinated to chromium(III) in a *cis* position, or whether a bulk solvent molecule is involved. The former is suggested by (a) the much greater acidity of bound water as compared to free and (b) the lack of steric deceleration along the series of alkyls (Table 7) in which k_{2A} decreases markedly. The transition state suggested is thus depicted as:

$$\left[\underset{\diagup \;|\;}{\overset{\diagdown \;|\;}{Cr^{2+}}} \overset{O \overset{\diagup H}{}}{\underset{\underset{\diagup \diagdown}{C} \text{---}}{\diagdown}} \cdots H \right]^{\ddagger}$$

† The alkyl complexes are regarded as a better guide on this point than the α-hydroxyalkyls where specific hydrogen-bonding interaction may influence the rate constants.

On the other hand, the acidolysis reactions of $[RCr(edta)]^{2-}$ complexes (Table 9), wherein no *cis* water molecule is present, also follows the same rate law.[61] It is notable that the acid-catalysed pathway for the edta complexes compared to $(H_2O)_5CrR^{2+}$ analogues is faster by $\sim 10^5$, perhaps reflecting the relative driving force toward the inorganic Cr(III) products. The rate constants for the acid-independent terms are comparable, however; since the Cr(III) stability should be felt in both, there may be a counterbalancing effect such as the unavailability of the internal (*cis*-water) electrophile in the $[RCr(edta)]^{2-}$ series.

TABLE 9

Rate constants[a,b] for acidolysis of $[RCr(edta)]^{2-}$ complexes

R	k_{1A} (s^{-1})	k_{2A} $(M^{-1} s^{-1})$
—CH$_2$OH	$2 \cdot 52 \times 10^{-4}$	$2 \cdot 56 \times 10^2$
—CH(CH$_3$)OH	$1 \cdot 35 \times 10^{-3}$	$7 \cdot 35 \times 10^1$
—C(CH$_3$)$_2$OH	$1 \cdot 38 \times 10^{-2}$	$1 \cdot 76 \times 10^2$

[a] Ref. [61]; at 25·0°C at 1·0 M ionic strength. The observed rate constant is $(k_{1A} + k_{2A}[H^+])/(1 + Q[H^+])$, Q being a protonation constant, 2×10^{-3} M at 25°C.
[b] Activation parameters are given in Table 8.

With the exception of $CrCHI_2^{2+}$,[99] the acidolysis reactions of $(H_2O)_5CrR^{2+}$ complexes do not show the inverse acid pathway found for the aquation reactions of every member of the family of inorganic analogues. That pathway is associated with a kinetic term $k'_A[(H_2O)_5CrX^{2+}][H_3O^+]^{-1}$. The conjugate base mechanism applicable to CrX^{2+} complexes yields a reactive intermediate complex $[(H_2O)_4Cr(OH)X^+]$ from which anionic X^- rapidly dissociates. This pathway would not be expected to be favourable for the organometallic complexes because the carbanion R^- will not be a suitable leaving group. Under more basic pH conditions, however, the CrR^{2+} complexes do decompose rapidly, $Cr(OH)_3$ being deposited.

It is interesting to note that acidolysis reactions have not been observed for aralkyl complexes such as $(H_2O)_5CrCH_2C_6H_5^{2+}$ or $(H_2O)_5Cr$-$CH_2C_5H_4NH^{3+}$. Homolysis reactions dominate the chemistry of these complexes containing resonance-stabilized radicals, with the possible exception of anion-accelerated reactions (Section V.D). In the presence of added Cr^{2+}, the rate of decomposition of $CrCH_2C_5H_4NH^{3+}$ is inversely proportional to $[Cr^{2+}]$, also indicative of homolytic reactions.[90]

V. ACCELERATED *TRANS* SUBSTITUTION

A. The coordination sphere of $Cr^{III}R$ complexes

Many arguments can be made in support of the *trans* position being the site at which ligand substitution occurs. It would appear that the only experimental evidence which addresses the point directly, however, is based on studies involving the complex $(H_2O)_5CrCH_2Cl^{2+}$ in water–methanol.[28] The principle behind the determination is explained in Scheme (I), which includes for purposes of comparison $(H_2O)_5CrBr^{2+}$, a complex which is not labile to substitution when placed in water.[101] (The explanation is cast in terms of the presumed five-coordinate intermediates $Cr(H_2O)_5^{3+}$ and $Cr(H_2O)_4(CH_3OH)^{3+}$, being formed upon reaction with Hg^{2+}, but that is not required for the argument to remain valid.)

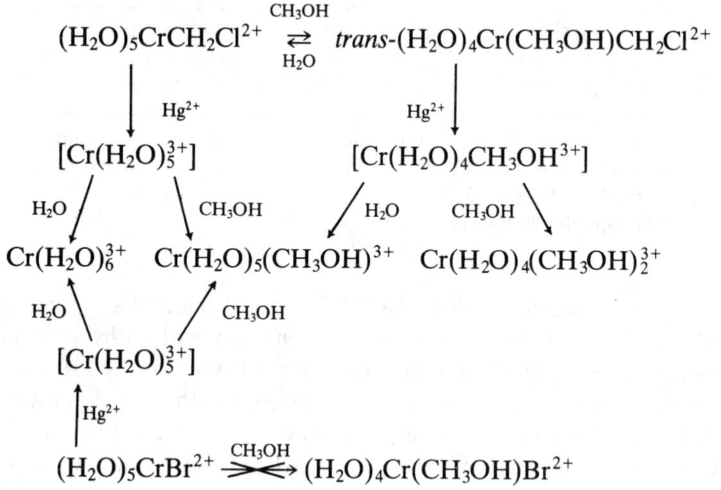

$$(H_2O)_5CrCH_2Cl^{2+} \underset{H_2O}{\overset{CH_3OH}{\rightleftarrows}} \textit{trans-}(H_2O)_4Cr(CH_3OH)CH_2Cl^{2+}$$

$$\big\downarrow Hg^{2+} \qquad\qquad\qquad Hg^{2+}\big\downarrow$$

$$[Cr(H_2O)_5^{3+}] \qquad\qquad\qquad [Cr(H_2O)_4CH_3OH^{3+}]$$

$$\overset{H_2O}{\swarrow}\quad\overset{CH_3OH}{\searrow}\qquad\overset{H_2O}{\swarrow}\quad\overset{CH_3OH}{\searrow}$$

$$Cr(H_2O)_6^{3+}\quad Cr(H_2O)_5(CH_3OH)^{3+}\quad Cr(H_2O)_4(CH_3OH)_2^{3+}$$

$$\overset{H_2O}{\searrow}\quad\overset{CH_3OH}{\swarrow}$$

$$[Cr(H_2O)_5^{3+}]$$

$$\big\uparrow Hg^{2+}$$

$$(H_2O)_5CrBr^{2+} \overset{CH_3OH}{\rightleftarrows} (H_2O)_4Cr(CH_3OH)Br^{2+}$$

Scheme (1)

If the starting $(H_2O)_5CrCH_2Cl^{2+}$ can be substituted by one or more molecules of methanol (one is suggested in Scheme (1)) *prior to* reaction with Hg^{2+}, then the composition of the solvent shell of the kinetically inert chromium(III) products will reflect that change. The experiments consist of separations and analyses[101] to determine the value of $\bar{n}$, the average number of methanol molecules bound in the coordination sphere of chromium(III):

$$\bar{n} = \frac{\text{total } [CH_3OH] \text{ in Cr(III) products}}{[Cr(III)]_{\text{total}}} \tag{38}$$

The variation of $\bar{n}$ with the mole-fraction of methanol is depicted in Fig. 5. For $CrBr^{2+}$, $\bar{n}$ approaches a limiting value of ~1 at unit mole fraction of methanol. This is as expected if the five water molecules remain unsubstituted by methanol. On the other hand, the limiting value of $\bar{n}$ approaches 2 for the organochromium complex. It is thus clear that *one* of the five water molecules in the parent $(H_2O)_5CrCH_2Cl^{2+}$ complex is unique with

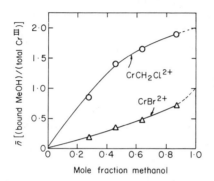

Fig. 5. The quantity $\bar{n}$, the number of methanol molecules bound to Cr(III) products, Equation (38), varies with the mole fraction of methanol. Data are shown for the complexes $CrCH_2Cl^{2+}$ [28] and $CrBr^{2+}$,[101] briefly equilibrated with methanol prior to reaction with Hg^{2+}.

respect to lability. (Thermodynamic data[101] would have $\bar{n}$ approach 6 if all positions were labile.) The most reasonable interpretation is that the one labile water molecule is the structurally unique one, that *trans* to the —CH$_2$Cl group. Kinetic data (Section V.B) and structural data (Section V.C) support this conclusion, but would not on their own be nearly as conclusive.

B. Kinetics of *trans* substitution reactions of $(H_2O)_5CrR^{2+}$ complexes

Qualitative evidence for reversible substitution of one water molecule by an anion X^- has been obtained in several systems. Only for X^- = —NCS$^-$ has extensive work been done, however;[28,102,103] some results are available for F^-.[22] The limitation to a single anion is somewhat unfortunate, since the distinctions between kinetically compatible mechanisms could be made more conclusively if data for other entering groups were available. Other anions attempted to date, however, have such feeble equilibrium constants that observations of reactions have not been possible under the reaction conditions employed (required to be acidic by the stability of CrR^{2+}). The reaction with thiocyanate ion produces a $1:1$ complex, judged by the position of the ligand field band to be coordinated via nitrogen. Higher complexes do not form, consistent with the notion that rapid substitution is limited to the *trans* positions but not proof of it since the stability constants decrease for successive addition of anions (unlike the neutral substitutions referred to earlier). The equilibrium reaction is written in the following form:

$$(H_2O)_5CrR^{2+} + SCN^- = trans\text{-}(H_2O)_4Cr(NCS)R^+ + H_2O \tag{39}$$

$$K = \frac{[(H_2O)_4Cr(NCS)R^+]}{[(H_2O)_5CrR^{2+}][SCN^-]} \tag{40}$$

The values of K ($25\cdot0°C$, $\mu = 1\cdot00$ M) range from $3\cdot5$ to $19\cdot1$ M^{-1}. They are reasonably insensitive to the particular group R of which a considerable number have now been examined (Table 10).

TABLE 10
Summary of the equilibrium and kinetic parameters[a] for the reaction of SCN^- with CrR^{2+} complexes according to Equations (39)–(49)

R	K_{eq} (M^{-1})	k_1 (s^{-1})
—CH_2OH	$13\cdot8 \pm 0\cdot3$	$>1\cdot52 \times 10^3$
—CH_2OCH_3	$17\cdot2 \pm 0\cdot3$	$2\cdot06 \times 10^1$
—$CH(CH_3)_2$	$19\cdot1 \pm 1\cdot7$	$3\cdot16 \times 10^0$
—CH_2CN	$3\cdot46 \pm 0\cdot15$	$>1\cdot35 \times 10^0$
—CH_2Cl	$10\cdot4 \pm 0\cdot6$	$2\cdot09 \times 10^{-1}$
—$CHCl_2$	$12\cdot7 \pm 0\cdot8$	$4\cdot62 \times 10^{-2}$

[a] At $25\cdot0°C$, $\mu = 1\cdot00$ M in $HClO_4$–$LiClO_4$ soilutions. Data from Refs. [28] and [103].

The kinetic data, which correspond to a reversible approach to equilibrium, obey the rate law,

$$\frac{d[(H_2O)_4Cr(NCS)R^+]}{dt}$$
$$= \frac{A[(H_2O)_5CrR^{2+}][SCN^-] - B[(H_2O)_4Cr(NCS)R^+]}{1 + C[SCN^-]} \tag{41}$$

A rate law of this form is a familiar one in the area of ligand substitution mechanisms. It is consistent with either: (a) a dissociative (D) or S_N1-limiting mechanism, or (b) an ion-pairing mechanism. These mechanisms, and the interpretation each would suggest for A, B, and C are as follows:

D mechanism

$$(H_2O)_5CrR^{2+} \overset{1}{\underset{-1}{\rightleftarrows}} (H_2O)_4CrR^{2+} + H_2O \tag{42}$$

$$(H_2O)_4CrR^{2+} + SCN^- \overset{2}{\underset{-2}{\rightleftarrows}} (H_2O)_4Cr(NCS)R^+ \tag{43}$$

$$\frac{d[Cr(NCS)R^+]}{dt} = \frac{(k_1k_2/k_{-1})[CrR^{2+}][SCN^-] - k_{-2}[Cr(NCS)R^+]}{1 + (k_2/k_{-1})[SCN^-]} \tag{44}$$

$$A = k_1k_2/k_{-1} \quad B = k_{-2} \quad C = k_2/k_1 \quad k_1 = A/C \quad K = A/B \tag{45}$$

Ion-pairing mechanism

$$(H_2O)_5CrR^{2+} + SCN^- \overset{K_{IP}}{\rightleftharpoons} (H_2O)_5CrR^{2+} NCS^- \tag{46}$$

$$(H_2O)_5CrR^{2+} NCS^- \overset{3}{\underset{-3}{\rightleftarrows}} (H_2O)_4Cr(NCS)R^+ + H_2O \tag{47}$$

$$\frac{d[Cr(NCS)R^+]}{dt} = \frac{(k_3 + k_{-3})K_{IP}[CrR^{2+}][NCS^-] - k_{-3}[Cr(NCS)R^+]}{1 + K_{IP}[SCN^-]} \tag{48}$$

$$A = (k_3 + k_{-3})K_{IP} \quad B = k_{-3} \quad C = K_{IP}$$

$$k_3 = (A/C) - B \quad K = A/B \tag{49}$$

The case for one of these dissociatively controlled mechanisms over the other is difficult to make convincingly from the data available.[28, 102, 103] The kinetic parameters for this reaction, which are independent of $[H^+]$ $(0·05–1\,M)$, are summarized in Table 10. The indicated references give complete tabulations, and the values here are limited to the rate constant for water dissociation, k_1 (since $k_{-3} \ll k_3$, the constant k_3 is very close in value to k_1[103]. It has been pointed out before[104] that k_1 or k_3 can be reasonably approximated as the rate of water exchange). The value of k_1 (or k_3) depends on the Hammett substituent parameter σ_I. A correlation is depicted in Fig. 6, which includes also the rate constants for the *trans*-water exchange of $(H_2O)_5CrX^{2+}$ ($X = I^-, Cl^-,$ and NCS^-).[105] It could also be argued[103] that the lack of steric variations in this series makes the Hammett substituent constant σ_p a suitable parameter. This approach, too, is shown in Fig. 6. Great significance should not be attributed to the details of the correlation, nor to the very negative value of the reaction constant $(\rho = -23)$ obtained from the latter approach. Rather, these results should be taken, at the present stage of development, simply to indicate that the

J. H. Espenson

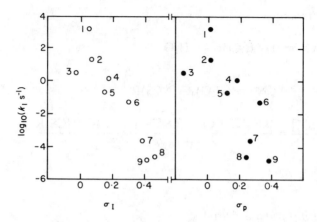

Fig. 6. The correlations of the rate constants for dissociation of the *trans*-water in the complexes $(H_2O)_5CrR^{2+}$ ($R = -CH_2OH$, 1; $-CH_2OCH_3$, 2; $-CH(CH_3)_2$, 3; $-CH_2CN$, 4; $-CH_2Cl$, 5; and $-CHCl_2$, 6) and $(H_2O)_5CrX^{2+}$ ($X = I$, 7; Cl, 8; and NCS, 9) with the Hammett substituent constants σ_I and σ_p are shown.

dissociation rates of water reflect polar effects in the direction expected and to a very pronounced extent.

A similar complex of F^- and $(H_2O)_5CrCF_3^{2+}$ has been observed,[22] but quantitative data are not available.

The accelerating effect of the group R on ligand exchange processes can best be compared by citing $t_{1/2}$ for the equilibration process under a given set of conditions. Values at $[SCN^-] = 0.100$ M and 25°C are as follows: $-CH_2OH$, 0.011 s; $-CH_2OCH_3$, 0.10 s; $-CH(CH_3)_2$, 5.4 s; $-CH_2Cl$, 42 s; $-CH_2CN$, 77 s; and $-CHCl_2$, 128 s. In contrast, the value of $t_{1/2}$ for anation of $Cr(OH_2)_6^{3+}$ is 9.3×10^6 s or $\sim 10^2$ days.[106] The halide groups produce acceleration, although not nearly as large, $t_{1/2}$ for water exchange being 2.6×10^3 s (I), 2.9×10^4 s (Cl), and 4.6×10^4 s (NCS).[105]

C. Structural data; the ground-state *trans* influence

What limited structural data are available show that there is a substantial lengthening of the chromium–ligand distance *trans* to the chromium–carbon bond. Table 11 summarizes the bond lengths for the few compounds examined to date. Three of the compounds are of the general family $[cis\text{-}(aryl)_2Cr(bipy)_2]I$. In every case the chromium–nitrogen bond length *trans* to a carbon is longer than that *trans* to a nitrogen.[80,107–109] The difference is some 0.05–0.08 Å, which is a very appreciable bond extension.

TABLE 11

Metal–ligand bond distances in organochromium complexes

Compound	Bond Lengths(Å)		Ref.
	Cr–N in C–Cr–N	Cr–N in N–Cr–N	
[*cis*-Ph₂Cr(bipy)₂]I	2·147	2·087	[107]
[(*cis*-Me₃SiCH₂)₂Cr(bipy)₂]I	2·156	2·103	[108]
[(*cis*-2-MeOC₆H₄)₂Cr(bipy)₂]I	2·156	2·071	[80]
cis-n-C₃F₇Cr(Me₂NCS₂)₂NC₅H₅	2·457ᵃ	2·392ᵃ	[109]

ᵃ CrS in C–Cr–S and Cr–S in S–Cr–S.

Such effects are not unique to organochromium(III) complexes. Kinetic and structural data for many metal alkyl and aryl complexes show similar effects. There are many examples in cobalt(III) complexes of labile groups *trans* to a Co–C bond. Structural data for these substances also support a lengthening of the metal–ligand bond *trans* to carbon. It is only reasonable to presume that the structural distortion is largely responsible for the increased rate of ligand dissociation, or in general a strong ground-state influence.

D. Anion effects in acidolysis reactions

Early indications were that the coordination sphere of CrR^{2+} complexes may be more labile to ligand substitution reactions than typical for inorganic chromium(III) complexes. Coordinating anions such as $CH_3CO_2^-$, $CH_2ClCO_2^-$, I^-, Br^-, Cl^-, N_3^- and NCS^- were found to accelerate the decomposition of $(H_2O)_5CrCH_2C_6H_5^{2+}$.[75] The interpretation offered then, and subsequently supported by other results (sections V.A, B) was that the effect was caused by penetration of the anion into the primary coordination sphere.

Regrettably no quantitative work has been done which would enable a sorting out of the two effects: ligand substitution and subsequent accelerated acidolysis. One presumes that the *trans* product, $(H_2O)_4Cr(X)R^+$, is subject to more facile attack by H_3O^+ on the α-carbon atom of R because it has been made more negative by the inductive effect of the good sigma donor X^-. One might also presume that the kinetically inert $(H_2O)_5CrX^{2+}$ would be the product, although entry of free X^- into the site being vacated by R could lead to *trans*-$(H_2O)_4CrX_2^+$. At the present these remain but presumptions.

VI. REACTIONS OF $Cr^{III}R$ COMPLEXES WITH ELECTROPHILES

A. Electrophilic displacement reactions and reaction products

A general reaction of alkylmetals including $Cr^{III}R$ complexes is the cleavage of the metal–carbon bond which occurs upon reaction with electrophiles.[110,111] The equation applicable to the specific case of $(H_2O)_5CrR^{2+}$ complexes is

$$(H_2O)_5CrR^{2+} + E^+ + H_2O = Cr(OH_2)_6^{3+} + E\!-\!R \tag{50}$$

where E^+ represents Hg^{2+}, RHg^+, Br_2, IBr, NO^+, Tl^{3+}, Hg_2^{2+}, and the previously considered case of H_3O^+ (Section IV). Before considering specific cases, mention of features applicable to the entire set is in order: (1) Each reaction (except H_3O^+) follows second-order kinetics; the mechanisms must be formulated as displacement processes, and the terminology of an S_E2 mechanism (bimolecular electrophilic substitution) will prove useful; (2) The system deemed most likely to show unimolecular kinetics (S_E1 mechanism), if any would, was $(H_2O)_5CrCH_2C_5H_4NH^{3+}$; no evidence for an electrophile-independent kinetic term was obtained;[112,113] (3) Many alkylmetals are prone to oxidation by the electrophilic reagents, which are often strong oxidizing species as well. It is not always easy to distinguish such oxidative processes, which tend to involve one-electron reactions, from two-electron electrophilic pathways.[114] As best as can be discerned, however, oxidative processes are unimportant for $(H_2O)_5CrR^{2+}$ complexes, and they thus afford systems in which the characteristics of authentic two-electron displacements can be explored for complexes with a wide range of X groups.

The kinetic characteristics of chromium(III) are such that the product composition can reflect structural details of the transition state. This has been very useful in ruling out four-centred transition states or S_{Ei} mechanisms. Reactions of $(H_2O)_5CrR^{2+}$ with HgX^+, HgX_3^-, or X_2 never form $(H_2O)_5CrX^{2+}$. This implies no Cr–X bond or bridge exists in the transition state.

B. Reactions with mercury(II) electrophiles

A considerable amount of kinetic data is now available on the reactions of $(H_2O)_5CrR^{2+}$ complexes with Hg^{2+}.[15,23,90,115,116] Less complete studies have also been conducted on related reactions, including $(H_2O)_5CrR^{2+}$ + CH_3Hg^+ (and other $R'Hg^+$ reagents), $[RCr([15]aneN_4)OH_2]^{2+}$ + Hg^{2+} and CH_3Hg^+,[117] and $(H_2O)_5CrR^{2+}$ + $Hg^{II}Cl_n^{2-n}$.[115] The net reactions and their laws follow the following patterns:

$$(H_2O)_5CrR^{2+} + Hg^{2+} + H_2O \longrightarrow Cr(OH_2)_6^{3+} + RHg^+ \tag{51}$$

$$-d[CrR^{2+}]/dt = k_{Hg}[CrR^{2+}][Hg^{2+}] \tag{52}$$

$$(H_2O)_5CrR^{2+} + R'Hg^+ + H_2O \longrightarrow Cr(OH_2)_6^{3+} + R'HgR \tag{53}$$

$$-d[CrR^{2+}]/dt = k_{R'Hg}[CrR^{2+}][R'Hg^+] \tag{54}$$

Table 12 gives the rate constants for various reactions. The activation parameters, in the cases where they have been determined, are given in Table 13. Some general features should be noted: (1) The rate constant is very sensitive to the extent of substitution on the alpha carbon atom. (2) The lower electrophilicity of $R'Hg^+$ as compared to Hg^{2+} is quite

TABLE 12

Rate constants[a] for reactions of mercury(II) electrophiles with $[L_5Cr^{III}R]^{2+}$ complexes according to Equations (51)–(54)

R	$(H_2O)_5CrR^{2+}$		Ref.	$[RCr([15]aneN_4)OH_2]^{2+d}$	
	k_{Hg} ($M^{-1} s^{-1}$)	$k_{CH_3Hg^+}$ ($M^{-1} s^{-1}$)		k_{Hg} ($M^{-1} s^{-1}$)	$k_{CH_3Hg^+}$ ($M^{-1} s^{-1}$)
(a) Alkyls					
$-CH_3$	$(1.0 \pm 0.1) \times 10^7$	$(1.00 \pm 0.02) \times 10^{4\,b}$	[15]	$(3.1 \pm 0.2) \times 10^6$	$(1.63 \pm 0.02) \times 10^3$
$-CH_2CH_3$	$(1.40 \pm 0.06) \times 10^5$	$(1.99 \pm 0.04) \times 10^2$	[15]	$(2.53 \pm 0.03) \times 10^3$	$(9.9 \pm 0.4) \times 10^0$
$-n\text{-}C_3H_7$	$(3.50 \pm 0.17) \times 10^4$	$(1.21 \pm 0.08) \times 10^2$	[15]	$(8.21 \pm 0.04) \times 10^1$	
$-n\text{-}C_4H_9$			[15]	$(4.88 \pm 0.17) \times 10^1$	
$-CH_2C(CH_3)_3$	$(4.9 \pm 0.2) \times 10^2$	$(5.8 \pm 0.6) \times 10^0$	[15]		
$-CH(CH_3)_2$	$(1.56 \pm 0.01) \times 10^0$		[62]	$(4.3 \pm 0.4) \times 10^{-3}$	
$-c\text{-}C_5H_9$	$(1.03 \pm 0.08) \times 10^0$			$(7.6 \pm 0.4) \times 10^{-3}$	
$-c\text{-}C_6H_{11}$				$(3.1 \pm 0.1) \times 10^{-3}$	
-1-adamantyl					
(b) Substituted alkyls					
$-CH_2Cl$	$(5.90 \pm 0.15) \times 10^{-1}$	6×10^{-4}	[15]		
$-CH_2Br$	$(4.68 \pm 0.26) \times 10^{-1}$		[15]		
$-CF_3$	$\sim 10^{-6}$		[15]		
$-CH_2CN$	$(9.8 \pm 0.3) \times 10^0$		[23]		
$-CH_2CH_2CN$	$(8.10 \pm 0.30) \times 10^1$		[23]		
$-CH_2CH(CH_3)CN$	$(2.54 \pm 0.01) \times 10^1$		[23]		
$-CH_2OH$	$(2.28 \pm 0.01) \times 10^2$		[116]		
$-CH_2OCH_3$	$(9.05 \pm 0.08) \times 10^1$		[116]		
(c) Aralkyls					
$-CH_2C_6H_5$	$(4.87 \pm 0.22) \times 10^4$	$(9.8 \pm 0.1) \times 10^{1\,c}$	[15]	$(1.14 \pm 0.03) \times 10^3$	$(5.2 \pm 0.1) \times 10^0$
$-p\text{-}CH_2C_6H_4CH_3$	$(5.22 \pm 0.27) \times 10^4$	$(1.21 \pm 0.05) \times 10^2$	[15]		
$-p\text{-}CH_2C_6H_4Br$	$(2.98 \pm 0.07) \times 10^4$	$(5.68 \pm 0.18) \times 10^1$	[15]		
$-p\text{-}CH_2C_6H_4CF_3$	$(2.10 \pm 0.06) \times 10^4$	$(3.47 \pm 0.08) \times 10^1$	[15]		
$-p\text{-}CH_2C_6H_4CN$	$(1.64 \pm 0.08) \times 10^4$	$(2.39 \pm 0.04) \times 10^1$	[15]		
$-p\text{-}CH_2C_6H_4CN$		1.66×10^1 (D_2O)	[94]		
$-2\text{-}CH_2C_5H_4NH^+$	$(3.0 \pm 0.2) \times 10^1$		[115]		
$-3\text{-}CH_2C_5H_4NH^+$	$(2.05 \pm 0.30) \times 10^2$		[115]		
$-4\text{-}CH_2C_5H_4NH^+$	$(5.0 \pm 0.3) \times 10^2$		[115]		
$-m\text{-}CH_2C_6H_4\text{-}O\text{-}m\text{-}C_6H_4CH_2Cr^{2+}$	$(4.74 \pm 0.02) \times 10^4$		[89]		
$-m\text{-}CH_2C_6H_4\text{-}O\text{-}m\text{-}C_6H_4CH_2Br$	$(2.09 \pm 0.09) \times 10^4$		[89]		

[a] At 25°C in water; Ionic strength was controlled at 0.50 M in data from Refs. [15], [62], [89], [115] and [117], and at 1.00 M in Refs. [23] and [116], except for $CrCF_3^{2+}$, $\mu = 1.7$ M. $[RCr([15]aneN_4)OH_2]^{2+}$, $\mu = 1.46$ M for secondary R groups. Values of k are independent of $[H^+]$, 0.01–0.5 (or 1.0) M.
[b] For other $R'Hg^+$ reagents the rate constant is 1.6×10^4 $M^{-1} s^{-1}$ (PhHgOAc) and 1.1×10^4 $M^{-1} s^{-1}$ (CH3HgOAc).
[c] For other $R'Hg^+$ reagents the rate constant is 40 $M^{-1} s^{-1}$ (PhHgOAc) and 65 $M^{-1} s^{-1}$ (CH3HgOAc) at $\mu = 0.1$ M.
[d] Ref. [117].

TABLE 13

Activation parameters for reactions of $[L_5Cr^{III}R]^{2+}$ with electrophiles

$[L_5CrR]^{2+}$	Electrophile	$\Delta H^{\ddagger}$ (kJ mol^{-1})	$\Delta S^{\ddagger}$ (J mol^{-1} K^{-1})	Ref.
(a) Mercury(II) electrophiles				
$[(H_2O)_5Cr\!-\!n\text{-}C_3H_7]^{2+}$	Hg^{2+}	$13\cdot8 \pm 0\cdot3$	-111 ± 11	[15]
$[H_2O)_5Cr\!-\!n\text{-}C_3H_7]^{2+}$	CH_3Hg^+	$28\cdot6 \pm 2\cdot4$	-109 ± 8	[15]
$[(H_2O)_5Cr\!-\!CH_2Cl]^{2+}$	Hg^{2+}	$39\cdot8 \pm 0\cdot8$	-116 ± 3	[15]
$[(H_2O)_5Cr\!-\!CH_2OCH_3]^{2+}$	Hg^{2+}	$38\cdot6 \pm 0\cdot3$	$-77\cdot8 \pm 0\cdot8$	[116]
$[(H_2O)_5Cr\!-\!CH_2CH_2CN]^{2+}$	Hg^{2+}	$28\cdot9 \pm 1\cdot9$	-111 ± 6	[23]
$CH_3CH_2Cr([15]aneN_4)OH_2]^{2+}$	Hg^{2+}	$30\cdot2 \pm 1\cdot2$	-77 ± 4	[117]
$n\text{-}C_3H_7Cr([15]aneN_4)OH_2]^{2+}$	Hg^{2+}	$48\cdot8 \pm 1\cdot5$	-45 ± 5	[117]
$n\text{-}C_4H_9Cr([15]aneN_4)OH_2]^{2+}$	Hg^{2+}	$33\cdot5 \pm 2\cdot1$	-100 ± 7	[117]
$C_6H_5CH_2Cr([15]aneN_4)OH_2]^{2+}$	Hg^{2+}	$33\cdot4 \pm 1\cdot6$	-75 ± 5	[117]
(b) Halogen electrophiles				
$[(H_2O)_5CrCH_2Cl]^{2+}$	Br_2	$33\cdot1 \pm 1\cdot8$	-134 ± 6	[100]
$[(H_2O)_5CrC_2H_5]^{2+}$	Br_2	$44\cdot8 \pm 3\cdot3$	15 ± 11	[100]
$[(H_2O)_5CrCH(CH_3)_2]^{2+}$	Br_2	$19\cdot6 \pm 2\cdot4$	$-99\cdot3 \pm 7\cdot8$	[62]

evident, k_{Hg} being 10^2–10^3 times larger than $k_{R'Hg}$ for a given CrR^{2+} complex, but different $R'Hg^+$ electrophiles ($R' = CH_3$, C_6H_5, and $C_6H_5CH_2$) show only minor differences. A similar trend is noted for $Hg^{II}Cl_n^{2-n}$ electrophiles, whose reactivity falls with increasing chloride substitution, especially the first.[115] (3) The substitution of electronegative substituents in the complex, and especially on the alpha carbon atom, lowers the reactivity. This is a feature expected of an electrophilic reaction, since such substitution renders the group R less carbanion-like. The ultimate situation is reached with $CrCF_3^{2+}$, which does not react with Hg^{2+}. (4) The rate increases mildly as electron-donating substituents are added at the *para* position of benzyl-chromium ion, and vice versa. The data are correlated well with the Hammett substituent constant σ_p, the reaction constants being $\rho = -0.62 \pm 0.05$ for Hg^{2+} amd -0.85 ± 0.05 for CH_3Hg^+.[15] The negative values of ρ are indicative of an activated complex in which the reaction centre (the benzylic carbon atom) is somewhat more positive in the activated complex following partial transfer to the cationic electrophile, than in the parent CrR^{2+} complex.

These observations are all consistent with the S_E2 mechanism. Further comparisons are best made in conjunction with results for other electrophilic reagents (Section VI.E).

C. Reactions with halogen electrophiles

The most extensive work has been done on the reactions of $(H_2O)_5CrR^{2+}$ complexes with aqueous bromine. Some results are also available for IBr and I_2.[100,118,119] The reactions occurring in the case of Br_2 and IBr are:

$$(H_2O)_5CrR^{2+} + Br_2 + H_2O \longrightarrow Cr(H_2O)_6^{3+} + RBr + Br^- \qquad (55)$$

$$(H_2O)_5CrR^{2+} + IBr + H_2O \longrightarrow Cr(H_2O)_6^{3+} + RI + Br^- \qquad (56)$$

where it is important to note that $Cr(H_2O)_6^{3+}$ and free bromide ions are produced rather than the kinetically inert $(H_2O)_5CrBr^{2+}$, which would have been isolable under the reaction conditions. Iodine monobromide produces $RI + Br^-$ rather than $RBr + I^-$, consistent with the S_E2 mechanism since the polarity $I^{\delta+} - Br^{\delta-}$ suggests that it is the positive end of the dipolar molecule which should attack the carbanion-like alkyl group.

The various halogens react with CrR^{2+} according to the rate equation

$$-d[CrR^{2+}]/dt = k_{XY}[CrR^{2+}][XY] \qquad (57)$$

Values of the rate constants k_{XY} are given in Table 14 and activation parameters for two reactions in Table 13. Bromine and IBr react at similar rates, and they react more rapidly than I_2. The trends in rate constant with

TABLE 14

Rate constants[a] for reactions of $(H_2O)_5CrR^{2+}$ complexes with halogen electrophiles according to Equations (55)–(57)

R	k_{Br_2} ($M^{-1}\,s^{-1}$)	Ref.	XY	k_{XY} ($M^{-1}\,s^{-1}$)	Ref.
(a) Alkyls					
—CH_3	$(2.1 \pm 0.2) \times 10^6$	[100]	I_2	$(8.5 \pm 1.1) \times 10^4$	[62]
—C_2H_5	$(4.9 \pm 0.5) \times 10^5$	[100]			
—$n\text{-}C_3H_7$	$(6.2 \pm 0.1) \times 10^5$	[100]			
—$CH_2C(CH_3)_3$	$(9.9 \pm 0.6) \times 10^3$	[100]			
—$CH(CH_3)_2$	$(1.70 \pm 0.05) \times 10^4$	[62]	IBr	$(3.54 \pm 0.22) \times 10^1$	[119]
—$c\text{-}C_5H_9$	$(1.13 \pm 0.10) \times 10^4$	[62]	I_2	8.8×10^0	[62]
(b) Substituted alkyls					
—CH_2Cl	$(1.06 \pm 0.06) \pm 10^0$	[100]	IBr	$(6.3 \pm 0.6) \times 10^{-1}$	[119]
	5.14×10^{-1} (D_2O)	[94]			
	$(3.5 \pm 0.3) \times 10^{-1}$	[100]			
—CH_2Br	$(7.13 \pm 0.06) \times 10^0$	[100]			
—CH_2I	$(6.8 \pm 0.3) \times 10^0$	[100]			
—$CH(Cl)CH_3$	$<3 \times 10^{-3}$	[100]			
—$CHCl_2$					
—CH_2COOH	6.8×10^{-3} (20°C)	[92]			
(c) Aralkyls					
—$CH_2C_6H_5$	8.3×10^5	[118]	I_2	4.20×10^3	[118]
			IBr	$(1.16 \pm 0.09) \times 10^6$	[119]
—$p\text{-}CH_2C_6H_4Br$	2.32×10^5	[118]	I_2	2.26×10^3	[118]
—$p\text{-}CH_2C_6H_4CF_3$	1.55×10^5	[118]	I_2	1.39×10^3	[118]
			IBr	$(2.21 \pm 0.12) \times 10^5$	[119]
—$p\text{-}CH_2C_6H_4CN$	9.6×10^4	[118]	I_2	1.06×10^3	[118]
—$p\text{-}CH_2C_6H_4CH_3$			I_2	4.76×10^3	[118]
			IBr	$(1.0 \pm 0.2) \times 10^6$	[119]
—$4\text{-}CH_2C_5H_4NH^+$	$(1.1 \pm 0.3) \times 10^3$	[100]			

[a] At 25.0°C and 1.00 M ionic strength.

TABLE 15

Rate constants (25°C) for pyridinomethyl(pentaaquo)chromium(III) ions and various electrophiles

Electrophile	k (M⁻¹ s⁻¹)			Ref.
	—2-CH$_2$C$_5$H$_4$NH$^+$	—3-CH$_2$C$_5$H$_4$NH$^+$	—4-CH$_2$C$_5$H$_4$NH$^+$	
Hg^{2+}	$3 \cdot 0 \times 10^1$	$2 \cdot 05 \times 10^2$	$5 \cdot 00 \times 10^2$	[115]
HgCl$^+$	$3 \cdot 3$	$3 \cdot 5 \times 10^1$	$1 \cdot 4 \times 10^2$	[113]
HgCl$_2$	$1 \cdot 7 \times 10^{-1}$	$1 \cdot 5$	$3 \cdot 2$	[113]
HgBr$_2$			$8 \cdot 7 \times 10^{-1}$	[113]
HgCl$_3^-$	$5 \cdot 0 \times 10^{-1}$	$6 \cdot 0$	$7 \cdot 3$	[113]
Hg$_2^{2+}$	$8 \cdot 3$	$1 \cdot 1 \times 10^2$	$1 \cdot 75 \times 10^2$	[120, 121]
TlCl$_3$	$0 \cdot 4$	$8 \cdot 4$	$6 \cdot 1$	[113]
Br$_2$			$1 \cdot 1 \times 10^3$	[100]

change in R group are remarkably similar to the changes in k_{Hg} among the same complexes. This is further evidence that oxidative processes are not involved. The latter is an important point since many alkylmetals react with halogens and Hg(II) by oxidation.[114] A series of *para*-substituted complexes $(H_2O)_5CrCH_2C_6H_4X^{2+}$ have been studied for the Br_2 and I_2 reactions.[118] The data correlate well with the Hammett equation, and the substantial negative values of the reaction constant—$\rho = -1\cdot29$ (Br_2) and $\rho = -0\cdot81$ (I_2)—support the assignment of the S_E2 mechanism.

D. Reactions with other electrophiles

No other electrophiles have been studied with an extensive series of CrR^{2+} complexes. However, data are available for numerous electrophiles reacting with 2-, 3-, and 4-pyridinomethylchromium(III) complexes. These values are given in Table 15. Even mercurous ion is electrophilic enough toward these complexes to react directly with them, rather than by the low concentration of Hg^{2+} in equilibrium with it. The latter often provides the major pathway for other alkylmetals.[120, 121]

It would seem that in every case the products and kinetics are consistent with an S_E2 mechanism. The transition state probably has an "open" structure, in the sense that groups on chromium, on the organic group R, or on the electrophile do not interact in its formation. The structure which suggests itself is:

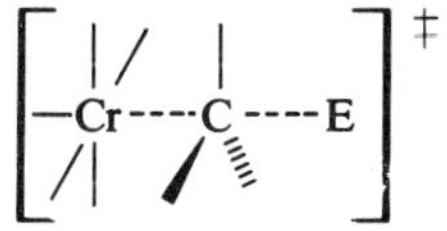

$$\left[\begin{array}{c} | \diagup \quad | \\ -Cr----C----E \\ \diagup | \quad \diagup \end{array} \right]^{\ddagger}$$

E. Stereochemistry of the S_E2 reactions of $[L_5Cr^{III}R]^{2+}$ complexes

As of the present time no organochromium complex of the sorts being considered in this review has been prepared having a chiral carbon bound to the metal. Thus not one determination of stereochemistry, nor any assessment of the stereospecificity, has been made for any reaction. The best that can be done at present is to compare the change in rate constant with variations in the structure of R for various reactions, including what are believed to be similar reactions proceeding by similar mechanisms for other alkylmetals.

This is not entirely satisfactory, for other assignments made on that basis[122] have later been shown to have been in error.[123] Nonetheless if the analogues are carefully chosen there may be some validity to it, especially if the known stereochemical extremes show distinctly different

TABLE 16

Relative rates[a] and stereochemistry of electrophilic substitution reactions of monoalkyl metal complexes

Reaction	Stereochemistry	$k/k_{C_2H_5}$ at 25°C				Ref.
		—CH$_3$	—n-C$_3$H$_7$	—CH$_2$C(CH$_3$)$_3$	—CH(CH$_3$)$_2$	
(H$_2$O)$_5$CrR^{2+} + Hg^{2+}	?	71	0·25	$3 \cdot 5 \times 10^{-3}$	$1 \cdot 1 \times 10^{-5}$	[15]
(H$_2$O)$_5$CrR^{2+} + CH$_3$Hg$^+$	?	50	0·61	$2 \cdot 9 \times 10^{-2}$		[15]
(H$_2$O)$_5$CrR^{2+} + Br$_2$	?	4·3	1·3	$2 \cdot 0 \times 10^{-2}$	$\sim 7 \times 10^{-5}$	[100, 119]
RCo(dmgH)$_2$OH$_2$ + Hg^{2+}	inversion	530	0·74	$7 \cdot 4 \times 10^{-2}$	$<5 \times 10^{-6}$	[123, 124]
RSn(CH$_2$C(CH$_3$)$_3$)$_3$ + Br$_2$	inversion	6·9	0·28	$4 \cdot 0 \times 10^{-3}$	$5 \cdot 2 \times 10^{-2}$	[125]
R$_2$Hg + HgBr$_2$	retention	2·4		0·78		[126, 127]
RHgBr + HCl	retention	0·16	0·62		0·68	[128]
"Typical S$_N$2"	inversion	33	0·04	10^{-6}	3×10^{-3}	[129]

[a] As given in Ref. [15].

trends in reactivity. Relative rates for a group of such reactions[15,100,119,123–129] are given in Table 16. The trends manifest in these results do indicate a different pattern for retention as opposed to inversion, and that the reaction of $(H_2O)_5CrR^{2+}$ complexes with Hg^{2+}, CH_3Hg^+, Br_2, and H_3O^+ conform more closely to the latter.

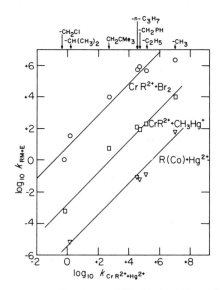

Fig. 7. The rate constants for electrophilic displacement of alkyl-metals correlate with one another. The plot shows the rate constants for three electrophilic reactions plotted on a logarithmic scale against log k for the series $(H_2O)_5CrR^{2+} + Hg^{2+}$.

An interesting linear free-energy relationship is found for several of these reactions. Figure 7 depicts a plot (on a logarithmic scale) showing the rate constant for each series plotted against one chosen as the standard.[130] The quality of the correlation is high and the lines shown are not necessarily the best fits, but were each drawn to have a slope of unity. The similarity of mechanism is strongly suggested, and it seems likely that this extends to stereochemistry as well.

VII. HOMOLYTIC DISPLACEMENT REACTIONS

The type of reaction to be considered here is known as bimolecular homolytic substitution, and is referred to as proceeding by the S_H2 mechanism. It is the one-electron reaction of a metal alkyl leading to alkyl transfer, formally alkyl radical transfer. The following pair of reactions shows the contrast between it and the two-electron transformation associated with the S_E2 mechanism:

$$CrR^{2+} + {}^*Cr^{2+} \longrightarrow Cr^{2+} + {}^*CrR^{2+} \qquad (S_H2 \text{ Mechanism}) \qquad (58)$$

$$CrR^{2+} + Hg^{2+} \longrightarrow Cr^{3+} + HgR^+ \qquad (S_E2 \text{ Mechanism}) \qquad (59)$$

Another example is the transalkylation reaction referred to earlier (Section II.E.1) which provides a route to CrR^{2+} complexes:

$$RCo(dmgH)_2OH_2 + Cr^{2+} \rightarrow CrR^{2+} + Co^{II}(dmgH)_2OH_2 \qquad (60)$$

A. Chromium atom exchange between Cr^{2+} and $(H_2O)_5CrR^{2+}$

The exchange between ${}^{51}Cr^{2+}$ and CrR^{2+} shown in Equation (58) takes place readily for $R = $ —4-$CH_2C_5H_4NH^{+}$[36] and —$CH_2C_6H_5$.[131] No exchange occurs between $CrCH_2Cl^{2+}$ $(2 \cdot 4 \times 10^{-3} \text{ M})$ and ${}^{51}Cr^{2+}$ $(2 \cdot 4 \times 10^{-2} \text{ M})$ over 90 min in 1 M $HClO_4$, and also none between $CrCHCl_2^{2+}$ $(6 \times 10^{-3} \text{ M})$ and ${}^{51}Cr^{2+}$ $(1 \cdot 5 \times 10^{-2} \text{ M})$ in the same time.[18] (The latter pair does react chemically to about 50% completion in that time—Section VIII.E.) As expected, none of the organochromium ions examined undergo exchange with $Cr(H_2O)_6^{3+}$.

In the two cases cited the rate of chromium exchange given by

$$R_{ex} = k_{ex}[Cr^{2+}][CrR^{2+}] \qquad (61)$$

with $k_{ex} = 5 \cdot 8 \times 10^{-2} \text{ M}^{-1} \text{ s}^{-1}$ for $R = $ —4-$CH_2C_5H_4NH^+$ at 55°C, 1·00 M $HClO_4$,[36] and $6 \cdot 0 \times 10^{-2} \text{ M}^{-1} \text{ s}^{-1}$ for $R = $ —CH_2Ph at 1·00 M $HClO_4$, extrapolated to 25°C $(\Delta H^{\ddagger} = 43 \cdot 4 \text{ kJ mol}^{-1}, \Delta S^{\ddagger} = -123 \text{ J mol}^{-1} \text{ K}^{-1})$.[131]

In view of the reversibility of the homolytic decomposition reactions of these two complexes—the respective rate constants being $5 \cdot 2 \times 10^{-5} \text{ s}^{-1}$ and $2 \cdot 6 \times 10^{-3} \text{ s}^{-1}$ under conditions identical with those cited above—should exchange not occur accordingly? There is every reason to believe that it does. The observed rate expression of Equation (61) implies that the bimolecular pathway is more favourable at the temperatures and chromium(II) ion concentrations used, and simply supersedes the unimolecular pathway.

Based on results in other systems shortly to be considered this exchange process should occur in many complexes. The value of k_{ex} is likely to be markedly affected by the steric bulk of the substituents on the alkyl group R.

B. Transfer of groups from alkylmetals to chromium(II)

One reaction leading to $(H_2O)_5CrR^{2+}$ complexes consists of the reaction of Cr^{2+} with a suitably chosen organometallic compound. Examples of this are the reactions occurring between organo-bis(dimethylglyoxi-mato)cobalt(III) complexes,[19] Equation (60). The reaction seems to be a quite general one for other organocobalt(chelate) complexes, and has been examined mostly for tetradenate macrocyclic ligands, including the cobalt corrins (cobalamins or Vitamin B_{12} derivatives[63]). The mechanism does *not* involve a unimolecular scission of the cobalt–carbon bond, which is totally negligible for these compounds. Rather, the rate follows second-order kinetics:

$$d[CrR^{2+}]/dt = k[Cr^{2+}][RCo(dmgH)_2OH_2] \qquad (62)$$

There is a mild dependence on $[H^+]$, since the oxime-protonated complex, in a rapid equilibrium with the parent complex, reacts with Cr^{2+} as well. The rate constants obtained for a series of organocobalt compounds are

TABLE 17
Rate constants[a] for the alkyl-transfer reactions between Cr^{2+} and $RCo(dmgH)_2OH_2$ according to Equations (60) and (62)

R	k ($M^{-1} s^{-1}$)
—CH_3	1.45×10^1 (3.6×10^2)[b]
—C_2H_5	1.3×10^{-2} (4.4×10^0)[b]
—n-C_3H_7	1.4×10^{-3}
—CH_2C(CH_3)_3	6.1×10^{-5}
i-C_3H_7	1.1×10^{-4}
—CH_2C_6H_5	5.0×10^0

[a] At 25·0°C in $HClO_4$–$LiClO_4$ medium having ionic strength 1·00 M; data from Ref. [19].
[b] For RCo(corrin); data from Ref. [63].

given in Table 17. The reactivity is greatest for methyl and benzyl, and drops off sharply for the more sterically hindered alkyl groups.

Although perhaps incidental to the main subject of the review, it should be noted that reactions of this type appear to be a fairly general process, occurring between Co(II) and RCo(III),[64,132–134] Sn(II) and RCo(III),[135] and perhaps other systems as well. The stability of the cobalt(II) products make them attractive one-electron leaving groups which is just the characteristic needed to favour homolytic displacement. Carbon-centred radicals may effect a similar displacement:[136]

$\cdot CCl_3 + PhCH_2Co(dmgH)_2NC_5H_5 \longrightarrow$

$$PhCH_2CCl_3 + Co(dmgH)_2NC_5H_5 \quad (63)$$

Transfer of R from mercury to chromium has been suggested to play a role in the reaction of RHg^+ and Cr^{2+}.[137] Proof of the suggested intervention of CrR^{2+} complexes in this reaction has not been obtained.

C. The S$_H$2 mechanism

In the terminology of organic displacement reactions, the description "S$_{H}$2 Mechanism" characterizes processes such as those in Equations (58), (60), and (63). In the terminology used for oxidation–reduction reactions in coordination chemistry, they might be referred to as inner-sphere electron transfers employing an electron-deficient bridging ligand. It has been argued[130] that these are equivalent descriptions, although they initially strike one as being quite different. An analysis of the energetics and dynamics of methyl exchange has been given.[64]

The data for Equation (60) in Table 17 shows the strong steric constraints. The data suggest that attack of the one-electron reagent occurs away from the metal–carbon bond, which would lead to inversion of configuration at carbon. This has been established for the Co-for-Co exchange,[134] but not for the Cr^{2+} reactions. It is interesting to note that Equation (60) should be capable of yielding chiral CrR^{2+} complexes, but the very low rates of the more highly substituted organocobalt complexes tried to date have precluded development of this theme.

VIII. OTHER REACTIONS OF ORGANOCHROMIUM(III) COMPLEXES

In this final section there are considered a number of other reactions of $(H_2O)_5CrR^{2+}$ complexes which have been examined from a mechanistic viewpoint. These reactions appear to be limited to particular R groups owing to the special features of reactivity involved in the individual cases.

A. Reaction with O$_2$

Primary alkyl organochromium(III) complexes are stable toward oxygen. Aralkyls react with O_2 only by prior, rate-limiting homolysis. For some (e.g. $CrCH_2Ph^{2+}$) the reaction is fairly rapid, for others (e.g. $CrCH_2C_5H_4NH^{3+}$) it is so slow that they were originally formulated as "air-stable" species. In either case, however, the reaction with O_2 proceeds at the identical rate as found for other reagents capable of oxidizing Cr^{2+} or $R\cdot$ (Section III).

The 2-propyl(pentaaquo)chromium(III) complex is quite different.[26,138] The cyclopentyl complex is as well,[62] and presumably so are other secondary and tertiary complexes not yet examined. The reaction of $(H_2O)_5CrCH(CH_3)_2^{2+}$ with O_2 is much faster than homolysis; the former requires a few minutes, the latter has $t_{1/2} \sim 1$ hour). There is evidence in the kinetic data, products, inhibition experiments, and concentration effects that the reaction follows a chain mechanism.[26,138] The situation can be summarized by noting that the approximate stoichiometric reaction occurring is:

$$CrCH(CH_3)_2^{2+} + O_2 + H^+ = Cr^{3+} + (CH_3)_2CO + H_2O \qquad (64)$$

The reaction rate (at $[CrCH(CH_3)_2^{2+}]_0 > \sim 10^{-4}\,M$) is given by:

$$-d[CrCH(CH_3)_2^{2+}]/dt = k_{exp}[CrCH(CH_3)_2^{2+}]^{3/2} \qquad (65)$$

with $k_{exp} = 0.49 \pm 0.06\,M^{-1/2}\,s^{-1}$ at 25°C and $\mu = 1.00\,M$, independent of $[O_2]$ and $[H^+]$. A chain mechanism consistent with the kinetic data is

Initiation: $CrCH(CH_3)_2^{2+} \xrightarrow{k_1} Cr^{2+} + \cdot CH(CH_3)_2 \qquad (66)$

Propagation: $\cdot CH(CH_3)_2 + O_2 \xrightarrow{k_2} (CH_3)_2CHOO\cdot \qquad (67)$

$(CH_3)_2CHOO\cdot + CrCH(CH_3)_2^{2+} \xrightarrow{k_3} CrOOCH(CH_3)_2^{2+} + \cdot CH(CH_3)_2 \qquad (68)$

$CrOOCH(CH_3)_2^{2+} + H^+ \xrightarrow{\text{fast}} Cr^{3+} + (CH_3)_2CO + H_2O \qquad (69)$

Termination: $2(CH_3)_2CHOO\cdot \xrightarrow{k_4}$

$$(CH_3)_2CHOH + (CH_3)_2CO + O_2 \quad (70)$$

The steady-state rate law for this mechanism is

$$\frac{-d[CrCH(CH_3)_2^{2+}]}{dt} = k_1[CrCH(CH_3)_2^{2+}] + k_3(k_1/2k_4)^{1/2}[CrCH(CH_3)_2^{2+}]^{3/2} \qquad (71)$$

which reduces, in the limit of long chain lengths, (i.e., $[CrCH(CH_3)_2^{2+}]_0 > \sim 10^{-4}\,M$, to Equation (65), the experimental rate constant being given by $k_{exp} = k_3(k_1/2k_4)^{1/2}$.

Arguments that can be formulated[26] to support this mechanism over others include specific inhibiting effects of Fe^{2+}, which reacts with $(CH_3)_2CHOO\cdot$, and of Cu^{2+}, which reacts with $\cdot CH(CH_3)_2$.[139,140]

The novel chemical step in the mechanism is the reaction of Equation (68), with $k_3 \sim 6 \times 10^4 \, \mathrm{M}^{-1} \mathrm{s}^{-1}$ at 25°C. It can be regarded as a bimolecular displacement process. Note the contrast between this S_H2 reaction and those discussed before (Section VII). The reaction here is radical attack at the metal with displacement of an alkyl radical, in contrast to the previous examples of displacement of a reduced metal by attack at a saturated carbon atom.

B. Oxidation of α-hydroxyalkylchromium(III) complexes

An extensive series of complexes, $CrCH_2OH^{2+}$, $CrCH(CH_3)OH^{2+}$, $CrC(CH_3)(C_2H_5)OH^{2+}$, etc., has been referred to in earlier sections. The existence of these as stable entities—as stable, that is, as their alkyl and other analogues; they are subject, as the others are, to acidolysis and homolysis reactions—is somewhat surprising. α-Hydroxyalkyl complexes are often not very stable even in organometallic series where the alkyl analogues are well known. The α-hydroxyalkyl group tends to be strongly reducing, as evidenced by many reactions including the notoriously high reducing strength of the free radical and the tendency of organometallic compounds to decompose by internal two-electron reactions:[141,142]

$$[(H_2O)Co^{III}(\text{chel})CH_2OH]^{2+} \rightarrow [H_2OCo^{I}(\text{chel})]^+ + HCHO + H^+ \qquad (72)$$

The inability of chromium to suffer the corresponding reduction to Cr^+ evidently stabilizes $(H_2O)_5CrCH_2OH^{2+}$ and similar species against the corresponding reaction. Nonetheless the complexes themselves are strong but selective reducing agents. Concurrent with the homolysis reactions, they react directly, and usually fairly rapidly, with Cu^{2+} and Fe^{3+}:[143,144]

$$CrCH_2OH^{2+} + Cu^{2+} = Cu^+ + Cr^{2+} + HCHO + H^+ \qquad (73)$$

$$CrCH_2OH^{2+} + Fe^{3+} = Fe^{2+} + Cr^{2+} + HCHO + H^+ \qquad (74)$$

There is no doubt that Cr^{2+} is formed quantitatively in this reaction. It is easily detected in both cases by conducting the reaction in the presence of a scavenger such as $(NH_3)_5CoF^{2+}$, which does not react with $CrCH_2OH^{2+}$ save by the indirect homolytic reaction. Without the scavenging reagent, Cr^{2+} is oxidized in a subsequent step by Cu^{2+} or Fe^{3+}.

The rates of these reactions show a *direct* dependence on $[Cu^{2+}]$ or $[Fe^{3+}]$, it now being assumed that proper allowance has been made for the (usually minor) contribution of the oxidant-independent homolysis and acidolysis reactions. The direct reactions show a strong inverse dependence on $[H^+]$, the rate being given by:[144,145]

$$\frac{-d[CrR^{2+}]}{dt} = \left(k + \frac{k'}{[H^+]}\right)[Ox][CrR^{2+}] \tag{75}$$

for R = an α-hydroxyalkyl group and Ox = Cu^{2+} or Fe^{3+}. The values of k and k' are summarized in Table 18. The latter term is by far the

TABLE 18

Rate constants[a] for the direct oxidation of α-hydroxyalkylchromium complexes by Cu^{2+} and Fe^{3+}

	Cu^{2+}		Fe^{3+}	
R	k (M^{-1} s^{-1})	k' (s^{-1})	k (M^{-1} s^{-1})	k' (s^{-1})
—CH_2OH	0·036	0·251	0·22	0·496
—$CH(CH_3)OH$	0·68	1·46	0·71	0·481
—$CH(C_2H_5)OH$	1·36	1·06	1·1	0·42
—$C(CH_3)_2OH$	0·77	0·574	3·8	1·90
—$C(CH_3)(C_2H_5)OH$	~0	1·46	1·4	13·1
—$C(C_2H_5)_2$	~0	3·3	60	30
—$C(CH_3)$ $(i-C_3H_7)OH$	13·5	11·4	~0	193
—$CH(CF_3)OH$	n.r.[b]		~0	0·13
—CH_2OCH_3	n.r.		0·006	0·013
—$CH(CH_3)OC_2H_5$	n.r.		0·08	0·040

[a] At 24·8–25·0°C and 1·0 M ionic strength in water containing 0·1–1·0 M organic cosolvent. Data from Refs. [144] and [145].
[b] n.r. = no reaction.

predominant one under the conditions employed. It has been suggested that it corresponds to a $[H^+]$-dependent pre-equilibrium reflecting the competition of H^+ and Cu^{2+} (or Fe^{3+}) for a single basic site, followed by an internal electron transfer step:

$$CrCH_2OH^{2+} + Cu^{2+} \overset{K}{\rightleftharpoons} CrCH_2OCu^{3+} + H^+ \tag{76}$$

$$CrCH_2OCu^{3+} \overset{k}{\rightarrow} Cr^{2+} + HCHO + Cu^+ \tag{77}$$

such that $k' = Kk$. Arguments given in favour of this particular site of proton dissociation over such alternatives as a water molecule coordinated to chromium or Cu^{2+} have been made,[144] but the point cannot be regarded as having been settled. The substitution process of Equation (76) suggests that an effective oxidant must be reasonably labile. Consistent with that postulate, Cu^{2+} and Fe^{3+} react, whereas $Co(NH_3)_5X^{2+}$ complexes (for example) do not.

Mercury(II) reacts with the same series of complexes by an array of complex processes.[116] The unsubstituted complexes (e.g. $CrCH_2OH^{2+}$, $CrCH_2OCH_3^{2+}$) react by S_E2 mechanisms (Section VI). Others involve one-electron oxidation processes analogous in stoichiometry and mechanism to the Cu^{2+} and Fe^{3+} reactions. Still others appear to involve two-electron redox processes.

Vanadium(IV) reacts with $CrCH_2OH^{2+}$:

$$VO^{2+} + CrCH_2OH^{2+} + H^+ = V^{3+} + Cr^{2+} + HCHO + H_2O \tag{78}$$

The reaction follows a second-order rate law

$$\frac{d[Cr^{2+}]}{dt} = k_{app}[VO^{2+}][CrCH_2OH^{2+}] \tag{79}$$

with k_{app} decreasing from $0.916 \, M^{-1} s^{-1}$ at $0.050 \, M \, H^+$ to $0.149 \, M^{-1} s^{-1}$ at $0.960 \, M \, H^+$.[146] The form of the hydrogen ion dependence suggests the involvement of steps like those in Equations (76)–(77). The reaction provides, incidentally, a convenient route for the homogeneous generation of Cr^{2+},[21] assuming VO^{2+} and V^{3+} do not interfere. Vanadium(IV) does not react directly with $CrC(CH_3)_2OH^{2+}$, although it does do so indirectly via homolysis (Section III and Fig. 1). The lack of a direct reaction with VO^{2+}, but its ready occurrence with Cu^{2+} and Fe^{3+}, has yet to be accounted for convincingly. It does suggest, however, as do the variety of reactions with Hg^{2+}, that a single mechanism may not be found which applies throughout.

C. Cr^{2+}-catalysed decomposition or rearrangement

The lack of effect of added Cr^{2+} on the decomposition of most $(H_2O)_5CrR^{2+}$ complexes has been noted (Section III.A and Fig. 1). An exception to this is the Cr^{2+}-catalysed linkage isomerization of the *C*-acetato (i.e., carboxymethyl) to *O*-acetato complex:[92]

$$(H_2O)_5CrCH_2COOH^{2+} \xrightarrow{Cr^{2+} \, cat} (H_2O)_5CrOCCH_3^{2+} \overset{\displaystyle O}{\overset{\displaystyle \|}{}} \tag{80}$$

The rate was evaluated at $0.50 \, M \, H^+$ only, and is given as $6.8 \times 10^{-3} \, X[Cr^{2+}][CrCH_2COOH^{2+}]$ although the first-order $[Cr^{2+}]$ dependence does not seem to be exact. It seems likely that the carbonyl oxygen can serve as a lead-in group for a conventional electron-transfer reaction. Proton addition to the α-carbon presumably is a part of the activation process, but whether the proton originates from a coordinated H_2O or from external H_2O is not known.

The complex of succinic acid, a more complicated species owing to chelation as well as incorporation of a second (inorganic, *O*-bound) Cr(III), also exhibits a Cr^{2+}-catalysed pathway for chromium-carbon cleavage reaction. It shows acid-independent and *acid-inverse* components:[147]

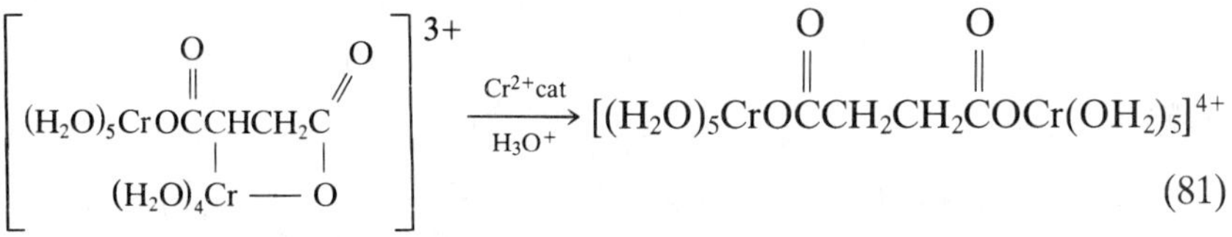

$$\left[\begin{array}{c} O \quad\quad\quad O \\ \| \quad\quad\quad\text{//} \\ (H_2O)_5CrOCCHCH_2C \\ | \quad\quad | \\ (H_2O)_4Cr \longrightarrow O \end{array} \right]^{3+} \xrightarrow[H_3O^+]{Cr^{2+}cat} [(H_2O)_5CrOCCH_2CH_2COCr(OH_2)_5]^{4+} \quad (81)$$

D. β-Elimination reactions

The general β-elimination reaction of metal alkyls containing a β-hydrogen,

$$M\!-\!\underset{|}{\overset{|}{C}}\!-\!\underset{|}{\overset{|}{C}}\!-\!H \rightarrow M\!-\!H + \;\diagdown\!C\!=\!C\!\diagup \quad (82)$$

has not been observed for $(H_2O)_5CrR^{2+}$ complexes. The reason for that may be the considerable instability of $(H_2O)_5CrH^{2+}$,[35,95] or it may be that these species are not amenable to the geometrical or electronic requirements envisaged for such reactions:[148]

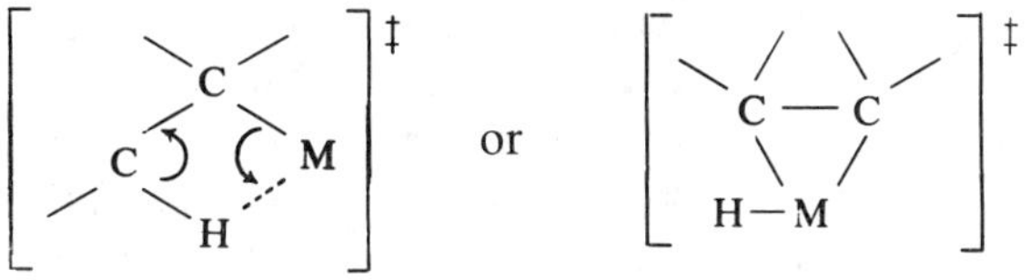

or

β-Haloalkyl complexes of Cr(III) have not been detected. Their formation has been inferred in the reaction of Cr(II) with 1,2-dihalides, but β-elimination is evidently too rapid to permit their isolation.[53,149,150] Stereochemical and product studies showing an appreciable yield of $CrBr^{2+}$ show that the cyclic, *cis*-elimination reaction,

$$[Cr\!-\!\underset{|}{\overset{|}{C}}\!-\!\underset{|}{\overset{|}{C}}\!-\!Br]^{2+} \rightarrow CrBr^{2+} + \;\diagdown\!C\!=\!C\!\diagup \quad (83)$$

is preferred over halide ion dissociation,

$$[Cr\!-\!\underset{|}{\overset{|}{C}}\!-\!\underset{|}{\overset{|}{C}}\!-\!Br]^{2+} \rightarrow Cr^{3+} + \;\diagdown\!C\!=\!C\!\diagup + Br^- \quad (84)$$

Applications of β-halide elimination and related reactions to organic synthesis have been noted.[52,54,151]

β-Hydroxyalkylchromium(III) ions have been observed only as transients. The complexes $CrCH(OH)CH_2OH^{2+}$, $CrC(CH_3)(OH)COOH^{2+}$, and $CrCH_2C(CH_3)_2OH^{2+}$ were prepared and detected pulse radiolytically,[25] and $CrCH_2CH_2OH^{2+}$ flash photolytically.[55] The complexes will decompose very rapidly by an acid-promoted pathway, such as

$$(H_2O)_5CrCH_2CH_2OH^{2+} + H^+ \rightarrow Cr(H_2O)_6^{3+} + C_2H_4 \qquad (85)$$

which has $k = 1 \cdot 4 \times 10^4 \, M^{-1} \, s^{-1}$ (24·1°C, 0·05 M ionic strength), or they will rearrange in a rapid step. The complex $CrCH_2C(OH)(CH_3)_2^{2+}$ reacts with H_3O^+ ($k = 1 \cdot 1 \times 10^3 \, M^{-1} \, s^{-1}$) to yield a new organochromium complex which has not been fully characterized, but of the two likely species shown, is probably the vinylic structure:[25]

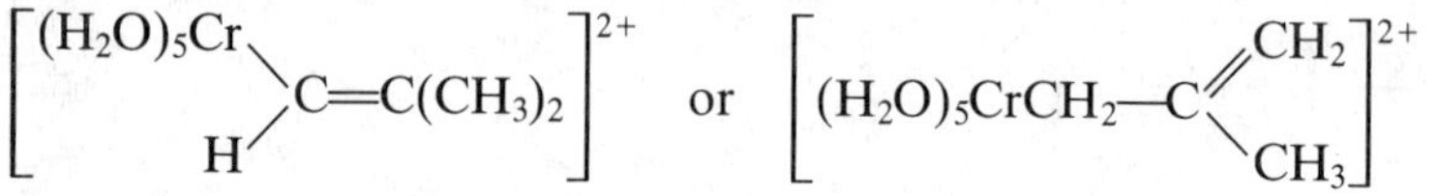

$$\left[\begin{array}{c} (H_2O)_5Cr \\ \diagdown \\ C=C(CH_3)_2 \\ H \diagup \end{array} \right]^{2+} \quad \text{or} \quad \left[(H_2O)_5CrCH_2-C \diagup^{\displaystyle CH_2}_{\displaystyle \diagdown CH_3} \right]^{2+}$$

E. Reactions of haloalkylchromium complexes with Cr²⁺

Abstraction of a halogen atom from a polyhalomethane by Cr^{2+} provides a convenient route to haloalkylchromium complexes, as considered earlier (Section II.B). Use of excess Cr^{2+} leads to continued reduction. Thus bromoform yields $CrCHBr_2^{2+}$ or $CrCH_2Br^{2+}$ depending on whether Cr^{2+} is present in stoichiometrically deficient or excess amount. In addition the separately isolated species $CrCHX_2^{2+}$ (X = Cl, Br, I) react directly with Cr^{2+},

$$CrCHX_2^{2+} + 2Cr^{2+} + H^+ = CrCH_2X^{2+} + Cr^{3+} + CrX^{2+} \qquad (86)$$

The stoichiometry and products shown have been confirmed.

The mechanism originally suggested[13] has been confirmed by experiments based on kinetics studies and ^{51}Cr-radiotracer determinations.[18,153] It also applies, with suitable modifications, to the conversion of $CrCH_2I^{2+}$ to $CrCH_3^{2+}$ by Cr^{2+}.[96] The reaction sequence is:

$$CrCHX_2^{2+} + Cr^{2+} \rightarrow CrX^{2+} + [Cr\dot{C}XH]^{2+} \qquad (87)$$

$$[Cr\dot{C}HX]^{2+} + Cr^{2+} \rightleftarrows Cr_2CHX^{4+} \qquad (88)$$

$$Cr_2CHX^{4+} + H^+ \rightarrow Cr^{3+} + CrCH_2X^{2+} \qquad (89)$$

The first step is rate-limiting, the rate constants at 25°C being $CrCHI_2^{2+}$, $11 \cdot 2 \, M^{-1} \, s^{-1}$,[153] $CrCHCl_2^{2+}$, $1 \cdot 6 \times 10^{-1} \, M^{-1} \, s^{-1}$,[18] and (for the modified version), $CrCH_2I^{2+}$, $2 \cdot 9 \times 10^{-2} \, M^{-1} \, s^{-1}$.[96] The order of halogen reactivity, I > Br > Cl, provides additional confirmation for the mechanism suggested. The radiotracer experiments[18,153] provide supporting evidence for the dichromium alkyl intermediate Cr_2CHX^{4+}. For both $X = Cl^{[18]}$ and $X = I^{[153]}$ there must be assumed to be a rapid *and reversible* step (Equation (88)) which reaches isotopic equilibrium prior to protonolysis (Equation (89)).

F. Conclusions

The mechanistic chemistry of organochromium(III) compounds, particularly the reactions of $(H_2O)_5CrR^{2+}$ species, has now developed to the point where some general patterns of reaction and reaction mechanism have emerged. As it happens these species often undergo competitive or concurrent reactions which exemplify fundamentally different kinds of chemistry (homolytic versus heterolytic cleavage, electrophilic cleavage versus electron transfer, etc.). These complexes would thus appear to be well constituted for studies designed to probe very subtle differences or gradual changes in mechanism.

Acknowledgements

This work was supported under Contract W-7405-ENG-82 by the US Department of Energy, Office of Basic Energy Sciences, Chemical Sciences Division. I should like to express my appreciation to those individuals who supplied results prior to publication. Thanks are due also to my co-workers, referenced herein, whose efforts enabled our own work to contribute to some of the developments in this area.

REFERENCES

[1] Herwig, W.; Zeiss, H.H. *J. Amer. Chem. Soc.* **1957**, *79*, 6561.
[2] Kurras, E.; Otto, J. *J. Organomet. Chem.* **1965**, *4*, 114.
[3] Mowat, W.; Shortland, H.; Yagupsky, G.; Hill, N.; Yagupsky, M.; Wilkinson, G. *J. Chem. Soc. Dalton Trans.* **1972**, 533
[4] Krausse, J.; Marx, G.; Schödl, G. *J. Organomet. Chem.* **1970**, *21*, 159.
[5] Anet. F.A.L.; LeBlanc, E. *J. Amer. Chem. Soc.* **1957**, *79*, 2649.
[6] Kochi, J.K.; Davis, D.D. *J. Amer. Chem. Soc.* **1964**, *86*, 5264.
[7] Nishimura, K.; Kuribayashi, H.; Yamamoto, A.; Ikeda, S. *J. Organomet. Chem.* **1972**, *37*, 317.
[8] Petrou, A.; Vrachnou-Astra, E.; Katakis, D. *Inorg. Chim. Acta* **1980**, *39*, 161.
[9] Loo, C.T.; Goh, L.-Y.; Goh, S.H. *J. Chem. Soc. Dalton Trans.* **1972**, 585.
[10] Samuels, G.J.; Espenson, J.H. *Inorg. Chem.* **1979**, *18*, 2587.

[11] Kochi, J.K. "Organometallic Mechanisms and Catalysis"; Academic Press: New York, 1978.
[12] Halpern, J. *Pure Appl. Chem.* **1979**, *51*, 2171.
[13] Dodd, D.; Johnson, M.D. *J. Chem. Soc. A* **1968**, 34.
[14] Ardon, M.; Woolmington, K.; Pernick, A. *Inorg. Chem.* **1971**, *10*, 2812.
[15] Leslie, J.P., II; Espenson, J.H. *J. Amer. Chem. Soc.* **1976**, *98*, 4839.
[16] Coombes, R.G.; Johnson, M.D.; Tobe, M.L.; Winterton, N.; Wong, L.-Y. *Chem. Commun.* **1965**, 251.
[17] Coombes, R.G.; Johnson, M.D. *J. Chem. Soc. A.* **1966**, 177.
[18] Espenson, J.H.; Leslie, J.P., II. *Inorg. Chem.* **1976**, *15*, 1886.
[19] Espenson, J.H.; Shveima, J.S. *J. Amer. Chem. Soc.* **1973**, *95*, 4468.
[20] Schmidt, W.; Swinehart, J.H.; Taube, H. *J. Amer. Chem. Soc.* **1971**, *93*, 1117.
[21] Bakač, A.; Espenson, J.H. *Inorg. Chem.* **1981**, *20*, 953.
[22] Malik, S.K.; Schmidt, W.; Spreer, L.O. *Inorg. Chem.* **1974**, *13*, 2986.
[23] Funke, L.A.; Espenson, J.H. *Inorg. Chem.* **1981**, *20*, 897.
[24] Nohr, R.S.; Espenson, J.H. *J. Am. Chem. Soc.* **1975**, *97*, 3392.
[25] Cohen, H.; Meyerstein, D. *Inorg. Chem.* **1974**, *13*, 2434.
[26] Ryan, D.A.; Espenson, J.H. *J. Amer. Chem. Soc.* **1982**, *104*, 704B.
[27] Jorgensen, C.K. *Prog. Inorg. Chem.* **1970**, *12*, 101.
[28] Bushey, W.R.; Espenson, J.H. *Inorg. Chem.* **1977**, *16*, 2772.
[29] Cohen, H.; Meyerstein, D. *J. Chem. Soc. Chem. Commun.* **1972**, 320.
[30] Dorfman, L.M.; Adams, G.E. "Reactivity of the Hydroxyl Radical in Aqueous Solutions"; National Bureau of Standards Report No. NSRDS-NBS-46, 1973.
[31] Neta, P. *Advances Phys. Org. Chem.* **1976**, *12*, 223.
[32] Farhataziz; Ross, A.B. "Selected Specific Rates of Reactions of Transients from Water in Aqueous Solutions III. Hydroxyl Radical and Perhydroxyl Radical and Their Radical Ions"; National Bureau of Standards Report No. NSRDS-NBS-59, 1977.
[33] Swallow, A.J. *Prog. Reaction Kinetics* **1978**, *9*, 195.
[34] Lilie, J.; Beck, G.; Henglein, A. *Ber. Bunsenges. Phys. Chem.* **1971**, *75*, 458
[35] Cohen, H.; Meyerstein, D. *J. Chem. Soc. Dalton Trans.* **1974**, 2559.
[36] Espenson, J.H.; Leslie, J.P., II. *J. Amer. Chem. Soc.* **1974**, *96*, 1954.
[37] Kochi, J.K.; Powers, J.W. *J. Amer. Chem. Soc.* **1970**, *92*, 137.
[38] Connick, R.W. Symposium on Relaxation Techniques; Buffalo, N.Y.; June 1965.
[39] Asmus, D.; Henglein, A.; Wigger, A.; Beck, G. *Ber. Bunsenges. Phys. Chem.* **1966**, *70*, 756.
[40] Simic, M.; Neta, P.; Hayon, E. *J. Phys. Chem.* **1969**, *73*, 3794.
[41] Lal, D.; Griller, D.; Husband, S.; Ingold, K.U. *J. Amer. Chem. Soc.* **1974**, *96*, 6355.
[42] Samuni, A.; Meisel, D.; Czapski, G. *J. Chem. Soc. Dalton Trans.* **1972**, 1273.
[43] Laurence, G.S.; Thornton, A.T. *J. Chem. Soc. Dalton Trans.* **1974**, 1142.
[44] Ref. 11, pp. 138–142.
[45] Chock, P.B.; Halpern, J. *J. Amer. Chem. Soc.* **1969**, *91*, 582.
[46] Cooper, T.A. *J. Amer. Chem. Soc.* **1973**, *95*, 4158.
[47] Gold, V.; Wood, D.L. *J. Chem. Soc. Dalton Trans.* **1981**, 2462A.
[48] Ilan, Y.A.; Czapski, G.; Ardon, M. *Israel J. Chem.* **1975**, *13*, 15.
[49] Sellers, R.M.; Simic, M.G. *J. Amer. Chem. Soc.* **1976**, *98*, 6145.

[50] Tamblyn, W.H.; Vogler, E.A.; Kochi, J.K. *J. Org. Chem.* **1980**, *45*, 3912.
[51] Castro, C.E.; Kray, W.C., Jr. *J. Amer. Chem. Soc.* **1966**, *88*, 4447.
[52] Ševčík, P. *Inorg. Chim. Acta* **1979**, *32*, L16.
[53] Kray, W.C., Jr.; Castro, C.E. *J. Amer. Chem. Soc.* **1964**, *86*, 4603.
[54] Mochida, I.; Noguchi, H.; Fujitsu, H.; Seiyama, T.; Takeshita, K. *Can. J. Chem.* **1977**, *12*, 2420.
[55] Ryan, D.A.; Espenson, J.H. *Inorg. Chem.* **1982**, *21*, 527.
[56] Kochi, J.K.; Mocadlo, P.E. *J. Org. Chem.* **1965**, *30*, 1134; *J. Am. Chem. Soc.* **1966**, *88*, 4094.
[57] Hyde, M.R.; Espenson, J.H. *J. Amer. Chem. Soc.* **1976**, *98*, 4488.
[58] Walling, C.; Padwa, A. *J. Amer. Chem. Soc.* **1963**, *85*, 1593, 2333.
[59] Asmus, K.-D.; Möckel, H.; Henglein, A. *J. Phys. Chem.* **1973**, *97*, 1218.
[60] Kirker, G.W.; Bakač, A.; Espenson, J.H. *J. Amer. Chem. Soc.* **1982**, *104*, 1249.
[61] Ogino, H.; Shimura, M.; Tanaka, N. *Inorg. Chem.* **1982**, *21*, 126.
[62] Connolly, P.; Espenson, J.H., unpublished observations.
[63] Espenson, J.H.; Sellers, T.D. *J. Amer. Chem. Soc.* **1974**, *96*, 94.
[64] Endicott, J.F.; Balakrishnan, K.P.; Wong, C.L. *J. Amer. Chem. Soc.* **1980**, *102*, 5519.
[65] Becket, A.; Porter, G. *Trans Faraday Soc.* **1963**, *59*, 2038.
[66] Zeldes, H.; Livingston, R. *J. Chem. Phys.* **1966**, *45*, 1946.
[67] Anpo, M.; Kubokawa, Y. *Bull. Chem. Soc. Japan* **1977**, *50*, 1913.
[68] Calvert, J.G.; Pitts, J.N. "Photochemistry"; Wiley: New York, 1966; Chapter 5.
[69] Malliaris, A.; Katakis, D. *J. Amer. Chem. Soc.* **1965**, *87*, 3077.
[70] Castro, C.E.; Stephens, R.D.; Mojé, S. *J. Amer. Chem. Soc.* **1966**, *88*, 4964.
[71] Castro, C.E.; Stephens, R.D. *J. Amer. Chem. Soc.* **1964**, *86*, 4358.
[72] Glockling, F.; Sneeden, R.P.A.; Zeiss, H.H. *J. Organomet. Chem.* **1972**, *40*, 163.
[73] Sneeden, R.P.A.; Throndsen, H.P. *J. Organomet. Chem.* **1966**, *6*, 542.
[74] Kurras, E. *Naturwiss.* **1959**, *46*, 171.
[75] Kochi, J.K.; Buchanan, D. *J. Amer. Chem. Soc.* **1965**, *87*, 853.
[76] Mueller, H. *Z. Chem.* **1969**, *9*, 311.
[77] Rusina, A.; Schröer, H.P.; Vlcek, A. *Inorg. Chim. Acta* **1969**, *3*, 411.
[78] Daly, J.J.; Sanz, F.; Sneeden, R.P.A.; Zeiss, H.H. *Chem. Commun.* **1971**, 243.
[79] Sneeden, R.P.A.; Zeiss, H.H. *J. Organomet. Chem.* **1973**, *47*, 125.
[80] Daly, J.J.; Sanz, F. *J. Chem. Soc. Dalton Trans.* **1972**, 2584.
[81] Seidel, W.; Fischer, K.; Schmiedeknecht, K. *Z. Anorg. Allg. Chem.* **1972**, *390*, 272.
[82] Sneeden, R.P.A. "Organochromium Compounds"; Academic Press: New York; 1975, pp. 28–82.
[83] Dey, K.; De, R.L. *J. Inorg. Nucl. Chem.* **1977**, *39*, 153.
[84] Goedken, V.I.; Peng, S.M.; Park, Y. *J. Amer. Chem. Soc.* **1974**, *96*, 284.
[85] Swaddle, T.W.; Guastalla, G. *Inorg. Chem.* **1968**, *7*, 1915.
[86] Woodruff, W.H.; Margerum, D.W. *Inorg. Chem.* **1973**, *12*, 963.
[87] Cohen, H.; Meyerstein, D. *J. Chem. Soc. Dalton Trans.* **1977**, 1056.
[88] Pohl, M.C.; Espenson, J.H. *Inorg. Chem.* **1980**, *19*, 235.
[89] Marty, W.; Espenson, J.H. *Inorg. Chem.* **1979**, *18*, 1246.
[90] Schmidt, A.R.; Swaddle, T.W. *J. Chem. Soc. A* **1970**, 1927.

[91] Shimura, M.; Espenson, J.H.; Bakač, A., unpublished observations.
[92] Ševčík, P.; Jakubcová, D. Collect. Czech. Chem. Commun. 1977, 42, 1776.
[93] Rüchardt, C.; Beckhaus, H.-D. Angew. Chem. Int. Ed. Engl. 1980, 19, 429
[94] Gold, V.; Wood, D.L. J. Chem. Soc. Dalton Trans. 1981, 2452.
[95] Ryan, D.A.; Espenson, J.H. Inorg. Chem. 1981, 20, 4401.
[96] Nohr, R.S.; Spreer, L.O. Inorg. Chem. 1974, 13, 1239.
[97] Ševčík, P.; Kresák, J. Collect. Czech. Chem. Commun. 1976, 41, 2198.
[98] Byington, J.I.; Peters, R.D.; Spreer, L.O. Inorg. Chem. 1979, 13, 3324.
[99] Akhtar, M.J.; Spreer, L.O. Inorg. Chem. 1979, 18, 3327.
[100] Espenson, J.H.; Williams, D.A. J. Amer. Chem. Soc. 1974, 96, 1008.
[101] Ferraris, S.D.; King, E.L. J. Amer. Chem. Soc. 1970, 92, 1215.
[102] Azran, J.; Cohen, H.; Meyerstein, D. J. Coord. Chem. 1977, 6, 249.
[103] Bakač, A.; Espenson, J.H.; Miller, L. Inorg. Chem. 1982, 21, 1557.
[104] Wilkins, R.G. "The Study of Kinetics and Mechanisms of Reactions of Transition Metal Complexes"; Allyn and Bacon, 1976; p. 188.
[105] Bracken, D.E.; Baldwin, H.W. Inorg. Chem. 1974, 13, 1325.
[106] Postmus, C.; King, E.L. J. Phys. Chem. 1955, 59, 1216.
[107] Daly, J.J.; Sanz, F.; Sneeden, R.P.A.; Zeiss, H. J. Chem. Soc. Dalton Trans. 1973, 73.
[108] Daly, J.J.; Sanz, F.; Sneeden, R.P.A.; Zeiss, H. Helv. Chim. Acta 1973, 56, 503.
[109] Marchese, A.L.; Scudder, M.; van den Bergen, A.M.; West, B.O. J. Organomet. Chem. 1976, 121, 63–71.
[110] Johnson, M.D. Rec. Chem. Prog. 1970, 31, 143.
[111] Johnson, M.D. Acc. Chem. Res. 1978, 11, 57.
[112] Coombes, R.G.; Johnson, M.D. J. Chem. Soc. A 1966, 1805.
[113] Coombes, R.G.; Johnson, M.D.; Vamplew, D. J. Chem. Soc. A 1968, 2297.
[114] Ref. 11, pp. 531–548.
[115] Dodd, D.; Johnson, M.D.; Vamplew, D. J. Chem. Soc. B 1971, 1841.
[116] Espenson, J.H.; Bakač, A. J. Amer. Chem. Soc. 1981, 103, 2728.
[117] Samuels, G.J.; Espenson, J.H. Inorg. Chem. 1980, 19, 235.
[118] Chang, J.C.; Espenson, J.H. Chem. Commun. 1974, 233.
[119] Espenson, J.H.; Samuels, G.J. J. Organomet. Chem. 1976, 113, 143.
[120] Dodd, D.; Johnson, M.D. Chem. Commun. 1970, 460.
[121] Dodd, D.; Johnson, M.D. J. Chem. Soc. Perkin Trans 2, 1974, 219.
[122] Abraham, M.H.; Grellier, P.L. J. Chem. Soc. Perkin Trans 2, 1973, 1132.
[123] Fritz, H.L.; Espenson, J.H.; Williams, D.A.; Molander, G.A. J. Amer. Chem. Soc. 1974, 96, 2378.
[124] Adin, A.; Espenson, J.H. Chem. Commun. 1971, 243.
[125] Jensen, F.R.; Madan, V.; Buchanan, D.H. J. Amer. Chem. Soc. 1971, 93, 5283.
[126] Hughes, E.D.; Ingold, C.K. J. Chem. Soc. 1961, 2359.
[127] Hughes, E.D.; Ingold, C.K.; Thorpe, F.G.; Vogler, H.C. J. Chem. Soc. 1961, 1133.
[128] Dessy, R.E.; Reynolds, G.F.; Kim, J.-Y. J. Amer. Chem. Soc. 1959, 81, 2683.
[129] Streitweiser, Jr., A. "Solvolytic Displacement Reactions"; McGraw-Hill: New York, 1962; p. 13.
[130] Espenson, J.H. ACS Symposium Series 1978, 82, 235.
[131] Parris, M.; Ashbrook, A.W. Can. J. Chem. 1979, 57, 1233.

[132] van der Bergen, A.; West, B.O. *Chem. Commun.* **1971**, 1371.
[133] van der Bergen, A.; West, B.O. *J. Organomet. Chem.* **1974**, *64*, 1125.
[134] Dodd, D.; Johnson, M.D.; Lockman, B.L. *J. Amer. Chem. Soc.* **1977**, *99*, 3664.
[135] Fanchiang, Y.-T.; Wood, J.M. *J. Amer. Chem. Soc.* **1981**, *103*, 5100.
[136] Bougeard, P.; Gupta, B.D.; Johnson, M.D. *J. Organomet. Chem.* **1981**, *206*, 211.
[137] Ouellette, R.J.; van Leuwen, B.G. *J. Org. Chem.* **1965**, *30*, 3967.
[138] Ryan, D.A.; Espenson, J.H. *J. Amer. Chem. Soc.* **1979**, *101*, 2488.
[139] Kochi, J.K.; Subramanian, R.V. *J. Amer. Chem. Soc.* **1965**, *87*, 4855.
[140] Kochi, J.K.; Bemis, A.; Jenkins, C.T. *J. Amer. Chem. Soc.* **1968**, *90*, 4616.
[141] Blackburn, R.; Kyaw, M.; Phillips, G.O.; Swallow, A.J. *J. Chem. Soc. Faraday Trans I* **1975**, *71*, 2227.
[142] Elroi, H.; Meyerstein, D. *J. Amer. Chem. Soc.* **1978**, *100*, 5540.
[143] Espenson, J.H.; Bakač, A. *J. Amer. Chem. Soc.* **1980**, *102*, 2488.
[144] Bakač, A.; Espenson, J.H. *J. Amer. Chem. Soc.* **1981**, *103*, 2721.
[145] Kirker, G.W. Ph.D. Thesis, Iowa State University, 1981.
[146] Bakač, A.; Espenson, J.H. *Inorg. Chem.* **1981**, *20*, 1621.
[147] Petrou, A.; Vrachnou-Astra, E.; Konstantatos, J.; Katsaros, N.; Katakis, D. *Inorg. Chem.* **1981**, *20*, 1091.
[148] Ref. 11, pp. 248–249.
[149] Singleton, D.M.; Kochi, J.K. *J. Amer. Chem. Soc.* **1967**, *89*, 6547.
[150] Kochi, J.K.; Singleton, D.M. *J. Amer. Chem. Soc.* **1968**, *90*, 1582.
[151] Kochi, J.K.; Singleton, D.M. *J. Org. Chem.* **1968**, *33*, 1027.
[152] Kochi, J.K.; Singleton, D.M.; Andrews, L.J. *Tetrahedron* **1968**, *24*, 3503.
[153] Nohr, R.S.; Spreer, L.O. *J. Amer. Chem. Soc.* **1974**, *96*, 2618.

Oxidation–reduction and Substitution Reactions of Iron–Sulphur Centres

Fraser Armstrong

Inorganic Chemistry Laboratory, University of Oxford

I. INTRODUCTION

The past two decades have witnessed some important developments in many areas that constitute the framework of coordination chemistry. Among these, improvements in x-ray crystal structure refinement and the successful exploitation of modern spectroscopic techniques to probe structural and dynamic features of metal complexes are particularly noteworthy. A natural consequence of progress in this direction has been the lucrative application of such physical methodology to the study of metal centres in biological systems, a task not readily undertaken using traditional approaches.[45] In reciprocal fashion, novel structural features and functional properties frequently displayed by such centres have inspired new challenges among preparative chemists who have endeavoured to synthesize satisfactory "model" compounds.[74] In the resulting profusion of activity, which has undoubtedly stimulated and sustained a close relationship between biochemists and coordination chemists, many categories of metal centre have been chemically identified and in many cases structurally characterized.

The development of the field of iron–sulphur (Fe–S) proteins is an example illustrating this multidisciplinary approach and in recent years we have witnessed their emergence in importance comparable to that of haemoproteins as regards functional diversity and the level of structural refinement.[31,62,98,124,166] Prior to the establishment of the chemical nature of Fe–S centres, such components were empirically identified in numerous biological samples through the application of low-temperature EPR spectroscopy.[18,19] In molecules ranging from the proteins known as rubredoxins and ferredoxins, to complex enzymes containing additional constituents such as molybdenum and flavin, the primary role of Fe–S centres appears to be to act as loci for inter- and intramolecular electron transfer. While the uncertainties and multicentre complications inherent in the large enzyme systems continue to occupy the attention of biochemists, the simpler Fe–S proteins now provide subject matter for an increasing number of chemists eager to investigate the intrinsic properties of individual Fe–S centres. In addition, these comparatively small biological molecules offer considerable scope for studies on the fundamental principles governing electron transfer between proteins. Consequently, ferredoxins have taken up position alongside blue-copper proteins and cyctochrome c as topics of scrutiny in this important yet poorly understood subject.[21] The study of Fe–S analogue systems has proved to be an extremely fruitful line of research, due largely to the extended efforts of Holm and co-workers, and compounds incorporating the various Fe–S core types, which display properties that are similar to or identical with corresponding centres in proteins, have been synthesized using relatively straightforward preparative routes.[13,69,74]

This review seeks to outline some of the chemical characteristics of Fe–S centres and discuss the use of simpler Fe–S proteins in evaluating mechanistic features of biological electron-transfer reactions.

II. STRUCTURAL CHARACTERISTICS OF Fe–S CENTRES

A. Classification

The diversity of proteins that contain Fe–S centres, as well as the variety of different types of centre, requires a level of classification that is descriptive and informative without being too inflexible. The nomenclature adopted for this purpose follows the guidelines of recent recommendations.[117]

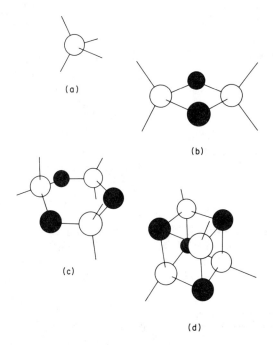

Fig. 1. Structures of the four types of Fe–S cluster identified in proteins. Fe and bridging S atoms are represented by open and solid circles respectively. (*a*) Monomeric Fe centre as found in Rd; (*b*) [2Fe–2S]; (*c*) [3Fe–3S]; (*d*) [4Fe–4S].

The major proportion of the content of this review concerns simple Fe–S proteins. The abbreviations Rd (rubredoxin), Fd (ferredoxin) and HiPIP (strictly reserved for the ferredoxin, "High-Potential Iron–Sulphur Protein", which is paramagnetic in the oxidized form, as isolated from photosynthetic bacteria) are used following clarifications in those instances where there is any ambiguity.

The term "centre" refers to the complete Fe coordination shell including cysteinyl sulphurs. It is therefore generally applicable, whereas the term "cluster" is reserved for the substructure of Fe and bridging "inorganic" S atoms, and consequently excludes monomeric Fe as found in the rub-redoxins (Fig. 1(a)). The other centres depicted in Fig. 1 are a fine example of the occurrence of mixed-valence systems in nature. In all cases only the atomic oxidation states Fe(II) and Fe(III) are involved but the presence of several such atoms in one integral unit renders possible (at least in theory) the attainment of more than one composite oxidation level. Individual formal oxidation states are used with the understanding that in many cases extensive delocalization can remove any clear distinction between Fe(II) and Fe(III).

For specific Fe–S centres it is convenient to describe the type of system by reference to the size of the cluster, the oxidation level as generally isolated (by summing the charges on each Fe, 2+ and 3+, and S, 2−) and (in a specific context) the redox couple in which the cluster normally operates. An example is given by $[2Fe–2S]^{2+(2+,1+)}$. In this case we have a two-Fe two-labile-S cluster normally found in the 2+ oxidation level, both Fe atoms being Fe(III). The superscript notation in round brackets refers to the oxidation levels utilized by this particular cluster, where in this case it is clear that the 2+ level can be reduced to 1+.

Alternatively in examples where, from the context, the nature of the cluster under discussion is unambiguous, the oxidation level of interest is written directly as in $[4Fe–4S]^{2+}$, which represents the state in which two iron atoms are formally Fe(III) and two are Fe(II).

The subscripts R and O are used to denote reduced and oxidized forms of Fe–S proteins under discussion, e.g. as in *Chromatium* HiPIP$_O$, parsley Fd$_R$.

In discussions on well characterized analogue compounds, the complete molecular formula is written out, e.g. as in $[Fe_4S_4(SCH_2Ph)_4]^{2-}$.

Salient structural features of the various types of Fe–S centres are outlined below. For more detailed accounts the reader is referred to several specialized reviews.[4,13,160]

B. Monomeric Fe centres

The centre comprising a single Fe atom in a distorted tetrahedral environment of cysteinyl sulphurs (Fig. 1(a)) is found in a group of low-MW proteins known as rubredoxins. These proteins, which are red in colour when oxidized, are generally isolated from anaerobic bacteria.[52] A related protein, desulforedoxin from *Desulfovibrio gigas*, which is a dimer of two identical subunits containing a single Fe centre, has also recently been characterized.[115] The function of rubredoxins is not generally clear, but the atypical protein from *Pseudomonas oleovorans*, which actually contains two Fe centres, is known to be an electron–transport component of the fatty acid and hydrocarbon hydroxylation system.[95] Reported reduction potentials range between −57 mV and +20 mV.[114,163] Consequently the proteins as isolated are normally in the Fe(III) state. In this form an EPR spectrum is obtained ($g = 4 \cdot 3$) which is attributable to Fe(III) in a low-symmetry environment. Mössbauer spectroscopy, which has proven to be an extremely powerful tool in the characterization of Fe–S centres, clearly shows high-spin Fe in both oxidation states.[48,126] This feature, which is as expected for Fe in a weak ligand field, appears to be without exception among Fe–S proteins so far examined. Rubredoxins have been the subject of several x-ray structure studies, in particular the protein from *Clostridium pasteurianum*, for which a recent determination has been carried out at $1 \cdot 2$ Å resolution.[155] The Fe–S bond lengths of $2 \cdot 33$, $2 \cdot 30$, $2 \cdot 29$ and $2 \cdot 24$ Å are in good agreement with EXAFS measurements which yield an average value of $2 \cdot 30$ Å with a deviation of $0 \cdot 06 \pm 0 \cdot 04$ Å.[136] Bond angles (S–Fe–S) given by the crystal structure analysis are in the range 104–114°, again indicating somewhat distorted tetrahedral symmetry. These results supersede an earlier study at $1 \cdot 5$ Å resolution where one Fe–S bond was found to be anomalously short at $2 \cdot 05$ Å.[154]

The synthesis and structure analysis of analogue compounds in which Fe is ligated by four mercaptide sulphurs has yielded useful comparative information. The Fe(III) complex anion [Fe(S$_2$—o-xyl)$_2$]$^-$ has approximate T_d symmetry with Fe–S bond lengths in the range $2 \cdot 26$–$2 \cdot 28$ Å and S–Fe–S angles ranging from 106° to 113°.[90] Restraints imposed by the peptide matrix are probably responsible for further distortion in the protein site. In addition, structural changes incurred upon reduction can be gauged from crystallographic data for the reduced state analogues [Fe(S$_2$—o-xyl)$_2$]$^{2-}$ and [Fe(SPh)$_4$]$^{2-}$.[43,90] For these compounds Fe–S bond lengths fall in the range $2 \cdot 32$–$2 \cdot 38$ Å, averaging $0 \cdot 09$ Å greater than in [Fe(S$_2$—o-xyl)$_2$]$^-$. The near-tetrahedral geometry is retained. The dimensional change accompanying reduction, which is of interest in the consideration of activation requirements for electron transfer, has also been estimated for Rd from *Peptococcus aerogenes* by the EXAFS (Extended X-ray Absorption Fine Structure) technique.[137,138] On reduction, the Fe–S bond length increases by an average of $0 \cdot 05$ Å.

C. [2Fe–2S] centres

The centre consisting of a [2Fe–2S] cluster coordinated to the protein by four cysteinyl sulphurs is shown in Fig. 1(*b*). It is the simplest Fe–S centre containing bridging acid-labile S atoms, a feature which differentiates rubredoxins from other Fe–S proteins. Although [2Fe–2S] centres have widespread occurrence amongst complex systems, characterization has naturally been pursued with the simplest examples, in this case the chloroplast ferredoxins. These molecules, for which considerable homology is conserved throughout photosynthetic organisms, are small proteins (MW ~ 10 000) of high negative charge containing a single [2Fe–2S] centre. While the structure of the [2Fe–2S] centre was deduced to an appreciable degree of certainty from spectroscopic information and comparison with model compounds several years ago; only recently has this been confirmed by an x-ray structure determination.[58,103]

Chloroplast ferredoxins function as electron carriers in the photosynthetic and respiratory systems, one example of involvement being with the coupling of redox processes involving pyridine nucleotides.[167] One electron is transferred per [2Fe–2S] centre[119] and reduction potentials are low, ~ −420 mV, similar to that of the hydrogen electrode at pH 7.[83,140] The oxidized protein is EPR-silent and reddish brown in colour, this being partially bleached upon reduction by suitable reagents such as dithionite. The reduced form is paramagnetic, displaying a characteristic EPR spectrum (average g value < 2) at low temperature attributable to a single unpaired electron.[120] This prominent feature, which is in addition a property of most [4Fe–4S] centres, has permitted the detection of these functional groups in intact tissue samples and complex enzyme systems.[18,19] Particularly concise information on the electronic and symmetry properties of Fe–S centres in chloroplast ferredoxins has been obtained through the use of Mössbauer spectroscopy.[17,30,51,78] The oxidized form of the cluster comprises two high-spin Fe(III) atoms that are not entirely equivalent, as indicated by significant spectral broadening, while the absence of any perturbation in the presence of an applied magnetic field is consistent with a diamagnetic ground-state arising from an antiferromagnetic exchange interaction.[60] On reduction, Mössbauer resonances attributable to discrete Fe(III) and Fe(II) atoms are observed, indicating localization of the unpaired electron on one of the Fe atoms. This overall picture receives further support with evidence from ENDOR (Electron Nuclear Double Resonance),[57] low-temperature optical spectroscopy,[130] low-temperature MCD (magnetic circular dichroism)[150] and by the observation of a linear electric field effect (LEFE) in a system that should, for complete electron delocalization, possess a centre of symmetry.[125] Referring to the nomenclature system described above, the two forms of the cluster can be written [2Fe–2S]$^{2+}$ and [2Fe–2S]$^{+}$.

The recent x-ray structure of blue-green algal *Spirulina platensis* Fd (oxidized form) reveals each of the Fe atoms in an essentially tetrahedral

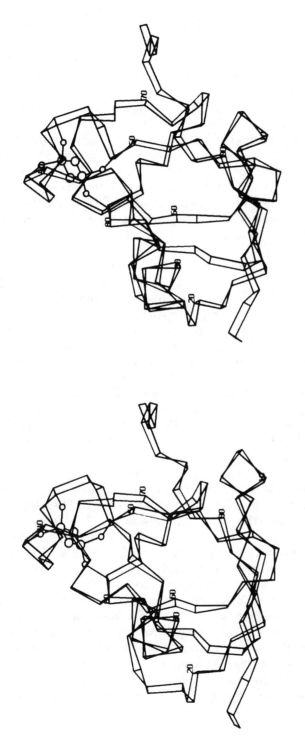

Fig. 2. Three-dimensional structure of *S. platensis* ferredoxin showing the protein backbone and the position of the [2Fe—2S] centre. (Original kindly supplied by Dr T. Tsukihara, Faculty of Engineering, Tottori University.)

environment of two cysteinyl and two mutually bridging sulphurs.[58,103] The $[2Fe-2S]^{2+}$ cluster is planar with dimensions that are in good agreement with those of the synthetic analogues $[Fe_2S_2(S_2-o\text{-xyl})_2]^{2-}$ and $[Fe_2S_2(S-p\text{-tolyl})_4]^{2-}$ [105] and the Fe–Fe distance of 2·72 Å suggests some measure of direct metal–metal interaction. Of interest from the standpoint of electron-transfer function is the protuberance above the molecular surface of two cysteinyl sulphurs (from residues 41 and 46) coordinating one of the Fe atoms (Fig. 2). The cluster is otherwise in a predominantly hydrophobic region. Homology comparisons between chloroplast ferredoxins from such diverse organisms as blue-green algae and higher plants indicate that the cluster binding cavity and nearby residues have been highly conserved.[103]

D. [4Fe–4S] centres

As with the [2Fe–2S] centre, the salient structural features of the [4Fe–4S] centre have been deduced from physicochemical investigations with simple examples, but there is no doubt that such centres are active components of more complex systems. Three small proteins containing [4Fe–4S] centres, all of them from bacterial sources, have been subjects of x-ray structure determination. These examples, from *Peptococcus aerogenes* (two [4Fe–4S]), *Chromatium vinosum* HiPIP in both normal oxidation levels (one [4Fe–4S]) and *Azotobacter vinelandii* (one [4Fe–4S], one [3Fe–3S]) reveal the essential geometry as shown in Fig. 1(d)[1,2,34–37,59,141] In addition, particularly enlightening information has been forthcoming from studies on synthetic [4Fe–4S] analogue compounds.[69]

A striking feature of [4Fe–4S] centres is the possible accessibility of at least three oxidation levels. This conclusion rationalizes the once-paradoxical observation that certain proteins known to contain [4Fe–4S] centres exhibit vastly different redox behaviour. As with other Fe–S systems, EPR spectroscopy has been an invaluable guide in the establishment of empirical behaviour. The great majority of [4Fe–4S] ferredoxins exhibit a diamagnetic ground-state in the form normally isolated, undergoing only reduction (one electron per [4Fe–4S] centre) to become paramagnetic with $S = \frac{1}{2}$. By contrast a small group of ferredoxins exemplified by the so-called High-Potential Iron-Sulphur Protein (HiPIP) from *Chromatium vinosum*, are diamagnetic in the reduced state, one-electron oxidation to a paramagnetic ($S = \frac{1}{2}$) form being the only redox process normally observed. The growing realization that the diamagnetic forms of Fe–S centre in each class of protein were not only structurally alike but comparable also by virtue of magnetic and spectroscopic properties suggested a means of unification within a scheme involving three empirical oxidation levels.[34,36] Furthermore, comparisons between the naturally occurring diamagnetic forms and the analogue compound $[Fe_4S_4(SCH_2Ph)_4]^{2-}$ demonstrated an isoelectronic relationship indicating a formal valence assignment of 2Fe(III)2Fe(II).[66] The scheme shown below depicts the three natural oxidation levels and the relationship with synthetic analogues.[48a]

	HiPIP couple	"Classical" Fd Couple	

Cluster $[4Fe–4S]^{3+} \underset{-e^-}{\overset{+e^-}{\rightleftharpoons}} [4Fe–4S]^{2+} \underset{-e^-}{\overset{+e^-}{\rightleftharpoons}} [4Fe–4S]^{+}$

Representative
Analogue $[Fe_4S_4(SR)_4]^{-} \underset{-e^-}{\overset{+e^-}{\rightleftharpoons}} [Fe_4S_4(SR)_4]^{2-} \underset{-e^-}{\overset{+e^-}{\rightleftharpoons}} [Fe_4S_4(SR)_4]^{3-}$

         $S = \frac{1}{2}$ $S = 0$ $S = \frac{1}{2}$

It must be stressed here that extension of the biological series to include the 4+ and "0" levels remains a likely possibility as more Fe–S proteins are characterized. Indeed several reports, based upon polarographic and kinetic investigations indicate that the $[4Fe–4S]^0$ level can be readily generated for analogue systems.[28,65,77,136a,146,153a]

The dichotomy displayed in the redox behaviour of the physiological systems is an intriguing example of the influence of extrinsic restraints on electrochemical properties. As previously noted, the majority of [4Fe–4S] ferredoxins operate between 2+ and 1+ oxidation levels and reduction potentials are generally low, around −400 mV, as found for chloroplast ferredoxins.[140] Ferredoxins in the diamagnetic 2+ level display broad absorption spectra with maxima around 390–400 nm, the olive-green colour of dilute solutions being considerably bleached upon reduction. The EPR spectrum of the 1+ level is (for ferredoxins containing single [4Fe–4S] centres, such as that from *Bacillus stearothermophilus*) similar to that of the chloroplast proteins with $g_{av} < 2$.[30,120] For the well characterized group of bacterial ferredoxins containing two [4Fe–4S] centres, the EPR spectrum is complicated by a triplet interaction between the two paramagnetic centres, these being situated some 12 Å apart.[102] Reversible oxidation of "classical" ferredoxins to the 3+ level has not been demonstrated. Instead, as is evident from kinetic studies using the reagents $Fe(CN)_6^{3-}$, $IrCl_6^{2-}$ and $Mn(cydta)^-$ (cydta = 1,2-diaminocyclohexanetetraacetate), irreversible degradation processes occur.[64] More precise information stems from the studies of Thomson *et al.*,[151] who have isolated the product formed upon prolonged treatment of *C. pasteurianum* Fd with $Fe(CN)_6^{3-}$ and examined the low-temperature MCD spectra. They conclude that species containing [3Fe–3S] clusters are formed, one Fe(II) per [4Fe–4S] being ejected as

indicated by the simultaneous formation of Prussian Blue. A similar degradation process possibly occurs with O_2 since small amounts of [3Fe–3S]
species, which can be detected by EPR and MCD, appear to be present
in samples of Fd immediately after isolation by normal (aerobic) procedures.[79,151] This behaviour is reflected in the chemistry of synthetic
[4Fe–4S] analogues since while the species $[Fe_4S_4(SR)_4]^{2-}$ and
$[Fe_4S_4(SR)_4]^{3-}$ have both been isolated and structurally characterized,
attempts to prepare the 3+ level analogue $[Fe_4S_4(SR)_4]^-$ have so far been
unsuccessful.

Reduction potentials for $[4Fe–4S]^{2+(3+,2+)}$ systems are generally higher,
E_{m7} (mid-point potential at pH 7) for *Chromatium* HiPIP being
+350 mV,[106] and the diamagnetic 2+ level ($HiPIP_R$) displays an absorption
spectrum similar to that of the oxidized bacterial ferredoxins. Upon oxidation, solutions become reddish in colour, $\lambda_{max} = 450$ nm, and an EPR
spectrum, $g \geq 2$, is obtained. Generation of the $[4Fe–4S]^+$ (super-reduced)
form of *Chromatium* HiPIP has been achieved under forcing nonphysiological conditions. The spectroscopic similarities with reduced (1+)
ferredoxins displayed by the form produced upon dithionite reduction in
partially denaturing medium (80% DMSO), serves to verify the validity
of the sequential oxidation level series.[29,49] Without prior unfolding of the
protein chain by solvent perturbation, pulse radiolysis, employing the
hydrated electron (reduction potential -2.7 V) is required to generate the
1+ level.[27]

Various attempts to rationalize the thermodynamic difference between
$[4Fe–4S]^{2+(3+,2+)}$ and $[4Fe–4S]^{2+(2+,1+)}$ systems have been made, one theory
receiving serious attention recently being the participation of H-bonding
between peptide NH and bridging or cysteinyl S atoms.[4,37] The number
of NH–S bonds per cluster in *P. aerogenes* (two [4Fe–4S]) Fd is almost
twice that observed for *Chromatium* HiPIP, suggesting that H-bonding
might stabilize a more negatively charged centre. Another theory considers
the effect of protein packing around the cluster, which could control redox
behaviour by allowing only specific nuclear configurational changes.[35,92]

Electrochemical properties have been examined for an extensive range
of [4Fe–4S] analogues.[48a,69,82] Despite considerable technical differences
between analogue potential determinations (in nonaqueous or partially
aqueous solution) and protein potentiometry (aqueous solution), it is clear
that analogue $[4Fe–4S]^{2+(2+,1+)}$ systems display lower potentials than do
their protein counterparts. The reasons for this are not clear, but factors
such as shielding of the Fe–S centre by the surrounding protein and
variations in solvent dielectric constant have been considered.[67,82]
Yet another possibility is the extent to which clusters are exposed to bulk
solvent, since the cluster in *Chromatium* HiPIP lies relatively buried in the

protein matrix,[34a] whereas in *P. aerogenes* Fd, both are relatively exposed.[1]

From the x-ray structure determinations on three ferredoxins, including both oxidized and reduced forms of *Chromatium* HiPIP, the [4Fe–4S] cluster can be generally visualized as two interpenetrating tetrahedra of four Fe and four (bridging) S atoms. The average Fe–Fe distances (2·75 Å) are smaller than the average S–S distance (3·50 Å), and consequently the geometry of the cluster deviates considerably from that of a simple cube.[36] It has been proposed that this represents a compromise between the tetrahedral geometry expected for Fe ligated by four S, and the normal (90°–105°) range for X–S–X bond angles.[34] For the synthetic analogues $[Fe_4S_4(SPh)_4]^{2-}$, $[Fe_4S_4(SCH_2Ph)_4]^{2-}$ and $[Fe_4S_4(S(CH_2)_2COO)_4]^{6-}$, x-ray structure determinations at resolutions representing an order of magnitude greater precision over those of the proteins, reveal further subtleties.[33,67,92,162] For all the 2+ level structures, overall tetragonal distortion is exhibited, four Fe–S bonds lying parallel to the cluster symmetry axis being shorter than the eight remaining Fe–S bonds. This must be regarded as an intrinsic property, and has been ascribed to Jahn–Teller effects.[92,162] Structure determinations on synthetic clusters in the 1+ level reveal a similar form of distortion. Dimensional alterations accompanying redox changes are discussed in greater detail in the following section.

Regarding the electronic states of [4Fe–4S] clusters, various theoretical models have been proposed (e.g. see Refs. [149,162]). The equivalence between Fe atoms in [4Fe–4S] clusters can be gauged by Mössbauer spectroscopy. For the 2+ oxidation levels, in which the cluster can be considered to be composed of two Fe(III), Fe(II) pairs, inequivalence is marginal, being most pronounced at the lowest temperatures.[30,107,108] Studies on the [4Fe–4S]³⁺ cluster in oxidized *Chromatium* HiPIP indicate that, at temperatures as low as 4·2 K, the hole created by electron loss is located on one of the Fe pairs, but this inequivalence is diminished with increasing temperature. For reduced ferredoxins at the 1+ level, a varying low level of inequivalence amongst Fe atoms is observed, but this in no way approaches the striking delocalization of the added electron that is seen with chloroplast [2Fe–2S]⁺ systems.[30]

E. [3Fe–3S] centres

Until comparatively recently, direct evidence for the existence of [3Fe–3S] centres was not forthcoming and now-established examples tended to be dogmatically categorized within the framework of [2Fe–2S] and [4Fe–4S] systems. However the recent x-ray structure determination, with refinement to 2·5 Å resolution, of a Fd (MW 14 500) from the nitrogen-fixing organism *Azotobacter vinelandii* clearly reveals the novel [3Fe–3S] cluster situated at ~12 Å from a [4Fe–4S] cluster.[59,141] Both centres are of the HiPIP type in as far as they are EPR-detectable only in the oxidized level ($S = \frac{1}{2}$, $g \geqslant 2$), but the reduction potentials differ by over 700 mV ([4Fe–4S], 320 mV; [3Fe–3S], −424 mV).[165] The [3Fe–3S] cluster, shown in Fig. 1(c), has a twist boat conformation and the three Fe atoms are coordinated to the protein by means of five cysteinyl sulphurs and one oxygen ligand which may be H_2O, the propensity of other (non-S) ligands to coordinate Fe–S clusters being clearly demonstrated. The Fe–Fe distance is 4·0 Å, significantly longer than is found in the case of [2Fe–2S] and [4Fe–4S] clusters. Mössbauer and MCD spectroscopy have yielded quantitative information regarding the electronic structure of the [3Fe–3S] centre in two small proteins, *A. vinelandii* Fd and *Desulfovibrio gigas* Fd II (which contains a single cluster per subunit) and can be used analytically to identify such centres in other biomolecules.[53,73,84,152] Mössbauer spectra of the reduced proteins (formally two Fe(III), one Fe(II)) show magnetic hyperfine interactions and in the case of *D. gigas* Fd II an intense temperature-dependent MCD spectrum is obtained. Such behaviour is consistent with a paramagnetic ground-state and data conform well to the assignment $S = 2$. As is usual for integer spin systems, an EPR spectrum is not displayed.

Evidence is accumulating for the existence of [3Fe–3S] centres in many other small and more complex proteins.[32,160] At the same time, however, the biological significance of these centres is under some debate. The recent finding that [4Fe–4S] centres in *C. pasteurianum* Fd are degraded to [3Fe–3S] centres upon prolonged treatment with $Fe(CN)_6^{3-}$ (or O_2) highlights the likelihood that many of these examples may represent artifacts of aerobic isolation procedures.[151] In this context it is interesting to note that ferredoxins I and II from *D. gigas* are identical in terms of subunit polypeptide chain (Fd I is a trimer, Fd II is a tetramer) but Fd I contains both [3Fe–3S] and [4Fe–4S] centres [79a]. The two holoproteins are easily separated. The implication is that interconversion between [4Fe–4S] and [3Fe–3S] centres might in many cases be particularly facile.† As is apparent from the much larger Fe–Fe bond distances and the increased number of coordinating ligands in the case of [3Fe–3S] centres, any such interconversion would require considerable conformational movement. Clearly this possibility could provide a fruitful subject for future investigations. A direct electron-transfer role for [3Fe–3S] ferredoxins is so far indicated only in the case of *D. gigas* Fd II where it appears that it is more reactive than Fd I as an electron carrier in the sulphite reductase system.[23,113]

† See Note Added in Proof, p. 114.

III. REDOX REACTIONS

A. General considerations

The quest towards a general theoretical basis for understanding metallo-protein single-electron-transfer processes has invoked much of the now-established formalism as well as uncovering problems requiring alternative explanation. A critical balance of reasoning has resulted, with retention of sufficient flexibility to be of widespread application. It is consequently of interest to review briefly some of the concepts that currently constitute this framework.

There is good reason to assume that most protein–protein single-electron-transfer reactions involving metalloproteins are of the outer-sphere type, no substitution of inner coordination sphere ligands occurring at the metal centre. One approach to the problem of rationalizing biological electron-transfer processes has therefore been to extend and develop the theory of Marcus.[99, 142, 147, 157] The Marcus cross-relations (1) and (2) relate the rate constant for a cross-reaction in terms of the overall thermodynamic driving force, as expressed by an equilibrium constant Q, and the intrinsic reactivities of the reactants as expressed by the respective electron self-exchange rate constants k_{11} and k_{22}. The term Z in (2) is the bimolecular collision frequency $10^{11}\,\mathrm{M}^{-1}\,\mathrm{s}^{-1}$.

$$k_{12} = (k_{11}k_{22}Qf)^{1/2} \tag{1}$$

$$\log f = (\log Q)^2/4 \log (k_{11}k_{22}/Z^2) \tag{2}$$

Through the use of this formalism, with refinement through iterative cycles on (1) and (2), values of k_{12} can be converted into quantities (k_{11}) that should be independent of driving force and inherent reactivity of redox partner. Protein self-exchange rate constants k_{11} derived from values of k_{12} measured for a range of redox partners should be similar (within an order of magnitude) if a common electron-transfer pathway is operative. By comparison with simpler inorganic reactions, for which the Marcus approach is now recognized as having considerable success in assignment of mechanism, extension to protein systems can be ambiguous, although there is little reason to suppose that fundamental principles are at fault. The arguments against drawing mechanistic conclusions from application of relative Marcus theory focus largely upon the optimistic assumption that large asymmetrical molecules can be regarded as "hard-spheres" for which bimolecular interaction parameters may be estimated and adequate com-pensation made. Uncertainty as to the magnitude of localized interactions between protein and redox partner places this assumption in jeopardy. The contribution to $\Delta G_{12}^{\ddagger}$ from these effects may in some cases be very large and consequently the use of a second-order rate constant for drawing mechanistic conclusions must be viewed with some caution. A similar objection applies to the use of overall activation parameters $\Delta H_{12}^{\ddagger}$ and $\Delta S_{12}^{\ddagger}$.

Recent attention has been given to close examination of ionic strength dependences of reaction rates with a view to extracting more meaningful data from kinetic studies. Koppenol[86] has proposed a procedure for identifying reaction sites on the surface of a protein with asymmetric charge distribution, thereby recognizing the limitations of interpretation within a "hard-sphere" model. The basis for this is an extension of the theories of Brønsted and Debye and Hückel, with special consideration for the dipole moments of the reactants and transition complex. Such an approach is applicable at low ionic strength, and is likely to be most useful in the analysis of small reagent–protein reactions in which one of the reactants may be treated as a point charge. For protein–protein reactions, such an assumption not always justified and some guess has to be made concerning the relative orientation of one of the partners in the transition state.

A contrasting approach to rate data analysis has been pursued by Wherland and Gray.[156] Using Marcus theory and terms for the coulombic interaction between reactants, an expression has been derived for correcting rate constants to infinite ionic strength, thereby attempting to compensate totally for interactions that are electrostatic in nature. This treatment requires the assumption that the two reactants are spherical with symmetrical charge distribution. Interestingly, the use of such electrostatically corrected rate constants has in several cases provided encouraging mechanistic insight, one topical example being in the analysis of reactions of *Chromatium* HiPIP,[116] for which the basic assumptions are compatible with established views on three-dimensional structures.

Inplicit in the consideration of bimolecular electron-transfer reactions is the formation of an encounter adduct between the two reactants, prior to electron transfer. If the formation of this adduct is sufficiently rapid compared with the actual rate of electron transfer, the second-order rate constant is given by

$$k_{12} = k_{et}K \tag{3}$$

where K is the equilibrium constant for precursor adduct formation and k_{et} is the (first-order) rate constant for electron transfer between the juxtaposed redox partners (including separation of free products). The approach is conceptually useful, since the overall process is conveniently divided into two components which may under favourable conditions be individually measured. The magnitude of the binding interaction, the origin of which, for example, might be electrostatic or hydrophohobic, is expressed in K. Precursor adduct formation, while possibly having limited influence in most small reagent–protein reactions, is a particularly important feature in the control of natural processes, reflecting *in vivo* substrate recognition. The rate constant k_{et} expresses the magnitude of activation energy contributions arising from the intrinsic Franck–Condon barriers for donor and acceptor centres, and, for long-range processes, probability terms dependent upon the distance of electron transfer. The Franck–Condon barrier which is the energy required to adjust the nuclear configurations of a reactant to that of the transition state can generally be considered as an intrinsic property of that system. For this reason, much insight can be obtained through consideration of structural changes accompanying electron transfer.

The large distance over which electrons are transferred in many biological systems popularly invokes the tunnelling concept in favour of alternatives such as direct orbital overlap between acceptor and donor centres and "hopping" via "accessible" radical formation sites in the protein matrix.[21] In view of this interest, considerable attention has been focused upon development of the theoretical background to the tunnelling problem and a particularly comprehensive survey is given by Chance *et al.*[38] Descriptions range from the quantum mechanical approach of Jortner[81] to the semi-classical theory of Hopfield,[71,72] although these are essentially equivalent at normal temperatures. Chien[39] has analysed reactions of native and Co-substituted cytochrome *c* in terms of contemporary tunnelling concepts and has shown that excellent agreement can be found between theory and observed behaviour. More recently a modified version of Hopfield's theory has been used in an attempt to determine effective electron-transfer distances for reactions of a range of metalloproteins including *Chromatium* HiPIP.[104] For proteins having a metal centre near the surface, as appears to be the case for many ferredoxins, it is reasonable to expect that a measure of direct orbital overlap with certain redox partners will be possible, thereby providing the most favourable pathway for electron transfer. Consequently, examination of three-dimensional structure, whenever possible, can provide excellent insight regarding the feasibility of various electron-transfer routes.

Most kinetic studies reported in this review are empirical investigations of small reagent–protein reactions. Justification for this approach in the face of criticism concerning the use of "synthetic" redox partners is upheld by the argument that natural electron donors or acceptors are usually large molecules about which little is established either structurally or with regard to intrinsic electron-transfer behaviour. On the other hand, by the use of transition metal complexes, whose structural integrity in solution may be relied upon, an extensive range of interaction situations may be explored and defined in terms of fundamental physicochemical principles.

B. Intrinsic electron-transfer reactivity of Fe–S centres

1. Structural features

Fundamental to the role of Fe–S centres as electron transfer loci is the ability to shuttle rapidly between relevant oxidation levels. Theoretical considerations show that the overall activation energy requirements for electron-transfer processes include contributions from the reorganization energy required to adjust the nuclear configuration of reactants to that of the transition state. Minimal reorganization of the nuclei involved is therefore to be equated with a lower intrinsic activation requirement and, excluding other factors, must facilitate rapid electron transfer at these centres. Since the relative energy of the transition state is related to the extent of differences in nuclear coordinates between reactant and product assemblies, precise structural information on Fe–S centres in different oxidation levels is of considerable value in rationalizing intrinsic electron-transfer reactivity. In practice, however, small structural changes are difficult to measure in the case of protein x-ray structure studies for which resolution is generally an order of magnitude lower than for most coordination compounds. In addition the low reduction potential of many Fe–S proteins hinders the preparation and stabilization of suitable crystals in the reduced state. Suitable synthetic analogues, for which the above restrictions are considerably relaxed, have provided useful information to complement that obtained with protein crystallography, revealing intrinsic properties that may or may not be applicable in the naturally occurring systems. An alternative approach is the use of the EXAFS technique, where measurements can be carried out on proteins in solution and for which the favourable back-scattering of electrons by nearest-neighbour S atoms renders it particularly suited to the study of Fe–S centres. Unlike x-ray crystallography the average Fe–S distance is obtained, but the spread of this value, as well as evidence for anomalously high site distortion can be gauged by analysis of the Debye–Waller factor.[148]

In the latter respect EXAFS experiments with rubredoxin have been of paramount importance. Reduction of *P. aerogenes* Rd in solution leads to an average lengthening of 0·05 Å in the four Fe–S (cys) bonds (2·27 to 2·32 Å).[138] This is to be compared with the 0·09 Å average increase for the analogue system $[Fe(S_2-o\text{-xyl})_2]^{1-/2-}$ (2·27 to 2·36 Å).[90] To the author's knowledge, no high-resolution x-ray structural data are available for the reduced protein.

Having a relatively high reduction potential, *Chromatium* HiPIP has been examined in both oxidation levels by x-ray crystallography, the isomorphous nature of $HiPIP_O$ and $HiPIP_R$ permitting Fourier difference analysis.[35,36] Such examination indicates that the Fe–S cluster contracts somewhat upon oxidation from the 2+ to 3+ level. The greatest changes in interatomic distance occur in the direction of four parallel Fe–S bonds where there is a mean contraction of 0·16 Å (2·38 to 2·22 Å). A second set of four parallel Fe–S bonds undergo a smaller contraction averaging 0·08 Å (2·33 to 2·25 Å) whereas in the remaining orthogonal direction there is a slight expansion of about 0·03 Å (2·25 to 2·28 Å). For Fe–S (cys) bonds, an average decrease of 0·02 Å is observed. Taken together, these values yield a value of 0·06 Å for the average Fe–S bond length contraction, and must therefore be treated with caution since EXAFS data actually suggest a mean increase of 0·01 Å (2·25 to 2·26 Å)[148]. The reasons for this discrepancy are not clear, although it would be reasonable to expect a less dramatic dimensional change to be incurred at a [4Fe–4S] centre (one electron per 4Fe) than for a single Fe. No data are currently available for $[4Fe–4S]^{3+}$ analogues, preparation attempts being unsuccessful owing to instability of this oxidation level in the synthetic series. Returning to the x-ray structure details, the dimensional changes obtained, if accepted as representing a reasonable picture, suggest that the overall effect accompanying oxidation of $HiPIP_R$ is the mutual approach of two opposite 2Fe–2S faces. Apart from internal cluster movements, changes in the cluster binding cavity might be expected to contribute to the Franck–Condon activation requirements and there is indeed evidence for small adjustments in the positions of certain groups, notably non-polar side chains and amide groups making NH—S contacts. The extent to which the configuration of the cluster influences the conformation of the polypeptide is also relevant although there is no crystallographic evidence to suggest that any significant conformational changes occur. Small but facile movements of the polypeptide might be expected to contribute to the reorganization energy, whereas larger changes involving very high activation energies could lead to the formation of intermediate high-energy states which would be reflected in alteration of the overall free-energy change.

Structure information pertaining to reduced bacterial ($[4Fe–4S]^+$) or plant ($[2Fe–2S]^+$) ferredoxins is limited to that obtained using EXAFS.[148] Upon reduction the average Fe–S bond distance in plant (rhubarb) Fd increases from 2·23 to 2·24 Å, comparable to that measured for *C. pasteurianum* 2[4Fe–4S] Fd, 2·25 to 2·26 Å. Again, these changes appear to be very small.

Holm and his associates have examined a range of synthetic [4Fe–4S] analogues by x-ray crystallography and compared the dimensions of 2+

and 1+ levels.[92] Such comparison with [2Fe–2S] analogues has not so far been successful since attempts to synthesize the reduced form invariably results in spontaneous dimerization.[28] For the [4Fe–4S] compounds, structural examination of the 2+ and 1+ levels serves to extend the 3+/2+ comparison made in the case of HiPIP. Efforts expended on this strategy have led to the proposal that the unconstrained idealized cluster structural change accompanying electron transfer is as indicated below:[93]

$$[Fe_4S_4(SR)_4]^{2-} \text{(compressed D}_{2d}) \underset{-e^-}{\overset{+e^-}{\rightleftharpoons}} [Fe_4S_4(SR)_4]^{3-} \text{(elongated D}_{2d})$$

Similar to evidence from HiPIP x-ray structure comparisons, the greatest change occurring upon reduction is elongation (2·27 to 2·35 Å for $[Fe_4S_4(SPh)_4]^{2-/3-}$) of four parallel Fe–S bonds, in this case along the $\bar{4}$ symmetry axis. Less pronounced elongation (2·26 to 2·29 Å) occurs along the four Fe–S(R) bonds whereas a slight contraction (2·30 to 2·29 Å) is evident for the remaining Fe–S bonds. The transition state geometry accordingly approximates to T_d symmetry.

In all the examples quoted above, and despite discrepancies between data obtained via different approaches, it is fairly clear that geometry changes involved are sufficiently small to indicate low Franck–Condon requirements. This feature, coupled with the absence of spin-multiplicity restrictions for essentially tetrahedral high-spin Fe(II) and Fe(III), conforms well to current concepts of requirements for electron-transfer reactivity (see e.g. Ref. [25]).

2. Dynamic features

Electron self-exchange reactions for some [4Fe–4S] analogue systems have been studied directly by ^{1}H NMR line broadening in acetonitrile solution.[133] For $[Fe_4S_4(SR)_4]^{2-/3-}$ (R = CH$_2$Ph, p-C$_6$H$_4$Me) the reactions conform to second-order kinetics, first-order each in oxidized and reduced clusters, and ambient temperature rate constants are in the range 10^6–10^7 M^{-1} s^{-1}. Activation parameters determined for the system $[Fe_4S_4(S-p-C_6H_4Me)_4]^{2-/3-}$ are $\Delta H^{\ddagger} = 3\cdot6$ kcal mol^{-1} and $\Delta S^{\ddagger} = -17$ cal K^{-1} mol^{-1} giving $\Delta G^{\ddagger}$, the total free-energy of activation, $= 8\cdot1$ kcal mol^{-1} at 18°C. From crude calculations based upon measured Fe–S distances, and relevant stretching force constants, $\Delta G^{\ddagger}_{reorg}$, the free-energy of "inner-shell" reorganization, is estimated to be $1\cdot5$ kcal mol^{-1}. That this value, albeit speculative, is considerably less than the kinetically observed quantity, demonstrates the superficiality of this approach. Other factors are clearly influential, perhaps adverse electrostatic effects stemming from 2–/3– interactions in solutions of low dielectric constant.

Nevertheless, the rapid electron exchange broadly inferred with the analogues is to be compared with contrasting observations made on protein systems. In general, two lines of approach have led to estimates for the electron self-exchange rate constants pertaining to simple Fe–S proteins. Firstly there is the application of Marcus theory using data from cross-reaction rate studies with inorganic partners, where as discussed earlier, cautious interpretation is required. With this line of reasoning, electrostatically corrected self-exchange rate constants have been calculated for *Chromatium* HiPIP [4Fe–4S]$^{3+/2+}$ ($1.3 \times 10^{-2}\,\mathrm{M^{-1}\,s^{-1}}$) and spinach Fd [2Fe–2S]$^{2+/1+}$ ($1.7 \times 10^{-3}\,\mathrm{M^{-1}\,s^{-1}}$) indicating a surprisingly low level of intrinsic reactivity.[44,132] The value of 10^8–$10^9\,\mathrm{M^{-1}\,s^{-1}}$ reported for *C. pasteurianum* Rd[76] serves to emphasize the diversities involved in these relative comparisons. The high level of reactivity indicated for the latter example may reflect the relative exposure of the monomeric Fe centre[155] as compared to that in *Chromatium* HiPIP[34–36] although the relative exposure of the [2Fe–2S] cluster in *S. platensis* Fd is not consistent with this rationale.[58,103] Alternatively, intrinsic metal site properties may be very influential. Using EXAFS and resonance Raman data for Rd, Reynolds *et al.*[133] estimate $\Delta G^{\ddagger}_{\mathrm{reorg}}$ to be $\simeq 1.3\ \mathrm{kcal\ mol^{-1}}$.

Secondly, qualitative studies of electron self-exchange processes operating for protein [4Fe–4S]$^{3+/2+}$ and [4Fe–4S]$^{2+/1+}$ systems, utilizing NMR line-broadening, have been reported. For *Chromatium* HiPIP and *Bacillus polymyxa* FdI (MW 9000, single [4Fe–4S]$^{2+/1+}$ cluster) the necessarily intermolecular electron transfer is sufficiently slow so that NMR spectra of half-reduced solutions are superimpositions of the spectra given by individual oxidized and reduced solutions.[127] This contrasts sharply with observations reported for partially reduced bacterial 2[4Fe–4S]$^{2+/1+}$ systems. Here ^{1}H and ^{13}C NMR spectra are exchange-averaged indicating rapid electron transfer between centres.[122,123,128,129] It is likely, though not established (since the concentration-dependence studies which are necessary in order to distinguish between first- and second-order processes have not been reported), that a rapid intramolecular electron transfer between the two centres is operative. There is no obvious direct electronic communication between the two clusters, $\sim 12\ \text{Å}$ apart, although a subtle magnetic interaction is apparent from EPR studies.[102] On the other hand the three-dimensional structure of *P. aerogenes* Fd shows that the two clusters lie close to the molecular surface[1]. Owing to the appreciable negative charge carried by these small ferredoxins, additional insight might be obtained through examination of the effects of ionic strength upon NMR exchange broadening. By virtue of the highly unfavourable electrostatics that might be expected to be particularly contributive in the case of intermolecular processes, rate constants should be greatly enhanced at higher ionic strength.

One conclusion that can be drawn from these observations taken together is that the surrounding polypeptide can significantly influence electron-transfer rates, as well as thermodynamic properties, a view that is of course well established in the field of enzyme structure and function. If effects arising from the energetics of bimolecular encounter (K) are not considered (a questionable oversight owing to the possible importance of specific interactions) it is likely that this modification can take the form of variations in the distance and route over which electron transfer occurs and/or steric constraints that are possibly imposed upon the cluster environment.

C. Kinetic studies with rubredoxins

To the author's knowledge there are few reports of physical kinetic studies involving small redox probes.[20,21,76] This is partly due to the low yields of rubredoxin which are obtained in many procedures. Kinetic parameters shown in Table 1, for the reduction of *C. pasteurianum* Rd by the reagents $Ru(NH_3)_6^{2+}$, $V(H_2O)_6^{2+}$ and $Cr(H_2O)_6^{2+}$ indicate that the protein has a high intrinsic reactivity. Reactions with these reagents are characterized by near-zero $\Delta H^{\ddagger}$ and large negative $\Delta S^{\ddagger}$ values, which, not forgetting the possible ambiguity arising from interpretation of overall parameters, very likely suggests a minimal barrier to thermal electron transfer invoking little reorganization of either the Fe centre, or the protein matrix. No evidence is found for limiting first-order kinetics at high reductant concentrations. The reduction by $Ru(NH_3)_6^{2+}$ is thermodynamically unfavourable and a large excess of reductant is required to drive the reaction over. Use of final absorbance values to determine an equilibrium constant yields a value in agreement with that calculated on the basis of known potentials.

The rate and activation parameters argue against an inner-sphere pathway for $V(H_2O)_6^{2+}$ and this is extended via interpretation of the k_V/k_{Cr} ratio of 13, which lies within the range 10–60 expected if both operate as outer-sphere reductants,[153] to exclude an inner-sphere mechanism for $Cr(H_2O)_6^{2+}$. This is somewhat surprising considering the location of the Fe centre near the molecular surface[154,155] and the demonstrated propensity of $Cr(H_2O)_6^{2+}$ to engage in inner-sphere processes, particularly if thiolate S can be utilized as a bridging ligand. Such a hydrophilic reagent might, however, have difficulties approaching the Fe site which is in a rather hydrophobic environment. An outer-sphere pathway is of course assured for $Ru(NH_3)_6^{2+}$ where no opportunity is afforded for formation of bridging intermediates on this time-scale.

D. Kinetic studies with chloroplast [2Fe–2S] ferredoxins

The low reduction potentials characteristic of chloroplast ferredoxins have naturally imposed restrictions upon the choice of experimental redox partner in kinetic investigations. There is, for example, the limitation regarding selection of reducing agents, sufficiently well characterized at physiological pH values, that have reduction potentials of around $-400\,mV$ or less. Reported physical studies on the reduction of these proteins are therefore restricted to investigations of the reaction with dithionite, for which rate constants show a dependence on $[S_2O_4]^{1/2}$ indicating participation of the SO_2^- radical[89] and the reaction with the electrochemically generated methylviologen cation radical where a second-order rate constant $10^5\,M^{-1}\,s^{-1}$ is obtained.[134] On the other hand, many of the one-electron oxidants familiar to chemists and biochemists have relatively high reduction potentials and low intrinsic kinetic barriers to electron transfer. Consequently oxidation reactions of reduced ferredoxins are frequently too fast to study by flow techniques.

TABLE 1

Summary of kinetic data for the reduction of *C. pasteurianum* Rd[a]

Reductant	k (25°C) $(M^{-1}\,s^{-1})$	$\Delta H^{\ddagger}$ (kcal mol^{-1})	$\Delta S^{\ddagger}$ (cal K^{-1} mol^{-1})
$Ru(NH_3)_6^{2+b}$	9.5×10^4	1.4	-31
$V(H_2O)_6^{2+c}$	1.1×10^4	0.1	-40
$Cr(H_2O)_6^{2+d}$	1.2×10^3	0	(-44)

[a] Ref. [76]. [b] pH 6.3–7.0, $I = 0.1$. [c] pH 3.5–4.5, $I = 0.5$. [d] pH 3.5–4.0, $I = 0.1$.

Many cobalt(III) complexes, particularly those with several nitrogen donor ligands, are for various reasons rather sluggish regarding electron-transfer reactivity and exhibit reasonably low reduction potentials, enabling conditions to be met under which oxidation reactions of reduced ferredoxins can be conveniently studied. A particularly attractive feature of cobalt(III) species is their inertness to substitution and the wide range of structural types that can be synthesized in a pure form. Thus the opportunity is afforded to investigate the effects of factors such as charge and ligand type on the interaction with the protein and subsequent electron transfer.

Sykes and his associates have undertaken a programme of study aimed in this direction, employing substitution-inert oxidants as diverse in charge and ligand type as $(NH_3)_5Co\,(NH_2)\,Co(NH_3)_5^{5+}$ $(Co(III)_2^{5+})$ and $Co(oxal)_3^{3-}$, in reactions with reduced parsley (and spinach) Fd.[9–11] A prominent feature in these investigations is the observation of saturation kinetics with the more positively charged oxidants. With oxidant in pseudo first-order excess, data conform to an empirical expression as in (5):

$$k_{obs} = \frac{[Oxidant]}{A + B[Oxidant]} \tag{5}$$

This can be written in the linear form (6):

$$\frac{1}{k_{obs}} = \frac{A}{[Oxidant]} + B \tag{6}$$

so that plots of $(k_{obs})^{-1}$ against $[Oxidant]^{-1}$ yield slope A and intercept B.

At least three mechanisms may be invoked to explain this dependence. These are outlined as follows:

Mechanism A

$$Fd_R + Ox \rightleftharpoons Fd_R:Ox \qquad K \tag{7}$$

$$Fd_R:Ox \rightarrow products \qquad k_{et} \tag{8}$$

$$k_{obs} = \frac{k_{et}K[Ox]}{1 + K[Ox]} \tag{9}$$

in which rate-determining electron transfer is preceded by kinetically detectable precursor adduct formation. Provided the condition $K[Ox] \ll 1$ holds, a first-order dependence of k_{obs} on $[Ox]$ is expected and (9) reduces to (3), where $k_{12} = k_{obs}/[Ox]$.

Mechanism B

$$Fd_R \rightleftharpoons Fd_R^* \qquad k_1, k_2 \tag{10}$$

$$Fd_R^* + Ox \rightarrow products \qquad k_3 \tag{11}$$

$$k_{obs} = \frac{k_1k_3[Ox]}{k_2 + k_3[Ox]} \tag{12}$$

in which reaction proceeds after prior reorganization or activation of Fd_R. This mechanism has been favoured in the $Cr(H_2O)_6^{2+}$ reduction of ferricytochrome c where the limiting rate constant at high $[Cr(II)]$ corresponds to the dissociation of a methionyl-S from Fe(III).[161] Interpretation in terms of such a mechanism requires that limiting rates for several reactions should be similar irrespective of the identity of the oxidant. As this is not the case with any of the reactions studied by the authors (see Table 2), mechanism B seems unlikely.

TABLE 2

Summary of kinetic data for the oxidation of chloroplast[a] [2Fe–2S] ferredoxins

Oxidant	Overall Parameters				Component Parameters					Ref.
	k (25°C) ($\text{M}^{-1}\,\text{s}^{-1}$)	$\Delta H^{\ddagger}$ (kcal mol^{-1})	$\Delta S^{\ddagger}$ (cal K^{-1} mol^{-1})	K (25°C) (M^{-1})	ΔH^{0} (kcal mol^{-1})	ΔS^{0} (cal K^{-1} mol^{-1})	k_{et} (s^{-1}) (25°C)	$\Delta H^{\ddagger}_{\text{et}}$ (kcal mol^{-1})	$\Delta S^{\ddagger}_{\text{et}}$ (cal K^{-1} mol^{-1})	
$(NH_3)_5Co(NH_2)Co(NH_3)_5^{5+}$	5.6×10^{6b}	17.0	29	26400^b	5.6	39	214^b	11.4	−10	c
$Pt(NH_3)_6^{4+}$	6.9×10^4	–	–	21000	–	–	3.3	–	–	c
$Co(NH_3)_6^{3+}$	1.9×10^4	18.7	24	998	10.2	48	19.2	8.5	−24	d
$Co(NH_3)_6^{3+}$	1.5×10^{3e}	–	–	77^e	–	–	19.9^e	–	–	d
$Co(en)_3^{3}$	1.6×10^3	21.0	26	597	11.0	50	2.7	10.0	−23	d
$Co(NH_3)_5Cl^{2+}$	4.1×10^5	8.4	−5	(194)	(2.6)	(19)	(2300)	(5.8)	−24	d
$Co(NH_3)_5C_2O_4^{+}$	5.7×10^3	8.0	−15	–	–	–	–	–	–	d
$Co(dmgH)_2(Ph\ NH_2)_2^{+l}$	7.4×10^5	6.7	−9	–	–	–	–	–	–	k
$Co(acac)_3$	4.3×10^3	6.3	−20	–	–	–	–	–	–	h
$Fe(hedta)^f$	2.5×10^{4g}	0.3	−37	–	–	–	–	–	–	h
$Co(edta)^-$	7.2×10^3	5.2	−23	–	–	–	–	–	–	d
$Fe(edta)^{2-f}$	2.9×10^{5h}	0.7	−31	–	–	–	–	–	–	h
$Co(C_2O_4)_3^{3-}$	3.9×10^3	3.2	−32	–	–	–	–	–	–	c
Ferricytochrome $c^{f,j}$	8.1×10^4	9.6	−4	–	–	–	–	–	–	h
Metmyoglobin^{f,j}	2.3×10^6	−0.9	−32	–	–	–	–	–	–	h

[a] Unless otherwise stated, parsley Fd, pH = 8.0 (Tris-Cl), $I = 0.1$ (NaCl).
[b] Temp = 7°C.
[c] Ref. [11].
[d] Ref. [9].
[e] $I = 0.5$ (NaCl).
[f] Spinach Fd, pH = 7.8 (Tris-Cl), $I = 0.1$.
[g] Temp = 26°C.
[h] Ref. [132].
[i] Temp = 12.5°C.
[j] $I = 0.1$, pH = 7.0 (phosphate) 25°C.
[k] Adzamli et al., unpublished results.
[l] dmgH = dimethylglyoxime.

F. Armstrong

Mechanism C

$$FdR + Ox \rightleftharpoons FdR:Ox \qquad K_4 \qquad (13)$$

$$FdR + Ox \rightarrow products \qquad k_5 \qquad (14)$$

(n.b. $FdR:Ox \nrightarrow$ products

$FdR:Ox + Ox \nrightarrow$ products)

$$k_{obs} = \frac{k_5[Ox]}{1 + K_4[Ox]} \qquad (15)$$

This is termed the "dead-end" mechanism since strong association of oxidant with protein occurs, but at a non-productive site to produce a redox-inactive adduct. The reaction can proceed only via a productive bimolecular encounter between free protein and reagent.

It is difficult to distinguish between mechanisms A and C directly, but a number of observations serve to argue against the latter interpretation. Firstly for mechanism A, the limiting rate at high oxidant concentration corresponds to k_{et}. The intraadduct electron-transfer rate would not be expected to be appreciably influenced by variations in ionic strength, and this is indeed borne out with studies involving $Co(NH_3)_6^{3+}$ and FdR (Table 2). At pH 8·0, 25°C, $I = 0·10$ M, interpretation in terms of this mechanism yields $K = 998$ M^{-1}, $k_{et} = 19·2$ s^{-1}, whereas for $I = 0·50$ M, $K = 77$ M^{-1}, $k_{et} = 19·9$ s^{-1}. On the other hand, for mechanism C, the limiting rate is k_5/K_4, a quotient that comprises bimolecular quantities that might both be expected to be influenced significantly by ionic strength variations. Similarity between limiting rates at two ionic strengths would have to be accounted for by identical changes in K_4 and k_5, an unlikely coincidence. Further argument against the "dead-end" interpretation arises from studies in which the redox-inactive analogue $Cr(NH_3)_6^{3+}$ competitively inhibits the reaction with $Co(NH_3)_6^{3+}$ but accelerates the reaction with $Co(edta)^-$. A complete and general inactivation, as required by mechanism C, is therefore not observed. The far-stretching requirement for a potentially redox-active precursor adduct to remain dormant must in addition be regarded with some scepticism. As a consequence of these considerations, as well as observations drawn from studies with blue-copper proteins,[91] preference has been given to mechanism A. Kinetic parameters from an extensive range of studies are shown in Table 2. No variation of rate constants with pH (7·0–9·0) is seen with either $Co(NH_3)_6^{3+}$ or $Co(edta)^-$ as oxidant. Although the amino-acid sequence of parsley Fd has not been reported, accumulation of such data for a wide range of [2Fe–2S] ferredoxins reveals that a single histidine, which might normally be expected to exhibit a pK_a in this pH region, is invariant at position 92[103].

The increasing magnitude of K, for precursor adduct formation, with reagent charge is indicative of a predominantly electrostatic interaction, and positive ΔS^0 values are consistent with lower solvation for an adduct of decreased charge. The reaction with $Co(NH_3)_5Cl^{2+}$ gives only marginal evidence for rate saturation, whereas $Co(NH_3)_5C_2O_4^+$ and increasingly negatively charged oxidants yield only overall rate constants, indicating little tendency to undergo significant association with the protein prior to electron transfer ($K[Ox] \ll 1$). From amino-acid analyses of chloroplast ferredoxins a significant negative charge is expected at pH 7·0, the iso-electric point for oxidized spinach Fd being <4.[94] Ignoring internal compensatory effects such as H-bonding, the overall charge could be as much as 17− in the case of reduced spinach Fd.[164] Consequently a favourable interaction with more positively charged redox partners is expected, but the question remains as to the relative importance of overall and localized charge. The redox-inactive analogues $Cr(NH_3)_6^{3+}$ and $Cr(en)_3^{3+}$ inhibit oxidation by the positively charged reagents according to (16):

$$k_{obs} = \frac{k_{et}K[Ox]}{1 + K_{Cr}[Cr]} \tag{16}$$

This is consistent with a scheme ((17)–(19)) in which a single $Cr(NH_3)_6^{3+}$ (or $Cr(en)_3^{3+}$) bound to the protein completely blocks the reaction.

$$Fd_R + Cr \rightleftharpoons Fd_R : Cr \qquad K_{Cr} \tag{17}$$

$$Fd_R + Ox \rightleftharpoons Fd_R : Ox \qquad K \tag{18}$$

$$Fd_R : Ox \rightarrow products \qquad k_{et} \tag{19}$$

Since only one Cr(III) is required, a single binding site, rather than a number of sites on the protein surface, appears to be used for all these oxidants. Some insight into the size of this area is suggested by the relative magnitudes of K for $Co(III)_2^{5+}$ (26 400 M^{-1}) and $Co(NH_3)_6^{3+}$ (998 M^{-1}). The binuclear complex can be viewed as a "dumb-bell" of two $Co(NH_3)_5^{2.5+}$, but the greatly increased stability constant indicates that more than just one end is "seen" by the protein. A fairly large zone, therefore, is probably involved in binding, but the region at which electron transfer occurs must be sharply defined, otherwise it is unlikely that a single redox-inert 3+ ion could completely inhibit the reaction with $Co(NH_3)_5C_2O_4^+$, for which a much milder electrostatic interaction is expected.

With $Co(edta)^-$ as oxidant, a non-linear increase in rate constants is observed in the presence of $Cr(NH_3)_6^{3+}$. This is consistent with reaction (20):

$$Fd_R : Cr + Ox \rightarrow Fd_R + Cr + product \qquad k_{Cr} \tag{20}$$

in which the $Fd_R : Cr$ adduct is more reactive toward $Co(edta)^-$ than Fd_R itself. In combination with (17)–(19), provided $K[Ox] \ll 1$ so that $k_{12} = k_{et}K$, the rate law obtained is (21), or the linear form (22):

$$\frac{k_{obs}}{[Ox]} - k_{12} = \frac{(k_{Cr} - k_{12})K_{Cr}[Cr]}{1 + K_{Cr}[Cr]} \tag{21}$$

$$\frac{[Ox]}{k_{obs} - k_{12}[Ox]} = \frac{1}{(k_{Cr} - k_{12})K_{Cr}} \cdot \frac{1}{[Cr]} + \frac{1}{(k_{Cr} - k_{12})} \tag{22}$$

The value of K_{Cr} ($459 \pm 10 \, \text{M}^{-1}$) is identical with values obtained from studies in which $Cr(NH_3)_6^{3+}$ inhibits the reaction, indicating that the same binding process is influential in both cases. The redox-inactive anions $Fe(CN)_6^{4-}$ and $Zr(C_2O_4)_4^{4-}$ do not inhibit oxidation by $Co(C_2O_4)_3^{3-}$, indicating little tendency of such negatively charged species to associate strongly with the protein.

With the neutral oxidants $Co(acac)_3$, $Co(NH_3)_3(NO_2)_3$, and $Co(acac)_2(NH_3)(NO_2)$, the binding of $Cr(NH_3)_6^{3+}$ (and also $Cr(en)_3^{3+}$ or $(en)_2Cr(OH, O_2CCH_3)Cr(en)_2^{4+}$, with $Co(acac)_3$) results only in partial inhibition (Adzamli *et al.*, unpublished results) which supersedes an earlier report that oxidation by $Co(acac)_3$ was unaffected by $Cr(NH_3)_6^{3+}$ association.[11] Fits to expressions (16) or (21) are not satisfactory but using Equation (23), which is an alternative form of (21), linear plots are obtained after inserting a known value for K_{Cr}.

$$\frac{k_{obs}}{Ox} \cdot (1 + K_{Cr}[Cr]) = k_{12} + k_{Cr}K_{Cr}[Cr] \tag{23}$$

For partial inhibition $k_{Cr} < k_{12}$. A summary of all data is given in Table 3.

Previous interpretation, for which the apparent insensitivity of $Co(acac)_3$ oxidation to $Cr(NH_3)_6^{3+}$ binding was crucial, involved three binding sites which are selected according to reagent charge and ligand type.[11] The more recent results, however, favour a much simpler explanation, namely that $Cr(NH_3)_6^{3+}$ can influence the reactivity of all oxidants, cationic, neutral and anionic, by binding in a locality utilized by all three. The term "functional zone" is used to describe this locality and the various interactions with incoming small reagents are shown schematically in Fig. 3. The "functional zone" incorporates a patch of negative charge, which constitutes the electrostatically favourable binding site for cations such as $Co(NH_3)_6^{3+}$ and $Cr(NH_3)_6^{3+}$, and an area at which electrons leave or enter the protein, the electron-transfer point. As implied earlier, the electron-transfer point is probably very localized, perhaps consisting of a bridging or cysteinyl sulphur atom, and must lie near to the negative patch in order to account for the complete inhibition of $Co(NH_3)_5C_2O_4^+$ in the presence

TABLE 3

Summary of data for the oxidation of reduced parsley and *C. pasteurianum* ferredoxins in the presence of redox-inactive Cr(III) complexes[a]

Oxidant	Cr(III) complex	K_{Cr} (M^{-1})	k (M^{-1} s^{-1})	k_{Cr} (M^{-1} s^{-1})	Ref.
A. Parsley Fd					
$Co(III)_2^{5+}$	$Cr(NH_3)_6^{3+}$	305^b	$5\cdot6 \times 10^{6b}$	–	c
$Pt(NH_3)_6^{4+}$	$Cr(NH_3)_6^{3+}$	474	$6\cdot9 \times 10^4$	–	c
$Co(NH_3)_6^{3+}$	$Cr(NH_3)_6^{3+}$	476	$1\cdot9 \times 10^4$	–	c
$Co(NH_3)_6^{3+}$	$Cr(en)_3^{3+}$	590	$1\cdot9 \times 10^4$	–	c
$Co(NH_3)_5Cl^{2+}$	$Cr(NH_3)_6^{3+}$	462	$4\cdot1 \times 10^5$	–	c
$Co(NH_3)_5C_2O_4^+$	$Cr(NH_3)_6^{3+}$	467	$5\cdot7 \times 10^3$	–	c
$Co(acac)_3$	$Cr(NH_3)_6^{3+}$	468^d	$4\cdot1 \times 10^3$	$1\cdot8 \times 10^3$	e
$Co(acac)_3$	$Cr(en)_3^{3+}$	590^f	$4\cdot3 \times 10^3$	$2\cdot1 \times 10^3$	e
$Co(acac)_3$	$Cr(III)_2^{4+}$	1100^g	$4\cdot3 \times 10^3$	$1\cdot8 \times 10^3$	e
$Co(NH_3)_3(NO_2)_3$	$Cr(NH_3)_6^{3+}$	468^d	$6\cdot7 \times 10^3$	$3\cdot4 \times 10^3$	e
$Co(acac)_2(NH_3)(NO_2)$	$Cr(NH_3)_6^{3+}$	468^d	$1\cdot3 \times 10^4$	$5\cdot1 \times 10^3$	e
$Co(edta)^-$	$Cr(NH_3)_6^{3+}$	459	$7\cdot2 \times 10^3$	$2\cdot2 \times 10^4$	c
B. *C. pasteurianum* Fd					
$Co(NH_3)_6^{3+}$	$Cr(NH_3)_6^{3+}$	212	$4\cdot6 \times 10^4$	–	h
$Co(NH_3)_6^{3+}$	$Cr(en)_3^{3+}$	318	$4\cdot6 \times 10^4$	–	h
$Co(NH_3)_6^{3+}$	$Cr(III)_2^{4+}$	326	$4\cdot6 \times 10^4$	–	h
$Co(acac)_3$	$Cr(NH_3)_6^{3+}$	212^d	$3\cdot3 \times 10^4$	$1\cdot8 \times 10^4$	h
$Co(edta)^-$	$Cr(NH_3)_6^{3+}$	212^j	$1\cdot1 \times 10^4$	$5\cdot2 \times 10^4$	h

[a] Unless otherwise stated, pH = 8·0 (Tris-Cl), I = 0·1 (NaCl), Temp = 25°C.
[b] Temp = 7°C.
[c] Ref. [11].
[d] Average of K_{Cr} values as determined experimentally.
[e] Adzamli *et al.*, unpublished results.
[f] Value for $Cr(en)_3^{3+}$ inhibition of $Co(NH_3)_6^{3+}$.
[g] Value for $(en)_2 Cr.\mu - (OH, O_2C.CH_3).Cr(en)_2^{4+}$ inhibition of $Co(NH_3)_6^{3+}$; Henderson and Sykes, unpublished results.
[h] Armstrong *et al.*, unpublished results.
[j] Independent determination, using expression (21) gives K_{Cr} = 221 M^{-1}, k_{Cr} = 5·1 × 10^4 M^{-1} s^{-1}.

of bound $Cr(NH_3)_6^{3+}$. That the electron-transfer point is not actually located within the cation binding area (and thereby physically obstructed during $Cr(NH_3)_6^{3+}$ occupancy) is clear from the results with neutral and anionic oxidants. With $Co(edta)^-$, the rate enhancement results from more favourable electrostatics, whereas with the neutral oxidants a mild steric interference is envisaged. The above model perhaps rationalizes the high activation enthalpies for electron transfer that are obtained with the more positively charged reagents, since vibrational motion will be required to provide an effective probability of encounter between bound oxidant and electron-transfer point. At the same time, attention is drawn to the view that binding, at least that often detected with small nonphysiological partners, may not necessarily occur in such a manner as to achieve optimal rates of electron transfer between centres. An ideal situation may be approached only in the case of physiological partners where specific binding interactions, which optimize the mutual orientation of both species for efficient electron transfer, provide a basis for the control of biological redox pathways.

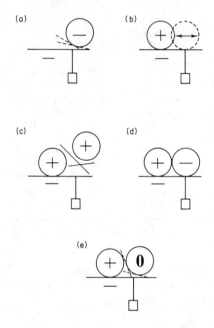

Fig. 3. Scheme depicting interactions of various reagents with the "functional zone" of parsley [2Fe–2S] (and *C. pasteurianum* 2[4Fe–4S]) Fd. The Fe–S cluster is represented by (□), while full and partial inhibition are indicated by ⟩⟨ and ⟩⟩⟨⟨ respectively. (*a*) Approach by anions such as Co(edta)⁻ (hindered by adverse electrostatics). (*b*) Binding of cations such as Co(NH₃)₆³⁺. Efficient electron-transfer communication with Fe–S cluster requires additional movement. (*c*)–(*e*) Interactions with "functional zone" in the presence of bound redox-inactive Cr(NH₃)₆³⁺.

Rawlings *et al.*[132] have studied the oxidation of spinach Fd_R by Fe(edta)⁻ and Fe(hedta) (hedta = *N*-hydroxyethylethylenediaminetriacetate) and the proteins horseheart cytochrome *c* and metmyoglobin. The rather low electrostatically corrected k_{11} value, $1 \cdot 7 \times 10^{-3} \, \mathrm{M^{-1} s^{-1}}$, calculated from data obtained with Fe(edta)⁻ is interpreted as indicating that the [2Fe–2S] centre is rather inaccessible to this reagent. Some scepticism has, however, been expressed by Armstrong and Sykes[9] who suggest that Marcus-type ionic strength corrections based upon the Fe(III) reagent (actually $Fe(edta)(H_2O)^-$ where H_2O occupies the seventh coordination site) are liable to be in error owing to deprotonation and dimerization equilibria producing $2-$ and $4-$ species at pH 7·8. These effects are probably responsible for a pH profile (pK 7·2) observed with this reagent.

Activation parameters display a reasonable isokinetic relationship.[11] However, there is certainly some doubt about the usefulness of such an approach since the "fit" obtained here is fortuitous, experimental rate measurement limitations necessarily confining $\Delta G^\ddagger$ within a narrow range. Previous criticism has been directed at this concept.[16] Nevertheless, it is worthy of note that the more cationic reagents (including cytochrome *c*) yield more positive overall $\Delta H^\ddagger$ and $\Delta S^\ddagger$ values, establishing in fact a general trend that is apparent from the data in Table 2.

At the present time the exact location of the "functional zone" remains uncertain, although it is worth mentioning means by which this information might be obtained. A particularly attractive approach has been demonstrated with the blue-copper protein plastocyanin. In this case, for the diamagnetic Cu(I) reduced form, specific binding sites for the redox-inactive species (active counterparts, where applicable, in parentheses) $Cr(CN)_6^{3-}$ ($Fe(CN)_6^{3-}$), $Cr(phen)_3^{3+}$ ($Co(phen)_3^{3+}$), and $Cr(NH_3)_6^{3+}$ have been assigned on the basis of high-resolution NMR line-broadening studies.[42,63] A paramagnetic Cr(III) complex, if associated with the protein, broadens resonances due to protons in the nearby vicinity. The magnitude of this effect is proportional to the inverse sixth power of the distance between proton and paramagnetic centre; consequently if the relevant proton resonances can be assigned to specific amino-acid residues, the locality of the Cr(III) binding site may be determined. In conjunction with three-dimensional structural data,[41] results indicate that $Cr(CN)_6^{3-}$ binds at a site (possibly positively charged) very near the Cu centre, whereas $Cr(phen)_3^{3+}$ and $Cr(NH_3)_6^{3+}$ share a more distant zone, described as a pocket of negative charge arising from five invariant aspartate and glutamate residues. A high specificity in binding location is therefore indicated and zones of predominantly acidic residues appear to function as binding sites for cationic species.

From the three-dimensional structure determination for *S. platensis* Fd, the Fe–S cluster is located on the inside of one arm of a "horseshoe"-shaped area at the top of the molecule, as shown in Fig. 2.[58, 103] Amino-acid sequences determined for a wide range of chloroplast ferredoxins from prokaryotes and eukaryotes indicate that this section comprises the larger proportion of invariant and semi-invariant (chemically similar) residues[103] which, besides their location near the cluster, are through evolutionary conservation those most likely to be involved in electron transfer. A mechanistic role for aromatic side-chains as suggested for bacterial (*P. aerogenes*) Fd[1] and *Chromatium* HiPIP[35] seems unjustified here in view of the absence of invariant aromatic residues adjacent to the cluster, although a single histidine is generally conserved at position 92. On the other hand, the location of the cluster near the molecular surface, with two cysteinyl S atoms exposed to solvent on one side, and a predominantly hydrophobic cavity on the other, supports the feasibility of direct orbital interaction with suitable redox partners. A search for invariant and semi-invariant acidic residues likely to provide a suitable binding site for cationic reagents such as $Co(NH_3)_6^{3+}$ reveals certain possibilities. One of these concerns the "horseshoe"-like cavity in which the Fe–S cluster is located. Glutamate (or aspartate) is highly conserved at positions 67, 68 and 69 at the end of the elongated segment forming one arm of the "horseshoe". The somewhat hydrophobic crevice consequently forms a pocket of negative charge, being lined by acid residues 67, 68 and 69, a highly conserved glutamate (94) adjacent to the cluster, as well as the Fe–S centre (contributing 3− in the reduced form). Such a zone or part of it might, by analogy with plastocyanin, form a binding site for cations such as $Co(NH_3)_6^{3+}$.

An important question that must be considered concerns the relevance of such localized interactions to physiological function, where the redox partners are generally large protein molecules. Electrostatic forces probably play an important role in controlling *in vivo* dynamics. One of the key functions of chloroplast Fd is the reduction of $NADP^+$, a process that requires Fd:$NADP^+$ oxidoreductase, a FAD-containing enzyme.[167] A 1 : 1 complex between Fd and enzyme is thought to be the catalytically active species, and a strong electrostatic interaction appears to be responsible for the high binding constant, $K = 2 \times 10^7$ at $I = 0$, high ionic strength resulting as expected in dissociation.[56] Electrochemical titrations performed on this system show that complex formation lowers the Fd reduction potential by 22 mV while raising the enzyme potential 23 mV,[139] a feature that results in a thermodynamic driving force significantly higher than that calculated for the isolated components. The observation that bacterial Fd from various sources is capable of replacing chloroplast Fd in the *in vivo* reduction of $NADP^+$ serves to support the assignment of low-specificity electrostatic interactions.[94, 144] While being structurally quite different from chloroplast ferredoxins, bacterial ferredoxins have similar reduction potentials and are appreciably negatively charged at physiological pH values.

Aside from this example, numerous other Fd:protein complexes are implicated in a variety of metabolic processes. Another important function of chloroplast Fd is in the reduction of nitrite to ammonia where a 1:1 complex between Fd and Fd:nitrite oxidoreductase is possibly involved.[85] It seems likely, but not established, that electrostatic interactions may be operative. A somewhat novel role for Fd is suggested by observations made on the cytochrome *c* reductase activity of Fd:NADP$^+$ oxidoreductase. Cytochrome *c* bound to spinach Fd is a much better substrate than cytochrome *c* alone, implying that Fd might in this case function merely to quench the positive charge on the haemoprotein.[46] The tetrameric [3Fe–3S] protein Fd(II) from *D. gigas* is thought to undergo complex formation with cytochrome c_3 as part of the sulphite reduction pathway. Specific electrostatic interactions are likely.[112] The [2Fe–2S] protein adrenodoxin forms a 1:1 complex with adrenodoxin reductase for which the ionic strength effects again indicate the involvement of dominant electrostatic interactions.[40]

These observations serve to emphasize the complementary value of small reagent protein studies with regard to protein–protein dynamics. The combination of small size and structural integrity allows evaluation of site localization and specificity that is often difficult to assess from examination of protein–protein systems. Clearly the "physiological" and "nonphysiological" approaches each have a place in this somewhat undeveloped field.

E. Kinetic studies with bacterial 2[4Fe–4S] ferredoxins

The small ferredoxins MW 5000–6000, containing two [4Fe–4S] clusters, which are easily isolated from several anaerobic microbes, are the best characterized examples of Fe–S proteins operating in the [4Fe–4S]$^{2+/1+}$ couple. The considerable sequence homology existing between the various ferredoxins of this class allows justifiable speculation on structural aspects based on the three-dimensional structure analysis at 2.8 Å (and more recently at 2 Å) for the Fd from *P. aerogenes*.[1, 2]

The two clusters are situated ~12 Å apart along the line of elongation of the molecule, as shown in Fig. 4, and an interesting feature is the approximate two-fold symmetry axis which relates the two cluster-binding halves of the molecule. Furthermore, the sequences for the first and second halves of these small proteins are related by an approximate 180° rotation.[135] This intriguing example of symmetry in a biological molecule has prompted the question of whether some form of cooperativity might exist between the two clusters.[36, 118] The manner of coordination of each cluster, by a "triplet" of cysteine residues from one half of the sequence and a single residue from the other, implies some measure of mechanical coupling whereby a geometry change concomitant with oxidoreduction at one site might perturb (thermodynamically or kinetically) the other. The space between the two clusters is occupied by amino-acid side-chains. A conformational change accompanying reduction of C. acidi-urici Fd is suggested by an observed decrease in the number of tritium-exchangeable sites.[70]

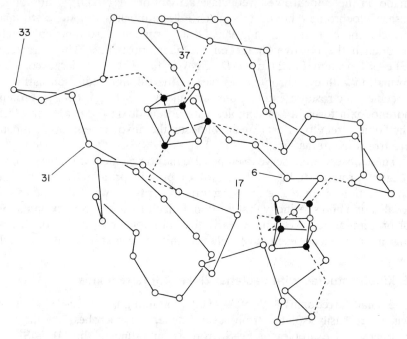

Fig. 4. Three-dimensional structure of *P. aerogenes* Fd (after Adman *et al.*,[1] showing the α-carbon atoms and positions of the two [4Fe–4S] clusters. Dotted lines indicate cysteinyl–S–Fe links and arrows depict the positions of invariant acidic residues.

From equilibrium measurements there is little doubt, from the Nernst coefficient $n = 1$, that electrons are transferred singly.[140] The presence, in most clostridial-type ferredoxins sequenced to date, of aromatic residues in the near vicinity of each cluster has permitted the monitoring of redox changes using ^{13}C NMR. In the case of examples for which the two aromatic amino-acids are different, *C. pasteurianum* Fd (phenylalanine and tyrosine), and the chemically modified protein *C. acidi-urici* (phe^2) Fd (phenylalanine and tyrosine), reduction at either cluster can be individually monitored.[122] Results indicate that the individual reduction potentials of the clusters within each example differ by as little as $10 \pm 5\,mV$ and $<10\,mV$ respectively. The average reduction potential for *C. pasteurianum* Fd determined by equilibration with the $H_2/2H^+$ couple via hydrogenase, is -403 mV at pH 7.0.[140] The equilibrium electron occupancy of the two sites has been further examined by EPR titration, exploiting the ability to distinguish between singly and doubly reduced molecules.[143] It is concluded that there is no evidence for any cooperative interaction. Likewise, employing pulse-radiolysis to rapidly generate the singly-reduced form and compare its rate of re-oxidation by $Co(NH_3)_5Cl^{2+}$ with that of the fully reduced form, no unusual kinetic reactivity is noted.[26] Possible communication but not cooperativity is therefore indicated for these bifunctional molecules.

Using small substitution-inert oxidants as probes, the electron-transfer reactivity of reduced *C. pasteurianum* 2[4Fe–4S] Fd has been studied.[12] With all the reagents used (see Table 4), single-stage kinetics are observed for the two-equivalent process. In view of the above overwhelming evidence against cooperativity, and the apparent absence of unusually high reactivity in the one-electron pulsed protein, the authors interpret this behaviour in terms of a statistically related biphasic scheme in which the fully reduced form (RR) reacts at twice the rate of the one-electron-reduced form (RO) (24):

$$Fd_{RR} \xrightarrow{k_A} Fd_{RO} \xrightarrow{k_B} Fd_{OO} \qquad (24)$$

If, as seems reasonable, equal absorbance changes $(\varepsilon_{OO} - \varepsilon_{RO}) = (\varepsilon_{RO} - \varepsilon_{RR})$ are observed for each cluster, and from a statistical standpoint $k_A = 2k_B$, substitution into the general equation for biphasic kinetics[24a] gives (25):

$$A_t = \varepsilon_{OO}C_0 + (\varepsilon_{RR} - \varepsilon_{OO}) C_0 e^{-k_A t}$$
$$+ (\varepsilon_{RO} - \varepsilon_{OO})[k_A C_0/(k_B - k_A)](e^{-k_A t} - e^{-k_A t}) \qquad (25)$$

in which C_0 is the initial concentration of Fd_{RR}. The absorbance changes A (for a 1 cm path length) are expressed as in (26):

$$A_\infty - A_t = 2(\varepsilon_{OO} - \varepsilon_{RO})C_0 e^{-k_B t} \qquad (26)$$

Consequently, rate constants k_{obs} obtained from the single-stage kinetics actually correspond to the true rate constants for the monofunctional species Fd_{RO}, and must be multiplied by the statistical factor 2 in order to obtain k_A.

As with studies on chloroplast ferredoxins, the more positively charged reagents (excluding the 5+ complex, for which high reaction rates limit oxidant concentration) show a less than first-order dependence at high concentration, and data conform well to expression (5). Kinetic parameters

TABLE

Kinetic data for the oxidation of reduced *C. pasteurianum* Fd^a

Oxidant	k (25°C)^c ($M^{-1} s^{-1}$)	$\Delta H^{\ddagger}$ (kcal mol^{-1})	$\Delta S^{\ddagger}$ (cal K^{-1} mol^{-1})	K (25°C) (M^{-1})	ΔH^0 (kcal mol^{-1})	ΔS^0 (cal K^{-1} mol^{-1})	k_{et} (25°C) (s^{-1})	$\Delta H^{\ddagger}_{et}$ (kcal mol^{-1})	$\Delta S^{\ddagger}_{et}$ (cal K^{-1} mol^{-1})
(NH$_3$)$_5$Co(NH$_2$)Co(NH$_3$)$_5^{5+}$	9·6 × 10^{5b}	–	–	–	–	–	–	–	–
Pt(NH$_3$)$_6^{4+}$	2·64 × 10^5	–	–	2400	–	–	111	–	–
Co(NH$_3$)$_6^{3+}$	4·6 × 10^4	15.8	15.3	466	0·3	13·4	98	15·3	1·9
Co(en)$_3^{3+}$	3·1 × 10^3	17.0	14.4	261	0·9	13·9	11·8	16·1	0·5
Co(acac)$_3$	3·1 × 10^4	–	–	–	–	–	–	–	–
Co(edta)$^-$	1·1 × 10^4	7·6	−14·4	–	–	–	–	–	–
Co(C$_2$O$_4$)$_3^{3+}$	4·8 × 10^3	–	–	–	–	–	–	–	–

^{a} pH = 8·0, (Tris-Cl) I = 0·1; Ref. [12].
^{b} Temp = 7°C.
^{c} Rate constant corresponds to reaction with Fd$_{RO}$ and must be multiplied by the statistical factor 2 to obtain the value for Fd$_{RR}$.

are shown in Table 4. Interpretation in terms of a scheme involving kinetically detectable precursor adduct formation followed by electron transfer, has been pursued as with previous studies. Values of K (M^{-1}), ΔH^0 (kcal mol^{-1}) and ΔS^0 (cal K^{-1} mol^{-1}) for $Co(NH_3)_6^{3+}$ and $C(en)_3^{3+}$ are respectively 466, 0·3, +13 and 261, 0·9, +14 (25°C, pH = 8, $I = 0·1$). A predominantly electrostatic interaction is indicated, but one that is milder than for comparable studies with parsley [2Fe–2S] Fd. Furthermore the near-zero ΔH^0 values suggest that considerably less conformational upheaval is incurred in adduct formation. From these activation parameters, and competition experiments with redox-inert Cr(III) analogues (see Table 3), it is concluded that cationic reagents such as $Co(NH_3)_6^{3+}$, $Co(en)_3^{3+}$ and $Cr(NH_3)_6^{3+}$ bind at the same site on the protein. Furthermore, while the cationic oxidants are inhibited ($k_{Cr} = 0$) by the binding of Cr(III) analogues, $Co(acac)_3$ and $Co(edta)^-$ respond by partial inhibition and rate enhancement respectively (Armstrong *et al.*, unpublished results). Rationalisation in terms of a functional zone analogous to that suggested above for parsley Fd must therefore be given consideration. No meaningful variation of rate constants for $Co(NH_3)_6^{3+}$ (K, k_{et}) or $Co(acac)_3$ and $Co(edta)^-$ (overall) is observed over the pH range 7·0–8·5 (Tris). This is reasonable in view of the small variation of reduction potential with pH in the region 6·7–7·75[140] and the absence of a histidine group, which is frequently responsible for pH-reactivity profiles in this pH range.

As with chloroplast ferredoxins, the considerable excess of acidic over basic residues ensures a significant overall negative charge at pH 8·0. From amino-acid analysis, calculations indicate a net charge of 12− for *C. pasteurianum* Fd_{RR}, but internal hydrogen-bonding would be expected to somewhat diminish this. Homology similarities between *P. aerogenes* and *C. pasteurianum* ferredoxins[164] allow some speculation regarding possible productive binding sites for cationic oxidants. For $Co(NH_3)_6^{3+}$ and $Co(en)_3^{3+}$, the near-zero $\Delta S_{et}^{\ddagger}$ values suggest that electron transfer is occurring within a far more compact assembly than with parsley Fd. The two clusters lie near (~5 Å) to the molecular surface and the exposure to solvent of cysteinyl —CH_2 groups (residues 11 and 38) at each end of the molecule suggests that (in a dynamic situation) direct orbital overlap with cysteinyl sulphur atoms might be feasible, consequently removing the requirement for longer-range tunnelling processes. In the vicinity of one of the clusters, three aspartate residues lying in fairly close sequence at positions 31, 33 and 37 might provide (with the formal 3− charge originating from the reduced centre) a compact zone of high negative charge, this being a possible area for the binding of cationic species.

The question remains as to whether one or two equivalent "functional zones" may be operative in this bifunctional protein. It is to be recalled that the first and second halves of the structure in *P. aerogenes* Fd may, to a considerable extent, be superimposed on each other.[135]

In cases for which $K[Ox] \ll 1$, the relationship $k = k_{et}K$ holds, but the statistical ratio $k_A = 2k_B$ can originate from either K or k_{et} depending upon whether electron transfer is directed towards one or two reaction sites on the protein. Four possibilities have been considered which include examples where rapid intramolecular electron transfer between the two clusters is operative[12]. These are shown schematically in Fig. 5. On present evidence no one of these alternatives can be favoured over the others.

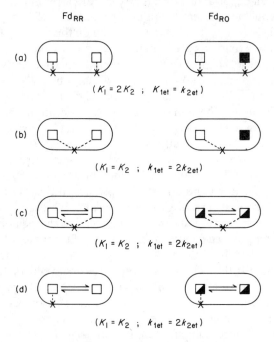

Fig. 5. Schematic representation of alternate ways in which clostridial-type ferredoxins might transfer electrons with involvement of one or two reaction sites (×) with and without communication between [4Fe–4S] clusters (□). Statistical values of K for association and k_{et} for electron transfer are indicated in each case.

The possible role of aromatic residues in the electron-transfer function of these ferredoxins has been debated for some time. In most clostridial-type ferredoxins an aromatic residue, tyrosine or phenylalanine, is conserved at positions 2 and 28, adjacent to each of the clusters. This speculation is, however, overshadowed by several notable observations. No loss of *in vivo* electron-transfer reactivity accompanies the chemical replacement of tyrosine-2 by leucine in *C. acidi-urici* Fd,[96] the naturally occurring protein *Clostridium M–E* Fd in which arginine replaces one of the aromatic residues possesses full biological activity[145] and most conclusive of all, full electron-transfer activity can be demonstrated in a chemically modified form of *C. M–E* Fd in which the sole aromatic residue tyrosine-2 is replaced by leucine.[97] Alternatively these groups have been proposed to act as a hydrophobic "shield" for the clusters.[96]

By tentative use of the Marcus relationships (1) and (2), some idea of the intrinsic reactivity of *C. pasteurianum* Fd can be obtained using the reaction with $Co(edta)^-$ for which the error introduced by neglecting unpredictable electrostatic interactions is likely to be minimal. With $E^0 = 380$ mV for $Co(edta)^-$,[68] $k_{22}(Co(edta)^-) = 4 \times 10^{-7} M^{-1} s^{-1}$,[75] and $E^0 = -403$ mV for Fd,[140] a value of $k_{11} = 2 \times 10^3 M^{-1} s^{-1}$ can be estimated for the self-exchange reaction (27):

$$Fd^*_{RR} + Fd_{RO} \rightarrow Fd^*_{RO} + Fd_{RR} \tag{27}$$

This value indicates a higher intrinsic reactivity for *C. pasteurianum* Fd than for the parsley [2Fe–2S] counterpart, where a similar approach using the $Co(edta)^-$ cross-reaction rate constant yields $k_{11} = 2 \times 10^2 M^{-1} s^{-1}$. The higher intrinsic reactivity does not stem from enthalpic effects since $\Delta H^{\ddagger}_{et}$ values for the reaction with $Co(NH_3)_6^{3+}$ and $Co(en)_3^{3+}$, and $\Delta H^{\ddagger}$ for the overall reaction with $Co(edta)^-$ are actually somewhat higher than for parsley Fd. Instead, the enhancement appears in all cases to arise from a more favourable entropy contribution.

F. Kinetic studies with high-potential [4Fe–4S] proteins

As indicated from the substantial number of literature references, kinetic properties of these simple Fe–S proteins have been extensively studied. [6, 8, 44, 55, 109–111, 116, 131] This interest stems in part from the availability of three-dimensional structure information on the protein from *Chromatium vinosum*[34–36] and from the congenial reduction potentials which permit investigation with a wide range of oxidants and reductants, in most cases without demanding anaerobicity requirements. For the purpose of forming comparisons between independent studies, relevant kinetic data are grouped together in Table 5.

By contrast with the structures of other simple Fe–S proteins, that of *Chromium HiPIP* (Fig. 6) clearly reveals a somewhat buried cluster. Intuitively, one might therefore expect this to be reflected in the protein's electron-transfer behaviour and several observations discussed below do in fact appear to bear this out.

Only for the oxidation of *Chromatium* HiPIP$_R$ by Co(4,7-DPSphen)$_3^{3-}$ (4,7-DPSphen = 4,7-di(phenyl-4'-sulphonate)-1,10-phenanthroline) is rate saturation observed at high reagent concentration, indicative of strong precursor adduct formation prior to electron transfer.[6] In all other cases,

TABLE 5

Summary of kinetic data for the reactions of *Chromatium vinosum* HiPIP with inorganic reagents

	k (25°C) ($M^{-1} s^{-1}$)	$\Delta H^\ddagger$ (kcal mol^{-1})	$\Delta S^\ddagger$ (cal K^{-1} mol^{-1})	Ref.
Oxidants				
Co(phen)$_3^{3+}$ [a]	$2 \cdot 8 \times 10^3$	14·9	7	b
Ru(NH$_3$)$_5$py^{3+} [c]	$1 \cdot 1 \times 10^3$	9·4	-13	d
Mn(cydta)$^-$ [a]	$1 \cdot 3 \times 10^3$	3·6	-28	e
Co(4,7-DPSphen)$_3^{3-}$ [a]	68^f	$7 \cdot 0^f$	-27^f	e
Fe(CN)$_6^{3-}$ [g]	$2 \cdot 5 \times 10^3$	0	-45	h
Fe(CN)$_6^{3-}$ [a]	$2 \cdot 0 \times 10^3$	$-0 \cdot 4$	-45	b
Fe(CN)$_6^{3-}$ [i]	$5 \cdot 3 \times 10^4$	0	-41	j
Reductants				
Fe(edta)$^{2-}$ [a]	$1 \cdot 6 \times 10^3$	0·8	-41	b
Fe(CN)$_6^{4-}$ [g]	152	4·2	-35	h
Fe(CN)$_6^{4-}$ [a]	240	–	–	e
Fe(CN)$_6^{4-}$ [i]	1×10^3	3.7	-33	j

[a] pH 7·0 (phosphate), $I = 0 \cdot 1$ (NaCl).
[b] Ref. [131].
[c] pH 6.5 (phosphate), $I = 0 \cdot 5$ (Na$_2$SO$_4$).
[d] Ref. [44].
[e] Ref. [6].
[f] Saturation kinetics observed, $K = 3420$ M^{-1}, $\Delta H^0 = -8 \cdot 9$ kcal mol^{-1}, $\Delta S^0 = -13.7$ cal K^{-1} mol^{-1}, $k_{et} = 0 \cdot 020$ s^{-1}, $\Delta H_{et}^\ddagger = 15 \cdot 9$ kcal mol^{-1}, $\Delta S_{et}^\ddagger = -12 \cdot 9$ cal K^{-1} mol^{-1}.
[g] pH 7·3, $I = 0 \cdot 1$ (NaCl), Temp = 20°C.
[h] Ref. [109].
[i] *Rhodopseudomonas gelatinosa* HiPIP, pH 7·0, $I = 0 \cdot 12$ (NaCl).
[j] Ref. [111].

strictly second-order behaviour is displayed. A noticeable feature is the large variation in activation parameters, possibly reflecting the utilization of different reagent binding sites and electron-transfer routes. Using the Marcus relationship (1) Gray and co-workers have calculated self-exchange rate constants for *Chromatium* HiPIP from cross-reaction studies with a number of reagents.[44, 131] Electrostatically corrected k_{11} values, $1 \cdot 4 \times 10^4$ M^{-1} s^{-1} (Co(phen)$_3^{3+}$), 2.1×10^3 M^{-1} s^{-1} (Ru(NH$_3$)$_5$py^{3+}), $2 \cdot 3$ M^{-1} s^{-1} (Ru(NH$_3$)$_6^{2+}$), and $1 \cdot 3 \times 10^{-2}$ M^{-1} s^{-1} (Fe(edta)$^{2-}$) span 6 orders of magnitude. Despite reservations concerning applicability of the Marcus approach to protein reactions, this variation is quite striking. Gray and his associates have proposed that these results can be interpreted in terms of a "kinetic accessibility" scale. The aromatic groups of Co(phen)$_3^{3+}$ and the

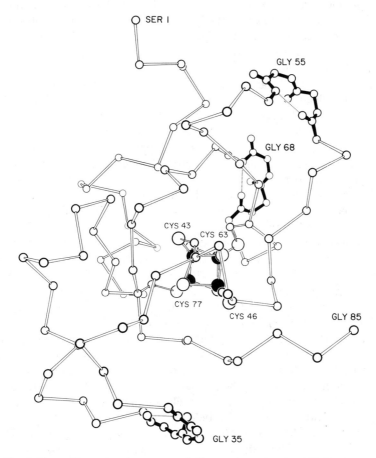

Fig. 6. Three-dimensional structure of *Chromatium vinosum* HiPIP showing the α-carbon atoms and the position of the [4Fe–4S] cluster (original kindly provided by Professor C.W. Carter, Jr.).

single pyridine ligand from Ru(NH$_3$)$_5$py^{3+} might be expected to penetrate the hydrophobic interior of HiPIP, thereby achieving direct orbital overlap with the buried Fe–S centre (it is to be noted that Ru(NH$_3$)$_6^{2+}$ is less reactive than Ru(NH$_3$)$_5$py^{3+} by a factor of 10^3). Such an interaction would require some movement of the peptide chains, accounting for the high $\Delta H^{\ddagger}$ values (14·9 and 9·4 kcal mol^{-1} respectively). Penetration by Ru(NH$_3$)$_5$py^{3+} would be expected to be subdued by comparison with Co(phen)$_3^{3+}$ because of the adverse interaction between the hydrophobic ammine ligands and the hydrophobic protein interior. Conversely the hydrophilic nature of Fe(edta)$^{2-}$ prohibits any penetration of the protein and electron transfer is forced to occur over a much longer distance. The near-zero $\Delta H^{\ddagger}$ and large negative $\Delta S^{\ddagger}$ values are consistent with this interpretation.

A modified version of Hopfield's equation,[71] which relates rate constants to electron-transfer distances, has been used with varying degrees of success to estimate distances from protein surface to metal centre.[104] For *Chromatium* HiPIP with Fe(edta)$^{2-}$ as reductant, this analysis yields a value of 5·8 Å. This is considerably more than the value of 1·6 Å obtained using data for Ru(NH$_3$)$_5$py^{3+}, supporting the above view that reagents with hydrophobic ligands are able to penetrate the protein core to shorten the distance of electron transfer. The estimate of 5·8 Å, even if considered somewhat qualitative, is supported by the three-dimensional structure[34–36] and evidence from electron spin-echo decay analysis which indicates no free access for deuterons to the Fe–S centre.[125]

Some insight regarding the existence of different electron-transfer pathways and binding sites has been achieved through studies involving simultaneous attack on *Chromatium* HiPIP$_R$ by Fe(CN)$_6^{3-}$ and Co(4,7-DPSphen)$_3^{3-}$ (the latter reagent associates strongly with the protein, $K = 3420$ M^{-1}, but intraadduct electron transfer is very slow, $k_{et} = 0.020$ s^{-1}).[6] Oxidation by Fe(CN)$_6^{3-}$ proceeds unaffected by the binding of Co(4,7-DPSphen)$_3^{3-}$, consequently a different site, and presumably an alternative electron transfer pathway, must be involved. Similarly, oxidation by Mn(cydta) is unaffected and must therefore utilize a different site also, although this may be the same as used by Fe(CN)$_6^{3-}$. It appears that overall charge might be relatively unimportant, as independently suggested by other authors (see below).

Cusanovich and his associates have studied the equilibration of HiPIP with Fe(CN)$_6^{3-/4-}$ in both directions[109, 111] and for the protein isolated from three organisms, *Chromatium*, *Rhodopseudomonas gelatinosa*, and *Thiocapsa pfennigii*, pH–rate constant profiles have been examined over a limited range (5–11). With *Rps gelatinosa* HiPIP good fits to pK values of 7·3 (oxidised) and 7·8 (reduced) are obtained. With oxidized and reduced forms of *Thiocapsa* and *Chromatium* HiPIP, rate increases are observed below pH 7, this effect being particularly dramatic with the *Thiocapsa* protein. In neither of the latter two cases can pK values be assigned (although as discussed below, Feinberg and his associates report pK assignments for *Chromatium* HiPIP on the basis of electrostatically corrected rate constants). The reduction of *Chromatium* and *Thiocapsa* HiPIP$_O$ by Fe(CN)$_6^{4-}$ is found to be independent of ionic strength ($0.008 < I < 0.208$), whereas both proteins exhibit rate increases at higher I for the oxidation reaction, plots of ln k against $I^{1/2}$ being linear. The authors interpret these results as suggesting a neutral protein binding site for the HiPIP$_O$–Fe(CN)$_6^{4-}$ reaction, and a small negatively-charged site for HiPIP$_R$ with Fe(CN)$_6^{3-}$. From amino-acid analyses, both of these proteins should carry a negative net charge at pH 7. For the oxidized forms, including a contribution of 1− for the Fe–S centre, these are calculated to be 4− (*Chromatium*, pI = 3·7) and 8− (*Thiocapsa*). Consequently, if it is considered that intrinsic H-bonding effects do not entirely remove this negative charge, then specific localized interactions must be operative between protein and reagent, the overall charge not being "seen" by Fe(CN)$_6^{4-}$. Such a proposal cannot be upheld in the case of *Rps gelatinosa* HiPIP, with which rate constants for both oxidation and reduction decrease with ionic strength. The net charge at pH 7 for the oxidized form is calculated to be 4+ (pI = 9·5), so that the experimentally determined plus–minus interaction could be explained simply in terms of overall charge. However, despite the obvious differences between *Chromatium* and *Rps gelatinosa* proteins, activation parameters (Table 5) are remarkably similar indicating that common mechanistic features are effective in both cases. The localized interactions may be dominant also in the positively charged protein. In all cases the apparent charge determined for the reduced protein is more negative than for the oxidized form. The authors propose that the Fe–S centre charge is "seen" by the Fe(CN)$_6^{3-/4-}$ reagent and have proposed likely zones on the protein surface within which this charge could be effectively "communicated" via carbonyl oxygen atoms. An area confined within residues 78–81, 47–48, 64–65, 31–34 and 16–17 is favoured.

Feinberg and co-workers have undertaken an intensive study of the oxidation of *Chromatium* HiPIP$_R$ by Fe(CN)$_6^{3-}$ as a function of pH and ionic strength.[55] Through examination of ionic strength dependences at various constant pH values, electrostatically corrected rate constants k^∞ have been calculated according to the equation derived by Wherland and Gray.[156] By this procedure, mechanistically relevant amino-acid deprotonations have been effectively partitioned from essentially electrostatic effects. The pH profile obtained by using k^∞ values is strikingly different from the zero dependence (pH 7–10) obtained using observed second-order rate constants. A maximum value of k^∞ occurs at pH 9 and two apparent pK values, 7 and 9 are resolvable. Furthermore, for pH values between 5·0 and 9·35, net protein charges Z calculated using the Wherland–Gray equation are in remarkably good agreement with corresponding values calculated on the basis of primary sequence data and standard pK assignments. It is found that for the reduced protein the effective charge becomes more negative as the pH is increased, reflecting deprotonation at one or more residues as expected. The observed increase in electrostatically corrected rate constants between pH 6 and 9 strongly suggests the participation of intrinsic factors in the regulation of electron transfer.

In an elegant investigation to determine the nature of this "pH effect", Nettesheim et al.[116] have examined perturbations in the UV (aromatic) and visible (Fe–S) spectral regions, incurred as a result of variation in pH. Quantitative analyses of the perturbation difference spectra, which in the UV aromatic region can be attributed to microenvironmental changes of trytophan residues, yield pK values of 6·9 and 6·7 for reduced and oxidized forms respectively. That the ionizable residue is in fact the sole histidine is demonstrated by modification of histidine-42 with the selective reagent diethylpyrocarbonate. Other residues are seemingly unaffected. Either deprotonation or chemical modificaton of histidine-42 in reduced HiPIP produces spectral perturbations (vs native) that resemble oxidized vs reduced difference spectra. The indication is that the environment in the hydrophobic interior (as "seen" from the Fe–S centre of either of the tryptophan residues at positions 76 and 80) is assuming a configuration closer to that of the oxidized form. The electrostatically corrected rate constant k^∞ for oxidation of modified HiPIP$_R$ ($6·0 \times 10^3$ M^{-1} s^{-1}) is in fact comparable to that of the unprotonated form ($\sim 6·7 \times 10^3$ M^{-1} s^{-1}). Viewed together these results suggest that modification or deprotonation of histidine-42 induces an equivalent effect, namely some displacement of the polypeptide structure resulting in a destabilization of the reduced form. A comparison of spectra for oxidized and reduced HiPIP clearly shows that a red shift of the aromatic bands occurs upon reduction. This effect is similar to that seen with model trytophan compounds upon raising the hydrophobicity of the solvent. It therefore appears that the modulation of the protein interior is in fact equivalent to an increase in hydrophobicity. This might be brought about by some expansion within the protein core, such an explanation being consistent with the finding that the Fe–S cluster becomes larger upon reduction. With this idea in mind, the authors draw attention to similarities with the "squeeze-effect" concept.[35] Examination of the three-dimensional structure of Chromatium HiPIP shows that the Fe–S cluster is located at an intramolecular interface which might be considered to bisect the molecule. The Fe–S bonds undergoing the greatest elongation upon reduction (2·22 to 2·38 Å) lie perpendicular to this interface so that the two halves might be expected to move apart. Intramolecular forces tend to constrain this movement providing some cluster compression in the reduced protein; however, the location of histidine-42 suggests that it could modulate this molecular strain. Hydrogen bonding between protonated histidine-42 and invariant asparagine-45 is suggested as a possible means of relieving this strain, such an influence being removed upon deprotonation or chemical modification.

Studies on the reactions of *Chromatium* and *Rps gelatinosa* HiPIP with *c*-type cytochromes have been reported. With cytochrome *c* (horse heart) and cytochrome c_2 from various bacterial sources, both types of HiPIP tend to display ionic strength dependences that are not expected on the basis of simple net charge considerations.[110] With certain c_2 cytochromes, biphasic behaviour has been noted and ascribed to variations in the orientation of the cytochrome with respect to HiPIP in the encounter complex. Such behaviour is not observed in reactions of these c_2 cytochromes with $Fe(CN)_6^{3-}$, indicating that intrinsic heterogeneity is not responsible. The results are consistent with the involvement of specific binding zones on the interacting proteins.

Aprahamian and Feinberg[8] have examined the reduction of *Chromatium* and *Rps gelatinosa* $HiPIP_O$ by native and modified (trinitrophenyllysine-13) horse heart cytochrome *c*. The trinitrophenyl (TNP) group is bulky and hydrophobic so that modification at lysine-13 might result in restricted access to the haem crevice. Using the Wherland–Gray equation, rate constants have been corrected to infinite ionic strength k^∞. Such treatment yields (for pH 7) k^∞ ($M^{-1} s^{-1}$) = 12.3×10^4 and 3.8×10^4 for *Chromatium* and *Rps gelatinosa* $HiPIP_O$ respectively with native cyt c^{2+}, and 17.5×10^4 and 5.46×10^4 with TNP-cyt c^{2+}. It is clear that partial blockage of the haem crevice does not impede reaction between the two proteins, resulting instead in a small but systematic increase in rates. The authors have proposed that modification could destabilize the haem crevice by disruption of a salt bridge between lysine-13 and glutamate-90. This might result in some increased flexibility of the haem edge. Alternatively, the insertion of an aromatic side-group would be expected to promote hydrophobic interactions between the two proteins. A region of conserved nonpolar residues, leucine-17, phenylalanine-48, leucine-65, phenylalanine-66 and serine-79, encircling a particularly accessible bridging S atom on the cluster, is suggested as a possible region for such an interaction.

An additional comment reflecting some of the various observations discussed above concerns the strong binding of $Co(4,7\text{-DPSphen})_3^{3-}$ to the reduced protein.[6] The association constant, $3420\ M^{-1}$, is in the same range as determined for its interaction with the blue-copper proteins[91] and demonstrates the ability of extended aromatic assemblies to "lock on" to protein structures. This provides further support for the importance of hydrophobic interactions in protein–protein reactions. It is to be noted however that no strong association is observed with $Co(phen)_3^{3+}$.[131]

G. Pulse radiolysis of Fe–S proteins

A number of recent reports describe studies on the reduction of Fe–S proteins by the hydrated electron e_{aq}^-.[7, 26, 27, 47] The ability to monitor optically both reduction of the protein chromophore (k_p) and decay of e_{aq}^- (k_e), $\lambda_{max} = 720$ nm (e = 18 500 M^{-1} cm^{-1}) at rates approaching the diffusion limit, permits the procurance of information pertaining to the existence of primary intermediates in the electron-transfer process. Furthermore, the reaction efficiency, which is the amount of protein chromophore reduced divided by the amount of e_{aq}^- that is actually available for reaction with the protein, can yield information on electron-transfer distances within the protein. Low efficiency is often associated with abortive capture of e_{aq}^- by intervening amino-acids and subsequent reaction with solvent.

Using this technique to produce small amounts of the one-electron reduced species *C. pasteurianum* Fd_{OR}, Butler et al.[26] have investigated the aspect of cluster–cluster cooperativity in terms of kinetic behaviour. With $Co(NH_3)_5Cl^{2+}$ as oxidant (at pH 7·0, $I = 0·1$, 18°C) the rate constant for reoxidation of "pulsed" Fd_{OR} (which corresponds to k_B of Equation (24)) is $5·1 \times 10^5$ $M^{-1}s^{-1}$. This is similar to the overall observed rate constant for oxidation of Fd_{RR}, $4·1 \times 10^5$ M^{-1} s^{-1}, measured by the stopped-flow technique, and it is therefore concluded that kinetic cooperativity is not inherent in these bifunctional molecules.

For the reduction of Fd_{OO} by e_{aq}^-, and by formate and propan-2-ol radicals, low overall efficiencies (30–40% for e_{aq}^- and CO_2^-, and 56% for $(CH_3)_2C\cdot OH$) along with marked differences between k_e ($3·4 \times 10^{10}$ M^{-1} s^{-1}) and k_p ($1·1 \times 10^3$ M^{-1} s^{-1}) were found. This was attributed to complex behaviour involving transient electron residence on aromatic side-chains. However, a more recent examination has yielded efficiencies varying from 35–96% with k_e and k_p essentially the same, thereby raising considerable doubt over the validity of previous data.[7] The authors express the view that variable contamination in protein preparations along with minor denaturation might provide alternative nonproductive sites for electron capture resulting in diminished efficiency and k_p. Recent identification of degradation products in *C. pasteurianum* Fd[151] lends considerable weight to this suggestion.

The same authors observe simple behaviour for the e_{aq}^- reduction of parsley Fd. The reaction efficiency is close to 100%, k_e and k_p are similar, and the second-order rate constant (pH 7–8, 25°C) is $9·7 \times 10^9$ $M^{-1}s^{-1}$. Again, possible artifacts are suggested to be responsible for complex behaviour previously reported.[47] Close agreement of k_e and k_p, with high reaction efficiency for both classes of Fd, is reasonable on the basis of representative three-dimensional structure information. For *P. aerogenes* 2[4Fe–4S] and *S. platensis* [2Fe–2S] ferredoxins the location of Fe–S clusters near to the surface and possible exposure of certain cysteinyl S atoms to solvent should provide ready access for e_{aq}^-.

Reduction of *Chromatium* $HiPIP_R$ by e_{aq}^- generates the super-reduced (SR) form ($[4Fe–4S]^+$).[27] The computed product spectrum, which is stable for at least 2 s at 21°C, is similar to that of *C. pasteurianum* Fd_{RR} and that obtained by Cammack[29] for HiPIP following dithionite reduction in 80% DMSO. Rate constants (pH 7·0, 25°C) for reduction of $HiPIP_O$ to $HiPIP_R$ ($1·7 \times 10^{10}$ $M^{-1} s^{-1}$) and $HiPIP_R$ to $HiPIP_{SR}$ ($1·8 \times 10^{10}$ $M^{-1} s^{-1}$) are close to the diffusion limit and $k_e \simeq k_p$ in both cases. However the highest efficiency obtained is only 50%, a feature that has (in the light of conflicting observations for *C. pasteurianum* Fd) been re-examined and substantiated.[7] A likely explanation is that a large proportion of the available electrons do not succeed in reaching the buried (~ 5 Å) cluster. This rationale receives support from similar observations made with azurin, for which the efficiency is as low as 20%.[54] The Cu centre in azurin is located 7–8 Å from the protein surface.[3,5]

H. Kinetic studies with analogue compounds

Compared with protein counterparts, reduction potentials for the $[4Fe–4S]^{2+/1+}$ analogue systems tend to be more negative and span a wider range. The nature of the solvent appears to be a particularly important factor influencing the electrochemical properties of these compounds, and whether by virtue of high dielectric constant or H-bonding propensity,[67,82,101] H_2O seems to provide the closest approach to physiological potential values. Water-soluble analogues therefore present the most suitable subjects for investigation, examples ($[4Fe–4S]^{2+}$ level) being $[Fe_4S_4(SCH_2CH_2CO_2)_4]^{6-}$[77] and $[Fe_4S_4(SCH_2CH_2OH)_4]^{2-}$ and the synthetic peptide complex $Fe_4S_4(S—(RS)—Cys(Ac)NHMe)_4]^{2-}$[67].

The species $[Fe_4S_4(SCH_2CH_2CO_2)_4]^{6-}$, for which an x-ray structure determination confirms the essential cluster geometry as found in other analogues,[33] displays thermodynamically reversible one-electron reduction with a potential of -580 mV.[77] Kinetics of its reduction by the powerful one-electron reagent $Cr(edta)^{2-}$ have been studied using the stopped-flow technique.[65] Reduction of the $[4Fe–4S]^{2+}$ oxidation level is fast and unresolved, but the subsequent reduction of $[Fe_4S_4(SCH_2CH_2CO_2)_4]^{7-}$, presumably to give the $[4Fe–4S]^0$ level, is slower and first-order in both reagents. The absorption spectrum of the product, which appears to undergo decomposition over periods of 1–2 min, was obtained from final absorbance values at pH 8·5 ($HSCH_2CH_2CO_2^-$). Second-order rate constants (20°C), $\Delta H^{\ddagger}$, and $\Delta S^{\ddagger}$ values are respectively, $2·2 \times 10^5$ $M^{-1} s^{-1}$, 10·3 kcal mol^{-1}, and 0·2 cal K^{-1} mol^{-1}, the reaction rate being independent of pH (8·0–9·4) and buffer ($HSCH_2CH_2CO_2^-$) concentration. With

$Cr(edta)^{2-}$ as reductant there is the possibility of an inner-sphere mechanism, but this was not tested for because of the difficulty of product isolation and ambiguity introduced as a result of the anomalous lability of the Cr(III)edta product.

Using polarographic techniques, reversible reduction of $[Fe_4S_4(SCH_2CO_2)_4]^{7-}$ is observed at $-930\,mV,$[65, 77] but apart from measurement of the final absorption spectrum from kinetic studies, no actual product examination has been reported. Further characterization of the product, employing techniques such as Mössbauer spectroscopy, is clearly desirable in order to confirm the assignment of $[4Fe{-}4S]^0$ ($= 4Fe(II)$).

IV. SUBSTITUTION AND RELATED PROCESSES

A. General behaviour

Although most extensively studied with [4Fe–4S] analogues, thiol exchange reactions (Equation (28)) are an important feature of Fe–S systems in general, providing the basis for the analytically useful cluster extrusion technique.

$$[Fe_4S_4(SR)_4]^{2-} + nR'SH \longrightarrow [Fe_4S_4(SR)_{4-n}(SR')_n]^{2-} + nRSH \tag{28}$$

The favourable replacement of alkyl thiol ligands in the analogue compounds $[Fe_4S_4(SR)_4]^{2-}$ (R = t-Bu, Et) by aryl thiols (R' = p-$C_6H_4NH_2$, p-tolyl, o-$C_6H_4NO_2$, and p-$C_6H_4NO_2$) has been quantitatively examined.[50] In acetonitrile solution the initial reaction (corresponding to replacement of the first thiol) is first-order in tetramer and first-order in added thiol, and addition of H_2O up to 20% solvent does not greatly affect kinetic behaviour. Second-order rate constants show a direct dependence upon the acidity of the incoming thiol (on the basis of pK measurements made in aqueous ethanol). The authors propose that ligand substitution proceeds via protonation of coordinated alkylthiolate followed by rapid separation of alkylthiol and binding of arylthiolate according to Equations (29) and (30):

$$Fe_4S_4(SR)_4^{2-} + R'SH \rightleftharpoons Fe_4S_4(SR)_3HSR^- + R'S^- \tag{29}$$

$$Fe_4S_4(SR)_3HSR^- + R'S^- \longrightarrow Fe_4S_4(SR)_3(SR')^{2-} + RSH \tag{30}$$

Accordingly, addition of organic acids such as benzoic acid accelerates the rate of ligand exchange. Steric effects within the reactant complex appear to be relatively unimportant as indicated by a close similarity of rate constants for Et and t-Bu tetramers.

Bruice and his associates have undertaken quantitative kinetic studies on the internal hydrolysis of [4Fe–4S] clusters with regard to the effects of pH and added thiol concentration.[24,77,100] A notable feature with general applicability for both model compounds and proteins is the susceptibility of clusters to hydrolytic scission at low pH, a property that is expressed in the marked instability of Fe–S proteins (except rubredoxins) in acid solution, as demonstrated by evolution of H_2S. Direct protonation of the cluster as in (31) is proposed as a prerequisite for this process, a feature that may be relevant to the mechanism of activation of hydrogenase.[14]

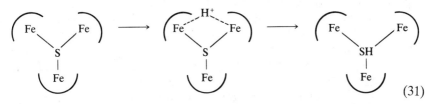

$$(31)$$

Consequently [4Fe–4S] clusters may be viewed as the conjugate base species for weak acids [4Fe–4S(H$^+$)] and pK_a values for the analogues $[Fe_4S_4(SR)_4]^{2-}$ (R = CH_3, $CH_2CH(CH_3)_2$, $C(CH_3)_3$) and $[Fe_4S_4(SCH_2CH_2CO_2)_4]^{6-}$ have been measured by absorbance–pH titration.[24,77] The values obtained, respectively ~3·9 (in mixed aqueous solution, back-extrapolation of absorbance to zero time) and 7·4 (direct measurement in H_2O) are independent of added thiol concentration, as is the rate of cluster hydrolysis. A related study on the destructive oxidation of clusters by O_2 indicates that the protonated form is most reactive, pK_a (kinetic) for $[Fe_4S_4(SCH_2CH(CH_3)_2)_4]^{2-}$ being 4·5.[24] The authors report that cluster hydrolysis occurs also at higher pH, but is now dependent upon ligand exchange by H_2O and OH^- and accordingly shows inhibition by excess thiol.[77] Between acid and alkaline catalysed cluster hydrolysis [4Fe–4S] systems both natural and analogue have varying degrees of stability. The clostridial-type ferredoxins retain a finite rate of hydrolysis, whereas *Chromatium* HiPIP is markedly stable.[100] This is probably attributable, in the latter case, to favourable shielding of the cluster from bulk solvent as apparent from the three-dimensional structure[34,35,36] and the experimentally observed restricted accessibility of deuterons to the cluster zone.[125]

Complete substitution of thiol by non-S ligands such as Cl^- and OAc^- has been demonstrated[158] and the x-ray structure determination of $(Et_4N)_2[Fe_4S_4Cl_4]$ confirms retention of the essential cluster dimensions.[22] Reaction of $[Fe_4S_4(SR_4)_4]^{2-}$ with electrophilic reagents CH_3COCl and $(CH_3CO)_2O$ in *N*-methyl-2-pyrrolidinone solution yields the complete (n = 1–4, R = Cl, OAc) series of substituted tetramers.[80] With the more electron-withdrawing ligands $CF_3CO_2^-$ and $CF_3SO_3^-$ (derived from the reagents $(CF_3CO)_2O$, $(CF_3SO_2)_2O$ and $CF_3SO_3CH_3$) only the $n = 1$ species are formed, further substitution apparently producing forms susceptible to decomposition. The authors draw attention to possible coordination of protein-bound Fe–S clusters by O-ligands such as glutamate or aspartate, a feature that now seems likely for partial coordination of the [3Fe–3S] cluster in *A. vinelandii* Fd.[59,141] The considerably enhanced rate of reaction of $(CH_3CO)_2O$ with the reduced species $[Fe_4S_4(SR)_4]^{3-}$ indicates that reduction activates the cluster towards substitution, a result that is quite reasonable from consideration of analogue Fe–S(R) bond length increases.[92] Such labilization could render the cluster capable of performing a catalytic role through facile inner-sphere complex formation with redox substrate, in which respect it is interesting to note that sequential substitution of thiolate by Cl^- or OAc^- results in a progressive increase in reduction potential. The magnitude of this effect is in the order of 100 mV per successive substitution. Consequently ligand exchange coupled with reduction could constitute a system for "pumping" centres down to lower potentials as originally proposed by Job and Bruice.[77] Such a concept could be important in the catalysis of low-potential processes such as N_2 reduction.

B. Cluster transformations

A number of analogue cluster interconversion reactions are of mechanistic interest besides being synthetically useful, and Cambray *et al.*[28] have examined the inter-relationship between 1-Fe, 2-Fe and 4-Fe systems. The progressive systematic assembly of synthetic Fe–S compounds begins with formation of the Rd_R analogue $[Fe(S_2-o-xyl)_2]^{2-}$ according to (32):[90]

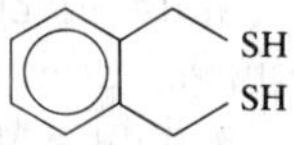

$$FeCl_4^- \xrightarrow[\text{NaOEt}]{\text{excess}} [Fe(S_2-o-xyl)_2]^{2-} \tag{32}$$

Controlled oxidation of the dianion yields the only Rd_O analogue $[Fe(S-o-xyl)_2]^-$, and subsequent formation of [2Fe–2S] species is accomplished via reaction (33) employing a 1:1 mixture of NaSH and NaOMe.

$$2[Fe(S_2-o-xyl)_2]^- + 2NaSH + 2NaOMe$$

$$\longrightarrow [Fe_2S_2(S_2-o-xyl)_2]^{2-} + 2Na_2(S_2-o-xyl) + 2MeOH \tag{33}$$

Conversion of $[Fe_2S_2(S_2-o-xyl)_2]^{2-}$ to $[Fe_2S_2(SPh)_4]^{2-}$ can be carried out by treatment with PhSH. Reduction of $[Fe_2S_2(SPh)_4]^{2-}$ and to a lesser extent $[Fe_2S_2(S_2-o-xyl)_2]^{2-}$ in DMF or acetonitrile results in dimerization of the $[2Fe-2S]^+$ product to form $[4Fe-4S]^{2+}$ species as in (34) and (35):

$$2[Fe_2S_2(SPh)_4]^{2-} + 2e^- \longrightarrow 2[Fe_2S_2(SPh)_4]^{3-} \tag{34}$$

$$2[Fe_2S_2(SPh)_4]^{3-} \longrightarrow [Fe_4S_4(SPh)_4]^{2-} + 4PhS^- \tag{35}$$

In the absence of a reducing potential $[2Fe-2S]^{2+}$ analogues are stable in aprotic solvents such as DMF, DMSO and hexamethylphosphoramide (HMPA). However, in aqueous mixtures of these solvents, $[4Fe-4S]^{2+}$ species are slowly formed according to (36), whereby

$$2[Fe_2S_2(SPh)_4]^{2-} \longrightarrow [Fe_4S_4(SPh)_4]^{2-} + 2PhS^- + PhSSPh \tag{36}$$

the reaction rate is decreased with increasing (aqueous) pH and added thiol concentration. This could indicate that ligand-exchange processes with H_2O or OH^- may be rate-determining events. The stability of $[2Fe-2S]^{2+}$ in necessarily mixed aqueous solution is important in ensuring the correct diagnosis in protein cluster extrusion experiments.

The notable absence of characterized [3Fe–3S] analogue systems indicates that such species may be somewhat unstable with respect to the other cluster structures. Such a situation is expected to influence the occurrence and properties of [3Fe–3S] centres in nature.

C. Cluster extrusion

The ease with which intact Fe—S clusters can be extruded from proteins and captured by thiol ligands has provided a novel means of determining the type of cluster present in a particular protein.[13,15,61,87,121,159] The effectiveness of this technique is dependent upon the displaced cluster, released by protein unfolding in mixed solvent systems, retaining its structural integrity for sufficient time to allow ligation by thiols. The "captured" clusters are identified by comparison with well characterized analogue compounds, usually employing optical, EPR or NMR spectroscopy.

An alternative to cluster extrusion into organic thiol systems, particularly if protein turbidity in mixed-solvent systems is to be avoided, is transfer into other apoproteins. Suitable acceptors allowing easy identification and quantitation of clusters are apoadrenodoxin ([2Fe–2S], reduced holoprotein has characteristic axial EPR spectrum instead of the normal rhombic type) and *B. polymyxa* apoferredoxin I ([4Fe–4S], reduced holoprotein yields EPR spectrum uncomplicated by triplet interaction with other cluster, as with clostridial-type ferredoxin).[121]

Using cluster displacement techniques, the Fe–S clusters in various enzymes including nitrogenase Mo/Fe protein have been identified.[88] However, the recent unambiguous identification of [3Fe–3S] clusters in several proteins, most notably the Fd from *A. vinelandii*, is consistent with reports of anomalous cluster displacement behaviour for this and other proteins.[15] It appears that the [3Fe–3S] cluster undergoes rearrangement during the displacement process, consequently emphasizing the need for considerable caution in the use of this procedure.

Note Added in Proof

Since the preparation of this manuscript, further examples of facile cluster inter-conversion processes have been reported. Mössbauer spectroscopy clearly shows that [3Fe–3S] clusters in *D. gigas* FdII are converted into [4Fe–4S] by incubation with $^{57}Fe(II)$ and S^{2-} in the presence of dithiothreitol (Kent, T.A.; Moura, I.; Moura, J.J.G.; Lipscomb, J.D.; Huynh, B.H.; LeGall, J.; Xavier, A.V.; Munck, E. *FEBS Lett.* **1982**, *138*, 55–58). This feature is echoed in the behaviour of aconitase for which activation of the isolated enzyme requires incubation with Fe(II) and dithiothreitol. Mössbauer and EPR data are consistent with a [3Fe–3S] to [4Fe–4S] conversion, the former state probably arising from oxidative damage during isolation (Kent, T.A.; Dreyer, J-L.; Kennedy, M.C.; Huynh, B.H.; Emptage, M.H.; Beinert, H.; Munck, E. *Proc. Natl. Acad. Sci. USA* **1982**, *79*, 1096–1100). Among the large family of Fe–S containing enzymes, aconitase is an intriguing example since its metabolic function, the interconversion of aconitase and *iso-*citrate, involves no obvious electron-transfer process.

Acknowledgments

I wish to thank Elinor T. Adman, Helmut Beinert, H. Allen, O. Hill and A. Geoffrey Sykes for helpful comments and criticisms. I am also grateful to Charles W. Carter, Jr., H. Matsubara and T. Tsukihara for providing illustrations of protein structures.

REFERENCES

[1] Adman, E.T.; Sieker, L.C.; Jensen, L.H. *J. Biol. Chem.* **1973**, *248*, 3987–3996.

[2] Adman, E.T.; Sieker, L.C.; Jensen, L.H. *J. Biol. Chem.* **1976**, *251*, 3801–3806.

[3] Adman, E.T.; Stenkamp, R.E.; Sieker, L.C.; Jensen, L.H. *J. Mol. Biol.* **1978**, *123*, 35–47.

[4] Adman, E.T. *Biochim. Biophys. Acta.* **1979**, *549*, 107–144.

[5] Adman, E.T.; Jensen, L.H. *Isr. J. Chem.* **1981**, *21*, 8–12.

[6] Adzamli, I.K.; Davies, D.M.; Stanley, C.S.; Sykes, A.G. *J. Amer. Chem. Soc.* **1981**, *103*, 5543–5542.

[7] Adzamli, I.K.; Buxton, G.V.; Ong. H.; Sykes, A.G. *J. Inorg. Biochem.* **1982**, in press.

[8] Aprahamian, G.; Feinberg, B.A. *Biochemistry* **1981**, *20*, 915–919.

[9] Armstrong, F.A.; Sykes, A.G. *J. Amer. Chem. Soc.* **1978**, *100*, 7710–7715.

[10] Armstrong, F.A.; Henderson, R.A.; Segal, M.G.; Sykes, A.G. *J. Chem. Soc. Chem. Commun.* **1978**, 1102–1103.

[11] Armstrong, F.A.; Henderson, R.A.; Sykes, A.G. *J. Amer. Chem. Soc.* **1979**, *101*, 6912–6917.

[12] Armstrong, F.A.; Henderson, R.A.; Sykes, A.G. *J. Amer. Chem. Soc.* **1980**, *102*, 6545–6551.

[13] Averill, B.A.; Orme-Johnson, W.H. *In* "Metal Ions in Biological Systems", Vol 7; Sigel, H., Ed.; Dekker: New York, 1978; pp. 127–183.

[14] Averill, B.A.; Orme-Johnson, W.H. *J. Amer. Chem. Soc.* **1978**, *100*, 5234–5236.

[15] Averill, B.A.; Bale, J.R.; Orme-Johnson, W.H. *J. Amer. Chem. Soc.* **1978**, *100*, 3034–3043.

[16] Banks, B.E.C.; Damjanovic, V.; Vernon, C.A. *Nature (London)* **1972**, *240*, 147–148.

[17] Bearden, A.J.; Dunham, W.R. *In* "Iron–Sulphur Proteins", Vol. II; Lovenberg, W., Ed.; Academic Press: New York and London, 1973; pp. 239–253.

[18] Beinert, H.; Heinen, W.; Palmer, G. *In* "Enzyme Models and Enzyme Structure", Brookhaven Symposia in Biology: No. 15; 1962; pp. 229–265.

[19] Beinert, H. *In* "Iron–Sulphur Proteins", Vol. I; Lovenberg, W., Ed.; Academic Press: New York and London, 1973; pp. 1–36.

[20] Bennett, L.E. *Prog. Inorg. Chem.* **1973**, *18*, 1–176.

[21] Bennett, L.E. *In* "Iron–Sulphur Proteins", Vol. III; Lovenberg, W., Ed.; Academic Press: New York and London, 1977; pp. 331–379.

[22] Bobrik, M.A.; Hodgson, K.O.; Holm, R.H. *Inorg. Chem.* **1977**, *16*, 1851–1858.

[23] Bruschi, M.; Hatchikian, E.C.; LeGall, J.; Moura, J.J.G.; Xavier, A.V. *Biochim. Biophys. Acta* **1976**, *449*, 275–284.

[24] Bruice, T.C.; Maskiewicz, R.; Job, R. *Proc. Natl. Acad. Sci. U.S.A.* **1975**, *72*, 231–234.

[24a] Buckingham, D.A.; Francis, D.J.; Sargeson, A.M. *Inorg. Chem.* **1974**, *13*, 2630–2639.

[25] Buhks, E.; Bixon, M.; Jortner, J.; Navon, G. *Inorg. Chem.* **1979**, *18*, 2014–2018.

[26] Butler, J.; Henderson, R.A.; Armstrong, F.A.; Sykes, A.G. *Biochem. J.* **1979**, *183*, 471–474.

[27] Butler, J.; Sykes, A.G.; Buxton, G.V.; Harrington, P.C.; Wilkins, R.G. *Biochem. J.* **1980**, *189*, 641–644.

[28] Cambray, J.; Lane, R.W.; Wedd, A.G.; Johnson, R.W.; Holm, R.H. *Inorg. Chem.* **1977**, *16*, 2565–2571.

[29] Cammack, R. *Biochem. Biophys. Res. Commun.* **1973**, *54*, 548–554.

[30] Cammack, R.; Dickson, D.P.E.; Johnson, C.E. *In* "Iron–Sulphur Proteins", Vol. III; Lovenberg, W., Ed.; Academic Press: New York and London, 1977; pp. 283–330.

[31] Cammack, R. *In* "Metalloproteins: Structure, Function and Clinical Aspects"; Weser, U., Ed.; Thieme Verlag: Stuttgart, 1979; pp. 162–184.

[32] Cammack, R. *Nature (London)* **1980**, *286*, 442.

[33] Carrell, H.L.; Glusker, J.P.; Job, R.; Bruice, T.C. *J. Amer. Chem. Soc.* **1977**, *99*, 3683–3690.

[34] Carter, C.W., Jr.; Kraut, J.; Freer, S.T.; Alden, R.A.; Sieker, L.C.; Adman, E.T.; Jensen, L.H. *Proc. Natl. Acad. Sci. U.S.A.* **1972**, *69*, 3526–3529.

[34a] Carter, C.W., Jr.; Kraut, J.; Freer, S.T.; Xuong, Ng.H.; Alden, R.A.; Bartsch, R.G. *J. Biol. Chem.* **1974**, *249*, 4212–4225.

[35] Carter, C.W., Jr.; Kraut, J.; Freer, S.T.; Alden, R.A. *J. Biol. Chem.* **1974**, *249*, 6339–6346.

[36] Carter, C.W., Jr. *In* "Iron–Sulphur Proteins", Vol. III; Lovenberg, W., Ed.; Academic Press: New York and London, 1977; pp. 157–204.

[37] Carter, C.W., Jr. *J. Biol. Chem.* **1977**, *252*, 7802–7811.

[38] Chance, B.; DeVault, D.C.; Frauenfelder, H.; Marcus, R.A.; Schrieffer, J.B.; Sutin, N. (Eds.) "Tunnelling in Biological Systems"; Academic Press: New York and London, 1979.

[39] Chien, J.C.W. *J. Phys. Chem.* **1978**, *82*, 2158–2171.

[40] Chu, J-W.; Kimura, T. *J. Biol. Chem.* **1973**, *248*, 5183–5187.

[41] Colman, P.M.; Freeman, H.C.; Guss, J.M.; Murata, M.; Norris, V.A.; Ramshaw, J.A.M.; Venkatappa, M.P. *Nature (London)* **1978**, *272*, 319–324.

[42] Cookson, D.J.; Hayes, M.T.; Wright, P.E. *Nature (London)* **1980**, *283*, 682–683. *Biochim. Biophys. Acta* **1980**, *591*, 161–176.

[43] Coucouvanis, D.; Swenson, D.; Baenziger, N.C.; Holah, D.G.; Kostikas, A.; Simopoulos, A.; Petroulaas, V. *J. Amer. Chem. Soc.* **1976**, *98*, 5721–5723.

[44] Cummins, D.; Gray, H.B. *J. Amer. Chem. Soc.* **1977**, *99*, 5158–5167.

[45] Darnall, D.W.; Wilkins, R.G. (Eds.) "Methods for Determining Metal Ion Environments in Proteins. 2. Structure and Function of Metalloproteins"; Elsevier/North Holland: Amsterdam, 1980.

[46] Davis, D.J.; San Pietro, A. *Arch. Biochem. Biophys.* **1977**, *182*, 266–272.

[47] Davydov, R.M.; Kuprin, S.P.; Fel, N.S.; Neznaiko, N.F.; Mukin, E.N.; Blyumenfeld, L.A. *Dokl. Akad. Nauk SSSR* **1978**, *239*, 220–222 (CA *88*, 147762).

[48] Debrunner, P.G.; Münck, E.; Que, L.; Schulz, C.E. *In* "Iron–Sulphur Proteins", Vol. III; Lovenberg, W., Ed.; Academic Press: New York and London, 1977; pp. 381–417.

[48a] DePamphillis, B.V.; Averill, B.A.; Herskovitz, T.; Que, L., Jr.; Holm, R.H. *J. Amer. Chem. Soc.* **1974**, *96*, 4159–4164.

[49] Dickson, D.P.E.; Cammack, R. *Biochem. J.* **1974**, *143*, 763–765.

[50] Dukes, G.R.; Holm, R.H. *J. Amer. Chem. Soc.* **1975**, *97*, 528–533.

[51] Dunham, W.R.; Bearden, A.J.; Salmeen, I.T.; Palmer, G.; Sands, R.H.; Orme-Johnson, W.H.; Beinert, H. *Biochim. Biophys. Acta* **1971**, *253*, 134–152.

[52] Eaton, W.A.; Lovenberg, W. *In* "Iron–Sulphur Proteins", Vol. II; Lovenberg, W., Ed.: Academic Press: New York and London, 1973; pp. 131–162.

[53] Emptage, M.H.; Kent, T.A.; Huynh, B.H.; Rawlings, J.; Orme-Johnson, W.H.; Münck, E. *J. Biol. Chem.* **1980**, *255*, 1793–1796.

[54] Faraggi, M.; Pecht, I. *Biochem. Biophys. Res. Commun.* **1971**, *45*, 842–848.

[55] Feinberg, B.A.; Johnson, W.V. *Biochem. Biophys. Res. Commun.* **1980**, *93*, 100–105.

[56] Foust, G.P.; Mayhew, S.G.; Massey, V. *J. Biol. Chem.* **1969**, *244*, 964–970.

[57] Fritz, J.; Anderson, R.; Fee, J.; Palmer, G.; Sands, R.H.; Tsibris, J.C.M.; Gunsalus, I.S.; Orme-Johnson, W.H.; Beinert, H. *Biochim. Biophys. Acta* **1971**, *253*, 110–133.

[58] Fukuyama, K.; Hase, T.; Matsumoto, S.; Tsukihara, T.; Katsube, Y.; Tanaka, N.; Kakudo, M.; Wade, K.; Matsubara, H. *Nature (London)* *286*, **1980**, 522–524.

[59] Ghosh, D.; Furey, W., Jr.; O'Donnell, S.; Stout, C.D. *J. Biol. Chem.* **1981**, *256*, 4185–4192.
[60] Gibson, J.F.; Hall, D.O.; Thornley, J.H.M.; Whatley, F.R. *Proc. Natl. Acad. Sci. U.S.A.* **1966**, *56*, 987–990.
[61] Gillum, W.O.; Mortenson, L.E.; Chen, J-S.; Holm, R.H. *J. Amer. Chem. Soc.* **1977**, *99*, 584–595.
[62] Hall, D.O.; Cammack, R.; Rao, K.K. *In* "Iron in Biochemistry and Medicine", Jacobs, A.; Worwood, M., Eds.; Academic Press: New York and London, 1974; Chapter 8.
[63] Handford, P.M.; Hill, H.A.O.; Lee, R.W-K.; Henderson, R.A.; Sykes, A.G. *J. Inorg. Biochem.* **1980**, *13*, 83–88.
[64] Harmer, M.A.; Sykes, A.G. *Biochem. Biophys. Res. Commun.* **1981**, *101*, 83–87.
[65] Henderson, R.A.; Sykes, A.G. *Inorg. Chem.* **1980**, *19*, 3103–3105.
[66] Herskovitz, T.; Averill, B.A.; Holm, R.H.; Ibers, J.A.; Phillips, W.D.; Weiher, J.F. *Proc. Natl. Acad. Sci. U.S.A.* **1972**, *69*, 2437–2441.
[67] Hill, C.L.; Renaud, J.; Holm, R.H.; Mortenson, L.E. *J. Amer. Chem. Soc.* **1977**, *99*, 2549–2557.
[68] Hin-Fat, L.; Higginson, W.C.E. *J. Chem. Soc. A* **1967**, 298–301.
[69] Holm, R.H.; Ibers, J.A. *In* "Iron–Sulphur Proteins", Vol. III; Lovenberg, W., Ed.; Academic Press: New York and London, 1977; pp. 205–281.
[70] Hong, J-S.; Rabinowitz, J.C. *J. Biol. Chem.* **1970**, *245*, 4995–5000.
[71] Hopfield, J.J. *Proc. Natl. Acad. Sci. U.S.A.* **1974**, *71*, 3640–3644.
[72] Hopfield, J.J. *Biophys. J.* **1977**, *18*, 311–321.
[73] Huynh, B.H.; Moura, J.J.G.; Moura, I.; Kent, T.A.; LeGall, J.; Xavier, A.V.; Münck, E. *J. Biol. Chem.* **1980**, *255*, 3242–3244.
[74] Ibers, J.A.; Holm, R.H. *Science* **1980**, *209*, 223–235.
[75] Im, Y.A.; Busch, D.H. *J. Amer. Chem. Soc.* **1961**, *83*, 3357–3362.
[76] Jacks, C.A.; Bennett, L.E.; Raymond, W.N.; Lovenberg, W. *Proc. Natl. Acad. Sci. U.S.A.* **1974**, *71*, 1118–1122.
[77] Job, R.C.; Bruice, T.C. *Proc. Natl. Acad. Sci. U.S.A.* **1975**, *72*, 2478–2482.
[78] Johnson, C.E.; Cammack, R.; Rao, K.K.; Hall, D.O. *Biochem. Biophys. Res. Commun.* **1971**, *43*, 564–571.
[79] Johnson, M.K.; Thomson, A.J.; Robinson, A.E.; Rao, K.K.; Hall, D.O. *Biochim. Biophys. Acta* **1981**, *667*, 433–451.
[79a] Johnson, M.K.; Hare, J.W.; Spiro, T.G.; Moura, J.J.G.; Xavier, A.V.; Le Gall, J. *J. Biol. Chem.* **1981**, *256*, 9806–9808.
[80] Johnson, R.W.; Holm, R.H. *J. Amer. Chem. Soc.* **1978**, *100*, 5338–5344.
[81] Jortner, J. *J. Chem. Phys.* **1976**, *64*, 4860–4867.
[82] Kassner, R.J.; Yang, W. *J. Amer. Chem. Soc.* **1977**, *99*, 4351–4355.
[83] Ke, B.; Bulen, W.A.; Shaw, E.R.; Breeze, R.H. *Arch. Biochem. Biophys.* **1974**, *162*, 301–309.
[84] Kent, T.A.; Huynh, B.H.; Münck, E. *Proc. Natl. Acad. Sci. U.S.A.* **1980**, *77*, 6574–6576.
[85] Knaff, D.B.; Smith, J.M., Malkin, R. *FEBS. Lett.* **1978**, *90*, 195–197.
[86] Koppenol, W.H. *Biophys. J.* **1980**, *29*, 493–507.
[87] Kurtz, D.M., Jr.; Wong, G.B.; Holm, R.H. *J. Amer. Chem. Soc.* **1978**, *100*, 6777–6779.
[88] Kurtz, D.M., Jr.; McMillin, R.S.; Burgess, B.K.; Mortenson, L.E.; Holm, R.H. *Proc. Natl. Acad. U.S.A.* **1979**, *76*, 4986–4989.

[89] Lambeth, D.O.; Palmer, G. *J. Biol. Chem.* **1973**, *248*, 6095–6103.

[90] Lane, R.W.; Ibers, J.A.; Frankel, R.B.; Papaefthymiou, G.C.; Holm, R.H. *J. Amer. Chem. Soc.* **1977**, *99*, 84–98.

[91] Lappin, A.G.; Segal, M.G.; Weatherburn, D.C.; Sykes, A.G. *J. Amer. Chem. Soc.* **1979**, *101*, 2297–2301, 2302–2306.

[92] Laskowski, E.J.; Frankel, R.B.; Gillum, W.O.; Papaefthymiou, G.C.; Renaud, J.; Ibers, J.A.; Holm, R.H. *J. Amer. Chem. Soc.* **1978**, *100*, 5322–5337.

[93] Laskowski, E.J.; Reynolds, J.G.; Frankel, R.B.; Foner, S.; Papaefthymiou, G.C.; Holm, R.H. *J. Amer. Chem. Soc.* **1979**, *101*, 6562–6570.

[94] Lee, S.S.; Travis, J.; Black, C.C., Jr. *Arch. Biochem. Biophys.* **1970**, *141*, 676–689.

[95] Lode, E.T.; Coon, M.J. In "Iron–Sulphur Proteins", Vol. I; Lovenberg, W., Ed.; Academic Press: New York and London, 1973; pp. 173–191.

[96] Lode, E.T.; Murray, C.L.; Sweeney, W.V.; Rabinowitz, J.C. *Proc. Natl. Acad. Sci. U.S.A.* **1974**, *71*, 1361–1365.

[97] Lode, E.T.; Murray, C.L.; Rabinowitz, J.C. *Biochem. Biophys. Res. Commun.* **1974**, *61*, 163–169.

[98] Lovenberg, W. (Ed.) "Iron–Sulphur Proteins", Vols. I–III; Academic Press: New York and London, 1973, 1973, 1977.

[99] Marcus, R.A. *Annu. Rev. Phys. Chem.* **1964**, *15*, 155–196.

[100] Maskiewicz, R.; Bruice, T.C. *Biochemistry* **1977**, *16*, 3024–3029.

[101] Maskiewicz, R.; Bruice, T.C. *J. Chem. Soc. Chem. Comm.* **1978**, 703–704.

[102] Mathews, R.; Charlton, S.; Sands, R.H.; Palmer, G. *J. Biol. Chem.* **1974**, *249*, 4362–4328.

[103] Matsubara, H.; Hase, T.; Wakabayashi, S.; Wada, K. In "The Evolution of Protein Structure and Function"; Sigman, D.S., Brazier, M.A.B., Eds.; Academic Press: New York and London, 1980; pp. 245–266.

[104] Mauk, A.G.; Scott, R.A.; Gray, H.B. *J. Amer. Chem. Soc.* **1980**, *102*, 4360–4363.

[105] Mayerle, J.J.; Denmark, S.E.; DePamphilis, B.V.; Ibers, J.A.; Holm, R.H. *J. Amer. Chem. Soc.* **1975**, *97*, 1032–1045.

[106] Dus, K.; DeKlerk, H.; Sletton, K.; Bartsch, R.G. *Biochim. Biophys. Acta* **1967**, *140*, 291–311.

[107] Middleton, P.; Dickson, D.P.E.; Johnson, C.E.; Rush, J.D. *Eur. J. Biochem.* **1978**, *88*, 135–141.

[108] Middleton, P.; Dickson, D.P.E.; Johnson, C.E.; Rush, J.D. *Eur. J. Biochem.* **1980**, *104*, 289–296.

[109] Mizrahi, I.A.; Wood, F.E.; Cusanovich, M.A. *Biochemistry* **1976**, *15*, 343–348.

[110] Mizrahi, I.A.; Cusanovich, M.A. *Biochemistry* **1980**, *19*, 4733–4737.

[111] Mizrahi, I.A.; Meyer, T.E.; Cusanovich, M.A. *Biochemistry* **1980**, *19*, 4727–4733.

[112] Moura, J.J.G.; Xavier, A.V.; Cookson, D.J.; Moore, G.R., Williams, R.J.P.; Bruschi, M.; LeGall, J. *FEBS Lett.* **1977**, *81*, 275–280.

[113] Moura, J.J.G.; Xavier, A.V.; Hatchikian, E.C.; LeCall, J. *FEBS Lett.* **1978**, *89*, 177–179.

[114] Moura, I.; Moura, J.J.G.; Santos, M.H.; Xavier, A.V.; LeGall, J. *FEBS Lett.* **1979**, *107*, 419–421.

[115] Moura, I.; Huynh, B.H.; Hausinger, R.P.; LeGall, J.; Xavier, A.V.; Munck, E. *J. Biol. Chem.* **1980**, *255*, 2493–2498.
[116] Nettesheim, D.G.; Johnson, W.V.; Feinberg, B.A. *Biochim. Biophys. Acta* **1980**, *593*, 371–383.
[117] Nomenclature Committee of the International Union of Biochemistry. *Eur. J. Biochem.* **1979**, *93*, 427–430.
[118] Orme-Johnson, W.H. *Annu. Rev. Biochem.* **1973**, *42*, 159–204.
[119] Orme-Johnson, W.H.; Beinert, H. *J. Biol. Chem.* **1969**, *244*, 6143–6148.
[120] Orme-Johnson, W.H.; Sands, R.H. *In* "Iron–Sulphur Proteins", Vol. II; Lovenberg, W., Ed.; Academic Press: New York and London, 1973; pp. 195–238.
[121] Orme-Johnson, W.H.; Holm, R.H. *Methods Enzymol.* **1978**, *53*, 268–274.
[122] Packer, E.L.; Sternlicht, H.; Lode, E.T.; Rabinowitz, J.C. *J. Biol. Chem.* **1975**, *250*, 2062–2072.
[123] Packer, E.L.; Sweeney, W.V.; Rabinowitz, J.C.; Sternlicht, H.; Shaw, E.N. *J. Biol. Chem.* **1977**, *252*, 2245–2253.
[124] Palmer, G. *In* "The Enzymes", Vol. 12B; Bayer, P.D., Ed.; Academic Press: New York and London, 1975; pp. 1–56.
[125] Peisach, J.; Orme-Johnson, N.R.; Mims, W.B.; Orme-Johnson, W.H. *J. Biol. Chem.* **1977**, *252*, 5643–5650.
[126] Phillips, W.D.; Poe, M.; Wieher, J.F.; McDonald, C.C.; Lovenberg, W. *Nature (London)* **1970**, *227*, 574–577.
[127] Phillips, W.D.; McDonald, C.C.; Stombaugh, N.A.; Orme-Johnson, W.H. *Proc. Natl. Acad. Sci. U.S.A.* **1974**, *71*, 140–143.
[128] Poe, M.; Phillips, W.D.; McDonald, C.C.; Lovenberg, W. *Proc. Natl. Acad. Sci. U.S.A.* **1970**, *65*, 797–804.
[129] Poe, M.; Phillips, W.D.; McDonald, C.C.; Orme-Johnson, W.H. *Biochem. Biophys. Res. Commun.* **1971**, *42*, 705–713.
[130] Rawlings, J.; Siiman, O.; Gray, H.B. *Proc. Natl. Acad. Sci. U.S.A.* **1974**, *71*, 125–127.
[131] Rawlings, J.; Wherland, S.; Gray, H.B. *J. Amer. Chem. Soc.* **1976**, *98*, 2177–2180.
[132] Rawlings, J.; Wherland, S.; Gray, H.B. *J. Amer. Chem. Soc.* **1977**, *99*, 1968–1971.
[133] Reynolds, J.G.; Coyle, C.L.; Holm, R.H. *J. Amer. Chem. Soc.* **1980**, *102*, 4350–4355.
[134] Rickard, L.H.; Landrum, H.L.; Hawkridge, F.M. *Bioelectrochem. Bioenerg.* **1978**, *5*, 686–696.
[135] Rossman, M.G.; Argos, P. *J. Mol. Biol.* **1976**, *105*, 75–95.
[136] Sayers, D.E.; Stern, E.A.; Herriot, J.R. *J. Chem. Phys.* **1976**, *64*, 427–428.
[136a] Schrauzer, G.N.; Kiefer, G.W.; Tano, K.; Doemeney, P.A. *J. Amer. Chem. Soc.* **1974**, *96*, 641–652.
[137] Shulman, R.G.; Eisenberger, P.; Blumberg, W.E.; Stombaugh, N.A. *Proc. Natl. Acad. Sci. U.S.A.* **1975**, *72*, 4003–4007.
[138] Shulman, R.G.; Eisenberger, P.; Teo, B-K.; Kincaid, B.M.; Brown, G.S. *J. Mol. Biol.* **1978**, *124*, 305–321.
[139] Smith, J.M.; Smith, W.H.; Knaff, D.B. *Biochim. Biophys. Acta* **1981**, *635*, 405–411.
[140] Stombaugh, N.A.; Sundquist, J.E.; Burris, R.H.; Orme-Johnson, W.H. *Biochemistry* **1976**, *15*, 2633–2641.

[141] Stout, C.D.; Ghosh, D.; Pattabhi, V.; Robbins, A.H. *J. Biol. Chem.* **1980**, 255, 1797–1800.
[142] Sutin, N. *In* "Inorganic Biochemistry"; Eichorn, G.L., Ed.; Elsevier: Amsterdam, 1973; pp. 613–653.
[143] Sweeney, W.V.; McIntosh, B.A. *J. Biol. Chem.* **1979**, 254, 4499–4501.
[144] Tagawa, K.: Arnon, D.I. *Nature (London)* **1962**, 195, 537–543.
[145] Tanaka, M.: Naniu, M.; Yasunobu, K.T.; Jones, J.B.; Stadtman, T.C. *Biochemistry* **1974**, 13, 5284–5289.
[146] Tano, K.; Schrauzer, G.N. *J. Amer. Chem. soc.* **1975**, 97, 5404–5408.
[147] Taube, H. "Electron Transfer Reactions of Complex Ions in Solution"; Academic Press: New York and London, 1970.
[148] Teo, B-K.; Shulman, R.G.; Brown, G.S.; Meixner, A.E. *J. Amer. Chem. Soc.* **1979**, 101, 5624–5631.
[149] Thomson, A.J. *J. Chem. Soc. Dalton Trans.* **1981**, 1180–1189.
[150] Thomson, A.J.; Cammack, R.; Hall, D.O.; Rao, K.K.; Briat, B.; Rivoal, J.C.; Badoz, J. *Biochim. Biophys. Acta* **1977**, 493, 132–141.
[151] Thomson, A.J.; Robinson, A.E.; Johnson, M.K.; Cammack, R.; Rao, K.K.; Hall, D.O. *Biochim. Biophys. Acta* **1981**, 637, 423–432.
[152] Thomson, A.J.; Robinson, A.E.; Johnson, M.K.; Moura, J.J.G.; Moura, I.; Xavier, A.V.; LeGall, J. *Biochim. Biophys. Acta* **1981**, 670, 93–100.
[153] Toppen, D.L.; Linck, R.G. *Inorg. Chem.* **1971**, 10, 2635–2636.
[153a] van Tamelin, E.E.; Gladysz, J.A.; Brulet, C.R. *J. Amer. Chem. Soc.* **1974**, 96, 3020–3021.
[154] Watenpaugh, K.D.; Sieker, L.C.; Herriot, J.R.; Jensen, L.H. *Acta Crystallogr. B* **1973**, 29, 943–956.
[155] Watenpaugh, K.D.; Sieker, L.C.; Jensen, L.H. *J. Mol. Biol.* **1979**, 131, 509–522.
[156] Wherland, S.; Gray, H.B. *Proc. Natl. Acad. Sci. U.S.A.* **1976**, 73, 2950–2954.
[157] Wherland, S.; Gray, H.B. *In* "Biological Aspects of Inorganic Chemistry"; Addison, A.W., Cullen, W., James, B.R., Dolphin, D., Eds.; Wiley: New York, 1977; pp. 289–368.
[158] Wong, G.B.; Bobrik, M.A.; Holm, R.H. *Inorg. Chem.* **1978**, 17, 578–584.
[159] Wong, G.B.; Kurtz, D.M., Jr.; Holm, R.H.; Mortenson, L.E.; Upchurch, R.G. *J. Amer. Chem. Soc.* **1979**, 101, 3078–3090.
[160] Xavier, A.V.; Moura, J.J.G.; Moura, I. *Structure and Bonding* **1981**, 23, 187–213.
[161] Yandell, J.K.; Fay, D.P.; Sutin, N. *J. Amer. Chem. Soc.* **1973**, 95, 1131–1137.
[162] Yang, C.Y.; Johnson, K.H.; Holm, R.H.; Norman, J.G., Jr.; *J. Amer. Chem. Soc.* **1975**, 97, 6596–6598.
[163] Yang, S.-S.; Ljungdahl, L.G.; Dervatanian, D.V.; Watt, G.D. *Biochim. Biophys. Acta* **1980**, 590, 24–33.
[164] Yasunobu, K.T.; Tanaka, M. *In* "Iron–Sulfur Proteins", Vol. II; Lovenberg, W., Ed.; Academic Press: New York and London, 1973; pp. 27–130.
[165] Yoch, D.C.; Carithers, R.P. *J. Bacteriol.* **1978**, 136, 822–824.
[166] Yoch, D.C.; Carithers, R.P. *Microbiol. Rev.* **1979**, 43, 384–421.
[167] Yocum, C.F.; Siedow, J.N.; San Pietro, A. *In* "Iron–Sulfur Proteins", Vol. I; Lovenberg, W., Ed.; Academic Press: New York and London, 1973; pp. 111–127.

Functional Properties of the Biological Oxygen Carriers

A.G. Sykes

Department of Inorganic Chemistry, The University, Newcastle upon Tyne

---

I. INTRODUCTION

Many simple living organisms including most insects, nematodes (i.e. parasitic worms) and jelly-fish, rely on the diffusion of O_2 and CO_2 between cells and the outer environment for their survival. A high surface area to volume ratio is clearly an advantage in such instances. With increasing size and complexity of the organism there becomes a need for more sophisticated forms of oxygen transport and storage. To meet this need three different protein types, haemoglobin (and myoglobin), haemerythrin, and haemocyanin have evolved. It is these proteins (and the manner in which they function) which provide the subject of this review. Two metals, Fe and Cu, are involved; see Table 1.

Haemoglobin (Hb) and myoglobin (Mb) are present in both vertebrate and invertebrate forms. The specific functional need for the tetramer and monomer forms of basically the same molecular unit in vertebrate Hb and Mb, to meet transport and storage needs respectively, is now well recognized. Higher, generally much higher, aggregates are present in invertebrate haemoglobins, and because of this greater complexity it has become customary to consider these proteins separately.[1] Invertebrate haemoglobins are extracellular and are often referred to as erythrocruorins. A few invertebrates have low MW aggregates (4 or 6 units) located within specialized blood cells, a situation which in the evolutionary context presumably relates to and carries through to the vertebrates. The active site in all Hb

TABLE 1

Summary of naturally occurring O_2 transport and storage proteins

Protein	Active site	MW/subunit	No. subunits	Colour (deoxy → oxy)
1. Vertebrate(porphyrin)				
Haemoglobin	Fe:O_2	17000	4[a]	purple → red
Myoglobin	Fe:O_2	17000	1	purple → red
2. Invertebrate(porphyrin)				
intracellular(haemoglobin)	Fe:O_2	17000[b]	4–8	purple → red
Extracellular-				
(erythrocruorin)[c]	Fe:O_2	17000	200[d]	purple → red
Chlorocruorin[e]	Fe:O_2	17000	High	red → green
Myoglobin	Fe:O_2	17000	1–2	purple → red
3. Plant(porphyrin)				
Leghaemoglobin	Fe:O_2	17000	1	purple → red
4. Invertebrate(non-porphyrin)				
Haemerythrin	2Fe:O_2	13500	8[f]	colourless → red-violet
Myohaemerythrin	2Fe:O_2	13900	1	colourless → red-violet
5. Invertebrate(non-porphyrin)				
Haemocyanin(arthropod)	2Cu:O_2	70000	48[d]	colourless → blue
Haemocyanin(mollusc)	2Cu:O_2	50000	160[d]	colourless → blue

[a] Hundreds of subunits in human haemoglobin sickle cell anaemia.
[b] A higher MW is known (40000).
[c] Also known as haemoglobin.
[d] Range of values; 200 is maximum for erythrocruorin.
[e] Contains modified protoporphyrin IX.
[f] Tetramer and dimer as well as trimer forms have been reported; see Ref. [118].

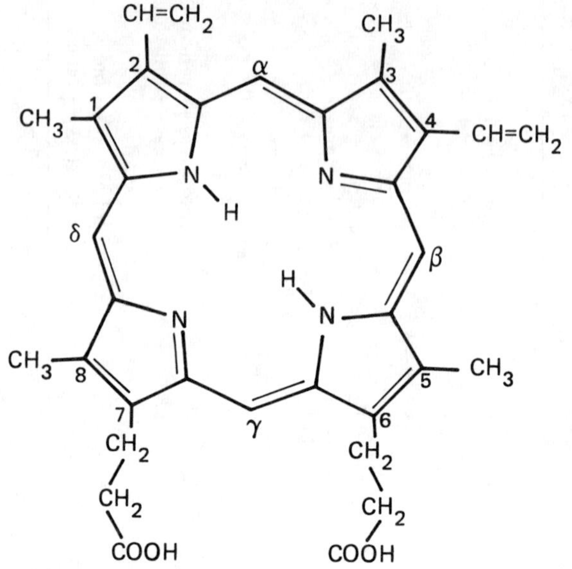

Fig. 1. Structure of protoporphyrin IX, the dianion of which coordinates via the four ring N-atoms. The 2 and 4 substituents are —C_2H_5 in mesoporphyrin and —H in deuteroporyphyrin.

and Mb forms consists of a single Fe(II) coordinated to a porphyrin macrocyclic ligand known as protoporphyrin IX (Fig. 1). Of the fifteen isomeric forms of protoporphyrin obtained by different positioning of the attached vinyl, methyl and propionic acid side chains, form IX appears to be the only one which is important in biology. Chlorocruorin, which is present in a few (invertebrate) polychaete annelid worms, contains a closely related porphyrin structure in which the vinyl at position 2 is replaced by a formyl group.[2] The name originates from the green colour of the oxy form. No chlorine is present.

Haemoglobins are also present in protozoa (single-celled organisms) but not in bacteria, and have been isolated as the monomer leghaemoglobin in root nodules of leguminous plants e.g. soy-beans,[3] where they most likely function as O_2 scavengers in a nitrogen-fixing environment. All vertebrates with very few exceptions (e.g. the antarctic fish cyclostomata) contain haemoglobin.[4]

Haemocyanin (Hc) and haemerythrin (Hr) have evolved separately, and are quite different from Hb and Mb in that they contain binuclear Cu(I) and binuclear Fe(II) active sites respectively. No porphyrin ring is present, and the metals are coordinated instead to amino-acid side chains.

It is one of the ironies of nature that a wide range of Co(II) complexes, including those with simple ligands e.g. NH_3, CN^- and amines, have the ability to bind and carry oxygen in a reversible manner without having any biological relevance.[5,6] Analogous complexes of Fe(II) and Cu(I), on the other hand, do not function as reversible carriers, irreversible oxidation being the more likely outcome. Even Fe(II) porphyrins, without the protective polypeptide chain present in Hb and Mb, undergo irreversible oxidation.[7] The study of both mononuclear and binuclear O_2 adducts of Co(II) complexes has provided much relevant and valuable insight into related inorganic chemistry.[6] The synthesis of stereochemically protected porphyrin ligands, which prevent the formation of binuclear Fe complexes and allow a mimic of reversible O_2 carrying properties, is an exciting and recent development.[8]

Although the blood cells of ascidian tunicates (i.e. sea-squirts) contain vanadium, which has at times been referred to as haemovanadin, it has now been demonstrated that these consist of a simple predominantly aquo-V(III) ion housed in vanadophores with no apparent capacity for reversible O_2 binding.[9]

The section below is concerned with the question of oxidation states and a description of the different modes of binding of O_2 to metals in inorganic complexes. This provides an introduction to the peroxo or superoxo terminology which has evolved in relation to different structure types, without which it becomes difficult to register fully the chemistry involved. The question of oxygen affinity and cooperativity is then considered. Subsequent sections are devoted to the different protein types.

The area of research concerned with the activation of O_2 (for redox purposes) by bonding to a metal[10] is not considered in this review.

II. CLASSIFICATION OF O_2 COMPLEXES

Although reference to O_2 as dioxygen is finding increasing usage, the still more widely used oxygen terminology is retained here. From an extensive range of inorganic studies two formal oxidation state descriptions, peroxo (O_2^{2-}) and superoxo (O_2^-), apply when O_2 is coordinated to a metal. From studies on the simplest possible inorganic compounds (O_2, H_2O_2, KO_2, etc.), O–O bond lengths as in Table 2 have been obtained. The same approximate peroxo and superoxo bond lengths are observed in x-ray crystal structures of transition metal coordination complexes, and together with supporting physicochemical measurements (including EPR, infrared and Raman spectroscopy, and more recently EXAFS) provide self-consistent interpretations. As an example of the use of infrared/Raman spectroscopy, O–O stretching frequencies of O_2 in different formal oxidation states are for molecular oxygen 1555 cm^{-1}, for complexed superoxide 1100–1200 cm^{-1}, and complexed peroxide 740–900 cm^{-1}.[11] Raman spectroscopy is required when the vibrational mode in question does not give rise to a change in dipole moment i.e. $\nu(O$–$O)$ in binuclear complexes when both O-atoms are bound to the metal atoms. As yet no case has

TABLE 2
Bond lengths for O_2 in different oxidation states

	Bond length (Å)
$O_2^+(g)$	1·12
$O_2(g)$	1·21
$KO_2(s)$	1·34
$H_2O_2(BaO_2)(s)$	1·48(1·49)

been established where the neutral O_2 description unequivocally applies to a coordinated O_2 group. An alternative viewpoint has been presented in which the use of superoxo and peroxo terminology is avoided.[10]

Different structure types which have been identified are illustrated in Fig. 2. When hydrogen peroxide reacts with d^0 transition metal aquo/oxo ions of Ti(IV), V(V), and Cr(VI) at pH ~ 1 (present initially as TiO^{2+}, VO_2^+ and CrO_4^{2-}) substitution reactions (assisted by H^+) result in the replacement of an oxo group by a peroxo ligand bound sideways as in (a).[12] Such examples are now well established. Complexes with more than one peroxo group $[V(O_2)_3(bipy)]^-$ and $[CrO(O_2)_2(bipy)]$ (bipy = 2,2'-bipyridine) have been isolated (O–O bond length 1·40 Å in latter) and structures of Cr(IV)(d^2) and Cr(V)(d^1) complexes, $[Cr(O_2)_2(NH_3)_3]$ and $[Cr(O_2)_4]^{3-}$, have also been determined (O–O 1·43 Å and 1·41 Å respectively). Although somewhat shorter than for peroxide in K_2O_2 or BaO_2 (1·49 Å), peroxo assignments are, it is believed, implied. Type (a) peroxo complexes of Zr(IV), Nb(V), Mo(VI) and W(VI) are also known.

Oxygen reacts reversibly with Vaska's complex [$trans$-Ir(PPh$_3$)$_2$(CO)(X)] ($X^- = Cl^-$, Br^-, I^-),

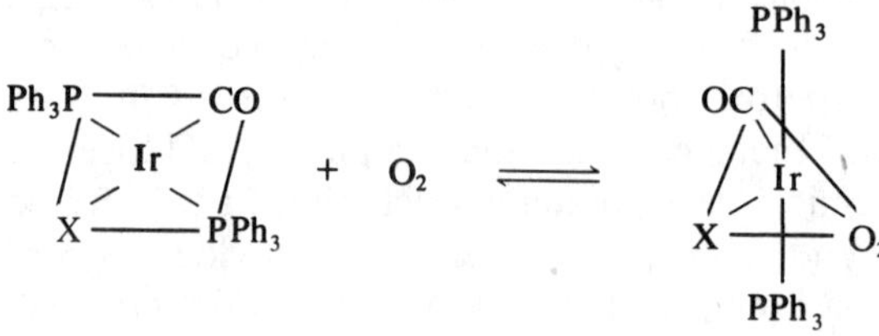

$$\tag{1}$$

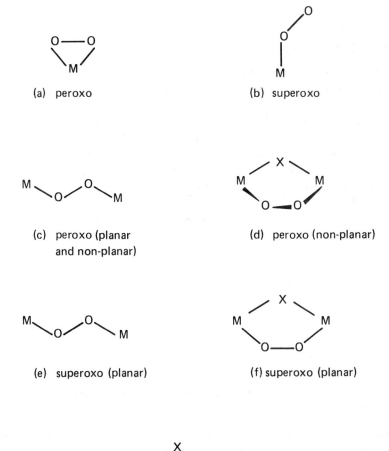

(a) peroxo

(b) superoxo

(c) peroxo (planar
and non-planar)

(d) peroxo (non-planar)

(e) superoxo (planar)

(f) superoxo (planar)

(g) hydroperoxo

Fig. 2. Structures of O_2 complexes and oxidation state assignments (peroxo or superoxo). Complex *(c)* can be planar or non-planar depending on anions (see Table 3).

The O_2 group is bound sideways as in (*a*) (both O-atoms are in the equatorial plane of the trigonal bipyramid), with O–O distances 1·45–1·50 Å.[13] The peroxo description again applies,[14] and the reaction is an example of oxidative addition, (2):

$$Ir(I) + O_2 \rightleftharpoons Ir(III)O_2^{2-} \qquad (2)$$

Other tertiary phosphine complexes of Ru(0), Rh(I) and Pt(0) behave in a similar fashion. Thus the complex $Pt(PPh_3)_3$ yields a square-planar Pt(II) adduct.

When O_2 binds to other metals which favour a one-equivalent change the bent M—O—O structure (*b*) is relevant and the superoxo terminology holds. Schiff-base complexes of Co(II) provide good examples, although only certain metal–ligand combinations provide the correct balance required for formation of 1:1 adducts. Thus salen Co(II) complexes and derivatives (Fig. 3) give 2:1 (metal to O_2) adducts except in the case of the 3-methoxy derivative.[15] The Co(II) complex of acacen, Fig. 3, is

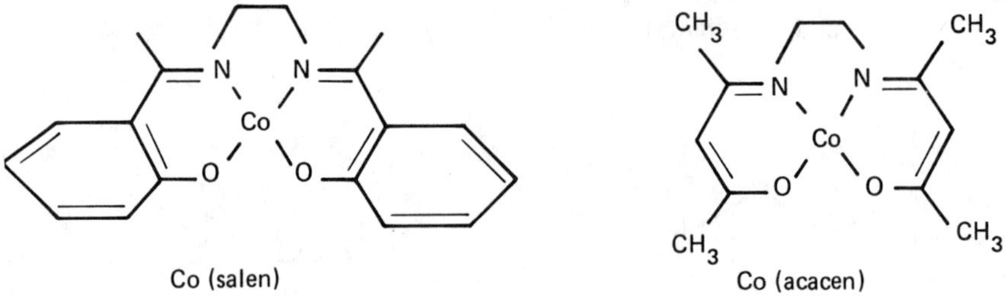

Co (salen)   Co (acacen)

Fig. 3. *N,N'*-ethylenebis(salicylideniminato)cobalt(II) and *N,N'*-ethylenebis-(acetylacetoniminato)cobalt(II) complexes, Co(salen) and Co(acacen) respectively.

known to give a 1:1 adduct at $\leqslant 0°C$ in coordinating solvents e.g. dimethylformamide (dmf), or alternatively in noncoordinating solvents (toluene) with added base B (e.g. pyridine),

$$Co(acacen)(B) + O_2 \longrightarrow Co(acacen)(B)(O_2) \qquad (3)$$

both in the solid state and in solution.[16] The solid has an IR band at 1140 cm^{-1}, corresponding to an O_2^- assignment, which disappears when the reaction is reversed by removal of O_2. EPR spectra support a 1:1 adduct (two Co, each with a 7/2 nuclear spin, would give 15 and not 8 hyperfine lines), and ~90% transfer of spin density from Co(II) to O_2 is indicated.[16] Magnetic resonance and magnetic moment data are consistent with an M—O—O angle of 120°. Cobalt(II) 1:1 complexes are also formed with porphyrins,[17,18] cobalamins (vitamin B_{12r}),[19,20] and phthalocyanin,[21] ligands. The $1:1$ $[Co(CN)_5O_2]^{3-}$ complex isolated using the large tetra-alkylammonium cation following oxygenation of $Co(CN)_5^{3-}$ solutions is an important example.[22] The O–O bond distance in this complex is 1.24 Å, consistent with a superoxo assignment.

Other Schiff-base ligands complexed to Co(II) yield $2:1$ (Co:O$_2$) adducts, as do many Co(II) complexes with simple ligands including NH$_3$, CN$^-$ (product isolated using small cations) and a range of amines. The O$_2$ group is bridging as in (c) and dicobalt(III) peroxo structures can be assigned, (4):

$$2Co(II) + O_2 \longrightarrow Co(III) . O_2^{2-} . Co(III) \qquad (4)$$

Tables 2 and 3 in the review by McLendon and Martell[6] give comprehensive listings of $1:1$ and $2:1$ complexes and relevant references. With a number of these complexes, e.g. with NH$_3$ as ligand, reversibility is only over a

TABLE 3
Dimensions obtained from crystal structures of $1:1$ and $2:1$ (cobalt to O$_2$) complexes

Complex	O–O Bond length (Å)	M—O—O Bond angle (degrees)
1:1 (superoxo)		
[Et$_4$N]$_3$[Co(CN)$_5$O$_2$]	1·24	153
[Co(bzacen)(py)O$_2$]^a	1·26	126
2:1 (superoxo)		
[(NH$_3$)$_4$Co(NH$_2$, O$_2$) . Co(NH$_3$)$_4$](NO$_3$)$_4$	1·32	121^b
[(en)$_2$Co . (NH$_2$, O$_2$) . Co(en)$_2$](NO$_3$)$_4$	1·36	119^b
[(NH$_3$)$_5$Co . O$_2$. Co(NH$_3$)$_5$]SO$_4$(HSO$_4$)$_3$	1·31	118^b
K$_5$[(CN)$_5$CoO$_2$Co(CN)$_5$]	1·26	121^{b,c}
2:1 (peroxo)		
[(NH$_3$)$_5$Co . O$_2$. Co(NH$_3$)$_5$](SO$_4$)$_2$. 4H$_2$O	1·47	112^d
[(NH$_3$)$_5$Co . O$_2$. Co(NH$_3$)$_5$](NCS)$_4$	1·47	111^b
[(en)$_2$Co . (NH$_2$, O$_2$) . Co(en)$_2$](NCS)$_3$. H$_2$O	1·46	110^e
[(salen)Co . O$_2$. Co(salen)](DMF)$_2$	1·34	120^{f,g}
K$_6$[(CN)$_5$Co . O$_2$. Co(CN)$_5$]	1·45	^{e}

^{a} Ligand bzacen is acacen ligand in Fig. 3 with two upper CH$_3$ replaced by C$_6$H$_5$.
^{b} Atoms CoO$_2$Co are planar.
^{c} Anion also present with torsion angle about O–O bond of 166°.
^{d} Torsion angle about O–O bond of 146°.
^{e} Atoms CoO$_2$Co are nonplanar.
^{f} Ligand salen is shown in Fig. 3.
^{g} Torsion angle about O–O bond of 110°; Ref. [15].

very limited number of cycles and mononuclear Co(III) products are readily formed. This property is used in the preparation of a wide range of mononuclear ammine Co(III) complexes which no longer contain bound O_2. A number of crystal structures have been determined and information relevant to the present discussion is given in Table 3.[23,24] When a second bridge is present, which is most often OH^- or NH_2^-, e.g. $[(trien)Co . (OH,O_2),Co(trien)]^{3+}$ (trien = triethylenetetraamine) and $[(en)_2Co . (NH_2,O_2) . Co(en)_4]^{3+}$ (en = ethylenediamine), it is necessary for the O_2^{2-} bridge to bond *cis* as in (d) rather than *trans*. The second bridge makes O_2 release more difficult.

Oxidation of 2:1 peroxo complexes as in Figs. 2(c) and (d) to superoxo complexes, (e) and (f), can be achieved using strong oxidants e.g. Ce(IV), $S_2O_8^{2-}$ and Cl_2.[4,25] An example of μ-peroxo disproportionation is known.[26]

Finally, there is one example of a hydroperoxo complex with bonding as in Fig. 2(g). This is obtained by protonation followed by isomerization of the complex $[(en)_2Co . (NH_2,O_2) . Co(en)_2]^{3+}$, which has a peroxo bridge as in (d).[27] Protonation is rapid and isomerization has a half-life of a few minutes.[25] An O–O distance of 1·42 Å has been obtained from the crystallographic study.[27]

No examples of complexes in which there is linear M—O—O bonding (180°) have yet been confirmed.

Schiff-base Co(II) complexes have found some use as a means of isolating oxygen from air.[6] Thus O_2 produced in this way on board a destroyer tender was used for welding and cutting over several months. The further application of synthetic oxygen carriers as catalysts for O_2 oxidations, and for use as blood substitutes is also possible. Perfluorochemicals e.g. perfluorodecalin as a 20% oil/water emulsion, are currently finding increasing use as blood substitutes.[28] Here, however, the high solubility of O_2 is the prime feature; no chemical binding of O_2 occurs as with the biological carriers. Thus H_2O dissolves 2·3% by volume of O_2 at 37°C and 1 atmosphere pressure, whereas perfluorochemicals dissolve 40% or more.

III. OXYGENATION AND COOPERATIVITY

Oxygenation curves are obtained by plotting the percentage saturation of available sites against partial pressure (p) of O_2, generally in mm of Hg (1 mm = 1 Torr). There are two possible shapes, hyperbolic and sigmoidal, as shown in Figure 4(a). The hyperbolic curve is readily explained in terms of O_2 binding to an active site X, (5):

$$X + O_2(g) \rightleftharpoons XO_2 \tag{5}$$

Equation (6) for the equilibrium constant K, (6),

$$K = \frac{[XO_2]}{[X]p} \tag{6}$$

can be alternatively expressed as (7),

$$f = \frac{Kp}{1 + Kp} \tag{7}$$

where f, the fraction of sites occupied ($\times 100$), is the percentage saturation. A plot of f against p is a hyperbolic shape. If the protein has several binding

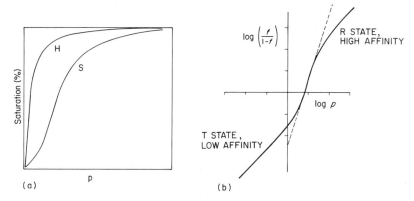

Fig. 4. *(a)* The variation of percentage saturation of metal sites with partial pressure of $O_2(p)$. Sigmoidal (S) or hyperbolic (H) shapes respectively are possible depending on whether cooperativity is or is not effective. *(b)* Case where cooperativity is observed. Plot enabling n (slope of line – – –) to be determined, Equation (9).

sites then the same relationship holds unless the different sites have different affinities. A good example is with haemoglobin, where there are four binding sites per molecule and cooperativity exists, that is the binding of the fourth O_2 occurs much more readily than its predecessors. Such positive cooperativity gives rise to a sigmoidal shape. An approximate expression, the Hill equation (8),

$$f = \frac{Kp^n}{1 + Kp^n} \tag{8}$$

now holds. This can be rearranged to (9):

$$\log\left(\frac{f}{1-f}\right) = n \log p + \log K \tag{9}$$

where a plot of the left-hand side against $\log p$ enables n to be evaluated (Fig. 4(b)). Although Equation (8) was derived following a wrong assumption, it describes the oxygenation curves quite well at pressures where the percentage saturation is not too close to 0 or 100. At 50% saturation K (equal to $1/p$) is a measure of the affinity of a protein for oxygen. The precise meaning of n is not always clear, but it is related to the degree of cooperativity. When $n = 1$, Equation (8) has the same form as (7) and there is no cooperativity. Proteins exhibiting cooperativity have n values as high as 5 with a value 9 reported for one haemocyanin.

When the pH of blood becomes more acidic due to the presence of CO_2 it is known that less O_2 binds to haemoglobin. This effect is known as the Bohr effect after Christian Bohr (father of the atomic physicist Niels Bohr). The sigmoidal O_2-binding curve in Fig. 4 moves to the right at the lower pH and release of O_2 is more efficient, as is required physiologically.

IV. VERTEBRATE HAEMOGLOBIN AND MYOGLOBIN

A. Occurrence

With very few exceptions vertebrate animals contain a circulatory tetrameric O_2-carrier haemoglobin (Hb), and a noncirculatory monomer myoglobin (Mb) which is used to store oxygen in muscles. Haemoglobin is contained in cells in a liquid medium called the plasma. It has been estimated that there are ~3 × 10^8 haemoglobin molecules in each red blood cell. Invertebrate animals have haemoglobin aggregates in solution in the plasma.

Haemoglobin is produced in the bone marrow. A feedback mechanism keeps production balanced in an individual; the normal life-time of a red blood cell is 120 days. When red cells cease to be functional, the haemoglobin is broken up and the Fe is salvaged and transported by the transferrins back to the bone marrow where it is reused. The remainder of the haemoglobin forms bilirubin which is excreted in bile.

B. Isolation

Crude haemoglobin (0·7 g) is washed with 1% NaCl, and haemolysed by addition of six times the volume of deionized water. The oxy form (HbO$_2$) can be converted to the Fe(III) met form by addition of potassium ferricyanide (7 ml of solution 1 g in 50 ml) at pH ~6. The reaction occurs by $Fe(CN)_6^{3-}$ oxidation of the deoxy form (Hb), which is withdrawn from the equilibrium (10):

$$Hb + O_2 \rightleftharpoons HbO_2 \tag{10}$$

After centrifuging it is possible to proceed with the clear solution. Reducing agents, e.g. dithionite, can be used to reduce the Fe(III) of the met form under anaerobic conditions, and regenerate the deoxy form. Relevant spectra, assumed to be the same for Hb and Mb, are shown in Fig. 5. The

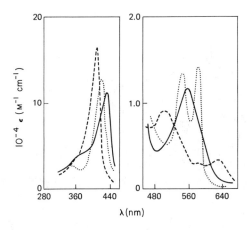

Fig. 5. UV–visible absorption spectra of Mb (—), MbO$_2$ (...) and met Mb (- - -). Intense Soret bands are observed ~ 400 nm.

spectrum of the met form is pH-dependent and a pK_a of ~8 for the axial H$_2$O ligand can be determined. Haemoglobin and myoglobin from various sources can be obtained commercially (e.g. Sigma Chemicals).

C. Active site

The active site consists of an Fe atom coordinated to the four pyrrole N atoms of the protoporphyrin IX macrocyclic ligand (Fig. 1). One of the axial Fe coordination positions is occupied by a histidine (sometimes

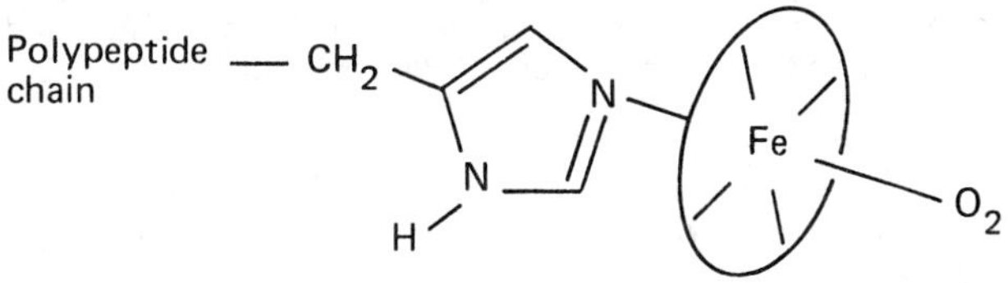

Fig. 6. Representation of the haem group and axial ligands in oxymyoglobin.

referred to as the proximal or F8 histidine, i.e. the eighth amino acid of the F-helix of the polypeptide chain). The Fe lies out of the porphyrin plane and towards the histidine in the 5-coordinate deoxy form. An H_2O may be weakly coordinated in the sixth position. Oxygen coordination occurs in the sixth position with movement of the Fe into the porphyrin plane (Fig. 6). The haem unit is referred to as the prosthetic group or cofactor. It is associated with and not (His-F8 apart) covalently bound to

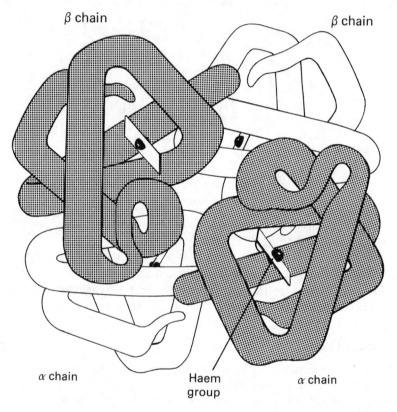

β chain β chain

α chain Haem α chain
group

Fig. 7. Quaternary structure of haemoglobin showing relative orientation of four polypeptide and haeme units. (Adapted from Dickerson R.E. and Geis I., "The Structure and Action of Proteins", Benjamin, California).

the polypeptide chain. For this reason it is relatively easy to remove and replace. The polypeptide is the globin part of the protein. Crystallographic information has been obtained for oxy and deoxy forms. (see below) The haem groups in Hb lie in isolated pockets on the surface of the subunits

(Fig. 7), with only the edge with two propionic acid side chains exposed. Folds in the peptide chain prevent close approach of the Fe atoms and formation of binuclear Fe(III) units.

D. Function

Haemoglobin (and myoglobin) combine readily and reversibly with O_2. Red blood cells (erythrocytes) of vertebrates transport O_2 from the lungs (arterial blood) to tissues. Myoglobin occurs in red muscle where it combines with O_2 released from the red cells, stores it and transports it to the mitochondria where energy is generated by combustion of glucose to CO_2 and H_2O. Myoglobin has a greater affinity for O_2 than haemoglobin, thus favouring transfer of O_2 in the capillaries of the muscle. Purple-blue venous blood consists of the deoxy form of haemoglobin. It carries away CO_2 and other waste materials from the muscles. The CO_2 (which is not coordinated to the Fe) is released in the lungs. Asphyxiation can occur due to the ability of CO to bind 150 times more strongly than O_2 to the Fe of haemoglobin. Heavy smokers can have as much as 20% of their haemoglobin bound to CO, one consequence being that the heart has to work harder to achieve the same efficiency. It is of interest here that the Fe—C—O unit is tilted in Hb and Mb due, it is believed, to the steric effect of distal His-E7 and Val-E11 groups.[29] Normally CO binds to a metal in a linear fashion; but for this effect the affinity for CO would be greater and the consequences of binding to Hb and Mb more damaging.

The concentration of O_2 in water normally provides a pressure of ~0·3 mm. With the help of haemoglobin, in human blood the overall uptake is equivalent to 9 mm.

E. Quaternary structure

Haemoglobin consists of a tetrahedral arrangement of four haem groups each surrounded by its polypeptide (globin) chain (Fig. 7). Normal adults have two α and two β type subunits and Hb can accordingly be represented as $\alpha_2\beta_2$. The α and β forms are distinguished by their different amino-acid sequences. In fetus and newly born babies the two β chains are replaced by γ chains, which have a lower affinity for the 2,3-diphosphoglycerate (DPG) regulator. This gives the $\alpha_2\gamma_2$ Hb a higher affinity for O_2 and facilitates the transfer of O_2 from the maternal to fetal circulation. Replacement of γ by β chains is generally complete within ~6 months after birth.

There are two different structural forms of tetrameric haemoglobin. The T (tense) state which is characteristic of the unligated form with the Fe atom five coordinate, and the R (relaxed) structure which is characteristic

```
                                                    10
Hb α    Val-      -Leu-Ser -Pro -Ala -Asp-Lys-Thr-Asn-Val -Lys-Ala -Ala -Trp-Gly
Hb β    Val -His -Leu-Thr-Pro -Glu -Glu-Lys-Ser -Ala -Val -Thr-Ala -Leu-Trp-Gly
Mb      Gly-      -Leu-Ser -Asx-Gly -Glx-Trp-Gln-      -Val -Leu-Asx-Val -Trp-Gly
            NA——|←————————— 5 ———— A——————10——————
```

```
                  20                                    30
Lys-Val -Gly -Ala -His -Ala -Gly-Glu-Tyr-Gly-Ala -Glu-Ala -Leu-Glu-Arg-Met-Phe-Leu
Lys-Val -Asn-          -Val -Asp-Glu-Val -Gly-Gly-Glu-Ala -Leu-Glu-Arg-Leu-Leu-Val
Lys-Val -Glu -Pro -Asp-Ile -Ala -Gly-His -Gly-Glx-Glx-Val -Leu-Ile -Arg-Leu-Phe-Lys
——15——→|   |←——————————— 5 ——————— B —— 10—————————— 15
```

```
                  40                                    50
Ser -Phe-Pro -Thr-Thr-Lys-Thr-Tyr-Phe-Pro -His -Phe-      -Asp-Leu-Ser -His -
Val -Tyr-Pro -Trp-Thr-Gln-Arg-Phe-Phe-Glu-Ser -Phe-Gly-Asp-Leu-Ser -Thr-Pro -Asp
Gly-His -Pro -Glu-Thr-Leu-Glu-Lys-Phe-Asp-Lys-Phe-Lys-His -Leu-Lys-Ser -Glu-Asp
——→|←——————— C ———— 5 —————→|←——————— CD——————————→|←—
```

```
                  60                                    70
      -Gly -Ser -Ala -Gln-Val -Lys-Gly -His -Gly-Lys-Lys-Val -Ala -Asp-Ala -Leu
Ala -Val -Met-Gly -Asn-Pro -Lys-Val -Lys-Ala -His -Gly-Lys-Lys-Val -Leu-Gly -Ala -Phe
Glu-Met-Lys-Ala -Ser -Glu-Asp-Leu-Lys-Lys-His -Gly-Ala -Thr-Val -Leu-Thr-Ala -Leu
—— 5———————————→|←——————— 5 ———— E ——— 10—————————— 15
```

```
                  80                                    90
Thr-Asn-Ala -Val -Ala -His -Val -Asp-Asp-Met-Pro -Asn-Ala -Leu-Ser -Ala -Leu-Ser -Asp
Ser -Asp-Gly -Leu-Ala -His -Leu-Asp-Asn-Leu-Lys-Gly -Thr-Phe-Ala -Thr-Leu-Ser -Glu
Gly -Gly -Ile -Leu-Lys-Lys-Lys-Gly -His -His -Glx-Ala -Glx-Ile -Lys-Pro -Leu-Ala -Glx
————————————— 20→|←——————— EF ——————————→|←·——————— F — 5——
```

```
                  100                                   110
Leu-His -Ala -His -Lys-Leu-Arg-Val -Asp-Pro -Val -Asn-Phe-Lys-Leu-Leu-Ser -His -Cys
Leu-His -Cys-Asp-Lys-Leu-His -Val -Asp-Pro -Glu-Asn-Phe-Arg-Leu-Leu-Gly -Asn-Val
Ser -His -Ala -Thr-Lys-His -Lys-Val -Pro -Ile -Lys-Tyr-Leu-Glu-Phe-Ile -Ser -Glu-Ser
————————————→|←——— FG ————————→|←——————— 5 ———— G ———— 10————
```

```
                  120                                   130
Leu-Leu-Val -Thr-Leu-Ala -Ala -His -Leu-Pro -Ala -Glu-Phe-Thr-Pro -Ala -Val -His -Ala
Leu-Val -Cys-Val -Leu-Ala -His -His -Phe-Gly-Lys-Glu-Phe-Thr-Pro -Pro -Val -Gln-Ala
Ile -Val -Asp-Val -Leu-Glu-Ser -Lys-His -Pro -Gly-Asx-Phe-Gly-Ala -Asp-Ala -Glx-Gly
—————————15————————→|←——— GH ————————→|←——————————— 5—
```

```
                  140
Ser -Leu-Asp-Lys-Phe-Leu-Ala -Ser -Val -Ser -Thr-Val -Leu-Thr-Ser -Lys-Tyr-Arg
Ala -Tyr-Gln-Lys-Val -Val -Ala -Gly-Val -Ala -Asn-Ala -Leu-Ala -His -Lys-Tyr-His
Ala -Met-Asx-Lys-Ala -Leu-Glu-Leu-Phe-Arg-Lys-Asp-Met-Ala -Ser -Asp-Tyr-Lys-Glu
————————————10————— H———————15————————————— 20→|
```

```
-    -    -    -    -
-    -    -    -    -
Leu-Gly -Phe-Gln-Gly
```

Fig. 8. The amino-acid sequences for the α and β polypeptide chains of human haemoglobin, and human myoglobin (Ref. [32]). Helical (single letter A–H) and non-helical (double letter) sections are indicated.

of all ligated forms. It has been demonstrated using x-ray crystallography that the principal difference is the arrangement of the four subunits in the two forms. The change from one to another involving relative shifts of up to 6 Å at subunit interfaces is essential for cooperative binding of O_2.[30] The 1962 Nobel Prize was shared by Kendrew and Perutz for their x-ray studies on the structures of myoglobin and haemoglobin respectively.

F. Amino-acid sequence

More than 20 myoglobins have been sequenced.[31] Some 80 of the residues are invariant of which 20 are involved in haemoglobin contact and 20 in inter-residue H-bonds. A comparison is made in Fig. 8 of the sequences of α and β chains of human haemoglobin and of myoglobin.[32] Sequence information for nearly 100 different polypeptide chains is available.[33] The size and structure of myoglobin is similar to that of the β subunit. The number of amino-acids are for $\alpha(141)$, $\beta(146)$ and myoglobin(152), where the α form has a molecular weight of ~ 16000. Other Hb amino-acid sequences which have been determined include sperm whale and horse. For horse as compared to human haemoglobin there are 18 and 25 changes respectively in the α and β sequences.

G. Secondary and tertiary structure

The peptide chains in haemoglobin and myoglobin have extensive helical structure. There are 7 helical segments in the α chains and 8 in the β and myoglobin forms (Fig. 9). These are linked by short nonhelical segments. Three-dimensional x-ray diffraction studies of globins from horse,[34] whale,[35] human,[36] seal,[37] tuna,[38] lamphrey,[39] midge,[40] and bloodworm[39] have been carried out. The tertiary structure is in all cases closely similar.

H. Oxygen affinity and Bohr effect

For Mb the graph of O_2 uptake against partial pressure of O_2 is hyperbolic, i.e. steep at the start and then levelling out (Fig. 10). Entirely different behaviour is observed with Hb, the curve increasing gently at first, then more steeply, and finally levelling out. It is sigmoidal in shape. Logarithmic plots (Equation (9)) give Hill coefficients of 2·8 for Hb and 1·0 for Mb, consistent with there being cooperativity in the case of Hb. The cooperativity stems from the tetrameric structure of Hb. The tetramer behaves in a coordinated manner whereby the binding of O_2 to one subunit increases the O_2 affinities of the others.

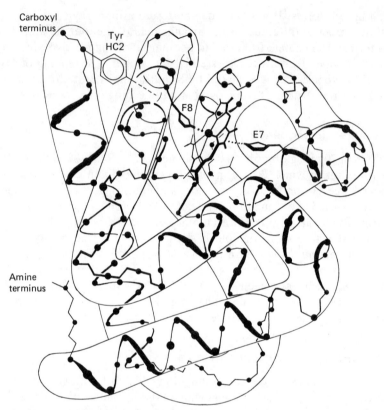

Fig. 9. Representation of the β subunit in haemoglobin. The black circles of the polypeptide chain represent α-carbon atoms. Movement of the side chains of the proximal F8 histidine (F helix) and HC2 tyrosine, it has been suggested may be a part of the triggering mechanism. (Reproduced with permission of Perutz, M., with modification as in Cotton, F.A. and Wilkinson, G., "Advanced Inorganic Chemistry", Wiley, New York, 4th Edn., 1980).

The magnitude of the Hill coefficient and O_2 affinity of Hb depend on levels in the red blood cells of H^+, CO_2, Cl^- and 2,3-diphosphoglycerate (DPG).[30] Increasing any one of these components shifts the O_2 curve to the right, as illustrated in Fig. 10 for pH 6·8. None of these factors affects the uptake of O_2 by myoglobin. At high partial pressures of O_2 (100 mm Hg in lungs) Hb is as good a binder as Mb, but at lower pressures, such as apply in muscle (~35 mm), Mb has significantly more affinity than Hb, which makes for efficient transfer between the two. As lactic acid and CO_2 are released in active muscle tissue, the pH decreases and O_2 transfer becomes more efficient in keeping with physiological needs. The reaction

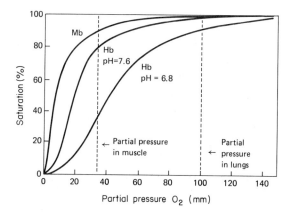

Fig. 10. Oxygenation curves for myoglobin (Mb) and haemoglobin (Hb). Different relative affinities at the two relevant physiological pH values (Bohr effect) are indicated.

of CO_2 with H_2O is catalysed by zinc carbonic anhydrase which is present in red blood cells:

$$H_2O + CO_2 \rightleftharpoons HCO_3^- + H^+ \qquad (11)$$

Two protons are taken up by Hb for every four O_2 released. The distal histidine (E7) is thought to protonate and exercise an influence by H-bonding to bound O_2. The HCO_3^- is transported back to the lungs (see below).

I. The mechanism of cooperativity in haemoglobin

An important observation that deoxy and oxy Hb have different crystal forms was made by Haurowitz in 1938. Crystals of deoxy and oxy Mb are, on the other hand, isomorphous. While x-ray crystallographic information has been forthcoming for deoxy Hb, crystals of fully oxygenated HbO_2 have only recently been isolated.[166,167] The closely related met Hb (H_2O in place of O_2) has been extensively studied, however, and information relating to the whole question of cooperativity obtained.

The arrangement of subunits and strength of bonds between them is thought to be important. Of the two forms of Hb, the R (relaxed) state binds O_2 to full capacity, whereas the T (tense) state exhibits less affinity. The transformation between the T and R forms is believed to take place after addition of 2 or 3 molecules of O_2. The deoxy form of Hb has the T-state structure and the met and oxy forms the R-state. Differences in structure are apparent in these two crystallographic forms. As Perutz has indicated,[30] there is extensive (an estimated 17–19 interactions) H-bonding within each $\alpha\beta$ pair in Hb, so that these subunit pairs behave as rigid entities in the T to R transition. Hydrogen-bonds are also formed between the two $\alpha\beta$ pairs. While different H-bonds are present for the T and R forms these do not appear to be more numerous (or stronger) in one than the other. A decisive feature is that the last amino acid in each polypeptide chain of the T structure forms a salt bridge ($-NH_3^+$ to $-CO_2^-$) with a neighbouring subunit. On interconversion of T and R forms the $\alpha\beta$ pairs rotate relative to each other by ~15° about a suitably placed axis, and there is a small shift along the same axis. Agents which lower the O_2 affinity either strengthen existing salt bridges or provide new ones. In other experiments it has been demonstrated that cooperativity disappears on splitting Hb into two $\alpha\beta$ pairs.

From the same crystallographic studies it is also clear that the Fe is displaced from the porphyrin plane towards the proximal coordinated histidine in the met form (R structure). The displacement is much greater in the deoxy form (T structure). The difference representing the movement of the Fe is now known to be less than the 0·75 Å originally suggested. Because the porphyrin ring is itself domed towards the Fe in the deoxy form, the movement of the Fe has to be clearly defined. The proximal histidine and F helix move away from the porphyrin plane when the deoxy form is produced. This shift is thought to serve as a trigger for conversion between T and R structures. However a full understanding of the way in which this movement is transmitted to contacts between the subunits and salt bridges is not yet certain. Various possibilities have been considered.[30]

J. Carbon dioxide transport

An additional function of Hb is transport of CO_2 back to the lungs. This is done by amine groups at the start of the polypeptide chains. At high CO_2 concentrations amine side chains combine with HCO_3^- to give $-NH-CO_2^-$ carbamino groups. These then form salt bridges with positively charged peptide groups in the T structure, which explains why CO_2 has more affinity for deoxy Hb than for oxy Hb which has the R structure. Back in the lungs with a plentiful supply of O_2, recombination with O_2 occurs with release of two protons for every four O_2 taken up. The release of H^+ results in the reformation of CO_2 (reverse of (11)) which is exhaled.

K. Model studies

This area has attracted considerable attention and there is an extensive literature.[41] Two areas are of interest in the present context. Firstly the chemistry exhibited by Fe(II) porphyrin complexes is considered. Secondly the much more esoteric and relevant chemistry resulting from the synthesis of sterically protected porphyrin ligands, the Fe(II) complexes of which give reversible O_2 uptake, is of interest.

A number of earlier predictions that high-spin Fe(II) has too big a radius and lies out of the porphyrin plane, whereas low-spin Fe(III) can fit into

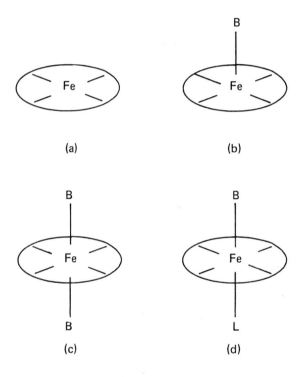

Fig. 11. Axial coordination to Fe(II) porphyrins, B = base, L = CO, O_2.

the plane of the porphyrin, have (in part) been confirmed. These ideas and the implied movement of the first Fe atom on increasing the coordination number from five to six have been incorporated into Perutz's explanation of cooperativity observed on binding O_2 to Hb.[42]

Figure 11 summarizes different Fe(II)–porphyrin complexes which can be studied. The unligated square-planar structure (a) is prepared by reduction of Fe(III) porphyrins in noncoordinating solvents.[43] On addition of base B, the initial product (b) (formation constant K_1) readily adds a second mole of B (K_2) to give (c). It is possible here that $K_2 > K_1$, since low-spin six-coordinate Fe(II) complexes will be favoured thermodynamically by crystal-field stabilization energy.[44] As a result it is generally more difficult to obtain five-coordinate complexes (b). One approach which has been explored has been to use the ligand 2-methylimidazole (2-MeIm), where (it was reasoned) following coordination of the N at position 3, the steric interaction between the methyl group and the porphyrin ring would prevent the Fe from moving into the porphyrin plane.[45]

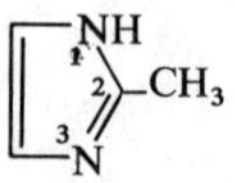

Thus the complex [Fe(TPP)(2-MeIm)] (see Fig. 12 for TPP ligand) has been prepared and from a crystal structure determination the Fe atom is 0·55 Å out of the mean haem plane.[46] Details of the crystal structure of

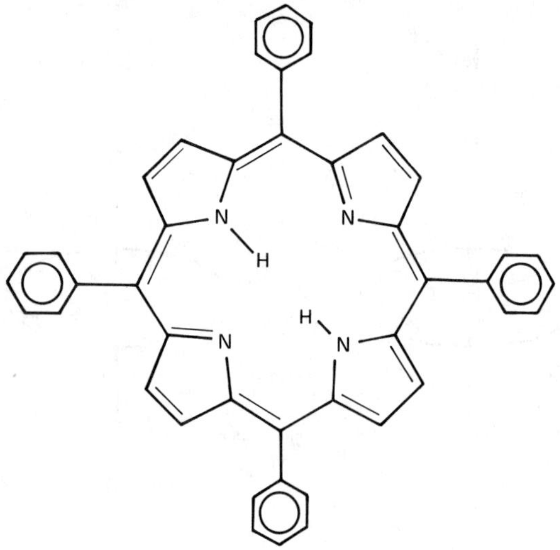

Fig. 12. Showing meso-tetraphenylporphyrin (= TPP). Note that the α, β, γ, δ positions in Fig. 1 contain phenyl substituents and the 1–8 pyrrole positions are unsubstituted.

the five-coordinate Fe(II) "picket-fence" complex (see Fig. 13) with 2-MeIm attached have also been reported (displacement 0·43 Å).[47] These values compare very well with recent estimates for the displacement of the Fe in deoxy Hb.[48] Doming of the porphyrin ring in the five-coordinate complexes appears to be variable. For the [Fe(TPP)(2-MeIm)] complex the Fe atom is 0·41 Å out of the mean N-atom porphyrin plane, compared with 0·55 Å as measured from the mean haem plane. This represents quite extensive doming (0·14 Å). The difference in the case of the "picket-fence" compound is much less (0·03 Å). A crystal structure of the low-spin six-coordinate Fe(II) complexes [Fe(TPP)(1-MeIm)$_2$] has been reported.[49] A recent development is the isolation of high-spin [Fe(TPP)(THF)$_2$], in which the Fe(II) is located in the porphyrin plane.[50] Magnetic susceptibility and Mössbauer measurements have confirmed that the complex is high-spin. It is suggested that this is a consequence of the weak crystal field of the THF (tetrahydrofuran) ligands. It appears that the porphyrin core radius is more variable than originally supposed, and can be as large as 2·1 Å with optimum size 2·01 Å.

Low-spin six-coordinate complexes (Fig. 11(d)) are obtained when CO binds to Fe(II) porphyrins. A crystal structure determination of the [Fe(TPP)(py)(CO)] complex has been carried out and the Fe—C—O unit shown to be linear.[51] When O$_2$ binds to Fe(II)–porphyrins in a reversible manner, low-spin diamagnetic complexes (d) are obtained. Although much of the earlier literature likewise refers to these oxy forms as Fe(II) complexes, an Fe(III)—O$_2^-$ assignment could well be a more accurate description, where the diamagnetism results from antiferromagnetic coupling of the Fe(III) and O$_2^-$. Of further interest in this context is the reaction of KO$_2$ (solubilized by a crown ether) with Fe(II)–porphyrin in e.g. toluene, when a new species best formulated as [Fe(III)(porph)(O$_2^{2-}$)] is obtained.[52]

Many simple unmodified Fe(II)–porphyrin complexes, of which protoporphyrin IX is a prime example, react with O$_2$ in an irreversible manner and the overall reaction may be summarized by (12):

$$4Fe(II) + O_2 \longrightarrow 2Fe(III) \cdot O_2^{2-} \cdot Fe(III) \qquad (12)$$

Using tetraphenylporphyrin complexes in toluene at −80°C a peroxo bridged intermediate has recently been detected by visible spectrophotometry and proton NMR.[53] It has been demonstrated that the intermediate reacts with two further moles of Fe(II):

$$Fe(III) \cdot O_2^{2-} \cdot Fe(III) + 2Fe(II) \longrightarrow 2Fe(III) \cdot O^{2-} \cdot Fe(III) \qquad (13)$$

or on warming (−22 to −40°C) decomposes as in (14):

$$2Fe(III) \cdot O_2^{2-} \cdot Fe(III) \longrightarrow 2Fe(III) \cdot O^{2-} \cdot Fe(III) + O_2 \qquad (14)$$

The kinetics of Equation (14) are first-order in the peroxo intermediate, and evidence supporting formation of Fe(IV)—O^{2-} has been presented.[53] It is of interest to compare this behaviour with that of μ-peroxo Co(III) complexes which are generally much more reluctant to proceed past the stage in which a μ-peroxo binuclear complex is formed. When they do so mononuclear Co(III) and not binuclear μ-oxo complexes are obtained.

The polypeptide (globin) component of Hb prevents the close approach of two haem units as required for reaction (12) to occur. Attempts to mimic the natural O_2-carrying process without a polypeptide require that formation of binuclear species be avoided. The challenge to synthesize modified porphyrins in which a steric hindrance has been created has produced much elegant work.[41] Initial attempts (1973) with Fe(II) macrocycle ligands,[54] and with Fe(II)–porphyrins having an imidazole (or pyridine) covalently attached ("tailbase" complexes) as in (i) of Fig. 13,[55]

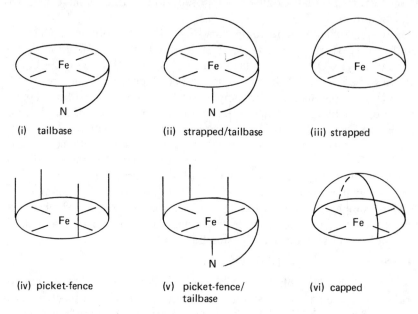

(i) tailbase   (ii) strapped/tailbase   (iii) strapped

(iv) picket-fence   (v) picket-fence/ tailbase   (vi) capped

Fig. 13. Different types of modification to Fe(II)–porphyrin complexes so that reversible O_2-binding is possible.

gave 1:1 O_2 adducts only at low temperatures ($-85°C$ and $-45°C$ respectively). The "strapped" complexes (ii)[56] and (iii)[57] with a hydrocarbon chain linked over the face of the porphyrin do not give reversible O_2 addition, almost certainly because of lack of rigidity of the chain, which can be pushed out of the way. The "picket-fence" structures (iv)[58] and (v)[59] and "capped" porphyrin (vi)[60], provide satisfactory steric protection and stabilize reversible O_2 addition at room temperature. Full formulae of (iv) and (vi) are shown in Fig. 14 and 15. A double "strapped" complex in the manner of (vi) has also been reported.[61] A wide range of studies on the "picket-fence" complexes, some of which are referred to below, have been carried out by Collman and colleagues.

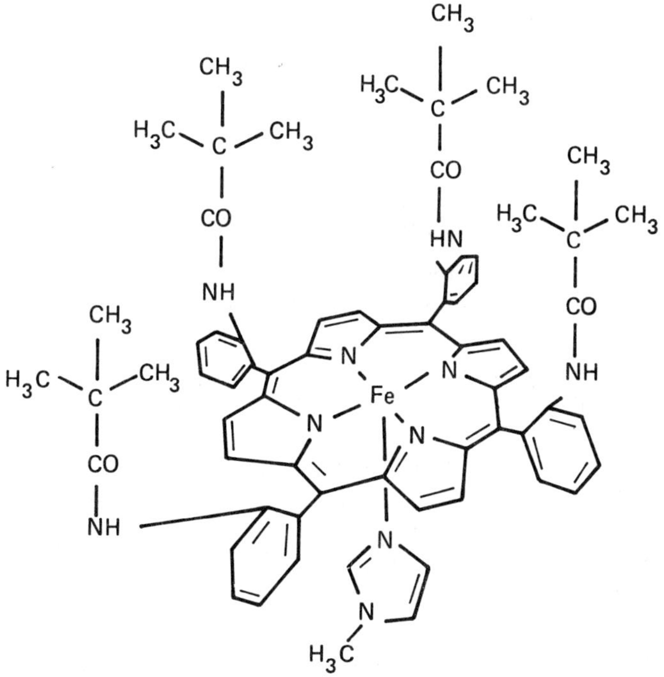

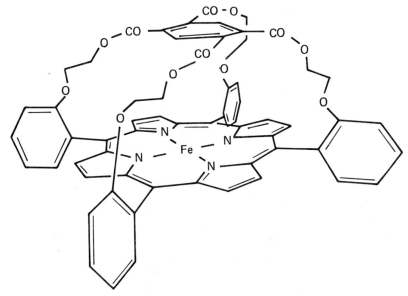

Fig. 14. Collman's "picket-fence" Fe(II)–porphyrin complex [Fe(TpivPP)(1-MeIm)] for reversible O_2-binding; H_2TpivPP is *meso*-tetra (α, α, α, α-*o*-pivalamidophenyl) porphyrin.

Fig. 15. Baldwin's "capped" Fe(II)–porphyrin for reversible O_2 binding.

A. G. Sykes

Also of interest are reversible systems in which Fe(II) porphyrins are attached to water-soluble polymers and rigid silica gel supports whereby dimerization processes are avoided.

L. Oxygen binding to Hb (Mb)

UV–visible spectra (Fig. 5) while providing a ready means of identifying O_2-binding, give no information as to the manner of the binding. Phillips has recently reported structural information for oxymyoglobin.[62] Structural information for partially (α_1 and α_2) and fully oxygenated Hb have now been obtained.[166,167] Deoxymyoglobin crystals grown under N_2 were exposed to air immediately before mounting on the diffractometer. Data collected at $-12°C$ and have been refined to $1·6$ Å resolution. The Fe–O–O bond angle is $115°$, and the O–O distance $1.22(6)$Å.[62] Similar dimensions have been reported for model complexes [Fe(O_2) (TpivPP) (2-MeIm)] ($1·22$ and $129°$), and [Fe(O_2) (TpivPP) (1-MeIm)] ($1·16$ and $131°$). An Fe–O–O angle of $156°$ is reported for Hb(O_2). The O–O distances do not provide a compelling case for the superoxo description (see Table

TABLE 4
Infrared assignments for 1 : 1 O_2 adducts to Fe(II) or Co(II) consistent with a superoxo assignment

Complex	ν(O–O)(cm^{-1})		
	$^{16}O^{16}O$	$^{18}O^{18}O$	$^{16}O^{18}O$
Mb(O_2)[a]	1107	1065	
CoHb(O_2)[b]	1105	1065	
[Fe(O_2)(TpivPP)(1-MeIm)][c]	1159	1075	
[Fe(O_2)(TpivPP)(2-MeIm)][a,c]	1158	1093	1121
[Co(O_2)(TpivPP)(1-MeIm)][c]	1150	1077	
[Co(O_2)(CN)$_5$]$^{3-}$	1138		

[a] A bent M–O–O unit has been demonstrated from crystallographic studies.
[b] A bent M–O–O unit has been inferred from EPR studies.
[c] TpivPP is the "picket-fence" ligand as in Fig 14.

2). Information as to the nature of the O_2 binding has also been obtained from resonance Raman spectra. The Fe–O stretching frequency at 568 cm^{-1} for the "picket-fence" complex[63] is identical to that for oxyhemoglobin (567 cm^{-1}).[64] When pure $^{16}O^{18}O$-labelled HbO$_2$ is used two peaks at ~550 cm^{-1} separated by ~20 cm^{-1} are observed. This is as expected for ν(Fe–$^{16}O^{18}O$) and ν(Fe$^{18}O^{16}O$) stretching modes if the O_2 is bound in an unsymmetrical end-on manner. Similarly from infrared studies ν(O–O) frequencies for MbO$_2$ compare with those previously obtained for Fe "picket-fence" complexes of known structure (Table 4). Structural information for coboglobin and other Co complexes have also been obtained. The narrow range of values displayed is consistent with the superoxo description.

A comparison has been made of Mössbauer spectra for Mb and Hb with the "picket-fence" complex. This technique is a probe for electron density at the Fe nucleus. An unusual temperature dependence of the quadrupole splitting for HbO$_2$, also observed for the "picket-fence" complex, has been attributed to a dynamic swivelling of the uncoordinated O-atom of the Fe—O—O unit about the coordinated Fe—O axis.[65] This explanation is acceptable providing paramagnetic states are not thermally accessible. However, recent magnetic susceptibility measurements over the temperature range 25–285 K now appear to support the belief that HbO$_2$ has a thermally populated paramagnetic state some 150 cm^{-1} above the diamagnetic ground state.[66] At 285 K the magnetic moment is reported to be 204 ± 0·3 BM.

EXAFS spectra of deoxy Hb and [Fe(TpivPP)(2-MEIm)] are very similar, consistent with similar Fe displacements from the plane on the porphyrin N-atoms.[168] An earlier study suggested that the displacement in Hb was much shorter (0.2 Å).[67]

From studies on the combination of O$_2$ with Fe(II)–porphyrins, the axial ligand need not necessarily be histidine. However, the π-donor properties of this ligand appear to enhance the Fe(II)(d$_{xy}$) to O$_2(\pi^*)$ interaction, and certainly as compared to other N-bases of similar basicity (e.g. substituted pyridines) help promote binding of O$_2$.

M. Thermodynamic and kinetic studies

The reversible formation of 1 : 1 O$_2$ adducts,

$$Mb + O_2 \rightleftharpoons MbO_2 \qquad (15)$$

has been studied using visible range spectrophotometry. Care is required in making comparisons as to whether O$_2$ is expressed in units of pressure (mm or atmospheres?) of concentration. The conversion factor will depend on the solubility of O$_2$ in a given solvent. The use of oxygen sensor electrodes is particularly helpful for the determination of O$_2$ in solution. Equilibrium constants for a number of myoglobins are close to 1·0 × 10^6 M^{-1} at 20°C.[68] Reactions are exothermic with $\Delta H°$ in the range −13 to −18 kcal mol^{-1}, and large negative $\Delta S°$ values, −45 to −60 cal K^{-1} mol^{-1}, consistent with the decrease in number of molecules.

Both stopped-flow and temperature-jump fast reaction techniques have been used to monitor the kinetics of O$_2$ addition. For myoglobin, linear

A. G. Sykes

plots of equilibration rate constants (k_{eq}) against equilibrium concentrations [Mb] + [O_2], are obtained:

$$k_{eq} = k_{on}([Mb] + [O_2]) + k_{off} \qquad (16)$$

The [Mb] term is small and can be neglected when O_2 is in excess. Whereas k_{on} is readily obtained from the slope of such plots, the intercept (k_{off}) is small and difficult to measure accurately. However in separate experiments dithionite can be used to induce dissociation of oxymyoglobin (it reacts rapidly with unbound O_2), and k_{off} can be determined directly therefore

TABLE 5

Rate constants (20°C) for formation (k_{on}) and dissociation (k_{off}) of oxy forms of myoglobin and haemoglobin at pH 7

	$10^{-7} k_{on}$ ($M^{-1} s^{-1}$)	k_{off} (s^{-1})	$\Delta H_{on}^{\ddagger}$ (kcal mol^{-1})	$\Delta H_{off}^{\ddagger}$ (kcal mol^{-1})
Mb(horse)	1·4	10	4·9[a]	18·4[b]
Mb(aplysia)	1·5	70	6·4	20·4
Leghaemoglobin	15[c]	11[c]		
Hb α-chain (human)[d]	4·8	28		
Hb β-chain (human)[d]	6·5	16		
Hb T-state (human)[e]	0·9	1080		
Hb R-state (human)[f]	4·0	48		
Tailbase porphyrin	2·9	24		

[a] $\Delta S_{on}^{\ddagger} = -37$.
[b] $\Delta S_{off}^{\ddagger} = 10$ cal K^{-1} mol^{-1}.
[c] 25°C.
[d] As monomer.
[e] First O_2 addition to tetramer.
[f] Final O_2 addition to tetramer.

using the stopped-flow method (Table 5).[69] An interesting recent development is to "flash" the carbon monoxide from the Mb and Hb adducts (high quantum yields are observed for the photodissociation) in the presence of a relative excess of O_2.[70] The rapid O_2 addition can be followed. Results obtained by this procedure are in agreement with other data. Rate constants for leghaemoglobin[71] (note the larger k_{on}), and for monomeric α and β components of haemoglobin,[72] are also shown in Table 5. The haemoglobin system is more complex with four on and four off rate constants to be taken into account in the fitting procedure.[73] Rate constants for the first (T-state) and last (R-state) stages of oxygenation are listed in Table 5. The higher k_{off} rate constant accounts for the lower O_2 affinity of the T-state. Traylor and colleagues[74] have reported k_{off} and k_{on} for a range of "tailbase" complexes in Fig. 13, which are closely similar to values obtained for Mb in Table 5.

N. Metal replacement[75]

The haem group gives blood its red colour. Colourless apoprotein can be obtained from either oxy or met Hb and Mb by the acidified acetone or acidified butanone procedure.[76] Both Hb and Mb can be reconstituted with the same (proto) or other (e.g. meso and haemato) porphyrins present, and porphyrins containing other oxidation state II metals can be introduced using standard methods.[77] Reconstitution with Co(II) porphyrin is in the presence of dithionite in aqueous pyridine solvent.[78,79]

The Co(II) substituted proteins can reversibly add O_2 as can the Co(II) porphyrins without the globin, a particularly useful observation and one which contrasts with the behaviour of Fe. Since EPR spectra are observed for the deoxy and oxy Co forms it has been possible to conclude that there is 80% transfer of spin density from Co(II) to O_2, consistent with Co(III) and O_2^- formal oxidation states.[78] Only a bent Co–O–O bond is consistent with observations made, the simplest model giving an angle of 120°.[80] A weaker Co–O bond makes this system less efficient than with Fe. The preparation of Hb hybrids with different Co and Fe occupancies of the α and β sites in the tetramer, permits an independent observation of O_2-binding. The different affinities of Co and Fe ensures that the first two O_2 groups go almost entirely to the Fe sites.[81]

Other metals, Mn(II) and Zn(II), have been incorporated into Hb and Mb. The Zn(II) does not react with O_2, and Mn(II) is oxidized to Mn(III), i.e. the met form, with H_2O probably bonded in the sixth coordination position. Of particular interest here is the comparison with the five-coordinate pyridine complex of Mn(II) tetraphenylporphyrin (Fig. 12), which combines reversibly with O_2 at $-79°C$ in toluene. Replacement of the axial nitrogenous pyridine ligand occurs and from EPR and optical spectra a (sideways-on) Mn(IV)–peroxo, rather than an Mn(III)–superoxo complex, is formed.[82] With the Mn(II) forms of Hb and Mb a similar reaction does not occur presumably because the O_2 is not able to compete with and replace the proximal histidine. Mixed Hb hybrids $\alpha_2^{Fe(II)}\beta_2^{Mn(II)}$ have also been prepared. The kinetics of CO binding to Mn(II), Zn(II) and Co(II) hybrid hemoglobins has been studied.[83]

O. Abnormalities

A fairly well understood example of Hb abnormality occurs in sickle-cell anaemia which is common in West and Central Africa, parts of India, the

Persian Gulf and Mediterranean. A characteristic of the disease is the more prominent bone structure of the forehead. The red blood cells have a reduced life-time and, particularly under conditions of fatigue caused by exercise, can assume an irregular crescent shape caused by semicrystalline haemoglobin aggregates at reduced O_2 pressures. When the parental genetic determinants are identical, the disease can be fatal during early years of life. It has survived natural selection because, with nonidentical determinants, the anaemia is not effective, but protection against malaria results. Although precise details of the protection are uncertain, the protozoan parasite of malaria is known to spend most of its life-cycle inside the red blood cell.

Sickle-cell anaemia is brought about by a single error, the replacement of a glutamic acid residue, normally present in the sixth position of the β chain of haemoglobin, by valine. The error is genetic in origin, and is the result of a single change of adenine for thymine in the three-base nucleotide coding for glutamic acid, giving instead the coding for valine. A slight change in the tertiary folding of the β-chain probably results from this replacement of the negatively charged glutamate. The blood type is also referred to as haemoglobin S.

V. INVERTEBRATE HAEMOGLOBIN AND MYOGLOBIN

A. Occurrence

A feature of these proteins is the wide variation of molecular size in going from one species to another. Work on the haemoglobins from certain annelids (e.g. segmented earth and marine worms), molluscs (e.g. snails, clams), and arthropods (shrimps and insect larvae have been investigated), has led to the proposal that molecular weights are simple multiples of a basic fundamental unit, and that quaternary structure is important.[84] Molecular weights range from 17000 for monomeric units containing a single haeme to aggregates with molecular weights as high as $3-4 \times 10^6$ for some annelid haemoglobins. The latter have ~200 binding sites. For comparison haemocyanin aggregates in gastropods, which are amongst the largest known protein molecules, have molecular weights as high as 9×10^6.[1]

In contrast to the giant extracellular annelid haemoglobins, additional haemoglobins of much lower molecular weights are sometimes encountered in coelomic cells of the polychaete annelids. A variety of oligomers are found including monomers and tetramers. In the mollusc family, while haemocyanins are fairly typical of gastropods and cephalopods, haemoglobins are also found. The reasons for these curious evolutionary divergences are not known. Monomeric (MW 17000), or more frequently dimeric, radular muscle myoglobin occurs in many gastropods in addition to the large extracellular haemoglobin. The occurrence of haemoglobin in arthropods is sporadic, and confined to a few insects and brachiopods (e.g. shrimps).

B. Size determination

Svedberg obtained a molecular weight of $2 \cdot 7 \times 10^6$ for the protein from the annelid *Lumbricus* earthworm by ultracentrifugation (sedimentation coefficient 60S).[84] A more recent value, nearer to 4×10^6, has been confirmed by low-angle x-ray scattering.[85,86] As with the haemocyanins, such proteins are good subjects for electron microscopy and some detail as to the structural arrangement of the subunits has been obtained.[87] A classification in terms of molecular size has been attempted (Table 5 in Ref. [85]). Although MWs of around 17000 seem fairly general, a notable exception is haemoglobin from a nematode (*Ascaris lumbricoides*) where a monomer form appears to have a molecular weight of 37000, and the subunit of an octamer form a molecular weight of 40600.[88]

C. Chlorocruorins

The chlorocruorins (or chlorohaemes) are found in a few polychaete annelid worms. They have high molecular weights and a marked similarity to annelid haemoglobins.[86] As previously mentioned, they are chemically different from haemoglobins, the 2-vinyl group of protoporphyrin IX having been replaced by a formyl group. This seems to have little effect on physical properties, apart from the green colour observed for the oxy form. The chlorocruorins will not be considered further as a separate category.

D. Oxygen-binding site

It seems likely that the mechanism of binding is closely similar to that of the vertebrate haemoglobins. X-ray data has been reported for the oxy and deoxy forms of monomeric haemoglobin from the larvae of the insect *Chironomus*.[89] Although the resolution is high ($1 \cdot 4$ Å), the electron density at the O_2 does not correspond well with that expected for a well defined molecule. There are, moreover, a number of unusual features. First, the

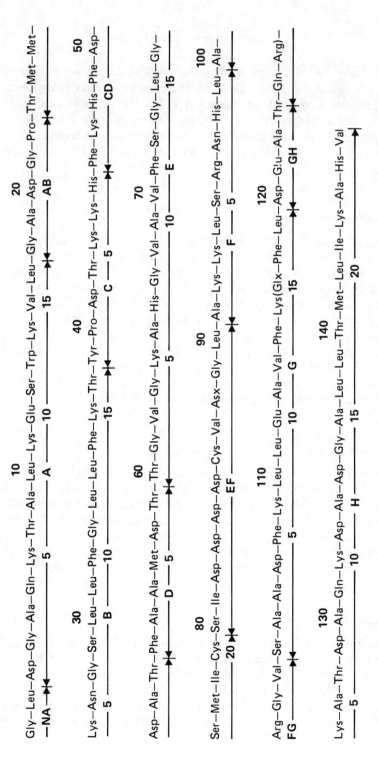

Fig. 16. Amino-acid sequence of the myoglobin from the invertebrate gastropod whelk *Busycon*. This mollusc contains haemocyanin as O₂ carrier.

Fe–O–O angle at 170° (possible error 30°) is close to linear, although no inorganic complexes exhibit this feature. Calculations indicate that a linear structure is energetically unfavourable.[90] Second, an H_2O is H-bonded to the bound O_2. Third, the Fe out-of-plane distance for the oxy form is anomalously large, as in vertebrate myoglobin (0·22 Å), with Fe displaced towards the coordinated histidine.

E. Amino-acid sequence

Some of the polypeptide chains of the annelid *Lumbricus* earthworm Hb have been separated and purified by ion-exchange chromatography in the presence of 8 M urea.[91] One of these has recently been sequenced and found to contain 157 residues (MW 18000). Homologies with vertebrate haemoglobins and myoglobins have been noted. Thus there is about 15% homology with the β-chain of human haemoglobin, and both proximal and distal haem binding histidine residues are present. The amino-acid sequence of radular muscle myoglobin dimer from the *Busycon* whelk has been reported (147 amino-acids)[92] (Fig. 16). A 25% homology with human haemoglobin (β-chain) has been noted.

F. Properties

It is not clear how the structural variations in invertebrate haemoglobins modify the O_2-binding properties of the haeme group to produce a wide range of variations in functional properties. The situtation is very like the haemocyanins where all possible variations occur with respect to O_2-affinity, cooperativity and the Bohr effect.[93] The Hb of arthropod clam shrimp *Cyzicus* for example (MW ~250 × 10^3)[94] is reported to bind O_2 cooperatively ($n = 2·3$), and to have an exceptionally high O_2-affinity (partial pressure for half saturation, $p_{1/2} = 0·035$ mm Hg). An annelid haemoglobin (from the tebellied polychaete), on the other hand, has low O_2-affinity, ($p_{1/2} = 36$ mm Hg), no significant cooperativity, and no Bohr effect. More generally, O_2-affinities are in the range $p_{1/2} = 5 ± 3$ mm Hg. Hill coefficients as high as $n = 4·8$ have been reported. Interestingly the myoglobin dimers from two gastropods have been reported to exhibit slight cooperativity ($n = 1·1$ and 1·5).[95] and in these relatively simple cases an understanding of the way in which this cooperativity is mediated would be of interest. Allosteric effects noted for vertebrate haemoglobins are not generally influential on the O_2 binding of extracellular invertebrate haemoglobins, although a mild depressant effect of ATP has been noted in some cases.[96,97]

VI. HAEMERYTHRIN

A. Occurrence

Haemerythrin has been found in an annelid, two brachiopods and two priapulid marine invertebrates. However, the sipunculid worms as listed in Table 6 are the major source and most extensively studied.[98] The sipunculids, unlike the haemoglobin-containing annelid worms do not have

TABLE 6
Origin of sipunculid worms as source of haemerythrins[a]

Name	Origin	Ref.
Phascolopsis (syn *Golfingia*) *gouldii*	East coast of USA (five species with minor, 1–5 amino-acid variations are known)	[108]
Phascolosoma agassizii[c]	Peninsula Marine Biologicals, Sand City, California, USA	[99]
Phascolosoma lurco[c]	Suva, Fiji	[100]
Sipunculus nudus[b]	Fishermen, Taranto, Italy	[104]
Themiste (syn *Dendrostomum*) *zostericola*[b,d,e]	Biomarine Supply, Venice, California, USA	[101]
Themiste (syn *Dendrostomum*) *dyscritum*[b]	Oregon Institute of Marine Biology, USA	[113]

[a] See also Ref. [98].
[b] Octamer.
[c] Trimer.
[d] Formerly *Themiste pyroides*.
[e] Also source of monomer.

segmented bodies. Lengths are variable (according to species) but are typically 10 cm and, although rare, locally they can be very common. They live on the sea bed and are to be found buried in the mud or sand between tide levels.

Haemerythrin, like vertebrate haemoglobin, is carried in blood cells (erythrocytes), where it exists as an octamer. It is however known to be present as a trimer in the blood cells of at least two sipunculid worms.[99,100] A monomer (myohaemerythrin) has been isolated from the retractor muscle of *Themiste zostericola*, which also has the octamer in the erythrocytes.[101] The situation appears similar, therefore, to that of haemoglobin and myoglobin in vertebrates. A review describing structural and spectroscopic properties has appeared.[102]

B. Isolation

Batches of 100 worms are generally required. Each worm is cut lengthwise and the coelomic fluid collected in a beaker.[101] The coelomic blood cells are separated and lysed by addition of an equal volume of distilled water. The oxyhaemerythrin obtained can be dialysed against a large volume of 20% ethanol, when a solid is deposited within a few hours. Alternatively the oxy form is dialysed against $0 \cdot 1$ M NaN_3 in order to convert to metazido haemerythrin, which is then precipitated by addition of 60% saturated $(NH_4)_2SO_4$ at pH $7 \cdot 0$. The entire procedure is generally carried out at ~5°C, and solid samples stored in a freezer (~−20°C). To obtain the monomer, two retractor muscles can be removed from each worm after collection of the coelomic fluid and careful washing. These are homogenized (using a blender) with buffer pH 8 in $0 \cdot 1$ M NaCl, and the haemerythrin separated by a procedure described.[101] The aquomet form can be obtained by oxidation of the deoxy form with, e.g., H_2O_2 or excess $Fe(CN)_6^{3-}$. It is unstable at pH > 10 denatures on decreasing the pH (~ 6) unless this is done slowly by dialysis. The octamer is more stable and easier to handle (and store) than the monomer. The UV–visible spectrum of haemerythrin varies with pH, and an approximate pK_a of ~9 for the aquo ligand has been suggested. Bubbling gases through rather than over haemerythrin solutions results in denaturing (a white flocculence is observed).

C. Function

Haemerythrin is involved in oxygen-binding and transport. It binds one mole of O_2 per active site containing two Fe(II) atoms in close proximity:

$$Fe(II)_2 + O_2 \rightleftharpoons Fe(III)_2O_2^{2-} \tag{16}$$

It has been demonstrated that a binuclear Fe(III) peroxo formulation applies (see below). There is no porphyrin, and in so far as haeme is synonymous with an Fe-porphyrin unit it could be argued that the haem-erythrin terminology is incorrect. However, the Greek origin, haem ($\alpha \iota \mu \alpha$) meaning blood (with its related functions), still applies. The peroxide group can be displaced and met forms obtained on addition of exogenous ligands $L^- = NCS^-$, N_3^-, CN^-, and F^-:

$$Fe(III)_2O_2^{2-} + L^- \longrightarrow Fe(III)_2L^- + O_2^{2-} \tag{17}$$

Unlike haemoglobin little or no cooperativity is observed for the extracted octameric form, and the Hill coefficient n is no greater than $1 \cdot 1$.[102] However, inside the coelomic cell haemerythrin has a lower O_2 affinity with $n > 3$ when cells are >50% saturated with O_2.[103] This suggests

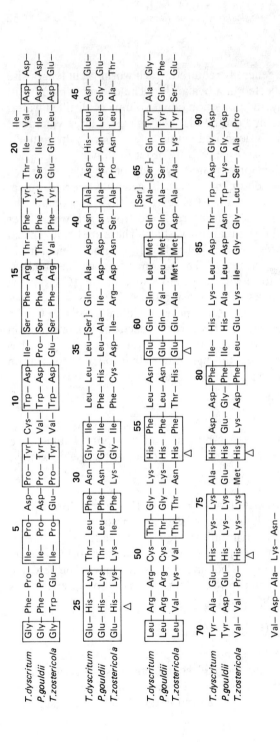

Fig. 17. Amino-acid sequences for haemerythrin from the octamers in *Themiste dyscritum*, in *Phascolopsis gouldii*, and from the monomer in *Themiste zostericola*. Invariant residues are enclosed in boxes. Residues identified as Fe ligands are indicated by △.

that there is a physiological effector. There appear to be no significant effects of pH (Bohr effect).[104–106]

D. Amino-acid sequence

Haemerythrin in the octamer consists of eight identical subunits. In addition to the sequences shown in Fig. 17, information is also available for the octamer from *Themiste zostericola*, some variants from *Phascolopsis gouldii*, and for segments of the trimer from *Phascolosoma agassizii*.[102,107–110] The octamer subunit has 113 amino-acids (MW 13500). The monomer with 118 amino-acids (MW 13900) has five extra amino-acids located between residues 90 and 91 (see Fig. 17). Invariant amino-acid residues are 42% of the total in the comparison made. Haemoglobin and myoglobin are also very similar, but with only 20% of the amino-acids invariant.

E. Secondary and tertiary structure

Each subunit consists of four approximately parallel sections 15–35, 46–60, 70–85 and 95–113, having α-helix structure, which accounts for 70% of the amino-acids.[111] A nonhelical 15-residue section containing the terminal NH_2 of the amino-acid chain is folded on one side of the helices (Fig. 18). The structures are very similar for monomer and octamer in spite of the five additional amino-acids in the monomer. The Fe ligands come from all four helical sections, which undoubtedly helps to stabilize the subunit.

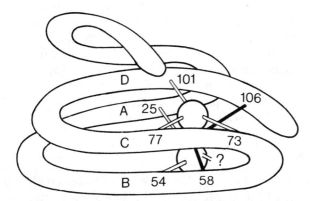

Fig. 18. A representation of the haemerythrin subunit, showing Fe atoms and the directions from which these are coordinated. The numbers refer to coordinated amino-acid residues in the octamer (see below). Side-chains to residues 58 and 106 are bridging ligands. The four α-helical sections A–D are indicated.

F. Quaternary structure

Earlier low resolution x-ray crystal structure information gave information regarding the arrangement of subunits in the octamer.[112,113] The subunits are in two layers (Fig. 19), overlapping like bricks, and in a doughnut shape with dimensions approximately $75 \times 75 \times 40$ Å. There is a large hole nearly 20 Å across, through the centre and coincident with the four-fold

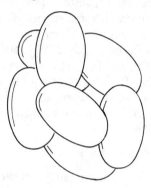

Fig. 19. The quaternary structure of octameric haemerythrin (Ref. [113]).

(C_4) axis of symmetry. Details of the surface amino-acid structure of different subunits presumably determine whether the monomer units aggregate to give octamer (or trimer) by electrostatic and/or H-bonding interactions. The octamer subunit contains a cysteine residue at position 50 which is not present in either monomer or trimer. If bulky reagents such as p-chloromercuribenzoate are attached to the S-atom of cysteine-50 then dissociation of the octamer occurs.[114,115] It is possible that the adjacent oppositely charged arginines (48 and 49) and lysine (53), which are conserved in the octamer but not in the monomer, are involved in association of subunits. Thus the close proximity of the large p-chloromercuribenzoate may be sufficient to disrupt such electrostatic associations.

G. Active site

From UV–visible spectra (Fig. 20), it can be concluded that no porphyrin ring is present, and therefore that the Fe atoms are coordinated directly to amino-acid residues. Prior to x-ray diffraction studies, eight histidine and tyrosine residues had been singled out as possible ligands. X-ray crystallographic studies by two groups at first gave worrying disagreement, but with further refinement now appear to be working towards a consensus.

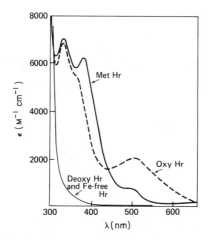

Fig. 20. UV–visible absorption spectra of deoxy, oxy and met forms of haemerythrin (ε values are per 2Fe unit). The absorbance $\sim$500 nm for Met Hr is probably due to traces of the oxy form.

There are no essential differences in active site structure of the monomer and octamer forms. Hendrickson and colleagues from studies on crystals of azidomethaemerythrin from the monomer of *Themiste zostericola* have reported an Fe–Fe distance of 3·44 Å,[116] and on the basis of crystallographic and magnetic susceptibility data suggested that the atoms are bridged by a μ-oxo ligand. Jenson and colleagues working with an aquomet form,[117] which they subsequently refer to as hydroxomet†, have recently reported data for azidomet,[118] all from *Themiste dyscritum* (octamer). They now agree that a single O-atom bridge (either μ-oxo or μ-hydroxo) is present. Other features which they describe for the azidomet, resolution 2·2 Å, are indicated in Fig. 21.[118] The complex consists of two octahedrally coordinated Fe atoms bridged by two carboxylato groups and the O-atom. The carboxylato groups bridge the Fe atoms with one O-atom of each RCO_2^- bound to each Fe as in inorganic analogue complexes. The other ligands are three histidines to one Fe, and two histidines and the azido to the other. There is no electron density connecting tyrosine-109 to the second Fe as previously proposed. The azide ligand clearly binds to only one Fe, which is consistent with predictions of Gay and Solomon[119] in their interpretation of polarized single-crystal spectra. At the same time refinement of the "aquomet" form to 2·0 Å has continued and similar structural features have been shown to hold.[118] The suggestion that in the

† Since the presence of a hydroxo ligand is not firmly established the simpler met designation is perhaps to be preferred.

absence of azide one of the Fe atoms is pentacoordinate is an interesting one requiring further investigation. In referring to the Hendrickson crystal structure papers on the monomer it has to be remembered that there are five extra amino-acids immediately following residue 90, and that numbers for coordinated amino-acids have to be adjusted accordingly.

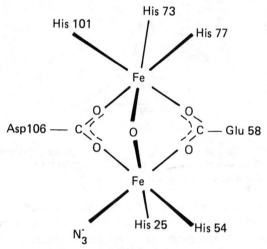

Fig. 21. The active site structure of haemerythrin from a recent x-ray diffraction study on the azidomet form of *Themiste dyscritum* (octamer). (Ref. [118]).

Comparative studies suggest that haemerythrin proteins from different sources have identical active sites.[120] Studies using the EXAFS technique, have indicated a preliminary Fe–Fe distance of $3 \cdot 0$ Å.[121] Further information using this technique is awaited with considerable interest.

H. Oxygen binding

The spectra of deoxy (colourless) and oxy (red-violet) haemerythrin are shown in Fig. 20. Similarities are to be noted in the spectra of oxy and met forms obtained by addition of exogenous ligands (e.g. NCS^- and N_3^-); Fig. 22. An assignment of transitions to the different electronic bands in oxy, met and deoxy forms has been reported.[122]

Deoxyhaemerythrin has a magnetic susceptibility corresponding to four unpaired electrons per Fe, as expected for high-spin Fe(II) ($t_{2g}^4 e_g^2$). Oxy and met forms become diamagnetic near absolute zero consistent with the ability of a μ-oxo ligand in simple inorganic compounds to couple two Fe(III) ions antiferromagnetically. Although other bridging ligands can give rise to antiferromagnetic coupling including O_2^{2-} as in oxyhaemocyanin (bonding Cu—O—O—Cu), it has been suggested that the magnitude of the coupling indicates involvement of a single O-atom.

Mössbauer spectra of several haemerythrins have also indicated high-spin Fe(II) for the deoxy form, and two antiferromagnetically coupled

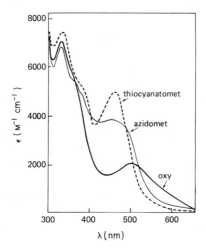

Fig. 22. UV–visible absorption spectra of oxy, azidomet and thiocyanatomet forms of haemerythrin (ε values are per 2Fe unit).

high-spin Fe(III) in the oxy and met forms.[123] However, whereas the deoxy and met forms give only a single doublet, oxyhaemerythrin has a pair of quadrupole-split doublets.[124] This suggests two different Fe environments in the oxy form.

Charge-transfer transitions for oxyhaemerythrin overlap several blue and green laser lines and make possible resonance Raman studies.[125] Peaks at 844 cm^{-1} and 540 cm^{-1} have been assigned to symmetric O–O and Fe–O stretching frequencies arising from bound O_2.[126] The ν(O–O) frequency at 844 cm^{-1} clearly indicates a peroxide assignment (i.e. in the range 740–900 cm^{-1}). These assignments are confirmed by noting the mass shifts resulting from the replacement of $^{16}O_2$ by $^{18}O_2$ e.g. the 844 cm^{-1} peak shifts to 798 cm^{-1}. With $^{16}O^{18}O$ spectra indicate that individual O-atoms are non-equivalent.[127] The data obtained, it has been suggested, leave two (of four) possible O_2-binding structures:

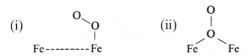

However (i) is not a recognized peroxide to metal structure, and (ii), while it is able to account for the antiferromagnetic coupling, is not compatible with Mössbauer findings (inequivalent Fe atoms in oxy but not deoxy and met forms). Again there is a need for further information.

I. Kinetics and thermodynamics

The kinetics of the on and off O_2 processes

$$\text{Hr} + O_2 \underset{k_{off}}{\overset{k_{on}}{\rightleftharpoons}} \text{HrO}_2 \tag{18}$$

for monomer and octamer forms have been studied by fast reaction techniques.[105, 128] Such studies indicate that the subunits of the octamer behave independently with only a single rate constant displayed (no cooperativity). Using stopped-flow and temperature-jump methods, details as previously for Mb, rate constants k_{on} and k_{off} have been determined. A wavelength 365 nm ($\varepsilon = 5 \cdot 8 \times 10^3 \text{ M}^{-1} \text{ cm}^{-1}$ for oxy and ~600 $\text{M}^{-1} \text{ cm}^{-1}$ for deoxy, both per Fe_2 unit) is used. Results for different haemerythrins are listed in Table 7. A result of note is that monomeric haemerythrin reacts with O_2 an order of magnitude faster than the octamer from *Themiste zostericola*, with the dissociation (k_{off}) also four times faster. The rate constant k_{on} for the monomer ($7 \cdot 8 \times 10^7 \text{ M}^{-1} \text{ s}^{-1}$) suggests a near diffusion-controlled process. Therefore as with haemoglobin it is likely that the deoxy form has an initially unoccupied coordination position or at least one occupied by a very weakly held group. Enthalpies of activation for k_{off} (Table 7) are to all intents identical to those reported for myoglobin (Table 5). Entropies of activation are again significantly positive. No uptake or release of protons is reported upon oxygenation. The 20 Å central cavity in the octamer does not appear to serve any specific function in O_2 binding and access to the binuclear Fe active site is believed to be from the outer surface.

Equilibrium constants (K) can be obtained directly by spectrophotometry (determination of HrO_2), and by using an O_2-sensor electrode to measure O_2 concentrations. Such electrodes (e.g. Beckman) are able to measure accurately low levels of O_2. Alternatively, K can be obtained from the ratio k_{on}/k_{off}. A comparison of rate and equilibrium constants for haemerythrin with haemoglobin and haemocyanin is made in Table 7. What is surprising is the remarkable similarity of the various parameters obtained. This is in spite of the different metals (Fe and Cu), porphyrin and non-porphyrin ligands, mononuclear and binuclear active sites, and superoxo and peroxo assignments for the bound O_2. It would appear that quite different O_2-binding proteins have evolved which are able to undergo reversible oxygenation with comparable efficiencies.

TABLE 7

A comparison of rate constants (25°C) for formation (k_{on}) and dissociation (k_{off}) of oxy forms of haemerythrin, myoglobin and haemocyanin, $I = 0.10$ M. (See Ref. [128] and references therein)

	$10^{-7} k_{on}$ ($M^{-1} s^{-1}$)	k_{off} (s^{-1})	10^{-5} K (M^{-1})	Conditions
Haemerythrin, *Therm. zost.* (monomer)	7·8	315[a]	2·5	25°C, pH 8·2
Haemerythrin, *Therm. zost.* (octamer)	0·75	82[b]	0·9	25°C, pH 8·2
Haemerythrin *Phas. gould.* (octamer)	0·74	51	1·5	25°C, pH 8·2
Haemerythrin, *Spin. nud.* (octamer)	2·6	120	2·2	25°C, pH 7·0
Myoglobin, sperm whale	1·9	11	17	21·5, pH 7·0
Haemoglobin, human (4th unit)	3·3	50	6·6	21·5, pH 7·0
Haemocyanin (*Helin. p*)(R-state)	0·38	10	3·8	20°C, pH 8·2
Haemocyanin (*Bucc. u.*) (R-state)	0·78	70	1·1	25°C, pH 7·3–8·2

[a] $\Delta H^{\ddagger}_{off} = 17$ kcal mol^{-1}; $\Delta S^{\ddagger}_{off} = 9$ cal K^{-1} mol^{-1} for k_{off}.
[b] $\Delta H^{\ddagger}_{off} = 19$ kcal mol^{-1}; $\Delta S^{\ddagger}_{off} = 15$ cal K^{-1} mol^{-1} for k_{off}.

J. Chemistry of the active site

Small anionic ligands displace the peroxo O_2^{2-} group from oxyhaemerythrin with the formation of met as in Equation (17). While exogenous ligands $L = NCS^-, N_3^-, CN^-$ and F^- are particularly efficient, Cl^- undergoes the reaction much less readily.[129] The substitution reaction which occurs gives only a single L ligand for each 2Fe active site, and the manner in which L is bonded is of interest. Although none of the met forms appear to be physiologically relevant, studies on substitution and electron-transfer reactions have attracted much attention. The area has been reviewed.[130]

From resonance Raman studies the thiocyanato met form is believed to be *N*-bonded with one of the structures shown below applying:

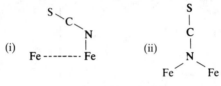

No inorganic complexes have yet been identified in which (ii) applies. With azide, using a labelled form $^{15}N^{14}N^{14}N^-$, it has likewise been concluded that the N atoms are in non-equivalent positions, and that two analogous structures are possible.[127] However structure (ii) is not consistent with recent x-ray information.[118] By conducting reduction and re-oxidation reactions in the presence of H_2 ^{18}O, it has been possible to make a tentative assignment of the azidomet band at $507\ cm^{-1}$ as originating from a μ-oxo ligand. The Fe–O (carboxylate) stretching mode could provide an alternative explanation.

The oxidative addition process accompanying O_2 uptake by deoxy haemerythrin apparently occurs in one stage, as does the oxidation of the deoxy form to the met with H_2O_2.[105] With the one-equivalent oxidant $Fe(CN)_6^{3-}$, on the other hand, a semi-met Fe(II, III) form of *Themiste zostericola* has been identified.[131] A slow intramolecular process then occurs ($t_{1/2}$ is a few minutes), and when sufficient oxidant is present further oxidation occurs. Possible explanations are that within the octamer disproportionation of the eight Fe(II, III) occurs yielding four Fe(II, II) and four Fe(III, III) units, or that each Fe(II, III) undergoes intramolecular change to give the nonidentical Fe(III, II). The first of these explanations is currently favoured since the mixed species formed behaves spectrophotometrically and kinetically like an equimolar mixture of deoxy and met forms with both O_2 and NCS^-. A half-reduced form is also prepared by one-electron reduction of methaemerythrin with dithionite, and again slow disproportionation ($t_{1/2}$ of 8 minutes) precedes further reduction. On addition of $Fe(CN)_6^{3-}$ prior to disproportionation rapid reoxidation occurs.

The two semi-met forms have quite distinct spectra (Fig. 23). Also at liquid He temperatures the semi-met forms have different EPR spectra with g values of 1·95 and 1·71 (the species generated from deoxy), and 1·93, 1·86 and 1·68 (the species from met). The met and deoxy forms are EPR-inactive. Both semi-met forms react with N_3^- to give a single semi-met azide adduct which is stable to disproportionation.[131]

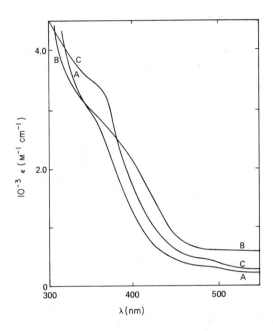

Fig. 23. UV–visible spectra of semi-met primary product forms of octameric haemerythrin generated by *(a)* $S_2O_4^{2-}$ reduction of met, and *(b)* $Fe(CN)_6^{3-}$ oxidation of the deoxy form. Spectrum *(c)* is that obtained by disproportion-ation of both semi-met forms and is the same as an equimolar mixture of the deoxy-met (Ref. [131]).

From x-ray crystallographic studies, the 2Fe active sites are separated by ~30 Å from an active site in the same layer and about the same distance from an active site in the second layer of the octamer. If the dispropor-tionation mechanism applies, electron transfer between these active sites has to occur. These are large distances for electron transfer, although the rate constant associated with the disproportionation is slow. Further infor-mation on the semi-met forms of the monomer and their behaviour might be helpful. What these studies do seem to confirm is that the two Fe at one site are nonidentical. *Phascolopsis gouldii* haemerythrin also gives two semi-met forms, but disproportionation is reported to be less effective.

K. Other anion binding sites

Evidence has been obtained for one or two additional sites on the protein at which association of anions such as ClO_4^-, NO_3^-, HCO_3^-, $H_2PO_4^-$ and Cl^- occurs.[130,132] Information as to the location of these sites using ClO_4^- has now been obtained from x-ray crystallographic studies.[133] The presence of such anions has the effect of decreasing the rate of formation and stability of methaemerythrin complexes with different L^- ligands. It also increases the affinity of the deoxy form for O_2.[134]

L. Inorganic model studies

A detailed analysis of UV–visible spectra of binuclear Fe(III) complexes having an oxo bridge and different terminal ligands has been carried out.[135] The similarity of spectra to those observed for oxy and met forms suggests that the μ-oxo ligand may be a common feature. Circular dichroic spectra are believed to support this view.[135] Further studies in this area are to be anticipated. Several small-molecule iron carboxylate structures have been reported.[136]

M. Further mechanistic considerations

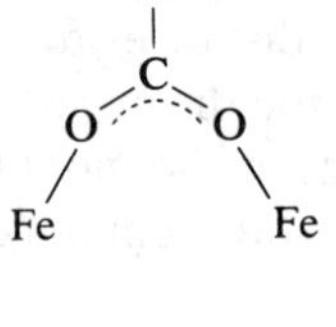

With the above information, in particular that from the recent x-ray crystal structure investigation, it is of interest to speculate further concerning the chemistry displayed by haemerythrin and the manner of O_2 binding. For the deoxy Fe(II)$_2$ state a hydroxo rather than an oxo bridge between the metals might seem more appropriate. However, no change in pH occurs on uptake of O_2. Certainly there is no precedent for an aquo ligand bridging two metals as a stable entity whether in the II or III state. The observation that the Fe(III) of the met form have nonidentical environments presumably carries through to the deoxy form, in which case the existence of dissimilar Fe(II, III)$_2$ and Fe(III, II)$_2$ semi-met forms is readily understood. Binding of O_2 (in place of N_3^- in Fig. 21) to a single Fe is perfectly reasonable since two μ-carboxylato ligands, with delocalized electron density, could provide a ready means of involving both Fe in the two-electron redox change. However binding of O_2^{2-} to a single Fe does require, in terms of known inorganic analogue chemistry, that this group be sideways-on to the metal. This is not consistent with infrared/Raman measurements previously referred to. Further studies will no doubt help in understanding these features.

VII. HAEMOCYANIN

A. Occurrence

Haemocyanins are high molecular weight O_2-carrying Cu proteins which occur in only two phyla of animals, molluscs and arthropods. Among the molluscs it is found in all cephalopods (octopus, squid, cuttlefish), and among arthropods in all decapod crustaceans (lobsters, crabs, shrimps).[137] For a listing of the different classes of molluscs and arthropods, and an indication as to which utilize haemocyanin, Fig. 1 of the article by Senozan should be referred to.[138] The distribution of haemocyanin elsewhere in these phyla is erratic. For example in the gastropods edible snails are known to contain large quantities, but related fresh-water species (*planorbis*) have large haemoglobins instead. Clams, oysters, scallops and other bivalve molluscs have no haemocyanin, and where they have respiratory proteins, use small dimeric or octameric intracellular haemoglobins. Some scorpions and spiders are known to contain haemocyanin, whereas other insects (the largest class of arthropod) do not appear to use this protein.

The reasons for the curious divergences between haemocyanins and haemoglobins are not known. There is no monomeric haemocyanin equivalent to myoglobin. Gastropods are known to have a myoglobin in their radular muscle regardless of whether the circulating respiratory protein is haemoglobin or haemocyanin.[139]

Unlike mammalian haemoglobin, haemocyanin is not confined to special cells but exists as a solute freely dissolved in the lymph. Concentrations can be appreciable, and in the horseshoe crab and octopus it is at a level 10 g/100 ml, i.e. about two-thirds that of haemoglobin in humans.[137,140] It has been noted, however,[141] that the concentration of haemocyanin varies not only among different species, but also among members of the same species.[137] There are differences between mollusc and arthropod haemocyanin (e.g. 0·25% as compared to 0·17% Cu respectively),[140] which are found also in spectroscopic investigations mentioned later. However, essentially the same fundamental O_2-carrying Cu unit is undoubtedly involved in all haemocyanins.

B. Isolation

Whelks (gastropod molluscs) are often used as a source of haemocyanin in the USA and UK. The American whelk (*Busycon*) is available from the Marine Biological Laboratories at Woods Hole, Massachusetts. *Buccinum* whelks are obtained from Marine Stations in Oban and Plymouth in the UK. By making a small opening in the shell the cardiac chamber can be exposed, the heart punctured, and the haemolymph syringed out.[142] The edible snail *Helix pomatia* (often referred to as the Rome or vineyard snail) is extensively used. The blood is cooled, centrifuged at low speed to remove

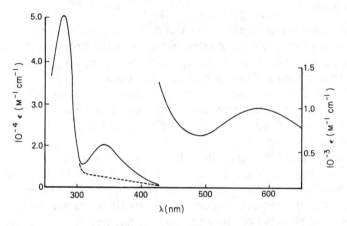

Fig. 24. UV–visible absorption spectrum of haemocyanin in the oxy (——), deoxy (– – –) forms. The absorption at ~ 280 nm is that observed for *L. pealei* haemocyanin.

debris, and exhaustively dialysed against water or buffer at 4°C. Concentrations can be estimated from the absorbance of the oxy form at 345 nm ($\varepsilon = 2 \cdot 0 \times 10^4 \, M^{-1} \, cm^{-1}$ per binuclear Cu active site; Fig. 24). The concentration obtained is $\sim 10^{-3} \, M$. Haemocyanin can be obtained from the *Limulus* horseshoe crab (arthropod) by bending the tail over and injecting a syringe into the "leather" belly. Up to 200 ml of blood can be withdrawn in this way. It gives a lower absorption at the 340 nm peak ($\varepsilon = 1700 \, M^{-1} \, cm^{-1}$ per active site).[142] Crab haemocyanin can be obtained by syringe from the leg joints. Octopus haemolymph can be purchased from Pacific Bio-Marine Laboratories in Venice, California. Though it is advisable to use fresh material, storage under CO at 4°C is possible.[143] The CO can be displaced with O_2 prior to use. In experiments where it is necessary to check the aggregation, this can be achieved by sedimentation velocity analysis using an ultracentrifuge.[144] The Cu in haemocyanin is tightly bound and is not removed by EDTA. Trace amounts of other metal ions e.g. Zn^{2+}, can therefore be removed by dialysis against several changes of 25 mM EDTA. The apo protein of *Busycon* can be prepared by dialysis against 10^{-2} M CN^- at pH 8·5.[142] Reconstitution procedures have been described.[142]

C. Oxygen-binding site

It has long been known that the binding site of haemocyanin contains two Cu atoms which bind one mole of O_2.[1] The deoxy form is colourless Cu(I), and the oxy form is blue, peak 570 nm ($\varepsilon \sim 10^3$ M^{-1} cm^{-1} per active site), with a band also at $\sim$340 nm ($\varepsilon \sim 2 \times 10^4$ M^{-1} cm^{-1}) (Fig. 24). Both these bands have been assigned to $O_2^{2-} \rightarrow Cu(II)$ charge transfer. At least

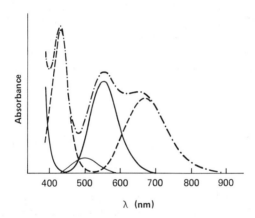

Fig. 25. A Gaussian resolution of the visible spectrum (– · – · –) of haemocyanin from the arthropod *Cancer borealis* at low temperature ($\sim$ 15 K) (Ref. [146]).

two other weak bands can be resolved at 15 K (Fig. 25). The shoulder at 425 nm is associated with a protein (possibly a phenolate or oxo bridge) to Cu(II) charge transfer, and that at $\sim$700 nm, to d–d transitions of the Cu(II).[145,146] Magnetic measurements indicate that the oxy form has no EPR signal, and it would appear that the two Cu(II) are antiferromagnetically coupled to an O_2^{2-} peroxo bridge. The equation for O_2-binding and the reverse may therefore be represented as

$$Cu(I)_2 + O_2 \rightleftharpoons Cu(II)_2O_2^{2-} \tag{20}$$

Resonance Raman spectra support the assignment of a peroxo group, which is thought to be nonplaner.[147] Use of the isotopically mixed $^{16}O^{18}O$ molecule has established[148] that the two ends of the bound O_2 molecule are essentially equivalent (which contrasts with findings for haemerythrin). Intensity patterns are somewhat different for arthropod and mollusc proteins, although different species within the same class show the same pattern.[149] The isotopic shifts observed using $^{63}Cu/^{65}Cu$ and H_2O/D_2O imply an asymmetric disposition of imidazole ligands, and frequencies are consistent with two imidazoles sharing a tetragonal plane with the two ligands bridging the Cu atoms and a third imidazole occupying an apical position.

Detailed spectroscopic (EPR and UV–visible) studies on a series of five mollusc and five arthropod oxyhaemocyanins,[146] support the view that the active sites of both phyla are similar. Significant differences are however observed, with indications that the arthropod active site is more distorted. It is of interest that ability to decompose H_2O_2 (i.e. catalase activity) by the active site of the deoxy form is much higher for the molluscs than the arthropods. Based on the spectroscopic studies it has been suggested that the effective active site of oxyhaemocyanins may be represented by the structure shown, where N represent a coordinated imidazole side chain of the polypeptide.[146]

A similar structure has been proposed from EXAFS studies on *Busycon canaliculatum*.[149] However a four-coordinated structure (no H_2O), has been proposed from EXAFS studies on oxyhaemocyanin from *Megathura crenulata* and *Helix pomatia*.[150] In both studies the EXAFS indicate that the Cu atoms in the deoxy protein are coordinated to two imidazoles with an average Cu–N distance of 1·95 Å. However, according to the model of Hodgson and colleagues[150] there is no evidence for a Cu–Cu interaction within 4 Å, and the model for the deoxy form proposed has two Cu atoms each coordinated to two histidines only. Upon oxygenation the two Cu atoms are pulled together to a separation of 3·55 Å, and are bridged by an atom of low atomic number (R in the above illustration), possibly a phenolate group from a tyrosine residue. The O_2 is bound end-to-end as peroxide to the two Cu atoms giving an approximately square-planar geometry at each.[150] This model, therefore, proposes a change in coordination number from 2 to 4 in going from the deoxy to oxy form.

Substantial rearrangement with a change in coordination number from 3 to 5 is also required by the alternative interpretation.[149] Whichever of these descriptions applies, clearly haemocyanin makes full use of the versatility in coordination numbers which is a hallmark of Cu chemistry. The utilization of (distorted) tetrahedral Cu(I) and Cu(II) geometries for the efficient functioning of blue Cu proteins as electron-transport agents is a further example of this adaptability.

D. Subunits

The most recent summary of the structure and assembly of haemocyanins is that given by the Bonaventuras.[151] As will be discussed below a binuclear Cu site binds single molecules of O_2. The proteins have high molecular weights which in arthropods are ~70000 per 2 Cu atoms. This is the minimum polypeptide chain. There are two Cu atoms for each 50000 in molecular weight of molluscs (the minimal functional unit), but eight such (nonidentical) subunits are covalently linked in a chain to give a minimum polypeptide of MW 400000. Proteolytic digestion is required to break such bonds and give subunits of MW ~50000. From electron microscopy on mollusc haemocyanin, it has been shown that in the gastropods 20, and in the cephalopods probably 10, of these polypepetide chains form giant cylindrical molecules. These are for the gastropod haemocyanins 380 Å long (half this in cephalopods), and 350 Å in diameter with MW ~9×10^6. Depending on the species, the haemocyanins of arthropods are present as aggregates containing 6, 12, 24 and 48 units. Six separate monomer poly-peptide chains each of MW ~70000 are present in each hexamer unit. Typically crustaceans and spiders have the 6 and 24 aggregates, shrimps 6 and 24, scorpions 24 and 48, and *Limulus* (horseshoe crabs) 48. The number of interacting subunits is in some cases dependent on pH and ionic composition. The development of ideas on the assembly of subunits is discussed elsewhere in the review by Wood.[1]

E. Amino-acid composition

These have appeared[152] for a number of molluscs (see Tables 2 and 4 of Ref. [1]), and some information regarding partial sequencing of fragments is available.[152] Haemocyanins are known to be glycoproteins with 1–8% carbohydrate content.

F. Allosteric effects

Haemocyanin generally exhibits cooperativity in O_2 binding,[1] although the reason for such large aggregates is far from clear. There are two effects which serve to control binding. Heterotropic effects are those resulting from the binding of, for example, H^+ (Bohr effect),[154] CO_2, and ions such as phosphate, Ca^{2+} and Mg^{2+}.[155] The homotropic effect is concerned with the effect of O_2 binding at one active site on the activity at other subunit active sites in the oligomer. The latter is the cooperativity effect which is illustrated by considering Hill plots. For the *Limulus* arthropod haemocyanin at 50% O_2 saturation, a value of 2 is obtained for the Hill coefficient (n).[151] More generally, gastropod mollusc haemocyanins have n in the range 2–4 and arthropod haemocyanins (especially spiders) as high as 9. An explanation of cooperativity in terms of low affinity T-state (tense) and high affinity R-state (relaxed) forms has been proposed.[156] Transition between the two occurs after a certain number of O_2 molecules become bound. The changeover between T- and R-states can be greatly influenced by heterotropic interactions. An alternative model has also been proposed.[157] Rate constants for the reaction of haemocyanin (R-state) with O_2 are listed in Table 7.[158,159]

G. Adducts to the Cu active site

Carbon monoxide coordinates to deoxyhaemocyanin. Unlike the reaction with O_2, no change in absorbance at 340 nm and 570 nm is observed (Fig. 24), and the Cu(I) oxidation state is retained. An analysis of infrared spectra of ^{13}C- and ^{18}O-labelled CO complexes is consistent with coordination of the C of the CO at one of the two Cu(I).[160] While O_2-binding is regulated by allosteric factors, CO-binding is not. It is possible that this is related to the need to vary the Cu–Cu distance on binding of O_2.

On treating the deoxy form with nitric oxide, a green-yellow solution of an EPR-detectable methaemocyanin is obtained.[145, 161] The coordination and redox chemistry of NO are complex since NO can coordinate as NO^+ and NO^-.[161] Here, resultant EPR spectra are consistent with monomeric Cu(II) together with (broad resonance) dipolar-coupled Cu(II).

H. Redox chemistry of the Cu active site

Just as methaemoglobin can be prepared, methaemocyanin has also been obtained with no O_2 attached. A dibridged Cu(II, II) structure has been proposed, where R is the same endogenous ligand as previously and L is an exogenous group.

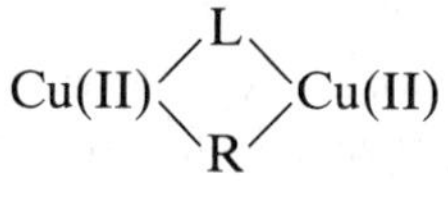

$$Cu(II) \overset{\diagup L \diagdown}{\underset{\diagdown R \diagup}{}} Cu(II)$$

There are two types of methaemocyanin to consider. From molluscs a met EPR-nondetectable form is obtained by treating oxyhaemocyanin with a 100-fold excess of N_3^- or F^- for 48 h at 37°C (pH 6·3),[145] while a similar form is obtained from arthropods by treating the deoxy form with a 5-fold excess of H_2O_2.[162] Ligand substitution can be effected by direct addition of different L groups (NO_2^-, $CH_3CO_2^-$ and halide ions). Interestingly, EPR-detectable met forms with L = CN^-, N_3^- and NCS^- can also be prepared,[163] where the difference it is sugested is that no endogenous R group is present. It is possible to isolate a semi-met Cu(I, II) form by treatment of oxyhaemocyanin with an excess of $NaNO_2$ and excess ascorbic acid.[145] In addition the preparations of so-called half-apo and met-apo forms[164] containing a single Cu(I) and a single Cu(II) respectively at the active site have been described. Using these various Cu active sites extensive chemical and spectroscopic comparisons have been possible.[146] It is concluded that the arthropod active site is distorted compared with that of mollusc.

REFERENCES

[1] Wood, E.J. *Essays in Biochemistry* **1980**, *16*, 1.
[2] Chung, M.C.M.; Ellerton, H.D. *Prog. Biophys. Mol. Biol.* **1979**, *35*, 53.
[3] Appleby, C.A. *Biochim. Biophys. Acta* **1962**, *60*, 226.
[4] Maclean, N. "Haemoglobin"; Edward Arnold: London, 1978; p. 3.
[5] Sykes, A.G.; Weil, J.A. *Progress in Inorganic Chemistry* **1971**, *13*, 1. Wilkins, R.G. *Advances in Chemistry Series*, No. 100, American Chemical Society, **1971**, 111.
[6] Basolo, F.; Hoffman, B.M.; Ibers, J.A. *Acc. Chem. Res.* **1975**, *8*, 384; McLendon, G.; Martell, A.E. *Coord. Chem. Rev.* **1976**, *19*, 1.
[7] James, B.R. *In* "The Porphyrins", Vol. V; Dolphin, D., Ed.; Academic Press: New York and London, 1978; p. 205.
[8] Collman, J.P.; Halbert, T.R.; Suslick, K.S. "Metal Ion Activation of Dioxygen"; Spiro, T.G., Ed.; Wiley: New York, 1980; p. 1.
[9] Biggs, W.R.; Swinehart, J.H. "Metal Ions in Biological Systems", Vol. 6; Sigel, H., Ed.; Dekker; New York, 1976, p. 141. Kustin, K.; McLeod, G.C. "Topics in Current Chemistry", Inorganic Biochemistry II, Vol. 6a; Springer: New York, 1977; p. 1.
[10] Drago, R.S.; Corden, B.B.; Zombeck, A. *Comments Inorg. Chem.*, **1981**, *1*, 53.
[11] Vaska, L. *Acc. Chem. Res.* **1976**, *9*, 175.
[12] Orhanović, M.; Wilkins, R.G. *J. Amer. Chem. Soc.* **1967**, *89*, 278.
[13] Laing, M.; Nolte, M.J.; Singleton, E. *J. Chem. Soc. Chem. Comm.* **1975**, 660.
[14] Valentine, J.S. *Chem. Rev.* **1973**, *73*, 235.
[15] Floriani, C.; Calderazzo, F. *J. Chem. Soc. A* **1969**, 946. Calligaris, M.; Nardin, G.; Randaccio, L.; Ripamonti, A. *J. Chem. Soc. A* **1969**, 1069.

[16] Crumbliss, A.L.; Basolo, F. *J. Amer. Chem. Soc.* **1979**, *92*, 55. Hoffman, B.M.; Diemente, D.L.; Basolo, F. *J. Amer. Chem. Soc.* **1970**, *92*, 61.

[17] Walker, F.A. *J. Amer. Chem. Soc.* **1973**, *95*, 1194.

[18] Stynes, D.V.; Stynes, H.C.; James, B.R.; Ibers, J.A. *J. Amer. Chem. Soc.* **1973**, *95*, 1796.

[19] Schrauzer, G.N.; Lee, L.P. *J. Amer. Chem. Soc.* **1970**, *92*, 1551.

[20] Bayston, J.H.; King, N.K.; Looney, F.D.; Winfield, M.E. *J. Amer. Chem. Soc.* **1969**, *91*, 2775.

[21] Abel, E.W.; Pratt, J.M.; Whelan, R.; *J. Chem. Soc. Chem. Comm.* **1971**, 449.

[22] Brown, L.O; Raymond, K.N. *Inorg. Chem.* **1975**, *14*, 2595.

[23] Schaefer, W.P. *Inorg. Chem.* **1968**, *7*, 725. Fronczek, F.R.; Schaefer, W.P.; Marsh, R.E. *Acta Cryst.* **1974**, *B30*, 117.

[24] Fronczek, F.R.; Schaefer, W.P.; Marsh, R.E. *Inorg. Chem.* **1975**, *14*, 611.

[25] Mori, M.; Weil, J.A. *J. Amer. Chem. Soc.* **1967**, *89*, 3732.

[26] Davies, R.; Sykes, A.G. *J. Chem. Soc. A* **1968**, 2840.

[27] Thewalt, U.; Marsh, R.E. *J. Amer. Chem. Soc.* **1967**, *89*, 6364.

[28] Geyer, R.P. *Bull. Parenter. Drug Association* **1974**, *28*, 88. Yokoyama, K.; Suyama, T.; Naito, R. "Oxygen and Life", 2nd B.O.C. Priestley Conference, Royal Soc. Chem. Spec. Publication No. 39, 1981, p. 142.

[29] Collman, J.P.; Brauman, J.I.; Halbert, T.R.; Suslick, K.S. *Proc. Natl. Acad. Sci. U.S.A.* **1976**, *73*, 3333.

[30] Perutz, M.F. *Sci. Amer.* **1978**, *239*, 68.

[31] Perutz, M.F. *Br. Med. Bull.* **1976**, *32*, 193, (195).

[32] Buse, G. *Angew; Chem. Int. Ed.* **1971**, *10*, 663.

[33] Dayhoff, M.O. (Ed.). "Atlas of Protein Sequence and Structure", Vol. 5; National Biomedical Research Foundation: Silver Spring, Maryland, 1972.

[34] Bolton, W.; Perutz, M.F. *Nature (London)* **1970**, *228*, 551.

[35] Kendrew, J.C.; Watson, H.C.; Strandberg, B.E.; Dickerson, R.E.; Phillips, D.C.; Shore, V.C. *Nature (London)* **1961**, *190*, 666.

[36] Muirhead, H.; Greer, J. *Nature (London)* **1970**, *228*, 516.

[37] Scouloudi, H. *J. Mol. Biol* **1968**, *40*, 353.

[38] Lattman, E.E.; Nockolds, C.E.; Kretsinger, R.H.; Love, W.E. *J. Mol. Biol.* **1971**, *60*, 271.

[39] Love, W.E.; Klock, P.A.; Lattman, E.E.; Padlan, E.A.; Ward, K.B.; Hendrickson, H.A. *Cold Spring Harbour Symm. Quant. Biol.* **1971**, *36*, 349. Hendrickson, W.A.; Love, W.E. *Nature (London)* **1971**, *232*, 197.

[40] Huber, R.; Epp, O.; Steigermann, W.; Formanek, H. *Eur. J. Biochem.* **1971**, *19*, 42.

[41] Perutz, M.F. *Nature (London)* **1970**, *228*, 726.

[42] Collman, J.R.; Halbert, T.R.; Suclick, K.S. "Metal Ion Activation of Dioxygen"; Spiro, T.G. Ed.; Wiley: New York, 1980; p. 1.

[43] Brault, D.; Rougee, M. *Biochem.* **1974**, *13*, 4598.

[44] Rougee, M.; Brault, D. *Biochem.* **1975**, *14*, 4100.

[45] Collman, J.P.; Reed, C.A. *J. Amer. Chem. Soc.* **1973**, *95*, 2048.

[46] Hoard, J.C.; Schiedt, W.R. *Proc. nat. Acad. Sci. U.S.A.*, **1973**, *70*, 3919.

[47] Jameson, G.B.; Molinaro, F.S.; Ibers, J.A.; Collman, J.P.; Brauman, J.I.; Rose, E.; Suslick, K. *J. Amer. Chem. Soc.* **1978**, *100*, 6769.

[48] Ten Eyck, L.F.; Arnone, A. *J. Mol. Biol.* **1976**, *100*, 3.

[49] Reed, C.A. "Metal Ions in Biological Systems", Vol. 7; Sigel, H. Ed.; Dekker: New York, 1978.

[50] Reed, C.A.; Mashiko, T.; Scheidt, W.R.; Spartalian, K.; Lang, G. *J. Amer. Chem. Soc.* **1980**, *102*, 2302.

[51] Peng, S.M.; Ibers, J.A. *J. Amer. Chem. Soc.* **1976**, *98*, 8032.

[52] McCandlish, E.; Miksztal, A.R.; Nappa, M.; Sprenger, A.Q.; Valentine, J.S.; Stong, J.D.; Spiro, T.G. *J. Amer. Chem. Soc.* **1980**, *102*, 4268.

[53] Chin, D.-H.; La Mar, G.N.; Balch, A.L. *J. Amer. Chem. Soc.* **1980**, *102*, 4344.

[54] Baldwin, J.E.; Huff, J. *J. Amer. Chem. Soc.* **1973**, *95*, 8477.

[55] Chang, C.K.; Traylor, T.G. *J. Amer. Chem. Soc.* **1973**, *95*, 5810.

[56] Battersby, A.R.; Hartley, S.G.; Turnbull, M.D. *Tetrahedron Letters* **1978**, *34*, 3109.

[57] Baldwin, J.E.; Klose, T.; Peters, M. *J. Chem. Soc. Chem. Comm.* **1976**, 881.

[58] Jameson, G. B.; Molinaro, F. S.; Ibers, J. A.; Collman, J. P.; Braumann, J. I.; Rose, E.; Suslick, K. S. *J. Amer. Chem. Soc.* **1980**, *102*, 3224.

[59] Jameson, G. B.; Rodley, G. A., Robinson, W. T.; Gagne, R. R.; Reed, C. A.; Collman, J. P. *Inorg. Chem.* **1978**, *17*, 850.

[60] Almog, J.; Baldwin, J.E.; Huff, J. *J. Amer. Chem. Soc.* **1975**, *97*, 227.

[61] Battersby, A.R.; Hamilton, A.D. *J. Chem. Soc. Chem. Comm.* **1980**, 117.

[62] Phillips, S.E.V. *J. Mol. Biol.* **1980**, *142*, 531.

[63] Maxwell, J.C.; Volpe, J.A.; Barlow, C.H.; Caughey, W.S. *Biochem. Biophys. Res. Comm.* **1974**, *58*, 166.

[64] Collman, J.P.; Brauman, J.I.; Halbert, T.R.; Suslick, K.S. *Proc. Natl. Acad. Sci. U.S.A.* **1976**, *73*, 3333.

[65] Spartalian, K.; Lang, G.; Collman, J.P.; Gagne, R.R.; Reed, C.A. *J. Chem. Phys.* **1975**, *63*, 5375.

[66] Cerdonio, M.; Castellano, A.C.; Calabrese, L.; Morante, S.; Pispisa, B.; Vitale, S. *Proc. Natl. Acad. Sci. U.S.A.* **1978**, *74*, 4916.

[67] Eisenberger, P.; Shulman, R.G.; Kincaid, B.M.; Brown, G.S.; Ogawa, S. *Nature (London)* **1978**, *274*, 30.

[68] Keyes, M.H.; Falley, M.; Lumry, R. *J. Amer. Chem. Soc.* **1971**, *93*, 2035.

[69] Antonini, E.; Brunori, M. "Hemoglobin and Myoglobin in Their Reactions with Ligands"; North Holland: Amsterdam, 1971.

[70] Noble, R.W.; Gibson, Q.H.; Brunori, M.; Antonini, E.; Wyman, J. *J. Biol. Chem.* **1969**, *244*, 3905.

[71] Imamura, T.; Riggs, A.; Gibson, Q.H. *J. Biol. Chem.* **1972**, *247*, 521.

[72] Brunori, M.; Schuster, T.M. *J. Biol. Chem.* **1969**, *244*, 4046.

[73] Ilgenfritz, G.; Schuster, T.M. *J. Biol. Chem.* **1974**, *249*, 2959.

[74] Geibel, J.; Cannon, J.; Campbell, D.; Traylor, T.G. *J. Amer. Chem. Soc.* **1978**, *100*, 3575.

[75] Hoffman, B.M. *In* "The Porphyrins", Vol. VII; Dolphin, D., Ed.; Academic Press: New York and London, 1979; p. 403.

[76] Rossi Fanelli, A.; Antonini, E.; Caputo, A. *Biochim. Biophys. Acta.* **1958**, *30*, 608. Yonetani, T. *J. Biol. Chem.* **1965**, *240*, 4509.

[77] Rossi Fanelli, A.; Antonini, E.; Caputo, A. *Biochim. Biophys. Acta.* **1959**, *35*, 95.

[78] Hoffman, B.M.; Petering, D.M. *Proc. Natl. Acad. Sci. U.S.A.* **1970**, *67*, 633.

[79] Yonetani, T.; Yamamoto, H.; Woodrow, G.V. *J. Biol. Chem.* **1974**, *249*, 682.

[80] Hoffman, B.M.; Diemente, D.L.; Basolo, F. *J. Amer. Chem. Soc.* **1970**, *92*, 61.

[81] Shulman, R.G.; Hopfield, J.J.; Ogawa, S. *Q. Rev. Biophys.* **1975**, *8*, 325.

[82] Hanson, L.K.; Hoffman, B.M. *J. Amer. Chem. Soc.* **1980**, *102*, 4602.

[83] Blough, N.V.; Zemel, H.; Hoffman, B.M.; Lee, T.C.K.; Gibson, Q.H. *J. Amer. Chem. Soc.* **1980**, *102*, 5685.

[84] Svedberg, T.; Pederson, K.O. "The Ultracentrifuge"; Clarendon Press: Oxford, 1940.

[85] Wood, E.J.; Mosby, L.J.; Robinson, M.S. *Biochem. J.* **1976**, *153*, 589.

[86] Chung, M.C.M.; Ellerton, H.D. *Prog. Biophys. Mol. Biol.* **1979**, *35*, 53.

[87] Terwilliger, R.C.; Terwilliger, N.B.; Schabtach, E.; Dangott, L. *Comp. Biochem. Physiol.* **1977**, *574*, 143.

[88] Terwilliger, R.C. *Amer. Zool.* **1980**, *20*, 53.

[89] Weber, E.; Steigemann, W.; Jones, T.A.; Huber, R. *J. Mol. Biol.* **1978**, *170*, 327. (See also Ref. [58].)

[90] Teo, B.K.; Li, W.K. *Inorg. Chem.* **1976**, *15*, 2005.

[91] Garlick, R.L.; Riggs, A. *Fed. Proc. Fed. An. Soc. Exp. Biol.* **1978**, *38*, 343.

[92] Bonner, A.G.; Lawson, R.A. *FEBS Lett.* **1977**, *73*, 201.

[93] Weber, R.E. *J. Comp. Physiol.* **1975**, *99*, 297.

[94] Ilan, E.; Daniel, E. *Comp. Biochem. Physiol.* **1979**, *63B*, 303.

[95] Geraci, G.; Sada, A.; Cirotto, C. *Eur. J. Biochem.* **1977**, *77*, 555.

[96] Harrington, J.P.; Suarez, G.; Bergese, T.A.; Nagel, R.L. *J. Biol. Chem.* **1978**, *253*, 6820.

[97] Weber, R.E.; Bol, J.F. *Comp. Biochem. Physiol.* **1976**, *53B*, 23.

[98] Gibbs, P.E. "British Sipunculans"; Academic Press: London and New York, 1977; pp. 1–35.

[99] Liberatore, F.A.; Truby, M.F.; Klippenstein, G.L. *Arch. Biochem. Biophys.* **1974**, *160*, 223.

[100] Addison, A.W.; Bruce, R.E. *Arch. Biochem. Biophys.* **1977**, *183*, 328.

[101] Klippenstein, G.L.; Van Riper, D.A.; Oosterom, E.A. *J. Biol. Chem.* **1972**, *247*, 5959.

[102] Loehr, J.S.; Loehr, T.M. "Advances in Inorganic Biochemistry", Vol. 1.; Eichhorn, G.L., Marzilli, L.G. (Eds.); Elsevier North Holland; New York, 1979; p. 235.

[103] Klippenstein, G.L.; Cote, J.L.; Ludlam, S.E. *Biochem.* **1976**, *15*, 1128.

[104] Bates, G.; Brunori, M.; Amiconi, G.; Antonini, E.; Wyman, J. *Biochem.* **1968**, *7*, 3016.

[105] Mangum, C.P.; Kondon, M. *Comp. Biochem. Physiol.* **1975**, *50A*, 777.

[106] Bradič, Z.; Harrington, P.C.; Wilkins, R.G. "Biochem. Clin. Asp. Oxygen"; Academic Press: London and New York, 1979; p. 557.

[107] Loehr, J.S.; Lammers, P.J.; Brimhall, B.; Hermodson, M.A. *J. Biol. Chem.* **1978**, *253*, 5726.

[108] Klippenstein, G.L.; Holleman, J.W.; Klotz, I.M. *Biochem.* **1968**, *7*, 3868.

[109] Klippenstein, G.L.; Cote, J.L.; Ludham, S.E.; *Biochem.* **1976**, *15*, 1128.

[110] Klippenstein, G.L. *Biochem.* **1972**, *11*, 372.

[111] Stenkamp, R.E.; Sieker, L.C.; Jensen, L.H.; McQueen, J.E. *Biochem.* **1978**, *17*, 2499.

[112] Ward, K.B.; Hendrickson, W.A.; Klippenstein, G.L. *Nature (London)* **1975**, *257*, 818.

[113] Stenkamp, R.E.; Sieker, L.C.; Jensen, L.H.; Loehr, J.S. *J. Mol. Biol.* **1976**, *100*, 23.

[114] Klotz, I.M. "Subunits in Biological Systems"; Timasheff, S.N., Fasman, G.D. Eds.; Dekker: New York, 1971; p. 55.
[115] Clarke, S.E; Sieker, L.C.; Stenkamp, R.E.; Loehr, J.S. *Biochem.* **1979**, *18*, 684.
[116] Hendrickson, W.A.; Klippenstein, G.L.; Ward, K.B. *Proc. Natl. Acad. Sci. U.S.A.* **1975**, *72*, 2160. Hendrickson, W.A. *Naval Res. Reviews* **1978**, *31*, 1.
[117] Stenkamp, R.E.; Sieker, L.C.; Jensen, L.H. *Acta Cryst.* **1978**, *A34*, 1014.
[118] Stenkamp, R.E.; Sieker, L.C.; Jensen, L.H.; Sanders-Loehr, J. *Nature (London)* **1981**, *291*, 263.
[119] Gay, R.R.; Solomon, E.I. *J. Amer. Chem. Soc.* **1978**, *100*, 1972.
[120] Dunn, J.B.R.; Addison, A.W.; Bruce, R.E.; Loehr, J.S.; Loehr, T.M. *Biochem.* **1977**, *16*, 1743.
[121] Stern, E.A., unpublished results quoted by Stenkamp, R.E.; Jensen, L.H. "Advances in Inorganic Chemistry", Vol. 1; Eichhorn, G.L., Marzilli, L.G. Eds.; Elsevier North Holland; New York, 1979; p. 230.
[122] Loehr, J.S.; Loehr, T.M.; Mauk, A.G.; Gray, H.B. *J. Amer. Chem. Soc.* **1980**, *102*, 6992.
[123] York, J.L.; Bearden, A.J. *Biochem.* **1970**, *9*, 4549. Okamura, M.Y.; Klotz, I.M.; Johnson, C.E.; Winter, M.R.C.; Williams, R.J.P. *Biochem.* **1969**, *8*, 1951.
[124] Moss, T.H.; Moleski, C.; York, J.L. *Biochem.* **1971**, *10*, 840. Garbett, K.; Johnson, C.E.; Klotz, I.M.; Okamura, M.Y.; Williams, R.J.P. *Arch. Biochem. Biophys.* **1971**, *142*, 574.
[125] Kurtz, D.M.; Shriver, D.F.; Klotz, I.M. *Coord. Chem. Rev.* **1977**, *24*, 145.
[126] Dunn, J.B.R.; Shriver, D.F.; Klotz, I.M. *Proc. Natl. Acad. Sci. U.S.A.* **1973**, *70*, 2582. Dunn, J.B.R.; Shriver, D.F.; Klotz, I.M. *Biochem.* **1975**, *14*, 2689.
[127] Kurtz, D.M.; Shriver, D.F.; Klotz, I.M. *J. Amer. Chem. Soc.* **1976**, *98*, 5033.
[128] Petrou, A.; Armstrong, F.A.; Harrington, P.C.; Wilkins, R.G.; Sykes, A.G. *Biochim. Biophys. Acta*, **1981**, *670*, 377.
[129] Rao, A.L.; Keresztes-Nagy, S. *Biochim. Biophys. Acta* **1973**, *313*, 249.
[130] Harrington, P.C.; Wilkins, R.G.; Muhoberac, B.B.; Wharton, D.C. "The Biological Chemistry of Iron"; Dunford, H.B., Dolphin, D., Raymond, K.N., Sieker, L.C. Eds.; Reidel: New York, 1982.
[131] Babcock, L.M.; Bradič, Z.; Harrington, P.C.; Wilkins, R.G.; Yoneda, G.S. *J. Amer. Chem. Soc.* **1980**, *102*, 2849. Harrington P.C.; Wilkins, R.G. *J. Amer. Chem. Soc.* **1981**, *103*, 550.
[132] Garbett, K.; Damall, D.W.; Klotz, I.M. *Arch. Biochem. Biophys.* **1971**, *142*, 455.
[133] Stenkamp, R.E.; Sieker, L.C.; Jensen, L.M. *J. Mol. Biol.* **1978**, *126*, 457.
[134] DePhillips, M.A. *Arch. Biochem. Biophys.* **1971**, *144*, 122.
[135] Garbett, K.; Darnell, D.W.; Klotz, I.M.; Williams, R.J.P. *Arch. Biochem. Biophys.* **1969**, *135*, 419.
[136] Thundathil, R.V.; Holt, E.M.; Holt, S.L.; Watson, K.J. *J. Amer. Chem. Soc.* **1977**, *99*, 1818.
[137] Van Holde, K.E.; Van Bruggen, E.F.J. "Subunits in Biological Systems Part A"; Timasheff, S.N., Fasman, G.D., Eds.; Dekker: New York, 1971; p. 1.
[138] Senozan, N.M. *J. Chem. Educ.* **1976**, *53*, 684.
[139] Bannister, W.H.; Bannister, J.V.; Micalle, H. *Comp. Biochem. Physiol.* **1968**, *24*, 1061.

[140] Ghiretti, F. "Physiology and Biochemistry of Hemocyanins", Academic Press: New York and London, 1968.
[141] Pilson, M.E.Q. *Biol. Bull.* **1965**, *128*, 459.
[142] Larrabee, J.A.; Spiro, T.G. *J. Amer. Chem. Soc.* **1980**, *102*, 4217.
[143] De Ley, M; Lontie, R. *FEBS Letters* **1970**, *6*, 125.
[144] Wood, E.J. *Biochim. Biophys. Acta* **1975**, *328*, 101.
[145] Eickman, N.C.; Himmelwright, R.S.; Solomon, E.I. *Proc. Natl. Acad. Sci. U.S.A.* **1979**, *76*, 2094.
[146] Himmelwright, R.S.; Eickman, N.C.; LuBien, C.D.; Solomon, E.I. *J. Amer. Chem. Soc.* **1980**, *102*, 5378.
[147] Freedman, T.B.; Loehr, J.S.; Loehr, T.M. *J. Amer. Chem. Soc.* **1976**, *98*, 2809.
[148] Thamann, T.J.; Loehr, J.S.; Loehr, T.M. *J. Amer. Chem. Soc.* **1977**, *99*, 4187.
[149] Brown, J.M.; Powers, L.; Kincaid, B.; Larrabee, J.A.; Spiro, T.G. *J. Amer. Chem. Soc.* **1980**, *102*, 4210.
[150] Co, M.S.; Hodgson, K.O.; Eccles, T.K.; Lontie, R. *J. Amer. Chem. Soc.* **1981**, *103*, 984. Co, M.S.; Hodgson, K.O. *J. Amer. Chem. Soc.* **1981**, *103*, 3200.
[151] Bonaventura, J.; Bonaventura, C. *Amer. Zool.* **1980**, *20*, 7.
[152] Markl, J.; Strych, W.; Schartau, W.; Schneider, H.J.; Schoeberl, P.; Linzen, B. *Hoppe-Seyler's Z. Physiol. Chem.* **1979**, *360*, 639.
[153] Schneider, H.J.; Schartau, W.; Linzen, B.; Lottspeich, F.; Henschen, A. *Hoppe-Seyler's Z. Physiol. Chem.* **1980**, *361*, 1211.
[154] Hall, R.L.; Wood, E.L.; Kamerling, J.P.; Gerwig, G.J.; Vliegenthart, J.F.G. *Biochem. J.* **1977**, *165*, 173.
[155] e.g. Van Driel, R.; Kuiper, H.A.; Antonini, E.; Brunori, M. *J. Mol. Biol.* **1978**, *121*, 431.
[156] Monod, J.; Wyman, J.; Changeux, J.-P. *J. Mol. Biol.* **1965**, *12*, 88.
[157] Koshland, D.; Nemethy, G.; Filmer, D. *Biochem.* **1966**, *5*, 365.
[158] Van Driel, R.; Antonini, E.; Brunori, M. *J. Mol. Biol.* **1974**, *89*, 103.
[159] Wood, E.J.; Cayley, G.R.; Pearson, J.S. *J. Mol. Biol.* **1977**, *109*, 1.
[160] Van der Deen, H.; Hoving, H. *Biophys. Chem.* **1979**, *9*, 169.
[161] Schoot-Uiterkamp, A.J.M.; Van der Deen, H,; Berendsen, H.J.C.; Boas, J.F. *Biochim. Biophys. Acta* **1974**, *372*, 407.
[162] Felsenfeld, G.; Printz, M.P. *J. Amer. Chem. Soc.* **1959**, *81*, 6259.
[163] Himmelwright, R.S.; Eickman, N.C.; Solomon, E.I. *Biochem. Biophys. Res. Comm.* **1979**, *86*, 628.
[164] Himmelwright, R.S.; Eickman, N.C.; Solomon, E.I. *Biochem. Biophys. Res. Comm.* **1978**, *81*, 243.
[165] Shigehara, K.; Shinohara, K.; Sato, Y.; Tsuchida, E. *Macromolecules* **1981**, *14*, 1153. (Fe porphyrins to polymers).
[166] Derewenda, Z. S.; Dodson, E. J.; Dodson, G. G.; Brzozowski, A. M. *Acta Cryst.* **1981**, *A37*, 407 and personal communication. (HbO_2)
[167] Shaanan, B. *Nature* **1982**, *296*, 683. (HbO_2)
[168] Perutz, M. F.; Hasnain, S. S.; Duke, P. J.; Sessler, J. L.; Hahn, J. E. *Nature* **1982**, *295*, 535. (Hb)
[169] Lamy, J.; Lamy, J. (eds.) "*Invertebrate Oxygen-binding Proteins*" (Proceedings Workshop Course, 1979), Dekker, New York, 1981. (Extensive Hc coverage).

Substitution Reactions of Oxo-Metal Complexes

Kazuo Saito and Yoichi Sasaki

Department of Chemistry
Tohoku University

Abbreviations of ligand names

Hacac	acetylacetone (2,4-pentanedione)	H₂ida	iminodiacetic acid
H₂aliz	alizaline (1,2-dihydroxyanthraquinone)	Hmd	mandelic acid
		H₂mal	malonic acid
H₃as	1,2-dihydroxyanthraquinone-3-sulphonic acid	H₂medda	*N,N'*-dimethylethylenediamine-*N,N'*-diacetic acid
H₂cat	catechol	H₂mida	*N*-methyliminodiacetic acid
H₃dhb	3,4-dihydroxybenzoic acid	H₆mtb	methyl thymol blue
H₂dipic	pyridine-2,6-dicarboxylic acid	nma	*N*-methylacetamide
Hdipiv	dipivaloylmethane	H₃nta	nitrilotriacetic acid
dce	1,2-dichloroethane	Hox	8-hydroxyquinoline (oxine)
dma	*N,N*-dimethylacetamide	H₂oxs	8-hydroxyquinoline-5-sulphonic acid
dmf	*N,N*-dimethylformamide		
dmmp	dimethyl methylphosphonate	H₃pg	pyrogallol (1,2,3-trihydroxybenzene)
dmso	dimethyl sulphoxide		
H₃dopa	L-dopa ((3,4-dihydroxyphenyl)alanine)	phen	1,10-phenanthroline
		H₂pmida	(2-pyridylmethyl)iminodiacetic acid
H₂edda	ethylenediamine-*N,N'*-diacetic acid		
		py	pyridine
H₃ep	L-epinephrine ((3,4-dihydroxyphenyl)-2-(methyl-amino)ethanol)	Hta	thioacetic acid
		H₂tart	tartric acid
		tep	triethylphosphate
H₄edta	ethylenediaminetetraacetic acid	Htfac	1,1,1-trifluoroacetylacetone
H₄ga	gallic acid (3,4,5-trihydroxybenzoic acid)	H₃thb	1,2,4-trihydroxybenzene
		thf	tetrahydrofuran
Hgly	glycine	tmp	trimethylphosphate
Hhfac	hexafluoroacetylacetone	tmu	tetramethylurea
H₃hedta	*N'*-(2-hydroxyethyl)ethylenedia-mine-*N,N',N'*-triacetic acid	Htta	thenoyltrifluoroacetone
		Hvmd	vanillomandelic acid

I. INTRODUCTION

A. Occurrence of oxo-metal ions

Most bi- and tervalent transition-metal ions give regular or slightly distorted octahedral complexes. On the other hand, quadrivalent and higher-valent ions of transition metals have a marked affinity towards the oxide anion and tend to form "oxo-metal ions" which are highly distorted.[1,2] There is an overall trend towards a greater number of M=O bonds with increase in the oxidation number of the metal ion. Among cations having a d^0 configuration, Ti(IV) and V(V) give octahedral TiO^{2+} and *cis*-$V(O)_2^+$ species, whereas Cr(VI) and Mn(VII) give tetrahedral CrO_4^{2-} and MnO_4^-, respectively. Oxo-metal complexes are well characterized for the early transition elements. Transition metal ions of Group 8 in the periodic table also give compounds with M=O bonds (e.g. OsO_4), but these are readily reduced and have been little studied in aqueous solutions. Second and third row transition-metal ions give oxo complexes which are more

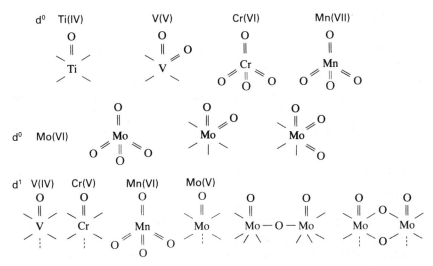

Fig. 1. Typical structural units for some metal elements of higher oxidation state.

stable towards reduction than their congeners in the first series. Very often transition-metal ions of higher oxidation numbers give di- or polynuclear species with oxide (or sometimes sulphide) bridges. Typical structures of such oxo-metal species are illustrated in Fig. 1.

B. Characteristics of the structure of oxo-metal ions

Most oxo-metal ions have coordination number 6 or 4. However, because of the very strong bonding between M^{n+} and O^{2-}, their structures are no longer regular octahedral or tetrahedral (except $M(O)_4^{m-}$ species). X-ray structural studies have demonstrated that in mono-oxo-metal complexes[1–5] the bonds *trans* (and apical) to M=O are longer than those *cis* to donors (i.e. equatorial) in a six-coordinate configuration with the central metal ion situated appreciably above the plane defined by the basal ligands. Sometimes the apical site remains vacant, making the coordination number 5. Whenever two oxo ligands are coordinated to a metal ion, they usually occupy the *cis* sites, exceptions being for *trans*-$[Mo(O)_2(CN)_4]^{4-}$, some rhenium(V) complexes, and the actinide elements.[1–6]

C. Ligand substitution reactions of metal complexes

Substitution reactions of bi- and tervalent metal ions have been extensively studied in aqueous and non-aqueous solutions. There are good reviews relating to substitution reactions of octahedral and square-planar complexes.[7-12] The rate of substitution of octahedral complexes is very much dependent on the number of d electrons, and the charge of the central metal ion. Both bi- and tervalent metal ions give similar dependence on d electron configuration, but the former give rate constants greater than the latter by 10^3 to 10^8.[8,13,14]

Most substitution reactions proceed as shown in Scheme (1) in aqueous solutions.

$$M—X + Y \underset{K_{OS}}{\rightleftharpoons} (M—X)(Y) \underset{k_s}{\longrightarrow} (M—Y)(X) \tag{1}$$

Here the ligands that remain coordinated throughout the reaction are omitted and (M—X)(Y) and (M—Y)(X) refer to "outer-sphere" complexes in which Y and X, respectively, are in the second coordination sphere. Whenever the charges of the complex and the reagent have opposite signs, they are called ion-pairs. The rate constant k_s is for the substitution process involving the outer-sphere precursor complex. The overall substitution rate constant is usually expressed as the product $K_{OS}k_s$. The k_s step is reckoned as an exchange between X and Y in the first and second coordination spheres. Hence the mechanism is referred to as an "interchange". The rate-determining step can be either dissociative, in which bond breaking between M and X precedes the formation of the M–Y bond; or associative, in which the M–Y bond is formed before the M—X bond is broken.[8,9,15] Hence interchange mechanisms are generally divided into two categories, I_d and I_a, depending on the rate-determining step. If there is sufficient evidence for the existence of "M" or "X–M–Y" as intermediate, the mechanism is classified as D or A, respectively. One viewpoint which has been generally accepted is that bivalent metal ions undergo substitution via an I_d mechanism, whereas tervalent metal ions react via an I_a mechanism.[8,9,14] Such a difference is explained by the difference in charge density of central metal ions.[9] However, it is now known that there are some exceptions: Mn(II) certainly from bivalent metal ions,[16,17] and Co(III) and Al(III) from the tervalent metal ions.[9] This suggests that the size of metal ions is an important deciding factor among ions of the same charge; smaller ions preferring more dissociative, and larger ions more associative pathways.

D. Substitution reactions of oxo-metal complexes

If the above information were directly extrapolated to the substitution reactions of complexes with higher oxidation number, a very small rate of reaction would be expected; e.g. a quadrivalent metal complex with d^1 configuration would have a second-order rate constant of 10^{-5} to $10^{-3} \, \text{M}^{-1} \text{s}^{-1}$ at room temperature. Mechanisms of substitution would moreover be associative for metals of higher oxidation number. However, oxo-metal complexes give much higher rates, and sometimes it is claimed they have dissociative mechanisms. Such behaviour may be compared to the fact that conjugate-base forms of aqua metal ions generally give much higher rates (and a greater tendency to dissociative mechanisms) than the parent complexes. For example, rate constants for substitution into $[Cr(H_2O)_6]^{3+}$ are 10^{-5} to $10^{-9} \, \text{M}^{-1} \, \text{s}^{-1}$ and the mechanism is I_a; those for $[Cr(OH)(H_2O)_5]^{2+}$ are $\sim 10^{-4} \, \text{M}^{-1} \, \text{s}^{-1}$ and a dissociative mechanism has been assigned. Oxo-metal ions may be regarded as exhibiting an extreme of conjugate-base behaviour.

Regioselectivity in substitution reactions has been extensively studied with square-planar complexes.[18,19] Information concerning mutual ligand influence in octahedral complexes is much less,[7,14,20–22] and regioselectivity is reckoned to be much more modest as compared with square-planar complexes. Oxo-complexes exhibit remarkable regioselectivity, which is believed to originate from the very strong M=O bonds.

Besides ordinary substitution reactions, oxo-metal complexes undergo significant polymerization in neutral and acidic solutions. They also exhibit characteristic reactions with hydrogen peroxide.

E. Outline of this review

To date only limited range of oxo-metal complexes have been the subject of kinetic studies. Attempts are made in this review to summarize the available data relating to the kinetics and mechanisms of substitution of oxo-metal complexes and to illustrate important features and trends. The aim is not necessarily of comprehensive coverage.

Oxo-metal complexes have various coordination geometries, and hence their substitution reactions involve various kinds of stereochemistry. This review is divided according to the number of d electrons, rather the steric structures. Oxo-metal ions with more than two d electrons will not be covered here since available data are not sufficiently extensive to lead to general conclusions. Kinetic data for substitution of $U(O)_2^{2+}$ complexes are included. There is currently no review article which deals with the kinetics of oxo-metal complexes; however, the reviews which have included data for substitution reactions of some oxo complexes are available.[23] It is planned that kinetic studies on exchange of oxide ions in oxo-metal ions with water will be covered in a review by Gamsjäger and Murmann[24] to appear in Volume 2 of this series.

II. SUBSTITUTION OF OXO-METAL COMPLEXES WITH d¹ CONFIGURATION

Only vanadium(IV) and molybdenum(V) have been studied extensively, and will be considered here.

A. Vanadium(IV) complexes

Vanadium(IV) complexes generally contain the VO^{2+} unit.[3,25] The structure is significantly distorted so that the V^{IV} metal is situated 0·1 to 0·3 Å above the plane defined by the four basal coordination sites. Ligands in the apical position are at rather long distances, and sometimes the position remains vacant. Early studies of the ligand substitution reactions showed very similar kinetic behaviour to those of Ni^{2+} complexes, and VO^{2+} was reckoned as a kind of bivalent metal ion. Recent studies, however, have made clear quite different characteristic behaviour of this cation, including a remarkable regioselectivity with apical ligand far more labile than the basal sites. Internal rearrangement from the apical to the basal site seems to play an important role in some cases. The exchange of O in the VO^{2+} moiety is very slow in water ($2·98 \times 10^{-5} \, s^{-1}$ at 0°C).[26] The oxo group remains unchanged during substitution reactions at other coordination sites.

Table 1 lists rate constants and activation parameters for solvent exchange and ligand exchange reactions. The water molecule at the apical site exchanges at diffusion controlled rates,[27,36] whereas those at the basal sites do so at much lower rates, of the order of $10^2 \, s^{-1}$ at 25°C.[27,28,37] Rate constants for other substitution reactions of $VO(H_2O)_5^{2+}$ at the basal site (Table 2) are mostly in the range from 10^2 to $10^3 \, s^{-1}$;[30–43] their $\Delta S^{\ddagger}$ values are negative and $\Delta H^{\ddagger}$ are small.[27–35] Results have been analysed by Scheme 1, the value of K_{OS} being estimated using the Fuoss equation.[47] The k_s values are similar to those for the water exchange at the basal site.

The acid dissociation constant of $[VO(H_2O)_5]^{2+}$ is of order 10^{-6} M at room temperature. Accordingly, participation of the hydroxo species $[VO(OH)(H_2O)_4]^+$ in anation reactions may be ignored at pH values below 3. Che and Kustin[42] have indicated that the hydroxo complex reacts with vmd⁻, md⁻ and ta⁻ some 50 times faster than the pentaaqua complex. They pointed out that some of the data in Table 2[33,41] should be reviewed carefully, since the participation of hydroxo species was not considered despite the high pH at which the rate was measured. The small rate constant for formation of the tartrate complex at low pH was claimed to be due to the slow chelation of the protonated unidentate ligand.[40] This accords with chelation of unidentate glycine as the zwitterion ($35 \, s^{-1}$ at 25°C) being much slower than the formation of the unidentate glycine complex.[48]

TABLE 1

Kinetic data for ligand exchange reactions of oxovanadium(IV)

Complex	Exchanging ligand	Solvent	k_{ex} (s^{-1}(25°C))	$\Delta H^{\ddagger}$ (kJ mol^{-1})	$\Delta S^{\ddagger}$ (J K^{-1} mol^{-1})	Ref.
[VO(H$_2$O)$_5$]$^{2+}$	H$_2$O	H$_2$O	$5 \cdot 2 \times 10^{2}$ ^{a}	55·9	−6·3	[27, 28]
	H$_2$O	H$_2$O	$\sim 10^{11}$ ^{b}			[27]
[VO(OH)$_3$(H$_2$O)$_2$]$^-$	(OH$^-$)	H$_2$O	$<1 \times 10^{4}$ ^{c}			[29]
[VO(dmf)$_4$]$^{2+}$	dmf	dmf	$5 \cdot 8 \times 10^{2}$	30·5	−88·0	[30]
[VO(CH$_3$CN)$_4$]$^{2+}$	CH$_3$CN	CH$_3$CN	$2 \cdot 85 \times 10^{3}$	29·6	−84	[31]
[VO(CH$_3$OH)$_4$]$^{2+}$	CH$_3$OH	CH$_3$OH	$5 \cdot 65 \times 10^{2}$	39·7	−59·6	[32]
[VO(gly)$_2$]	gly$^-$	H$_2$O	$3 \cdot 6 \times 10^{2}$	33·6	−84·0	[33]
[VO(mal)$_2$]$^{2-}$	Hmal$^-$	H$_2$O	$1 \cdot 1 \times 10^{3}$ M^{-1}	36·1	−68·0	[34]
[VO(acac)$_2$]	Hacac	dce	$7 \cdot 1 \times 10^{-2}$ M^{-1} ^{d}	46·7	−61·9	[35]

^{a} Basal water.
^{b} Axial water.
^{c} At 65°C.
^{d} At −33°C.

TABLE 2

Kinetic data for complex formation (k_f) and aquation (k_d) reactions of oxovanadium(IV) in water[a]

Ligand	k_f (M^{-1} s^{-1})	$\Delta H^{\ddagger}$ (kJ mol^{-1})	$\Delta S^{\ddagger}$ (J K^{-1} mol^{-1})	k_d(s^{-1})	$\Delta H^{\ddagger}$ (kJ mol^{-1})	$\Delta S^{\ddagger}$ (J K^{-1} mol^{-1})	Ref.
			(i) [VO(H$_2$O)$_5$]$^{2+}$				
SO$_4^{2-}$	$1\cdot5 \times 10^{3}$ [b]			$6\cdot0 \times 10^{2}$			[38]
NCS$^-$	$1\cdot15 \times 10^{4}$	45·4		60 ± 20	60		[39]
Htart$^-$	$1\cdot70 \times 10^{2}$						[40]
	3×10^{4}			34 ± 3			[41]
mal^{2-}	$\sim2 \times 10^{4}$			$\sim2\cdot5 \times 10^{-2}$			[41]
C$_2$O$_4^{2-}$	$\sim4 \times 10^{4}$			$\sim2\cdot3 \times 10^{-3}$			[41]
Hgly	$1\cdot3 \times 10^{3}$	50·4	$-16\cdot8$	$4\cdot6 \times 10^{3}$	55·0	$-10\cdot1$	[33]
vmd$^-$	$1\cdot13 \times 10^{3}$						[42]
md$^-$	$1\cdot09 \times 10^{3}$						[42]
ta$^-$	$6\cdot76 \times 10^{2}$						[42]
tta$^-$	$3\cdot6 \times 10^{3}$						[43]
tfac$^-$	2×10^{2}						[43]
Htta	7·6						[43]
Htfac	3·5						[43]
Hacac	4·4						[43]
			(ii) [VO(pmida)(H$_2$O)]				
NCS$^-$	0·26	61·4	-61	0·061	48·9	-90	[44]
N$_3^-$	3·7	63·5	-47	0·13	47·2	-75	[44]
NO$_2^-$	$1\cdot0$[c]	65	-48				[45]
			(iii) [VO(nta)(H$_2$O)]$^-$				
NCS$^-$	0·62	41	-112	0·17	69	-25	[45]
N$_3^-$	4·1	54	-52	0·48	53	-75	[45]
NO$_2^-$	$0\cdot20$[c]	66	-48				[45]
[VO$_2$(nta)]$^{2-}$	1·36	62	-33	0·051	56	-79	[45, 46]

[a] Rate constants at 25°C.
[b] First-order rate constant within the ion-pair of [VO(H$_2$O)$_5$]$^{2+}$ and SO$_4^{2-}$.
[c] At 45°C.

On the other hand, the anation reaction of aqua–pmida and aqua–nta complexes (Fig. 2) in which the apical site is blocked by the tertiary amino nitrogen group is much slower (rate constants are 10^0 to 10^{-1} M s^{-1} at room temperature) in the pH region from 3 to 5. The acid hydrolysis of these complexes to give pentaaqua species is observed only in acid solutions of $[H^+] \geqslant 0.1$ M,[50] and the x-ray crystal structure must therefore be preserved

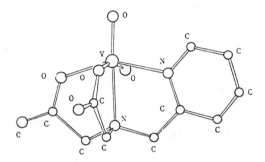

Fig. 2. The X-ray structure of [V^{IV}O(pmida)(H$_2$O)] (from Ref. [49], reproduced by permission of the Chemical Society of Japan).

in the pH range 3 to 5. Hence the given values seem to represent the real rate of basal substitution, while the other reported "basal substitutions" must reflect the rate at which the ligand at the very labile apical site migrates to the basal site.[44,45,50,51] Thus the ratio of rates of substitutions at the apical and basal sites is greater than 10^8. Since nta^{3-} and pmida^{2-} are expected to accelerate the substitution of the sixth ligand more than (H$_2$O)$_4$ does, the real regioselectivity ratio, apical/basal, may be even larger. The early report of the absence of observation by ^{1}H NMR technique of water exchange in the nta complex[52] can now be explained by the slow basal water substitution.

Substitution at the basal sites involving apical–basal migration of the substituting ligand has been verified in Mo^V=O complexes (*vide infra*), as well as the Mo^{II} complex which has strong Mo–Mo bonds.[53] It seems that such a mechanism may be common for the substitution reactions of complexes exhibiting marked regioselectivity.

The anation and aquation of [VO(nta)(H$_2$O)]$^-$ and [VO(pmida)(H$_2$O)] are considered to proceed by an associative mechanism on the basis of the negative $\Delta S^{\ddagger}$ and the different rate constants obtained by use of different nucleophiles as reagent.

The exchange of bridging tartrate in the dinuclear complex [V$_2$O$_2$(tart)$_2$]$^{4-}$ was studied using optical activity. The independence of rate constants $(0.0112$ s^{-1} at 25°C, $I = 3.0$ M (LiClO$_4$)) on the free tartrate

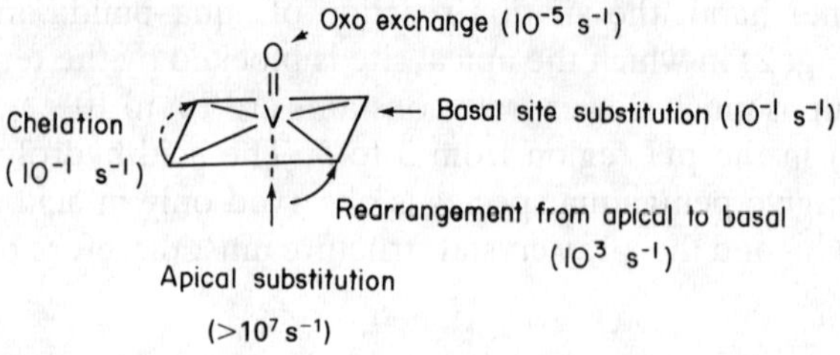

Fig. 3. Different substitution rates at various coordination sites of oxovanadium(IV) ion (approximate first-order rate constants at room temperature in parenthesis).

concentration and the large $\Delta H^{\ddagger}$ (105 kJ mol^{-1}) and positive $\Delta S^{\ddagger}$ (+71 J K^{-1} mol^{-1}) suggest a dissociative reaction mechanism.[54]

As a summary, the various kinds of substitution proposed for oxovanadium(IV) are illustrated in Fig. 3.[51]

B. Molybdenum(V) complexes

Molybdenum(V)[1,4,5] gives stable MoO^{3+} cations in organic solvents, but the stable form in aqueous solution is a doubly bridged dinuclear species Mo$_2$O$_4^{2+}$ [55] in which each Mo^V has one terminal oxo group. Singly bridged Mo$_2$O$_3^{4+}$ complexes are known but their kinetic behaviour has not yet been investigated.[4]

1. Mononuclear complexes

Monomeric MoO^{3+} ions are readily hydrolysed in water. Garner and colleagues have studied the substitution reactions of bromide,[56] nitrite[57,58] and nitrate[59,60] for OPPh$_3$ in [MoOCl$_3$(OPPh$_3$)$_2$] using dichloromethane as solvent. The substitution of bromide ($X^- = Br^-$) proceeds in two steps: substitution at the apical site is followed by internal rearrangement of the bromide to the basal site (Scheme 2):

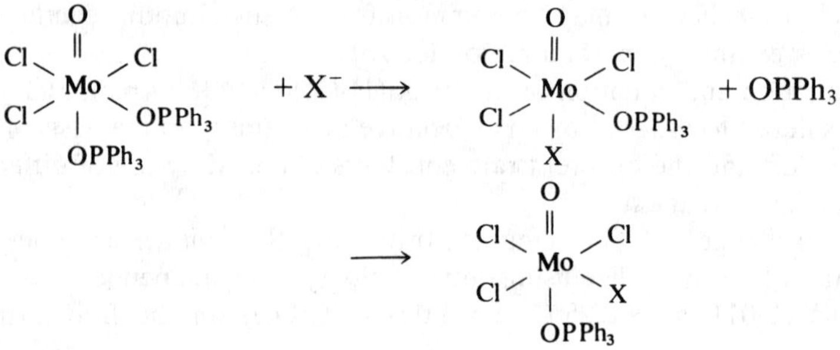

(2)

Nitrite and nitrate give similar substitution reactions, which are followed by rapid oxidation of Mo^V to Mo^{VI}. The first step, the substitution at the apical site, proceeds by a D (S_N1 limiting) mechanism[56,61]:

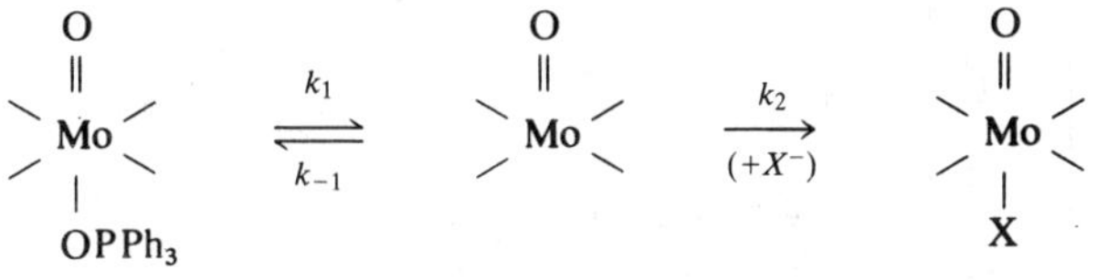

$$
\begin{array}{ccccc}
\text{O} & & \text{O} & & \text{O} \\
\| & k_1 & \| & k_2 & \| \\
\diagdown\text{Mo}\diagup & \rightleftharpoons & \diagdown\text{Mo}\diagup & \xrightarrow{(+X^-)} & \diagdown\text{Mo}\diagup \\
\diagup\ |\ \diagdown & k_{-1} & \diagup\ \diagdown & & \diagup\ |\ \diagdown \\
\text{OPPh}_3 & & & & \text{X}
\end{array} \qquad (3)
$$

Table 3 shows k_1 and k_2/k_{-1} values. The independence of k_1 values on the nucleophile indicated a dissociative rate-determining step. The k_2/k_{-1} values indicate an order of nucleophilicity for X^- towards the intermediate with

TABLE 3
Rate constants k_1 and k_2/k_{-1}, as defined in Equation (3), for substitution reactions of monomeric molybdenum(V) complexes in 1,2-dichloroethane (L is the leaving and X the incoming ligand)

Complex	L	X	k_1 (s^{-1})	k_2/k_{-1}	Ref.
[Mo(O)Cl$_3$(OPPh$_3$)]	OPPh$_3$	Br$^-$	41·6	8	[56]
	OPPh$_3$	Cl$^-$	42·0	27	[56]
	OPPh$_3$	NO$_2^-$	51.8	47	[57]
	OPPh$_3$	NO$_3^-$	40·3	31	[59]
[Mo(O)Cl$_3$(OP{N(CH$_3$)$_2$}$_3$)$_2$]	OP(N(CH$_3$)$_2$)$_3$	Br$^-$	9·9	5·5	[61]
	OP(N(CH$_3$)$_2$)$_3$	Cl$^-$	7·5	3·6	[61]
	OP(N(CH$_3$)$_2$)$_3$	NO$_3^-$	10·6	2·1	[61]

coordination number 5. It is noted that the k_1 value for substitution at the apical site is significantly smaller than that for the isoelectronic cation $V^{IV}O^{2+}$. The difference may originate in the difference in the oxidation state of the central metal atoms.

2. Dinuclear complexes

Table 4 lists kinetic data for substitution of a series of unidentate ligands for an aqua ligand in the doubly-bridged Mo(V) species.[62–64] The oxalato complexes have the structure[65,66] shown in Fig. 4. If this structure is retained in aqueous solutions, the kinetic data correspond to substitution at the basal site, and the data given are to be so understood. The rate constant for 1:1 substitution of NCS$^-$ into [Mo$_2$O$_4$(H$_2$O)$_n$]$^{2+}$ [62] is similar

TABLE 4

Kinetic data for complex formation (k_f) and aquation (k_d) of $Mo_2^VO_2(\mu\text{-}X)_2$-type complexes in water

Complex	Ligand	k_f (M^{-1} s^{-1}) or k_d (s^{-1})	$\Delta H^\ddagger$ (kJ mol^{-1})	$\Delta S^\ddagger$ (J K^{-1} mol^{-1})	Ref.
(i) Complex formation					
[Mo$_2$O$_2(\mu$-O)$_2$(H$_2$O)$_n$]$^{2+}$ ^{a}	NCS$^-$	2.9×10^4	47.5 ± 3.8	-1.3 ± 13.0	[62]
[Mo$_2$O$_2(\mu$-O)$_2$(C$_2$O$_4$)$_2$(H$_2$O)$_2$]$^{2-}$	NCS$^-$	5.0×10^3	47.0	-17.6	[63]
	py	3.0×10^3	45.4	-27.3	[63]
[Mo$_2$O$_2(\mu$-S)$_2$(C$_2$O$_4$)$_2$(H$_2$O)$_2$]$^{2-}$	NCS$^-$	2.1×10^5	31.5	-38.6	[64]
(ii) Aquation					
[Mo$_2$O$_2(\mu$-O)$_2$(NCS)(H$_2$O)$_{n-1}$]$^+$	NCS$^-$	1.2×10^2	57.5 ± 10.5	-12.6 ± 33.6	[62]
[Mo$_2$O$_2(\mu$-O)$_2$(C$_2$O$_4$)$_2$(NCS)(H$_2$O)]$^{3-}$	NCS$^-$	9.16×10^2	63.4	23.5	[63]
[Mo$_2$O$_2(\mu$-O)$_2$(C$_2$O$_4$)$_2$(H$_2$O)(py)]$^{2-}$	py	48.7	68.4	16.0	[63]
[Mo$_2$O$_2(\mu$-S)$_2$(C$_2$O$_4$)$_2$(NCS)(H$_2$O)]$^{3-}$	NCS$^-$	3.5×10^4	42.4	-17.2	[64]

^{a} n is assumed to be 6.

to that for the oxalato complex. Therefore, it was reasoned, the process observed corresponds to substitution at the basal site,[63] and a dissociative mechanism seems likely. The aqueous solutions of the oxalato complex, however, give only one sharp ^{13}C NMR signal,[67] indicating that in solution the aqua ligand is at the apical site or that the apical–basal rearrangement

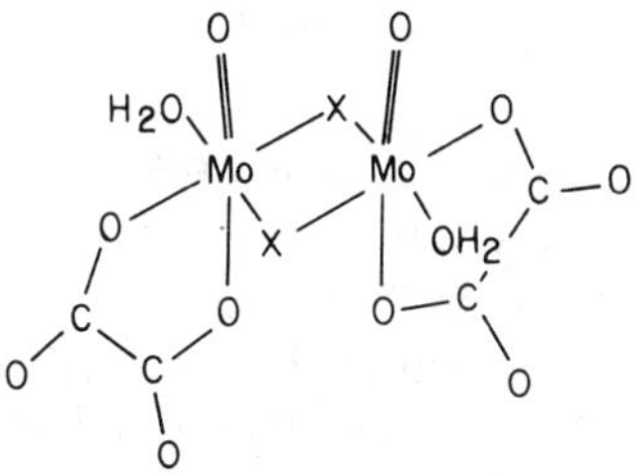

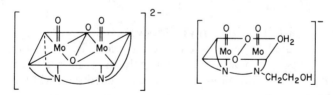

(X = O or S)

Fig. 4. Structures of $[Mo_2^VO_2X_2(C_2O_4)_2(H_2O)_2]_{2-}$ (X = O or S) (Refs. [65, 66]).

proceeds very rapidly in solution. Hence the given kinetic data do not necessarily correspond to substitution at the basal site. Comparison with data for the substitution reactions of mononuclear Mo^VO^{3+} and $V^{IV}O^{2+}$ complexes suggests that the apical sites in the dinuclear complexes may also be very labile. More data are certainly needed for unambiguous conclusion to be reached. It is seen that replacement of the bridging oxide by sulphide increases the lability.[64]

Fig. 5. Structures of $[Mo_2^VO_4(edta)]^{2-}$ and $[Mo_2^VO_4(hedta)H_2O]^-$. (Refs [68, 69], reproduced by permission of the Royal Chemical Society and the Chemical Society of Japan.)

The $Mo_2O_4^{2+}$ species involving multidentate ligands such as edta^{4-} and related ligands (Fig. 5) have also been studied. The rate of substitution of the chelated ligand decreases significantly as the dentate number of the ligand increases.[69] This trend is exemplified by studies on acid hydrolysis (i.e. aquation reactions) in 0·1 M HClO$_4$ at 25°C.

$$[Mo_2O_4(edta)]^{2-[68]} \approx [Mo_2O_4(hedta)(H_2O)]^{-[69]} <$$
$$(10^{-3}\,s^{-1}) \qquad\qquad (10^{-3}\,s^{-1})$$

$$[Mo_2O_4(ida)_2]^{2-[70]} < [Mo_2O_4(C_2O_4)_2(H_2O)_2]^{2-[70]} <$$
$$(10^{-2}\,s^{-1}\ at\ 0°C) \qquad\qquad (10^0\,s^{-1})$$

$$[Mo_2O_4(NCS)(H_2O)_5]^{+[62]}$$
$$(10^2\,s^{-1})$$

$$(4)$$

Such a difference is characteristic of $Mo_2O_4^{2+}$ species. It appears that if partially aquated species play important roles, recombination would be more favourable than further dissociation.

The exchange of the oxo group at the terminal site with solvent water has a half-life of ~4 min at 40°C, while that at the bridging site is 400 hours at 40°C.[71] Conversion of the doubly bridged species into the singly bridged form is believed to be effective in the outer-sphere oxidation of $[Mo_2O_4(H_2O)_6]^{2+}$ with $[Ir^{IV}Cl_6]^{2-}$,[72] $[Fe^{III}(phen)_3]^{3+}$,[72] and $(NH_3)_5Co(O_2)Co(NH_3)_5^{5+}$.[73] The rate constant is of the order of $10^{-6}\,s^{-1}$ at 25°C, and is in good accord with the rate constant for exchange of bridging oxo groups.

Only one study is available concerning the substitution of a W^V complex. Acid hydrolysis of $[W_2O_4(edta)]^{2-}$ exhibits a lower rate constant than that for $[Mo_2O_4(edta)]^{2-}$ by a factor of 60 times.[74]

III. SUBSTITUTION OF OXO-METAL COMPLEXES WITHOUT d ELECTRONS

Reactions of Ti(IV), V(V), Cr(VI), Mo(VI), and W(VI) have been fairly extensively studied and will be considered below. Besides simple substitution reactions, two types of reaction, polymerization–depolymerization and peroxo complex formation, have been studied, and will be reviewed in separate sections.

A. Titanium(IV) complexes

The oxotitanium(IV) ion, TiO^{2+}, is stable in aqueous solutions only at pH < 2,[75] and the kinetics of substitution reactions of its complexes have been studied in such acid media.[76,77] Table 5 indicates that there is only a modest difference between the complex formation rate constants (k_f), and an I_d mechanism is suggested.[76]

TABLE 5

Kinetic data for complex formation (k_f) and aquation (k_d) of oxotitanium(IV), $[TiO(H_2O)_n]^{2+}$, in water[a]

Ligand	k_f ($M^{-1}\,s^{-1}$)	$\Delta H^\ddagger$ (kJ mol⁻¹)	$\Delta S^\ddagger$ (J K⁻¹ mol⁻¹)	k_d (s⁻¹)	$\Delta H^\ddagger$ (kJ mol⁻¹)	$\Delta S^\ddagger$ (J K⁻¹ mol⁻¹)	I^b (M)	[H⁺] (M)	Ref.
NCS⁻	$(6{\cdot}06 \pm 1{\cdot}2)$ $\times 10^3$			$(1{\cdot}98 \pm 0{\cdot}05)$ $\times 10^3$			0·10		[76]
$H_4P_2O_7$	$2{\cdot}21 \times 10^3$	49·1	−16·8	$7{\cdot}2 \times 10^2$	62.6	+19·3	0·50	0·10–0·35	[76]
$H_3P_2O_7^-$	$1{\cdot}10 \times 10^3$						0·50	0·10–0·35	[76]
$H_2P_2O_7^{2-}$	$0{\cdot}95 \times 10^3$						0·50	0·10–0·35	[76]
HF	$3{\cdot}60 \times 10^3$						0·50	0·10–0·35	[76]
HF	$1{\cdot}86 \times 10^3$	44·5	−33·6				0·50	0·11–0·48	[76]
H_4mtb^{2-}	$3{\cdot}2 \times 10^2$			$(1{\cdot}3 \times 10^{-3})$			0·50	0·35–1·85 (pH)	[77]

[a] Rate constants at 25°C.
[b] Adjusted with LiClO₄ (except H_4mtb^{2-}).

TABLE 6

Rate constants (25°C) for complex formation reactions of vanadium(V) in water

Reactions	k_f (M^{-1} s^{-1})	I (M)	pH or [H$^+$] (M)	Ref.
VO$_2^+$ + H$_2$edta^{2-} ^{a}	3·84 × 10^6	3·0 (NaClO$_4$)	1·5–2·0 (pH)	[78]
+ Hnta^{2-}	1·93 × 10^5	3·0 (NaClO$_4$)	1·5–2·0 (pH)	[79]
+ H$_2$nta$^-$	3·26 × 10^5	3·0 (NaClO$_4$)	1·5–2·0 (pH)	[79]
+ Hmida$^-$	2·46 × 10^3	1·0 (NaClO$_4$)	1·43–1·98 (pH)	[80]
+ Hedda$^-$	1·07 × 10^8	1·0 (NaClO$_4$)	2·16–2·89 (pH)	[80]
+ H$_2$cat	1·84 × 10^4	1·0 (LiClO$_4$)	0·2–1·0 ([H$^+$])	[81]
+ H$_3$pg	4·36 × 10^4	1·0 (LiClO$_4$)	0·2–1·0 ([H$^+$])	[81]
+ H$_3$thb	9·91 × 10^4	1·0 (LiClO$_4$)	0·2–1·0 ([H$^+$])	[81]
+ H$_3$dopa	1·12 × 10^4	1·0 (LiClO$_4$)	0·2–1·0 ([H$^+$])	[81]
+ H$_3$ep	1·70 × 10^4	1·0 (LiClO$_4$)	0·2–1·0 ([H$^+$])	[81]
VO$_2$(OH)$_2^-$ + H$_2$edta^{2-}	2·34 × 10^4	0·5 (NH$_4$Cl)	8·13–8·76 (pH)	[82]
+ Haliz$^-$	2·28 × 10^4	0·5 (NH$_4$Cl)	8·33–9·23 (pH)	[82]
VO$_2$(OH)$_3^{2-}$ + H$_2$edta^{2-}	2·4 × 10^3	0·5 (NH$_4$Cl)	8·13–8·76 (pH)	[82]
+ Haliz$^-$	1·2 × 10^3	0·5 (NH$_4$Cl)	8·33–9·23 (pH)	[82]

^{a} Rate = ab[H$_2$edta^{2-}][VO$_2^+$]/(1 + b[H$_2$edta^{2-}]), $k_f = ab$.

B. Vanadium(V) complexes

1. Complex formation

Since vanadium(V) polymerizes in basic solutions, most studies have been made in acidic solution. The two oxide ions are *cis* to each other and the complex remains hexa-coordinated even in the more deprotonated species such as $[V(O)_2(OH)_2(H_2O)_2]^-$ and $[V(O)_2(OH)_3(H_2O)]^{2-}$. Hence there is no change in the coordination number on substitution reaction. Available kinetic data are summarized in Table 6.[78–82] Rate constants for complex formation reactions of VO_2^+ range between 10^4 and 10^6 M^{-1} s^{-1} except for the reactions with Hedda$^-$ and Hmida$^-$. The observed rate constant k_f is the product of the precursor formation constant and the rate constant for substitution within the precursor. The former seems to account for the small difference in k_f among the ligands with different charges. The rate-determining step common to all of them is probably of dissociative nature.

Yamada and Tanaka reckoned that the k_f value ($1 \cdot 07 \times 10^8$ M^{-1} s^{-1}) for Hedda$^-$ is the rate constant for loss of water from VO_2^+, and that the smaller k_f for Hmida$^-$ and H$_2$nta$^-$ may reflect the rate of deprotonation from NH in the rate determining step.[80] An overall view of Table 6, however, suggests that the rate for Hedda$^-$ might be rather exceptional.

The deprotonated species, $[VO_2(OH)_2]^-$ and $[VO_2(OH)_3]^{2-}$, give more or less similar k_f values on reaction with negatively charged reagents to those obtained for VO_2^+ with chargeless reagents.[82] The rate constant for oxygen exchange on VO_4^{3-} has been reported to be of the order of 10^{-1} s^{-1} at 0°C,[83] and the difference in rate here may be partly due to the difference in coordination number. When bis-chelate type complexes are formed with tiron, norepinephrine and 6,7-dihydroxo-2-napthalenesulphonate, rate constants increase with increasing pH from 8 to 9.[84] This is the opposite trend to that for mono-ligand complex formation, and the same trend as is observed for the pH dependence of bis-ligand type complexes of Mo^{VI}.[85]

2. Acid- and base-hydrolysis

Acid hydrolysis of VO_2^+-complexes has been kinetically studied with multidentate aminocarboxylates and polyhydric phenols as shown in Table 7.[80,81] Within the given pH range the dependence of rate constants on hydrogen-ion concentration is rather simple. Reactions of the complexes of polyhydric alcohols give no pH dependence,[81] whereas those of aminocarboxylate complexes seem to be initiated by protonation prior to bond breaking.[80]

TABLE 7
Rate constants for the aquation (i.e. acid-hydrolysis) of dioxovanadium(V) complexes†

Complex	Rate-law dependence	k	$[H^+]$ range	Ref.
$[V(O)_2(edda)]^-$ [a]	$[H^+]$	1.45×10^3 M^{-1} s^{-1}	0.0013–0.0069	[80]
$[V(O)_2(mida)]^-$ [a]	$[H^+]$	5.75×10^2 M^{-1} s^{-1}	0.011–0.037	[80]
$[V(O)_2(ida)]^-$ [a]	$[H^+]^2$	5.02×10^2 M^{-2} s^{-1}	0.071–0.252	[80]
$V(O)_2$-cat[b]	$[H^+]^0$	41.9 s^{-1}	0.2–1.0	[81]
$V(O)_2$-pg[b]	$[H^+]^0$	8.39 s^{-1}	0.2–1.0	[81]
$V(O)_2$-thb[b]	$[H^+]^0$	10.8 s^{-1}	0.2–1.0	[81]
$V(O)_2$-dopa[b]	$[H^+]^0$	55.2 s^{-1}	0.2–1.0	[81]
$V(O)_2$-ep[b]	$[H^+]^0$	66.6 s^{-1}	0.2–1.0	[81]

[a] $I = 1.0$ (NaClO$_4$).   † Exact chemical formulae are not given.
[b] $I = 1.0$ (LiClO$_4$).

Data for base hydrolysis are available only for the dissociation of multidentate aminocarboxylates.[86] The rate is commonly expressed by equation (5):

$$k_{obs} = (k_1 + k_2 K_{OS}[OH^-]^2)/(1 + K_{OS}[OH^-]^2) \qquad (5)$$

Here K_{OS} is for the outer-sphere association between the complex and

TABLE 8
Kinetic data for the base-hydrolysis of dioxovanadium(V) complexes[a]

Complex	k_1 (s^{-1})	k_2 (s^{-1})	K_{OS} (M^{-2})	$[OH^-]$-range	Ref.
$V(O)_2$-bis(ida)	14.3	1.85	6.10×10^5	0.00117–0.0456	[86]
$[V(O)_2(edda)]^-$	2.80	160	1.50×10^2	0.00294–0.0914	[86]
$[V(O)_2(nta)]^{2-}$	0.80	85.2	1.52×10^6	0.000114–0.0277	[86]
$[V(O)_2(edta)]^{3-}$	0.0060	0.0303	1.82×10^8	0.0000604–0.0368	[86]

[a] Rate law, $-d[\text{complex}]/dt = (k_{obs})$; $I = 3.0$ M (NaClO$_4$); 25°C.

hydroxide ion. The small rate constant for the edta system is accounted for by the fact that the free acetate branches of edta can coordinate to the vacant coordination site following partial dissociation resulting in retardation of the overall rate of dissociation.[86]

3. Other reactions

Kinetics of the alcohol exchange for the ester complexes, $V(O)(OR)_3$ (R = Pr^n, Bu^n, neo-pentyl, and Pr^i) by NMR techniques gave small $\Delta H^\ddagger$

and negative $\Delta S^{\ddagger}$ values, which suggest an associative mechanism.[87] With quinoline derivatives (Q) as ligands, characteristic dimers of the general formula $[Q_2(O)V-O-V(O)Q_2]$ are formed.[88] This dinuclear species reacts slowly with alcohols in chloroform to give $V(O)(OR)Q_2$ with a rate constant of 10^{-3} to $10^{-2} M^{-1} s^{-1}$ at 25°C.[89] The rate decreases as the basicity of Q increases and the R becomes more bulky.[89]

C. Chromium(VI) complexes

Since chromate is a strong oxidizing reagent, not many data have been accumulated for the substitution of Lewis bases for the oxide in CrO_4^{2-}.[90–96] Coordination number 4 is retained on substitution. Haim has analysed the available data in terms of equation (6)

$$\text{Rate} = k_f[HCrO_4^-][X][H^+] \tag{6}$$

and found that k_f is of the order of $10^5 M^{-2} s^{-1}$ and is virtually independent of the nature of X.[97] He presumed a diffusion-controlled protonation on $HOCrO_3^-$, followed by a rate-determining loss of water through a disso-ciative mechanism.[97] He also discussed the possibility that the rate law could be interpreted by considering a concerted mechanism, in which H^+ and X^- simultaneously interact with $HOCrO_3^-$.

Halogen exchange on CrO_3F^- is very slow in DMSO ($<10^{-5} M^{-1} s^{-1}$), but CrO_2F_2 and CrO_2Cl_2 exchange their halogen ions within time-scales observable using NMR techniques.[98] A difference in coulombic interac-tion, as estimated by the Fouss equation,[47] does not seem to be responsible for such a big difference. The lower number of oxo groups in CrO_2X_2 makes the metal centre less electronegative and results in a greater tendency towards nucleophilic attack.

D. Molybdenum(VI) and tungsten(VI) complexes

1. Complex formation

Anation reactions of catechols and aminocarboxylates to molydbate and tungstate have been studied in the pH range from 5 to 9.[85,99–103] Substitution reactions are accompanied by change in coordination number, from 4 to 6. The rate of reaction generally increases with a decrease in pH. There are "proton ambiguities"; thus the pH dependence can be accounted for by either the reactions of variously protonated species of MoO_4^{2-} (or WO_4^{2-}) or those of variously protonated ligands. Gilbert and Kustin have estimated the maximum rate constants for individual reactions of variously protonated species on the assumption that a particular reaction takes place

TABLE 9

Maximum second-order rate constants ($M^{-1} s^{-1}$) for MoO_4^{2-} and HMO_4^- (M = Mo, W) complex formation at 25°C in water

Ligand	Complex				Ref.
	MoO_4^{2-}	WO_4^{2-}	$HMoO_4^-$	HWO_4^-	
Hox	$4 \cdot 1 \times 10^2$	$2 \cdot 4 \times 10^3$	$4 \cdot 5 \times 10^6$	$\sim 5 \cdot 4 \times 10^6$	[99, 100]
ox⁻			$1 \cdot 5 \times 10^8$	$\sim 2 \cdot 6 \times 10^9$	[99, 100]
Hoxs⁻	$2 \cdot 5 \times 10^3$	$1 \cdot 3 \times 10^4$	$\sim 3 \cdot 9 \times 10^6$	$< 3 \times 10^6$	[100]
oxs²⁻			$4 \cdot 0 \times 10^7$	$\sim 6 \cdot 2 \times 10^8$	[100]
Hcat⁻	$3 \cdot 0 \times 10^2$	$1 \cdot 2 \times 10^2$	$4 \cdot 8 \times 10^7$	$1 \cdot 7 \times 10^7$	[101]
cat²⁻			$3 \cdot 0 \times 10^{10}$	$1 \cdot 3 \times 10^{10}$	[101]
H₂thb⁻	$7 \cdot 6 \times 10^1$		$6 \cdot 6 \times 10^7$		[85]
Hthb²⁻			$5 \cdot 3 \times 10^9$		[85]
H₂pg⁻	$1 \cdot 3 \times 10^2$	$5 \cdot 6 \times 10^2$	$2 \cdot 1 \times 10^8$	$7 \cdot 5 \times 10^8$	[85]
Hpg²⁻			$3 \cdot 6 \times 10^9$	$4 \cdot 7 \times 10^{10}$	[85]
Hep²⁻	$3 \cdot 8 \times 10^2$	$3 \cdot 8 \times 10^2$	$3 \cdot 6 \times 10^7$	$5 \cdot 8 \times 10^7$	[85]
ep³⁻			$3 \cdot 8 \times 10^8$	$1 \cdot 2 \times 10^9$	[85]
Hdopa²⁻	$3 \cdot 3 \times 10^2$	$3 \cdot 3 \times 10^2$	$4 \cdot 0 \times 10^7$	$7 \cdot 0 \times 10^7$	[85]
dopa³⁻			$2 \cdot 1 \times 10^8$	$6 \cdot 6 \times 10^8$	[85]
H₂edta²⁻			$2 \cdot 3 \times 10^5$		[102]
H₂ga²⁻		$1 \cdot 4 \times 10^3$			[85]
Hga³⁻					[85]
HS⁻			$1 \cdot 3 \times 10^6$	$6 \cdot 6 \times 10^7$	[106]
[Co(NH₃)₅(H₂O)]³⁺			$3 \cdot 2 \times 10^5$	$1 \cdot 4 \times 10^{10}$	[104]
cis-[Co(en)₂(OH)₂]⁺				$3 \cdot 2 \times 10^7$	[105]
cis-[Co(en)₂(OH)(H₂O)]²⁺				$1 \cdot 0 \times 10^7$	[105]

exclusively and that there is no contribution from other reaction paths.[85] Table 9 indicates that $HMoO_4^-$ gives much greater rates than MoO_4^{2-}. If the oxo-anion is protonated, the more basic ligands are more reactive; if the oxo-anion is not protonated the less basic ligands are more reactive.[85] Honig and Kustin have suggested that the protonated species $HMoO_4^-$ is in fact the octahedral complex $[MoO_2(OH)_3(H_2O)]^-$ [107] (there is an argument that two protons are required for the complex to become octahedral[108]), and that the hydrogen bonding between this anion and the basic ligand facilitates the reactions. Therefore it is tacitly suggested that the rate-determining step is of the associative kind.

In further studies Funahashi *et al.* have interpreted their data in terms of a general rate law[103]:

$$k_{obs} = k_f'[MoO_4^{2-}][L'][H^+] \tag{7}$$

Whenever a term containing $[H^+]^2$ is observed the second H^+ is placed on the ligand. When values of k_f' are plotted against $\log(K_{L'H})$, where $K_{L'H}$ is for the acid dissociation constant of $L'H$, a linear relationship is observed (Fig. 6), except for $L' = [Co(NH_3)_5(OH)]^{2+}$ and nta.[103] They have proposed a mechanism in which MoO_4^{2-} undergoes a weak interaction with L' to give a complex of coordination number 5, followed by a proton-assisted configurational change and bond formation as the rate-determining

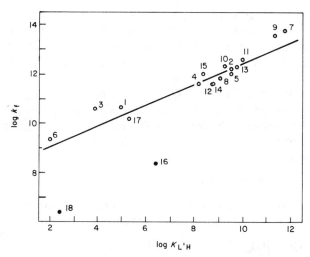

Fig. 6. Relationship between $\log(k_f)$ and $\log(K_{L'H})$ for Mo(VI) complex formation. L' = Hox(1), ox⁻(2), Hoxs⁻(3), oxs²⁻(4), Hcat⁻(5), H_2edta²⁻(6), Hthb²⁻(7), H_2thb⁻(8), Hpg²⁻(9), H_2pg⁻(10), ep³⁻(11), Hep²⁻(12), dopa³⁻(13), Hdopa²⁻(14), H_2ga²⁻(15), [Co(NH₃)₅(OH)]²⁺(16), Has(17), and Hnta²⁻(18) (from Ref. [103], reproduced by permission of the American Chemical Society).

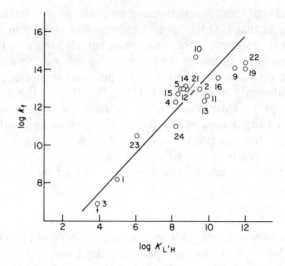

Fig. 7. Relationship between $\log(k_f)$ and $\log(K_{L'H})$ for W(VI) complex formation. (L' = Hox(1), ox⁻(2), Hoxs⁻(3), oxs²⁻(4), Hcat⁻(5), H₂edta²⁻(6), Hthb²⁻(7), H₂thb⁻(8), Hpg²⁻(9), H₂pg⁻(10), ep³⁻(11), H₂ep²⁻(12), dopa³⁻(13), Hdopa²⁻(14), H₂ga²⁻(15), cat²⁻(19), Hga³⁻(20), H₂dhb⁻(21), Hdhb²⁻(22), *cis*-[Co(en)₂(OH)(H₂O)]²⁺(23), *cis*-[Co(en)₂(OH)₂]⁺(24).

step.[103] When Gilbert and Kustin's data on tungstate[85] are analysed in accordance with Funahashi's suggestion (Fig. 7), a linear plot is observed, although the fluctuation is slightly bigger than that for molybdate. The larger gradient for tungstate than for molybdate suggests that the substitution reactions on tungstate are more ligand-sensitive.

A series of thiomolybdates $MoO_xS_{4-x}^{2-}$ have been prepared. Rate constants for interconversion substitution reactions of S- and O-forms decrease with increasing number of S atoms.[106] The more bulky sulphur atom may sterically retard the associative rate-determining step.

2. Acid- and base-hydrolysis

Rates of aquation of aminocarboxylate complexes of Mo^{VI} and W^{VI} are listed in Table 10.[86,103,109] The rate expression is

$$k_{obs} = (k_1 + k_2 K_{OH}[OH^-])/(1 + K_{OH}[OH^-]) \qquad (8)$$

where K_{OH} is the association constant between the complex and OH^-. The K_{OH} values in Table 10 suggest that the association involves some special interaction rather than a simple electrostatic effect. Most k_1 values differ by less than one order of magnitude. It is seen that ida^{2-} without free

TABLE 10

Kinetic data for base-hydrolysis of Mo(VI) and W(VI) complexes, as defined by the rate equation (8), at 25°C

Complex	k_1 (s^{-1})	k_2 (s^{-1})	K_{OH} (M^{-1})	[OH$^-$] (M) or pH	I (M)	Ref.
[Mo(O)$_3$(ida)]$^{2-}$	79	660	7·93	0·00694–0·0907 M	3·0 (NaClO$_4$)	[86]
[Mo(O)$_3$(nta)]$^{3-}$	0·020	4·40	4·79	0·0218–0·135 M	3·0 (NaClO$_4$)	[86]
	0·061	4·16	4·55	0·05–0·2 M	0·5 (NaClO$_4$)	[109]
	0·0018			pH 6·1–7·0	1·0 (NaClO$_4$)	[103]
[Mo(O)$_3$(edda)]$^{2-}$	0·82	1·90	23·0	0·00464–0·0884 M	3·0 (NaClO$_4$)	[86]
[Mo(O)$_3$(edta)]$^{4-}$	0·26	3·60	4·90	0·00896–0·183 M	3·0 (NaClO$_4$)	[86]
[W(O)$_3$(ida)]$^{2-}$	8·4	38·0	12·1	0·00695–0·0889 M	3·0 (NaClO$_4$)	[86]
[W(O)$_3$(nta)]$^{3-}$	0·0030	0·0870	57·9	0·0102–0·115 M	3·0 (NaClO$_4$)	[86]
[W(O)$_3$(edda)]$^{2-}$	0·021	0·400	5·46	0·00797–0·0917 M	3·0 (NaClO$_4$)	[86]
[W(O)$_3$(edta)]$^{4-}$	0·020	0·0870	35·9	0·00877–0·183 M	3·0 (NaClO$_4$)	[86]
Mo^{VI}-ox	1·95			pH 7·92–8·91	0·2 (NaClO$_4$)	[103]
Mo^{VI}-oxs	0·85			pH 7·50–8·50	0·2 (NaNO$_3$)	[103]
Mo^{VI}-cat	7·76			pH 7·30–7·80	0·1 (KNO$_3$)	[103]
Mo^{VI}-edta	7·59			pH 7·25–8·49	0·1 (NaNO$_3$)	[103]
[Mo(O)$_2$(OH)$_2$(as)]$^{3-}$	0·9			pH 7·4–8·1	1·0 (NaClO$_4$)	[103]

acetate gives a greater rate than when an uncoordinated acetate is present. Free acetate "arms" may coordinate to the site made vacant by partial dissociation of a ligand and decrease the overall rate. Rate constants for molybdenum complexes are an order of magnitude greater than those for tungsten.

3. Intramolecular rearrangement

Since the two oxo groups in monomeric Mo(VI) complexes are *cis* to each other, the two methyl groups on a given acac⁻ ligand in [Mo(O)$_2$(acac)$_2$] are not equivalent. Two methyl proton peaks coalesce at 313°C in benzene.[110] The activation parameters for the exchange are given in Table 11.[110,111] There is no intermolecular exchange with free Hacac, and so the exchange process must be intramolecular.[110]

TABLE 11

Activation parameters for the intramolecular rearrangement of Mo(VI) β-diketonate complexes

Complex	Solvent	$\Delta H^{\ddagger}$ (kJ mol^{-1})	$\Delta S^{\ddagger}$ (J K^{-1} mol^{-1})	Ref.
Mo(O)$_2$(acac)$_2$	benzene	69	+18·5	[110]
	chloroform	52	+58·8	[110]
Mo(O)$_2$(dipiv)$_2$	dichloromethane	69		[111]

E. Summary

Dissociative mechanisms have been proposed for the oxo-metal ions Ti(IV), V(V) and Cr(VI) in the first transition series, while associative mechanisms appear to operate for Mo(VI) and W(VI). The rate of substitution is much greater for the di-oxo complex of V(V) than for mono-oxo complex of Ti(IV). A characteristic feature of complex formation of Cr(VI), Mo(VI) and W(VI) is the increase in the rate as [H$^+$] increases; this occurs despite the proposal that the mechanism for Cr(VI) is different. The H$^+$ assisted mechanism (possibly a concerted mechanism) may be more general for substitution of tetrahedral oxo-metal ions. The role of H$^+$ has still to be clarified. If rate constants are compared on the basis of rate laws (6) and (7), it is clearly seen that HCrO$_4^-$ is much less reactive than MoO$_4^{2-}$ and WO$_4^{2-}$.

IV. DECOMPOSITION OF POLYACIDS[112]

A. Vanadium(V) polyacids

The decavanadate(V) ion $V_{10}O_{28}^{6-}$ is dominant in aqueous solutions of pH 2 to 6.[113] It decomposes on addition of acid or base to give VO_2^+ and VO_4^{3-} respectively. In acid solutions of more than 0·2 M, the Scheme (9) has been proposed:[114]

$$H_2V_{10}O_{28}^{4-} + H^+ \overset{K_1}{\rightleftharpoons} H_3V_{10}O_{28}^{3-} \overset{K_2}{\rightleftharpoons} H_4V_{10}O_{28}^{2-} \overset{k_a}{\rightarrow} \quad (9)$$

The k_aK_2 value is $0·132\ M^{-1}s^{-1}$ at 25°C and $I = 1·3\ M$ (NaNO$_3$). Large cations such as R_4N^+ and R_3S^+ retard the acid decomposition by forming stable ion-pairs with the decavanadate ion.[114]

In basic solutions the rate is expressed by a two-term equation (10):

$$k_{obs} = k_a + k_b[OH^-] \quad (10)$$

Rate constants are very much dependent on the ionic strength, and on the kind of neutral salt (particularly of cation) used for adjusting the ionic strength.[115, 116] Values of k_a and k_b give reverse dependences on the kind of cation:

k_a: $K^+ < Na^+ \sim Li^+ < R_4N^+$

k_b: $K^+ > Na^+ > Li^+ > R_4N^+$

The ion-pair formation constants with $V_{10}O_{28}^{6-}$ decrease in the order $K^+ > Na^+ > R_4N^+$. It appears as if k_a and k_b involve participation of the free acid anion and the ion-pair respectively.[116] Decavanadate ions are also decomposed by the attack of nucleophiles. The kinetics of the decomposition by 7-iodo-8-hydroxyquinoline-5-sulphonate have been studied.[117] At pH > 7 vanadium(V) is present in various forms including dimer, trimer, and tetramer. The kinetics of the formation of these species has also been reported.[118,119]

B. Molybdenum(VI) and tungsten(VI) polyacids

Molybdate ions MoO_4^{2-} are stable in basic solutions, but polymerize at pH < 7 to give $Mo_7O_{24}^{6-}$ and $Mo_8O_{26}^{4-}$.[1,2] The temperature-jump technique has been used to measure the rate constants for the equilibration between monomer and heptamer, and between monomer–heptamer and octamer at pH 5·50 to 6·75.[120] Higher polymers are formed at lower pH values.[2]

TABLE 12

Kinetic data for the base decomposition of homo- and hetero-polyacids of Mo(VI) and W(VI) (k_a and k_b are defined by the rate equation (10))

Polyanion	k_b (25°C) (M^{-1} s^{-1})	$\Delta H_b^{\ddagger}$ (kJ mol^{-1})	$\Delta S_b^{\ddagger}$ (J K^{-1} mol^{-1})	k_a (25°C) (s^{-1})	Medium	Ref.
$Mo_7O_{24}^{6-}$	$1\cdot96 \times 10^4$	64 ± 8	$+54 \pm 12$	20 ± 5	2·0 M LiCl	[123]
	$1\cdot03 \times 10^4$	56 ± 4	$+21 \pm 4$	9 ± 2.5	2·0 M NaCl	[123, 124]
	$8\cdot2 \times 10^3$	59 ± 4	$+21 \pm 4$	$2\cdot5 \pm 5$	2·0 M KCl	[123]
	$1\cdot43 \times 10^4$	61.7		$12\cdot7$	1·0 M NaCl	[124, 125, 126]
	$9\cdot80 \times 10^3$	58.4		$7\cdot59$	2·0 M NaCl	[124, 125, 126]
	$8\cdot50 \times 10^3$	54.2		$4\cdot72$	3·0 M NaCl	[124, 125, 126]
	$6\cdot20 \times 10^3$	50.0		$3\cdot04$	4·0 M NaCl	[124, 125, 126]
$Mo_8O_{26}^{4-}$				$7\cdot5 \pm 3.8$	1·0 M $NaNO_3$	[120]
$P_2Mo_5O_{23}^{6-}$	$16\cdot7$			$4\cdot9 \times 10^3$	1·0 M $NaNO_3$	[120]
$H_4GeMo_{12}O_{40}$					3·0 M $NaClO_4$	[127]
$H_2W_{12}O_{40}^{6-}$	$0\cdot124^b$			$8\cdot4 \times 10^{-5a}$		[128]
$BW_{12}O_{40}^{5-}$	$0\cdot64$				1·0 M NaCl	[129]
	$0\cdot86$				1·0 M NaCl	[130]
	$1\cdot30$				1·0 M KCl	[130]
$SiW_{12}O_{40}^{4-}$	114	39 ± 4	-71 ± 13		1·0 M LiCl	[130]
	160	33 ± 4	-88 ± 13		1·0 M NaCl	[131]
	203	39 ± 2	-71 ± 4		1·0 M KCl	[131]
$SiW_{11}O_{39}^{8-}$	$1\cdot95 \times 10^{-4}$	77 ± 12	-59 ± 9	1.33×10^{-4}	1·0 M LiCl	[131]
$SiW_9O_{34}^{10-\,c}$	$4\cdot2 \times 10^{-2}$	80 ± 13	-4 ± 14	7.5×10^{-5}	1·0 M KCl	[131]
	$7\cdot8 \times 10^{-3}$	51 ± 4	-113 ± 9		1·0 M NaCl	[131]
	$1\cdot4 \times 10^{-3}$	65 ± 4	-84 ± 5		1·0 M NaCl	[131]
$Te^{VI}\text{-}W_4^{\,d}$	$0\cdot211$ M s^{-1}	39			1·0 M Et_4NCl	[176]

ᵃ Acid-decomposition.
ᵇ At 26°C.
ᶜ Rate constants at 25·8°C.
ᵈ At 41°C. Rate constant for the intermediate species of the decomposition of twelve acids.

In strongly acid solution (0·2 to 3·0 M HClO$_4$), monomer and dimer forms are believed to be in equilibrium, although the precise structure of these is unknown.[121] Rate constants for forward and back reactions in

$$2HMoO_3^+ \rightleftharpoons H_2Mo_2O_6^{2+} \tag{11}$$

have been measured and are $(1·71 \pm 0·01) \times 10^5\,\text{M}^{-1}\,\text{s}^{-1}$ and $(3·20 \pm 0·20) \times 10^3\,\text{s}^{-1}$ at 25°C and $I = 3·0$ M.[122] The participation of further protonated species such as H$_2$MoO$_3^{2+}$ and H$_3$Mo$_2$O$_6^{3+}$ was also indicated.[122] Tungsten forms stable WO$_4^{2-}$ in basic solution, but polymerizes to give dodecatungstate ions at lower pH.[1,2] In the presence of borate, silicate and phosphate, Mo(VI) and W(VI) form stable hetero-polyacids. Table 12 gives the rate of decomposition of homo- and heteropolyacids;[120,123–131] the rates are very different from one species to another. The greater the charge of the polyanion (including dichromate, $\Delta H^{\ddagger} = 20$ kJ mol^{-1})[132], the greater is $\Delta H^{\ddagger}$. Heptamolybdate ions Mo$_7$O$_{24}^{6-}$ give a unique mode of base decomposition among other polyanions including dichromate and decavanadate. Its $\Delta S^{\ddagger}$ is positive and the influence of the cation on the decomposition rate is different from that of others; i.e. K$^+$ < Na$^+$ < Li$^+$ for Mo$_7$O$_{24}^{6-}$.[123] The free anion is much more reactive than is the ion-pair. The size and negativity of the cavity of the polyanion is different from that observed in other cases.[123] Polyanions also decompose in the presence of various nucleophiles such as ammonia and pyridine. Associative attack by nucleophile was proposed for the decomposition of Cr$_2$O$_7^{2-}$ and V$_{10}$O$_{28}^{6-}$ on the basis of negative $\Delta S^{\ddagger}$,[123,124] and similarly for Mo$_7$O$_{24}^{6-}$ on the basis of the relation of decomposition rate to the pK_a of nucleophiles,[126,133] although in this latter case $\Delta S^{\ddagger}$ is positive. The formation of Cr$_2$O$_7^{2-}$ was claimed by Haim to be dissociative on the basis of a free-energy relationship.[97] Further information is required to help settle such a contradictory situation and enable the mechanism to be assigned unequivocally.

Other kinetic studies on the formation and dissociation of hetero-polyanions containing more than three cations have been reported.[135–139]

V. FORMATION OF PEROXO COMPLEXES

Oxo-metal complexes without d electrons, including Cr^{VI}, V^V, Mo^{VI} and Ti^{IV}, react with hydrogen peroxide in aqueous solution, and oxo ligands are replaced by peroxide. The rate of peroxo complex formation is proportional to the concentration of the complex and H$_2$O$_2$ at a constant [H$^+$]. Its dependence on H$^+$ concentration is, however, rather complicated. Table 13 gives rate constants which are independent of H$^+$ concentration as well

TABLE 13

[H⁺]-independent rate constants k_1 and [H⁺]-first-order dependent rate constants k_2 for the formation of peroxo complexes at 25°C

Reactant complex	k_1 (M⁻¹ s⁻¹)	$\Delta H_1^\ddagger$ (kJ mol⁻¹)	$\Delta S_1^\ddagger$ (J K⁻¹ mol⁻¹)	k_2 (M⁻² s⁻¹)	$\Delta H_2^\ddagger$ (kJ mol⁻¹)	$\Delta S_2^\ddagger$ (J K⁻¹ mol⁻¹)	Ref.
Ti(O)$_{aq}^{2+}$	1.2×10^2			50			[141]
Ti^{IV}-ida	176						[145]
Ti^{IV}-nta (tetramer)	170						[145]
Ti^{IV}-dipic	164						[145]
[Ti(O)(edta)]$^{2-}$	53.3^a						[146]
V(O)$_{2(aq)}^+$	4.0×10^{2b}			1.6×10^{3b}			[141]
V^V-dipic	0.39	46 ± 2	-97 ± 9	4.1×10^2	24 ± 1.5	-114 ± 9	[142]
(trimer)	1.1			7.2×10^{3d}	$(23.5)^d$	$(-97)^d$	[143]
[V(O)$_2$(nta)]$^{2-c}$	7.41	39 ± 1	-96 ± 9	1.86×10^4	39 ± 1	-32 ± 9	[142]
[V(O)$_2$(edta)]$^{3-}$				1.5×10^6	47 ± 4	29 ± 8	[144]
[V(O)$_2$(Hedta)]$^{2-}$				4.6×10^4	36 ± 8	-17 ± 10	[144]
[V(O)$_2$(edda)]$^-$	0.27	49 ± 3	-90 ± 5	2.8×10^{4e}			[144]
[V(O)$_2$(medda)]$^-$				2.0×10^3			[144]
HCrO$_4^-$				1.5×10^4			[175]

^{a} Second-order rate constant at pH 4·57.

^{b} At 6°C.

^{c} $\Delta V_1^\ddagger = -3.4 \pm 0.5$ cm³ mol⁻¹, $\Delta V_2^\ddagger = 1.5 \pm 0.5$ cm³ mol⁻¹.

^{d} $k_2 = k_a K : k_{obs} = k_a K[H^+][V(V)]/(1 + K[H^+])$, $\Delta H^\ddagger$ and $\Delta S^\ddagger$ are for k_a.

^{e} $k_2 = K_{OS} k_2'$ (see Equation (12)).

as those which are proportional to it (there are also terms proportional to $[H^+]^2$ and $[H^+]^{-1}$).[141-147]

The structure of the reactant is not always clear. Some are clearly not monomeric; e.g. the vanadium(V) complex of dipic is believed to be a trimer,[143] the complex of Ti(IV) with dipic a polymer, and that with nta^{3-} to be a tetramer in the solid state.[145] It is noted here that the species reacting are not necessarily those found in the solid state; thus a monomer form is the reactant in the case of the Ti^{IV}–dipic complex.[145] The peroxo complexes which are formed are monomeric.

Funahashi *et al.* have analysed the kinetic data for the reaction of $[VO_2(edda)]^-$ and $[V(O)_2(medda)]^-$ and excess H_2O_2.[144] A plot of rate constants k_{obs} against $[H_2O_2]$ deviates from linearity to give saturation at high H_2O_2. From such a relationship k_2 can be expressed by

$$k_2 = k_2' K_{OS}[H_2O_2]/(1 + K_{OS}[H_2O_2]) \qquad (12)$$

where K_{OS} is the formation constant for the precursor species. These were estimated to be 20 and 300 M^{-1} for the medda and edda complexes, respectively, and independent of $[H^+]$. Hence, the precursor species are not simple outer-sphere complexes and the first-order rate constant, k_2', is responsible for the H^+ dependence. It has been presumed that H^+ attaches to one of the oxo ligands of the precursor species, and that H_2O_2 associates with V^V first as a unidentate ligand. The ligating O-atom of H_2O_2 then

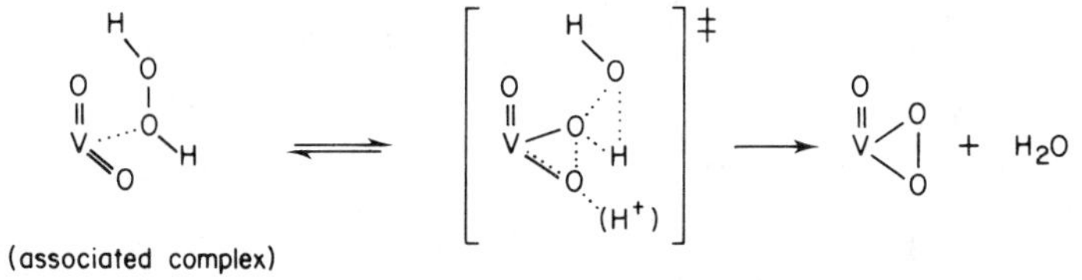

(associated complex)

Fig. 8. A proposed mechanism for peroxo-complex formation of vanadium(V) (from Ref. [147]).

interacts with the protonated oxo with the release of H_2O to give the triangular VO_2 moiety. Confirmation of such a mechanism using ^{18}O labelling techniques would be of interest.

VI. OXO-METAL COMPLEXES WITH MORE THAN TWO d ELECTRONS

These ions have not been studied extensively, and available data are not sufficient to formulate any general ideas of the mechanism of substitution.

TABLE 14

Kinetic data for the ligand exchange reactions of dioxouranium(VI), $trans$-U(O)$_2$L$_n$

L	n	Solvent	k_{ex} (s^{-1})[a]	T (°C)	$\Delta H^{\ddagger}$ (kJ mol^{-1})	$\Delta S^{\ddagger}$ (J K^{-1} mol^{-1})	Ref.
(H$_2$O)$_4$	4	H$_2$O/acetone-d^6	$9 \cdot 80 \times 10^5$	25	41·6 2·1	+8·8 10·9	[153]
(H$_2$O)$_x$(dmso)[b]	–	H$_2$O/dmso	$8 \cdot 42 \times 10^4$	25	24·8 0·4	−68·0 2·5	[153]
(H$_2$O)$_x$Cl[b]	–	H$_2$O/acetone-d^6	$2 \cdot 97 \times 10^4$	25	25·6 0·0	−73·9 0·8	[153]
(H$_2$O)$_x$Br[b]	–	H$_2$O/acetone-d^6	$8 \cdot 49 \times 10^4$	25	28·1 1·7	−56·7 7·6	[153]
dmf	5	CD$_2$Cl$_2$	179	−53	32·3	−52·4	[154]
nma	5	CD$_2$Cl$_2$	176	0	67	+46	[155]
	5	CD$_3$CN	335	0	55·4	+7·0	[155]
tmu	5	CD$_2$Cl$_2$	68	0	80	+83	[156]
	5	CD$_2$CN	77	0	78	+78	[156]
dmso	5	acetone-d^6	273 14	−13	38·9	−47·5	[157]
tmp	5	CD$_2$Cl$_2$	103	−13	24·7	−111	[158]
tep	5	CD$_2$Cl$_2$	32·6	−13	42·3	−52·7	[158]
dmmp	5	CH$_2$Cl$_2$	76	−5	57·9	+8·0	[159]
dma	5	CD$_2$Cl$_2$	83	−13	41·3	−40·7	[160]
Np^V(O)$_2$(CH$_3$OH)$_4^+$	4	CD$_3$OH	$9 \cdot 1 \times 10^4$	0	31·5 1·7	−37·0 2·5	[161]

[a] Values of k_{ex} from Refs. [154–160] are average values of k_{ex} in various reactant concentrations.
[b] H$_2$O exchange.

Trinuclear molybdenum(IV) species, $Mo_3O_4^{4+}$,[148,149] dinuclear oxo-bridged molybdenum(III) complexes,[150,151] and rhenium(IV)[152] have been the subject of recent investigations. Oxygen-exchange studies have provided important information on the behaviour of oxo-metal ions in this category, and will be discussed elsewhere.[24]

VII. SUBSTITUTION OF URANIUM(VI) COMPLEXES

A. Ligand exchange

Among the actinide elements quinque- and sexa-valent cations of U, Np, Pu and Am have MO_2^+ and MO_2^{2+} species, respectively, in which the oxo groups are *trans* to each other and the other ligands occupy the basal site (coordination number, 6–8). Rate constants for oxo exchange, it seems,

TABLE 15
Formation, k_f, and dissociation, k_d, rate constants for dioxouranium(VI) complexes in aqueous solution

Ligand	T (°C)	k_f ($M^{-1} s^{-1}$)	k_d (s^{-1})	Ref.
SO_4^{2-}	20	180	3·6	[162]
CH_2ClCOO^-	20	110	4·4	[162]
NCS^-	20	290		[162]
CH_3COO^-	20	1050	4·4	[162]
PAR	25	$3·64 \times 10^5$		[163]
Htta	25	$\geqslant 1 \times 10^4$		[164]
tta^- (enolate)	25	$\geqslant 3 \times 10^5$		[164]
Hacac (keto)	25	3·6		[165]
Hacac (enol)	25	5330		[165]
Htfac (enol)	25	$\geqslant 1·3 \times 10^3$		[165]
$tfac^-$ (enolate)	25	$\geqslant 1·6 \times 10^4$		[165]
UO_2^+	25	116		[166]

have not been investigated, and substitution at the basal site has been most studied with U^{VI}; see the summary in Tables 14[153–161] and 15[162–166]. Rate constants for ligand exchange (Table 14) are in the range from 10^2 to $10^5 s^{-1}$ at room temperature and are independent of concentration of free ligand.[153–160] A purely dissociative mechanism is proposed for the substitution of complexes with coordination number 7.[154–160] Exchange of a water, however, is believed to proceed by an I_d mechanism, since an intermediate with a trigonal bipyrimidal structure is not feasible.[153] Independence of the rate on water concentration ($1 \cdot 80$–$3 \cdot 50$ M) was explained by saturation of outer-sphere complex formation.[153]

For the reactions of complexes with coordination number 7, an isokinetic relationship holds between $\Delta H^{\ddagger}$ and $\Delta S^{\ddagger}$.[155,158] However, no correlation is seen between donor number and other solvent parameters, and kinetic parameters such as k_{ex} and $\Delta H^{\ddagger}$ which are obtained.[155] The isokinetic plot lies between those for Al^{3+} and bivalent cations such as Ni^{2+}. It has been suggested that the surface charge at the basal site of UO_2^{2+} is between that of Al^{3+} and divalent cations, and is similar to that of $V^{IV}O^{2+}$.[153]

B. Complex formation

Substitution rate constants in aqueous solution (Table 15) have a range of 10^4, and the rate law is rather complicated. Hence k_f values should be compared with some care. Exchange of water suggests a dissociative rate-determining step.[153] However, when second-order rate constants are compared, $k_f = K_{OS}k_s$; k_s values are smaller than for water exchange by a few orders for both uni- and bi-valent anions.

Substitution of $UO_2(\text{tributylphosphine})_2(NO_3)_2$ with dimethylcarbazone and oxine in benzene solvent gives second-order rate constants of the order of magnitude 10 M^{-1} s^{-1} for both forward and back reactions.[167,168] These reactions are accelerated by the addition of water and alcohols.[169] The formation of β-diketonate complexes is also accelerated in mixtures of water/methanol[165] as compared with pure methanol.

The complex $UO_2(\text{thf})(\text{hfac})_2$ gives two ^{19}F NMR signals at room temperature, indicating that both organic ligands occupy the basal sites to give coordination number 7. The peaks coalesce at higher temperatures in a mixture of CD_2Cl_2 (90%), methylcyclohexane and isopentane. The rate constant is $\sim 10^3$ s^{-1} at 30°C, and an intramolecular migration mechanism is suggested.[170]

Rate constants for substitution on UO_2^{2+} are fairly large despite the high charge of U^{VI}. The oxo groups seem to have a big influence by neutralizing the high charge and providing some kind of labilizing effect.

VIII. SUMMARY

The presence of oxo ligands has not only labilizing effect, but also characteristic regioselectivity as has been most clearly demonstrated for the reactions of V(IV) and Mo(V). Oxo-metal complexes reveal quite different features in their ligand substitutions as compared to low-valent metal ions.

Figure 9 shows the relationship between apparent second-order rate

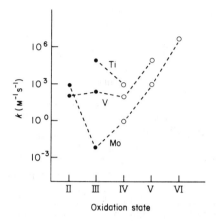

Fig. 9. Relationship between the substitution rate and the oxidation state for titanium, vanadium, and molybdenum. Data sources other than those mentioned in the text are Ti(III) (Ref. [171]), V(II) (Ref. [172]), V(III) (Ref. [173]), Mo(II) (Ref. [53]), and Mo(III) (Ref. [174]). Open circles indicate oxo species.

constants and oxidation number of the central metal atoms for three metals Ti, V and Mo. Complexes of $V^{IV}O^{2+}$ exhibit a marked regioselectivity, when rate constants for anation of unidentate ligands at the "basal site" are considered. This possibly represents the rate of migration from the apical to the basal site. The data for $Ti^{IV}O^{2+}$ may be similarly understood. The result indicated for Mo^{IV} is for a ternuclear species bridged by oxo groups, whereas data for Mo^{V} are for dinuclear species with two oxo bridges. The reaction of Mo(VI) involves substitution of an oxo ligand, while other oxo-metal ions involve replacement of other than oxo ligands.

Figure 9 shows general tendencies; substitution rate constants decrease initially as the oxidation number increases giving the smallest values for the quadrivalent state (except for Mo^{III} with d^3 configuration), and then increase again as the oxidation number increases further. This increase of substitution rate constants clearly parallels the increase in number of oxo ligands coordinated to the metal.

REFERENCES

[1] Cotton, F.A.; Wilkinson, G. "Advanced Inorganic Chemistry", 4th edn.; Wiley, New York, 1980.

[2] Kepert, D.L. "The Early Transition Metals"; Academic Press, New York and London, 1972.

[3] Selbin, J. *Chem. Rev.* **1965**, *65*, 153; *Coord. Chem. Rev.* **1966**, *1*, 293; Syamal, A. *Coord. Chem. Rev.* **1975**, *16*, 309.

[4] Stiefel, E.I. *Progr. Inorg. Chem.* **1976**, *22*, 1.

[5] Spivack, B.; Dori, Z. *Coord. Chem. Rev.* **1975**, *17*, 99.

[6] Rouschias, G. *Chem. Rev.* **1974**, *74*, 531.

[7] Basolo, F.; Pearson, R.G. "Mechanism of Inorganic Reactions"; Wiley: New York, 1967.

[8] McAuley, A.; Hill, J. *Quart. Rev.* **1969**, *23*, 18.

[9] Swaddle, T.W. *Coord. Chem. Rev.* **1974**, *14*, 217.

[10] Edwards, J.O.; Monacelli, F.; Ortaggi, G. *Inorg. Chim. Acta* **1974**, *11*, 47.

[11] Martin D.S. *Inorg. Chim. Acta Rev.* **1967**, *1*, 87.

[12] Cattalini, L. *Progr. Inorg. Chem.* **1970**, *13*, 263.

[13] Ohtaki, H.; Tanaka, M.; Funahashi, S. "Yoekihanno no Kagaku (Chemistry of Reactions in Solution)"; Gakkaishuppan-center, Tokyo, 1977.

[14] Saito, K; Sasaki, Y.; Kido, H.; Nagasawa, A.; Ogino, K; In "Mukikagaku-zensho; Coordination Compounds"; Yamatera H. and Yamasaki K., Eds; Maruzen: Tokyo, 1981; Part II, p. 227.

[15] Langford, C.H.; Gray, H.B. "Ligand Substitution Process"; Benjamin: New York, 1965.

[16] Ducommun, Y.; Newman, K.E.; Merbach, A.E. *Inorg. Chem.* **1980**, *19*, 3696.

[17] Meyer, F.K.; Newman, K.E.; Merbach, A.E. *J. Am. Chem. Soc.* **1979**, *101*, 5588.

[18] Yatsimirskii, K.B. *Pure Appl. Chem.* **1974**, *38*, 341.

[19] Hartley, F.R. *Chem. Soc. Rev.* **1973**, *2*, 163.

[20] Tobe, M.L. "Inorganic Reaction Mechanisms"; Nelson: London, 1972.

[21] Wilkins, R.G. "The Study of Kinetics and Mechanisms of Reactions of Transition Metal Complexes"; Allyn and Bacon: Boston, 1974.

[22] Poon, C.K. *Coord. Chem. Rev.* **1973**, *10*, 1.

[23] Margerum, D.W.; Cayley, G.R.; Weatherburn, D.C.; Pagenkopf, G.K. In "Coordination Chemistry"; Martell A.E., Ed.; American Chemical Society, 1978; Vol. 2, p. 1.

[24] Gamsjäger, H.; Murmann, R.K. Review to be published in this series.

[25] Rosseinsky, R.D. *Chem. Rev.* **1972**, *72*, 215.

[26] Murmann, R.K. *Inorg. Chim. Acta* **1981**, *49*, 11.

[27] Reuben, J.; Fiat, D. *Inorg. Chem.* **1977**, *25*, 443.

[28] Wüthrich, K.; Connick, R.E. *Inorg. Chem.* **1967**, *6*, 583.

[29] Copenhafer, W.C.; Rieger, P.H. *Inorg. Chem.* **1977**, *16*, 2431.

[30] Jordan, R.B.; Angerman, N.S. *J. Chem. Phys.* **1968**, *48*, 3983.

[31] Angerman, N.S.; Jordan, R.B. *Inorg. Chem.* **1969**, *8*, 65.

[32] Angerman, N.S.; Jordan, R.B. *Inorg. Chem.* **1969**, *8*, 1824.

[33] Tomiyasu, H.; Dreyer, K.; Gordon, G. *Inorg. Chem.* **1972**, *11*, 2409.

[34] Tomiyasu, H.; Ito, S.; Tagami, S. *Bull. Chem. Soc. Japan.* **1974**, *47*, 2843.

[35] Nishizawa, M.; Saito, K. *Bull. Chem. Soc. Japan* **1978**, *51*, 483.

[36] Walker, F.A.; Carlin, R.L.; Rieger, P.H. *J. Chem. Phys.* **1966**, *45*, 4181.

[37] Zeltmann, A.H.; Morgan, L.O. *Inorg. Chem.* **1971**, *10*, 2739.

[38] Strehlow, H.; Wendt, A. *Inorg. Chem.* **1963**, *2*, 6.

[39] Schlund, A.; Wendt, H. *Ber. Bunsenges. Phys. Chem.* **1968**, *72*, 652.

[40] Kustin, K.; Pizer, R. *Inorg. Chem.* **1970**, *9*, 1536.

[41] Hoffman, H.; Ulbricht, W. *Ber. Bunsenges. Phys. Chem.* **1972**, *76*, 1052.

[42] Che, T.M.; Kustin, K. *Inorg. Chem.* **1980**, *19*, 2275.
[43] Hynes, M.J.; O'Regan, B.D. *J. Chem. Soc., Dalton Trans.* **1980**, 7.
[44] Nishizawa, M.; Saito, K. *Inorg. Chem.* **1978**, *17*, 3676.
[45] Nishizawa, M.; Saito, K. *Inorg. Chem.* **1980**, *19*, 2284.
[46] Nishizawa, M.; Nirotsu, K.; Ooi, S.; Saito, K. *J. Chem. Soc., Chem. Commun.* **1979**, 707.
[47] Fuoss, R.M. *J. Am. Chem. Soc.* **1958**, *80*, 5059.
[48] Tomiyasu, H.; Gordon, G. *Inorg. Chem.* **1976**, *15*, 870.
[49] Ooi, S.; Nishizawa, M.; Matsumoto, K.; Kuroya, H.; Saito, K. *Bull. Chem. Soc. Japan.* **1979**, *52*, 452.
[50] Nishizawa, M.; Saito, K. *Bull. Chem. Soc. Japan.* **1980**, *53*, 664.
[51] Saito, K. *In* "Coordination Chemistry-20 (IUPAC)", Banerjea, D. Ed.; Pergamon Press: Oxford, 1980; p. 173.
[52] Wüthrich, K., Connick, R.E. *Inorg. Chem.* **1968**, *7*, 1377.
[53] Teramoto, K.; Sasaki, Y.; Migita, K.; Iwaizaumi, M.; Saito, K. *Bull. Chem. Soc. Japan.* **1979**, *52*, 446.
[54] Anaya, T.M.; Tapscott, R.E. *Inorg. Chim. Acta* **1981**, *49*, 11.
[55] Ardon, M.; Pernick, A. *Inorg. Chem.* **1973**, *12*, 2484.
[56] Garner, C.D.; Hyde, M.R.; Mabbs, F.E.; Routledge, V.I. *J. Chem. Soc., Dalton Trans.* **1975**, 1175.
[57] Hyde, M.R.; Garner, C.D. *J. Chem. Soc., Dalton Trans.* **1975**, 1186.
[58] Garner, C.D.; Hyde, M.R.; Mabbs, F.E. *Nature* **1975**, *253*, 623.
[59] Garner, C.D.; Hyde, M.R.; Mabbs, F.E.; Routledge, V.I. *J. Chem. Soc., Dalton Trans.* **1975**, 1180.
[60] Garner, C.D.; Hyde, M.R.; Mabbs, F.E.; Routledge, V.I. *Nature* **1974**, *252*, 579.
[61] Garner, C.D.; Hyde, M.R.; Mabbs, F.E.; Routledge, V.I. *J. Chem. Soc., Dalton Trans.*, **1977**, 1198.
[62] Sasaki, Y.; Taylor, R.S.; Sykes, A.G. *J. Chem. Soc., Dalton Trans.* **1975**, 396.
[63] Cayley, G.R.; Sykes, A.G. *Inorg. Chem.* **1976**, *15*, 2882.
[64] Armstrong, F.A.; Shibahara, T.; Sykes, A.G. *Inorg. Chem.* **1978**, *17*, 189.
[65] Cotton, F.A.; Morehouse, S.M. *Inorg. Chem.* **1965**, *4*, 1377.
[66] McDonald, W.S. *Acta Cryst.* **1978**, B*34*, 2850.
[67] Sasaki, Y. **1976**; unpublished observation.
[68] Sasaki, Y.; Sykes, A.G. *J. Chem. Soc., Dalton Trans.* **1974**, 1468.
[69] Sasaki, Y.; Morita, T.S. *Bull. Chem. Soc. Japan.* **1977**, *50*, 1637.
[70] Sasaki, Y.; Sykes, A.G. *J. Less-Common Metals* **1974**, *36*, 125.
[71] Murmann, R.K. *Inorg. Chem.* **1980**, *19*, 1765.
[72] Cayley, G.R.; Taylor, R.S.; Wharton, R.K.; Sykes, A.G. *Inorg. Chem.* **1977**, *16*, 1377.
[73] Sasaki, Y. *Bull. Chem. Soc. Japan.* **1977**, *50*, 1939.
[74] Soares, A.B.; Taylor, R.C.; Sykes, A.G. *J. Chem. Soc., Dalton Trans.* **1980**, 1101.
[75] Ellis, J.D.; Thompson, G.A.K.; Sykes, A.G. *Inorg. Chem.* **1976**, *15*, 3172.
[76] Thompson, G.A.K.; Taylor, R.S.; Sykes, A.G. *Inorg. Chem.* **1977**, *16*, 2880.
[77] Mal'kova, T.V.; Fomina, L.A. *Russ. J. Inorg. Chem.* **1974**, *19*, 377.
[78] Lagrange, J.; Lagrange, P. *Bull. Soc. Chim. Fr.* **1972**, 19.
[79] Lagrange, J.; Lagrange, P. *Bull. Soc. Chim. Fr.* **1975**, 1460.
[80] Yamada, S.; Ukei, Y.; Tanaka, M. *Inorg. Chem.* **1976**, *15*, 964.

[81] Kustin, K.; Liu, S.-T.; Nicolini, C.; Toppen, D.L. *J. Am. Chem. Soc.* **1974**, *96*, 7410.

[82] Kustin, K.; Toppen, D.L. *J. Am. Chem. Soc.* **1973**, *95*, 3564.

[83] Murmann, R.K. *Inorg. Chem.* **1977**, *16*, 46.

[84] Ferguson, J.H.; Kustin, K. *Inorg. Chem.* **1979**, *18*, 3349.

[85] Gilbert, K.; Kustin, K. *J. Am. Chem. Soc.* **1976**, *98*, 5502.

[86] Zare, K.; Lagrange, J.; Lagrange, P. *Inorg. Chem.* **1979**, *18*, 568.

[87] White, P.J.; Kaus, M.J.; Edwards, J.O.; Rieger, P.H. *J. Chem. Soc., Chem. Commun.* **1976**, 429.

[88] Yuchi, A.; Muranaka, H.; Yamada, S.; Tanaka, M. *Bull. Chem. Soc. Japan.* **1980**, *53*, 1560.

[89] Yuchi, A.; Yagishita, S.; Yamada, S.; Tanaka, M. *Bull. Chem. Soc. Japan.* **1981**, *54*, 200.

[90] Frennesson, S.A.; Beattie, J.K.; Haight, Jr., G.P. *J. Am. Chem. Soc.* **1968**, *90*, 6018.

[91] Frennesson, S.A.; Beattie, J.K.; Haight, Jr., G.P. *Acta Chem. Scand.* **1969**, *23*, 3277.

[92] Lin, C.; Beattie, J.K. *J. Am. Chem. Soc.* **1972**, *94*, 3011.

[93] Muirhead, K.A.; Haight, Jr., G.P.; Beattie, J.K. *J. Am. Chem. Soc.* **1972**, *94*, 3006.

[94] Pladziewicz, J.; Espenson, J.H. *Inorg. Chem.* **1971**, *10*, 634.

[95] Swinehart, J.H.; Castellan, G.W. *Inorg. Chem.* **1974**, *3*, 278.

[96] Okumura, A.; Kitani, M.; Toyomi, Y.; Okazaki, N. *Bull. Chem. Soc. Japan.* **1980**, *53*, 3143.

[97] Haim, A. *Inorg. Chem.* **1972**, *11*, 3147.

[98] Akena, A.M.; Brown, D.S.; Tuck, D.G. *Can. J. Chem.* **1971**, *49*, 1505.

[99] Knowles, P.F.; Diebler, H. *Trans. Faraday Soc.* **1968**, *64*, 977.

[100] Diebler, H.; Timms, R.E. *J. Chem. Soc. A* **1971**, 273.

[101] Kustin, K.; Liu, S.-T. *J. Am. Chem. Soc.* **1973**, *95*, 2487.

[102] Honig, D.S.; Kustin, K. *J. Am. Chem. Soc.* **1973**, *95*, 5525.

[103] Funahashi, S.; Kato, Y.; Nakayama, M.; Tanaka, M. *Inorg. Chem.* **1981**, *20*, 1752.

[104] Taylor, R.S. *Inorg. Chem.* **1977**, *16*, 116.

[105] Gamsjäger, H.; Thompson, G.A.K.; Sagmüller, W.; Sykes, A.G. *Inorg. Chem.* **1980**, *19*, 997.

[106] Harmer, M.A.; Sykes, A.G. *Inorg. Chem.* **1980**, *19*, 2881.

[107] Honig, D.S.; Kustin, K. *J. Phys. Chem.* **1972**, *76*, 1575.

[108] Cruywagen, J.J. *Inorg. Chem.* **1980**, *19*, 552; Cruywagen, J.J.; Rohwer, E.F.C.H. *Inorg. Chem.* **1975**, *14*, 3136.

[109] Collin, J.-P.; Lagrange, P. *Bull. Soc. Chim. Fr.* **1976**, 1304.

[110] Craven, B.M.; Ramey, K.C.; Wise, W.B. *Inorg. Chem.* **1971**, *10*, 2626.

[111] Pinnavaia, T.J.; Clements, W.R. *Inorg. Nucl. Chem. Lett.* **1971**, *7*, 1127.

[112] Tytko, K.-H.; Glemser, O. *Adv. Inorg. Radiochem.* **1976**, *19*, 139.

[113] Schwarzenbach, G.; Geier, G. *Helv. Chim. Acta* **1963**, *46*, 906.

[114] Clare, B.W.; Kepert, D.L.; Watts, D.W. *J. Chem. Soc., Dalton Trans.* **1973**, 2479, 2481.

[115] Druskovich, D.M.; Kepert, D.L. *J. Chem. Soc., Dalton Trans.* **1975**, 947.

[116] Goddard, J.B.; Gonas, A.M. *Inorg. Chem.* **1973**, *12*, 574.

[117] Voissat, B. *Bull. Soc. Chim. Fr.* **1975**, 1111.

[118] Heath, E.; Howarth, O.W. *J. Chem. Soc., Dalton Trans.* **1981**, 1105.

[119] Whittaker, M.P.; Asay, J.; Eyring, E.M. *J. Phys. Chem.* **1966**, *70*, 1005.

[120] Honig, D.S.; Kustin, K. *Inorg. Chem.* **1972**, *11*, 65.
[121] Krumenacker, L. *Ann. Chim.* **1972**, *7*, 425.
[122] Ojo, J.F.; Taylor, R.S.; Sykes, A.G. *J. Chem. Soc.*, *Dalton Trans.* **1975**, 500.
[123] Druskovich, D.M.; Kepert, D.L. *Aust. J. Chem.* **1975**, *28*, 2365.
[124] Lagrange, P.; Schwing, J.-P. *Bull. Soc. Chim. Fr.* **1970**, 1340.
[125] Collin, J.-P.; Lagrange, P. *Bull. Soc. Chim. Fr.* **1974**, 777.
[126] Collin, J.-P.; Lagrange, P.; Lagrange, J.-P. *J. Less-Common Metals* **1974**, *36*, 117.
[127] Mellstrom, R.; Ingri, N. *Acta Chem. Scand.* **1974**, A*28*, 703.
[128] Biquard, M.; Souchay, P. *Ann. Chim.* **1975**, *10*, 163.
[129] Glemser, O.; Holznagel, W.; Holtje, W. *Z. Anorg. Allg. Chem.* **1966**, *342*, 75.
[130] Kepert, D.L.; Kyle, J.H. *J. Chem. Soc.*, *Dalton Trans.* **1978**, 1781.
[131] Kepert, D.L.; Kyle, J.H. *J. Chem. Soc.*, *Dalton Trans.* **1978**, 137.
[132] Clare, B.W.; Druskovich, D.M.; Kepert, D.L.; Kyle, J.H. *Aust. J. Chem.* **1977**, *30*, 211.
[133] Collin, J.-P.; Lagrange, P. *Bull. Soc. Chim. Fr.* **1974**, 773.
[134] Moore, P.; Kettle, S.F.A.; Wilkins, R.G. *Inorg. Chem.* **1966**, *5*, 220.
[135] Smith, D.P.; Pope, M.T. *Inorg. Chem.* **1973**, *12*, 331.
[136] Hunt, Jr., R.W.; Hargis, L.G. *Anal. Chem.* **1977**, *49*, 779.
[137] Cadiot, M.; Volfovsky, C. *Rev. Chim. Min.* **1975**, *12*, 493.
[138] Dauzonne, D.; Fournier, M. *Compt. Rend.* **1974**, *279*, C, 37.
[139] Souchay, P.; Salamon-Bertho, G. *Compt. Rend.* **1972**, *274*, C, 1677.
[140] Connor, J.A.; Ebsworth, E.A.V. *Adv. Inorg. Chem. Radiochem.* **1964**, *6*, 279.
[141] Orhanovič, M.; Wilkins, R.G. *J. Am. Chem. Soc.* **1967**, *89*, 278.
[142] Funahashi, S.; Haraguchi, K.; Tanaka, M. *Inorg. Chem.* **1977**, *16*, 1349.
[143] Wieghardt, K. *Inorg. Chem.* **1978**, *17*, 57.
[144] Funahashi, S.; Midorikawa, T.; Tanaka, M. *Inorg. Chem.* **1980**, *19*, 91.
[145] Wieghardt, K.; Quilitzsch, U.; Weiss, J.; Nuber, B. *Inorg. Chem.* **1980**, *19*, 2514.
[146] Kristine, F.J.; Shepherd, R.E. *J. Chem. Soc.*, *Chem. Commun.* **1980**, 132.
[147] Funahashi, S.; Ishihara, K.; Tanaka, M. *Inorg. Chem.* **1981**, *20*, 51; *Inorg. Chim. Acta* **1979**, *35*, L351.
[148] Ojo, F.; Sasaki, Y.; Taylor, R.S.; Sykes, A.G. *Inorg. Chem.* **1976**, *15*, 1006.
[149] Murmann, R.K.; Shelton, M.E. *J. Am. Chem. Soc.* **1980**, *102*, 3984.
[150] Wajda, S.; Kurzak, B. *Bull. Acad. Polon. Sci.*, *Ser. Sci. Chim.* **1978**, *26*, 709; *Polish J. Chem.* **1980**, *54*, 179, 2131.
[151] Wajda, S.; Bezak, E. *Bull. Acad. Polon. Sci.*, *Ser. Sci. Chim.* **1975**, *23*, 943; *ibid.* **1977**, *25*, 101.
[152] Wajda, S.; Hyla-Kryspin, I. *Nukleonika* **1974**, *19*, 511.
[153] Ikeda, Y.; Soya, S.; Fukutomi, H.; Tomiyasu, H. *J. Inorg. Nucl. Chem.* **1979**, *41*, 1333.
[154] Bowen, R.P.; Honan, G.J.; Lincoln, S.F.; Spotwood, T.M.; Williams, E.H. *Inorg. Chem. Acta* **1979**, *33*, 235.
[155] Honan, G.J.; Lincoln, S.F.; Williams, E.H.; Spotwood, T.M. *J. Chem. Soc.*, *Dalton Trans.* **1979**, 1220.
[156] Honan, G.J.; Lincoln, S.F.; Williams, E.H. *J. Chem. Soc.*, *Dalton Trans.* **1979**, 320.
[157] Honan, G.J.; Lincoln, S.F.; Williams, E.H. *J. Solution Chem.* **1978**, *7*, 443.

[158] Crea, J.; Digiusto, R.; Lincoln, S.F.; Williams, E.H. *Inorg. Chem.* **1977**, *16*, 2825.
[159] Crea, J.; Lincoln, S.F.; Williams, E.H. *Aust. J. Chem.* **1976**, *29*, 2183.
[160] Bowen, R.P.; Lincoln, S.F.; Williams, E.H. *Inorg. Chem.* **1976**, *15*, 2126.
[161] Sheppard, J.C.; Burdett, J.L. *Inorg. Chem.* **1966**, *5*, 921.
[162] Hurwitz, P.; Kustin, K. *J. Phys. Chem.* **1967**, *71*, 324.
[163] Ekstrom, A.; Johnson, D.A. *J. Inorg. Nucl. Chem.* **1974**, *36*, 2549.
[164] Hynes, M.J.; O'Regan, B.D. *J. Chem. Soc., Dalton Trans.* **1976**, 1200.
[165] Hynes, M.J.; O'Regan, B.D. *J. Chem. Soc., Dalton Trans.* **1980**, 1502.
[166] Whittaker, M P.; Eyring, E.M.; Dibble, E. *J. Phys. Chem.* **1965**, *69*, 2319.
[167] Egozy, Y.; Weiss, S. *J. Inorg. Nucl. Chem.* **1976**, *38*, 1717.
[168] Mazurek, K.; Egozy, Y.; Weiss, S. *J. Inorg. Nucl. Chem.* **1979**, *41*, 1023.
[169] Mazurek, K.; Egozy, Y.; Weiss, S. *J. Inorg. Nucl. Chem.* **1976**, *38*, 1335.
[170] Kramer, G.M.; Dines, M.B.; Kastrup, R; Melchior, M.T.; Maas, Jr., E.T. *Inorg. Chem.* **1981**, *20*, 3.
[171] Chmelnick, A.M.; Fiat, D. *J. Chem. Phys.* **1969**, *51*, 4238.
[172] Olson, M.; Kanazawa, Y.; Taube, H. *J. Chem. Phys.* **1969**, *51*, 289.
[173] Chmelnick, A.M.; Fiat, D. *J. Magn. Reson.* **1972**, *8*, 325.
[174] Sasaki, Y.; Sykes, A.G. *J. Chem. Soc., Dalton Trans.* **1975**, 1048.
[175] Furahashi, S.; Uchida, F.; Tanaka, M. *Inorg. Chem.* **1978**, *27*, 2784.
[176] Babnova, L.A.; Nikitina, T.K.; Ganelina, E.Sh. *Russ. J. Inorg. Chem.* **1977**, *22*, 707.

Rates and Mechanism of Reaction for Elements in Groups I–III

J.C. Lockhart

Department of Inorganic Chemistry
The University of Newcastle upon Tyne

I. INTRODUCTION

A comparison of the outline of this review on reactions of Main Group elements with an overview of mechanistic work on the three lightest elements Li, Be, B made in 1974 shows the profile of published work to have altered dramatically. The emphasis previously[1] was almost entirely

217

on boron, and kinetic data for alkali metals heavier than lithium were almost nonexistent. Interestingly, mechanistic distinctions were based on spectroscopic, stereochemical and isotopic labelling as much as on kinetics. Now the emphasis is on the alkali and alkaline earth metals and there is much more kinetic work, the natural result of the increasing availability of fast reaction techniques which can be applied to the alkali metals and their generally labile coordination spheres, and of the boost given by discoveries of ionophoric ligands (natural and synthetic)[2,3] to the chemistry of Groups I and II. The lack of spectroscopic features of the s block elements, in contrast to the d block metals, as detailed by Williams[4] (and bewailed by alkalophiles), is amply made up by those of the ligands. Indeed, direct NMR studies of the alkali metals themselves, based on improved understanding of the basis of quadrupolar relaxation,[5–7] and greatly improved NMR technology, today form a major investigating technique. The accessibility of computers likewise has had its impact on the calculation of potential energy surfaces by molecular orbital methods, particularly for the light s and p block elements, which are more reliably parametrized. It was certainly timely that so many new techniques for the determination of mechanism should find application in this somewhat neglected area of the Periodic Table.

This chapter ranges over the elements Li–Cs, Mg–Ba, B–Tl and includes other M^{3+} ions (Eu^{3+}, Gd^{3+}) where a comparison is relevant. In addition to work on macrocycles and alkali cations, it also covers aspects of Group III chemistry, such as free radical substitutions, hydroboration and elimination reactions, new departures in the complex story of the alkyl-lithium aggregates and Grignard formation. Work reported on octahedral substitution at Group III centres is more naturally treated as a facet of octahedral substitution and has been omitted. Mechanistic papers on biological aspects of Ca and Mg chemistry are not in general included. Much of the report is arranged by Periodic Table grouping, except where work for several elements with particular ligands is more conveniently discussed in one place.

Recent reviews pertinent to this general area are on boron photochemistry (Porter and Turbini),[8] four-centre reactions, including boron redistributions (Bauer),[9] application of NMR of the quadrupolar nuclei ^{43}Ca and ^{25}Mg (Forsen and Lindman)[7] and ^{23}Na (Laszlo)[10] to chemical problems, solution studies of alkali cations (Popov)[11] and aspects of macrocyclic chemistry (Reinhoudt and de Jong),[12] including kinetic studies (Liesegang and Eyring)[14] and kinetic studies involving the alkali metal cations (Burgermeister and Winkler-Oswatitsch).[13] A new series reviewing macrocyclic chemistry has appeared.[15]

II. RATES AND MECHANISM IN GROUP IA CHEMISTRY

A. Macrocyclic ligands

A number of macrocyclic and other ligands are represented in Formulae I–XXX. The correct IUPAC nomenclature for many of these systems is rather pedantic. The simplest ligand shown (I) is strictly known as 1,4,7,10-tetraoxacyclododecane, and a more complex one such as XII should be called 15,15′-nonamethylenedinitrilodimethylidynebis-(2,3,5,6,8,9,11,12-octahydro-1,4,7,10,13-benzopentaoxacyclopentadecin).

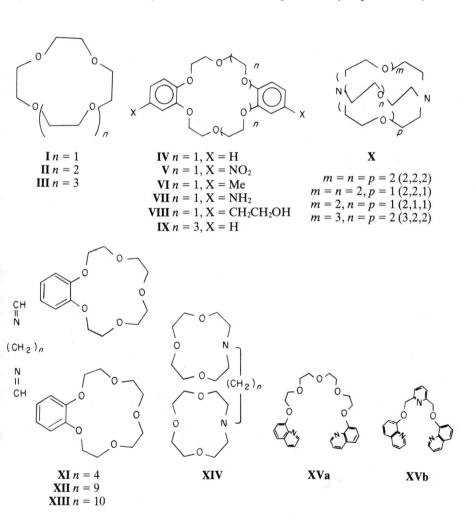

I $n = 1$
II $n = 2$
III $n = 3$

IV $n = 1, X = H$
V $n = 1, X = NO_2$
VI $n = 1, X = Me$
VII $n = 1, X = NH_2$
VIII $n = 1, X = CH_2CH_2OH$
IX $n = 3, X = H$

X

$m = n = p = 2\ (2,2,2)$
$m = n = 2, p = 1\ (2,2,1)$
$m = 2, n = p = 1\ (2,1,1)$
$m = 3, n = p = 2\ (3,2,2)$

XI $n = 4$
XII $n = 9$
XIII $n = 10$

XIV

XVa

XVb

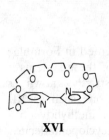

XVI

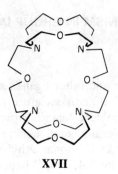

XVII

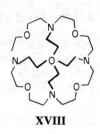

XVIII

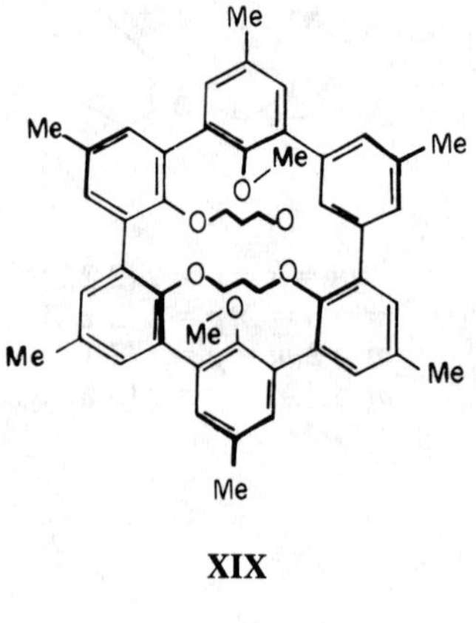

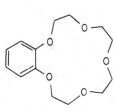

XIX

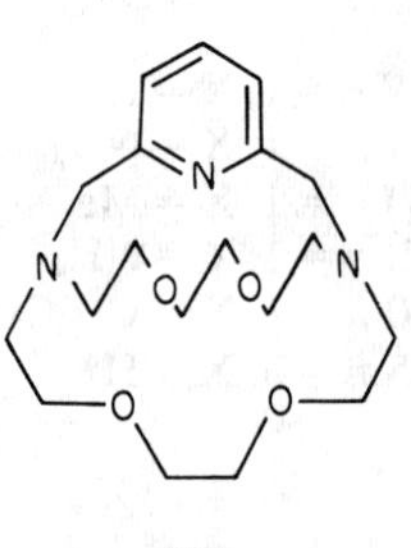

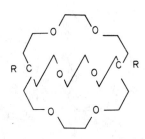

XX

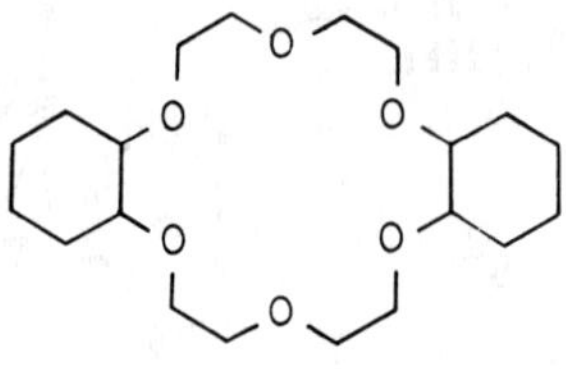

XXI

XXII

XXIV R = PhCH₂OCH₂

XXIII R = Me

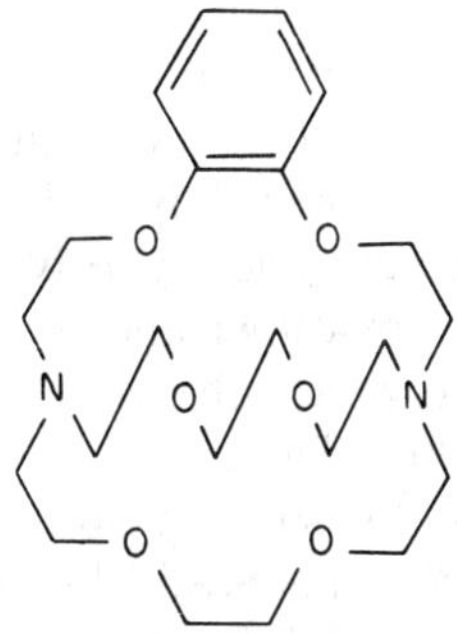

XXV

(2, 2, 2)B

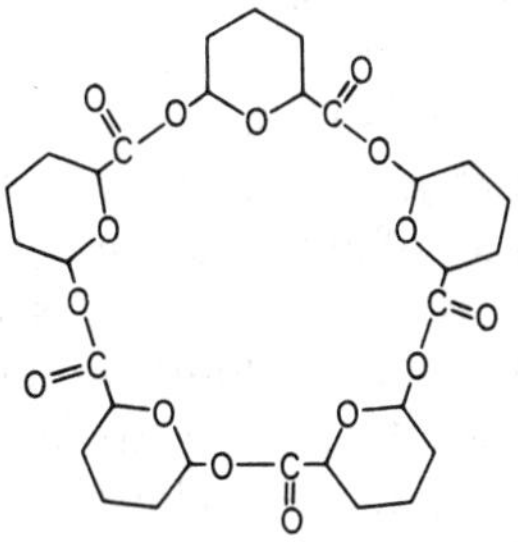

XXVI

cyclo-(L-Lac-L-Val-D-Hyv-D-Val)$_3$ cyclo-(L-Pro-L-Val-D-Pro-D-Val)$_3$

cyclo-(L-Pro-L-Val-D-Ala-D-Val)$_3$

XXVII   **XXIX**

XXVIII

XXX

Understandably, only those with a penchant for nomenclature care to use these forms. Trivial names, often descriptive of the overall shape suggested by molecular models, have been devised for many ligands, after the example set by Pedersen,[2] who named ligand IV a "crown" compound. Compounds I–IX, XXI and XXII are crowns. Compounds such as X, XVII, XVIII, XX, XXIII–XXV were called cryptands by Lehn, to describe their potential to provide a three-dimensional cavity (which, with oxygen dipoles inward, and metal *englobé* (enclosed) was then termed metal cryptate). Compounds XI–XIV are known as clams, or sometimes, bis-crowns, while XVIII and XIX are spherands. Compounds XXVII–XXIX are often referred to by trivial names, XXVII being a naturally occurring cyclodepsipeptide, known as valinomycin. The trivial names, accompanied by reference to the formula number, are used in this review.

1. Interactions with macrocyclic ligands

The problems addressed here are to explain the behaviour of alkali cations, not merely in a single solvent phase, but also in multiple phases, a fundamental question being the role of biological membranes in maintaining the K^+/Na^+ discrimination in living cells. The answers being sought are structural, thermodynamic and kinetic. While the functioning of, for example, the Na^+/K^+ ATPase of the "sodium pump" is understood in a stoichiometric sense, even the structure of the enzyme is poorly established and the sites of alkali cation involvement are not known and are the subject of much speculation. This is a system for which chemical models are advantageous in building a preliminary picture. The Pedersen discovery[2] of the crown ligands for the alkali metals and the subsequent development of ranges of macrocyclic and macropolycyclic ligands,[15–17] mostly with oxygen donors, have provided a multitude of models for carrier or receptor sites on proteins, and for the mechanism of transport. A massive build-up of data has provided information on several angles, particularly of selectivity in a single phase (as measured by the extent of complexation), which is often the first information provided on any new ligand, selectivity in solvent extraction, and increasingly the dynamics of cation complexation in a single phase and the rates of cation transfer between phases.

The reaction of alkali metal cations with ligands in solution is very fast, complexation rates often being within a factor of 100 or so of the diffusion-controlled rate, and a common rate-determining step is observed in many systems. A variety of techniques has been used to determine rates, confidence in the data being engendered by agreement between (i) rates from diverse kinetic methods obtained in widely different concentration ranges, and (ii) equilibrium constants derived from a ratio of forward and reverse rate constants and those determined by direct thermodynamic methods. A selection of kinetic parameters is given in Tables 1–10 for the reaction of alkali cations with crowns (I–IX, XXI), clams (XI–XIV), podands (XV) and cryptands (X, XVII, XVIII). In drawing comparisons from these tables it should be remembered that NMR parameters were obtained at high substrate concentration (as high as 0.5 M Na^+ for ^{23}Na NMR, in at least two-fold molar excess over ligand,[18] or decimolar ligand for ^1H or ^{13}C NMR in at least two-fold molar excess over alkali cation[19]), while for stopped-flow[20] or temperature-jump measurements[21] monitored by UV spectrophotometry or conductivity[22] data are obtained typically at 10^{-4}–10^{-5} M cation and ligand concentration in a high ionic strength background. The ultrasonic data are typically at ~ 0.05 M cation and ligand concentrations,[23] cyclic voltammetry[24] at $\sim 10^{-3}$ M while ~ 0.0035—0.05 M was used for calorimetric stopped-flow work.[25]

Of the sequence of steps (Equations (1–4) where C stands for crown, clam, cryptand, i.e. the macrocycle) to be considered in the context of mechanism, the rate-determining step is frequently thought to be the complexation shown in Equation (2), for which values of k_{-2}, or k_2 and

TABLE 1

Rate parameters for dissociation of Na^+ from its macrocyclic complexes

Salt	Ligand	Solvent	k_{-2}^a (s^{-1})	E_a (kcal mol^{-1})	$\Delta G^\ddagger$ (kcal mol^{-1})	Method	Ref.
NaSCN	IV	DMF	4.8×10^3	12.6			[18]
NaSCN	IV	MeOH	8.0×10^2	11.7			[18]
NaBPh$_4$	IV	DME	5.4×10^2	13.3		^{23}Na NMR linewidth	[18]
NaSCN	V	DMF	9.2×10^3	12.5			[18]
NaSCN	VII	DMF	7.6×10^3	13.1			[18]
NaI	VIII	MeOH	9.7×10^2 ^{b}	11.4			[36]
NaF^c	VI	THF	5.5×10^2 ^{d}	12.5		^{1}H NMR coalescence^e	f
NaSCN^g	I	CDCl$_3$			11.0	^{13}C NMR coalescence^h	[29]
NaSCN^g	I	MeOH			10.6	^{23}Na NMR	
NaBPh$_4$	XXII	THF, dioxolan	slow^i				j
NaCl	IX	MeOH	1.3×10^5 ^{k}			T-jump	[21]
NaCl	III	H$_2$O	3.4×10^7 ^{k}			ultrasonic	[14]^l
NaCl	II	H$_2$O	4.8×10^7 ^{k}			ultrasonic	[14]^l
NaSCN	XXI	MeOH	5.2×10^4 ^{k}	8.3		^{23}Na NMR linewidth	[18]

^{a} At $-13°$C unless otherwise stated, refers to step 2.

^{b} At 5°C.

^{c} Fluorenyl.

^{d} At $-18°$C.

^{e} Several temperatures.

^{f} Wong, K.H.; Konizer, G.; Smid, J. *J. Amer. Chem. Soc.* **1970**, *92*, 666.

^{g} 2:1 ligand:metal complex.

^{h} $-40°$C.

^{i} Rate was anion-dependent, fast for ClO$_4^-$, I$^-$.

^{j} Lin, J.D.; Popov, A.I. *J. Amer. Chem. Soc.* **1981**, *103*, 3773.

^{k} At 25°C.

^{l} Liesegang, G.W.; Farrow, M.M.; Arce Vasquez, F.; Purdie, N.; Eyring, E.M. *J. Amer. Chem. Soc.* **1977**, *99*, 3240.

TABLE 2

Rate parameters for dissociation of K^+ from macrocyclic complexes

(A) Salt	Ligand	Solvent	k_{-2}^{a} (s^{-1})	E_a	$\Delta G^{\ddagger}$	Method	Ref.
				(kcal mol^{-1})			
KI	IV	MeOH	$6\cdot1 \times 10^{2}$ [b]	$12\cdot6$		^{39}K NMR	[26]
KI	VIII	MeOH	[c]	$10\cdot9$			[36]
KI	XXIII	CDCl$_3$	$12\cdot0^{d}$		$12\cdot2^{d}$	^{1}H NMR	[19]
KSCN	XXIV	CDCl$_3$/CS$_2$	$16\cdot2^{e}$	$15\cdot9$	$12\cdot2^{e}$	^{1}H NMR	[19]
KSCN	XIV	CD$_3$CN			<13	^{13}C NMR	[f]

(B) Salt	Ligand	Solvent	k_{2}^{a} $(M^{-1}\,s^{-1})$	k_{-2}^{a} (s^{-1})	Method	Ref.
KCl	IX	MeOH	6×10^{8}	$1\cdot6 \times 10^{4}$	T-jump	[21]
KCl^{g}	III	H$_2$O	$4\cdot3 \times 10^{8}$	$3\cdot7 \times 10^{6}$	ultrasonic	[14^{h}]
KCl	II	H$_2$O	$4\cdot3 \times 10^{8}$	$7\cdot8 \times 10^{7}$		[14^{i}]
KBr	XVa	MeOH	$1\cdot1 \times 10^{8}$	4×10^{3}		[43]
KBr	XVb	MeOH		10^{5}		[43]
KBr	XI	MeOH	$3\cdot7 \times 10^{5}$	$2\cdot5 \times 10^{1}$	T-jump	[j]
KBr	XII	MeOH	$5\cdot4 \times 10^{5}$	$1\cdot2 \times 10^{1}$		[j]
KBr	XIII	MeOH	$1\cdot2 \times 10^{5}$	$1\cdot0 \times 10^{1}$		[j]

[a] For step 2, all at 25°C unless otherwise noted.
[b] −34°C.
[c] Not determined.
[d] −45°C.
[e] −43°C.
[f] Temperature not stated. Calverley, M.J.; Dale, J. J.C.S. Chem. Comm. **1981**, 684.
[g] $\Delta H^{\ddagger} = 10\cdot2$ kcal m^{-1}, $\Delta S^{\ddagger} = 3\cdot1$ cal K^{-1} mol^{-1}.
[h] Liesegang, G.W.; Farrow, M.M.; Purdie, N.; Eyring, E.M. J. Amer. Chem. Soc. **1976**, 98, 6905.
[i] Liesegang, G.W.; Farrow, M.M.; Vazquez, F.A.; Purdie, N.; Eyring, E.M. J. Amer. Chem. Soc. **1977**, 99, 3240.
[j] Rao, P.V.S.; Lockhart, J.C., unpublished work.

TABLE 3

Rate parameters for dissociation of Cs$^+$ from macrocyclic complexes

Salt	Ligand	Solvent	k_{-2} (25°C) (s^{-1})	k_2 ($M^{-1}\,s^{-1}$)	E_a (kcal mol^{-1})	Method	Ref.
CsCl	IX	MeOH	4.7×10^4	8×10^8		T-jump	[21]
CsCl	III	H$_2$O	4.4×10^7	4.3×10^8		ultrasonic	[14]
CsBPh$_4$	III	pyridine	9.5×10^3		8.4	^{133}Cs NMR lineshape	[46]
CsBPh$_4$	XXI	PC	11×10^3		8.5		a
CsBF$_4$	III	CHF$_2$Cl/CHFCl$_2$			7.0 ± 0.3^b	^{1}H, ^{13}C NMR coalescence	[30]

^{a} Mei, E.; Popov, A.I.; Dye J.L. *J. Phys. Chem.* **1977**, *81*, 1677. PC = propylene carbonate.

^{b} $\Delta G^{\ddagger}$ from coalescence temperature −130°C.

TABLE 4

Rate parameters for reaction of Rb$^+$ with macrocycles

Salt	Ligand	Solvent	k_2^a ($M^{-1}\,s^{-1}$)	k_{-2}^a (s^{-1})	Method	Ref.
RbCl	III	H$_2$O		1.2×10^7	ultrasonic	[14]^b
RbCl	II	H$_2$O		1.2×10^8	ultrasonic	[14]^c
RbBr	XI	MeOH	5.8×10^5	9	T-jump	d
RbBr	XII	MeOH	5.4×10^5	15	T-jump	d
RbBr	XIII	MeOH	2.5×10^5	6	T-jump	d

^{a} 25°C, refers to step 2.

^{b} Liesegang, G.W., Farrow, M.M.; Purdie, N.; Eyring, E.M. *J. Amer. Chem. Soc.* **1976**, *98*, 6905.

^{c} Liesegang, G.W.; Farrow, M.M.; Vasquez, F.A.; Purdie, N.; Eyring, E.M. *J. Amer. Chem. Soc.* **1977**, *99*, 3240.

^{d} Rao, P.V.S.; Lockhart, J.C., unpublished work.

TABLE 5

Rate parameters for reaction of Li$^+$ with macrocycles

Salt	Ligand	Solvent	k_2^a ($M^{-1} s^{-1}$)	k_{-2}^a (s^{-1})	$\Delta G^{\ddagger}$ (kcal mol^{-1})	Method	Ref.
LiClO$_4$	III	dioxolan	—	$5 \cdot 4 \times 10^7$		ultrasonic	[23]
LiCl	III	H$_2$O	8×10^7	6×10^7		ultrasonic	[14][b]
LiCl	II	H$_2$O		fast[c]		ultrasonic	[14][d]
LiClO$_4$	XIV	CD$_3$CN			$<13^d$	^{1}H NMR coalescence	
LiSCN	I	1:2 CHCl$_2$F: CHClF$_2$			$8 \cdot 2^e$	^{1}H NMR coalescence	[27]

[a] 25°C unless stated otherwise.
[b] Liesegang, G.W.; Farrow, M.M.; Vasquez, F.A.; Purdie, N.; Eyring, E.M. *J. Amer. Chem. Soc.* **1977**, *99*, 3240.
[c] Too fast to measure.
[d] Calverley, M.J.; Dale, J. *J.C.S. Chem. Comm.* **1981**, 684; temperature not stated.
[e] At 96°C.

k_{-2} have been measured:

$$C' \underset{k_{-1}}{\overset{k_1}{\rightleftharpoons}} C \tag{1}$$

$$M^+(solv)_n + C \underset{k_{-2}}{\overset{k_2}{\rightleftharpoons}} MC^+ + n(solv) \tag{2}$$

$$MC^+ \underset{k_{-3}}{\overset{k_3}{\rightleftharpoons}} (MC'')^+ \tag{3}$$

$$M^{*+} + MC^+ \underset{k_{-4}}{\overset{k_4}{\rightleftharpoons}} M^*C^+ + M^+ \tag{4}$$

Scheme (1)

as indicated in Tables 1–10. In this scheme, C, C' and C'' represent different conformational forms for free or complexed ligand. Step 4, involving exchange of cation directly with complex, has been ruled out in several studies.[18,26]

2. Rapid pre-equilibria involving the ligand (Equation (1))

With ligands of this complexity there are naturally many possible conformational changes—it is necessary to assess the rate of these changes relative to the rate of complexation (Equation (2)), and the probable involvement in mechanism. Conformational changes in the ligand while complexed (represented by Equation (3)) are also important (see II.A.4).

Much attention has been given to possible ligand conformational equilibria preceding the complexation step. Chock, in his careful temperature-jump studies of the reaction of K^+ with dibenzo-30-crown-10 (IX),[21] discovered that the temperature dependence of the relaxation amplitudes for the potassium complexation was inconsistent with Equation (2) as the sole step in the mechanism, and proposed the rapid pre-equilibrium in Equation (1) (referred to in the literature as the Chock mechanism). In the Chock studies only one relaxation time, that for step 2, was found within the range of the instrumentation, but ultrasonic relaxation experiments with 18-crown-6 (III) in the absence of alkali cations in dioxolan at −19·8°C show a Debye relaxation not observed at room temperature, which is attributed to a conformational change of the crown.[23] The smaller 15-crown-5 (II) shows an additional relaxation in H_2O at 25°C which is likewise attributed to Equation (1).[14]

NMR studies[27–31] of the fate of the ligand using ligand nuclei (^1H and ^{13}C) frequently give evidence of a faster process corresponding to Equation

(1). The single-line ^{1}H and ^{13}C NMR spectra of the simple crowns I–III observed at room temperature are clear evidence of a conformational exchange in the free ligands, with rapid averaging.[27-29] Dale and coworkers have succeeded in detecting more than one conformational process by observing the NMR spectra of I–III in Freon solvents down to very low temperatures (−165°C). They deduce the free ligand I has two major conformers, the quadrangular form IA and the biangular form IB shown in Fig. 1 (see also Table 10). These forms (and others) are found in crystal structures,[32-34] the IB form for uncomplexed crown[34] and the IA form which has four coplanar oxygens, in sandwich and other metal complexes.[33] Dale *et al.* interpret the changes in the NMR spectra in terms of equilibrium between IA and IB, present in the ratio 2:1 at −165°C, and a lower energy process within each of these two conformers, fortuitously having the same activation energy. In the 2:1 sandwich complex with NaSCN, ^{13}C NMR shows a high energy barrier (supposed to be for the decomplexation step, reverse of Equation 2), while *within* the complex, the conformational changes in the ligand have a lower free-energy barrier, showing that it is not necessary for the ligand to become completely detached from the metal in order to change conformation. Energy differences between the two

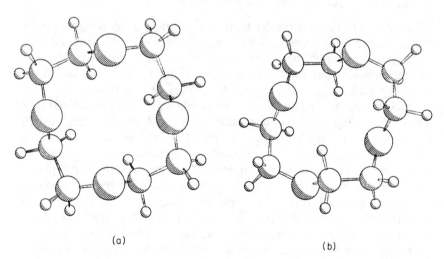

(a)   (b)

Fig. 1. (A) View perpendicular to the plane of the oxygen atoms for 12-crown-4 in the square conformation (drawn from atomic coordinates for C and O given in F.P. Remoortere and F.P. Boer, *Inorg. Chem.* **1974**, *13*, 2071).

(B) Biangular conformation viewed perpendicular to the plane containing three oxygens (drawn from the atomic coordinates given in M.A. Neuman, E.C. Steiner, F.P. van Remoortere and F.P. Boer, *Inorg. Chem.* **1975**, *14*, 734). Plotted using PLUTO courtesy of Dr. S. Motherwell and Dr. W. Clegg.

forms IA and IB calculated from molecular mechanics[35] and CNDO methods[36] are compared in Table 10 with the free energy barriers found in the NMR work for I and its 2:1 NaSCN and 1:1 LiSCN complexes.

Although the conformational averaging of simple polyether crowns is very fast, it can be detected by NMR methods at extremely low temperatures or by ultrasonics, and in solvents in which many substituted crowns, podands, clams, etc., are insoluble. However, the substituted versions often provide spectroscopic signposts[30,31,37] which enable conformational changes to be detected more readily. Moreover rigidity in a ring (as for instance in the bipyridyl series XVI) makes for a higher activation energy and slower switching.[38] The *anti* form of XVI is present in the crystal and at room temperature in solution, but at low temperature in solution the *syn* form is found.

Lehn, Sauvage and Dietrich[39] described the cryptands X as mixtures of three types of conformer,† depending on the orientation of the nitrogen "lone pair" with respect to the molecular cavity, usually represented as *i* (pointing inward) or *o* (pointing outward), hence the three possibilities (*i,i*), (*o,i*) or (*o,o*). Direct evidence for conformers of the (*i,i*) type is

$$(i,i) \qquad\qquad (o,i) \qquad\qquad (o,o)$$

obtained from crystal structures, and for rapid conformational change from NMR spectra. Very recently ultrasonic absorption studies of the cryptand (2,2,2) (that is, X with $n = m = p = 2$) have been carried out in water over the temperature range 25–55°C, and at 0·15–0·4 M concentration of cryptand, and a frequency range of 1–300 MHz. The absorption corresponded to a sum of two Debye relaxation processes as would be expected for the multiple equilibria shown in Equation (5). The authors[40] declined to identify the observed relaxations with either specific process shown in Equation (5), but point out that ligand rearrangement cannot be the rate-determining step for complexation (Equation (2)). The rate constants

---

† Many conformers are actually possible for each type, based on the free rotation of OCH_2CH_2O segments, and a number of different conformational arrangements of the ligand strands is apparent in crystal structures,[17] which usually contain cryptands of the *i,i* type, prevalent for most metal cryptates in the solid state.

TABLE 6
Rates of reaction of cryptands with alkali cations at 25°C for spontaneous acid-catalysed dissociation

Cryptand X — m	n	p	Cation	log K_2[a]	k_{-2}[b] (s⁻¹)	k_{H^+}[c] (M⁻¹ s⁻¹)	k_{H^+}/k_{-2}	Solvent	Ref.
2	1	1	Li	5.5	2.5×10^{-2}	21.0	850	H_2O	[22]
2	2	1	Na	5.4	14.5	180.0	12.4	H_2O	[22]
2	2	2	K	5.4	7.5^d	0	0	H_2O	[22]
					5.5^e	590.0	107	H_2O	[20]
2	1	1	Li	8.0	4.4×10^{-3}	4.9×10^{-1}	1.1×10^2		[62]
2	1	1	Na	6.1	2.5	0			[62]
2	2	1	Li	5.4	7.5×10			MeOH	[62]
2	2	1	Na	9.7	2.35×10^{-2}	2.1×10^3	28		[62]
2	2	1	K	8.5	1.09	3.7×10^{-1}	16		[62]
2	2	1	Rb	6.7	7.5×10				[62]
2	2	1	Cs	4.3	2.3×10^4				[62]
2	2	2	Li	2.6	3×10^2				[62]
2	2	2	Na	8.0	2.87				[62]
2	2	2	K	10.4	1.8×10^{-2}	4.2×10^2	1.46×10^2	MeOH	[62]
2	2	2	Rb	9.0	8.0×10				[62]
2	2	2	Cs	4.4	4×10^4				[62]
XX			Na	4.2	2.5×10^4				[43]
XX			K	—	10^5				[43]

[a] K for Equation (2) in units of mol⁻¹ dm³.
[b] Dissociation rate, Equation (2) (compare footnote f).
[c] Acid-catalysed dissociation rate, from Equation (10).
[d] Value by extrapolation to zero ionic strength.
[e] $I = 0.2$ M $Et_4N^+Cl^-$.

[f] Two ligand conformational changes for X (2,2,2) cryptand in water have $k = 4.4 \times 10^8$ s⁻¹ and 4.4×10^7 s⁻¹ at 25°C with $\Delta H^{\ddagger} = 1.6 \pm 0.04$ and 5.4 ± 0.5 kcal mol⁻¹ and $\Delta S^{\ddagger} = -13.4 \pm 0.14$ cal K⁻¹ mol⁻¹ and -5.5 ± 1.6 cal K⁻¹ mol⁻¹ respectively (Ref. [40]).

and activation parameters deduced for the two steps are shown in Table 6.

3. The complexation step (Equation (2))

The forward step (complexation) in Equation (2) is usually very fast (10^6–10^8 M^{-1} s^{-1}) although rather less than the expected encounter-controlled rate for cation/neutral complex.[41] Slower complexation steps are found for cryptands with a cavity too small for the cation concerned,[42] and also when the cation charge is increased (as will be seen in Section III, alkaline earths and lanthanides(II) and (III)), and where considerable reorganization of the ligand is required first (valinomycin,[41] clams,[36]

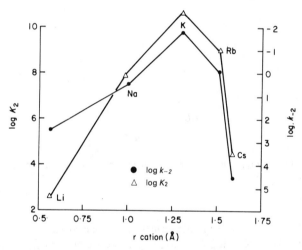

Fig. 2. Comparison of the equilibrium constant and back reaction rate for Equation (2) as cation radius is varied, for reaction with cryptand X (2,2,2). Data from Ref. [42].

podands[43]). These slow steps may of course conceal rapid pre- and post-equilibria, not resolved with the instrumental method employed. For any one ligand the rate constant k_2 changes very slightly with metal (usually within a factor of about 10 for singly charged cations). The decomplexation rate constants k_{-2}, however, show a much greater range and are seen to be the principal factor discriminating between metals. This is probably best displayed on a diagram such as Fig. 2, wherein $\log k_{-2}$ and $\log K_2$ are plotted versus the ionic radius of the cation, the vertical axes being adjusted to bring out the similarities. The correlation of thermodynamic stability with decomplexation rate is clear. A number of similar correlations of k_{-2} and K_2 have been noted—indeed plots of k_{-2} against log K_2 for individual ligands have been found to be straight lines of unit slope when either cation or solvent is changed (water being a notable exception among solvents,[42] see Fig. 3). That log k_{-2} should correlate with log K_2 where the

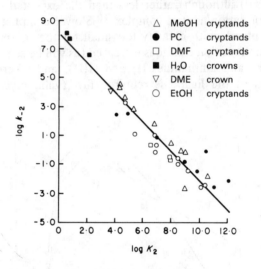

Fig. 3. Plot of log k_{-2} against log K_2 for several ligands and solvents. Data from Tables 1–6.

values of the complexation rate constant k_2 are virtually the same is no surprise, since log $K = \log k_2 - \log k_{-2}$ is the equation of the straight line with log K and log k_{-2} the variables and log k_2 the constant. That the correlation should have the same slope and intercept for a range of different ligands and solvents is arresting. The correlation where the complexation rates are of a different order of magnitude (e.g. for the clams and Group I metals, cryptands and Group II metals) simply has the same unit slope, but the intercept on the log k_{-2} axis corresponds to the value of log k_2, the complexation rate. The striking feature of the correlation is that the formation rates should be so similar in different solvents, the scatter of about two log units corresponding to the factor of ~100 difference in complexation rate constants. Ligands for which the data points lie below the line of unit slope present higher barriers to the complexation reaction. The similarity of complex formation rates for so many different solvents can only mean that substantial desolvation of the cation takes place after

TABLE 7

Kinetic parameters for the benzo-substituted cryptand XXV with alkali salts at 25°C (from Ref. [64]) MeOH solvent

Cation	log K_2[a] ±0·05	k_{-2} (s⁻¹)	$\Delta G_{-2}^{\ddagger}$ (kcal mol⁻¹)	$\Delta H_{-2}^{\ddagger}$ (kcal mol⁻¹)	$\Delta S_{-2}^{\ddagger}$ (cal K⁻¹ mol⁻¹)	$\Delta G_2^{\ddagger b}$ (kcal mol⁻¹)
Li	2·19	fast				
Na	7·5	2·74 ± 0·17 (250 M⁻¹ s⁻¹)[c]	16·9	13·2	−12·4	6·7
K	9·2	0·158 ± 0·007	18·5	18·4	−0·7	6·0
Rb	7·19	20·4 ± 0·24	15·7	16·8	−1·7	5·9
Cs	2·99	fast				

[a] K_2 in M⁻¹.

[b] Free energy of activation for formation reaction: k_2 may be obtained, $k_2 = K_2 k_{-2}$.

[c] Acid-catalysed rate constant k_{H^+}: no acid catalysis for Rb⁺ or K⁺ up to 6×10^{-3} M added CF_3SO_3H.

the rate-determining encounter, which is consistent also with higher complex formation rates for the larger cations with small solvation energies, and rather smaller formation rates for the more strongly solvated doubly charged alkaline earth cations. It is a strong presumption that the transition state resembles the reactants. Cox, Garcia-Rosas and Schneider[42] have examined this idea quantitatively, calculating hypothetical free-energies of transfer between solvents for both the transition state and the reactants, using established procedures. A plot of $\Delta G_{tr}^{\ddagger}$ versus ΔG_{tr} for the formation of $K(2,2,2)^+$ cryptate in a series of solvents is a straight line with a slope of 0·75, with a good correlation except for H_2O, which appears to be a rogue solvent in many respects. The transition state is thus seen to be slightly less sensitive to solvent variation than the reagents. No correlation whatsoever was found for an analogous plot with the free-energies of transfer of the product cryptate. Dissociation rates were also found to correlate well with the solvent donor number[44] for any one metal cryptate in a series of solvents, the dissociation rate increasing sharply with donor number of solvent, while the corresponding formation rates decreased slightly.

Another interesting feature of the decomplexation step arises for the substituted dibenzo-18-crown-6 derivatives, IV–VIII, for which the acti-

TABLE 8

Dissociation rate constants (k_{-2}), acid-catalysed rate constants, k_{HA}, and formation constants K_2 in propylene carbonate at 25°C for some alkali cation cryptates (from Ref. [63])

Cryptand X			Cation	$k_{-2}{}^a$ (s^{-1})	$k_{HA}{}^b$ $(M^{-1} s^{-1})$	k_{HA}/k_{-2}	$\log K_2{}^c$
m	n	p					
2	1	1	Li	10^{-5}	d		12·4
2	1	1	Na	$3·6 \times 10^{-2}$	1·6	44	8·7
2	2	1	Na	10^{-2}	$9·2 \times 10$	>9000	12·0
2	2	1	K	$3·7 \times 10^{-2}$	$2·9 \times 10$	783	9·8
2	2	1	Rb	7·5	0	0	7·0
2	2	1	Cs	$\sim 4 \times 10^2$			4·9
2	2	2	Na		$3·3 \times 10^4$	>30000	10·5
2	2	2	K	$3·1 \times 10^{-3}$	$1·5 \times 10$	5000	11·1
2	2	2	Rb	$1·7 \times 10^{-1}$	$2·4 \times 10$	142	9·0
2	2	2	Cs	3×10^2			4·1

a Dissociation rate as per Equation (2).

b General acid-catalysed rate constant obtained from observed rate at different [HA] where $k_{obs} = k_{-2} + k_{HA} [HA]$.

c Values of K_2 for equation (2) in M^{-1}.

d Very strongly acid-catalysed.

vation energy for the k_{-2} step has almost the same value for all the examples so far studied, despite changes of metal (Na^+ or K^+), change of substituents on the aromatic rings, and the solvent (see Tables 1 and 2). Most of the examples were investigated using quadrupolar line-broadening of NMR signals of the alkali cation, but one study used ^1H NMR.[45] Such NMR studies of line-broadening have been interpreted in terms of the two-site exchange in Equation (2), but in situations where complexes of different stoichiometries (as in the 1:1 and 2:1 complexes of ligand III with caesium)[46] are known to exist, more precise studies are needed to give information on Equation (6) as well as Equation (2).[5–7] The complex of

TABLE 9

Free energies of activation obtained from single coalescence temperature measurements in NMR spectra for the dissociation of macrotricycle

Ligand	Solvent	Cation	$\Delta G^{\ddagger}$ (kcal mol^{-1})	Temp (°C)	log $K_2{}^a$	Ref.
XVIII	CDCl$_3$	K	15·5	28	3·4	[48]
XVIII	CDCl$_3$	Rb	16·7	51	4·2	[48]
XVIII	CDCl$_3$	Cs	16·1	41	3·4	[48]

^{a} K_2 for Equation 2 in M^{-1} in H_2O at 25°C; cf. log K_2 values for X (2,2,2) 5·4, 4·2, 1·5 for K, Rb, Cs, in H_2O at 25°C.[42].

$CsBF_4$ with III gave evidence[30] for the dissociative process in Equation (6) (^1H and ^{13}C NMR studies, see Table 3).

$$C + MC^+ \underset{k_{-6}}{\overset{k_6}{\rightleftharpoons}} MC_2^+ \tag{6}$$

Among the curios of the cryptand range are the six-stranded macrotricycles, XVII and XVIII, which provide cylindrical and spheroidal cavities respectively.[47,48] The spherand XVIII has an estimated cavity radius of 1·8 Å (in the (i,i,i,i) topology). It looks like a potential sink for alkali cations of the correct dimension, but only the stability constant for the caesium complex is higher than for cryptand X (2,2,2); see Table 9. Measurements of the dissociation of alkali cations from the cavity (obtained from the coalescence temperatures of signals for free and complexed spherand) indicate a very slow release of cation (Table 9). The formation rates must also be slow however and should be a most interesting study. The Cram group has also synthesized a spherand, (XIX), designed to give a rigid cavity of roughly spherical shape in mimicry of valinomycin,[49] which is selective only for Li^+ or Na^+. Lithium can replace sodium in the complex, the reaction having a half-life greater than 72 hours at ambient temperature in $CDCl_3$ containing ~6% by volume of $(CD_3)_2SO$. These ligands would seem to model strong biological receptor sites.

4. Equilibria after the rate-determining step

The possibility of conformational change in the complex (step 3 of Scheme 1) was not always realised, due to its inaccessiblity to kinetic investigation. Enough favourable cases have now been dealt with to show its importance, but it has not been fully assessed and more data are needed. The consensus of opinion on the formation step (Equation (2), Scheme 1) is that very little desolvation of the cation, and very little reorganisation of the ligand occurs in the rate-determining step—the structure of the transition state resembles more closely that of the reactants. At some stage, then, the cation must be desolvated and coordinated to the ligand in its stable configuration. A conformational equilibrium involving the complex was proposed to explain the slow complexing rate for valinomycin and sodium ions.[41] A process of this type has been identified for caesium cryptand systems,[46,59] where an exchange between two forms of the cryptate (as in Equation (3)) is much faster than exchange via Equation (2). Separate relaxation times for steps (2) and (3) have been observed in

TABLE 10

Activation free energy for exchange[a] between A and B isomers of 12-crown-4. Calculated binding energy differences[b,c]

Process	$\Delta G^{\ddagger a}$ (kcal mol^{-1})	T (°C)[a] (coalescence)	Ref.
A↔B	6·5		[28]
B↔B' A↔A'	5·5	−140	[28]
A↔B (LiSCN)	6·8, 5·6	−126, −160	[27]
A↔B (NaSCN)	8, 7	−105, −112	[29]
	Δ Binding energy (kcal mol^{-1})		
	2·9[b]		[35]
	12·5[c]		[36]

[a] Obtained at NMR coalescence temperature.

[b] From molecular mechanics calculation; A more stable than B.

[c] From CNDO calculation; A more stable than B.

temperature-jump studies of the pyridinophane[43] (XX); and with a thermal stopped-flow method, Liesegang found the complexation of Ca^{2+} ions with cryptand (2,1,1) to proceed in two steps according to Equations (2) and (3).[25] The conformational change of ligand I in its LiSCN and NaSCN complexes has been referred to in Section II.A.2 and the activation parameters are in Table 10. Ions can apparently bounce from end to end of the cylindrical cavity of macrotricycle XVII, in a fast intramolecular process, with concomitant fluxional movement of the ligand. This process has been hailed by the authors[47] as a possible model for a metal shuttle in biology. The inclusion complexes of the macrotricycle were examined by ^{13}C NMR. The most interesting ones contained alkaline earth metals and are mentioned in Section III.A.

5. Acid catalysis of the dissociation step

Macrocycles with a basic nitrogen atom are potentially proton-acid sensitive. Acid catalysis of the dissociation of metal cryptates is attributable to this basicity. pK_a values of the typical cryptand (2,2,2) (X) are $pK_1 = 7.3$ and $pK_2 = 9.6$ in water[50] at 25.0°C. The stoichiometry of the overall reaction is given in Equation (7),

$$MC^{n+} + 2H^+ \xrightarrow{k_e} CH_2^{2+} + M^{n+} \tag{7}$$

Assuming the mechanism in Equations (8, 9) the proposed protonation step (Equation (9)) is known to be very fast so the observed rate constant, the forward rate constant for Equation (8), essentially k_d,

$$MC^{n+} \underset{k_f}{\overset{k_d}{\rightleftharpoons}} M^{n+} + C \tag{8}$$

$$C + H^+ \xrightarrow{fast} CH^+ \tag{9}$$

is equal to k_e (Equation (7)) the overall rate of cryptate dissociation. For some cryptate systems e.g. the best known potassium cryptate $K(2,2,2)^+$, k_d is found to be independent of acid and alkali cation concentration at low concentration. The large changes in conductance which arise when reaction takes place according to Equation (7) are the basis for the detection of metal dissociation rates in the stopped-flow analysis used by Cox and Schneider.[22] The cryptate dissociation rate constants (k_{-2}) given in Tables 6–8 refer to situations in which the free cryptand is present entirely as the free base (i.e. high pH ranges where Equation (2) is valid). Acid catalysis by strong acids in water is, however, observed for dissociation of many metal cryptates,[17,51] with the rate dependence shown in Equation (10):

$$k_e = k_d + k_{H^+}[H^+] \tag{10}$$

(where k_e and k_d are as defined in Equations (7) and (8) and $k_d = k_{-2}$). For instance, for the $Ca(2,2,2)^+$ cryptate in water containing HCl up to 0·02 M concentration, a plot of k_e against [HCl] is a straight line whose slope and intercept give k_{H^+} and k_d respectively. There is also general acid catalysis in some systems[42], with $k_e = k_d + k_{H^+}[H^+] + k_{HA}[HA]$. The questions arise, why are some of the ligand–metal cryptate combinations subject to acid catalysed dissociation and some not? And what is the nature of the catalysis?

In Section II.A.2 we noted the three topologies possible for the cryptand ligands, based on the inversion of configuration of the bridgehead nitrogens (Equation (5)).[52] The cryptates also potentially have these topologies available,[53] but the (i,i) form should be stabilized by the presence of a positively charged cation *inside* the cavity (the inclusive type of complex).[46] Direct evidence for this form is found in the crystalline metal cryptates for many of which x-ray analyses have been performed.[54–57] Cox and Schneider hypothesize that direct dissociation from the inclusive (i,i) form is unlikely to be acid-catalysed, but that sites for attack by acid are provided by the o configuration in the (i,o) or (o,o) forms.[22,58]

The present knowledge of cryptate crystal structures together with detail provided by the powerful probe of alkali metal NMR in solution has contributed enormously to our understanding of the cryptate systems, giving considerable insight into the subtle ways in which the ligands adapt to fit the metal cation. It is here that the understanding of the acid catalysis must lie. The original idea for a globe-like molecule with hydrophobic exterior surface and polar interior cavity provided with oxygen dipoles to interact with the positively charged cation is marvellous in its simplicity. How must it be modified to account for the variation in reactivity? In the macrobicyclic cryptands X there is a supposed "best fit" cation for which the optimum ligand cavity radius (estimated from models) matches the cation radius. For the potassium cryptate $K(2,2,2)^+$ estimated cavity and cation radii are 1·4 Å, 1·33 Å. The actual value[57] of the average cavity radius obtained from the crystal structure is 1·38 Å. However for the smaller cation sodium, the (crystal) cavity radius shrinks to 1·2 Å, and for the larger rubidium cation the same ligand provides a cavity radius of 1·5 Å, presumably with some strain. The ligand can apparently "stretch" or "wrinkle" to provide the optimum location of the dipoles on its interior surface. For cryptands where the three strands are not of equal length some symmetry is lost. The (2,2,1) cryptand forms its most stable complex with sodium rather than potassium. It provides seven coordination sites for sodium and the crystal structure shows the cavity radius to be 1·1 Å. For the KSCN complex, the crystal cavity radius expands to 1·4 Å and the crystal structure indicates interaction of K^+ with the thiocyanate anion. The potassium ion is a tight fit, but even with the optimized fit the cation could not be symmetrically coordinated. A clear discussion of these effects in the crystal structures is given by Mathieu, Metz, Moras and Weiss.[57] There would appear to be three situations—the "perfect fit" in which interaction of cation and dipole is maximized by size-matching, and in which one would suppose the cation is well shielded from the solvent, the "very tight fit" complexes in which the metal protrudes slightly to interact with extra-ligand entities, and the "loose fit" complexes. The fluxional change of topology at the nitrogen bridgehead from an *i* to an *o* form would seem to be favoured for the "loose fit" complexes.

These three situations may be examined in solution by alkali metal NMR.[11]

Alkali cation shifts are extremely sensitive to their immediate environment and may indicate the degree of isolation of cation from solvent.[46] Considering the inclusive type of complex one would expect the shift to be relatively independent of solvating factors external to the ligand and this is found to be so in many instances. The caesium complex of cryptand[46] (3,2,2) and the potassium complex of (2,2,2) which are of the best fit type are thought to be inclusive in solution.[59] Popov *et al.* denote several tight fit complexes as exclusive,[46,59,60] based on the operational definition of exclusive as showing sensitivity to solvent and/or anion influences external to the ligand. Of course the metal might be in a range of locations ranging from inside the cavity but projecting, to outside the cavity and interacting with one donor site only. The caesium complexes of (2,2,2) and its benzo derivative XXV and the potassium complexes of the (2,2,1) and (2,1,1) cryptands are evidently exclusive on this NMR definition, yet the crystal structures of the caesium (2,2,2) and the potassium (2,2,1) cryptates show them to be inclusive and with *i,i* topology. For the Cs complex of XXV no inclusive form was found in solution at all. For $Cs(2,2,2)^+$ there is an equilibrium between inclusive and exclusive forms, which favours the inclusive form at low temperatures.

While a spherical alkali cation may initially attack at one dipole of a polyether strand to form a transitory exclusive type of complex, it will ultimately end up in an inclusive situation, surrounded by its optimal complement of oxygen dipoles. To identify important features of the transitory complex, one must use a Lewis acid other than a spherical cation. One can form a stable exclusive complex from a Lewis acid with only one (or perhaps two) vacant coordination sites. The lanthanide shift reagents fulfil this criterion and have been used to demonstrate the most basic ether groupings of a crown polyether strand.[61] Evidence for two modes of complexing was found. Valuable structural information inherent in the shifts themselves might be obtained. This technique would be applicable to cryptands also. The simplest Group III Lewis acid, BH_3 has been found to give an (i,o) monoborane complex with the (1,1,1) cryptand (X, $m = n = p = 1$), and the (o,o) topology in its bis complex with (2,2,2) cryptand (X, $m = n = p = 2$).[17] The borane of course is bonded to the nitrogen donors as would be the proton; harder acids are required to complex the oxygens preferentially.

The problems posed by acid catalysis have pin-pointed the need for a fuller understanding of cryptate conformation. The available data on cryptate dissociation suggest that the very tight fit and the loose fit cryptates are more susceptible to acid catalysis than the "best fit" cryptates. An obvious mechanism for attack by H^+ on the "loose fit" complexes is via an intermediate with the (i,o) topology,[22,58] which should here be more readily accessible. It is less obvious why the very tight fit complexes are also subject to acid catalysis. The answer may lie in a greater tendency to form "exclusive" complexes. The exclusive form of the complex might provide a sufficient concentration of an exposed nitrogen site which could be acid-sensitive. The small cations do, however, show the greatest tendency to specific and general acid catalysis even in best fit systems. Susceptibility is evident in at least two ways, even from the relatively small amount of data available (Tables 6–8): at low acid concentrations, larger cations show no susceptibility to acid concentration (no acid catalysis for Rb^+ and K^+ at added CF_3SO_3H concentrations up to 6×10^{-3} M, cf. Table 7) where it is already clear for the smaller cations; when acid catalysis does set in (see Ref. [20]) the ratio k_{H^+}/k_{-2} or k_{HA}/k_{-2} describes the tendency to acid-catalysis of the dissociation step. A different facet of acid sensitivity is probed by each of these features and mechanistic complexity is to be expected. Acid catalysis has provided a useful perturbation of the cation–cryptand interaction which should provide great insight into the whole question of metal encapsulation.

6. Rate of transport of alkali cations between phases

The important biological role of both alkali and alkaline earth cations Na^+, K^+, Mg^{2+} and Ca^{2+} has prompted many studies of the way in which these small positively charged ions are able to move through the nonpolar interior of a biological membrane, both with a view to interpreting the process and exploiting it in analytical and industrial applications. It is generally accepted that molecules with lipophilic exteriors can function as carriers, loading and unloading metal ions at the membrane interface and transporting the encapsulated ions across the membrane interior by diffusion. Where the rate of loading and unloading of the cation is very fast compared to the rate of diffusion (called by Eisenman *et al.*[65] the "equilibrium domain") the overall rate of transport is controlled by the equilibrium between carrier and cation. Eisenman defines the "kinetic domain" as that situation in which rates of loading and unloading are comparable to the rate of shuttling of cation within the membrane.

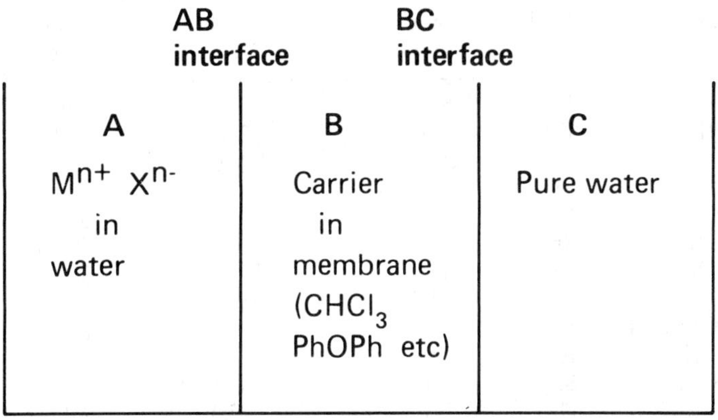

AB interface		BC interface	
A		**B**	**C**
M^{n+} X^{n-} in water		Carrier in membrane ($CHCl_3$ PhOPh etc)	Pure water

Fig. 4. Three-compartment transport system to measure carrier efficiency.

A very simple three-compartmental model for a membrane (Fig. 4) has been used in many studies of passive transport, with a middle apolar phase (B) e.g. $CHCl_3$, diphenylether as liquid membrane, in contact with each of two aqueous phases in the outer compartments. Synthetic crowns and cryptands have been used as carriers in the middle compartment, displaying yet another facet of their remarkable selectivity for cations. The general inference from several detailed studies, was that selectivities in rate of transport of cation from one aqueous phase to another depended on the value of the stability constant (Equation (2)) (provided that the rate of crossing the membrane was slow relative to the rates of complexing and decomplexing, placing these carriers firmly in the "equilibrium domain"). The relative selectivities were quite different from those in a single phase, and from those in solvent extraction (partition between two phases). Lamb *et al.*[66,67] have found that the rate of transport is at its highest for carrier/cation systems in which the log of the stability constant for complexation (Equation (2), log K_2) in methanol is betwen 5 and 8. This is a remarkable correlation, considering that the values of the decomplexing rate constant for carriers giving the same rate of transport varied by factors of up to 10^5. Some data are given in Table 11. It is to be expected that very

TABLE 11

Comparison of rate of transport through a CHCl$_3$ membrane with log K_2 for the carrier-cation equilibrium, and the aqueous dissociation rate

Carrier	Cation	log K_2 (MeOH)[a]	k_{-2} (H$_2$O)[b] (s^{-1})	Transport rate[c]
III	K	6·06	3·7 × 10^6	280
III	Rb	5·32	1·2 × 10^7	210
III	Cs	4·79	4·4 × 10^7	34
III	Sr	5·8		320
XXI	K	5·7		340
XXI	Sr	6·4		490
XXI	Ba	6·9		300
X (2,2,1)	Na	8·94	14·5	130
X (2,2,1)	K	7·55	2·0 × 10^3	290
X (2,2,1)	Rb	5·9		550
X (2,2,1)	Sr	10·75	1·5 × 10^{-3}	3·0
X (2,2,2)	Na	7·3	1·47 × 10^2	240
X (2,2,2)	K	9·85	7·5	88
X (2,2,2)	Rb	8·5	1·4 × 10^2	205
X (2,2,2)	Cs	7·07		3·1

[a] Log K_2 values for 1:1 complexes in methanol, reported in ref. [66].
[b] Carrier cation dissociation rates in water, taken from ref. [14] (III) and Ref. [58] (X (2,2,1) and X (2,2,2)).
[c] Rate given in mmoles transported × 10^4 per 24 hours, from aqueous source 1·0 M in nitrate salt, of carrier complex through CHCl$_3$, taken from Ref. [66].

slow dissociation rates would affect the transport rate, e.g. for lanthanide(III) complexes.[24] Consider any one ligand. Crown III provides the best spread of stability constants available and in Fig. 5 it can be seen that the rate of transport reaches a maximum at a log K value of ~5·8. The position of the maximum changes on the log K scale when the ligand is varied (see curve 2 for dicyclohexylcrown 6, ligand XXI, maximum carrier efficiency is at log K ~6·4). If a plot is made for any one cation with various carrier molecules, the curve is not nearly so smooth (Fig. 6). Clearly the factor not included here is the solvent interaction of each metallated ligand.

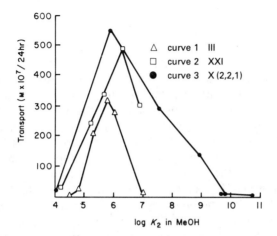

Fig. 5. Maxima in transport efficiency through a bulk chloroform membrane (see Fig. 4) displayed as a function of log K_2 in MeOH.

Cryptand X (2,2,1) emerges as the prince of crowns in this manifestation of selectivity and dicyclohexylcrown 6 (XXI) is a good second, while the cryptand with the greatest complexing power X (2,2,2) is a relatively inefficient carrier. The general explanation of the maximum in plots of carrier efficiency against log K_2 is similar to the Hansch treatment of hydrophobicity in pharmacology, where too hydrophobic a drug sinks in

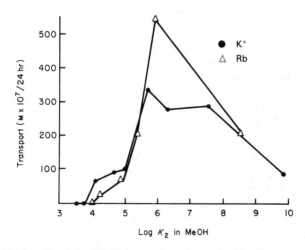

Fig. 6. Maxima in transport efficiency through a bulk chloroform membrane (see Fig. 4) displayed as a function of log K_2 in MeOH.

the first membrane and is released too slowly, while too hydrophilic a drug stays in the aqueous phase: the median hydrophobicity works best.[68,69] Here the stability constant must in some measure relate to extracting efficiency—the best extractant is not the best carrier because insufficient of the cation is released at the membrane interface with the second aqueous phase. Too low a stability constant means a low concentration of cation passing from the first aqueous phase into the membrane. The median situation (here log $K_2 \sim$ 5–8) is the best compromise. The analogy between hydrophobicity and stability constant in this case is not too far-fetched since for this particular type of ligand, the hydrophobic character of the exterior surface in the complexed form is an important feature of the complexing power. No quantitative relation between the Hansch hydrophobicity values for the macrocycles and other properties is evident although it has been sought.[70,71] Lamb et al. have modified the Reusch–Cussler[72] expression for the flux of cation carrier through the interfaces to account for the maximum values observed.

New macrolides have been synthesized containing four or five tetrahydropyran rings alternating with ester links, of which XXVI, a 25-membered ring, proved to be a better carrier of cations through an organic membrane than 18-crown-6 (III),[73] although in simple two-phase partition experiments it is less effective. The ion-extracting efficiencies were Cs^+ > Rb^+ > K^+ > Na^+ > Li^+ (2-phase partition) and the relative transport rates through CH_2Cl_2 membrane were Cs^+ > Rb^+ > K^+ > Ba^{2+} > Ca^{2+} > Na^+ > Li^+. Separate measurements of uptake and release of ions at organic membranes suggest that uptake at the membrane interface is rate-determining for XXVI in the membrane studies.

The cyclodepsipeptide valinomycin XXVII remains the best carrier of the potassium cation to date.[74] Synthetic efforts to make all-peptide and depsipeptide analogues have produced some curious results which help put the transport data for the crown and cryptand macrocycles in perspective.[75–79] A lucid discussion of the stereochemical and kinetic factors involved in the carrier mechanism for the peptide analogues XXVIII and XXIX has been made.[74] The cation structures of all three are of the "bracelet" type, in which the backbone is held with its dipolar amide or ester oxygen pointing at the cation. The free ligands have a more open "basket" conformation in which the cation approach on the open face is enabled. The peptide complexes are $\sim 10^3$ more stable than those of valinomycin,[75,76] but the cation dissociation of XXIX is too slow for carrier function ($k_{-2} \sim 3 \cdot 7 \times 10^{-4}$ s^{-1} at 25°C in D_2O).[74] XXVIII captures the cation in the aqueous phase and crosses the membrane as a hydrophobic ion. Valinomycin is almost insoluble in water; it captures its cation at the water–membrane interface and the rates of cation uptake are comparable to the rate of transport through the membrane, so that valinomycin falls into the "kinetic domain" as defined by Eisenman *et al.*[65] It has a moderately high k_{-2} in MeOH of $1{\cdot}2 \times 10^3$ s^{-1}, and has a stability constant (log K_2 in MeOH $\sim 3 \times 10^4$) outside the optimum range noted by Lamb for equilibrium-dominated carriers. But is still the most selective carrier for potassium to date, despite all the synthetic carriers which have been matched against it, by virtue of its carrier mechanism.

B. Alkyllithium compounds

The alkyl derivatives of lithium are usually polymeric. They are known to form aggregates up to hexamer in the gas phase and in noncoordinating solvents, which undergo inter- and intramolecular switching of alkyl and lithium.[1] The electronic structures of the methyl alkyls ($(LiMe)_n$, where $n = 1$–6) and ethyl alkyls ($(LiEt)_n$, where $n = 1,2$) can now be better understood as a result of MO studies by the PRDDO† approximation.[80] Condensed tetramer and hexamer are indicated to be stable, and bonding is described in terms of localized MOs, closed three-centre LiCLi and closed four-centre Li_3C bonds. The ethyl group gives very similar results. At least two stable configurations were calculated to exist for the hexamer, one of which resembles two weakly interacting D_{3h} trimers, which may be relevant to recent mechanistic studies on the propyllithium system. New studies show that propyllithium apparently forms more fully condensed oligomers $(LiR)_8$ and $(LiR)_9$ (the nonamer believed to have at least three isomers) at temperatures below 250 K in noncoordinating solvents.[81]

The dynamic behaviour of the propyllithium system has been reassessed using the greater sensitivity and resolution available with high-field NMR and new permutations of the possible isotopes. Although ^{13}C–^{7}Li coupling patterns can, in principle, define the stoichiometry of alkyllithium aggregates, the quadrupolar relaxation rates of the ^{7}Li nucleus (naturally 92·58% abundant; spin quantum number $I = 3/2$) have made this impractical for n-propyllithium (of normal isotopic abundance) in cyclopentane. The ^{7}Li NMR spectrum of ^{13}C-enriched n-propyllithium disappointingly shows considerable broadening on cooling (260–280 K) in hydrocarbon solvents, but the coupling between carbon and lithium is not resolved as it would be in ether solvents.[82] The isotopic variant $CH_3CH_2{}^{13}CH_2{}^6Li$ exhibits lithium splitting patterns in high-resolution ^{13}C NMR since the quadrupolar relaxation rate of ^{6}Li (spin $I = 1$) is too slow to average out the couplings. Octamers and monomers are identified[81] below 253 K. Temperature-dependent spectra have been interpreted as showing exchange between

---

† Partial retention of diatomic differential overlap.

aggregates, slowing on the ^{13}C NMR time scale at 269 K (^{13}C at 67·89 MHz) and below 259 K on the ^6Li time-scale (observed at 39·73 MHz), together with a faster intra-aggregate process, still fast on these scales at 180 K. Density matrix methods were used to predict the line-shapes for a ^{13}C nucleus coupled equally to each of six ^6Li nuclei (which the authors used as a model for the intramolecularly averaged hexamer) and the comparison of calculated with experimental linewidths for the ^{13}C spectra gave activation parameters $\Delta H^{\ddagger} = 4\cdot3$ kcal mol^{-1} and $\Delta S^{\ddagger} = -36$ cal K^{-1} mol^{-1} in good agreement with previous values from high-field ^1H NMR, while the ^6Li line-shapes, treated likewise by density matrix methods (the model was an ALi $\rightleftarrows$ BLi exchange), gave $\Delta H^{\ddagger} = 4\cdot0$ kcal mol^{-1} and $\Delta S^{\ddagger} = -37$ cal K^{-1} mol^{-1}. The relevant Eyring plots show overlapping lines for the ^{13}C NMR data (ranging over 205–298 K) and the ^6Li data (ranging over 180–259 K), remarkable but perhaps fortuitous agreement, since the different temperature ranges employed necessarily mean that the composition of the aggregates between which exchange is occurring alters with temperature. However, the result may indicate a similar mechanism for exchange of alkyl and of lithium even in the (potentially) different set of aggregates. The line-shape analysis does not of course define mechanism but merely provides kinetic data. The large negative entropy obtained implies a bimolecular step between aggregates.[81] Earlier work has usually been interpreted in terms of a rate-determining dissociation of the weakest aggregate.[83,84] This work takes full advantage of the enormous improvement both in technical and theoretical aspects of NMR. Consequently the data can be regarded as more reliable. It does of course refer to exchange between larger aggregates, which may be more weakly tethered, but the activation energies are considerably less than previously obtained (for systems with different alkyl groups).

C. Ligands other than macrocycles

1. Solvent exchange studies

In relation to the general problem of solvent exchange in the coordination sphere of cations, Rode, Reibnegger and Fujiwara[85] report on a new model for the transition state of water exchange, based on calculated values for the binding energy of water in the first and second hydration spheres. The MESQUAC (Mixed Electrostatic Quantum Chemical MO) approach was used to calculate the binding energies of water in the first, second, and third hydration spheres of twelve cations (including Li$^+$, Na$^+$, K$^+$, Mg^{2+}, Ca^{2+}) using ligand net atomic charges obtained from previous *ab initio* studies. The binding energies were then compared with enthalpies of hydration (for which there was an excellent correlation) and with the free-energies of activation ($\Delta G^{\ddagger}$) for aquo exchange. The first correlation found for $\Delta G^{\ddagger}$, with the binding energy for water molecules in the first hydration shell, was $\Delta G^{\ddagger}_{exp} = 0 \cdot 118 E_1 + 1 \cdot 3$ (where E_n is the binding energy, in kJ mol^{-1}, of the nth hydration shell). This is consistent with I_A or A mechanisms, but not with dissociative steps. Better correlation is obtained with a model involving water in the first and second hydration shells. A model was adopted in which the incoming and outgoing water molecules are assumed to be equidistant from the metal ion in the transition state, and to lie between the first and second hydration spheres. The stabilization energy for each of the two critical water molecules is then the same. This energy for the two ligands together was postulated to be a composite of the binding energies for water in the first and second shells, $E = k(E_1 + E_2)$. The activation energy for the exchange was then postulated to be given by $E - E_1$. These postulates gave a correlation of calculated $\Delta G^{\ddagger}$ with the experimental activation energies for the series of twelve cations, with a constant value of $k = 0 \cdot 86 \pm 0 \cdot 03$. This constant was interpreted as a measure of the location of the two water molecules between hydration shells. Since the k obtained was less than 1, the water molecules should be closer to the second shell. This stresses the need for consideration of the second hydration shell in interpretations of solvent exchange.

The ligand XXX, nonamethylimidodiphosphoramide (NPA) can operate as bidentate, simulating a first coordination shell, when the solid complex Li(NPA)$_2^+$ perchlorate is dissolved in nonhydroxylic solvents such as nitromethane, propylene carbonate and methylene chloride–nitromethane mixtures. When free ligand was added, exchange of ligand between bound and free sites could be followed by ^{31}P NMR. Temperatures of coalescence of ^{1}H NMR signals were much higher than for unidentate complexes of the same type. Second-order kinetics ($\Delta H^{\ddagger}$ for Li = 7·9 kcal mol^{-1}, $\Delta S^{\ddagger} = 12 \cdot 9$ cal K^{-1} mol^{-1}, $k = 1 \cdot 34 \times 10^4$ M^{-1} s^{-1} at 25°C) were obtained and a simple S$_N$2 mechanism proposed.[86]

III. GROUP IIA METALS

A. Interactions with macrocyclic ligands

1. Introduction

The general reaction of macrocycles and related ligands with alkaline earth cations is much like that described in Section II.A for alkali cations, suitably modified for the main differences in size and charge. Data on triply charged

TABLE 12

Rates of reaction of alkaline earth and related cations with macro-cycles in water at 25°C, for Equation (2)

Ligand	Cation	k_2 $(\mathrm{M}^{-1}\,\mathrm{s}^{-1})$	k_{-2} (s^{-1})	Ref.
III	Ca^{2+}	$<1 \times 10^8$	$>3\cdot2 \times 10^7$	[23b]
III	Sr^{2+}	$0\cdot77 \times 10^8$	$1\cdot5 \times 10^5$	[14, 87]
III	Ba^{2+}	$1\cdot3 \times 10^8$	$0\cdot17 \times 10^5$	[14, 87]
II	Sr^{2+}	$0\cdot65 \times 10^8$	$7\cdot3 \times 10^5$	[14, 87]
II	Ba^{2+}	$1\cdot2 \times 10^8$	23×10^5	[14, 87]

ions will be discussed in Section III.A.2 to provide further comparisons of size and charge effects. A few kinetic studies have been made for alkaline earth cations with crowns, and more with cryptands, and the general mechanistic features closely resemble those laid out in the scheme in Section II.A.1 (Equations (1–3)). The discussion will centre on this as before. The conformational step in Equation (1) would be unaffected by the metal cation and can be taken to have the same import as before. In the complexation step (Equation (2)) it is immediately clear on inspection of Table 12 that the complexation with crowns II and III is very weak[87] and that both complexation and decomplexation rates are fast in water.

TABLE 13

Rate parameters for cryptates of doubly and triply charged cations in water at 25°C

Cation	Ligand $X\,n\,m\,p$	k_{-2} (s^{-1})	k_2 $(\mathrm{M}^{-1}\,\mathrm{s}^{-1})$	$\Delta H^{\ddagger}_{-2}$ $(\mathrm{kcal\,mol}^{-1})$	$\Delta S^{\ddagger}_{-2}$ $(\mathrm{cal\,mol}^{-1}\,\mathrm{K}^{-1})$	Ref.
Ca^{2+}	2,2,1	$6\cdot6 \times 10^{-4}$	$5\cdot9 \times 10^3$	13·4	−28·2	[22]
	2,2,1	$2\cdot2 \times 10^{-3}$	$1\cdot6 \times 10^4$	15·1	−20	[88]
Sr^{2+}	2,2,1	$1\cdot45 \times 10^{-3}$	$3\cdot3 \times 10^4$	14·6	−22·5	[22]
Ba^{2+}	2,2,1	$6\cdot1 \times 10^{-2}$	$1\cdot22 \times 10^5$	15·0	−13·8	[22]
Eu^{2+}	2,2,1	$2\cdot0 \times 10^{-4}$	4×10^5	15·1	−25	[24]
Eu^{3+}	2,2,1	$4\cdot1 \times 10^{-7}$	0·35	19·2	−23·5	[24]
Yb^{3+}	2,2,1	$1\cdot3 \times 10^{-6}$		22·3	−10·7	[24]
Ca^{2+}	2,2,2	0·21	$5\cdot5 \times 10^3$	10·8	−25·8	[22]
	2,2,2	0·26	$7\cdot3 \times 10^3$	8·4	−33	[88]
Sr^{2+}	2,2,2	$7\cdot5 \times 10^{-5}$	$7\cdot5 \times 10^3$	18·9	−14·1	[22]
	2,2,2	$1\cdot0 \times 10^{-4}$	$1\cdot0 \times 10^4$	17·7	−17	[88]
Ba^{2+}	2,2,2	$1\cdot8 \times 10^{-5}$	$9\cdot0 \times 10^4$	21·0	−9·8	[22]
Eu^{2+}	2,2,2	$3\cdot0 \times 10^{-5}$	$9\cdot5 \times 10^5$	18·8	−16	[24]
Eu^{3+}	2,2,2	$1\cdot1 \times 10^{-3}$	2·5	13·8	−26	[24]

No other crown data are available, in part because NMR technology has until recently been unable to cope with the alkaline earth cations. This situation is expected to improve[7] in the near future. However, there have been a number of studies of cryptation of alkaline earth cations;[88,89,90] see Tables 13–16, which show clearly that the rate constants are a factor of

TABLE 14
Direct comparison of charge effect for ions of similar size. Rate constants for Equation (2) in water at 25°C. Comparison of crown and cryptand[a]

Cation	Radius[b] (Å)	Ligand	k_{-2} (s^{-1})	k_2 (M^{-1} s^{-1})
Na$^+$	0·95	III	$3·4 \times 10^7$	$2·2 \times 10^8$
Ca^{2+}	0·99	III	$>3·2 \times 10^7$	$<1·0 \times 10^8$
Na$^+$	0·95	X (2,2,2)	$1·5 \times 10^2$	$1·9 \times 10^6$
Ca^{2+}	0·99	X (2,2,2)	0·22	7×10^3
Eu^{3+}	0·95	X (2,2,2)	$1·1 \times 10^{-3}$	2·5

[a] Data from Tables 1, 11 and 12.
[b] From Cotton, F.A.; Wilkinson, G. "Advanced Inorganic Chemistry"; 3rd Edition; Interscience: New York, 1972.

$\sim 10^2$–10^3 smaller for cryptation, and $\sim 10^3$–10^4 smaller for decryptation than those for alkali cations of similar size. The stability constants are correspondingly larger for the Group IIA cations. The activation parameters in Table 13 indicate enthalpies are not markedly different, but activation entropies are correspondingly more negative.

TABLE 15
Coalescence temperatures in ^{13}C NMR and exchange parameters for inclusion complexes (150–200 mM in D$_2$O) of XVII and alkaline earth cations (Ref. [47])

Cation	Coalescence temp (°C)	k^a s^{-1})	$\Delta G^{\ddagger}$ (kcal mol^{-1})	Process
Ca^{2+}	40	107	15·4	intramolecular[b]
Sr^{2+}	27	171	14·5	intramolecular[b]
Ba^{2+}	<3	>155	13·3	intramolecular[b]
La^{3+}	>93	<58	18·6	intramolecular[b]
Ca^{2+}	~105	~47[c]	~19·5	intermolecular

[a] Exchange rate.
[b] For these inclusion complexes the coalescence temperature for decomplexation is well above 100°C, $\Delta G^{\ddagger} \geqslant 19$ kcal mol^{-1}.
[c] This corresponds to the decomplexation step.

TABLE 16

Acid catalysis displayed by doubly and triply charged cation cryptates in the dissociation step (Equation (2))

Ligand X m	n	p	Cation	$k_{-2}{}^a$ (s^{-1})	$k_{H^+}{}^b$ (M^{-1} s^{-1})	k_{H^+}/k_{-2}	Conditions	Ref.
2	1	1	Ca^{2+}	0·82	c	—	d	[22]
2	2	1	Ca^{2+}	$6\cdot6 \times 10^{-4}$	$1\cdot95 \times 10^{-2}$	29·6	d	[22]
2	2	1	Eu^{3+}	3×10^{-7}	1×10^{-6}	~3	e	[24]
2	2	1	Sr^{2+}	$1\cdot47 \times 10^{-3}$	c	—	d	[22]
2	2	1	Eu^{2+}	1×10^{-4}	$2\cdot5 \times 10^{-3}$	40	e	[24]
2	2	1	Ba^{2+}	$6\cdot1 \times 10^{-2}$	c	—	d	[22]
2	2	2	Ca^{2+}	0·21	550	2600	d	[22]
2	2	2	Eu^{3+}	$1\cdot0 \times 10^{-3}$	0·2	200	f	[24]
2	2	2	Sr^{2+}	$7\cdot5 \times 10^{-5}$	$2\cdot13 \times 10^{-2}$	284	d	[22]
2	2	2	Eu^{2+}	5×10^{-5}	$7\cdot5 \times 10^{-3}$	150	f	[24]
2	2	2	Ba^{2+}	$1\cdot75 \times 10^{-5}$	$1\cdot4 \times 10^{-3}$	80	d	[22]

^{a} Dissociation step of Equation (2).
^{b} Slope of plot of k_c against [H$^+$], Equation (10).
^{c} Independent of [H$^+$] up to 2×10^{-2} M.
^{d} Acid HCl, zero ionic strength.
^{e} 1 M LiClO$_4$/HClO$_4$.
^{f} 0·1 M LiClO$_4$/HClO$_4$.

A process corresponding to Equation (3), in which the first-formed metal cryptate complex rearranges, has not been established except for the macrotricyclic ligand XVII (see Table 15). The inclusion complexes of this ligand are believed to be asymmetric, with the cation located nearer one end of the cylindrical cavity. An intramolecular switch in which the cation bounces from end to end of the cylinder was proposed to explain the NMR spectra. For the weakest of the complexes in Table 15, a dissociation process occurred at higher temperature (higher $\Delta G^{\ddagger}$), assigned to process (2) in the scheme.[47]

Solvent effects have been studied only for calcium cryptates. Moderate acid catalysis in water has been noted[22] (Table 16). The larger cations Sr^{2+} and Ba^{2+} have a reduced tendency to acid-catalysed dissociation.

2. Comparison of Group II with Groups I and III cations

The series Na^+, Ca^{2+}, Eu^{3+} provides variation in charge but close similarity in cation size (Table 14). Rates show little variation in crown complexes, but for cryptate (2,2,2) there is a factor of $\sim 10^2$–10^4 difference in both cryptation and decryptation rate constants for each unit of charge. The rate constants for Eu^{3+} are extremely small.[51,24] These were measured by cyclic voltammetry[24,51] and show pH dependence. Although the cryptates of Eu^{2+} aquate faster, they are much more thermodynamically stable than those of Eu^{3+}. More data on this point may be adduced from Tables 12–16. The Eu^{2+} cation behaves in the same way as the alkaline earths, the comparison with Sr^{2+}, which is the same size, being particularly valuable (see Table 16). The increased stability of 2^+ cryptates relative to 1^+ cryptates does not extrapolate to the Eu^{3+} cryptates.

The smaller cations show a greater tendency to acid catalysis, which (i) sets in at a lower concentration of acid, and (ii) gives a larger ratio of k_{H^+}/k_{-2}. There is no clear effect of increased charge over the range of data available (Table 16). It should be noted that for the triply charged lanthanide cations which aquate with a half-life of ~ 27 days at 25°C, small anions accelerate the reaction dramatically (OH^- reducing the half-life to 22 min and F^- to 2·8 days). The high residual charge on the lanthanide cation must be responsible. The CNDO-calculated residual charge on Na in a complex with ligand I $(NaL)^+$ is $\sim 0·3$–$0·4$, while for Ca in the same situation $(CaL)^{2+}$ it is $1·4$–$1·5$. The ion–dipole attraction of the lanthanide cryptate for anions outside the cryptand skin should be significant. The importance of this observation is that it opens up the possibility of adding further anionic reporter groups, perhaps to asymmetric cryptates, as probes of the interaction.

B. Other ligands

Ultrasonic absorption of EDTA complexes of the divalent metal ions Ca^{2+}, Sr^{2+} and Ba^{2+} (also Co^{2+}) at concentrations of ~0·2–0·6 M in aqueous solution was studied[89] with a view to verifying the pentacoordinate–hexacoordinate equilibrium (Equation (11)) which has been the subject of much work,[90–93] and obtaining rate data k_f and k_r for forward and reverse steps, plus ΔV, the volume change for the reaction

$$MY'^{2-} \underset{k_r}{\overset{k_f}{\rightleftharpoons}} MY''^{2-} \tag{11}$$

Additional data for the related PDTA and CyDTA ligands for which the equilibrium position of Equation (11) will differ was also obtained. A single absorption was observed which was dependent on ionic strength but independent of pH > 5 for Ca, pH > 7 for Sr and pH > 10 for the Ba system, and the derived values of k_f all at pH 12·0 (based on the assumption that $K = k_f/k_r = $ [hexacoord]/[pentacoord] = 7/3) are about an order of magnitude less than the water substitution process for the alkaline earth cations (Table 17). Rapid pre-equilibria are also discussed.

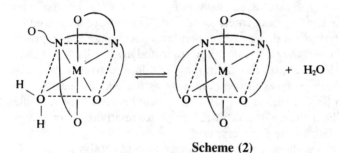

Scheme (2)

A foretaste of the contribution likely to emanate from direct NMR studies on the alkaline earth nuclei is given in a paper[94] on ^{43}Ca and ^{25}Mg NMR studies of processes occurring in rabbit skeletal muscle troponin C (TnC) in vitro.† The contraction of muscle develops when calcium ions flow into the sarcoplasm and bind to TnC, setting in motion the regulatory mechanism of the troponin–tropomyosin complex and enabling the thin and thick filaments to interact.‡ This occurs *in vivo* on the millisecond

---

† Biological papers are not in general surveyed for inclusion in this chapter unless they are of strong chemical interest.

‡ For a recent discussion of the role of Ca^{2+} in muscle contraction, see McCubbin, W.D.; Kay, C.M. *Acc. Chem. Res.*, **1980**, *13*, 185.

TABLE 17

Kinetic parameters for Equation (11) obtained
at 0·2–0·6 M MY, pH 12·0 and 25·0°C

Cation	$10^{-7} k_f$ (s^{-1})	$10^{-7} k_r$ (s^{-1})	ΔV $(cm^3 \, mol^{-1})$
Ca	3·6	1·5	5·3
Sr	9·2	3·9	3·6
Ba	14·5	6·2	5·4

time scale. The rate of exchange of Ca^{2+} and/or Mg^{2+} from their TnC complexes was measured using enriched samples (60% ^{43}Ca and 98% ^{25}Mg) and the observed rates were correlated with rates of changes observed using fluorescence probes on the TnC.

$$2M + TnC \underset{k_{-1}}{\overset{k_1}{\rightleftharpoons}} M_2TnC \underset{k_{-2}}{\overset{k_2}{\rightleftharpoons}} M_2TnC^*$$
$$\quad\quad\quad\quad (1) \quad\quad\quad\quad (2)$$

$$2M + M_2TnC^* \underset{k_{-3}}{\overset{k_3}{\rightleftharpoons}} M_4TnC^* \underset{k_{-4}}{\overset{k_4}{\rightleftharpoons}} M_4TnC^{**}$$
$$\quad\quad\quad\quad\quad (3) \quad\quad\quad\quad (4)$$

Scheme (3)

Of the four Ca^{2+} binding sites for TnC, two are high-affinity sites, $K_1 = 2 \times 10^7 \, M^{-1}$, and two are the regulatory sites with lower affinity, $K_3 = 3 \times 10^5 \, M^{-1}$. Mg^{2+} can bind to the Ca^{2+} high-affinity sites—$K = 5 \times 10^3 \, M^{-1}$—and also perhaps to other low affinity sites.

Scheme (3) indicates four processes for the interaction of metal ions with TnC (steps 1 and 3 are the filling of the high- and low-affinity sites) and subsequent conformational change of the protein (steps (2) and (4)). Fluorescence measurements indicate $k_{-2} = 1 \, s^{-1}$ and $k_{-4} = 300 \, s^{-1}$ for Ca^{2+}, which suggests step (4) to be the most important step in muscle control, and $k_{-2} \doteq 8 \, s^{-1}$ and $k_2 = 100 \, s^{-1}$ for Mg^{2+}. The NMR experiments measured the Ca^{2+} exchange at the regulatory sites only, the rate constant $k_{off} = k_{-3} = 1 \times 10^3 \, s^{-1}$, a factor of ten faster than the conformational change. The Mg^{2+} release was 10^3 times faster ($k_{off} = 8 \pm 5 \times 10^3 \, s^{-1}$) than the conformational change in step (2). While the Ca^{2+} exchange rate in the absence of Mg^{2+} is approximately equal at each of the two regulatory sites, in the presence of Mg^{2+} the rate at one site becomes a factor of ~10 greater than that at the other site. It is thus possible that Mg^{2+} may play a role in modifying Ca^{2+} exchange rates *in vivo*.

C. Grignard formation

A fresh look at one of the most familiar of all laboratory reactions,

$$RX + Mg \longrightarrow RMgX \qquad (R = alkyl, aryl, X = halide)$$

the formation of Grignard reagent, is recounted in a series of papers.[95–100] For alkyl iodides, the rate of this heterogeneous reaction is limited only by the rate of encounter of the reagents (i.e. controlled by the diffusion rate and the rate of mass transport across phase boundaries) and not by chemical factors. The rate for alkyl chlorides, and for some of the less reactive alkyl bromides, is controlled by chemical factors, and is proportional to the concentration of RX and the surface area of the magnesium. The rates of reaction for certain alkyl and aryl halides have been determined. Extensive use was made of structure–reactivity profiles to eliminate from the list of possible intermediates carbanions and carbocations, and to discount the S_N2 and direct insertion mechanisms. The two most likely steps were considered to be electron transfer to the organic halide from Mg, and/or halogen abstraction from the organic halide by Mg. Structure–reactivity profiles for Grignard formation for aryl bromides compared well with those for known free radical reactions of the substrate. Previous NMR studies[99] show the anomalous signal intensities characteristic of chemically induced dynamic nuclear polarisation (CIDNP), demonstrating free radical intermediates in Grignard mixtures. The difficulty of trapping such free radicals in the presence of Grignard reagents which are themselves most efficient scavengers, has been overcome by using a nitroxide as radical trapping agent together with t-BuOH which traps the Grignard as it is formed.[100] The relative rates of trapping of the Grignard by t-BuOH and the nitroxide spin-trap are such that very little of the Grignard reacts with the spin-trap. The reaction of cyclopentyl bromide

with Mg was studied, and the cyclopentyl radical was trapped by 2,2,6,6-tetramethylpiperidine nitroxyl (XXXI) as O-cyclopentylhydroxylamine (XXXII). Scheme (4) shows the sequence of reactions. More than 80% of the original cyclopentylbromide could be trapped as XXXII, indicating that the free radical is the precursor of most of the Grignard formed in the cyclopentyl bromide–magnesium reaction under the conditions used.[100]

$$RBr \xrightarrow{\text{Mg}} \underset{\text{transient}}{[R \cdot]} \longrightarrow RMgBr$$

$$R \cdot \xrightarrow[\text{XXXI}]{\text{fast}} XXXII$$

$$RMgBr \xrightarrow[\text{XXXI}]{\text{slow}} XXXII$$

$$RMgBr \xrightarrow[\text{tBuOH}]{\text{fast}} \text{cyclo-}C_5H_{10}$$

Scheme (4)

IV. GROUP IIIB ELEMENTS

A. Hydrometallation

The hydrometallation of olefins is extremely important in organic synthesis. Mechanisms of the reactions are of great concern to practising chemists both in industrial and academic research. Some relevant studies including recent theoretical approaches, are grouped here.

1. Hydroboration

The hydroboration reaction[101,102] which provides a striking example of the contribution of theoretical chemistry to the elucidation of mechanism, has proved too complicated for detailed kinetic investigation in solution except in special cases,[103–105] while the gas-phase reaction kinetics[106] posed very great practical problems. A number of molecular orbital calculations relating to the potential energy surface of the reaction have been made recently and these, while they do not reproduce experimental activation energies, help considerably in the understanding of the transition state and other features of the reaction.

Kinetic studies in solution are complicated by a number of alternative and additional reactions. For instance the solvent, if it is a Lewis base, may complex with borane. A plurality of steps is possible subsequent to the first addition of olefin, exemplified in Scheme (5) for the ethylene reaction. The three hydrogens of the BH_3 unit can be successively involved. There are three possible redistribution equilibria, and five possible monomer–dimer reactions of the first-formed products.[103,104] The first stage of the reaction, formation of thexyl borane, **XXXIII**, is possible for the hindered olefin $Me_2C{=}CMe_2$, and subsequent reactions can be blocked, except for the formation of the hydrogen-bridged dimer.

$$Me_2CH . CMe_2BH_2$$
$$\textbf{XXXIII}$$

Equilibria possible in the addition of BH$_3$ to olefins,† exemplified by ethylene

Hydroborations

$$CH_2 = CH_2 + BH_3 \rightleftharpoons EtBH_2$$

$$CH_2 = CH_2 + EtBH_2 \rightleftharpoons Et_2BH$$

$$CH_2 = CH_2 + Et_2BH \rightleftharpoons Et_3B$$

Redistributions

$$Et_3B + BH_3 \rightleftharpoons Et_2BH + EtBH_2$$

$$2EtBH_2 \rightleftharpoons Et_2BH + BH_3$$

$$2Et_2BH \rightleftharpoons EtBH_2 + Et_3B$$

Monomer-dimer equilibria (hydrogen-bridged dimers)

$$2BH_3 \rightleftharpoons B_2H_6$$

$$EtBH_2 + BH_3 \rightleftharpoons EtHBH_2BH_2$$

$$Et_2BH + BH_3 \rightleftharpoons Et_2BH_2BH_2$$

$$EtBH_2 + Et_2BH \rightleftharpoons EtHBH_2BEt_2$$

$$2Et_2BH \rightleftharpoons Et_2BH_2BEt_2$$

$$2EtBH_2 \rightleftharpoons EtHBH_2BHEt$$

Scheme (5)

† Equilibria in the addition of AlH_3 to olefins are even more complex, since higher oligomers can be formed, and the alkyl groups can act as bridges as well as the hydrogen.

For this first stage reaction, second-order kinetics, first-order in borane and in olefin, were obtained, with an E_a of 9.2 ± 0.4 kcal mol^{-1} and $\Delta S^{\ddagger} = -27 \pm 1$ cal K^{-1} mol^{-1}. The hydrogen–deuterium kinetic isotope effect was found to be 1·18, and the data were held to imply an early, asymmetric transition state with no evidence for the π-complex suggested by Streitwieser.[105] Fehlner determined the activation energy of the ethylene–borane reaction as 2 ± 3 kcal mol^{-1} in the gas-phase, and the transition state was thought to be a loosely bound ethylborane, rather than a π-complex.[106] Substituents are also known to affect the steric course of the reaction, anti-Markownikoff (AM) addition to the double bond for alkyl substituted olefins, while Markownikoff (M) addition can occur for electron-withdrawing substituents on the olefin. These also suggest a loosely bound transition state.

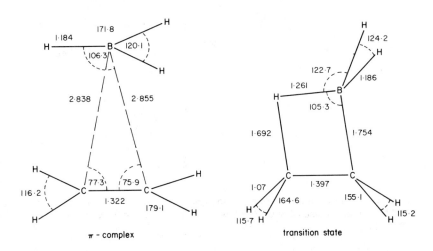

Fig. 7. Geometries calculated at the 4-31G SCF level, given in Angstroms and degrees. Reproduced with permission from Ref. [111].†

Theoretical approaches to the hydroboration of olefins using different levels of approximation have been made. These include a CNDO (complete neglect of differential overlap) approach,[107] the Dewar MNDO approximation[108] (modified neglect of differential overlap), PRDDO (partial retention of diatomic differential overlap) approach, coupled with more refined calculations of critical points along the reaction coordinate,[110,111] and further *ab initio* studies at more refined levels.[109,112] The more refined

† For explanation of basis sets, e.g. 4–31G, see the original papers.

calculations suggest that a π-complex is formed at a local minimum, early in the reaction,[112] and that both AM and M steric paths proceed from the π-complex,[111] the M path being favoured by $1 \cdot 1$ kcal mol^{-1} for cyanoethylene, and the AM path being favoured by $1 \cdot 1$ kcal mol^{-1} for propylene. The actual transition state is now thought to be a concerted, asymmetric,

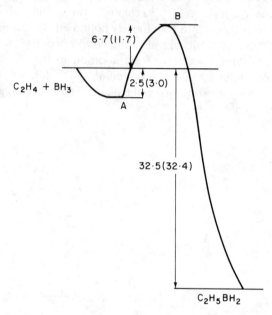

Fig. 8. Energy profile for the reaction $C_2H_4 + BH_3$. Values in kcal mol^{-1} for 6-31G** (parentheses 4-31G) SCF levels. Reproduced with permission from Ref. [111].

four-centre one. The optimized geometries obtained for the π-complex and the transition state by Nagase, Ray and Morukuma[112] (at the 4-31G SCF level) are shown in Fig. 7, and a potential energy profile for selected points calculated using the basis sets 4-31G and 6-31G**, is shown in Fig. 8.

2. Hydroalumination

A kinetic study of the reaction of diisobutylalane with 4-octyne $(i\text{-}Bu_2AlH)_3 + PrC{\equiv}CPr \rightarrow (i\text{-}Bu_2Al)PrC{=}CPrH$ was made by Eisch and Rhee,[113] who found two reaction steps, firstly the dissociation of trimer to monomer alane, secondly the rate-determining addition of alane to octyne. The activation energy for the rate-determining step was $4 \pm$

$2 \, \text{kcal mol}^{-1}$ in hexane solution. The kinetic isotope effect k_H/k_D was determined to be 1.68.

A SCF MO study of the hydroalumination reaction in Equation (12),

$$H_2AlH^* + HC\equiv CH \rightarrow H_2AlCH\!=\!CHH^* \tag{12}$$

using a contracted basis set of Gaussian-type orbitals has been made. Energies of the reactants, products, symmetric π-complex, and several points potentially along the reaction path were calculated. The results are qualitatively similar to those for the hydroboration reaction in IV.A.1, suggesting a concerted reaction in which the four reacting atoms of the asymmetric transition state (cf. Fig. 7) are joined by fractional bonds. The calculated activation energy was rather high at $14 \, \text{kcal mol}^{-1}$ compared to the experimental estimate of Eisch and Rhee. The π-complex was described as a shallow minimum like the hydroboration one described above.[114]

B. Reactions of borohydride and amine boranes

The mechanism of hydrolysis of BH_4^- in acetonitrile, as catalysed by acetic acid,[115] has been reassessed[116] following the discovery (via ^{11}B NMR[117] studies) that the kinetics measured previously were not those for BH_4^- but those of the fast-formed $BH_3O_2CCH_3^-$ (Scheme (6)). The first step, Equation (13) is fast and the

$$BH_4^- + CH_3CO_2H \overset{\text{fast}}{\rightleftharpoons} [CH_3CO_2H_2BH_3^-] \overset{\text{fast}}{\rightleftharpoons} CH_3CO_2BH_3^- + H_2 \tag{13}$$

$$CH_3CO_2BH_3^- + CH_3CO_2H \overset{K}{\rightleftharpoons} CH_3C \begin{array}{c} \diagup O^-\!\!-\!BH_3 \\ \diagdown \cdots HOCOCH_3 \end{array} \tag{14}$$

$$\text{rds} \diagup \quad \text{H-bonded complex}$$

$$k_{H_2O} \qquad\qquad\qquad \text{rds} \quad\Big\downarrow\, k_0$$

$$BH_3OH_2 + (CH_3CO_2)_2H^- \qquad BH_3(\text{solvent}) + (CH_3CO_2)_2H^-$$

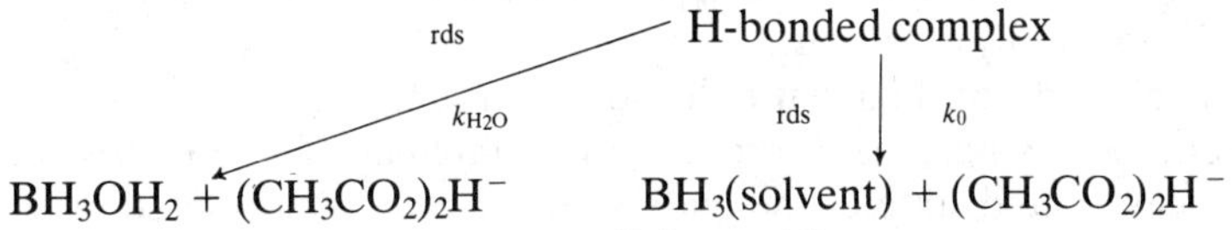

Scheme (6)

equilibrium constant K for Equation (14) is ~ 160. The loss of the next hydrogen from the BH_3 fragment of the H-bonded complex is after the rate-determining step. A variety of other intermediates was found in the NMR studies, believed to occur after the rate-determining step. The rate constants varied with water concentration, and a plot of the observed rate versus the water concentration gave the parameters k_0 (the "spontaneous" rate) and k_{H_2O}. Isotope effects on k_0 and k_{H_2O} were measured, with considerable uncertainty, but the effect on k_{H_2O} is very similar to the known isotope effects for acid hydrolysis of BH_4^- in water solvent.[118]

The isotope distribution of hydrogen formed in reaction of BH_4^- with aqueous acid, and the anhydrous reactions of $NaBH_4$ with H_2SO_4 and $HF^{[119]}$ in various isotopic combinations has been re-examined employing a permutational analysis of the assumed BH_5 intermediate on the reaction path.[120] The sequence in Equation (15) is assumed:

$$BH_4^- + H^+ \rightarrow [BH_5] \rightarrow BH_3 + H_2 \qquad (15)$$

Experimental results obtained by earlier workers for appropriate mixtures of BH_4^- and DX or BD_4^- and HX were interpreted in terms of a rigid C_s intermediate BH_5 for the aqueous acid results, edge attack on a tetrahedral face of BH_4^- by H_2SO_4 followed by axial–equatorial loss from a trigonal bipyramid BH_5, while the HF reaction was supposed to proceed via a fluxional BH_5 of undetermined structure. The interpretation is very dependent on the accuracy of the experimental observations, and on the assumed intermediate. The experimental data correspond to the loss of only one hydrogen per BH_4^- unit, and were obtained by reacting metal borohydride with an appropriate molar deficit of acid. Very similar experimental data for the AlH_4^- system are available.[119]

The mechanism of acid-catalysed hydrolysis of $NH_3 \cdot BH_3$ has been examined in an attempt to detect any species analogous to the BH_5 intermediate.[121] Hydrolysis was found to be faster than hydrogen exchange of B–H hydrogen, and to have a normal solution isotope effect (k_{H_2O}/k_{D_2O}) of ~1·5. The previously suggested mechanism[122] with electrophilic attack of the proton at the amino nitrogen, and *cis* displacement of the BH_3 is perfectly consistent with the data obtained, while the possibility of a five-coordinate intermediate is hard to reconcile with substitution effects, although it is not firmly ruled out.

A theoretical study of fluxional behaviour of $NaBH_4$ and H_2AlBH_4 by *ab initio* methods has been carried out, with a minimal STO-3G basis set of orbitals. The ground state of the $NaBH_4$ molecule was calculated to be most stable in the tridentate form XXXIV, that of the AlH_2BH_4 molecule was calculated to be most stable as the bidentate form XXXV. Tetradentate or unidentate forms were much higher in energy. Transition states for fluxional rearrangements were also examined, and the lowest energy for the $NaBH_4$ transition state was found for a bidentate configuration, while for the AlH_2BH_4, a tridentate geometry was the most likely for the transition state. Mechanisms corresponding to Berry pseudorotation were found to be unlikely because of the very high activation energies calculated for such paths.[123]

tridentate

XXXIV

bidentate

XXXV

C. Further reactions in Group III

1. Free radical reactions at boron centres

In the late 1960s a remarkable surge of information relating to homolytic substitution at boron centres formed part of a revival of interest in reactions of free radicals in solution.[124] A range of free radicals, such as peroxy, butoxy, alkylthiyl, could be reacted with triorganoboranes to displace an organic radical from boron. The reactions were very fast, and rates of radical attack on substrate were obtained by elegant competition techniques.[124] Equimolar mounts of borane and another substrate, usually cyclopentane, were allowed to compete for the attacking free radical, and the resultant displaced radicals (R· from the alkylborane, and cyclopentyl· from the cyclopentane) were sufficiently long-lived for their relative concentrations to be measured by integration of ESR signals, or, after quenching, by GLC. The rate constants for t-BuO· radical attack on some representative borane substrates R_3B are shown in Table 18. It is usually

TABLE 18
Rate constants for attack of t-BuO· on organoboranes at room temperature

R_3B	k ($M^{-1}\ s^{-1}$)	Method
Ph_3B	$1{\cdot}0\ 10^8$	laser photolysis[126]
n-Bu_3B	$1{\cdot}5\ 10^8$	competition with cyclopentane[a]
i-Bu_3B	$5{\cdot}1\ 10^6$	competition with cyclopentane[a]
sec-Bu_3B	$1{\cdot}5\ 10^6$	competition with cyclopentane[a]
$(MeBO)_3$	$1{\cdot}0\ 10^7$	competition with cyclopentane[a]

[a] New values, derived from those described in Ref. [124] (using new absolute rate data for cyclopentane taken from Paul, H.; Small, R.D.; and Scaiano, J.C. *J. Amer. Chem. Soc.* **1978**, *100*, 4520), as recalculated by the authors of Ref. [126].

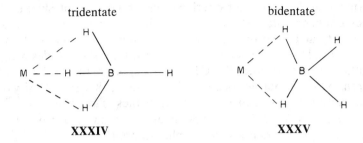

uncertain if the homolytic substitution is synchronous or not, since evidence has seldom been obtained for any free radical intermediate with unpaired spin density at the boron. Models for a possible four-coordinate boron-containing radical have been prepared by reaction of nitroxides with BCl_3 and other boron substrates $(R_2NOBCl_3\cdot)$. Coupling of the residual unpaired electron to the ^{11}B nucleus (spin $I = 3/2$), with ~5–8% spin density on the boron can be identified in ESR spectra of these model radicals.[125] The alkoxy radical t-BuO$\dot{\text{B}}$Ph$_3$ has now been observed as a product of the reaction of t-butoxy radicals with triphenylboron.[126]

$$\text{t-BuO·} + \text{BPh}_3 \xrightarrow{k_a} \underset{\text{XXXI}}{\text{t-BuO}\dot{\text{B}}\text{Ph}_3} \xrightarrow{k_d} \text{t-BuOBPh}_2 + \text{Ph·}$$

Butoxy radical was generated by flash photolysis and reacted to give a transient species, attributed as XXXI, with a rate constant $k_a = 1 \times 10^8 \, \text{M}^{-1}\text{s}^{-1}$ at 22°C. The transient decayed with a half-life of 15 μs. The mechanism of the reaction had been established previously but the hitherto elusive boron-centred radical had not been detected. Knowledge of its decay rate may make possible its detection by ESR.

Brindley, Hodgson, and Scotton[127] report that thermal decomposition of peroxy boron compounds $n\text{BuOOB}n\text{Bu}_2$, $(n\text{BuOO})_2\text{B}n\text{Bu}$ and $(s\text{BuOO})_2\text{B}s\text{Bu}$ is predominantly non-radical, but with a minor homolytic path. The activation parameters observed for the major path were:

	$\Delta H^{\ddagger}$ (kcal mol^{-1})	$\Delta S^{\ddagger}$ (cal K^{-1} mol^{-1})
$n\text{BuOOB}n\text{Bu}_2$	$13 \cdot 6 \pm 1 \cdot 07$	$-39 \cdot 5$
$(n\text{BuOO})_2\text{B}n\text{Bu}$	$15 \cdot 2 \pm 0 \cdot 4$	$-34 \cdot 1$
$(s\text{BuOO})_2\text{B}s\text{Bu}$	$10 \cdot 5 \pm 0 \cdot 53$	$-43 \cdot 1$

2. Elimination reaction of an alane

This is one of the fundamental synthetic routes in Group III chemistry, elimination of the elements of hydrogen, hydrogen halide or alkane being particular examples.[128] The proposed reaction sequence is shown in Equations (16) and (17), for dimethylalane and *N*-methylaniline.[129]

$$\text{Me}_2\text{AlH} + \text{PhNMeH} \underset{}{\overset{K_a}{\rightleftharpoons}} \text{Me}_2\text{AlH} \cdot \text{PhNMeH} \tag{16}$$

$$\text{Me}_2\text{AlH} + \text{PhNMeH} \xrightarrow{k} \text{H}_2 + \text{Me}_2\text{AlNMePh} \tag{17}$$

The reaction, in toluene solution at -63°C, was found to be second-order, the equilibrium Equation (16) being a "dead-end" path. The value of K_a was found to be $110 \, \text{M}^{-1}$ and $k = 6 \cdot 01 \times 10^{-3} \, \text{M}^{-1}\text{s}^{-1}$. Subsequent formation of a dimer, with 4:1 ratio of *cis*:*trans* isomers was thought to be a fast cycloaddition between monomers ($_2\pi_s + _2\pi_a$). Elimination of hydrogen is again rate-determining in the similar kinetic behaviour of the more basic primary amine benzylamine in reaction in toluene at −63°C with dimethylalane.[130] An additional equilibrium, with the four-coordinate adduct (see Equation (16)) adding a second mole of amine to give five-coordinate aluminium is a complicating step prior to the rate-determining one, and there are other more complex equilibria than in the *N*-methylaniline reaction, which complicate steps after the hydrogen elimination. The composite constant kK_a (see Equations (16) and (17)) was found to be $1·8 \times 10^{-4}\,s^{-1}$, but separate values of k and K_a could not be obtained. Again the stable product (under the kinetic conditions) was a dimer. Dissociation of the adduct appears to be a pre-requisite for the elimination reaction, as was found for the comparable studies of elimination of hydrogen halide from boron halide–amine adducts en route to borazole formation in studies over a decade ago.[1]

3. Redistribution of mixed halometallates

NMR studies on the central nucleus (^{115}In or ^{71}Ga) have been made for the mixed halometallates of In and Ga.[131, 132] The results show the scrambling reaction (Equation (18)) for indium to be complete on mixing, while the gallium reaction is sufficiently slow that the initial build-up of GaX_3Y^- prior to $GaX_2Y_2^-$ can be seen. This may be compared with data on the haloborates,[133] which were examined mechanistically by Hartman and Schrobilgen some years ago.

$$MX_4^- + MY_4^- \rightarrow MX_3Y^- + MX_2Y_2^- + MXY_3^- \tag{18}$$

REFERENCES

[1] Lockhart, J.C. "MTP Review", Vol. 9, Series Two; Tobe, M.L., Ed.; Butterworths: London, 1974; p. 1.
[2] Pedersen, C.J. *J. Amer. Chem. Soc.* **1967**, *89*, 7017.
[3] Dietrich, B.; Lehn, J.M.; Sauvage, J.P. *Tetrahedron Letters*, **1969**, *34*, 2885, 2889.
[4] Williams, R.J.P. *Q. Rev. Chem. Soc.* **1970**, *24*, 331.
[5] Delville, A.; Detellier, C.; Laszlo, P. *J. Mag. Resonance* **1979**, *34*, 301.
[6] Venkatachalam, C.M.; Urry, D.W. *J. Mag. Resonance* **1980**, *41*, 313.
[7a] Bull, T.E.; Forsèn, S.; Turner, D.L. *J. Chem. Phys.* **1979**, *70*, 3106.
[7b] Forsèn, S.; Lindman, B. *Ann Rep. NMR Spectroscopy* **1981**, *11A*, 183.
[8] Porter, R.F.; Turbini, L.J. "Topics in Current Chemistry", Vol. 96; Inorganic Chemistry; Springer-Verlag: Berlin, 1981; p. 1.

[9] Bauer, S.H. *Ann. Rev. Phys. Chem.* **1979**, *30*, 271.

[10] Laszlo, P. *Progress in NMR* **1979**, *13*, 257.

[11] Popov, A.I. *Pure Appl. Chem.* **1979**, *51*, 101.

[12] Reinhoudt, D.N.; de Jong, F. "Advances in Physical Organic Chemistry", Vol. 17; Gold, V., Bethell, D, Eds.; Academic Press: London, 1980; p. 279.

[13] Burgermeister, W.; Winkler-Oswatitsch, R. "Topics in Current Chemistry", Vol. 69; Springer-Verlag: Berlin, 1977; p. 91.

[14] Liesegang, G.W.; Eyring, E.F. *In* "Synthetic Multidentate Macrocyclic Compounds"; Izatt, R.M., Christensen, J.J. Eds.; Academic Press: New York, 1978; Chapter 5.

[15] "Progress in Macrocyclic Chemistry"; Izatt, R.M., Christensen, J.J. Eds.; Wiley: New York, 1979; Vol. 1.

[16] Cram, D.J.; Cram, J.M. *Acc. Chem. Res.* **1978**, *11*, 8.

[17] Lehn, J.M. *Acc. Chem. Res.* **1978**, *11*, 49.

[18] Shchori, E.; Jagur-Grodzinski, J.; Shporer, M. *J. Amer. Chem. Soc.* **1973**, *95*, 3842.

[19] Coxon, A.C.; Stoddart, J.F. *J. Chem. Soc., Perkin I* **1977**, 767.

[20] Gresser, R.; Boyd, D.W.; Albrecht-Gary, A.M.; Schwing, J.P. *J. Amer. Chem. Soc.* **1980**, *102*, 651.

[21] Chock, P.B. *Proc. Nat. Acad. Sci. U.S.A.* **1972**, *69*, 1939.

[22] Cox, B.G.; Schneider, H. *J. Amer. Chem. Soc.* **1977**, *99*, 2809.

[23a] Farber, H.; Petrucci, S. *J. Phys. Chem.* **1981**, *85*, 1396.

[23b] Liesegang, G.W.; Farrow, M.M.; Vazquez, F.A.; Purdie, N.; Eyring, E.M. *J. Amer. Chem. Soc.* **1977**, *99*, 3240.

[24] Yee, E.L.; Gansow, O.A.; Weaver, M.J. *J. Amer. Chem. Soc.* **1980**, *102*, 2278.

[25] Liesegang, G.W. *J. Amer. Chem. Soc.* **1981**, *103*, 953.

[26] Shporer, M.; Luz, Z. *J. Amer. Chem. Soc.* **1975**, *97*, 665.

[27] Anet, F.A.L.; Krane, J.; Dale, J.; Daasvatn, K.; Kristiansen, P.O. *Acta Chem. Scand.* **1973**, *27*, 3395.

[28] Borgen, G.; Dale, J.; Daasvatn, K.; Krane, J. *Acta Chem. Scand.* **1980**, *B34*, 249.

[29] Krane, J.; Amble, E.; Dale, J.; Daasvatn, K. *Acta Chem. Scand.* **1980**, *B34*, 255.

[30] Krane, J.; Dale, J.; Daasvatn, K. *Acta Chem. Scand.* **1980**, *B34*, 59.

[31] Lockhart, J.C.; Robson, A.C.; Thompson, M.E.; Tyson, P.D.; Wallace, I.H.M. *J. Chem. Soc., Dalton* **1978**, 611.

[32] Hughes, B.B.; Haltiwanger, R.C.; Pierpont, C.G.; Hampton, M.; Blackmer, G.L. *Inorg. Chem.* **1980**, *19*, 1801.

[33] North, P.P.; Steiner, E.C.; Remoortere, F.P.; Boer, F.P. *Acta Cryst.* **1976**, *B32*, 370.

[34] Groth, P. *Acta Chem. Scand.* **1978**, *A32*, 279.

[35] Bovill, M.J.; Chadwick, D.T.; Sutherland, I.O.; and in part, Watkin, D. *J. Chem. Soc., Perkin II* **1980**, 1529.

[36] Lockhart, J.C., unpublished work.

[37] Shinkai, S.; Nakaji, T.; Nishida, Y.; Ogawa, T.; Manabe, O. *J. Amer. Chem. Soc.* **1980**, *102*, 5860.

[38] Newkome, G.R.; Nayak, A.; Fronczek, F.; Kawato, T.; Taylor, H.C.R.; Meade, L.; Mattice, W. *J. Amer. Chem. Soc.* **1979**, *101*, 4472.

[39] Lehn, J.M.; Sauvage, J.P.; Dietrich, B. *J. Amer. Chem. Soc.* **1970**, *92*, 2916.

[40] Schneider, H.; Rauh, S.; Petrucci, S. *J. Phys. Chem.* **1981**, *85*, 2287.
[41] Winkler, R. *Structure and Bonding*, **1972**, *10*, 1.
[42] Cox, B.G.; Garcia-Rosas, J.; Schneider, H. *J. Amer. Chem. Soc.* **1981**, *103*, 1054, 1384.
[43a] Tümmler, B.; Maass, G.; Weber, E.; Wehner, W.; Vögtle, F. *J. Amer. Chem. Soc.* **1977**, *99*, 4683.
[43b] Tümmler, B.; Maass, G.; Vögtle, F.; Sieger, H.; Heimann, U.; Weber, E. *J. Amer. Chem. Soc.* **1979**, *101*, 2588.
[44] Gutmann, V. "Coordination Chemistry in Non-Aqueous Solvents"; Springer-Verlag: Vienna, 1968.
[45] Wong, J.H.; Konizer, G.; Smid, J. *J. Amer. Chem. Soc.* **1970**, *92*, 666.
[46] Mei, E.; Dye, J.L.; Popov, A.I. *J. Amer. Chem. Soc.* **1977**, *99*, 5308.
[47] Lehn, J.M.; Stubbs, M.E. *J. Amer. Chem. Soc.* **1974**, *96*, 4011.
[48] Graf, E.; Lehn, J.M. *J. Amer. Chem. Soc.* **1975**, *97*, 5022.
[49] Cram, D.J.; Kaneda, T.; Lein, G.M.; Helgeson, R.G. *J.C.S. Chem. Comm.* **1979**, 948; Helgeson, R.C.; Mazaleyrat, J.P.; Cram, D.J. *J. Amer. Chem. Soc.* **1981**, *103*, 3929.
[50] Lehn, J.M.; Sauvage, J.P. *J. Amer. Chem. Soc.* **1975**, *97*, 6700.
[51] Gansow, O.A.; Kausar, A.R.; Triplett, K.M.; Weaver, M.J.; Yee, E.L. *J. Amer. Chem. Soc.* **1977**, *99*, 7087.
[52] Dietrich, B.; Lehn, J.M.; Sauvage, J.P.; Blanzat, J. *Tetrahedron* **1973**, *29*, 1629.
[53] Dietrich, B.; Lehn, J.M.; Sauvage, J.P. *Tetrahedron* **1973**, *29*, 1647.
[54] Moras, D.; Weiss, R. *Acta Cryst.* **1973**, *B29*, 396, 400.
[55] Moras, D.; Metz, B.; Weiss, R. *Acta Cryst.* **1973**, *B29*, 383, 388.
[56] Fischer, J.; Mellinger, M.; Weiss, R. *Inorg. Chim. Acta* **1977**, *21*, 259.
[57] Mathieu, F.; Metz, B.; Moras, D.; Weiss, R. *J. Amer. Chem. Soc.* **1978**, *100*, 4412.
[58] Cox, B.G.; Schneider, H. *J. Amer. Chem. Soc.* **1980**, *102*, 3628.
[59] Kauffman, E.; Dye, J.L.; Lehn, J.M.; Popov, A.I. *J. Amer. Chem. Soc.* **1980**, *102*, 2274.
[60] Shih, J.S.; Popov, A.I. *Inorg. Chem.* **1980**, *19*, 1689.
[61] Lockhart, J.C.; Atkinson, B.; Marshall, G.; Davies, B. *J. Chem. Research*, S. **1979**, 32.
[62] Cox, B.G.; Schneider, H.; Stroka, J. *J. Amer. Chem. Soc.* **1978**, *100*, 4746.
[63] Cox, B.G.; Garcia-Rosas, J.; Schneider, H. *J. Phys. Chem.* **1980**, *84*, 3178.
[64] Cox, B.G.; Knop, D.; Schneider, H. *J. Phys. Chem.* **1980**, *84*, 320.
[65] Eisenman, G.; Krasne, S.; Ciani, S. *Ann. N.Y. Acad. Sci.* **1975**, *264*, 34.
[66] Lamb, J.D.; Christensen, J.J.; Oscarson, J.L.; Nielsen, B.L.; Asay, B.W.; Izatt, R.M. *J. Amer. Chem. Soc.* **1980**, *102*, 6820.
[67] Lamb, J.D.; Christensen, J.J.; Izatt, S.R.; Bedke, K.; Astin, M.S.; Izatt, R.M. *J. Amer. Chem. Soc.* **1980**, *102*, 3399.
[68] Lindenbaum, S.; Rytting, J.H.; Sternson, L.A., Chapter 5 in Ref. [15].
[69] Hansch, C. *Acc. Chem. Res.* **1969**, *2*, 232.
[70] Morf, W.E.; Amman, D.; Bissig, R.; Pretsch, E.; Simon, W., Chapter 1 in Ref. [15].
[71] Lehn, J.M. *Structure and Bonding*, **1973**, *16*, 1.
[72] Reusch, C.F.; Cussler, E.L. *A.I. Ch. E. Journal* **1973**, *19*, 736; **1975**, *21*, 160.
[73] Tajima, I.; Okada, M.; Sumitomo, H. *J. Amer. Chem. Soc.* **1981**, *103*, 4096.

[74] Davis, D.G.; Gisin, B.F. J. Amer. Chem. Soc. 1979, 101, 3755.

[75] Benz, R.; Gisin, B.F.; Ting-Beall, H.P.; Tosteson, D.C.; Läuger, P. Biochim. Biophys. Acta 1976, 455, 665.

[76] Gisin, B.F.; Ting-Beall, H.P.; Davis, D.G.; Grell, E.; Tosteson, D.C. Biochim. Biophys. Acta 1978, 509, 201.

[77] Ovchinnikov, Y.A.; Ivanov, A.M.; Schrob, A.M. "Membrane-Active Complexones"; Elsevier: Amsterdam, 1974.

[78] Stark, G.; Benz, R. J. Membrane Biology 1971, 5, 133.

[79] Funck, T.; Eggers, F.; Grell, E. Chimia 1972, 26, 637.

[80] Graham, G.; Richtsmeier, S.; Dixon, D.A. J. Amer. Chem. Soc. 1980, 102, 5759.

[81] Fraenkel, G.; Henrichs, M.; Hewitt, J.M.; Su, B.M.; Geckle, M.J. J. Amer. Chem. Soc. 1980, 102, 3345.

[82] Fraenkel, G.; Fraenkel, A.M.; Geckle, M.J.; Schloss, F. J. Amer. Chem. Soc. 1979, 101, 4745.

[83] Brown, T.L. Acc. Chem. Res. 1968, 1, 23.

[84] Wakefield, B.J. "Chemistry of Organolithium Compounds"; Pergamon Press: Oxford, 1974.

[85] Rode, B.M.; Reibnegger, G.J.; Fujiwara, S. J. Chem. Soc. Faraday II 1980, 76, 1268.

[86] Rubini, P.R.; Rodehüser, L.; Delpuech, J.J. Inorg. Chem. 1979, 18, 2962.

[87] Rodriguez, L.J.; Liesegang, G.W.; Farrow, M.M.; Purdie, N.; Eyring, E.M. J. Phys. Chem. 1978, 82, 647.

[88] Loyola, V.M.; Pizer, R.; Wilkins, R.G. J. Amer. Chem. Soc. 1977, 99, 7185.

[89] Harada, S.; Funaki, Y.; Yasunaga, T. J. Amer. Chem. Soc. 1980, 102, 136.

[90] Brunetti, A.P.; Nancollas, G.H.; Smith, P.N. J. Amer. Chem. Soc. 1969, 91, 4680.

[91] Wilkins, R.G.; Yelin, R.E. J. Amer. Chem. Soc. 1970, 92, 1191.

[92] Grant, M.W.; Dodgem, H.W.; Hunt, J.P. J. Amer. Chem. Soc. 1971, 93, 6828.

[93] Eigen, M.; Maass, G. Z. Phys. Chem. (Frankfurt am Main) 1966, 49, 163.

[94] Andersson, T.; Drakenberg, T.; Forsen, S.; Thulin, E. FEBS Letters 1981, 125, 39.

[95] Rogers, H.R.; Hill, C.L.; Fujiwara, Y.; Rogers, R.J.; Mitchell, H.L.; Whitesides, G.M. J. Amer. Chem. Soc. 1980, 102, 217.

[96] Rogers, H.R.; Deutch, J.; Whitesides, G.M. J. Amer. Chem. Soc. 1980, 102, 226.

[97] Rogers, H.R.; Rogers, R.J.; Mitchell, H.L.; Whitesides, G.M. J. Amer. Chem. Soc. 1980, 102, 231.

[98] Barber, J.J.; Whitesides, G.M. J. Amer. Chem. Soc. 1980, 102, 239.

[99] Schaart, B.J.; Bodewitz, H.W.H.J.; Blomberg, C.; Bickelhaupt, F. J. Amer. Chem. Soc. 1976, 98, 3712.

[100] Lawrence, L.M.; Whitesides, G.M. J. Amer. Chem. Soc. 1980, 102, 2493.

[101] Burg, A.B. Chemtech. 1977, 7, 50.

[102] Brown, H.C. "Hydroboration"; Benjamin: New York, 1962.

[103] Pasto, D.J.; Lepeska, B.; Cheng, T.C. J. Amer. Chem. Soc. 1972, 94, 6083.

[104] Pasto, D.J.; Lepeska, B.; Balasubramaniyan, V. J. Amer. Chem. Soc. 1972, 94, 6090.

[105] Streitwieser, A.; Verbit, L.; Bittman, R. J. Org. Chem. 1967, 32, 1530.

[106] Fehlner, T.P. J. Amer. Chem. Soc. 1971, 93, 6366.

[107] Dasgupta, S.; Datta, M.K.; Datta, R. *Tetrahedron Letters* **1978**, 1309.
[108] Dewar, M.J.S.; McKee, M.L. *Inorg. Chem.* **1978**, *17*, 1075.
[109] Clark, T.; Schleyer, P. v. R. *J. Organomet. Chem.* **1978**, *156*, 191.
[110] Sundberg, K.R.; Graham, G.D.; Lipscomb, W.N. *J. Amer. Chem. Soc.* **1979**, *101*, 2863.
[111] Graham, G.D.; Freilich, S.C.; Lipscomb, W.N. *J. Amer. Chem. Soc.* **1981**, *103*, 2546.
[112] Nagase, S.; Ray, N.K.; Morokuma, K. *J. Amer. Chem. Soc.* **1980**, *102*, 4536.
[113] Eisch, J.J.; Rhee, S.G. *J. Amer. Chem. Soc.* **1974**, *96*, 7276.
[114] Gropen, O.; Haaland, A. *Acta Chem. Scand.* **1981**, *A35*, 305.
[115] Modler, R.F.; Kreevoy, M.M. *J. Amer. Chem. Soc.* **1977**, *99*, 2271.
[116] Meeks, B.S.; Kreevoy, M.M. *Inorg. Chem.* **1979**, *18*, 2185.
[117] Meeks, B.S.; Kreevoy, M.M. *J. Amer. Chem. Soc.* **1979**, *101*, 4918.
[118] Kreevoy, M.M.; Hutchins, J.E.C. *J. Amer. Chem. Soc.* **1972**, *94*, 6371.
[119] Olah, G.A.; Westerman, P.W.; Mo. Y.K.; Klopman, G. *J. Amer. Chem. Soc.* **1972**, *94*, 7859.
[120] Willem, R. *J. Chem. Soc., Dalton Trans.* **1979**, 33.
[121] Kelly, H.C.; Marriott, V.B. *Inorg. Chem.* **1979**, *18*, 2875.
[122] Kelly, H.C.; Underwood, J.A. *Inorg. Chem.* **1969**, *8*, 1202.
[123] Barone, V.; Dolcetti, G.; Lelj, F.; Russo, N. *Inorg. Chem.* **1981**, *20*, 1687.
[124] Davies, A.G.; Roberts, B.P. *Acc. Chem. Res.* **1972**, *5*, 387.
[125] Eames, T.B.; Hoffman, B.M. *J. Amer. Chem. Soc.* **1971**, *93*, 3141.
[126] Griller, D.; Ingold, K.U.; Patterson, L.K.; Scaiano, J.C.; Small, R.D. *J. Amer. Chem. Soc.* **1979**, *101*, 3780.
[127] Brindley, P.B.; Hodgson, J.C.; Scotton, M.J. *J. Chem. Soc. Perkin II* **1979**, 45.
[128] Lockhart, J.C. "Introduction to Inorganic Reaction Mechanisms", Butterworths: London, 1966; Chapter 7.
[129] Beachley, O.T.; Tessier-Youngs, C. *Inorg. Chem.* **1979**, *18*, 3188.
[130] Beachley, O.T. *Inorg. Chem.* **1981**, *20*, 2825.
[131] McGarvey, B.R.; Taylor, M.J.; Tuck, D.G. *Inorg. Chem.* **1981**, *20*, 2010.
[132] McGarvey, B.R.; Trudell, C.O.; Tuck, D.G.; Victoriano, L. *Inorg. Chem.* **1980**, *19*, 3432.
[133] Hartman, J.S.; Schrobilgen, G.J. *Inorg. Chem.* **1972**, *11*, 940.

REFERENCES ADDED IN PROOF

[134] Wang, K.K.; Scouten, C.G.; Brown, H.C. *J. Amer. Chem. Soc.* **1982**, 104, 531. Kinetics of hydroboration of alkynes. Section IVA.
[135] Bouquant, J.; Delville, A.; Grandjean, J.; Laszlo, P. *J. Amer. Chem. Soc.* **1982**, 104, 686. Na complexes with Spiro (bis-crown) ethers. Kinetics and thermodynamics via ^{23}Na NMR. Section IIA.
[136] Smith, P.B.; Dye, J.L.; Cheney, J.; Lehn, J.M. *J. Amer. Chem. Soc.* **1981**, 103, 6044. Kinetics and thermodynamics of protonation of cryptand X (1,1,1). Section IIA.5.
[137] Cox, B.G.; Murray-Rust, J.; Murray-Rust, P.; van Truong, N.; Schneider, H. *J. Chem. Soc., Chem. Comm.* **1982**, 377. Kinetics and crystal structure for (*i,i*) diprotonated cryptand X (2,1,1). Section IIA.5.

[138] Lein, G.M.; Cram, D.J. *J. Chem. Soc., Chem. Comm.* **1982**, 301. Complexation and decomplexation rates for spherands with Na and Li picrates. Section II.A.3.

[139] Anderson, T.; Drakenberg, T.; Forsen, S.; Thuline, E.; Sward, M. *J. Amer. Chem. Soc.* **1982**, 104, 576. ^{43}Ca NMR studies of binding sites for parvalbumin, troponin C, calmodulin. Section III.B.

[140] Aalmo, K.M.; Krane, J. *Acta Chem. Scand.* **1982**, *A*36, 219. Multinuclear dynamic NMR studies of Li complexes of 1,5,9,13-tetraoxacyclohexadecanes. Section II.A.

Mechanistic Aspects of Transition Metal Complexes Containing Coordinated Sulphur

Edward Deutsch†, Michael J. Root and Dennis L. Nosco

Department of Chemistry
University of Cincinnati

† Author to whom correspondence should be addressed.

I. INTRODUCTION

In his classic 1965 review of Group VI donor atoms, Livingstone[1] noted that the most-studied ligands were the halide ions, cyanide ion, and ligands having oxygen or nitrogen as the donor atom. Ligands with sulphur as the donor atom had been much less investigated, primarily because of difficulties encountered in synthesizing appropriate metal complexes by direct means. However, in recent years the development of new, often indirect, synthetic routes has provided a variety of robust metal complexes containing coordinated sulphur. One class of such complexes is especially suited for detailed mechanistic studies since the first coordination sphere of its members consists of a unique "soft" sulphur atom and five "hard" nitrogen or oxygen atoms. Specifically, thiolato complexes of chromium(III), cobalt(III), iron(III) and ruthenium(III) may be prepared by the metal(II) reduction of organic disulphides.[2–6,8] For example,

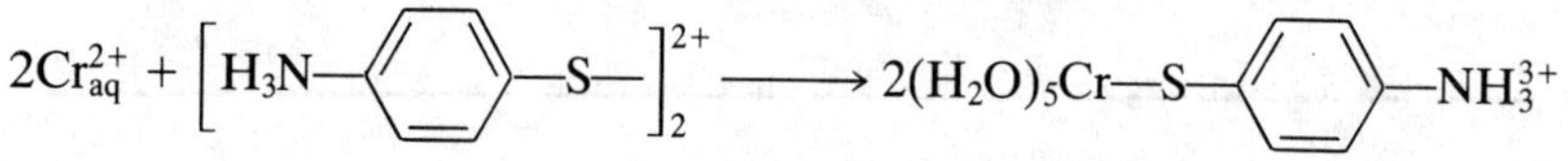

$$2Cr^{2+}_{aq} + \left[H_3N-\underset{}{\bigcirc}-S- \right]^{2+}_2 \longrightarrow 2(H_2O)_5Cr-S-\underset{}{\bigcirc}-NH_3^{3+}$$

$$4en + 2Co^{2+}_{aq} + [H_2NCH_2CH_2S-]_2 \longrightarrow 2\,(en)_2Co(SCH_2CH_2NH_2)^{2+}$$

Subsequent investigations into the chemistry of coordinated thiols have led to routes for the conversion of the initial class of thiolato complexes into other thiolato complexes as well as into complexes containing other types of coordinated sulphur[4,9–12]. For example

$$Cr^{2+}_{aq} + (en)_2Co(SCH_2CH_2NH_2)^{2+} \longrightarrow (H_2O)_5CrSCH_2CH_2NH_3^{3+}$$

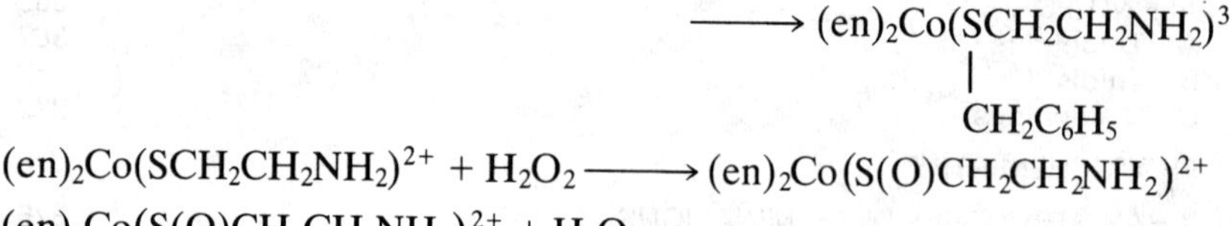

$$H_2S + (H_2O)_5CrS-\underset{}{\bigcirc}-NH_3^{3+} \longrightarrow$$

$$(H_2O)_5CrSH^{2+} + HS-\underset{}{\bigcirc}-NH_3^{+}$$

$$(en)_2Co(SCH_2CH_2NH_2)^{2+} + C_6H_5CH_2Br$$

$$\longrightarrow (en)_2Co(SCH_2CH_2NH_2)^{3+}$$
$$|$$
$$CH_2C_6H_5$$

$$(en)_2Co(SCH_2CH_2NH_2)^{2+} + H_2O_2 \longrightarrow (en)_2Co(S(O)CH_2CH_2NH_2)^{2+}$$

$$(en)_2Co(S(O)CH_2CH_2NH_2)^{2+} + H_2O_2$$

$$\longrightarrow (en)_2Co(S(O)_2CH_2CH_2NH_2)^{2+}$$

$$2\,(en)_2Co(SCH_2CH_2NH_2)^{2+} + Co^{3+}_{aq}$$

$$\longrightarrow (en)_2Co(SCH_2CH_2NH_2)^{4+} + 2Co^{2+}_{aq}$$
$$|$$
$$SCH_2CH_2NH_3$$

These reactions illustrate the greater diversity available within Group VI donor ligands relative to Group VII ligands. For all practical purposes the Group VII ligands are just the monofunctional halide anions, and therefore within Group VII only gross variations in ligand properties can be obtained by jumping from one period to the next. However, within the Group VI donor ligands these large jumps can be fine-tuned by varying both the oxidation state of, and the nature of the groups bonded to, the coordinated Group VI element.

In the last ten years there has been an upsurge of interest in the chemistry of coordinated sulphur, partly because of the prevalence of this species in biological systems, and partly because of the distinct metal and ligand properties conferred by coordination of sulphur. Various aspects of this chemistry have been reviewed, the two most recent surveys providing a complete listing of previous reviews.[13,14] This article is concerned with the mechanistic aspects of sulphur coordination, i.e. how the reactivity of the sulphur-containing species is affected by the metal centre, how the reactivity of the metal is affected by the sulphur-donating ligand, and how metal–sulphur bonding effects new reactivity patterns. The reactivity of square planar complexes has been treated in several reviews (e.g. Ref. [15]) and thus emphasis in this article is placed on octahedral complexes, largely those of cobalt, chromium, ruthenium and iron. Organometallic complexes have been excluded from consideration since very few mechanistic studies have been conducted on these species. Complexes containing 1,1- and 1,2-dithiolate ligands are not included since they have recently been reviewed[16,17] and since only a few mechanistic studies on these species have been reported. In several areas, most notably metal–sulphur inter-actions in biological systems and *trans* effects in square planar complexes, the earlier literature is adequately covered by other review articles; in these cases the earlier reviews are referenced and only the more recent literature is surveyed. Every effort has been made to systematically cover the literature through 1980, and where appropriate selected references published through October, 1981 have been included. While every attempt has been made to include all relevant literature references, the wide scope of this article virtually ensures that some references have been inadvertently omitted, and we apologise in advance to the authors of these articles.

This review is organized into sections and subsections dealing with various aspects of the reactivity of metal–sulphur systems. Each section, or major sub-section, consists of a relatively critical discussion followed by a non-critical, comprehensive, table of kinetic data. The distinctions between sections are relatively arbitrary, but the major distinction between redox and substitution reactions has been made in accordance with the accepted definition of oxidation state. This distinction can lead to some confusion; e.g. the first of the following reactions is a redox reaction whereas the second, obviously related, reaction is a substitution reaction:

$$M—SR + R'S—I \longrightarrow M—S(R)—SR' + I^-$$

$$M—SR + R'—I \longrightarrow M—S(R)—R' + I^-$$

To minimize confusion, reactions such as these are cross-referenced within each appropriate section. Sections dealing with the affinities of sulphur ligands for metal ion centres, x-ray structural characterizations of metal–sulphur systems, electrochemistry, and photochemistry, are focused on the relevance of these topics to mechanistic aspects of complexes containing coordinated sulphur.

II. OXIDATION-REDUCTION REACTIONS

A. Reductions of metal complexes

1. Electron transfer through coordinated thiolates and thioethers

Coordinated thiolates mediate electron transfer from chromium(II) to cobalt(III) more efficiently than do the analogous coordinated alcoholates. For the chromium(II) inner-sphere reductions of various thiolate[2, 18, 19] and alkoxide[2, 19] cobalt(III) complexes the ratio of specific rate constants for sulphur- and oxygen-containing bridging ligands range from $k_S/k_O = 35$ to 3400. This rate enhancement has been attributed to the greater Lewis basicity of coordinated thiolate which thus stabilizes the binuclear precursor complex; for example, during the copper(I) reduction of $(en)_2Co(SCH_2COO)^+$, a binuclear Cu^I–$S(R)$–Co^{III} cluster is rapidly formed which subsequently undergoes intramolecular decay to yield Cu(II) and Co(II).[20] However, it is unlikely that this explanation accounts for the rapid reduction of thiolato complexes by chromium(II) since Cr_{aq}^{2+} is a much harder Lewis acid than is Cu_{aq}^+ and thus it is not clear that sulphur coordination to chromium(II) is favoured over oxygen coordination. It has also been proposed that the enhanced rate of reduction of thiolate–cobalt(III) complexes arises from the sulphur-induced structural *trans* effect (STE) present in these complexes;[21] the STE presumably lowers the Franck–Condon barrier for Co(III) reduction in both inner-sphere reductions by chromium(II) and outer-sphere reductions by $Ru(NH_3)_6^{2+}$.[19]

Interestingly, for sulphur-bridged inner-sphere electron transfer from chromium(II) to chromium(III), large k_S/k_O values can be qualitatively correlated with the presence of a STE in the sulphur–chromium(III) complex. Thus, for the complexes $(H_2O)_5CrSR^{n+}$ where $R = H$, $C_6H_4NH_3^+$ and $CH_2N(CH_3)_3^+$,[22] electron transfer through sulphur is much more rapid than is electron transfer to $(H_2O)_5CrOH^{2+}$; these sulphur–chromium(III) complexes have been shown to exhibit a sulphur-induced kinetic *trans* effect (KTE) which is correlated with the presence of a STE.[23,24] However, a STE is not observed in $(en)_2Cr(SCH_2COO)^+$ and the chromium(II) reduction of this complex is not unusually rapid.[21,25] The difference in the two classes of compounds may arise from the fact that water is a weaker ligand than the chelating ethylenediamine and is thus more affected by the *trans*-situated sulphur ligand, allowing both a direct KTE and an indirect lowering of the Franck–Condon barrier for electron transfer.

Thiolato–chromium(III) complexes containing pendant carboxylate groups are reduced very rapidly due to the ability to form a stabilized, O,S-chelated, precursor complex with chromium(II).[18,26]

The chromium(II) reduction of bis(ethylenediamine)cobalt(III) complexes containing chelating thioether ligands, i.e. $(en)_2Co(S(R)CH_2CH_2NH_2)^{3+}$, have also been studied.[19,27,28] Contrary to earlier results, Kennard and Deutsch showed that these reactions proceed by inner-sphere electron transfer through sulphur. In the transition state the sulphur atom thus achieves four-coordination, somewhat similar to the four-coordinate sulphur atom in $(NH_3)_5RuS(CH_3)_3^{2+}$.[29] The smaller Group VI congener, oxygen, is apparently unable to achieve four-coordination in an inner-sphere electron transfer transition state; Linck[30] has shown that water does not function as an electron transfer bridge for the reduction of $(NH_3)_5CoOH_2^{3+}$ by chromium(II). Not surprisingly, chromium(II) reduction of the thioether complexes proceeds much more slowly than reduction of the corresponding thiolate complexes, the effect being manifested largely in the activation enthalpies. If the thioether complex contains a pendant carboxylate group the rate of reduction increases markedly, and shows an inverse acid dependence, presumably because of O,S-chelation of the reductant in the precursor complex.[28]

$$(en)_2Co\underset{NH_2}{\overset{S-CH_2-\overset{\overset{OH}{|}}{C}=O}{\bigg\langle}}\Bigg.^{3+} + Cr_{aq}^{2+} \xrightarrow{-H^+} \left[(en)_2Co\underset{NH_2}{\overset{CH_2-C=O}{\bigg\langle}}S{=}Cr{\overset{O}{\big\backslash}}\right]^{4+} \quad (1)$$

2. Electron transfer through coordinated thiocyanate

In 1955 Taube[31] noted that the chromium(II) reduction of $(NH_3)_5CoN_3^{2+}$ was more rapid than the reduction of the corresponding isothiocyanato complex, and this has been offered[32] as evidence for

TABLE 1

Rate parameters for the reductions of thiolate, thioether and related complexes of Co(III) and Cr(III)

Complex	Reductant	k_2 $(\text{M}^{-1}\,\text{s}^{-1})^a$	ΔH^* (kcal mol^{-1})	ΔS^* (eu)	Conditions^b	Ref.
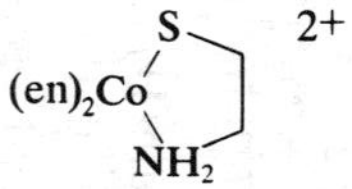 $\text{(en)}_2\text{Co}{-}S{\cdots}\text{NH}_2$ $2+$	$\text{Cr}^{2+}_{\text{aq}}$	3.3×10^4	7.3	-14		[19]
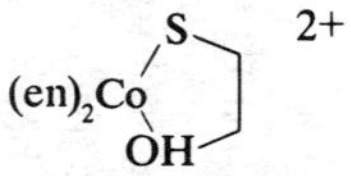 $\text{(en)}_2\text{Co}{-}S{\cdots}\text{OH}$ $2+$	$\text{Cr}^{2+}_{\text{aq}}$	6.0×10^6	—	—	18·6°C, $I = 0.10$ M	[19]
$\text{(en)}_2\text{Co}{-}S{\cdots}\text{O}{=}$ $+$	$\text{V}^{2+}_{\text{aq}}$	6.5	12.0	-14		[19]
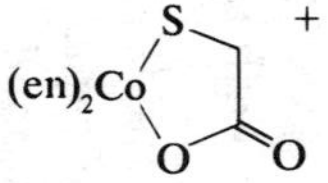	$\text{Cr}^{2+}_{\text{aq}}$	6.4×10^6	$\cong 1$	$\cong -24$	18·6°C, $I = 0.10$ M	[19]
	$\text{V}^{2+}_{\text{aq}}$	9.6	11.6	-15	$I = 0.10$ M (H/NaCl)	[19]
	$\text{Ru(NH}_3\text{)}_6^{2+}$	0.15	—	—		[19]
	Cu^+_{aq}	2×10^{-3}	21.4	1	$I = 0.10$ M (HClO$_4$)	[20]

	Reductant	k				Ref.
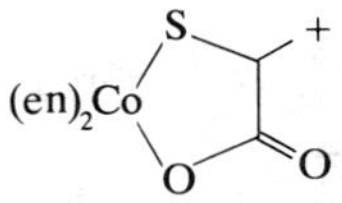 (en)$_2$Co S / C=O (+)	Cr$^{2+}_{aq}$	1.5×10^5	1.1	−31	$I = 0.1$ M	[19]
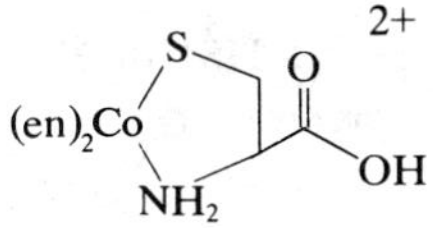 (en)$_2$Co S / NH$_2$ / C(=O)OH (2+)	Cr$^{2+}_{aq}$	2.4×10^5	—	—		[18]
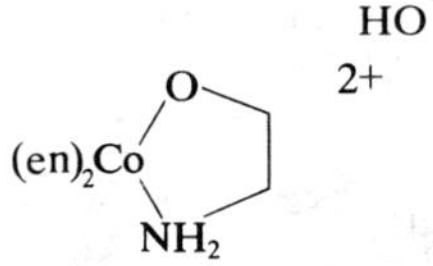 (en)$_2$Co O / NH$_2$ (2+)	Cr$^{2+}_{aq}$	9.4×10^2	5.1	−28		[19]
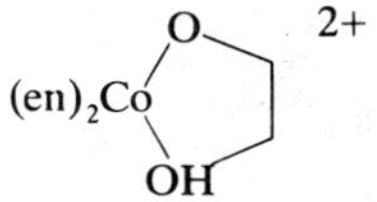 (en)$_2$Co O / OH (2+)	Cr$^{2+}_{aq}$	7.2×10^3	—	—		[19]
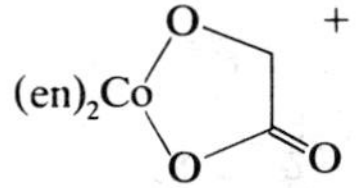 (en)$_2$Co O / O (+)	Cr$^{2+}_{aq}$	1.91×10^3	≈ 2.2	≈ -36		[19]
	Ru(NH$_3$)$_6^{2+}$	$<10^{-2}$	—	—		[19]
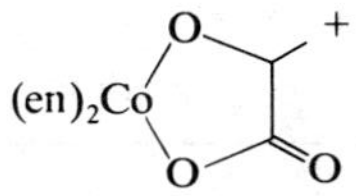 (en)$_2$Co O / O (+)	Cr$^{2+}_{aq}$	50	≈ 2	≈ -43		[19]

TABLE 1 (cont.)

Complex	Reductant	k_2 ($\text{M}^{-1}\,\text{s}^{-1}$)[a]	ΔH^* (kcal mol^{-1})	ΔS^* (eu)	Conditions[b]	Ref.
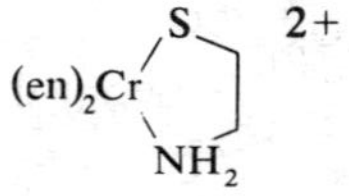 (en)₂Cr〈S, NH₂〉 ring, 2+	Cr^{2+}_{aq}	1.12×10^{-4}	—	—		[25]
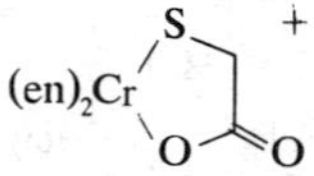 (en)₂Cr〈S, C(=O)O〉 ring, +	Cr^{2+}_{aq}	$1\cdot2 \times 10^{-3}$	$18\cdot4$	-10		[25]
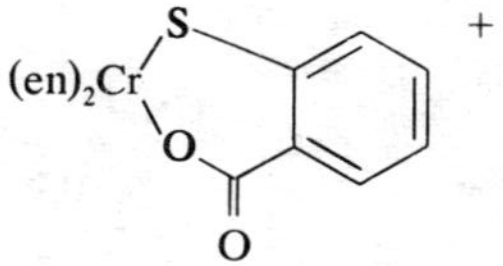 (en)₂Cr〈S, O–C(=O)–C₆H₄〉, +	Cr^{2+}_{aq}	$2\cdot5 \times 10^{-4}$	—	—		[25]
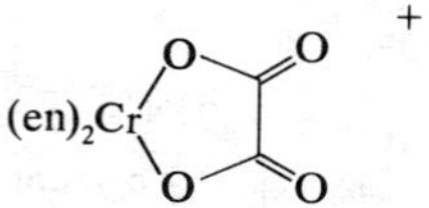 (en)₂Cr〈O₂C–CO₂〉 oxalate, +	Cr^{2+}_{aq}	$2\cdot8 \times 10^{-3}$	—	—		[25]
$(H_2O)_5CrSH^{2+}$	Cr^{2+}_{aq}	>120	—	—	4°C, $I = 2\cdot0$ M (H/NaClO₄) [H⁺] = 1·7 M	[22]
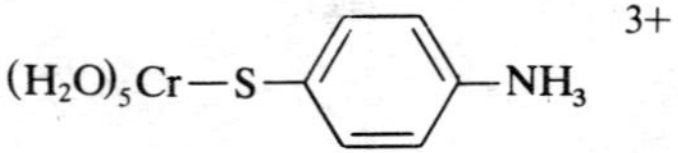 $(H_2O)_5Cr{-}S{-}C_6H_4{-}NH_3$, 3+	Cr^{2+}_{aq}	>40	—	—	4°C, $I = 2.3$ M (HClO₄)	[22]

Complex	Reductant	k			Conditions	Ref.
$(H_2O)_5CrSCH_2N(CH_3)_3^{3+}$	Cr_{aq}^{2+}	$\cong 10$	—	—	4°C, $I = 2\cdot6$ M (H/NaClO₄)	[22]
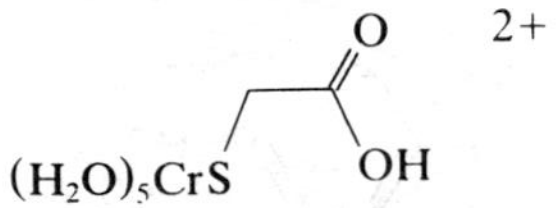 $(H_2O)_5CrS\,(CH_2COOH)^{2+}$	Cr_{aq}^{2+}	$>2 \times 10^4$	—	—		[26]
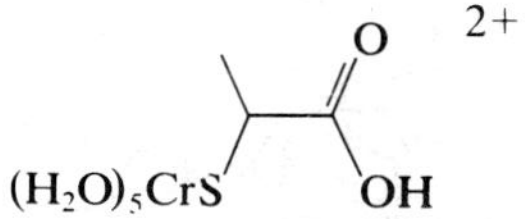 $(H_2O)_5CrS\,(CH(CH_3)COOH)^{2+}$	Cr_{aq}^{2+}	$>2 \times 10^4$	—	—		[26]
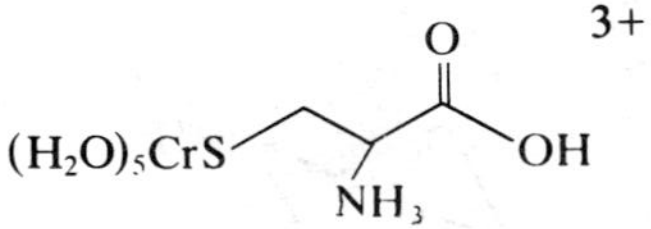 $(H_2O)_5CrS\,(CH_2CH(NH_3)COOH)^{3+}$	Cr_{aq}^{2+}	6×10^3	—	—		[18]
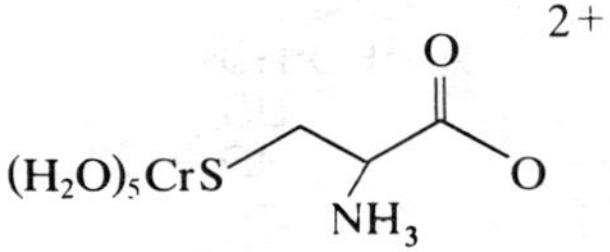 $(H_2O)_5CrS\,(CH_2CH(NH_3)COO)^{2+}$	Cr_{aq}^{2+}	$1\cdot6 \times 10^7$	—	—		[18]
$(H_2O)_5CrOH^{2+}$	Cr_{aq}^{2+}	$2\cdot3$	—	—		[288]
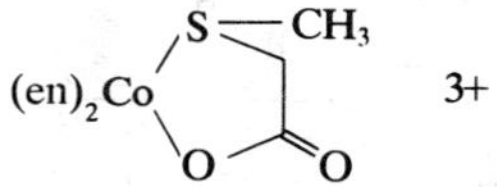 $(en)_2Co(S(CH_3)CH_2COO)^{3+}$	Cr_{aq}^{2+}	274	$8\cdot4$	-19		[19]

TABLE 1 (cont.)

Complex	Reductant	k_2 $(\text{M}^{-1}\ \text{s}^{-1})^a$	ΔH^* (kcal mol^{-1})	ΔS^* (eu)	Conditions^b	Ref.
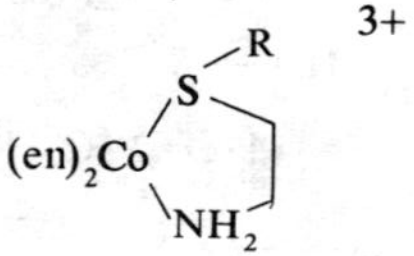 (en)$_2$Co with S–R, NH$_2$ (3+)						
R = CH$_3$	$\text{Cr}^{2+}_{\text{aq}}$	0.381	5·5	−42		[19]
CH$_3$	$\text{Cr}^{2+}_{\text{aq}}$	0·337	4·9	−44		[28]
CH$_2$CH$_3$	$\text{Cr}^{2+}_{\text{aq}}$	$2·7 \times 10^{-2}$	6·5	−44		[28]
 (cyclohexyl)CH$_2$	$\text{Cr}^{2+}_{\text{aq}}$	$1·26 \times 10^{-2}$	7·6	−42		[28]
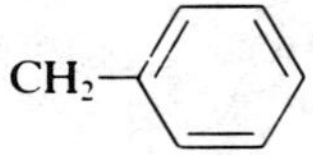 (phenyl)CH$_2$	$\text{Cr}^{2+}_{\text{aq}}$	$3·45 \times 10^{-2}$	7·4	−42		[28]
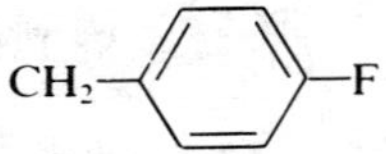 (F-phenyl)CH$_2$	$\text{Cr}^{2+}_{\text{aq}}$	$3·56 \times 10^{-2}$	—	—		[28]
 (CH$_3$-phenyl)CH$_2$	$\text{Cr}^{2+}_{\text{aq}}$	$3·3 \times 10^{-2}$	—	—		[28]

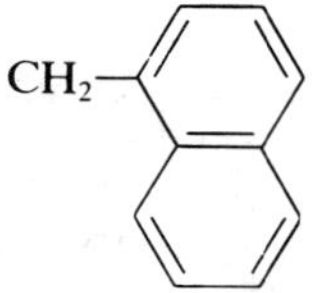 CH$_2$	Cr$_{aq}^{2+}$	4.4×10^{-2}	—	—	[28]
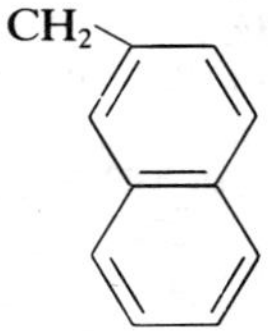 CH$_2$	Cr$_{aq}^{2+}$	3.3×10^{-2}	—	—	[28]
R = CH$_2$COOCH$_3$	Cr$_{aq}^{2+}$	0.193	—	—	[28]
CH$_2$COOH^c	Cr$_{aq}^{2+}$	$a = 19$ M^{-1} s^{-1} $b = 4.92 \times 10^3$ M^{-1}	—	—	[28]
CH$_2$CH$_2$COOH^d	Cr$_{aq}^{2+}$	$a = 0.03$ M^{-1} s^{-1} $b = 0.114$ s^{-1}	13·0 8·5	−22 −34	[28]
CH$_2$CH$_2$CH$_2$COOH^d	Cr$_{aq}^{2+}$	$a = 0·04$ M^{-1} s^{-1} $b = 7 \times 10^{-4}$ s^{-1}	8·3 13·9	−37 −26	[28]

^{a} Rate = k_2[oxidant][reductant].
^{b} $T = 25°C$ and $I = 1.0$ M (H/LiClO$_4$) unless otherwise noted.
^{c} $k_2 = a/(1 + b[H^+])$.
^{d} $k_2 = a + b/[H^+]$.

TABLE 2

Rate parameters for the reductions of isothiocyanate, thiocyanate and azide complexes

Complex	Reductant	k_2 (M^{-1} s^{-1})[a]	ΔH^* (kcal mol^{-1})	ΔS^* (eu)	Conditions[b]	Ref.
$(NH_3)_5CoNCS^{2+}$	Cr^{2+}_{aq}	19	6·9	−32	$I = 1·0$ M (H/NaClO$_4$)	[33]
	V^{2+}_{aq}	0·3			$I = 1·0$ M (H/NaClO$_4$)	[33]
	Eu^{2+}_{aq}	$\cong0·7$			$I = 1·0$ M (H/NaClO$_4$)	[33]
	Eu^{2+}_{aq}	$4·95 \times 10^{-2}$	7·5	−40	$I = 1·0$ M (H/LiClO$_4$)	[36]
	Fe^{2+}_{aq}	$<3 \times 10^{-3}$			$I = 1·0$ M (H/LiClO$_4$)	[34]
	Ti^{3+}_{aq}	$<3 \times 10^{-4}$			$I = 0·50$ M (H/LiClO$_4$/Cl)	[37]
					$[H^+] = 0.13$ M	
	Ti^{3+}_{aq}	$\cong2·3 \times 10^{5}$			$I = 0·50$ M (H/LiClO$_4$/Cl)	[37]
					$[H^+] = 0.31$ M	
	$Co(CN)_5^{3-}$	$1·1 \times 10^{6}$			$I = 0·2$ M	[40]
	$Co(CN)_5^{3-}$	$1·0 \times 10^{6}$			$I = 0·1$ M (NaClO$_4$)	[46]
	$Cr(bpy)_3^{2+}$	$1·0 \times 10^{4}$			$I = 1·0$ M (H/NaClO$_4$)	[33]
	$Ru(NH_3)_6^{2+}$	0·74	14·9	−10	$I = 0·2$ M (H/LiCl)	[51]
	$Ru(en)_3^{2+}$	0·15				[51]
$(H_2O)_5CrNCS^{2+}$	Cr^{2+}_{aq}	$1·8 \times 10^{-4}$				[38]
	V^{2+}_{aq}	$4·4 \times 10^{-5}$	23·1	−1	27°C	[45]
$(H_2O)_5FeNCS^{2+}$	Cr^{2+}_{aq}	$\geq2 \times 10^{7}$			$I = 3·0$ M (H/MgClO$_4$)	[44]
	V^{2+}_{aq}	$6·6 \times 10^{5}$				[53]
	Fe^{2+}_{aq}	27·8			$I = 1·0$ M (H/LiClO$_4$)	[48]
$(NH_3)_5RuNCS^{2+}$	Ti^{3+}_{aq}	840	8·4	17	$I = 0·5$ M	[50]
	$Ti(HEDTA)$	$2·8 \times 10^{4}$				[50]
$trans$-$(en)_2Co(OH_2)NCS^{2+}$	Cr^{2+}_{aq}	$1·4 \times 10^{3}$				[49]
cis-$(en)_2Co(OH_2)NCS^{2+}$	Cr^{2+}_{aq}	45				[49]
$trans$-$(en)_2Co(NH_3)NCS^{2+}$	Cr^{2+}_{aq}	3·8				[49]
cis-$(en)_2Co(NH_3)NCS^{2+}$	Cr^{2+}_{aq}	3·1				[49]
$trans$-$(en)_2Co(NCS)_2^+$	Cr^{2+}_{aq}	28				[49]
cis-$(en)_2Co(NCS)_2^+$	Cr^{2+}_{aq}	30				[49]
$(NH_3)_5CoSCN^{2+}$	Cr^{2+}_{aq}	8×10^{4} [c]			$I = 2$ M (LiCl)	[42]
	Cr^{2+}_{aq}	$1·9 \times 10^{5}$ [d]			$I = 2$ M (LiCl)	[42]
	V^{2+}_{aq}	30				[41]
	Fe^{2+}_{aq}	0·12				

Oxidant	Reductant	k_2	$\Delta H^\ddagger$	$\Delta S^\ddagger$	Conditions[b]	Ref.
Ti^{3+}_{aq}		35	—	—	$I = 1\cdot0$ M $(H/LiClO_4/Cl)$ $[H^+] = 0.35$ M	[43]
	$Co(CN)_5^{3-}$	$>10^8$	—	—	$I = 0\cdot1$ M $(NaClO_4)$	[46]
	$Cr(bpy)_3^{2+}$	$\geq7 \times 10^6$	—	—	$I = 0\cdot2$ M $(H/LiCl)$	[51]
	$Ru(NH_3)_6^{2+}$	379	6·4	−25	$I = 0\cdot2$ M $(H/LiCl)$	[51]
	$Ru(en)_3^{2+}$	45·3	—	—	$I = 0\cdot2$ M $(H/LiCl)$	[51]
$(H_2O)_5CrSCN^{2+}$	Cr^{2+}_{aq}	4·2	—	—	$I = 3\cdot0$ M $(H/MgClO_4)$	[44]
	V^{2+}_{aq}	8·0	13·0	−11		[45]
	V^{2+}_{aq}	7·1	—	—		[53]
$(CN)_5CoSCN^{3-}$	V^{2+}_{aq}	138	—	—	$I = 1\cdot0$ M $(H/LiClO_4)$	[47]
	V^{2+}_{aq}	256	—	—	$I = 0\cdot20$ M	[47]
$PCo(OH_2)(SCN)^{4+}$[e]	$Ru(NH_3)_6^{2+}$	$3\cdot6 \times 10^6$	—	—	$I = 0\cdot5$ M $(NaCl)$	[52]
$(NH_3)_5CoN_3^{2+}$	Cr^{2+}_{aq}	$\cong3 \times 10^5$	—	—	$I = 1\cdot0$ M $(H/NaClO_4)$	[33]
	V^{2+}_{aq}	13	11·7	−14	$I = 1\cdot0$ M $(H/NaClO_4)$	[33]
	Eu^{2+}_{aq}	$1\cdot9 \times 10^2$	5·5	−30	$I = 1\cdot0$ M $(H/NaClO_4)$	[33]
	Fe^{2+}_{aq}	$8\cdot7 \times 10^{-3}$	—	—	$I = 0.89(ClO_4^-)$	[35]
	Ti^{3+}_{aq}	10·9	—	—	$I = 0\cdot50$ M $(H/LiClO_4/Cl)$ $[H^+] = 0.13$ M	[37]
Ti^{3+}_{aq}		6.28	—	—	$I = 0.50$ M $(H/LiClO_4/Cl)$ $[H^+] = 0.30$ M	[37]
	$Co(CN)_5^{3-}$	1.6×10^6	—	—	$I = 0.2$ M	[33]
	$Ru(NH_3)_6^{2+}$	1·82	9·4	−26	$I = 0.2$ M $(H/LiCl)$	[51]
	$Ru(en)_3^{2+}$	0.26	—	—	$I = 0.2$ M $(H/LiCl)$	[51]
$(H_2O)_5CrN_3^{2+}$	Cr^{2+}_{aq}	4·68	9·6	−23	$I = 0.5$ M $(HClO_4)$	[39]
$(H_2O)_5FeN_3^{2+}$	Cr^{2+}_{aq}	$\geq2 \times 10^7$	—	—		[44]
	V^{2+}_{aq}	$5\cdot2 \times 10^5$	—	—	$I = 1\cdot0$ M $(H/LiClO_4)$	[53]
$(CN)_5CoN_3^{3-}$	V^{2+}_{aq}	112	—	—	$I = 1\cdot0$ M $(H/LiClO_4)$	[47]
$PCo(OH_2)N_3^{4+}$[e]	$Ru(NH_3)_6^{2+}$	$1\cdot5 \times 10^4$	—	—	$I = 0\cdot5$ M $(NaCl)$	[52]

[a] Rate = k_2[oxidant][reductant].
[b] $T = 25°C$ and $I = 1\cdot0$ M$(HClO_4)$ unless otherwise noted.
[c] Adjacent attack.
[d] Remote attack.
[e] P = tetrakis(4-N-methylpyridyl)porphine.

inner-sphere electron transfer. Since then there have been many studies on the rates of reduction of analogous isothiocyanato and azido complexes in order to elucidate mechanistic details. These include the reduction of $(NH_3)_5CoX^{2+}$ (X $=N_3^-$ and $-NCS^-$) by $Cr_{aq}^{2+},^{[33]}$ $V_{aq}^{2+},^{[33]}$ $Fe_{aq}^{2+},^{[34,35]}$ $Eu_{aq}^{2+},^{[33,36]}$ and $Ti_{aq}^{3+},^{[37]}$ as well as the reduction of $(H_2O)_5CrX^{2+}$ complexes by $Cr_{aq}^{2+}.^{[38,39]}$ In each of these studies the ratio of specific rate constants k_{N_3}/k_{-NCS} is greater than one, a result which can be used to support an inner-sphere mechanism.[32] This conclusion arises from application of the hard–soft acid-base theory to estimate the relative stabilities of the precursor complexes; the "hard" reductants Cr_{aq}^{2+}, V_{aq}^{2+}, Eu_{aq}^{2+} and Ti_{aq}^{3+} bind preferentially to a "hard" nitrogen atom rather than to a "soft" sulphur atom when forming the inner-sphere precursor complex, and thus the azido complex reacts more rapidly than the isothiocyanato complex. (In all systems, adjacent attack at the coordinated nitrogen atom is discounted because of electronic and steric constraints.) On the other hand, the "soft" reductant $Co(CN)_5^{3-}$ reacts with the azido and isothiocyanato complexes $(NH_3)_5CoX^{2+}$ at about the same rate[40] indicating a greater affinity of this reductant for the "soft" sulphur atom.

Inclusion of the thiocyanato complexes $(NH_3)_5CoSCN^{2+}$ [36,41–43] and $(H_2O)_5CrSCN^{2+}$ [41,44,45] extends the ordering of specific rates to $k_{-SCN} > k_{N_3} > k_{-NCS}$. The large value of k_{-SCN} arises largely from adjacent attack at the coordinated sulphur atom; the "hard" reductant Cr_{aq}^{2+} reduces $(NH_3)_5CoSCN^{2+}$ by both adjacent and remote attack pathways,[42] while the "softer" reductant $Co(CN)_5^{3-}$ reduces $(NH_3)_5CoSCN^{2+}$ by adjacent attack alone.[46] Thus, as is true for the coordinated sulphur atom of thiolato and thioether complexes (vide supra), the coordinated sulphur atom of thiocyanato complexes efficiently mediates inner-sphere electron transfer to cobalt(III). It should be noted that a contribution to the enhanced values of k_{-SCN} may also arise from the ease of stretching a cobalt–sulphur bond relative to a cobalt–nitrogen bond.

Other reported electron transfer reactions in which thiocyanate functions as a bridge include the V_{aq}^{2+} reductions of $Co(CN)_5SCN^{3-},^{[47]}$ the Cr_{aq}^{2+} [44] and Fe_{aq}^{2+} [48] reductions of $FeNCS^{2+}$, and the Cr_{aq}^{2+} reductions of various cis- and trans-$(en)_2Co(NCS)(X)^{n+}$ complexes where X $= OH_2$, NH_3 and NCS^-.[49] More recently the inner-sphere reductions of $(NH_3)_5RuNCS^{2+}$ by Ti_{aq}^{3+} and Ti(HEDTA) (HEDTA = N-(hydroxyethyl)ethylene-diaminetriacetic acid) have been reported;[50] as expected, the Ti_{aq}^{3+} reductions of $(NH_3)_5RuNCS^{2+}$ is faster than that of $(NH_3)_5CoNCS^{2+}$ [37] because of the different symmetries of the acceptor orbitals on Ru(III) and Co(III) and because of the larger Franck–Condon barrier associated with cobalt(III) complexes.

Reported outer-sphere electron transfer reactions include the reductions of $(NH_3)_5CoX^{2+}$ $(X = -SCN^-, N_3^-, -NCS^-)$ by $Cr(bipy)_3^{2+}$ [33] and by $Ru(NH_3)_6^{2+}$ and $Ru(en)_3^{2+}$,[51] as well as the reductions of *trans*-$PCo(OH_2)(X)^{4+}$ complexes $(X = N_3^-, -SCN^-; P = $ tetrakis(4-*N*-methyl-pyridyl)porphine) by $Ru(NH_3)_6^{2+}$.[52] As is true for the inner-sphere reactions, the ordering of specific rates is $k_{-SCN} > k_{N_3} > k_{-NCS}$. The most dramatic effect occurs for the *S*-bonded species, k_{-SCN}/k_{N_3} being 40–200 times larger than k_{N_3}/k_{-NCS}, presumably because the metal–sulphur bond is weaker than the metal–nitrogen bond and therefore can be more readily stretched to attain the transition state configuration. The effect is manifested in the activation enthalpy. The V_{aq}^{2+} reduction of $FeNCS^{2+}$ [53] is presumed to proceed by an outer-sphere mechanism, since the observed rate is faster than the rate of substitution on V_{aq}^{2+} [32] and is approximately the same as the rate of V_{aq}^{2+} reduction of other FeX^{2+} complexes $(X = OH^-, Cl^-, N_3^-)$.

3. Electron transfer through coordinated sulphur oxyanions

Several studies involving electron transfer through sulphate, sulphite, or thiosulphate have been reported; however, the early work by Fraser and co-workers[54,55] should be discounted since these results have proven to be irreproducible. Of the three ligands, sulphate has been the most extensively investigated, since the sulphato complexes are the easiest to prepare. Also, it should be noted that when functioning as an electron transfer bridge sulphate must be *O*-bonded to both metal centres (i.e., an *O,O*-bridge); however, sulphite can be an *O,O*- or *O,S*-bridge, and thiosulphate can be an *O,O*-, *O,S*-, or *S*-bridge.

The reductions of amminecobalt(III) complexes containing coordinated sulphate by the "hard" reductants Cr_{aq}^{2+}, V_{aq}^{2+}, Eu_{aq}^{2+} and Ti_{aq}^{3+} [33,54–57] apparently proceed by an inner-sphere mechanism with coordination by one of the "hard" oxygen atoms of the sulphate ligand to the reductant. However, the reduction of $(NH_3)_5CoSO_4^+$ by the "soft" reductant $Co(CN)_5^{3-}$ (in the presence of excess CN^-) evidently proceeds *via* formation of $Co(CN)_6^{4-}$ and subsequent outer-sphere electron transfer.[40] Thus, coordination of a "hard" sulphato oxygen atom to $Co(CN)_5^{3-}$ is so unfavourable that the normally less efficient outer-sphere pathway becomes the dominant route for electron transfer.

The reductions of binuclear amminecobalt(III) complexes containing a bridging sulphate or selenate group have been studied. The chromium(II) reduction of $(NH_3)_8(\mu\text{-}NH_2)(\mu\text{-}SO_4)Co_2^{3+}$ [58] proceeds by an initial fast reaction yielding a Cr(III)–Co(III) binuclear product, and then the subsequent, slower reduction of this species. Only the first step could be monitored for the selenato analog, this rate being ~50 times faster than that observed for the sulphato complex. It is presumed that the rate

TABLE 3

Rate parameters for the reductions of Co(III) complexes containing coordinated sulphur oxyanions

Complex	Reductant	k_2 ($\text{M}^{-1}\,\text{s}^{-1}$)[a]	ΔH^* (kcal mol⁻¹)	ΔS^* (eu)	Conditions	Ref.
$(NH_3)_5CoOSO_3$	Cr_{aq}^{2+}	18	6.2	−32	$I = 1.0$ M (H/NaClO₄)	[33]
	Eu_{aq}^{2+}	1.4×10^2	6.7	−26	$I = 1.0$ M (H/NaClO₄)	[33]
	V_{aq}^{2+}	25.5	11.6	−13	$I = 2.0$ M (H/LiClO₄)	[56]
	$TiOH_{aq}^{2+}$ [b]	$1.98 \times 10^{-2}\,\text{s}^{-1}$	—	—	$I = 0.5$ M (H/LiCl)	[57]
	$Co(CN)_5^{3-}$ [c]	$4 \times 10^4\,\text{M}^{-2}\,\text{s}^{-1}$	—	—	$I = 0.2$ M	[40]
	$Cr(bpy)_3^{3+}$	4.5×10^4	—	—	$I = 0.1$ M (H/NaClO₄)	[33]
	$Ru(NH_3)_6^{2+}$	12.9	—	—	$I = 0.1$ M (H/LiClO₄)	[57]
$(NH_3)_4Co \begin{smallmatrix} NH_2 \\ O-O \\ \ \ \ \ SO_2 \\ O \end{smallmatrix} Co(NH_3)_3^{3+}$	Cr_{aq}^{2+}	7.4	8.7	−25	$I = 2.0$ M (H/LiClO₄)	[58]
	V_{aq}^{2+}	7.94	11.2	−17	$I = 2.0$ M (H/LiClO₄)	[56]
$(NH_3)_4Co \begin{smallmatrix} NH_2 \\ O-O \\ \ \ \ \ SeO_2 \\ O \end{smallmatrix} Co(NH_3)_3^{3+}$	Cr_{aq}^{2+}	372	7.2	−23	$I = 2.0$ M (H/LiClO₄)	[58]
$(NH_3)_5CoSO_4Cr(OH_2)_4^{+}$ [d]	V_{aq}^{2+}	15.3	11.7	−14	$I = 2.0$ M (H/LiClO₄)	[56]
	Cr_{aq}^{2+} [e]	$a = 0.256\ \text{M}^{-1}\,\text{s}^{-1}$; $b = 0.192\ \text{s}^{-1}$	14.6 ; 13.9	−12 ; −15	$I = 2.0$ M (H/LiClO₄)	[58]
$(NH_3)_5CoS_2O_3^{+}$	Cr_{aq}^{2+}	850	9.4	−14	$I = 1.0$ M (H/LiClO₄)	[59]

[a] Rate = k_2[oxidant][reductant].

[b] $k_2 = k_1/(K_a + [\text{H}^+])$.

[c] Rate = k_2[Co(III)][Co(II)][CN⁻].

[d] Presumed intermediate in the stepwise reduction of $(NH_3)_5(\mu\text{-}NH_2)(\mu\text{-}SO_4)Co_2^{3+}$ by Cr_{aq}^{2+}.[58]

[e] $k_2 = a + b/[\text{H}^+]$.

difference (manifested in the activation enthalpy) arises from the greater oxidizing power of selenate relative to sulphate. The rates of vanadium(II) reduction[56] of these sulphato- and selenato-bridged dimers are nearly identical and thus appear to be controlled by substitution on vanadium.[32]

The chromium(II) reductions of the S-bonded complexes $(NH_3)_5CoSO_3^+$ and $(NH_3)_5CoSSO_3^+$ are of interest since they can give additional information on the ability of sulphur to mediate electron transfer. Unfortunately, the early work by Fraser[55] on $(NH_3)_5CoSSO_3^+$ has been shown to be incorrect,[59] it being probable that Fraser's preparation contained significant amounts of $(NH_3)_5CoOH_2^{3+}$. Given this background, it is only prudent to also discount Fraser's results on $(NH_3)_5CoSO_3^+$.[55] Single-crystal x-ray structural analysis of $(NH_3)_5CoSSO_3^+$ shows that it is S-bonded; inner-sphere chromium(II) reduction occurs by remote attack on a pendant oxygen atom and thus in this system thiosulphate functions as an O,S-bridge.[59] The rate of chromium(II) reduction of $(NH_3)_5CoSSO_3^+$ is 45 times greater than the corresponding rate of reduction of $(NH_3)_5CoOSO_3^+$;[33] this may arise from the enhanced ability of sulphur to mediate electron transfer, or from the weaker Co–S bond making it easier to surmount the Franck–Condon barrier. The lower activation enthalpy associated with reduction of the sulphato complex is more than offset by the more positive activation entropy for the thiosulphato analogue.

4. Electron transfer to complexes with pendant thioethers

Pendant thioether groups can also enhance the rate of electron transfer from chromium(II) to cobalt(III); thus, the Cr_{aq}^{2+} reductions of $(NH_3)_5Co(OOCCH_2SR)^{2+}$ complexes[60,61] are slightly faster than the reductions of analogous alkyl and oxygen-containing complexes. This effect was ascribed to O,S-chelation of chromium(II) in the precursor complex, similar to the O,S-chelation of chromium(II) observed in the reduction of the linkage isomer complexes $(en)_2Co(S((CH_2)_nCOOH)CH_2CH_2NH_2)^{3+}$ wherein the thioether functionality is coordinated and the carboxylate group is pendant.[28] The chromium(II) reduction of $(NH_3)_5Co(OOCCH(NH_3)CH_2CH_2SCH_3)^{3+}$ is not especially rapid,[61] presumably because O,S-chelation in the precursor complex would require formation of the less stable seven-membered ring (however, the higher formal charge and greater steric requirements of the complex may also contribute to the slower rate of reduction). In a related study,[18] complexes derived from $(en)_2Co(NH_2CH_2COO)^{2+}$, but with pendant thioether groups, were shown to be reduced by chromium(II) more slowly than the parent glycinato complex; this effect was ascribed to the electron-withdrawing

TABLE 4

Rate parameters for the chromium(II) reductions of Co(III) complexes containing pendant thioethers and related complexes

Complex	k_2 ($M^{-1} s^{-1}$)[a]	ΔH^* (kcal mol^{-1})	ΔS^* (eu)	Conditions[b]	Ref.
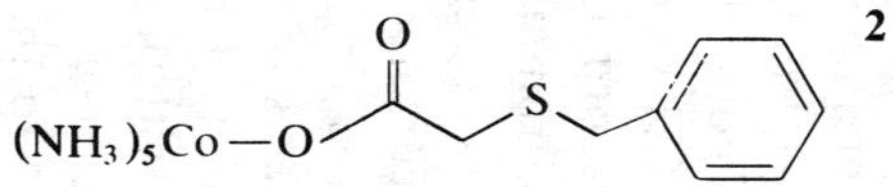 $(NH_3)_5Co$—O—...—S—CH$_2$—C$_6$H$_5$ **2**	5·2	—	—		[60]
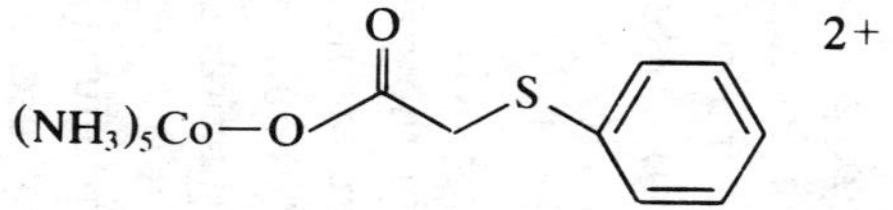 $(NH_3)_5Co$—O—...—S—C$_6$H$_5$ **2+**	0·91	—	—		[61]
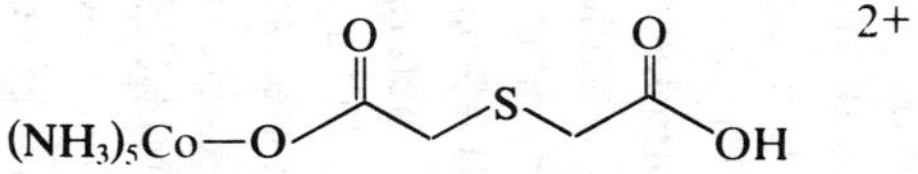 $(NH_3)_5Co$—O—...—S—CH$_2$—COOH **2+**	$a = 9\ M^{-1} s^{-1}$ $b = 14\ s^{-1}$	— —	— —		[61]
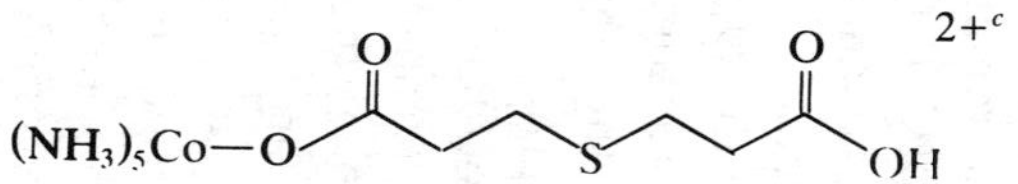 $(NH_3)_5Co$—O—...—S—...—COOH **2+c**	11	—	—		[61]
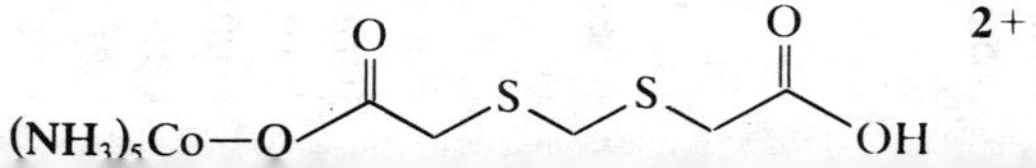 $(NH_3)_5Co$—O—...—S—CH$_2$—COOH **2+**	1·6	—	—		[61]

Complex				Conditions	Ref.
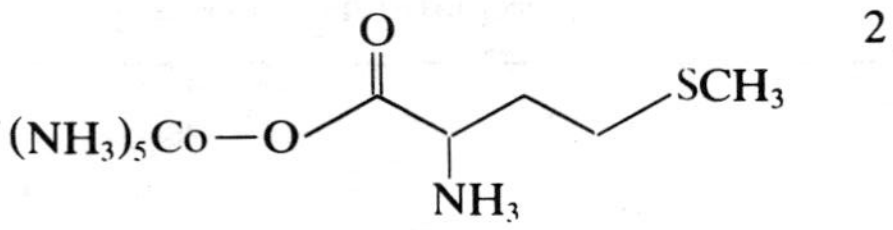 $(NH_3)_5Co-O-C(=O)-CH_2CH_2-SCH_3$, $-NH_3$ 2+	1.1×10^{-2}	—	—	—	[61]
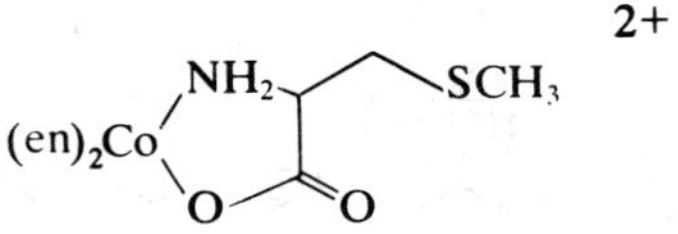 $(en)_2Co$ (NH$_2$, SCH$_3$, O–O chelate) 2+	0.56	9	−28	$I = 1.0$ M (H/LiClO$_4$)	[18]
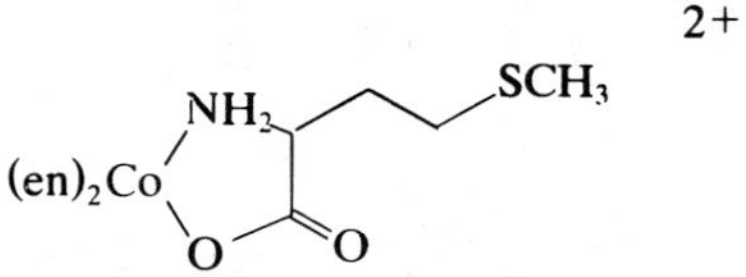 $(en)_2Co$ (NH$_2$, SCH$_3$ chelate) 2+	0.416	9.7	−28	$I = 1.0$ M (H/LiClO$_4$)	[18]
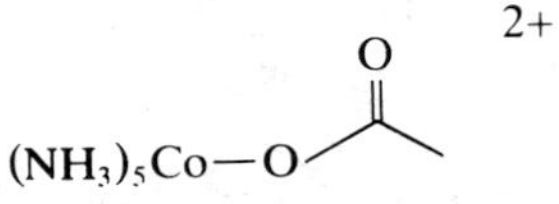 $(NH_3)_5Co-O-C(=O)CH_3$ 2+	0.36	—	—	—	[61]
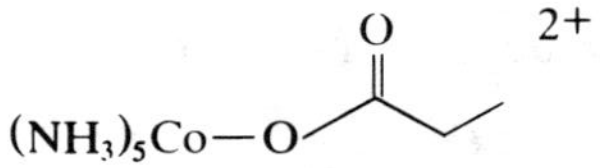 $(NH_3)_5Co-O-C(=O)CH_2CH_3$ 2+	0.14	—	—	—	[61]
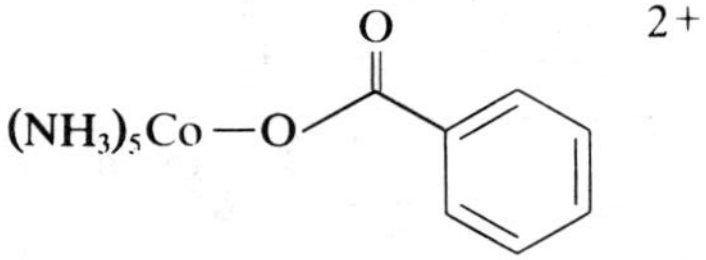 $(NH_3)_5Co-O-C(=O)C_6H_5$ 2+	0.14	—	—	—	[61]

TABLE 4 (cont.)

Complex	k_2 (M⁻¹ s⁻¹)ᵃ	ΔH^* (kcal mol⁻¹)	ΔS^* (eu)	Conditionsᵇ	Ref.
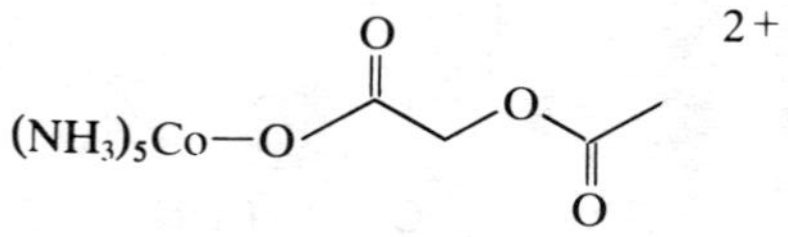 $(NH_3)_5Co-O-$ acetoxyacetate, 2+	0·17	—	—		[61]
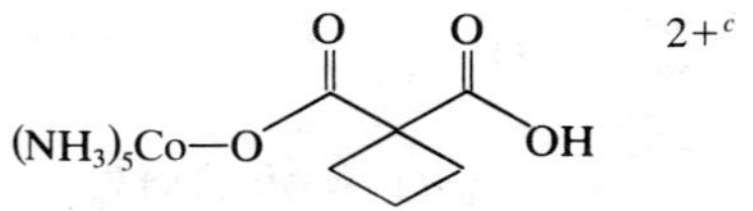 $(NH_3)_5Co-O-$ cyclobutane-1,1-dicarboxylate, 2+ᶜ	$a = 0.20$ M⁻¹ s⁻¹ $b = 0.093$ s⁻¹	— —	— —		[60]
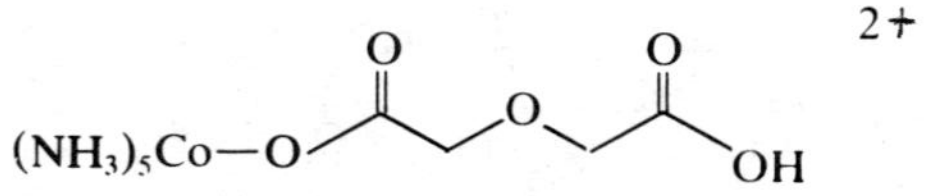 $(NH_3)_5Co-O-$ (diglycolate), 2+	0·17	—	—		[60]
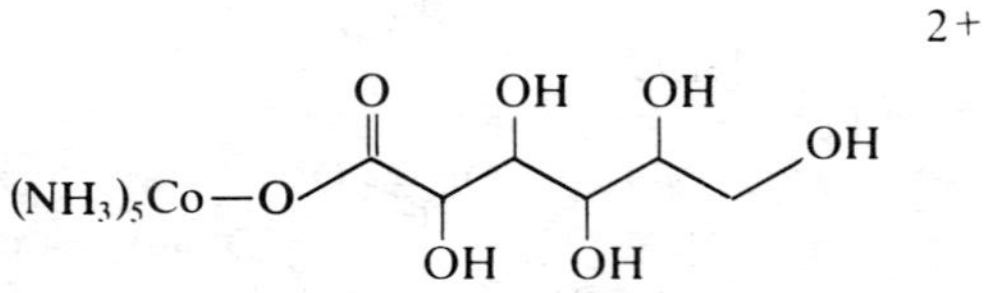 $(NH_3)_5Co-O-$ (keto-sugar carboxylate), 2+	2·7	—	—		[60]
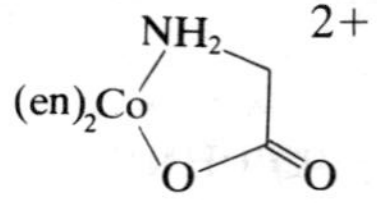 $(en)_2Co$ (glycinato/keto), 2+	2·22	8·9	−27	$I = 1{\cdot}0$ M (H/LiClO₄)	[19]

ᵃ Rate $= k_2$[oxidant][reductant].
ᵇ $T = 25°C$, $I = 1{\cdot}5$ M (H/NaClO₄) unless otherwise noted.
ᶜ $k_2 = a + b/[H^+]$.

ability of the pendant thioether causing a decrease in the stability of the carboxylato-bridged precursor complex.

5. Nonbridging ligand effects

Nonbridging, sulphur-containing ligands can affect the rate of electron transfer to cobalt(III) complexes. In assessing this phenomenon it is important to compare complexes of the same formal charge; thus, early examples involving complexes such as $(en)_2Co(Cl)(NCS)^+$ and $(en)_2Co(Cl)(NH_3)^{2+}$ [62] do not provide a direct measure of the nonbridging ligand effect. Worrell and co-workers have prepared a series of thioether–cobalt(III) complexes which, when compared to analogous ammine complexes, directly probe the nonbridging ligand effect of a coordinated thioether. In the complexes *cis*-(1,8-diamino-3,6-dithiaoctane)CoX$_2^+$ where X = Cl,[63,64] X = Br,[64] and X$_2$ = C$_2$O$_4$,[65] reduction occurs 10^3 times faster than in the analogous *cis*-(en)$_2$CoX$_2^+$ complexes. This rate enhancement is attributed to the ease of stretching the Co–S bond, and the concomitant lowering of the Franck–Condon barrier, despite the greater degree of chelation of the thioether ligand. The ordering of specific rates $k_{Cl} \cong k_{C_2O_4} > k_{Br}$ is reflected in the activation enthalpies, the relatively high $k_{C_2O_4}$ value possibly implying electron transfer through a double bridge.[32]

The situation is less clear when the bridging ligand is azide. Thus, the complexes *cis*-(1,8-diamine-3,6-dithiaoctane)Co(N$_3$)$_2^+$ and *cis*-(NH$_3$)$_4$Co(N$_3$)$_2^+$ are reduced at about the same rate,[66] as are the complexes QCoN$_3^{2+}$ and QSCoN$_3^{2+}$ (Q = 7-methyl-4,10-dithia-1,7,13-triazatridecane; QS = 1,11-diamine-3,6,9-trithiaundecane.[67]

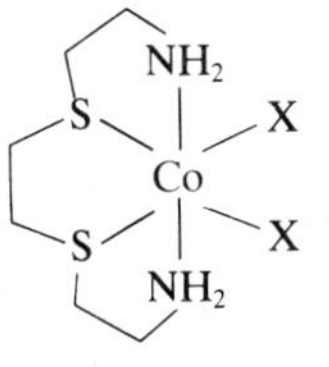

(1,8-diamino-3,6-dithiaoctane)CoX$_2^+$ 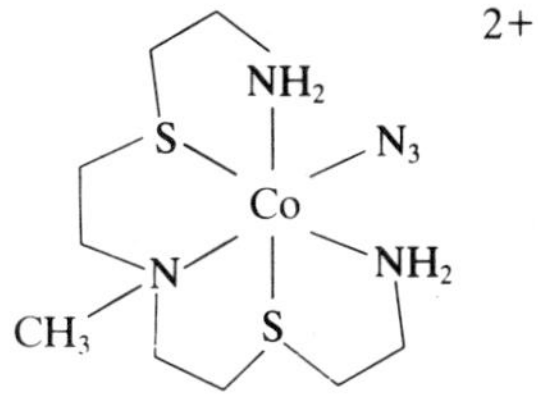   QCoN$_3^{2+}$ 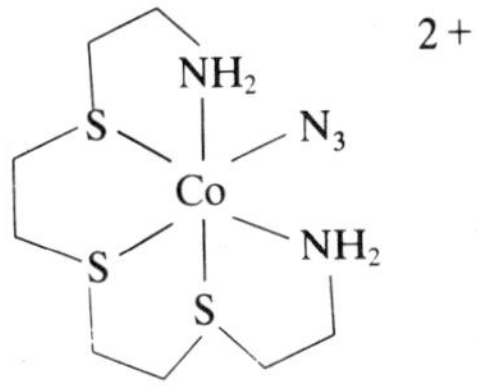   QSCoN$_3^{2+}$

Also, QCoN$_3^{2+}$ and QSCoN$_3^{2+}$ undergo reduction only slightly faster than does the analogous complex *cis*-(NH$_3$)$_4$Co(N$_3$)(OH$_2$)$^{2+}$. These several comparisons indicate that the reduction of azido complexes may be influenced by effects not present in the reduction of the halo and oxalato complexes.

TABLE 5

Rate parameters for the iron(II) reductions of coordinated thioether and related complexes: nonbridging ligand effects

Complex	k_2 $(\text{M}^{-1}\,\text{s}^{-1})^a$	ΔH^* (kcal mol^{-1})	ΔS^* (eu)	Conditions^b	Ref.
X = Cl⁻	1·35	9·2	−35	$I = 1\cdot0$ M (H/NaClO₄)	[63]
Cl⁻	1·66	10·4	−23		[64]
Br⁻	$9\cdot7 \times 10^{-2}$	12·1	−23		[64]
N₃⁻	0·145	17·1	−5	$I = 1\cdot15$ M	[66]
1/2C₂O₄²⁻	1·65	10·7	−22		[65]
	1·35	14·1	−11		[67]
	0·914	13·2	−15		[67]
cis-(en)₂CoCl₂⁺	$1\cdot6 \times 10^{-3}$	—	—	$I = 1\cdot06$ M	[62]
cis-(NH₃)₄(CoN₃)₂⁺	0·185	—	—	$I = 0\cdot26$ M	[35]
(NH₃)₄CoC₂O₄⁺	$4\cdot16 \times 10^{-4}$	18.5	−12	$I = 0.89$ M	[289]
(NH₃)₅CoN₃²⁺	$8\cdot7 \times 10^{-3}$	—	—		[35]

^{a} Rate $= k_2$[oxidant][reductant].

B. Oxidation of coordinated sulphur

The oxidation of coordinated sulphur-containing ligands is an important aspect of many biological redox systems.[68] Interestingly, these oxidations can often lead to coordination-stabilized moieties that exist only transiently when noncoordinated (e.g. sulphenic acids and sulphenyl iodides). In this context considerable research has recently been aimed at elucidating the chemistry involved during the oxidation of coordinated thiols, and at delineating the chemistry of coordination-stabilized species derived from thiol oxidations.

1. One-equivalent oxidation

All but one of the studies reported on the reaction of coordinated thiols with one-equivalent oxidants can be interpreted as proceeding through the radical-ion intermediate $RSSR^-$, either coordinated or noncoordinated. The one clear exception to $RSSR^-$ participation involves a special case wherein net oxidation occurs at carbon rather than sulphur (*vide infra*). While in some instances other mechanistic interpretations also adequately describe the observed data, none of these alternative interpretations are as generally applicable as is this unifying view of $RSSR^-$ participation. The radical ion dimer $RSSR^-$ is, of course, a well known species that is readily generated in pulse radiolysis experiments by either oxidation of thiols with $OH^{\cdot}$

$$RSH + OH^{\cdot} \longrightarrow RS^{\cdot} + H_2O \qquad (2a)$$

$$RS^{\cdot} + RSH = RSSR^- + H^+ \qquad (2b)$$

or reduction of disulphides with e_{aq}^-:[69–71]

$$RSSR + e_{aq}^- \longrightarrow RSSR^- \qquad (3)$$

The clearest evidence for $RSSR^-$ participation in the one-equivalent oxidation of a coordinated thiol arises from the stoichiometry observed for the reaction of the prototype thiolato complex $(en)_2Co(SCH_2CH_2NH_2)^{2+}$ with $Np(VI)$ (NpO_2^{2+} is a one-equivalent oxidant of $E^° = 1·15$ V; other one-equivalent oxidants such as Co_{aq}^{3+} and cerium(IV) give equivalent stoichiometries).[9,72]

$$2\,Co–SR + Np(VI) \longrightarrow Co–(RSSR) + Np(V) + Co_{aq}^{2+} \qquad (4)$$

The addition of one equivalent of $Np(VI)$ oxidant results in the net *reduction* of one equivalent of cobalt(III) and the generation of one mole of the coordinated disulphide $(en)_2Co(S(SCH_2CH_2NH_3)CH_2CH_2NH_2)^{4+}$. The two equivalents of oxidizing power necessary to convert two coordinated thiols to a coordinated disulphide thus arise from one $Np(VI) \rightarrow Np(V)$ and one $Co(III) \rightarrow Co(II)$, and this is a relatively rare example of an induced electron transfer reaction. It is important to note that in the starting thiolato complex just one sulphur atom is associated with each cobalt(III) centre, but in the quantitatively generated disulphide product there are two sulphur atoms associated with each cobalt(III) centre. Thus the reaction must proceed by a mechanism that efficiently brings both sulphur atoms together; such a mechanism can readily be based upon participation of RSSR⁻ in analogy to Equations (2a) and (2b):

$$Co-SR + Np(VI) \longrightarrow Co-\dot{S}R + Np(V) \tag{5a}$$

$$Co-\dot{S}R + Co-SR = Co-(RSSR^-)-Co \tag{5b}$$

$$Co-(RSSR^-)-Co \longrightarrow Co-(RSSR) + Co_{aq}^{2+} \tag{5c}$$

The first step is the coordinated analog to generation of a thiyl radical (Equation (2a)), the second step is the coordinated analogue of RSSR⁻ formation (Equation (2b)), and the last step is intramolecular electron transfer from the coordinated RSSR⁻ radical to cobalt(III) yielding cobalt(II) and the coordinated disulphide product. The initial oxidation step appears to be rate-limiting since the rate law is simply first-order in coordinated thiol and first-order in oxidant (oxidation by cobalt(III) shows the expected inverse acid dependence associated with the $Co_{aq}^{3+}/CoOH^{2+}$ equilibrium) and thus the kinetics do not reveal any mechanistic details.[9] Interestingly, the thiolato–chromium(III) analogues are oxidized much more rapidly than are the thiolato–cobalt(III) complexes, there yet being no satisfactory explanation for this phenomenon.[73]

A similar induced electron transfer reaction, with participation of a coordinated RSSR⁻ intermediate, can readily account for observations on the Ce(IV) oxidation of the thiolato–ruthenium(III) complex $(NH_3)_5RuS(CH_2)_4SH^{2+}$.[8] Addition of one equivalent of Ce(IV) leads to net *reduction* of Ru(III) to Ru(II) and formation of a coordinated, cyclic disulphide:

$$Ru^{III}-S(CH_2)_4SH + Ce(IV) \longrightarrow Ru^{III}-\dot{S}(CH_2)_4SH + Ce(III) \tag{6a}$$

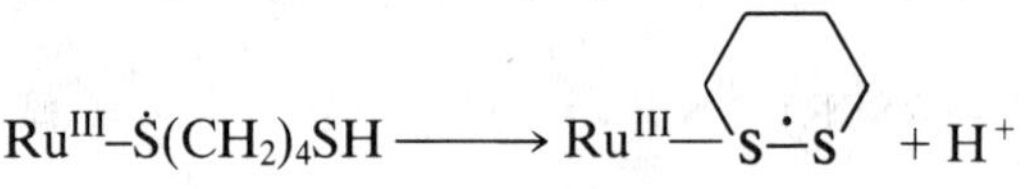

$$Ru^{III}-\dot{S}(CH_2)_4SH \longrightarrow Ru^{III}-\langle S\dot{-}S \rangle + H^+ \tag{6b}$$

$$Ru^{III}-\langle S\dot{-}S \rangle \longrightarrow Ru^{II}-\langle S-S \rangle \tag{6c}$$

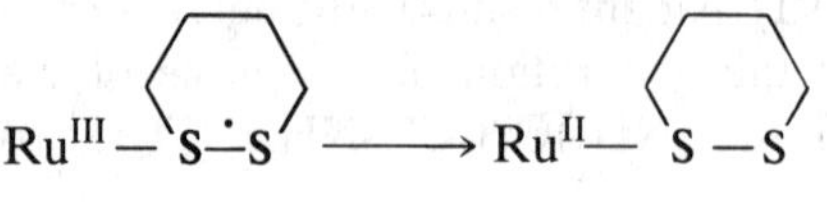

In this sytem there is no requirement for a bimolecular step to produce disulphide since there are two thiol sulphur atoms associated with each ruthenium centre. As originally proposed,[8] it is possible that this reaction proceeds through a Ru(IV) intermediate which then undergoes intramolecular decay to yield the disulphide–ruthenium(II) product; however, even this decay could possibly proceed by one-equivalent steps involving a coordinated RSSR$^-$ intermediate. It is interesting that the weaker oxidants Fe^{3+}_{aq} and $cis\text{-}(NH_3)_4Ru(NCC_6H_5)_2^{3+}$ do *not* oxidize $(NH_3)_5RuS(CH_2)_4SH^{2+}$ to the cyclic disulphide, but rather to an unidentified 4+ charged product which is possibly $(NH_3)_5RuS(CH_2)_4SS(CH_2)_4SRu(NH_3)_5^{4+}$. This implies that one step of the reaction sequence to form the cyclic disulphide is energetically demanding, and this could be either oxidation of the coordinated thiol (relative to oxidation of the pendant thiol) or oxidation of Ru(III) to Ru(IV).

The aquation of the thiolato–chromium(III) complex $(H_2O)_5CrSC_6H_4NH_3^{3+}$ is promoted by molecular oxygen, this complicated reaction being catalysed by noncoordinated thiol;[3] since noncoordinated thiol is the product of the net aquation reaction, the process follows autocatalytic kinetics. A reasonable mechanism for this autocatalytic, oxygen-induced, aquation reaction can be based on the intermediacy of coordinated RSSR$^-$:

$$RSH + O_2 \longrightarrow RS^{\cdot} \tag{7a}$$

$$Cr\text{–}SR + RS^{\cdot} \longrightarrow Cr\text{–}(RSSR^-) \tag{7b}$$

$$Cr\text{–}(RSSR^-) \longrightarrow Cr^{3+}_{aq} + RSSR^- \tag{7c}$$

$$RSSR^- = RS^{\cdot} + RS^- \tag{7d}$$

In the first step, noncoordinated 4-mercaptoaniline is oxidized by molecular oxygen to yield a thiyl radical; this thiyl radical then converts coordinated RS$^-$ to coordinated RSSR$^-$ which aquates relatively rapidly (coordinated disulphides are known to aquate much more rapidly than coordinated thiolates). While other reaction pathways are certainly possible, the kinetic observations suggest RS$^{\cdot}$ oxidative catalysis of Cr–SR bond cleavage and this in turn strongly implies the existence of a RSSR$^-$–Cr(III) intermediate. Relatively stable RSSR$^-$–Cr(III) intermediates have also been proposed to account for structural[74] and kinetic[5] observations on the chromium(II) reduction of disulphides; Lane and co-workers[75] have presented preliminary EPR evidence characterizing a remarkably stable RSSR$^-$–Cr(III) complex resulting from the chromium(II) reduction of dithiodiglycolic acid.

The reaction of Fe(III) with $(H_2O)_5CrSC_6H_4NH_3^{3+}$ leads to simple cleavage of the Cr–S bond according to the rate law $k(Fe^{III})(CrSR^{3+})$; the mechanism presumably involves initial, rate-determining, oxidation of the coordinated thiol to a coordinated thiyl radical.[3] The stoichiometry of the reaction of Fe(III) with $(H_2O)_5CrSH^{2+}$ [76] is more complex since the H–S bond is more labile than the Cr–S bond, and thus the Cr–S bond is maintained during the oxidation process. However, the reaction can still be understood in terms of initial oxidation of a coordinated hydrosulphide to a coordinated sulphydryl radical, followed by stabilization of this radical through formation of a sulphur–sulphur bond (Equations (2a and b)). The oxidation rate law is again simply $k(Fe^{III})(CrSH^{2+})$, but the sulphur-containing products are the dimeric species $Cr^{III}S_2Fe^{II4+}$ (>80%) and $Cr^{III}S_2Cr^{III4+}$ (<20%). Presumably initial, rate determining, Fe(III) oxidation of $(H_2O)_5CrSH^{2+}$ yields the binuclear radical $Cr^{III}S–Fe^{II4+}$ which is then stabilized by interaction with another $CrSH^{2+}$ moiety; these two reactions are analogous to the two-step formation of $RSSR^-$ by the one-equivalent oxidation of RSH (Equations (2a and b)).

$$CrSH^{2+} + Fe^{III} = Cr\text{–}\dot{S}\text{–}Fe^{II4+} + H^+ \tag{8a}$$

$$Cr\text{–}\dot{S}\text{–}Fe^{II4+} + CrSH^{2+} = Cr\text{—}S\text{—}\underset{\diagdown Cr}{\overset{H \atop |}{\dot{S}}}{\diagup}^{Fe^{II6+}} \tag{8b}$$

This trinuclear intermediate can then be oxidized to a trinuclear product which in turn can dissociate to form CrS_2HFe^{4+} and Cr_{aq}^{3+}, and, to a lesser extent, CrS_2Cr^{4+} and Fe_{aq}^{2+}. The dichromium product further reacts with Fe_{aq}^{2+} to yield the more stable CrS_2HFe^{4+} product.

The one example of coordinated thiol oxidation by one-equivalent reagents which clearly does not involve a $RSSR^-$ intermediate is reaction of the thioglycolate complexes $(en)_2M(SCH_2COO)^+$ (M = Co^{III}, Cr^{III}) with Np(VI), Co_{aq}^{3+}, Ce(IV) etc.[68,73,77,78] In all cases the predominant product is $(en)_2M(SC(O)COO)^+$, the monothiooxalate complex in which net oxidation has occurred at carbon and not at sulphur; this product has been definitively identified by single-crystal x-ray structural analysis.[77,78] While the detailed mechanism of this net four-equivalent oxidation process is still abstruse, it is clear that the initial step involves oxidation at the coordinated sulphur atom; at some later stage in the reaction, net oxidizing power is transferred from the sulphur atom to the adjacent carbon atom. Evidence for initial oxidation occurring at sulphur rather than carbon comes from several sources. In pulse radiolysis experiments involving $OH^{\cdot}$ oxidation of thiolato–chromium(III) complexes,[79] only the thioglycolate complex yields a transient spectrum and this spectrum is similar to that observed for complexes containing the S-bonded sulphenato $(RS=O^-)$ ligand.[12] In addition, the analogous glycolato complex $(en)_2Co(OCH_2COO)^+$ which does not contain a coordinated sulphur atom also does not undergo oxidation at carbon. Finally, a host of two-equivalent oxidants (*vide infra*), which are known to attack the sulphur atom of coordinated thiols, also react with $(en)_2Co(SCH_2COO)^+$ to yield $(en)_2Co(SC(O)COO)^+$.[77] A possible dehydration mechanism for transferal of oxidizing power from coordinated sulphur to the adjacent carbon atom has been proposed.[79]

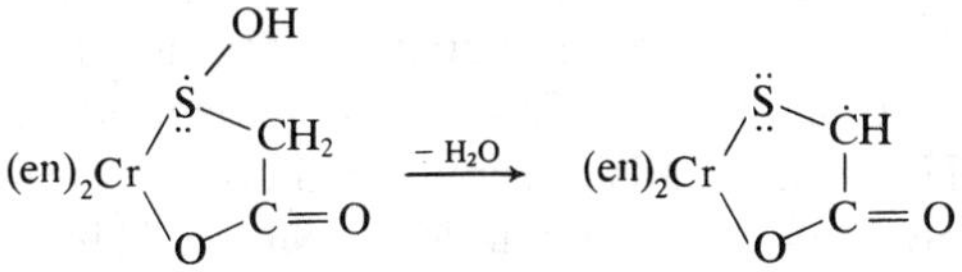

2. Two-equivalent oxidation

Two-equivalent oxidations of coordinated sulphur can generally be understood in terms of the nucleophilicity of low-valent sulphur towards species such as H_2O_2, I^+, RS^+, etc. It should be understood that the difference between nucleophilic attack and two-equivalent oxidation is merely a formalism based on the arbitrary definition of oxidation state. For example, nucleophilic attack by a coordinated thiolate (RS^-) on CH_3I leads to a coordinated thioether $(RS—CH_3)$ and this *is not* formally a redox reaction since carbon is less electronegative than sulphur; however, nucleophilic attack by a coordinated thiol on H_2O_2 leads to a coordinated sulphenic acid $(RS—OH)$ and this *is* formally a redox reaction since oxygen is more electronegative than sulphur. Coordinated sulphur atoms, especially those derived from thiols, retain considerable nucleophilicity and are therefore generally very reactive towards two-equivalent oxidants. These reactions are synthetically very fruitful, and recently some of the better-defined systems have been subject to kinetic analysis.

The H_2O_2 oxidation of thiolato–cobalt(III) complexes leads directly to sulphenato–cobalt(III) complexes by oxygen atom transfer; e.g.

$$(en)_2Co(SCH_2CH_2NH_2)^{2+} + H_2O_2$$

$$\longrightarrow (en)_2Co(S(O)CH_2CH_2NH_2)^{2+} + H_2O$$

and in several cases the sulphenato product has been characterized by single-crystal x-ray structural analysis.[12, 80–84] The H_2O_2 oxidation of the analogous thiolato–chromium(III) complexes leads to Cr–S bond fission via a presumed unstable sulphenato–chromium(III) intermediate:[83]

$$(en)_2Cr(SCH_2CH_2NH_2)^{2+} + H_2O_2$$

$$\longrightarrow [(en)_2Cr(S(O)CH_2CH_2NH_2)^{2+} + H_2O$$

$$(en)_2Cr \underset{NH_2CH_2CH_2S-OH}{\overset{OH_2^{3+}}{<}} \longrightarrow products$$

The greater lability of Cr–S bonds relative to Co–S bonds is well established by studies on thiolato[85] and thioether[28] complexes, and thus it is not unreasonable to assign the instability of the sulphenato–chromium(III) intermediate to the inherent instability of the Cr–S bond. Reaction of $(H_2O)_5CrSR^{n+}$ complexes with H_2O_2 also leads to rapid Cr–S bond fission by a process that presumably involves a similar labile sulphenato–chromium(III) intermediate;[83] the originally proposed[3] free radical mechanism for this reaction now appears implausible.

The mechanism of these H_2O_2 oxidation reactions is taken to be nucleophilic attack by coordinated sulphur on the O–O peroxide bond, coordinated thiols being as potent nucleophiles as thiosulphate and thiourea.[83] Interestingly, when bonded to cobalt(III), thiols are significantly better nucleophiles than when bonded to chromium(III), presumably due to greater π back-bonding in the cobalt system (d^6 against d^3). The rate law for all oxidations is $(Nuc)(H_2O_2)(a + b(H^+))$, the acid dependence reflecting oxidation by both H_2O_2 and $H_3O_2^+$.[86] Since the rate term b reflects attack on $H_3O_2^+$ while a reflects attack on H_2O_2, simple electrostatic arguments predict that the ratio b/a should be largest for anionic nucleophiles, intermediate for neutral nucleophiles, and smallest for cationic nucleophiles. Table 6 collects the available data[83] on the acid dependence of H_2O_2 oxidation of sulphur-containing nucleophiles, and it is seen that the expected trend in b/a values is realized if the two complexes with coordinated isothiocyanate are discounted. The isothiocyanate complexes become concordant if one accepts the view that they fall more naturally into the classification of neutral nucleophiles, since in these complexes the remote sulphur atom carries a formal charge of zero.

The rate of H_2O_2 oxidation of a coordinated thiol is relatively insensitive to the nature of the thiolato complex (thiolato chelate ring size or steric requirements, ancillary ligands, etc.) implying that reorganization of the inner coordination sphere does not contribute significantly to the activation barrier. In fact, for the two complexes $L_4Cr(SCH_2COO)^+$, oxidation of the bis(ethylenediamine) complex is actually 2·5 times faster than is oxidation of the tetraaquo analogue. This is consistent with the nucleophilic attack scheme, since ethylenediamine is a better electron donor than is

TABLE 6

Summary of available kinetic data describing the acid dependence of the H_2O_2 oxidation of sulphur-containing nucleophiles[a,b]

Nucleophile	a (M^{-1} s^{-1})	b (M^{-2} s^{-1})	b/a (M^{-1})
Anionic			
$S_2O_3^{2-}$	0·025	1·7	68
SCN^-	$5·2 \times 10^{-4}$	0.025	48
Neutral			
$(HOCH_2CH_2)_2S$	$2·2 \times 10^{-3}$	0·023	10
$O(CH_2CH_2)_2S$	$2·6 \times 10^{-3}$	0·035	14
$(NH_2)_2C{=}S$	0·07	1.42	20
$(NHCH_3)_2C{=}S$	0·094	0·60	6
$(NHCH_2CH_3)_2C{=}S$	0·086	0·53	6
Cationic			
$[(en)_2Co(NO_2)(NCS)]^+$	$4·6 \times 10^{-5}$	$1·3 \times 10^{-3}$	28
$[(NH_3)_5Co(NCS)]^{2+}$	$5·3 \times 10^{-5}$	$9·8 \times 10^{-4}$	19
$[(en)_2Co(S(O)CH_2CH_2NH_2)]^{2+}$	$3·4 \times 10^{-4}$	$5·1 \times 10^{-4}$	1.6
$[(en)_2Co(SCH_2CH_2NH_2)]^{2+}$	1·18	1·8	1.5
	0·94	$\cong 1·2$	$\cong 1·3$
$[(en)_2Co(SCH_2CH(COOH)NH_2)]^{2+}$	0·24	0.54	2·2
$[(en)_2Cr(SCH_2CH_2NH_2)]^{2+}$	0·36	0·90	2·5
$[(en)_2Cr(SCH_2CO_2)]^+$	0·38	0.80	2.1
$[(en)_2Cr(SCH_2CH_2CO_2)]^+$	0.50	1.00	2.0
$[(en)_2Cr(SC(CH_3)_2CO_2)]^+$	0·036	0.11	3.0

[a] Conditions: 25°C, H_2O solvent, variable ionic strength.[83]
[b] Rate = $(a + b[H^+])[\text{nucleophile}][H_2O_2]$.

water, but is opposite to what would be expected if rearrangement of the chromium(III) coordination sphere contributed significantly to the energetics of the oxidation process. Thus it is the energetics of O–O bond fission that dominate the reaction.[83]

The sulphenato–cobalt(III) complexes are further oxidized by H_2O_2 to yield the corresponding sulphinato–cobalt(III) complexes;[12,80] e.g.

$(en)_2Co(S(O)CH_2CH_2NH_2)^{2+} + H_2O_2$

$$\longrightarrow (en)_2Co(S(O)_2CH_2CH_2NH_2)^{2+} + H_2O$$

and in this prototype system the sulphinato product has been characterized by single-crystal x-ray structural analysis.[10] Again, the mechanism of this oxidation reaction is taken to be nucleophilic attack by the coordinated sulphenato sulphur atom on the O–O peroxide bond. Sulphenato sulphur is a much poorer nucleophile than is thiolato sulphur, the thiolato complex

$(en)_2Co(SCH_2CH_2NH_2)^{2+}$ reacting with H_2O_2 about 3500 times more rapidly than the sulphenato complex $(en)_2Co(S(O)CH_2CH_2NH_2)^{2+}$. This is as expected on the basis of both steric and electronic arguments: the sulphenato sulphur atom is three-coordinate, whereas the thiolato sulphur atom is two-coordinate; and the sulphenato sulphur atom is bonded to an electron-withdrawing oxygen atom, whereas the thiolato sulphur atom is not.

The H_2O_2 oxidation of the isothiocyanato complex $(NH_3)_5CoNCS^{2+}$ deserves mention at this point.[87-89] This interesting reaction leads to a number of products, most notably $(NH_3)_6Co^{3+}$, $(NH_3)_5CoCN^{2+}$, SO_4^{2-} and CO_2. These results indicate net oxidation of both sulphur and carbon, subsequent hydrolysis reactions, and the intriguing possibility of a coordinated nitride intermediate. The rate law is the usual $(Co^{III})(H_2O_2)(a + b(H^+))$, and the addition of mercury(II) to form the $(NH_3)_5CoNCSHg^{4+}$ adduct retards the rate of oxidation. These observations are consistent with a mechanism analogous to that discussed above for H_2O_2 oxidation of coordinated sulphur, i.e. rate-determining nucleophilic attack by the pendant sulphur atom on the O–O peroxide linkage.

Oxidation of a coordinated thiol to a coordinated sulphenic acid by H_2O_2 is an example of a group transfer reaction wherein the "group" being transferred is an oxygen atom. Oxidation of coordinated thiols by *N*-(alkylthio)- and *N*-(arylthio)phthalimides involves transfer of a RS^+ group to yield a coordinated disulphide,[90] while oxidation by *N*-iodosuccinimide can be viewed as an I^+ transfer.[91]

$$(en)_2Co(SCH_2CH_2NH_2)^{2+} + H_2O_2 \longrightarrow (en)_2Co(S(O)CH_2CH_2NH_2)^{2+}$$

$$(en)_2Co(SCH_2CH_2NH_2)^{2+} + RS-N$$

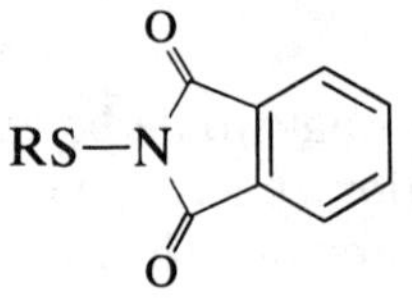

$$\longrightarrow (en)_2Co(S(SR)CH_2CH_2NH_2)^{3+}$$

$$(en)_2Co(SCH_2CH_2NH_2)^{2+} + I-N$$

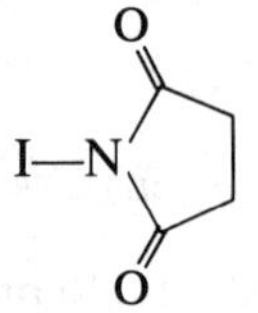

$$\longrightarrow [(en)_2Co(NH_2CH_2CH_2)]_2I]^{5+}$$

Even though the assignment of oxidation states in the binuclear iodine product is not definitive, it is clear that all three reactions involve oxidation of the coordinated thiol. Also, all three reactions clearly proceed by nucleophilic attack of the coordinated sulphur atom on the O–O, S–N or I–N linkage of the substrate. The binuclear iodine product can be formally viewed as a two-coordinate complex of I^+ wherein the thiolato–cobalt(III) moieties function as stabilizing, sulphur-donating, ligands analogous to thiourea in the bis(thiourea)iodine(I) complex $(tu)_2I^+$.[92] However, it is probably more useful to view the binuclear product as a derivative of a coordinated sulphenyl iodide (RS–I) since many of the reactions of this species mimic the reactions of noncoordinated sulphenyl iodides; e.g.

$$((en)_2Co(SCH_2CH_2NH_2))_2I^{5+} \rightleftharpoons$$

$$(en)_2Co(S(I)CH_2CH_2NH_2)^{3+} + (en)_2Co(SCH_2CH_2NH_2)^{2+}$$

$$(en)_2Co(S(I)CH_2CH_2NH_2)^{3+} + RSH$$

$$\longrightarrow (en)_2Co(S(SR)CH_2CH_2NH_2)^{3+} + HI$$

$$(en)_2Co(S(I)CH_2CH_2NH_2)^{3+} + H_2C{=}CH{-}C(O)NH_2$$

$$\longrightarrow (en)_2 Co(SCH_2CH_2NH_2)^{3+}$$
$$|$$
$$CH_2{-}CH{-}C(O)NH_2$$
$$|$$
$$I$$

Because of the lability of the S–H bond, oxidation of $(H_2O)_5CrSH^{2+}$ by molecular iodine leads simply to the persulphide bridged complex $(H_2O)_5CrSSCr(H_2O)_5^{4+}$.[23,76] It is likely that this reaction proceeds through the "sulphenyl iodide" intermediate $(H_2O)_5CrSI^{2+}$ in analogy to the reaction of organic thiols with iodine;[93]

$$RSH + I_2 \longrightarrow RSI + HI$$

$$RSI + RSH \longrightarrow RSSR + HI$$

$$(H_2O)_5CrSH^{2+} + I_2 \longrightarrow [(H_2O)_5CrSI]^{2+} + HI$$

$$[(H_2O)_5CrSI]^{2+} + (H_2O)_5CrSH^{2+} \longrightarrow (H_2O)_5CrSSCr(H_2O)_5^{4+} + HI$$

The I_2 oxidation of *cis*-$(en)_2Co(S_2O_3)_2^-$ produces one equivalent of sulphate and a complex formulated as *trans*-$(en)_2Co(OH_2)(S_3O_3)$,[94] i.e. a complex containing the disulphane monosulphonate, $-S(S)SO_3$, ligand.

Two-equivalent oxidation at coordinated sulphur has also been effected by some unusual reagents. Oxidation of the *S,N*-cysteine complex $(en)_2Co(SCH_2CH(COOH)NH_2)^{2+}$ by trityl chloride or *p*-nitrobenzenesulphonyl chloride in dimethylsulphoxide leads to the corresponding sulphenato complex $(en)_2Co(S(O)CH_2CH(COOH)NH_2)^{2+}$. These reactions presumably proceed via nucleophilic attack of the coordinated thiolato sulphur atom on cationic species such as $(CH_3)_2S^+$ or $(CH_3)_2S—OR^+$ to yield unstable adducts which then hydrolyse to form the sulphenato complex.[81] A similar oxidation of the S,N-cysteine complex by mixture of acetic anhydride and dimethylsulphoxide leads to cleavage of the Co–S bond and formation of an unusual sulphenamide complex.[78] Again, the initial step of this reaction presumably involves nucleophilic attack of the coordinated sulphur atom on an O-acylated sulphoxonium species generated from dimethylsulphoxide and acetic anhydride; this attack yields a coordinated $RSS(CH_3)_2^+$ intermediate which presumably undergoes successive Co–S bond fission, condensation of the pendant sulphur atom with an adjacent ethylenediamine (with loss of dimethyl sulphide), and formation of a new carboxylate-cobalt(III) bond:

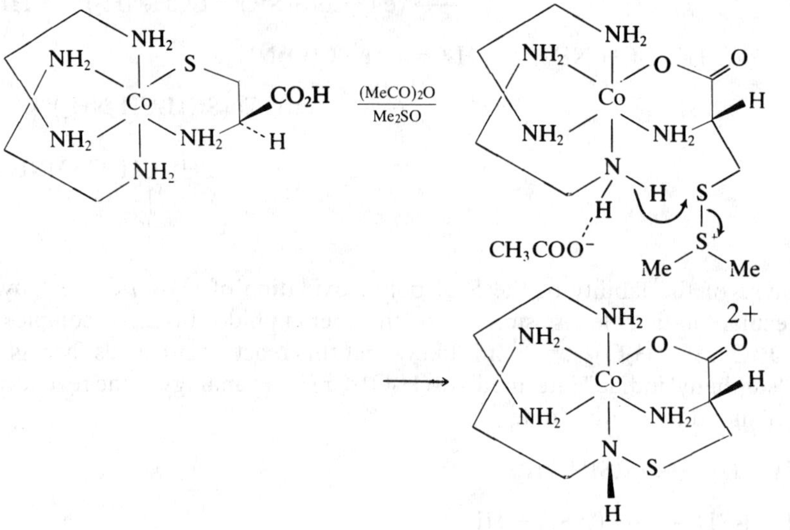

Oxidation of the sulphenamide complex with N-bromosuccinamide or H_2O_2 yields the sulphinamide and sulphonamide complexes.[95]

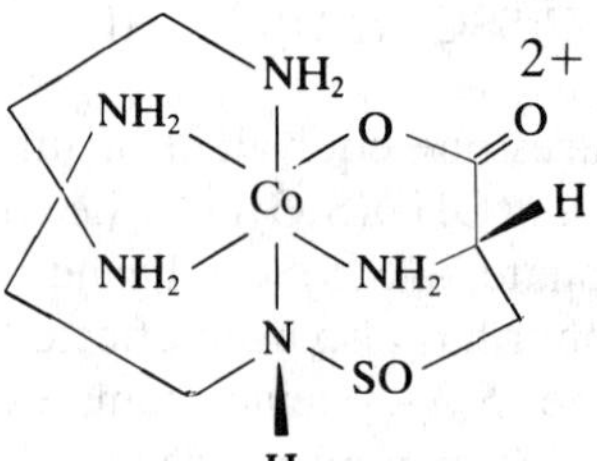

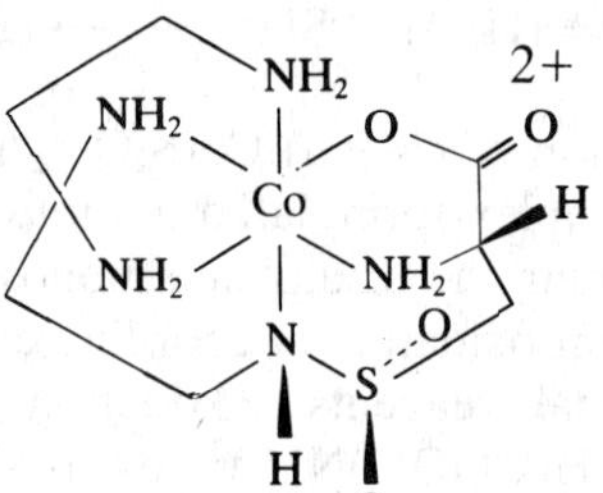

The structure of the sulphenamide and sulphinamide products have been verified by single-crystal x-ray structural analysis.[78,95]

Reduction of the sulphenamide complex with dithionite or borohydride leads to S–N bond cleavage and formation of the *N,O*-bound cysteine complex.[96] The pendant thiol of this product is available for further reaction, e.g. methylation or oxidation to the sulphenamide complex. Reaction of the product thiol with the parent sulphenamide complex yields the cysteine-bridged dimer.

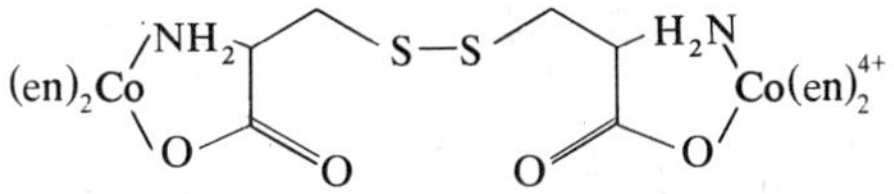

The reaction of the sulphenamide complex with CN^- leads to a 2-aminothiazoline complex.[97]

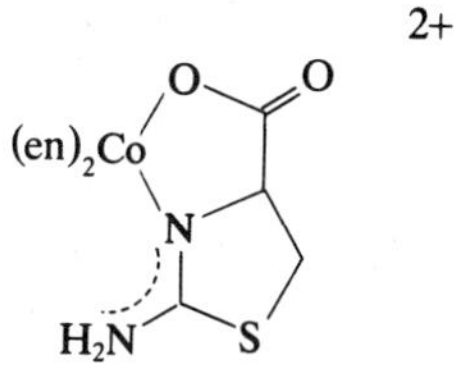

A few two-equivalent oxidations of sulphur-containing amineruthenium complexes have been qualitatively investigated. The *trans* labilizing ability of *S*-bonded sulphite[11,98] makes $trans\text{-}(NH_3)_4Ru(SO_3)(H_2O)^+$ a valuable synthetic intermediate.[99] After the desired ligand replaces the labilized water molecule, the resulting $trans\text{-}(NH_3)_4Ru(SO_3)(L)^{n+}$ complex is oxidized with H_2O_2 to convert the coordinated sulphite to sulphate, the resulting sulphato–ruthenium(III) complex being substitution-inert. Oxidation of the coordinated sulphur(IV) presumably occurs by initial conversion of coordinated SO_3^{2-} to coordinated SO_2 and subsequent nucleophilic attack by this species on the O–O bond of H_2O_2.[98] This mechanism is similar to that proposed for the H_2O_2 oxidation of noncoordinated SO_2.[100] Molecular oxygen converts the ruthenium(II) complex $(NH_3)_5RuSH_2^{2+}$ to the dimeric species $(NH_3)_5RuSSRu(NH_3)_5^{4+}$ [101] via an intermediate which has been postulated to be the ruthenium(III) species $(NH_3)_5RuSH^{2+}$.[102] The $(NH_3)_5RuSSRu(NH_3)_5^{4+}$ dimer is of considerable interest, largely because of the ambiguity in assigning oxidation states to the Ru and S atoms, and has been the subject of a single-crystal x-ray structural analysis.[103]

The oxidation of $(en)_2Co(SCH_2COO)^+$ to $(en)_2Co(SC(O)COO)^+$ by one-equivalent reagents which is unusual and was noted in the previous section is also effected by two-equivalent reagents such as *N*-iodosuccini-

TABLE 7
Oxidation of coordinated sulphur

Complex	Oxidant	Major products	k_2 (M⁻¹ s⁻¹)[a]	ΔH^* (kcal mol⁻¹)	ΔS^* (eu)	Conditions [b]	Ref.
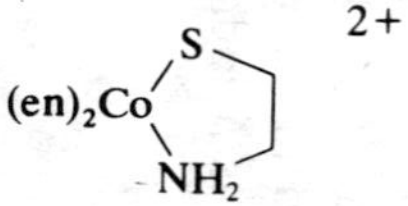 $(en)_2Co(S\!-\!CH_2CH_2\!-\!NH_2)$ 2+	NpO_2^+	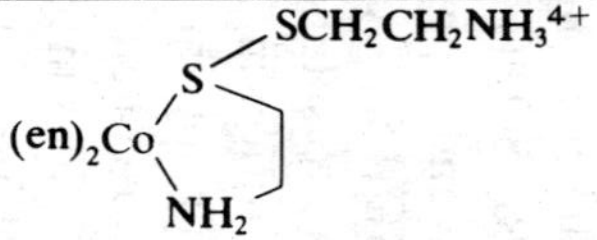 $(en)_2Co(S\!-\!CH_2CH_2\!-\!NH_3)^{4+}$, Co_{aq}^{2+}	2842	7.6	−17		[9]
	Co_{aq}^{3+}	Co_{aq}^{2+}	$a = 933$ M⁻¹ s⁻¹[c] $b = 1152$ s⁻¹	12.5 18.0	−3 16		[9]
$(H_2O)_5CrSH^{2+}$	Fe_{aq}^{3+}	$(H_2O)_5CrS_2HFe(OH)_3^{4+}$ $(H_2O)_5CrSSCr(H_2O)_5^{4+}$	$a = 1.50 \times 10^{-2}$ s⁻¹[d]	—	—		[76]
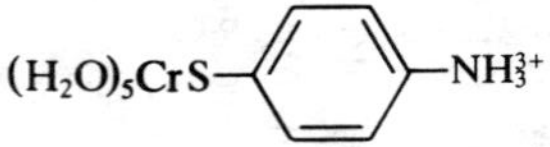 $(H_2O)_5CrS\!-\!C_6H_4\!-\!NH_3^{3+}$	Fe_{aq}^{3+}	Cr_{aq}^{3+}, $H_3NC_6H_4SSC_6H_4NH_3^{4+}$	3×10^{-2}	—	—	$I = 2.0$ M (H/NaClO₄)	[3]
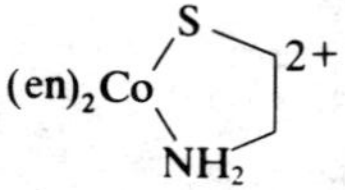 $(en)_2Co(S(\!=\!O)\!-\!CH_2CH_2\!-\!NH_2)$ 2+	H_2O_2	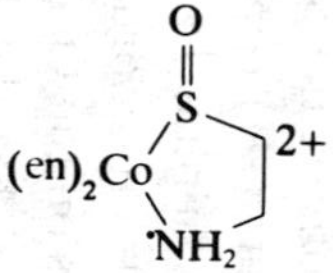 $(en)_2Co(O\!=\!S\!-\!CH_2CH_2\!-\!NH_2)$ 2+	3.20^e $a = 1.18$ M⁻¹ s⁻¹ $b = 1.8$ M⁻¹ s⁻¹	7.3	−32	$I = 1.0$ M (HClO₄)	[83]
$(en)_2Co(S\!-\!CH_2\!-\!C(\!=\!O)\!-\!O)$ ring	H_2O_2	$(en)_2Co(O\!=\!S\!-\!CH_2\!-\!C(\!=\!O)\!-\!O)^+$	0.86	—	—	20–3°C, pH 5–7	[82]
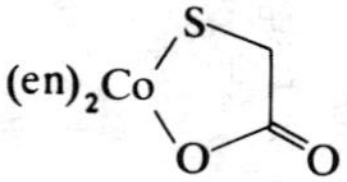 $(en)_2Co(S\!-\!CH_2\!-\!C(\!=\!O)\!-\!O)$ 2+	H_2O_2	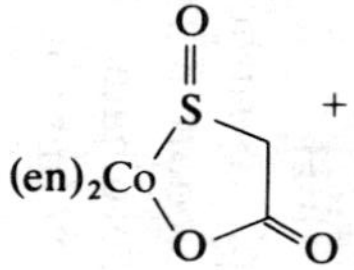 $(en)_2Co(O\!=\!S\!-\!CH_2\!-\!C(\!=\!O)\!-\!O)^+$	2.54	10.2	−22	$I = 1.0$ M (HClO₄)	[83]
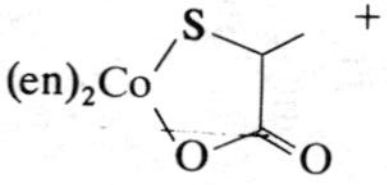 $(en)_2Co(S\!-\!CH(CH_3)\!-\!C(\!=\!O)\!-\!O)^+$	H_2O_2	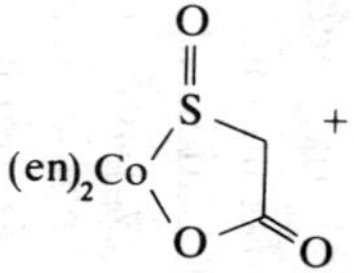 $(en)_2Co(O\!=\!S\!-\!CH_2\!-\!C(\!=\!O)\!-\!O)^+$	2.20	9.7	−25	$I = 1.0$ M (HClO₄)	[83]

Reactant	Oxidant	Products	k		$\Delta S^{\ddagger}$	Conditions	Ref.
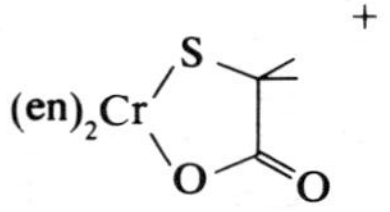 (en)$_2$Cr–S–C(CH$_3$)$_2$–C(=O)–O ring, +	H$_2$O$_2$	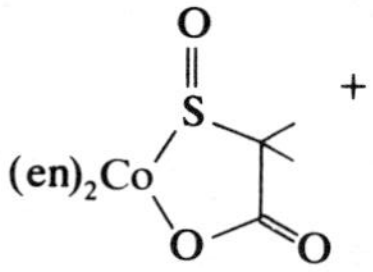 (en)$_2$Co–S(=O)–C(CH$_3$)$_2$–C(=O)–O ring, +	0·52	9·2	−29	$I = 1·0$ M (HClO$_4$)	[83]
(en)$_2$Cr–S–C(CH$_3$)$_2$–CH(NH$_2$)(COOH), 2+	H$_2$O$_2$	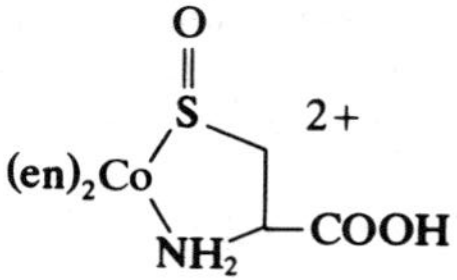 (en)$_2$Co–S(=O)–C(CH$_3$)$_2$–CH(NH$_2$)(COOH), 2+	0·40	9·6	−28	20·3°C, $I = 1·0$ M (H/NaClO$_4$), pH 6·9 (Phosphate)	[82]
(en)$_2$Co–S–C(CH$_3$)$_2$–CH(NH$_2$)(COOH), 2+	H$_2$O$_2$	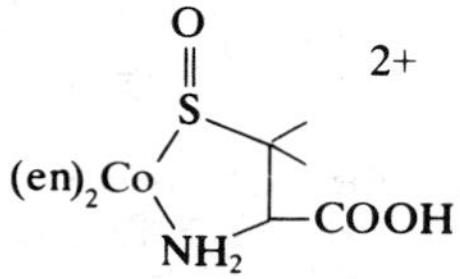 (en)$_2$Co–S(=O)–C(CH$_3$)$_2$–CH(NH$_2$)(COOH), 2+	0·14	—	—	20·3°C, $I = 1·0$ M (H/NaClO$_4$), pH 6·9 (phosphate)	[82]
(en)$_2$Cr–S–CH$_2$CH$_2$–NH$_2$, 2+	H$_2$O$_2$	various aquation products	1·13^e $a = 0·36$ M^{-1} s^{-1} $b = 0·90$ M^{-2} s^{-1}	9·7 — —	−26 — —	$I = 1·0$ M (HClO$_4$)	[83]
(en)$_2$Cr–S–CH$_2$–C(=O)–O, +	H$_2$O$_2$	various aquation products	1·13^e $a = 0·38$ M^{-1} s^{-1} $b = 0·80$ M^{-2} s^{-1}	9·3 — —	−27 — —		[83]
(en)$_2$Cr–S–CH$_2$CH$_2$–C(=O)–O, +	H$_2$O$_2$	various aquation products	1·19^e $a = 0·50$ M^{-1} s^{-1} $b = 1·00$ M^{-2} s^{-1}	10·0 — —	−25 — —		[83]
(en)$_2$Cr–S–C(CH$_3$)$_2$–C(=O)–O, +	H$_2$O$_2$	various aquation products	0·16^e $a = 0·036$ M^{-1} s^{-1} $b = 0·11$ M^{-2} s^{-1}	10·6 — —	−27 — —		[83]

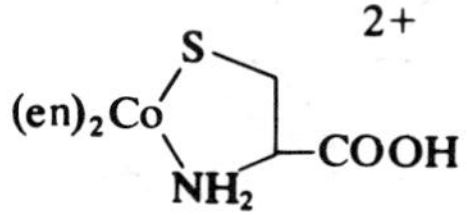

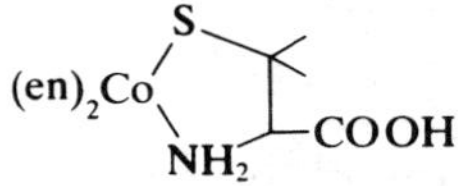

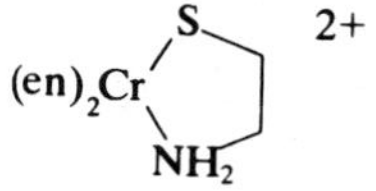

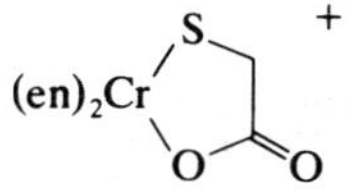

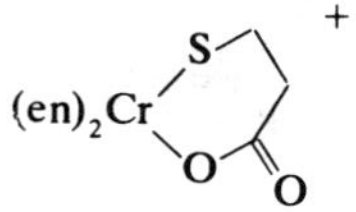

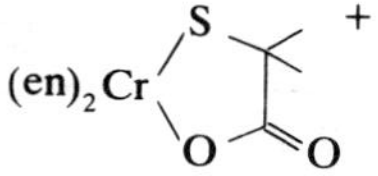

TABLE 7 (cont.)

Complex	Oxidant	Major products	k_2 $(\text{M}^{-1}\,\text{s}^{-1})^a$	ΔH^* (kcal mol^{-1})	(eu)	Conditions ^{b}	Ref.
$(H_2O)_4Cr$ (cyclic S,O complex, +)	H_2O_2	various aquation products	0·445	10·4	-27	26·6°C, $I=1·0$ M (HClO$_4$)	[83]
$(H_2O)_5Cr–SCH_2CH_2NH_3^{3+}$	H_2O_2	Cr_{aq}^{3+}	0·176	10·6	-26	25·5°C, $I=1·0$ M (HClO$_4$)	[83]
$(H_2O)_5Cr–SC_2H_4\cdot NH_3^{3+}$	H_2O_2	Cr_{aq}^{3+}	0·045	10·8	-28	26·0°C, $I=1·0$ M (HClO$_4$)	[83]
$(en)_2Co$ (sulfinate ring, NH$_2$) 2+	H_2O_2	$(en)_2Co$ (sulfonate ring, NH$_2$) 2+	$a=3\cdot35\times10^{-4}$ M^{-1} s^{-1e} $b=5\cdot09\times10^{-4}$ M^{-2} s^{-1}	14·6 14·4	-26 -25		[12]
$(NH_3)_5CoNCS^{2+}$	H_2O_2	$Co(NH_3)_6^{3+}$, Co_{aq}^{2+}, SO_4^{2-}, CO_2, CN^-	$a=1\cdot3\times10^{-3}$ M^{-1} s^{-1e} $b=8\cdot3\times10^{-3}$ M^{-2} s^{-1}	17·4 —	-17 —	65°C, $I=0·5$ M (H/NaClO$_4$)	[87]
$(en)_2Co$ (thiazolidine ring, =O) 2+	H_2O_2	$Co(NH_3)_6^{3+}$, $(NH_3)_5CoCN^{3+}$, SO_4^{2-}	$a=5\cdot26\times10^{-5}$ M^{-1} s^{-1e} $b=9\cdot9\times10^{-4}$ M^{-2} s^{-1}	15·3 —	— —	$I=0·5$ M (H/NaClO$_4$)	[88]
$tr\text{-}(en)_2Co(OH_2)(SO_3)^+$	f	Co_{aq}^{2+}	$3\cdot61\times10^{-4}$ s^{-1g}	32·8	9	73°C, $I=2·36$ M (HClO$_4$)	[107]
$(en)_2Co$ (thiazolidine ring, NH$_2$) 2+	f	Co_{aq}^{2+}	$2\cdot91\times10^{-5}$ s^{-1}	33	15	75°C	[113]

^{a} $-d[\text{complex}]/dt = ([\text{complex}][\text{oxidant}])$

^{b} $T=25°C$, $I=1·00$ M (H/LiClO$_4$) unless otherwise noted.

^{c} $k_2=a+b/[\text{H}^+]$.

^{d} $k_2=a/[\text{H}^+]$.

^{e} $k_2=a+b[\text{H}^+]$.

^{f} Intramolecular electron transfer.

^{g} $k_2=ka_{\text{H}_2\text{O}}$.

mide.[77] Again, oxidation of the coordinated sulphur atom is likely to be the initial step in these reactions since the analogous glycolato complex $(en)_2Co(OCH_2COO)^+$ is not oxidized to the corresponding oxalato complex under similar conditions. Transfer of oxidizing power from the sulphur atom to the adjacent carbon atom presumably depends upon the marked acidity of the α-methylene protons in coordinated thioglycolic acid. When the α-methylene protons are *not* acidic, as in $(en)_2Co(SCH_2CH_2NH_2)^{2+}$, oxidizing power is *not* transferred and the observed product contains an oxidized sulphur atom (e.g. $[(en)_2Co(NH_2CH_2CH_2S)]_2I^{5+}$.[91]

3. Intramolecular electron transfer

Oxidation of a coordinated sulphur atom can also occur by intramolecular electron transfer (IET) from the coordinated sulphur atom to the metal centre. However, there are only a few examples of this reaction, and all involve the strong oxidant cobalt(III) and either coordinated sulphite (either *S*- or *O*-bonded) or coordinated thiolate. In these cases IET yields labile cobalt(II) and the one-equivalent oxidized sulphur radical which then undergoes subsequent reactions which are difficult to monitor.

The reactions involving coordinated sulphite are complicated by isomerization (*S*-bonded and *O*-bonded) and aquation (*S*-bonded sulphite is a powerful *trans* labilizing ligand) processes and thus often do not directly reflect IET. For example, it has been proposed that the redox-decomposition of *trans*-$(NH_3)_4Co(OH_2)(SO_3)^+$ proceeds through rate-determining *trans–cis* isomerization followed by fast loss of an ammine ligand and finally IET.[104] The kinetic parameters observed for this reaction therefore do not describe the IET step. Similarly, although the redox decomposition of $(NH_3)_5CoOSO_2^+$ is purported to proceed by IET,[105] the observed activation entropy is higher than that expected for IET processes (*vide infra*) and thus it is probable that decomposition occurs through a rate-determining dissociation step. It should be noted that rate-determining isomerization of *S*-bonded sulphite has also been proposed in the bimolecular oxidation of $(CN)_5FeSO_3^{5-}$ by $IrCl_6^{2-}$ and Br_2.[106] The one sulphito–cobalt(III) complex that truly appears to undergo redox decomposition by rate determining IET is *trans*-$(en)_2Co(OH_2)(SO_3)^+$; the activation entropy for this reaction is only 9 e.u., consistent with the small amount of solvent reorganization expected for an IET transition state.[107]

More recently the well defined IET decomposition of the thiolato complex $(en)_2Co(SCH_2CH_2NH_2)^{2+}$ has been investigated.[113] As expected, addition of CH_3Hg^+ to form the $(en)_2Co(S(HgCH_3)CH_2CH_2NH_2)^{3+}$ adduct markedly decreases the rate of IET by decreasing the polarizability of the coordinated sulphur atom and making it a poorer reductant. In the presence of CH_3Hg^+, the IET reaction is probably carried through the small amount of free thiolato complex in equilibrium with the adduct.[111] Further decreasing the polarizability of the coordinated sulphur by converting $(en)_2Co(SCH_2CH_2NH_2)^{2+}$ to the thioether complex $(en)_2Co(S(CH_3)CH_2CH_2NH_2)^{3+}$ totally inhibits the IET reaction. The activation parameters governing the IET decomposition of $(en)_2Co(SCH_2CH_2NH_2)^{2+}$ are surprisingly similar to those governing the IET decomposition of $trans$-$(en)_2Co(OH_2)(SO_3)^+$. This is taken to result from a fortuitous cancellation of effects; the thiolato complex should react faster since S(II) is a better reductant than S(IV), but the sulphito complex should react faster because the weak $trans$ aquo ligand generates a smaller Franck–Condon barrier than does the strong-field ethylenediamine ligand. Both activation entropies are small, as expected for IET reactions which involve only minimal solvent reorganization.

C. Oxidation–reduction reactions of noncoordinated sulphur compounds

1. Reduction of disulphides

The reduction of organic disulphides by one-equivalent reagents plays a key role in the metal-ion-promoted thiol–disulphide interconversions which are the basis of many biological energy transfer cycles. In addition, the one-equivalent reduction of disulphides provides a convenient synthetic route to thiolato complexes of Co(III), Cr(III), Fe(III) and Ru(III) that are not readily accessible by substitution routes.[2,3,6,8,85] However, in spite of the importance of this reaction the kinetics of the metal ion reduction of disulphides has not been well studied, only one detailed kinetic analysis having been reported.[5]

The chromium(II) reduction of p-aminophenyl disulphide has been investigated in detail, under concentration conditions ranging from pseudo-first-order excess of chromium(II) to pseudo-first-order excess disulphide (diS).[5] In the presence of excess chromium(II) the stoichiometry is

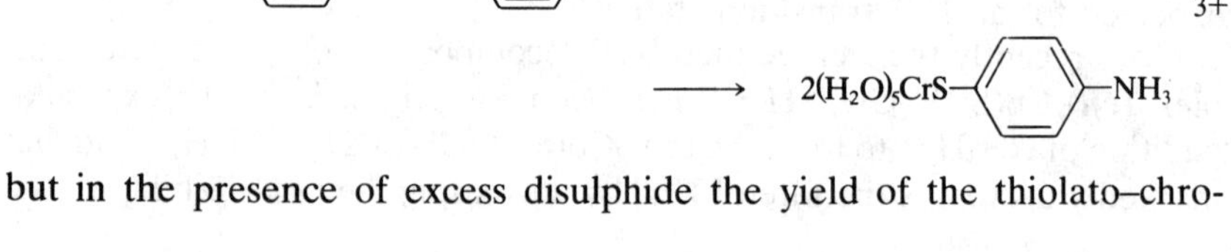

$$2Cr_{aq}^{2+} + H_3N\!-\!\langle\bigcirc\rangle\!-\!S\!-\!S\!-\!\langle\bigcirc\rangle\!-\!NH_3^{2+}$$

$$\longrightarrow 2(H_2O)_5CrS\!-\!\langle\bigcirc\rangle\!-\!NH_3^{\,3+}$$

but in the presence of excess disulphide the yield of the thiolato–chromium(III) product complex is less than 90%. For all concentration conditions the rate law is

$$\frac{d(Cr-SC_6H_4NH_3^{3+})}{dt} = \frac{a(Cr^{2+})(diS)}{1 + b(diS)}$$

and it is the $b(diS)$ term in the denominator that causes the yield of the product complex to decrease in the presence of excess disulphide. All kinetic and stoichiometric observations can be explained by a mechanism which features the radical ion dimer $RSSR^-$ coordinated to chromium(III). This species is generated by the initial inner-sphere reduction of RSSR by chromium (II), the relatively stable $RSSR^-$ radical being trapped in the substitution inert coordination sphere of chromium(III). The $Cr^{III}-RSSR^-$ intermediate can react with chromium(II) to yield two moles of the thiolato–chromium(III) product complex, and this is the predominant reaction mode in the presence of excess chromium(II). Or, the $Cr^{III}-RSSR^-$ intermediate can react with free disulphide to yield products which rapidly undergo Cr–S bond fission; this reaction pathway becomes important in the presence of excess disulphide. These observations indicate that the synthesis of thiolatometal complexes *via* the reductive cleavage of disulphides should *not* be conducted in the presence of excess disulphide (as would normally be done in syntheses based on a substitution route).

As noted in a previous section on the one-equivalent oxidation of thiols, both free $RSSR^-$ and coordinated $RSSR^-$ can have considerable stability, and it is likely that coordinated $RSSR^-$ species play important roles in many redox processes.[5,9,72,74,112] Direct evidence for the existence of a relatively stable $Cr^{III}-RSSR^-$ species has been briefly presented.[75] In the chromium(II) reduction of various chelating disulphides such as 2,2'-dithiodiacetic acid and 2,2'-dithiodipropionic acid, a long-lived, EPR active, intermediate is observed; the EPR spectrum of this intermediate is consistent with a $Cr^{III}-RSSR^-$ species. Also, these reactions proceed via a rate law that is first-order in disulphide but second-order in chromium(II); this implies that the rate-determining step is chromium(II) reduction of the $Cr^{III}-RSSR^-$ intermediate.

2. Oxidation of thiols

While a large number of studies on the metal ion oxidation of free thiols have been reported, many are not of high quality and several are seriously deficient in that they do not establish the stoichiometry of the reaction being investigated. Careful studies[73,114] have shown that the stoichiometry of thiol oxidation often depends upon the ratio of thiol/oxidant; while clean stoichiometries are observed at high ratios, low ratios lead to "over oxidation" wherein excess equivalents of oxidant are consumed. This phenomenon is readily understood in terms of Danehy's pioneering work on the iodine oxidation of thiols.[93] The initial oxidation step often leads to a reactive sulphur-containing intermediate (e.g. a thiyl radical or a sulphenyl iodide) which in the presence of excess thiol subsequently reacts to stoichiometrically yield a disulphide; however, at low thiol concentrations this intermediate can be intercepted by the oxidant and thereupon be converted to an "over-oxidized" product (e.g. a sulphinic or sulphonic acid). In addition, most studies have been conducted in the presence of molecular oxygen; this is inappropriate since it has been established[114] that molecular oxygen can also intercept reactive intermediates and seriously affect both observed stoichiometries and observed reaction rates.

The mechanism of thiol oxidation by metal ion reagents is markedly dependent on the nature of the oxidant. However, for one-equivalent oxidants a continuing theme appears to be generation of the reactive thiyl radical (RS·) and stabilization of this radical either by coordination or by conversion to the radical ion dimer $RSSR^-$. As noted several times previously, the $RSSR^-$ dimer is relatively stable and can be further stabilized by coordination to a metal ion.[5,75]

Early studies on the oxidation of thiols by the outer-sphere reagent $Fe(CN)_6^{3-}$ are somewhat confused,[115–117] but later work indicates that the reaction has simple 1:1 stoichiometry (yielding a disulphide) and proceeds by simple outer-sphere electron transfer.[118,119] The cerium(IV) oxidation of various 2-thiocarboxylic acids, and the 2-hydroxy analogues, have been studied in some detail.[114,120,121] Observed activation enthalpies are lower for the thiols than for the alcohols, presumably reflecting the greater stability of the thiyl radical. The activation enthalpy governing the neptunium(VI) oxidation of 2-thioacetic acid is also comparatively[73] low presumably for the same reason. The cerium(IV) and neptunium(VI), oxidations exhibit large negative activation entropies implying that these reactions involve a high degree of associative character; coordination of the thiocarboxylic acid substrate to the metal centre prior to electron transfer is an attractive explanation for this phenomenon. The cobalt(III) oxidations of 2-thiosuccinic acid[122] and 2-hydroxysuccinic acid[120d] purportedly follow a different pattern than that observed for Ce(IV), i.e. the observed activation enthalpies are lower for the alcohol than for the thiol. This result appears anomalous and may be associated with the experimental difficulties involved with using Co_{aq}^{3+} as an oxidant.

Oxidations of thiols by the weaker one-equivalent reagents Cu_{aq}^{2+} and Fe_{aq}^{3+} involve dimeric intermediates,[112,123,124] presumably because such dimers allow disulphide formation (a net two-equivalent oxidation) without involvement of a high-energy radical species. In general, a thiol coordinates to a metal centre and then two such adducts form a dimer; for iron(III) electron transfer then takes place within the dimer, but for copper(II) the dimer is reduced by a free thiol. The rate of iron(III) oxidation of 2-thioacetic acid, 2-thiopropionic acid, 2-thiosuccinic acid, and 2-thio-2-methylpropionic acid decreases with increasing substitution at the carbon atom adjacent to the thiol group, indicating that steric effects are important in the activation process. However, the rate differences are not large, higher ΔH^* values being offset by less negative ΔS^* values.

The reaction of one-equivalent oxidants with thiols to produce disulphides must either proceed through radical intermediates, or through a dimeric precursor complex which brings two metal centres together. Contrariwise, multi-equivalent oxidants can in principle directly form disulphides without radical intermediates and without the formation of binuclear precursor complexes. For the multi-equivalent oxidants VO_2^{+} [125] and $HCrO_4^{-}$ [126] two pathways appear to function, only one of which avoids formation of a radical intermediate: (1) formation of a thiol–metal complex followed by intramolecular electron transfer to yield the one-equivalent reduced metal ion and a thiyl radical, and (2) formation of a thiol–metal complex followed by bimolecular reaction of this complex with a free thiol to yield the two-equivalent reduced metal and the disulphide product. A third pathway, which also involves a radical intermediate, has been proposed for the Mo(VI) oxidation of thiols:[127] formation of a thiol–metal complex followed by bimolecular reaction of this complex with a free thiol to yield the one-equivalent reduced metal ion and a thiyl radical.

3. Oxidation of thiocyanate

The metal ion oxidation of thiocyanate is complicated by the ability of thiocyanate to form both N-bonded and S-bonded precursor complexes, the instability of thiocyanate in aqueous acid, and the complicated decomposition reactions of thiocyanogen (the oxidation product of thiocyanate). In aqueous solutions thiocyanogen rapidly hydrolyses to CN^{-}, SO_4^{2-} and SCN^{-}. Despite these difficulties a large number of studies have been reported, and from this work it is clear that many of the mechanistic and stoichiometric aspects of thiol oxidations are also important in thiocyanate oxidations. To be especially noted are the stability of the $(SCN)_2^{-}$ radical ion dimer and the stoichiometric necessity of combining two SCN moieties (either SCN^{-} or $SCN^{\cdot}$) somewhere in the reaction sequence.

The outer-sphere oxidations of thiocyanate by the one-equivalent agents $Fe(phen)_3^{3+}$ and some analogous phenanthroline-substituted complexes,[128] $Os(bpy)_3^{3+}$ and $Os(phen)_3^{3+}$,[129] and $IrCl_6^{2-}$ [130] have been studied in some detail. All reactions exhibit a term which is second-order in thiocyanate and which most likely arises from oxidation of SCN⁻ by an oxidant ·SCN ion pair; this pathway presumably generates the relatively stable $(SCN)_2^-$ radical ion dimer and the reduced metal centre. The reactions of the Os(III) and Ir(IV) oxidants also exhibit a term which is first-order in thiocyanate and which presumably arises from electron transfer within the oxidant ·SCN ion pair to yield the monomeric SCN⁺ radical. As noted previously for thiol oxidations, weaker oxidants tend to utilize reaction pathways wherein two sulphur centres are associated with the oxidant at the moment of electron transfer in order to generate a more stable dimeric radical; stronger oxidants can also utilize pathways wherein a less stable monomeric radical is generated. The rates of the Os(III) and Fe(III) oxidations are adequately correlated within the Marcus theory for outer-sphere electron transfer reactions.

The oxidations of thiocyanate by the one-equivalent agents Fe_{aq}^{3+},[131,132] Co_{aq}^{3+},[133] and Mn_{aq}^{3+} [134] are apparently inner-sphere. While these "hard" metal centres undoubtedly complex thiocyanate predominantly through nitrogen, it is certainly possible that the reaction proceeds through a small, equilibrium-controlled, amount of an S-bonded precursor complex. The multi-equivalent oxidant Cr(VI) also reacts by an inner-sphere pathway, higher-order terms in SCN⁻ reflecting either (1) reaction of free thiocyanate with a Cr(VI) · SCN adduct, or (2) coordination of several thiocyanate ligands to Cr(VI) prior to electron transfer.[135] In this latter possibility, reduction of chromium(VI) would actually occur by intramolecular electron transfer (IET) from the coordinated thiocyanate. The Au(III) oxidation of thiocyanate to yield the Au(I) complex $Au(SCN)_2^-$ also proceeds by an inner-sphere pathway, although the observed kinetics are rather complicated.[136] A likely precursor complex of importance to this reaction is $Au(SCN)_4^-$. Several redox reactions involving catalysis by thiocyanate have been postulated to proceed through inner-sphere or outer sphere thiocyanato–metal complexes.[52,137–141]

The several observations noted above prompt an alternative mechanistic interpretation for the production of cobalt(II) from the H_2O_2 oxidation of $(NH_3)_5CoNCS^{2+}$. Since H_2O_2 is well known to react predominantly by two-equivalent pathways, the production of cobalt(II) from this reaction is somewhat confusing. However, the yield of cobalt(II) is known to increase as the reaction temperature increases.[87] Thus it is possible that at elevated temperatures IET from coordinated thiocyanate to cobalt(III) becomes effective. This process yields cobalt(II) and a SCN⁺ radical which could react with another $(NH_3)_5CoNCS^{2+}$ centre to yield a coordinated thiocyanogen radical; IET of this species would then yield thiocyanogen and a second mole of cobalt(II).

4. Oxidation of thiourea

Many of the mechanistic and stoichiometric aspects of thiol and thiocyanate oxidations noted above also apply to the metal ion oxidations of thiourea. In addition, there has been some confusion about the origin of the inverse acid dependence often observed in thiourea oxidations. However, once any acid dependence controlling the form of the oxidant is accounted for, it is now clear that the inverse acid pathway arises from deprotonation of thiourea to form the $H_2NC(S)NH^-$ anion. This result[142] arises from consideration of relevant aqueous pK_a values.[143]

The oxidation of thiourea and various *N*- and *N,N'*-substituted derivatives (including thiouracil, thiosemicarbazide, and simple alkyl derivatives) generally yields the formamidine disulphide product, and with one-equivalent oxidants it is generally presumed that a thiourea radical is an important reaction intermediate. Oxidations by a variety of metal ions have been reported: Cu(III),[144–147] Ce(IV),[148,149] Co(III),[150,151] Mn(III),[134,143] Cr(VI),[152] V(V),[121] Os(VIII),[153] and $IrCl_6^{2-}$.[142] Inner-sphere intermediates have been identified in the Cr(VI) and V(V) reactions, and reactions of Ce(IV), Co(III) and Mn(III) appear to be substitution-controlled. The outer-sphere oxidation by $IrCl_6^{2-}$ is a second-order in thiourea, presumably resulting from reaction of thiourea with a thiourea · $IrCl_6^{2-}$ adduct. Association of two thiourea molecules in the transition state allows formation of a relatively stable dimeric radical; this is similar to the reaction of thiourea with the inner-sphere thiourea · V(V) and thiourea · Cr(VI) intermediates, although in these cases two-electron transfer produces the final formamidine disulphide product rather than a dimeric radical intermediate. Copper(II) catalyses the $IrCl_6^{2-}$ oxidation of thiourea,[142] presumably through the intermediacy of a thiourea · Cu(II) complex.

5. Oxidation of other sulphur-containing species

The gold(III) oxidation of sulphur-containing molecules of biological interest has recently received attention because of the purported toxicity of Au(III) and the use of thiolato–Au(I) complexes for the treatment of rheumatoid arthritis.[154] An intriguing observation on the stoichiometry of the Au(III) oxidation of thiols and disulphides has appeared.[110] While $AuBr_4^-$ reacts with excess thiol to yield disulphides and thiolato–Au(I) complexes, it reacts with excess disulphide to yield Au(0) and sulphonic acids. Thus thiols reduce Au(III) to Au(I), but disulphides, which are weaker reductants than thiols, reduce Au(III) to Au(0). This apparent anomaly is easily understood when the great thermodynamic stability of thiolato–Au(I) complexes is taken into account; in the presence of excess

Sulphur compound	Oxidant or reductant	Rate law
$H_3N-\underset{}{\bigcirc}-S-S-\bigcirc-NH_3^{2+}$	Cr_{aq}^{2+}	$\dfrac{a[\text{disulphide}]}{1+b[\text{disulphide}]}[\text{Cr(II)}]$
HSCH$_2$COOH	NpO$_2^{2+}$	$(a+b/[\text{H}^+])[\text{thiol}][\text{Np(VI)}]$
HSCH$_2$COOCH$_3$	NpO$_2^{2+}$	$(a+b/[\text{H}^+])[\text{thiol}][\text{Np(VI)}]$
HSCH$_2$COOH	Ce$_{aq}^{4+}$	$a[\text{thiol}]\,[\text{Ce(IV)}]$
HSCH(CH$_3$)COOH	Ce$_{aq}^{4+}$	$a[\text{thiol}]\,[\text{Ce(IV)}]$
HOOCCH(SH)CH$_2$COOH	Ce$_{aq}^{4+}$	$a[\text{thiol}]\,[\text{Ce(IV)}]$
	Co$_{aq}^{3+}$	$(a+b/[\text{H}^+])[\text{thiol}][\text{Co(III)}]$
	VO$_2^+$	$(a+b[\text{thiol}])[\text{V(V)}]^c$
HSCH$_2$CH(NH$_2$)COOH	HCrO$_4^-$	$\dfrac{K(a[\text{H}^+]+b[\text{thiol}])[\text{thiol}][\text{Cr(VI)}]^c}{1+K[\text{thiol}]}$
	Mo(VI)	$a[\text{thiol}]^2\,[\text{Mo(VI)}]$
glutathione	Mo(VI)	$a[\text{thiol}]$
HSCH$_2$COOH	Mo(V)	$a[\text{thiol}]\,[\text{Mo(V)}]^2\ ^c$
	Mo(VI)	$a[\text{thiol}][\text{Mo(VI)}]^c$
SCN$^-$	Fe(phen)$_3^{3+}$	$a[\text{SCN}^-]^2\,[\text{Fe(III)}]$
	Fe(phen)$_3^{3+}$	
	Fe(5–CH$_3$–phen)$_3^{3+}$	
	Fe(4,7-(CH$_3$)$_2$-phen)$_3^{3+}$	
	Fe(5–Cl–phen)$_3^{3+}$	
	Fe(5–Br–phen)$_3^{3+}$	
	Fe(5–NO$_2$–phen)$_3^{3+}$	
	Os(phen)$_3^{3+}$	$(a[\text{SCN}^-]+b[\text{SCN}^-]^2)[\text{Os(III)}]$
	Os(bpy)$_3^{3+}$	$(a[\text{SCN}^-]+b[\text{SCN}^-]^2)[\text{Os(III)}]$
	IrCl$_6^{2+}$	$(a[\text{SCN}^-]+b[\text{SCN}^-]^2)[\text{Ir(IV)}]$
	Co$_{aq}^{3+}$	$(a+b/[\text{H}^+])\,[\text{SCN}^-]\,[\text{Co(III)}]$
	CrO$_4^{2-}$	$a[\text{H}^+]^3\,[\text{SCN}^-]^2\,[\text{Cr(VI)}]\,/(1+K[\text{SCN}^-]\,[$
	AuBr$_4^-$	$a[\text{SCN}^-][\text{Au(III)}]$
	Au(SCN)$_4^-$	$a[\text{SCN}^-][\text{Au(III)}]$
S=C(NH$_2$)$_2$	Ce$_{aq}^{4+}$	$a[\text{thiourea}]\,[\text{Ce(IV)}]$
S=C(NHCH$_3$)$_2$	Ce$_{aq}^{4+}$	$a[\text{thiourea}]\,[\text{Ce(IV)}]$
S=C(NHCH$_2$CH$_3$)$_2$	Ce$_{aq}^{4+}$	$a[\text{thiourea}]\,[\text{Ce(IV)}]$
S=C(NHCH$_2$CH$_2$NH)	Ce$_{aq}^{4+}$	$a[\text{thiourea}]\,[\text{Ce(IV)}]$
S=C(NH$_2$)(NHNH$_2$)	Ce$_{aq}^{4+}$	$a[\text{thiourea}]\,[\text{Ce(IV)}]$

parameters	ΔH^* (kcal mol^{-1})	ΔS^* (eu)	Conditions[a]	Ref.
$\cdot 103$ M^{-1} s^{-1}	9·4	−33	$I=2\cdot0$ M (H/ZnClO$_4$)	[5]
$4\cdot5$ M^{-1}			[H$^+$]$=1\cdot0$ M	
$.5$ M^{-1} s^{-1}	6	−37	$I=1\cdot0$ M (H/LiClO$_4$)	[73]
$34\cdot2$ s^{-1}	14·2	−4		
8 M^{-1} s^{-1}	—	—	$I=1\cdot0$ M (H/LiClO$_4$)	[73]
$\cdot7$ s^{-1}				
$\cdot9\times10^{-3}$ M^{-1} s^{-1}	7·3	−27	22·9°C, [H$^+$]$=0\cdot5$ M	[120]
$.66\times10^{-3}$ M^{-1} s^{-1}	6·2	−31	25·2°C, [H$\cdot$]$=0\cdot5$ M	[120]
$\cdot10\times10^{-2}$ M^{-1} s^{-1}	7·0	−30	22·0°C, [H$^+$]$=0\cdot5$ M	[120]
$\cdot05$ M^{-1} s^{-1}	37·1[b]	—	12·7°C, $I=1\cdot0$ M	[122]
$\cdot27$ s^{-1}	—	—		
$\cdot0$ s^{-1}	—	—	15°C	[125]
0 M^{-1} s^{-1}	—	—		
$\cdot2\times10^{-2}$ M^{-2} s^{-1}	12	−27		[126]
$\cdot4\times10^{-2}$ M^{-2} s^{-1}	10·8	−27		
$\cdot599$ M^{-2} min^{-1}	—	—	60°C, $I=1\cdot71$ M, pH 7·5 (phosphate)	[127]
$\cdot34\times10^{-4}$ min^{-1}	—	—	60°C, $I=1\cdot71$ M, pH 7·5 (phosphate)	[127]
$.35$ M^{-2} s^{-1}	8·0[b]	−17[b]	60°C, $I=1\cdot71$ M, pH 6·0 (phosphate)	[290]
$\cdot81$ M^{-1} s^{-1}	11·3	−16		[290]
$\cdot5\times10^3$ M^{-2} s^{-1}	—	—	$I=1\cdot0$ M (HClO$_4$)	[128]
$\cdot8\times10^4$ M^{-2} s^{-1}	—	—	$I=1\cdot0$ M (H$_2$SO$_4$)	[128]
$\cdot4\times10^4$ M^{-2} s^{-1}	—	—		[128]
$\cdot2\times10^2$ M^{-2} s^{-1}	—	—		[128]
$\cdot74\times10^5$ M^{-2} s^{-1}	—	—		[128]
$\cdot50\times10^5$ M^{-2} s^{-1}	—	—		[128]
$\times10^6$ M^{-2} s^{-1}	—	—		[128]
$\cdot4$ M^{-1} s^{-1}	—	—	$I=1\cdot0$ M (H/NaCl)	[129]
$\cdot1\cdot6$ M^{-2} s^{-1}	—	—		
$0\cdot024$ M^{-1} s^{-1}	—	—	$I=1\cdot0$ M (H/NaCl)	[129]
$\cdot8$ M^{-2} s^{-1}	10·5	−18		
$\cdot1\times10^{-3}$ M^{-1} s^{-1}	15·2	−16	$I=0\cdot1$ M (NaClO$_4$), pH 2	[130]
$\cdot93$ M^{-2} s^{-1}	8·7	−30		
$\cdot6\cdot5$ M^{-1} s^{-1}	20·6	20	$I=3\cdot0$ M (H/NaClO$_4$)	[133]
$\cdot9\cdot6$ s^{-1}	25·6	37		
$\cdot30\times10^3$ M^{-5} s^{-1}	—	—	$I=0\cdot71$ M (H/NaClO$_4$)	[135]
$\times10^4$ M^{-1} s^{-1}	—	—	$I=1\cdot0$ M (H/NaClO$_4$)	[136]
$\cdot4\times10^3$ M^{-1} s^{-1}	—	—		[136]
63 M^{-1} s^{-1}	7·4	−33	23·9°C, [H$^+$]$=0\cdot5$ M	[148]
90 M^{-1} s^{-1}	8·5	−29	25·5°C, [H$\cdot$]$=0.5$ M	[148]
$\cdot03$ M^{-1} s^{-1}	8·3	−28	24·7°C, [H$^+$]$=0\cdot5$ M	[148]
$\cdot7\cdot0$ M^{-1} s^{-1}	9·0	−25	26·3°C, [H$^+$]$=0\cdot5$ M	[148]
$\cdot27$ M^{-1} s^{-1}	9·2	−29	23·7°C, [H$^+$]$=0\cdot5$ M	[148]

Sulphur compound	Oxidant or reductant	Rate law
$S\!=\!C(NH_2)_2$	Co^{3+}_{aq}	$(a+bK/[H^+])[\text{thiourea}][\text{Co(III)}]$
$S\!=\!C(NHCH_3)_2$	Co^{3+}_{aq}	$(a+bK/[H^+])[\text{thiourea}][\text{Co(III)}]$
$S\!=\!C(NHCH_2CH_3)_2$	Co^{3+}_{aq}	$(a+bK/[H^+])[\text{thiourea}][\text{Co(III)}]$
$S\!=\!C(NHCH_2CH_2NH)$	Co^{3+}_{aq}	$(a+bK/[H^+])[\text{thiourea}][\text{Co(III)}]$
$S\!=\!C(NH_2)_2$	Co^{3+}_{aq}	$(a+b/[H^+])[\text{thiourea}][\text{Co(III)}]$
$S\!=\!C(NHCH_3)(NH_2)$	Co^{3+}_{aq}	$(a+b/[H^+])[\text{thiourea}][\text{Co(III)}]$
$S\!=\!C(NHCH_3)_2$	Co^{3+}_{aq}	$(a+b/[H^+])[\text{thiourea}][\text{Ci(III)}]$
$S\!=\!C(NHCH_2CH_3)_2$	Co^{3+}_{aq}	$(a+b/[H^+])[\text{thiourea}][\text{Co(III)}]$
$S\!=\!C(NHCH_2CH_2NH)$	Co^{3+}_{aq}	$(a+b/[H^+])[\text{thiourea}][\text{Co(III)}]$
$S\!=\!C(NH_2)_2$	CrO_4^{2-}	$(a+b[H^+][\text{thiourea}]+c[H^+]^2\,[\text{thiourea}]$ $K[H^+][\text{thiourea}][\text{Cr(VI)}]/(1+[H^+][\text{thio}$
$S\!=\!C(NHCH_2CH_2NH)$		$\{(a+b[H^+]^2\,[\text{thiourea}])K[H^+]$ $[\text{thiourea}][\text{Cr(VI)}]\}/$ $\{(1+K[\text{thiourea}]\,[H^+])\}^c$
$S\!=\!C(NH_2)_2$	VO_2^+	$(a+b[\text{thiourea}])\,[H^+]^2\,[\text{thiourea}]^2[V(V$
	$IrCl_6^{2-}$	$a[\text{thiourea}][\text{Ir(IV)}]$
$S\!=\!C(NHCH_3)_2$	$IrCl_6^{2-}$	$a[\text{thiourea}][\text{Ir(IV)}]$
$S\!=\!C(NHCH_2CH_2NH)$	$IrCl_6^{2-}$	$a[\text{thiourea}][\text{Ir(IV)}]$

[a] $T=25°C$ unless otherwise noted.
[b] Activation energy.
[c] Rate law for redox decomposition of metal ion–sulphur compound intermediate.

parameters	ΔH^* (kcal mol^{-1})	ΔS^* (eu)	Conditions[a]	Ref.
M^{-1} s^{-1}	8·6[b]	−29	I=0.8 M (H/NaClO$_4$)	[150]
80 M^{-1} s^{-1}	9·0[b]	−22		
2 M^{-1} s^{-1}	7·6[b]	−26	I=1·1 M (H/NaClO$_4$)	[150]
000 M^{-1} s^{-1}	9·8[b]	−14		
6 M^{-1} s^{-1}	7·8[b]	−29	I=1·0 M (H/NaClO$_4$)	[150]
600 M^{-1} s^{-1}	10·6[b]	−12		
0 M^{-1} s^{-1}	7·8[b]	−30	I=1·1 M (H/NaClO$_4$)	[150]
60 M^{-1} s^{-1}	10·9[b]	−19		
63 M^{-1} s^{-1}	19·9	20	I=1·50 M (H/NaClO$_4$)	[151]
82 s^{-1}	26·3	43		
61 M^{-1} s^{-1}	21·2	26	I=1·50 M (H/NaClO$_4$)	[151]
67 s^{-1}	24·2	36		
63 M^{-1} s^{-1}	18·8	18	24·9°C, I=1·50 M	[151]
18 s^{-1}	25·3	39	(H/NaClO$_4$)	
48 M^{-1} s^{-1}	15·6	7	25·5°C, I=1.50 M	[151]
67 s^{-1}	24·1	35	(H/NaClO$_4$)	
30 M^{-1} s^{-1}	21·7	23	24·9°C, I=1·50 M	[151]
41 s^{-1}	26·5	41	(H/NaClO$_4$)	
			24·9°C, I=1·0 M (H/NaClO$_4$)	[152]
020 s^{-1}	—	—		
5·6 M^{-2} s^{-1}	10·7	−19		
3 M^{-3} s^{-1}	≤1	−45		
3 s^{-1}	15	−9	24·9°C, I=1·0 M	[152]
7·5 M^{-3} s^{-1}	≤1·5	−45	(H/NaClO$_4$)	
59 M^{-1} s^{-1}	—	—	I=1·5 M	[291]
6 M^{-2} s^{-1}	—	—	I=0.15 M (H/NaClO$_4$),	
68 M^{-2} s^{-1}	6·1	−26	pH 1·1	[142]
94 M^{-2} s^{-1}	5.8	−27		[142]
97 M^{-2} s^{-1}	7.5	−22		[142]

thiol, Au(I) is stabilized by the "soft-soft" interactions of the thiolato–Au(I) linkage. However, in the absence of thiols, Au(I) is unstable with respect to reduction to Au(0), and disulphides are capable of effecting this reduction. Gold(III), as $AuCl_4^-$, also oxidizes methionine (a thioether) to the corresponding sulphoxide in aqueous media;[156] this reaction proceeds by an inner-sphere mechanism.

The oxidation of H_2S to S^0 can be effected by $(NH_3)_5Rupy^{3+}$ (py = pyridine) and similar complexes.[157] Contrariwise, reflecting the great sensitivity of the Ru(III)/Ru(II) couple to the nature of the coordinating ligands, $(NH_3)_6Ru^{2+}$ reduces SO_2 to S^0.[158]

D. Electrochemistry

The techniques of electrochemistry have been profitably applied to a variety of coordination complexes, but there have been only a few electrochemical studies on well defined, sulphur-containing complexes. This situation obtains largely for two reasons: (1) Most sulphur-containing species undergo strong adsorption on mercury and noble metal electrodes, and therefore do not yield interpretable electrochemical data. However, Anson and co-workers[159] have utilized this adsorption phenomenon to probe the chemistry of isothiocyanato–chromium(III) complexes. (2) Most well defined complexes with sulphur ligands involve the substitution-inert cobalt(III) centre, and reduction of these complexes leads to labile cobalt(II) and consequently to irreversible electrochemical behaviour. This section surveys some selected electrochemical studies on substitution-inert complexes that contain sulphur ligands. Specifically excluded from this survey are studies of labile metal ions in the presence of excess ligand (e.g. SCN^-), and studies wherein only the oxidation state of the central metal changes and thus the only effect of the sulphur containing ligand is on the $E^{\circ\prime}$ of this process (e.g. electrochemistry of $(NH_3)_5RuSH_2^{2+/3+}$).

Isothiocyanato complexes of chromium(III) are strongly adsorbed on mercury electrodes,[159–161] as is expected from the known reaction of $(H_2O)_5CrNCS^{2+}$ with mercury(II) to yield the $CrNCSHg^{4+}$ adduct.[162] In general, the adsorption on mercury increases with increasing number of NCS^- ligands on the chromium(III) centre.[161,163] The rate of reduction of the adsorbed complexes is faster than the rate of reduction of the corresponding nonadsorbed complex,[161,164–166] this effect presumably arising because bridging —NCS— is a weaker ligand than monodentate —NCS. Thus, adsorption on mercury weakens the Cr–N bond and concomitantly decreases the Franck–Condon barrier to electron transfer. Within the various isothiocyanato complexes studied, for those with *trans*-situated aquo, ammine and isothiocyanato ligands, the rate of electrochemical reduction parallels the rate of Fe(II) reduction of the *trans*-(en)$_2$Co(Cl)X^{n+} (X = H$_2$O, NCS$^-$, NH$_3$) complexes,[62] i.e. $k_{H_2O} > k_{NCS} > k_{NH_3}$.[166] This ordering reflects the relative ease of stretching of the bond to the *trans*-situated ligand in the activated complex.

Studies on chromium(III) complexes of the potentially heptadentate ligand S(CH$_2$CH$_2$N(CH$_2$COOH)$_2$)$_2$ (TEDTA) have recently been reported.[167] There appear to be two dominant complexes, one with a coordinated thioether (II) and one with a pendant thioether(I):

Isomer I   Isomer II

The electrochemistry of this system is complicated by several pH-dependent equilibria, the equilibrium between Isomer I and Isomer II (which appears to be catalysed by chromium(II)), and the inherent lability of the thioether–Cr(III) bond.[28] However, it is clear that both isomers are absorbed on mercury, and surprisingly the isomer containing the coordinated thioether (Isomer II) is much more strongly adsorbed.[168] Adsorption occurs presumably through the sulphur atom since the oxygen-containing analogue (i.e. the chromium(III) complex of O(CH$_2$CH$_2$N(CH$_2$COOH)$_2$)$_2$) is not adsorbed. Thus, when Isomer II is adsorbed the sulphur atom attains four-coordination (i.e. it is bonded to Cr, Hg, and two carbon atoms), a situation which has been previously observed in an electron transfer transition state (sulphur bonded to Cr, Co and two carbon atoms[28]) and in a ground state complex (sulphur bonded to Ru and three carbon atoms[29]). No satisfactory explanation is available for why the three-coordinate sulphur atom of Isomer II should bind more strongly to mercury than does the two-coordinate sulphur atom of Isomer I, although back-donation of π-electron density from chromium to sulphur within Isomer II has been proposed as a possibility.[167]

The difficulties inherent in studying the electrochemical reduction of cobalt(III) complexes are exemplified by observations made on the polarographic reduction of *trans*-(en)$_2$Co(OH$_2$)(NCS)$^{2+}$ and *trans*-(en)$_2$Co(NCS)$_2^+$.[169] Initial reduction of an isothiocyanato complex gives rise to labile cobalt(II), free ethylenediamine and free NCS$^-$, the cobalt(II) and ethylenediamine being in equilibrium with $Co(en)_3^{2+}$. At the potential at which the isothiocyanato complexes are reduced, $Co(en)_3^{2+}$ is oxidized to $Co(en)_3^{3+}$; as the sweep is extended to more negative potentials, this $Co(en)_3^{3+}$ formed *in situ* is subsequently reduced. Thus, reduction of a single, well defined, complex gives rise to two distinct polarographic waves. Further complications can arise when the sulphur-containing ligand labilizes the cobalt(III) centre. Both these situations obtain for sulphito–cobalt(III) complexes.[170] Reduction of $(en)_2Co(OH_2)(SO_3)^+$ or *cis*-$(en)_2Co(SO_3)_2^-$ in acidic solution gives rise to a wave which can be ascribed to the reduction of free SO_3^{2-} produced when the cobalt(III) complex is reduced to labile cobalt(II). Moreover, polarography of $(en)_2Co(OH_2)(SO_3)^+$ gives rise to a wave characteristic of $(en)_2Co(SO_3)_2^-$ which is presumably formed by reaction of free SO_3^{2-} with the aquo complex which is labilized by the presence of *S*-bonded sulphite.[11]

III. SUBSTITUTION REACTIONS

A. Making and breaking metal-sulphur bonds

1. Sulphides and hydrosulphides

Surprisingly few mechanistic studies concerning the HS^- and S^{2-} ligands have been reported, undoubtedly because of the complicated, and often intractable, chemistry of metal sulphides. However, in recent years a few systems have been encountered wherein the sulphido–metal linkage is well defined and the kinetics of metal–sulphur bond breaking and making are well behaved. Much of this chemistry has been developed in response to the growing interest in molybdenum- and iron-containing metalloenzymes which are known to contain sulphido–metal linkages.

In a pioneering study on the replacement of oxo (O^{2-}) groups by sulphido (S^{2-}) groups, detailed kinetics of the interconversion of $MoO_xS_{4-x}^{2-}$ species were monitored in aqueous media.[171] For the formation reactions the rate law is of the form $k(Mo^{VI})(HS^-)(H^+)$ and this is interpreted as representing reaction of HS^- at a protonated molybdenum centre. It is likely that protonation of the molybdenum centre enhances conversion from four-coordinate to six-coordinate molybdenum(VI); acid catalysed, transient expansion of the molybdenum coordination sphere is a recognized reaction pattern for substitution at tetrahedral molybdenum(VI).[172] Consistent with this associative substitution scheme, the rates of interconversion of $MoO_xS_{4-x}^{2-}$ species decrease as the number of larger sulphido ligands in the coordination sphere increases. Not surprisingly, in this associatively activated, tetrahedral system the sulphido ligand does not induce any special labilizing effect.

Two other, less detailed, studies on the interaction of sulphido ligands with a tetrahedral metal centre have been reported in connection with the $Fe_2S_2(SR)_4^{2-}$ and $Fe_4S_4(SR)_4^{2-/3-}$ clusters developed by Holm and co-workers[172a,172b] as ferredoxin protein active site analogues. The acid-induced hydrolysis of the $Fe_4S_4(SR)_4^{2-}$ cluster[173] was found to be rapid below pH 6·5 ($t_{1/2}$ = 4 min at pH 5·75 and 40 sec at pH 0·50) and independent of the steric bulk of the R group (R = methyl or t-butyl). Hydrolysis presumably proceeds by rapid protonation of sulphido groups followed by Fe–S bond cleavage to yield products such as

and

The very slow equilibration of sulphido clusters with their selenido analogues has recently been studied in acetonitrile by ^{1}H NMR techniques.[108] Within any of the three congeneric cluster pairs $Fe_2X_2(SR)_4^{2-}$, $Fe_4X_4(SR)_4^{2-}$ and $Fe_4X_4(SR)_4^{3-}$ (R = p-toluyl, X = S, Se) S^{2-} and Se^{2-} ligands are exchanged to achieve a statistical distribution of mixed chalcogenido clusters. The $Fe_4X_4(SR)_4^{3-}$ species achieve equilibrium much more rapidly (41 h) than do the $Fe_4X_4(SR)_4^{2-}$ species (51 days), an effect that is attributed to the longer (and therefore weaker) Fe–S bonds in the reduced 3$^-$ cluster. The mechanism of this complicated exchange reaction is not at all clear. However, since X^{2-} ligands are exchanged individually rather than in pairs, the mechanism does *not* appear to involve simple cleavage of the longer bonds of the Fe_4X_4 core to yield two Fe_2X_2 clusters; such cleavage and recombination would lead to exchange of X^{2-} ligands in pairs.

There have been only two detailed kinetic studies concerned with the interaction of H_2S/HS^- with octahedral metal centres. In an extensive effort to delineate the chemistry of ammineruthenium(II) complexes containing coordinated sulphur, the equilibria between H_2S and the two complexes $(NH_3)_5RuOH_2^{2+}$ and *trans*-$(NH_3)_4(isn)RuOH_2^{2+}$ were investigated.[102] In both cases the approach to equilibrium follows the rate law $(Ru^{II})(k_{-1} + k_1(H_2S))$; since the acid dependencies of k_1 and k_{-1} were not determined, there is no information as to whether H_2S or HS^- is the attacking nucleophile. The observations that k_1 is larger for the penta-ammine complex, whereas k_{-1} is larger for the isonicotinamide complex are readily understood in terms of the π-acid character of isonicotinamide which decreases the ability of the ruthenium(II) centre to donate π electron density to sulphur. The aquation and anation rates are manifested in the overall formation constant of the H_2S complex being about 200 times greater when NH_3 is the *trans*-situated ligand.

While the $(H_2O)_5CrSH^{2+}$ ion was first reported in 1967,[174] it wasn't until 1976 that a well defined synthetic procedure was developed for this material and the aquation kinetics were investigated in detail.[184] The rate law for aquation is of the usual two-term form observed for ligands derived from weak acids: rate = $(CrSH^{2+})(k_0 + k_1(H^+))$. There is also some indication of the influence of the expected inverse acid term, $k_{-1}/(H^+)$, but this term is not well defined by the observed data. The k_0 term is of the same magnitude as that observed for aquation of $(H_2O)_5CrSR^{n+}$ complexes[3,4] and may represent loss of HS^- from $(H_2O)_5Cr^{3+}$ or the tautomeric loss of H_2S from $(H_2O)_4(OH)Cr^{2+}$.[4] The k_1 term clearly reflects loss of H_2S from $(H_2O)_5Cr^{3+}$, even though coordinated HS^- is a very weak base. By conservatively estimating that the K_a of coordinated H_2S in $(H_2O)_5CrSH_2^{3+}$ is less than 1 M, it is calculated that at 40°C the rate of Cr–S bond fission in $(H_2O)_5CrSH_2^{3+}$ is at least ten times faster than the rate of water exchange in $(H_2O)_6Cr^{3+}$. The greater lability of coordinated H_2S relative to coordinated H_2O is entirely consistent with the tenets of the hard–soft acid–base theory[237].

2. Thiols, thioethers and related ligands

A larger number of mechanistic studies have been reported in this area, however the field is still limited by the number of well defined, substitution-inert, complexes that are synthetically accessible. For mono-dentate ligands, in addition to the square planar, d^8 systems, well char-acterized, kinetically tractable, complexes are known only for ruthen-ium(II) and chromium(III). The iron–sulphur clusters such as $Fe_4S_4(SR)_4^{2-}$ comprise a unique class of complexes containing monodentate thiols. For chelating ligands the list extends to cobalt(III) which is so inert that essentially no data are available on the lability of Co–S bonds, and to copper(II) for the special case of macrocyclic thioether complexes.

In their extensive investigation on ammineruthenium(II) complexes of sulphur-containing ligands, Kuehn and Taube[102] described one of the few systems wherein both the rates of metal–sulphur bond breaking and making are in principle assessible for monodentate ligands. Unfortunately, the rates of ligation of $(NH_3)_5RuOH_2^{2+}$ by $(CH_3)_2S$ and C_2H_5SH are the same as the rates of ligation by a variety of ligands that do not contain sulphur; thus these ligation rates appear to be controlled by the lability of the Ru–OH$_2$ bond and do not yield any information on the relative nucleophilicities of the sulphur ligands. Also unfortunately, the rates of Ru–S bond fission for $(NH_3)_5RuS(CH_3)_2^{2+}$, $(NH_3)_5RuS(H)C_2H_5^{2+}$, *trans*-$(NH_3)_4(isn)RuS(CH_3)_2^{2+}$ and *trans*-$(NH_3)_4(isn)RuS(H)C_2H_5^{2+}$ are so slow that interference by other reactions (presumably loss of the ligand situated *trans* to sulphur) prevents accurate determination of the aquation rates. The specific rate governing loss of ethanethiol from the pentaamineruthenium(II) centre is estimated to be less than $3 \times 10^{-5} s^{-1}$. However, loss of thiophene from the pentaamineruthenium(II) centre is much faster ($t_{1/2} \sim 85 s$), and in this case the formation constant for the thiophene complex from $(NH_3)_5RuOH_2^{2+}$ can be estimated as $10 M^{-1}$. Formation constants for the more inert thioether and thiol complexes are greater than $10^3 M^{-1}$.

The rates of aquation of the dimethylchalcogenide complexes of ruthenium(III), $(NH_3)_5Ru(X(CH_3)_2)^{3+}$ with X = S, Se and Te, increase in the order S < Se ⩽ Te.[7] This order presumably results from a decrease in s–p hybridization along the series S > Se > Te which results in a corresponding decrease in metal–chalcogen orbital overlap.

The rate of Cr–S bond breaking when a monodentate thiol is lost has been measured for the $(H_2O)_5CrSR^{3+}$ complexes where SR represents the zwitterionic ligands $^-SC_6H_4NH_3^+$ and $^-SCH_2CH_2NH_3^+$. The observed kinetics define the usual three-term rate law (CrSR) $(k_{-1}/(H^+) + k_0 + k_1(H^+))$ for aquation of pentaaquochromium(III) complexes derived from anions of weak acids.[3,4] Because of the different Bronsted acidities of aliphatic and aromatic thiols, these two kinetic studies allowed an analysis of k_0 and k_1 terms that could be extended to a variety of $(H_2O)_5CrX^{n+}$ complexes. It was shown that for complexes of weak acid anions pk_0 is linearly dependent on pk_1 implying that for both the k_0 and k_1 paths the leaving group is protonated before bond fission occurs. This supports the operation of a "tautomeric" mechanism for the k_0 path; i.e. for weak acid anions k_0 describes loss of HX from $(H_2O)_4(OH)Cr^{2+}$ rather than X^- from $(H_2O)_5Cr^{3+}$.[4] As is readily seen in Fig. 1, the switch from

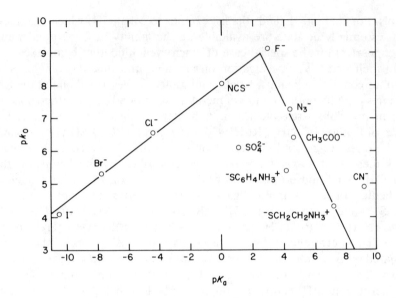

Fig. 1. Value of pk_0 for aquation of $(H_2O)_5CrX^{n+}$ against pK_a of HX.

the "tautomeric" mechanism for loss of weak acid anions to the "normal" mechanism for loss of strong acid anions occurs for acids of pK_a values around 1–2.

The rate of Cr–S bond breaking as the first step in thiolato chelate ring opening has been monitored in both bis(ethylenediamine)chromium(III)[85] and tetraaquochromium(III) systems;[26,175] typical complexes are $(en)_2Cr(SCH_2CH_2NH_2)^{2+}$, $(en)_2Cr(SCH_2COO)^+$ and $(H_2O)_4Cr(SCH_2COO)^+$. As expected, the rate of Cr–S bond fission is acid-catalysed reflecting the fact that RSH is a better leaving group than RS$^-$. Acid-independent Cr–S bond fission can also be detected, although in the bis(ethylenediamine)chromium(III) complexes acid-independent Cr–N bond fission becomes competitive. In general, Cr–S bond fission is favoured for those complexes containing a *cis* carboxylate group, and for complexes containing ammine ligands; both observations are consistent with previously established kinetic patterns for aquation of chromium(III) complexes. While Cr–S bond formation can be detected qualitatively after adding base to solutions of aquated bis(ethylenediamine) complexes, competing reactions prevent the accumulation of accurate rate data.[85] However, Cr–S bond formation can be monitored more precisely during the rechelation reactions of aquo-chromium(III) complexes;[26] from these studies it is clear that a pendant thiolato group very efficiently substitutes onto chromium(III). For analogous $(en)_2M(SCH_2COO)^+$ and $(en)_2M(SCH_2CH_2NH_2)^{2+}$ complexes, where M = cobalt(III) or chromium(III), the rate of Cr–S bond fission is at least 10^4 times greater than the rate of Co–S bond cleavage. The kinetic stability of $(en)_2Co(SCH_2CH_2NH_2)^{2+}$ is remarkable, no aquation being detected after 4 months in $1 M HClO_4$ at 25°C, or after four days in $1 M NaOH$ at 45°C. The great difference in lability between comparable Cr–S and Co–S bonds is not readily explicable in terms of crystal field arguments or bond length/strength arguments, but may be due to the different Bronsted basicity of thiolato sulphur when coordinated to cobalt(III) or chromium(III).[85]

For analogous chromium(III) complexes the rate of Cr–S bond fission is much greater for thioether ligands than for thiolato ligands.[28] For example, the half-life for Cr–S bond cleavage in the benzyl thioether complex $(en)_2Cr(S(CH_2C_6H_5)CH_2CH_2NH_2)^{3+}$ is ~2 h[28] while the comparable half-life for Cr–S bond cleavage in the thiolato complex $(en)_2Cr(SCH_2CH_2NH_2)^{2+}$ is ~96 h (calculated at $0·1 M HClO_4$, where approximately 60% of the reaction proceeds by the acid-independent path).[85] This lability of the thioether–chromium(III) bond is consistent with the observation of strong acid catalysis of thiolato–chromium(III) bond fission, since the neutral ligands RSH and RSR' are both presumably better leaving groups than the anionic ligand RS^-. It is anticipated that the cleavage of thioether-chromium(III) bonds is *not* acid-catalysed, although this point has yet to be verified experimentally. From the relative rates of Cr–S bond fission in $(en)_2Cr(SCH_2CH_2NH_2)^{2+}$, $(H_2O)_5Cr(SCH_2CH_2NH_3)^{3+}$ and $(en)_2Cr(S(CH_2C_6H_5)CH_2CH_2NH_2)^{3+}$, the half-life for aquation of the monodentate thioether complex $(H_2O)_5Cr(S(CH_2C_6H_5)CH_2CH_2NH_3)^{4+}$ is estimated to be about 14 min at 22°C.[28] The greater lability of the monodentate complexes, relative to the chelated analogues, is exactly as expected.

A further slow chelation process involving the making and breaking of thioether–chromium(III) bonds has been qualitatively described.[167] The interaction of the potentially heptadentate thioether ligand $S(CH_2CH_2N(CH_2COOH)_2)_2$ with chromium(III) gives rise to two complexes, both of which are hexacoordinate but only one of which contains a Cr–S bond. The structures of these two complexes are given in Section II.D. These species appear to be related by an equilibrium which requires four months to be achieved.

The very complicated kinetics of RS^- displacement from $Fe_4S_4(SR)_4^{n-}$ clusters $(RS = {}^-SCH_2CH_2COO^-)$ has been investigated in aqueous media.[176] Below pH 6·5 the cluster decomposes by hydrolytic scission of the Fe_4S_4 core (*vide supra*) while above pH 6·5 the RS^- ligands exchange with other lyate species (including H_2O, OH^-, alchohols, other thiols,

Reaction	I (M)	T (°
	H₂S, Hydrosulp	
$MoO_3S^{2-} + H_2O \rightleftharpoons MoO_4^{2-} + HS^- + H^+$	2·0 (NaCl)	2.
$MoOS_3^{2-} + H_2O \rightleftharpoons MoO_2S_2^{2-} + HS^- + H^+$	2·0 (NaCl)	2.
$MoS_4^{2-} + H_2O \rightleftharpoons MoOS_3^{2-} + HS^- + H^+$	2·0 (NaCl)	2.
$(H_2O)_5CrSH^{2+} + H_3O^+ \rightleftharpoons (H_2O)_6Cr^{3+} + H_2S$	1·0 (LiClO₄)	4
$(NH_3)_5Ru(SH_2)^{2+} + H_2O \rightleftharpoons$ $(NH_3)_5Ru(H_2O)^{2+} + H_2S$	0·21 ([H⁺]=0·1 M)	2.
$tr\text{-}(NH_3)_4Ru(isn)(H_2S)^{2+} + H_2O \rightleftharpoons$ $tr\text{-}(NH_3)_4Ru(isn)(H_2O)^{2+} + H_2S$	0·5 (HTFA)^q	2.
	Thiols, thiolates, thioe	
$(NH_3)_5Ru(X)^{2+} + H_2O \rightleftharpoons (NH_3)_5Ru(OH_2)^{2+} + X$		
X = $(CH_3)_2S$	0·1 (HTFA)^q (13% ethanol in H₂O)	2.
X = CH_3CH_2SH	0·1 (HTFA)^q (13% ethanol in H₂O)	2.
X = thiophene	0·1 (HTFA)^q (13% ethanol in H₂O)	2.
$tr\text{-}(NH_3)_4Ru(isn)(X)^{2+} + H_2O \rightleftharpoons$ $tr\text{-}(NH_3)_4Ru(isn)(H_2O)]^{2+} + X$		
X = $(CH_3)_2S$	0·5 (HTFA)^q	2.
X = CH_3CH_2SH		2.
$(NH_3)_5Ru(S(CH_3)_2)^{3+} + H_2O \rightleftharpoons$ $(NH_3)_5Ru(H_2O)^{3+} + (CH_3)_2S$	0·2 (Li/HCl)	2.
$(H_2O)_5Cr(SCH_2CH_2NH_3)^{3+} + H_3O^+ \rightleftharpoons$ $(H_2O)_6Cr^{3+} + HSCH_2CH_2NH_3^+$	1·0 (NaClO₄) 2·0 (LiClO₄)	2. 2.

$(H_2O)_5Cr(NH_2CH_2CH_2SH)^{3+}$ with $1·0$ (LiClO₄) at 2.

	1·0 (LiClO₄)	25
	4·0 (LiClO₄)	25

	0·25 (LiClO₄)	25
	2·0 (LiClO₄)	25

^{a}	k_1 $(M^{-1} s^{-1})^a$	k_{-0} $(M^{-1} s^{-1})^b$	k_{-1} $(M^{-2} s^{-1})^b$	ΔH^* (kcal/mol)^c	ΔS^* (eu)^c	Ref.
ulphides						
$\times 10^{-3}$	—	—	$4\cdot0\times10^9$	—	—	[171]
$)\times10^{-5}$	—	—	$1\cdot2\times10^9$	—	—	[171]
$\times 10^{-6}$	—	—	$<1\cdot6\times10^6$	—	—	[171]
$\times10^{-5}$	3.82×10^{-5}	—	—	$27\cdot7$	9.4	[184]
$\times10^{-5}$	—	$0\cdot100^e$	—	—	—	[102]
$\times10^{-3}$	—	6.78×10^{-3}	—	—	—	[102]
elated ligands						
$\times10^{-2}$	—	$<4\cdot2\times10^{-6g}$	—	—	—	[102]
$\times10^{-2}$	—	$\leqslant3\times10^{-5g}$	—	—	—	[102]
$\times10^{-2f}$	—	8.2×10^{-3}	—	—	—	[102]
0^{-6}	—	—	—	—	—	[102]
0^{-3}	—	—	—	—	—	[102]
$\times10^{-7}$	—	—	—	—	—	[7]
$\times10^{-5}$	$8\cdot0\times10^{-5}$	—	—	—	—	[26]
$\times10^{-5}$	1.31×10^{-4}	—	—	$27\cdot6^h$ $20\cdot6^i$	$14\cdot0^h$ $-7\cdot1^i$	[4]
$\times10^{-6}$	$7\cdot57\times10^{-6}$	$1\cdot41\times10^{-6}$	0.359×10^{-6}	—	—	[26]
$\times10^{-6j}$	$7\cdot.6\times10^{-6}$	—	—	$16\cdot2$	$-17\cdot6$	[85]
$\times10^{-5j}$	$3\cdot42\times10^{-5}$	—	—	—	—	
10^{-7}	$7\cdot0\times10{-6}$	$6\cdot8\times10^{-6}$	8×10^{-2}	—	—	[26]
	$2\cdot6\times10^{-4}$	—	—	—	—	[26]

TABLE 9

Reaction	I (M)	T (°C)

$(H_2O)_4Cr \overset{S}{\underset{O}{\diagup}} \overset{+}{\diagdown}_{O} \; + \; H_3O^+ \; \rightleftharpoons \; (H_2O)_5Cr-O\overset{O}{\overset{\|}{C}}CH(CH_3)SH$

| 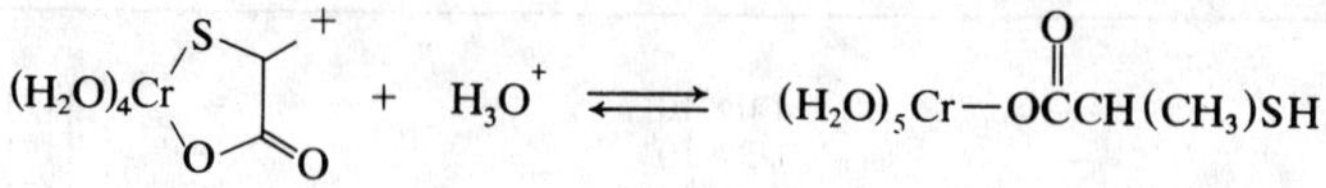 | 2·0 (LiClO$_4$) | 25 |

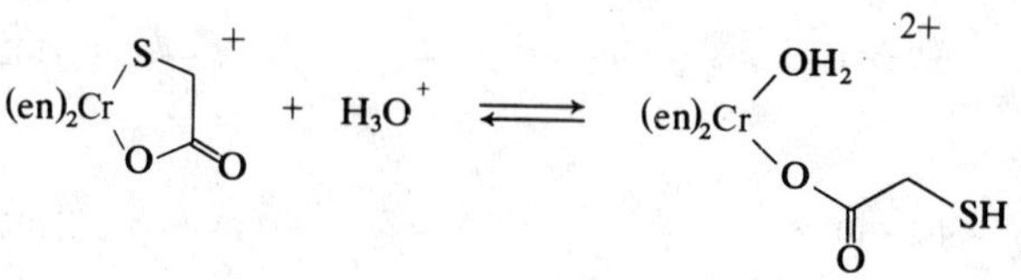

$(en)_2Cr \overset{S}{\underset{O}{\diagup}} \overset{+}{\diagdown}_{O} \; + \; H_3O^+ \; \rightleftharpoons \; (en)_2Cr \overset{OH_2}{\diagdown} \cdots \overset{2+}{}$ ... $O-C(=O)-CH_2-SH$

| | 1·0 (LiClO$_4$) | 25 |
| | 4·0 (LiClO$_4$) | 25 |

$(H_2O)_5Cr-S-\!\!\bigcirc\!\!-NH_3^{3+} \; + \; H_3O^+ \; \rightleftharpoons$

$(H_2O)_6Cr^{3+} \; + \; HS-\!\!\bigcirc\!\!-NH_3^+$

| 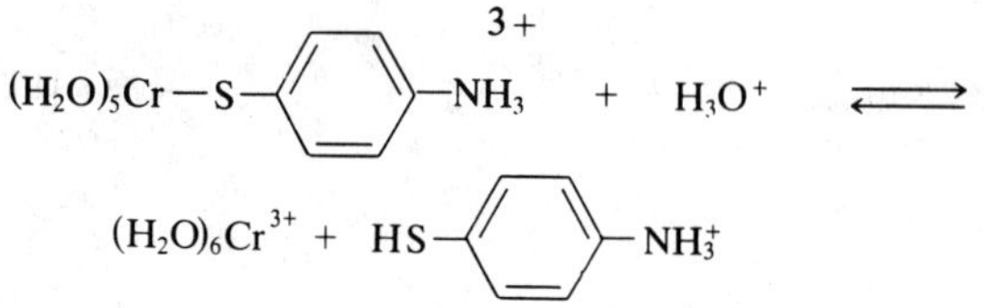 | 2·00 (LiClO$_4$) | 25 |

$(H_2O)_5CrSCN^{2+} + H_2O \rightleftharpoons (H_2O)_6Cr^{3+} + SCN^-$

| | 1·0 (HClO$_4$) | 25 |

$(en)_2Cr(S(CH_2C_6H_5)CH_2CH_2NH_2)^{3+} + H_3O^+ \rightleftharpoons$

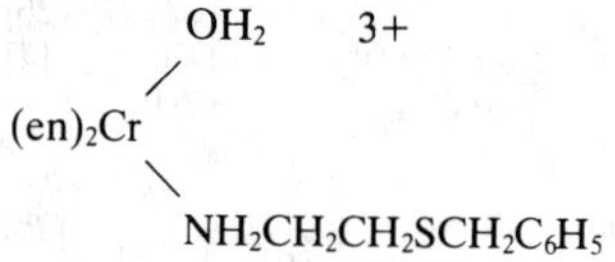

$(en)_2Cr \overset{OH_2}{\diagup} \; {}^{3+}$
$\diagdown \; NH_2CH_2CH_2SCH_2C_6H_5$

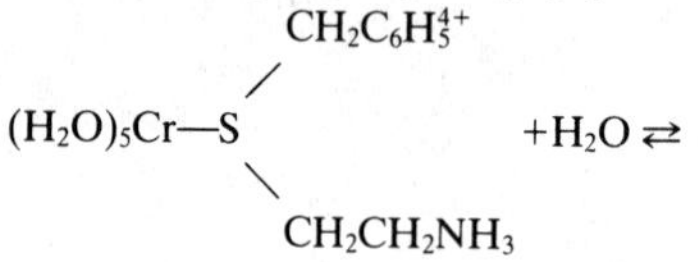

| | 0·1 (HClO$_4$) | 22 |

$CH_2C_6H_5^{4+}$
$(H_2O)_5Cr-S \overset{\diagup}{\diagdown} \; + H_2O \rightleftharpoons$
$CH_2CH_2NH_3$

$(H_2O)_6Cr^{3+} + C_6H_5-CH_2S-CH_2CH_2NH_3^+$

| | 0·1 (HClO$_4$) | 22 |

$CuX^{2+} \; \overset{H_3O^+}{\rightleftharpoons} \; Cu^{2+} + X^1$

$X = $

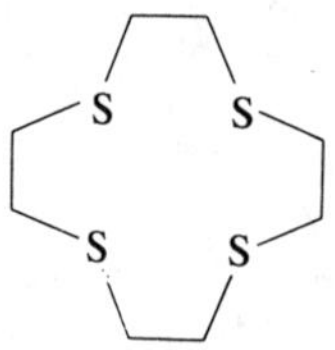

| | 0·1 (HClO$_4$) | 25 |

$s^{-1})^a$	k_1 $(M^{-1} s^{-1})^a$	k_{-0} $(M^{-1} s^{-1})^b$	k_{-1} $(M^{-2} s^{-1})^b$	ΔH^* (kcal/mol)^c	ΔS^* (eu)^c	Ref.
-0	7.7×10^{-5}	~ 0	7.1×10^{-7}	—	—	[26]
-5 × 10^{-5j}	1.11×10^{-3}	—	—	15·8	−18·5	[85]
-	9.3×10^{-3}	—	—	—	—	[85]
0 × 10^{-6}	1.10×10^{-6}	—	—	29·8^h	16·7^h	[85]
				23·6^i	−2·1^i	
8 × 10^{-5}	—	—	—	—	—	[44]
$_2 = 2.3$ h	—	—	—	—	—	[28]
$_2 = 14$ min	—	—	—	—	—	[28]
6	—	6.5×10^3	—	—	—	[178]

Reaction	I (M)
X =	0·1 (HClO₄)
	0·1 (HClO₄)
	0·1 (HClO₄)
	0·1 (HClO₄)
	0·1 (HClO₄)
R = CH₃ R = CH₂CH₃	0·1 (HClO₄) 0·1 (HClO₄)

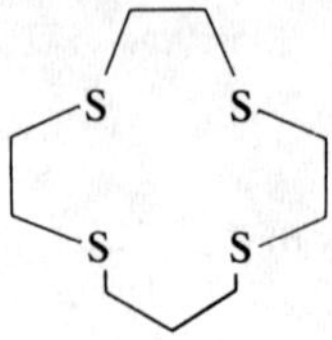

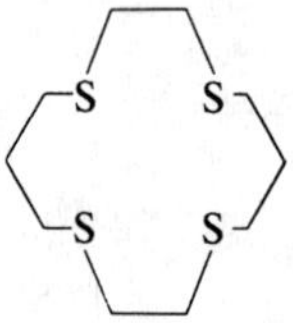

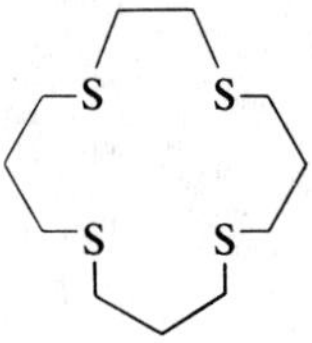

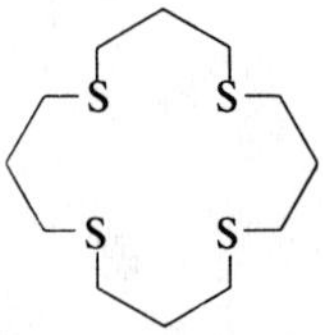

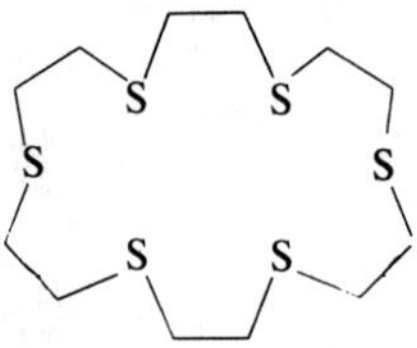

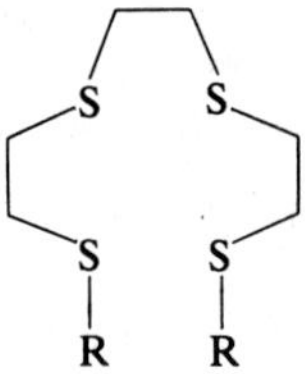

	k_1 $(\text{M}^{-1}\,\text{s}^{-1})^a$	k_{-0} $(\text{M}^{-1}\,\text{s}^{-1})^b$	k_{-1} $(\text{M}^{-2}\,\text{s}^{-1})^b$	ΔH^* (kcal/mol)^c	ΔS^* (eu)^c	Ref.
10^1	—	$7\cdot4 \times 10^4$	—	—	—	[178]
10^1	—	$1\cdot3 \times 10^5$	—	$\begin{matrix}10\\6\cdot1^p\end{matrix}$	$\begin{matrix}-13\\-11^p\end{matrix}$	[178]
0^1	—	$2\cdot35 \times 10^5$	—	—	—	[178]
10^3	—	$1\cdot7 \times 10^5$	—	—	—	[178]
0^1	—	$7\cdot5 \times 10^5$	—	—	—	[178]
0^3	—	$1\cdot3 \times 10^6$	—	—	—	[178]
0^4	—	$4\cdot2 \times 10^6$	—	—	—	[178]

Reaction	I (M)
$(EDTA)RuS_2O_3^{3-} + H_2O \rightleftharpoons (EDTA) RuOH_2^- + S_2O_3^{2-}$	$0 \cdot 1^m$
$[Co(DH)_2(H_2O)X]^{n+1} + H_2O \rightleftharpoons$ $[Co(DH)_2(H_2O)_2]^+ + X^n$	
$\quad X = S_2O_3^{2-}$	$4 \cdot 04$ (NaClO$_4$)
$\quad X = S = C(NH_2)$	$4 \cdot 04$ (NaClO$_4$)

[a] Values of k_0 and k_1 apply to aquation reaction. k_0 applies to acid-independent path and k_1 applies to an acid-dependent path. k_0 is used where the acid-dependency was not measured.

[b] k_{-0} and k_{-1} apply to anation by sulphur species. k_{-0} applies to acid-independent path and k_{-1} applies to an acid-dependent path. k_{-0} is used where the acid-dependency is not mentioned.

[c] Activation parameters are for aquation unless otherwise specified.

[d] Electrolyte not given.

[e] Ionic strength $= 0 \cdot 1 =$ acid strength (trifluoroacetic acid).

[f] Estimated from values for $HSCH_2CH_3$ and $S(CH_3)_2$.

[g] Loss of ammonia *trans* to X allows only an upper limit to be calculated.

[h] Values for k_0 path.

k_1 $(M^{-1} s^{-1})^a$	k_{-0} $(M^{-1} s^{-1})^b$	k_{-1} $(M^{-2} s^{-1})^b$	ΔH^* $(kcal/mol)^c$	ΔS^* $(eu)^c$	Ref.
—	2·94	—	$8·82^{n,p}$	—	[242]
—	$3·8 \times 10^{-1o}$	—	—	—	[182]
—	$2·7 \times 10^{-2o}$	—	—	—	[182]

es for k_1 path.

ved from k_{obs} against $[H^+]$ plot. Intercept may result from

$^{-1}$.

es determined in varying ratios of methanol/H_2O and
olated to 100% H_2O.

strength controlled by buffer concentration using acetate,
hate, carbonate or borate buffers.

d on experimental rate equation $k_{anation} = (a[L])/(b+[L])$,
$L = S_2O_3^{2-}$ ($a = 0·012 s^{-1}$, $b = 1·6 M$) and $S = C(NH_2)_2$ ($a =$
s^{-1}, $b = 0·45 M$).

vation parameters for anation.

uoroacetic acid.

Cl^-, etc.). The kinetics of the ligand exchange reactions are interpreted in terms of prior equilibria involving cores with only three thiol ligands $(Fe_4S_4(SR)_3)$ and cores with no thiol ligands (Fe_4S_4);

$$Fe_4S_4(SR)_4 \rightleftarrows Fe_4S_4(SR)_3 \rightleftarrows Fe_4S_4$$
$$\downarrow \qquad \downarrow$$
$$products \quad products$$

these species then react with nucleophiles by means of specific acid and base catalysed routes to yield the ligand-substituted clusters. In this system the observed rate is not determined by the lability of the Fe–SR bond, but it is clear that thiol groups dissociate from the cluster with great facility; Holm and co-workers[177] have used this facile ligand exchange reaction to prepare clusters containing a variety of thiol ligands

$$Fe_4S_4(SR)_4^{n-} + 4R'S = Fe_4S_4(SR')_4^{n-} + 4RS^-$$

Relative nucleophilicities towards the core go in the order $Cl^- \cong Br^- \ll OH^- < CN^-$ as expected for substitution on an iron centre.

The rapid complexations of copper(II) by macrocylic and open-chain polythioethers have been measured in aqueous methanol by T-jump and stopped-flow methods.[178] The observed kinetics are as expected for an approach to equilibrium, the rate of complexation correlating directly with the percentage of $Cu(H_2O)_6^{2+}$ present (this percentage decreases as the concentration of methanol in the solvent increases). Thus, over the range 0–60% methanol, $Cu(H_2O)_6^{2+}$ is the only species of solvated Cu(II) that is reactive towards the thioether ligands and the observed data can be used to calculate formation and dissociation rate constants (and the associated equilibrium constant) for pure aqueous media. For all the polythioether ligands it appears that the rate of formation of the first Cu–S bond is very fast and formation of the second Cu–S bond is rate-determining. Thus it is the variable difficulty in achieving closure of the first chelate ring that accounts for most of the observed differences in formation rate constants. The size of the macrocyclic ring and the thermodynamic macrocyclic effect are manifested in the later steps of the complexation process, being associated with the final circumscription of the metal ion by the cyclic ligand; consequently, the macrocyclic effect tends to parallel the dissociation rate constants. Comparisons among six macrocyclic and two open-chain polythioether ligands confirms that the flexibility of the macrocycle plays an important part in the complexation and dissociation of these ligands, although patterns of stabilities are not consistent among macrocycles of different chelate ring size. As expected, the stability constant for the open chain polythioethers are much smaller than those observed for the macrocycles.

The reactions of various square planar, d^8 metal centres with thioethers have recently been reviewed.[13,14] However, it should be noted that recent work implicates "non-specific" solvation in substitution reactions of d^8 metal centres.[179] Also, data supporting the accepted associative mechanism for reaction of thiourea with Pt(II) complexes has recently appeared.[180]

In very recent work[155] the half-life for ligand exchange in bis(thio-glucose)gold(I) is shown to be very rapid (≤ 2.2 msec by ^{1}H NMR). This result implies that such thiolato–gold(I) drugs used for treatment of rheumatoid arthritis undergo rapid exchange of ligands *in vivo*, and thus after injection all such drugs will achieve a common chemical form dictated by the availability and distribution of biological ligands.

3. Other sulphur-containing ligands

The kinetics of several miscellaneous reactions involving formation of metal–sulphur bonds have been reported. The reactions of a variety of organosulphur ligands (e.g. thiols) with aquo(ethylenediaminetetra-acetato)ruthenate(III) are too rapid to be conveniently monitored, but the anionic ligand thiosulphate reacts at a more moderate rate[242]. The anation is first-order in both thiosulphate and complex, and is independent of pH in the region 4 to 6; the rate decreases at both lower and higher pH values, presumably because the reactivities of $(edta)(OH)Ru^{2-}$ and $(Hedta)(OH_2)Ru^0$ are less than that of $(edta)(OH_2)Ru^-$. In a much more complicated system the reaction of SO_3^{2-} with $Co(CO_3)_3^{3-}$ was reported to proceed in two steps to yield monosulphito and then bis(sulphito) complexes, although no information was given as to whether SO_3^{2-} is *S*-bonded or *O*-bonded in these product complexes.[181] A very brief report on the ligation of *trans*-$Co(OH_2)_2(DH)_2^+$ (DH = monoanion of dimethylglyoxime) by thiourea and thiosulphate has been presented,[182] again no information being given as to which isomeric products are formed. The reactions of thiourea and some of its derivatives with $(CN)_5Fe(OH_2)^{3-}$ were briefly investigated as part of a larger study to elucidate the reactivity of various pentacyanoferrate(II) complexes.[183] Finally, the reactions of a variety of sulphur-containing ligands with *trans* labilized metal centres have been investigated in the context of elucidating the nature of the *trans* labilization phenomenon, and are therefore more naturally discussed in terms of the kinetic *trans* effect (*vide infra*).

B. Protonation at coordinated sulphur

Many types of coordinated sulphur atoms, especially those derived from thiolato and sulphido ligands, retain considerable Bronsted basicity. This proton affinity is most prominently manifested in acid catalysis of metal–sulphur bond fission processes. For example, the rate laws governing aquation of the chromium(III) complexes $(H_2O)_5CrSR^{n+}$, $(H_2O)_5CrSH^{2+}$, $(H_2O)_4Cr(SCH_2COO)^+$, $(en)_2Cr(SCH_2COO)^+$, and $(en)_2Cr(SCH_2CH_2NH_2)^{2+}$ all exhibit terms first-order in acid.[3,4,19,26,85,184] In some cases the pK_a value for the protonated complex can be indirectly estimated from the acid-dependent kinetic data. However, the inherent importance of the protonation of coordinated sulphur both to the chemical description of metal–sulphur species and to a variety of kinetic processes involving the metal–sulphur bond has generated several more direct determinations of protonation constants.

The protonation of the coordinated thiolato ligand in the cobalt(III) complex $(en)_2Co(SCH_2CH_2NH_2)^{2+}$ is firmly established by visible–UV spectral changes induced in aqueous perchloric acid media.[185] As the concentration of $HClO_4$ is increased the spectrum of $(en)_2Co(SCH_2CH_2NH_2)^{2+}$ reversibly changes to resemble the spectra of $(en)_2Co(S(CH_3)CH_2CH_2NH_2)^{3+}$, $(en)_2Co(S(Ag)CH_2CH_2NH_2)^{3+}$ and $(en)_2Co(S(SCH_3)CH_2CH_2NH_2)^{3+}$, all species in which the coordinated sulphur atom has been modified by further coordination to an electropositive centre (all these species have been characterized by other techniques, including single-crystal x-ray structural analysis). Therefore, in analogy to these related systems, and because there are no other atoms in $(en)_2Co(SCH_2CH_2NH_2)^{2+}$ that can interact with protons, addition of $HClO_4$ to $(en)_2Co(SCH_2CH_2NH_2)^{2+}$ must result in protonation of the coordinated sulphur atom.

$$(en)_2Co(SCH_2CH_2NH_2)^{2+} + H^+ = (en)_2Co(S(H)CH_2CH_2NH_2)^{3+}$$

Analysis of the acid-dependent visible–UV spectral data leads to the pK_a value listed in Table 10. This value is just about the same as that of a coordinated carboxylic acid; i.e. coordinated RCOOH and coordinated RSH have about the same acidity even though noncoordinated carboxylic acids are much stronger acids than are noncoordinated thiols. This coordination-induced levelling effect presumably arises since in coordinated RSH both the metal centre and the proton are bonded to the same sulphur atom and thus the proton is directly influenced by the inductive effect of the metal; however, in coordinated RCOOH the metal centre and the proton are most likely bonded to different oxygen atoms and the inductive effect of the metal is correspondingly reduced. Because of the similarity in pK_a values for coordinated thiols and coordinated carboxylic acids, it cannot be certain whether $(en)_2M(SCH_2COO)^+$ ($M = Cr^{III}$ or Co^{III}) is protonated on the sulphur atom or on the carboxylate group.[85,185]

When coordinated to cobalt(III) the thiolato sulphur atom is only weakly

Values of pK_a for various sulphur-containing species

Compound	pK_a	Conditions [$I(M)$, $T(°C)$, solvent]	Ref.
C_6H_5SH	6·62	~0, 25, CH_2Cl_2	[186]
$H_2NCH_2CH_2SH$	8·67[a]	–, 25, H_2O	[202]
$-O_2CCH_2CH_2SH$	10·21	0·1 ($LiClO_4$), –[f] H_2O	[176]
CH_3CH_2SH	12	–, 25, H_2O	[102]
H_2S	7	—	[102]
H_2O	15·7	—	[102]
$[(NH_3)_5Ru^{III}(SH_2)]^{3+}$	–10[b]	—	[102]
$[(NH_3)_5Ru^{II}(SH_2)]^{2+}$	4·0	~0·25 ($NaClO_4$), –[f] H_2O	[102]
$[(NH_3)_5Ru^{II}(OH_2)]^{2+}$	13·1	0·45 ($NaClO_4$), –[f] H_2O	[102]
tr-$[(isn)(NH_3)_4Ru^{II}(OH_2)]^{2+}$	11·7	0·475 (NaTosyl), 25, H_2O	[102]
tr-$[(isn)(NH_3)_4Ru^{II}(SH_2)]^{2+}$	3·25 ± 0·2	0·5 (NaTosyl), 25, H_2O	[102]
tr-$[(isn)(NH_3)_4Ru^{II}(SH)]^{2+}$	>14[b]	—	[102]
$[(NH_3)_5Ru^{II}(S(H)CH_2CH_3)]^{2+}$	9·2	0·1 (Na/HCl), –, H_2O	[102]
$[(NH_3)_5Ru^{III}(S(H)CH_2CH_3)]^{3+}$	–7[b]	—	[102]
$[(H_2O)Cr(SH_2)]^{3+}$	≤–1[b]	—	[23]
$[(en)_2Co(S(H)CH_2CH_2NH_2)]^{2+}$	–0·81 ± 0·08	8·0 (Na/HClO_4), 25, H_2O	[185]
$[H^+][(en)_2Co(SCH_2CO_2)]^{+g}$	0·39 ± 0·10	8·0 (Na/HClO_4), 25, H_2O	[185]
$[H^+][(en)_2Cr(SCH_2CO_2)]^{+g}$	0·06 ± 0·01[d]	4·0 (Li/HClO_4), 25, H_2O	[85]
$[(en)_2Co(S(OH)CH_2CH_2NH_2)]^{3+}$	–0·1	4·0 (Li/HClO_4), 25, H_2O	[12]
$[Fe_4S_4(SR)_4]^{n-}$			
R = —$CH_2CH(CH_3)_2$ ($n = 2$)	3·92	0·1, 30, 60/40 NMP[h]/H_2O	[173]
R = —$C(CH_3)_3$, —CH_3 ($n = 2$)	~3·9	0·1, 30, 60/40 NMP[h]/H_2O	[173]
R = —$CH_2CH_2CO_2^-$ ($n = 6$)	7·4	0·1 ($LiClO_4$), –[f] H_2O	[176]
$Fe(C_5H_5)(CO)_2(C_6H_5SH)$	≤–2·0[b,e]	~0, –, CH_2Cl_2	[186]

[a] $\overset{\oplus}{H_3N}$—$CH_2CH_2SH \overset{K_a \oplus}{\rightleftharpoons} NH_3CH_2CH_2S^\ominus + H^+$.
[b] Estimate.
[c] Postulated to be protonation of carboxylate.
[d] Determined by analysis of kinetic data.
[e] Determined in CH_2Cl_2. pK_a represents *estimate* based on pK_{assoc}, data. $A - H + B \overset{K_{assoc}}{\rightleftharpoons} [A \ldots HB]$.
[f] Data not given.
[g] Site of protonation not given.
[h] N-methylpyrrolidone.

basic, a $6 \cdot 5 \, M \, HClO_4$ medium being required to convert 50% of $(en)_2Co(SCH_2CH_2NH_2)^{2+}$ to the protonated form. Thus, coordination to cobalt(III) increases the acidity of a thiol by $\sim 10 \, pK_a$ units, this enhancement resulting simply from the inductive effect of the metal centre. In marked contrast, coordination of a thiol to the pentaammineruthenium(II) centre increases its acidity by only about 3 units,[102] the pK_a value of $(NH_3)_5Ru(S(H)C_2H_5)^{2+}$ being just about equal to that of noncoordinated $H_2NCH_2CH_2SH$. This difference in behaviour between cobalt(III) and ruthenium(II) complexes is ascribed to extensive π back-bonding in the ruthenium(II) system which places electron density on the coordinated sulphur atom. Apparently, in the ruthenium(II) system donation of π electron density to the coordinated sulphur atom just about cancels out the inductive effect resulting from coordination to a 2+ metal centre. Consistent with this back-bonding argument, substitution of the π-acid ligand isonicotinamide (isn) *trans* to coordinated sulphur causes *trans*-$(NH_3)_4(isn)RuSH_2^{2+}$ to be much more acidic than $(NH_3)_5RuSH_2^{2+}$.[102] Ruthenium(III), like cobalt(III), does not undergo extensive π back-bonding and concomitantly thiols coordinated to ruthenium(III) are very acidic. A pK_a value of -7 has been estimated for $(NH_3)_5Ru(S(H)C_2H_5)^{3+}$,[102] but this seems unrealistically low when compared to the pK_a value of -1 measured for $(en)_2Co(S(H)CH_2CH_2NH_2)^{3+}$ (even after taking into account the different ionic strengths used in the two systems). In any case, the acidities of thiols coordinated to cobalt(III), chromium(III) and ruthenium(III) appear to be determined largely by the inductive effect of the metal centre, whereas in ruthenium(II) complexes this effect is counteracted by extensive donation of π electron density from the metal to the coordinated sulphur. While the inductive effect will, of course, be operative to some extent in all metal systems, it remains to be seen whether or not π back-bonding plays a role in determining the basicity of coordinated sulphur in low-valent metal centres other than ruthenium(II) (e.g. Fe(II)).

The considerations noted above are relevant to observations on the protonation of $Fe_4S_4(SR)_4^{2-}$ clusters.[173,176] When R is a simple alkyl group the 2− charged cluster has a pK_a about $3 \cdot 9$ (extrapolated to aqueous media), and when R is $CH_2CH_2COO^-$ the 6− charged, water-soluble, cluster has a pK_a of 7. Bruice and co-workers argue that these values are too low to represent protonation of either the coordinated thiolate or the bridging sulphido ligand, and propose instead that it is the face of the cube that is being protonated. However, the data accumulated in Table 10 indicate that these pK_a values are entirely reasonable for protonation of coordinated thiolates, especially considering the overall negative charge of the cluster (which will increase the basicity of the coordinated sulphur by reducing the overall inductive effect of the electropositive metal centre) and the low oxidation state of the iron atoms in the cluster (mixed $Fe(II)$ and $Fe(III)$) which will promote π back-bonding. Given that the $2+$ charged complex $(NH_3)_5Ru(S(H)C_2H_5)^{2+}$ has a pK_a of $9\cdot2$,[102] it is not at all unreasonable that the coordinated thiol of $Fe_4S_4(SR)_3(HSR)^-$ could have a pK_a of $3\cdot9$. There is thus no reason to propose a special mode of protonation of the iron–sulphur clusters and it is likely that the chemistry of these species can be understood in terms of the chemistry of simpler, monomeric complexes.

Some other, miscellaneous, observations on the Bronsted basicity of coordinated sulphur-containing ligands have been reported. The coordinated thiol of $(C_5H_5)Fe(CO)_2(HSC_6H_5)^+$ is a strong acid in a variety of organic solvents.[186] In CH_2Cl_2 it is 8% associated with tetrahydrofuran, 62% associated with dimethyl sulfoxide and 72% associated with diphenylamine. The data do not directly yield a pK_a value (the low dielectric constant of CH_2Cl_2 promotes association between acid and base rather than proton transfer), but it is not unreasonable to estimate the pK_a as being equal to that of tetrahydrofuran (i.e. ~ -2). The coordinated sulphenato ligand of $(en)_2Co(S(O)CH_2CH_2NH_2)^{2+}$ undergoes 50% protonation in $1\,\text{M}\,HClO_4$[12], although protonation undoubtedly occurs on the pendant oxygen atom rather than on the coordinated sulphur atom.[185] The pK_a of $(H_2O)_5CrSH_2^{3+}$[184] is certainly less than 0 and so $(H_2O)_5CrSH^{2+}$ is the predominant species in aqueous solution. Deprotonation of $(H_2O)_5CrSH^{2+}$ could yield either $(H_2O)_5CrS^+$ or $(H_2O)_4(OH)CrSH^+$, but the pH region in which this deprotonation occurs is experimentally inaccessible due to olation of the chromium(III) centre.

C. Lewis basicity of coordinated sulphur

Coordinated sulphur atoms have affinity for acids other than the proton, and not surprisingly this affinity is very high for "soft" acids such as $Ag(I)$, CH_3Hg^+ and $Cu(I)$. The resultant sulphur-bridged, binuclear adduct is of interest as a model for the precursor complex in sulphur-bridged innersphere electron transfer reactions. In such a precursor complex, the coordinated sulphur atom of one complex functions as a ligand to a second metal centre.

Significant observations on the Lewis basicity of coordinated sulphur have been reported only for thiolato complexes, the one quantitative study available being concerned with the prototype cobalt(III) complexes $(en)_2Co(SCH_2CH_2NH_2)^{2+}$ and $(en)_2Co(SCH_2COO)^+$.[111] These species bind strongly to Ag^+ and CH_3Hg^+, the binding constants being about the same as observed for ligation of thioethers to these "soft" metal centres.

Comparisons among binding constants (Table 11), plus observations on the nucleophilicity of coordinated thiols towards H_2O_2,[83] lead to the following generalization: it is the number of covalent bonding interactions involving sulphur (and not the formal charge of the sulphur compound or the chemical identity of the sulphur species) which primarily determines

TABLE 11

Selected equilibrium constants governing Ag^+ and CH_3Hg^+ adduct formation with sulphur-containing species in aqueous media[a,b]

Adduct	K_f (consecutive) (M^{-1})	I (M)
$(Cocys)Ag^{3+}$	$(4\cdot0 \pm 0\cdot2) \times 10^4$	$0\cdot065^c$
$(Cocys)_2Ag^{5+}$	$(3\cdot1 \pm 0.2) \times 10^3$	$0\cdot065^c$
$(Cotga)Ag^{2+}$	$(4\cdot8 \pm 0.7) \times 10^4$	$0\cdot058^c$
$(Cotga)_2Ag^{3+}$	$(1\cdot3 \pm 0.2) \times 10^3$	$0\cdot058^c$
$(HOCH_2CH_2S)Ag$	$1\cdot6 \times 10^{13}$	$0\cdot1^d$
$((HOCH_2CH_2)_2S)Ag^+$	$3\cdot4 \times 10^3$	$0\cdot5^e$
$((HOCH_2CH_2)_2S)_2Ag^+$	$1\cdot9 \times 10^2$	$0\cdot5^e$
$(Cocys)HgCH_3^{3+}$	$(4.6 \pm 0.1) \times 10^4$	$0\cdot13^c$
$(Cocys)_2HgCH_3^{5+}$	$(5\cdot3 \pm 0\cdot5) \times 10^2$	$0\cdot13^c$
$(Cotga)HgCH_3^{2+}$	$(3\cdot3 \pm 0.1) \times 10^5$	$0\cdot11^c$
$(HOCH_2CH_2S)HgCH_3$	$1\cdot3 \times 10^{16}$	$0\cdot1^d$
$(HOCH_2CH_2S(HgCH_3))HgCH_3^+$	$1\cdot9 \times 10^6$	$0\cdot1^d$

[a] Cocys $\equiv [(en)_2Co(SCH_2CH_2NH_2)]^{2+}$;
  Cotga $\equiv [(en)_2Co(SCH_2COO)]^+$.
[b] Ref. [111].
[c] $LiClO_4$, 22°C.
[d] KNO_3, 20°C.
[e] $NaClO_4$, 25°C.

the Lewis basicity of the sulphur. Thus, the coordinated thiolato sulphur atom of $(en)_2Co(SCH_2CH_2NH_2)^{2+}$ is more similar to a noncoordinated thioether sulphur atom (RSR') than it is to a noncoordinated thiolato sulphur atom (RS^-). An additional interesting result of this work is the apparent high formation constant of $[(en)_2Co(NH_2CH_2CH_2S)]_2HgCH_3^{5+}$ wherein the mercury atom and the bridging sulphur atoms are all three-coordinate. The trinuclear adduct $[(en)_2Co(OOCCH_2S)]_2Ag^{3+}$ has been characterized by single-crystal x-ray structural analysis.[188]. This analysis shows that neither the Co–S nor the *trans* Co–N bond are lengthened with respect to the comparable bonds in the mononuclear complex $(en)_2Co(SCH_2COO)^+$. Thus, this trinuclear adduct does *not* reflect the bond lengthening thought to be necessary in order to attain the transition state for inner-sphere electron transfer. However, it is likely that the structural changes in the $(en)_2Co(SCH_2COO)^+$ centre observed upon its coordination to Ag(I) do model the structural changes that occur upon formation of an electron transfer precursor complex.

In related research Lane and co-workers have shown that $(en)_2Co(SCH_2CH_2NH_2)^{2+}$ and $(en)_2Co(SCH_2COO)^+$ form strong adducts with Cu(I).[20] Subsequent structural work demonstrates that these adducts are tetrameric with two Cu(I) centres bridging two thiolato–cobalt(III) complexes:[189]

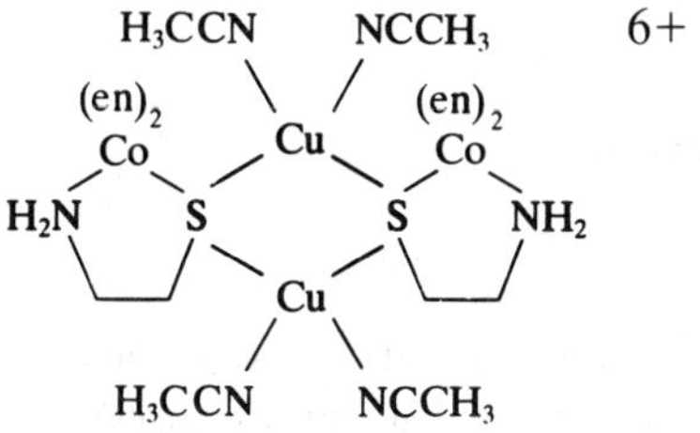

$$
\begin{array}{c}
H_3CCN \quad\quad NCCH_3 \quad\quad 6+ \\
(en)_2 \quad \diagdown \diagup \quad (en)_2 \\
Co \quad\quad Cu \quad\quad Co \\
H_2N \quad S \quad\quad S \quad NH_2 \\
\diagdown Cu \diagup \\
H_3CCN \quad\quad NCCH_3
\end{array}
$$

and thus the earlier estimate[20] given for the binding constant of the hypothesized one-to-one adduct should be discounted.

Qualitative observations on the binding of the thiolato complexes **A** and **B** to various metal centres have been reported.[190–195]

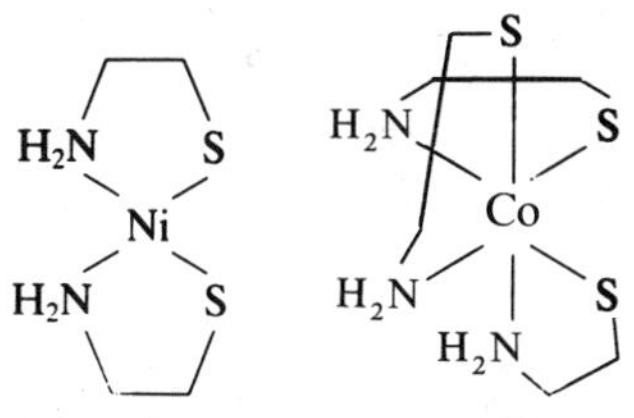

$$
\begin{array}{cc}
\begin{array}{c}
H_2N \quad S \\
\quad Ni \\
H_2N \quad S
\end{array}
&
\begin{array}{c}
S \\
H_2N \quad\quad S \\
\quad Co \\
H_2N \quad\quad S \\
H_2N
\end{array}
\\
\mathbf{A} & \mathbf{B}
\end{array}
$$

The neutral complex **A** functions as a bidentate ligand to metals such as Ni(II) and Pd(II) to form trinuclear adducts such as

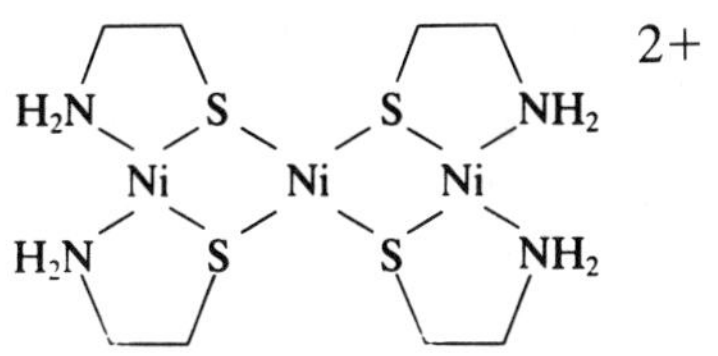

$$
\begin{array}{c}
\quad\quad\quad\quad\quad\quad 2+ \\
H_2N \quad S \quad\quad S \quad NH_2 \\
\quad Ni \quad Ni \quad Ni \\
H_2N \quad S \quad\quad S \quad NH_2
\end{array}
$$

The overall formation constant for this trinuclear nickel(II) adduct appears to be of the order of 10^7 M^{-2}.[196] The neutral complex **B** functions as a tridentate ligand to metals such as Ni(II), Fe(III), Co(III), and Ru(III) to form trinuclear adducts such as

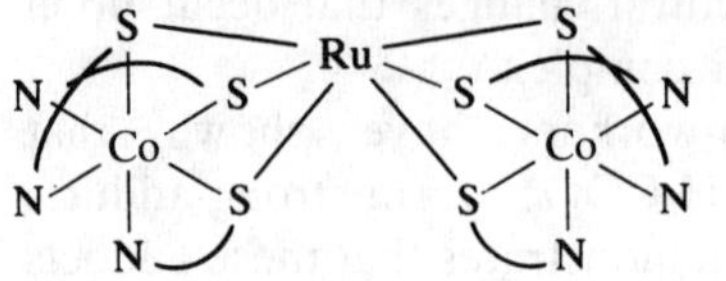

There is EPR evidence for metal–metal interaction when **B** is coordinated to Fe(III) or Ru(III).[194]

D. *S*-alkylation and *S*-dealkylation reactions

1. Alkylation of coordinated thiols

The coordinated sulphur atom of thiolato complexes retains considerable nucleophilicity, and this property has great synthetic utility as shown in Scheme I.[109]

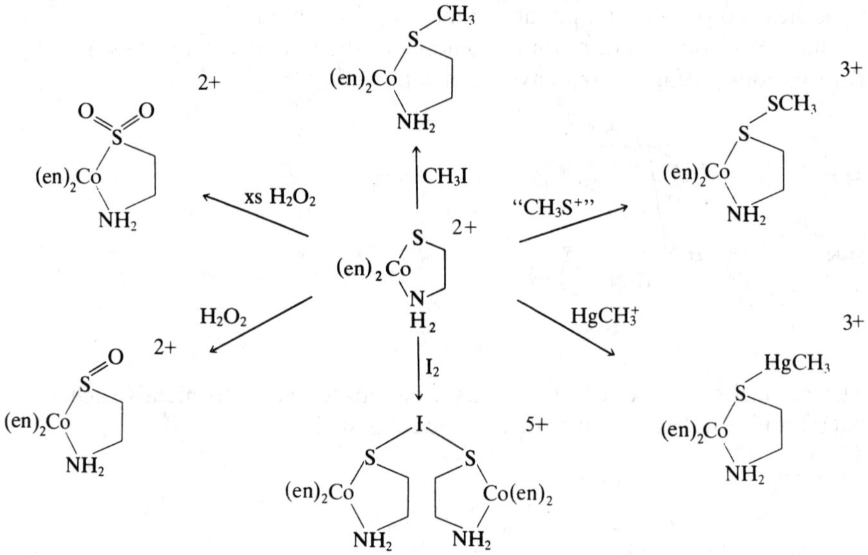

Scheme I

Synthetic aspects of the alkylation of coordinated thiols to yield coordinated thioethers (e.g. reaction with RX in Scheme I) have been reviewed by Livingstone[1] and more recently by Murray and Hartley[14]. Of more mechanistic interest is the fact that his reaction provides a probe for gauging the nucleophilicity of coordinated thiols.[109] Only two systems have been investigated in any detail: (1) alkylation of square planar thiolatonickel(II) complexes and (2) alkylation of octahedral thiolatocobalt(III) complexes and, to a much lesser extent, octahedral thiolato–chromium(III) complexes (Table 13).

Alkylation of the square planar thiolato–nickel(II) complex **C** occurs

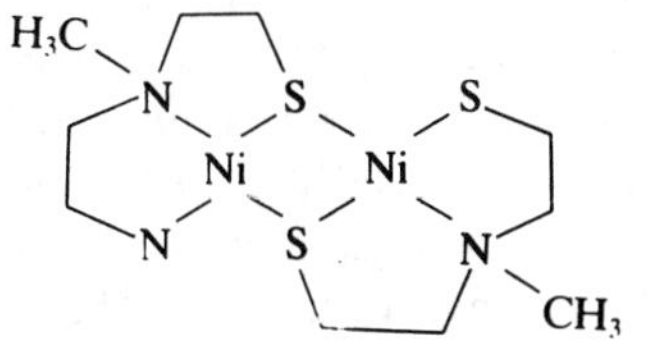

C

only on the terminal sulphur atoms, the second sulphur atom being alkylated more rapidly than the first.[196] Thus the rate law is simply $k(RX)(Ni_2L_2)$. The substitution-inert Pd(II) trimer **D** has no terminal sulphur atoms and does not undergo alkylation at any measurable rate. The very low reactivity of bridging thiolato sulphur atoms is readily understood from consideration of both steric and electronic factors.[196]. The more labile Ni(II) trimer **E**

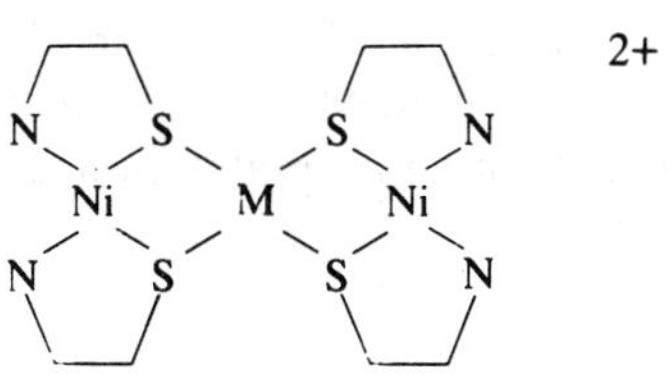

D: M = Pd   E: = M = Ni

undergoes dissociation into Ni^{2+} and two moles of $Ni(SCH_2CH_2NH_2)_2$, the terminal sulphur atoms of which then react with the alkylating agent.[196] This prior dissociation is reflected in the observed rate law $k(RX)(Ni_3L_4)/(Ni^{2+})^{1/2}$. The rate of alkylation decreases in the usual order $C_6H_5CH_2Br > CH_3I > CH_3Br > CH_3Cl$.

An analysis of activation parameters for the alkylation of square planar thiolato–nickel(II) complexes indicates an associative process which presumably involves the prior equilibrium

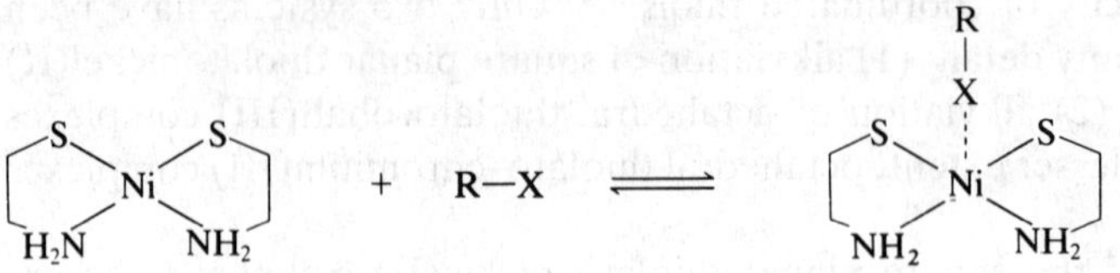

Prior coordination of the alkyl halide presumably weakens the R–X bond and facilitates nucleophilic attack by the coordinated sulphur atom. The existence of such an adduct is supported by the isolation of related thioether complexes with axially coordinated ligands (e.g. Ref. [197]) and by the observation of a nonlinear (RX) dependence in the benzyl bromide alkylation of certain N-substituted complexes.[198] Additional studies[199–201] have confirmed these general findings and provided some new information. The

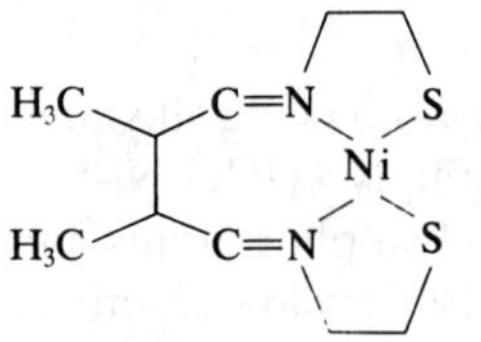

F

complex F is unusual in that the second alkylation reaction is slower than the first, and thus the monoalkylated product can be isolated. The aromatic 8-mercaptoquinoline complex G reacts slower than does the aliphatic analogue reflecting the greater steric requirements of an aromatic thiolato

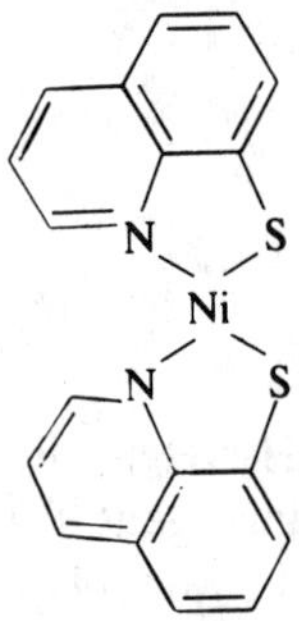

G

group. Systematic substitutions on the aromatic rings of complex G leads to a Hammett parameter $\rho = -2.9$ indicating that the thiolato moiety adds electron density to the transition state; this is entirely consistent with nucleophilic attack by the coordinated thiol. More recent work[202] has shown that the rate of alkylation of complex **H** is dependent on the chain length of the alkyl halide; for CH_3—$(CH_2)_n$—X the rate decreases along the series $n = 0 > 1 > 2 > 3 > 4$ confirming the expected order for nucleophilic displacement of X.

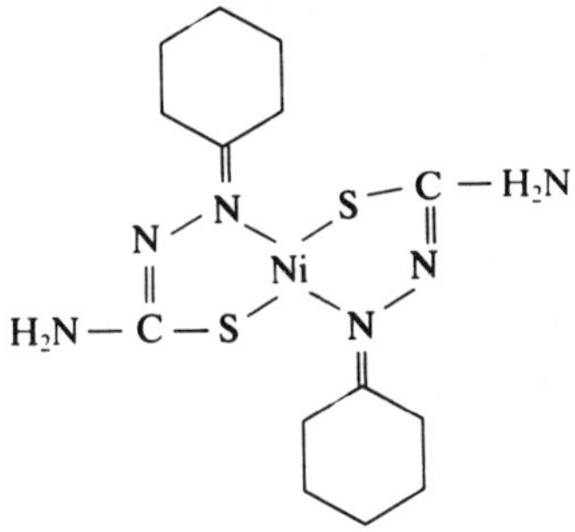

H

Since alkylation of four coordinate nickel(II) complexes proceeds by prior coordination of the alkyl halide to the metal centre, the rates of these reactions do not directly reflect the relative nucleophilicities of coordinated thiols. Rather, the net rate is determined additionally by the affinity of the central metal for the alkyl halide and the energy required to distort the five-coordinate intermediate. A more direct measure of the nucleophilicity of coordinated thiols and selenols has recently been obtained using coordinatively *saturated* octahedral complexes, rather than coordinatively

TABLE 12

Nucleophilicity constants for the reaction of chalcogen nucleophiles with iodomethane[a]

Nucleophile	$^nCH_3I$
$(C_6H_5CH_2)_2S$	4·84
$(C_6H_5CH_2)_2Se$	5·23
$(CH_3)_2S$	5·54
$(CH_3)_2Se$	6·32
C_6H_5SH	5·70
$C_6H_5S^-$	9·92
$C_6H_5Se^-$	~10·7
$[(en)_2Co(SCH_2CH_2NH_2)]^{2+}$	5·7

[a] Data from Ref. [109]. Conditions: 25°C, 100% methanol, no ionic strength control.

TABLE 13

Rates of alkylation of sulphur-containing compounds and metal complexes[a]

Compound (or complex)	Alkylating agent	Solvent	k_2 ($M^{-1}\,s^{-1}$)	ΔH^* (kcal mol^{-1})	Ref.
cis-Ni[Ni(SCH$_2$CH$_2$NH$_2$)$_2$]$^{2+b}$	CH$_3$I	CH$_3$OH	$1 \cdot 43 \times 10^{-3}$	$11 \cdot 7^c$	[196]
	C$_6$H$_5$CH$_2$Br	CH$_3$OH	9×10^{-3}	$10 \cdot 9^c$	[196]
cis-[Ni$_2$(CH$_3$N((CH$_2$CH$_2$S)$_2$)$_2$]^d	CH$_3$I	CHCl$_3$	$4 \cdot 2 \times 10^{-3}$	$10 \cdot 7^c$	[196]
	C$_6$H$_5$CH$_2$Br	CHCl$_3$	$2 \cdot 5 \times 10^{-3}$	$6 \cdot 91^c$	
cis-[Ni(SCH$_2$CH$_2$N = C(CH$_3$))$_2$]	C$_6$H$_5$CH$_2$Br	ClCH$_2$CH$_2$Cl	$0 \cdot 353^e$ / $9 \cdot 85 \times 10^{-3e}$	10	[198]
tr-[Ni(SCH$_2$CH$_2$N(CH$_3$)$_2$)$_2$]	C$_6$H$_5$CH$_2$Br	ClCH$_2$CH$_2$Cl	$0 \cdot 105$	$8 \cdot 8$	[199]
tr-[Ni(SCH$_2$CH$_2$NH(C$_3$H$_7$))$_2$]	C$_6$H$_5$CH$_2$Br	ClCH$_2$CH$_2$Cl	$0 \cdot 278$	$9 \cdot 4$	[199]
tr-[Ni(SCH$_2$CH$_2$NH(C$_8$H$_{17}$))$_2$]	C$_6$H$_5$CH$_2$Br	ClCH$_2$CH$_2$Cl	$0 \cdot 270$	—	[199]
tr-[Ni(SCH$_2$CH$_2$NH(C$_{10}$H$_{21}$))$_2$]	C$_6$H$_5$CH$_2$Br	ClCH$_2$CH$_2$Cl	$0 \cdot 312$	$10 \cdot 7$	[199]
cis-[Ni( )$_2$] 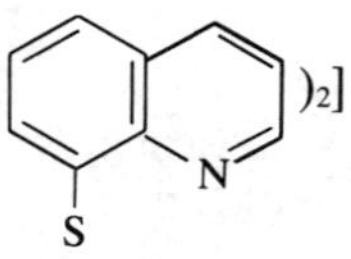	C$_6$H$_5$CH$_2$Br	CHCl$_3$	$4 \cdot 05 \times 10^{-3f}$	11	[200]
	C$_2$H$_5$CH$_2$Cl		$2 \cdot 55 \times 10^{-3f}$	11	
	CH$_3$I		$2 \cdot 12 \times 10^{-4}$	13	
cis-[Ni( )$_2$] 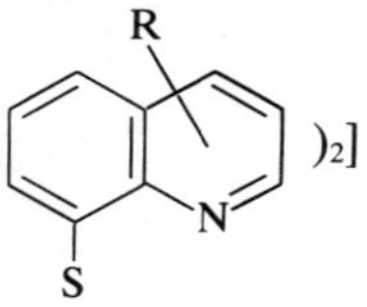					[201]

R = 5-chloro	CH_3I	$CHCl_3$	5.36×10^{-5g}	—	[109]
R = 5-nitro	$C_6H_5CH_2Br$		1.65×10^{-3g}	—	[109]
	CH_3I		$1\cdot48 \times 10^{-6g}$	—	[109]
	$C_6H_5CH_2Br$		4.73×10^{-4g}	—	[109]
$(en)_2Co(SCH_2CH_2NH_2)^{2+}$	CH_3I	65% DMF in H_2O	$8\cdot2 \times 10^{-3h}$	—	[109]
$(en)_2Co(SCH_2CO_2)^{+}$	CH_3I	65% DMF in H_2O	8.3×10^{-3h}	—	[109]
$(en)_2Cr(SCH_2CH_2NH_2)^{2+}$	CH_3I	65% DMF in H_2O	$6\cdot6 \times 10^{-3h}$	—	[109]
$(en)_2Co(SC_6H_4NH_2)^{2+}$	CH_3I	65% DMF in H_2O	$5\cdot1 \times 10^{-4h}$	—	[109]
$(en)_2Co(SeCH_2CH_2NH_2)^{2+}$	CH_3I	65% DMF in H_2O	$2\cdot5 \times 10^{-2h}$	—	[109]
CH_3CH_2SH	ethylene oxide	—	$7\cdot0 \times 10^{-2}$	—	[109]
$HOCH_2CH_2SH$	ethylene oxide	—	$4\cdot1 \times 10^{-2}$	—	[109]
C_6H_5SH	ethylene oxide	—	$2\cdot1 \times 10^{-2}$	—	[109]

[a] Rate constants at 25°C except where noted. Rate law = k[RX] [complex] except where noted. Rate constant for first alkylation step except where noted.

[b] Rate law = k[RX][Ni_3L_4]/[Ni^{2+}]$^{1/2}$.

[c] Actually E_a values.

, only terminal thiolates are alkylated.

[e] Rate constants for first and second alkylation steps, $k_1 > k_2$.

[f] 30°C.

[g] 30.4°C.

[h] [$HClO_4$] = 1·0 M.

unsaturated square planar complexes.[109] In a simple S_N2 mechanism the relative ordering of nucleophilicities toward CH_3I is

$$(en)_2Co(S(O)CH_2CH_2NH_2)^{2+} < (en)_2Co(SC_6H_4NH_2)^{2+}$$

$$< (en)_2Cr(SCH_2CH_2NH_2)^{2+} \cong (en)_2Co(SCH_2COO)^+$$

$$\cong (en)_2Co(SCH_2CH_2NH_2)^{2+} < (en)_2Co(SeCH_2CH_2NH_2)^{2+}.$$

Thus the nucleophilicity of the coordinated thiol is not affected by the central metal ($k_{Cr} = k_{Co}$), but is affected by the nature of the sulphur atom itself. Coordinated aromatic thiols are less nucleophilic than coordinated aliphatic thiols, consistent with what is known for noncoordinated thiols and with observations on thiolato–nickel(II) complexes.[200] The three-coordinated sulphur atom of the sulphenato complex $(en)_2Co(S(O)CH_2CH_2NH_2)^{2+}$ is much less nucleophilic than the two-coordinate sulphur atom of the thiolato complex $(en)_2Co(SCH_2CH_2NH_2)^{2+}$ as would be expected on the basis of steric and electronic considerations. Data in Table 12 show that noncoordinated thiols (RSH), noncoordinated thioethers (RSR′) and coordinated thiolates (RS—M) all have comparable nucleophilicities, and that these nucleophilicities are much less than that of a noncoordinated thiolate (RS⁻). Thus, the nucleophilicity of sulphur is strongly dependent on the number of groups bonded to sulphur but is relatively independent of the nature of the groups bonded to sulphur. This result is in harmony with observations on the H_2O_2 oxidation of thiolato complexes and related complexes.[83]

2. Dealkylation of coordinated thioethers

The dealkylation of coordinated thioethers to yield coordinated thiols has recently been reviewed,[14] this reaction being well documented only for square planar, d^8 metal centres. The mechanism is presumably the microscopic reverse of that delineated by Busch and co-workers[196] for the alkylation of coordinate thiols.

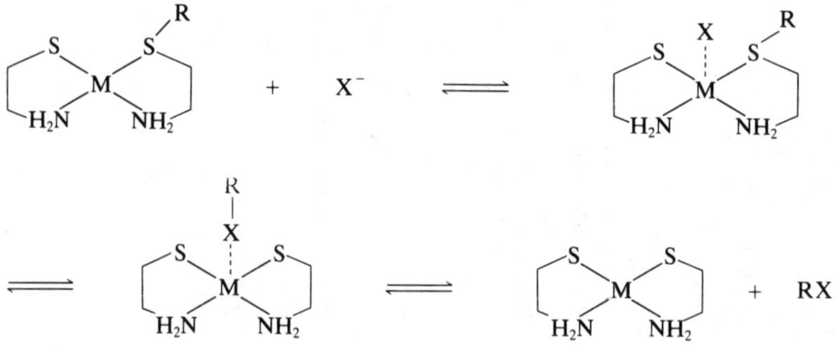

In this scheme the attacking nucleophile X first adds to the coordinatively unsaturated square planar metal centre and then the alkyl group R migrates from the coordinated sulphur atom to X; dissociation of RX to yield a thiolato complex completes the reaction sequence. While very few kinetic data have been obtained, the following observations concerning the nature of the dealkylation reaction are consistent with this scheme: (1) For various metal centres, rates decrease along the series Ni(II) > Pd(II) > Pt(II) reflecting the relative lability of the d^8 centre and thus the relative ease of generating the initial five-coordinate intermediate. (2) For different X groups, rates decrease along the series I^- > Br^- > Cl^- reflecting the relative nucleophilicities of the halide anions. (3) Dealkylation occurs, but dearylation does not occur; i.e. the migrating group must be aliphatic. (4) Dealkylation proceeds at a reasonable rate only when the nonmigrating group of the thioether is aromatic, and the rate is further enhanced if this group is perfluorinated; these factors promote cleavage of the S–R bond by destabilizing the R–S bond.

Kinetic observations on the dealkylation of $PdX_2(o\text{—}CH_3SC_6H_4PPh_2)$ by X^- (X^- = SCN^-, I^-) have recently been reported[203] and the results are consistent with the above scheme[292]. The observed rate law is $k(Pd)(X)$ and when X^- = SCN^- the reaction proceeds to completion in DMF to yield $CH_3\text{—}SCN$ rather than $CH_3\text{—}NCS$. Thus, initial attack on the coordinated thioether is by the more nucleophilic sulphur atom of NCS^-.

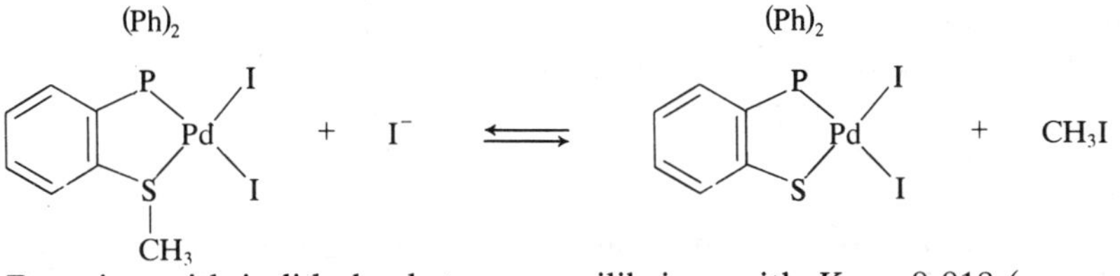

Reaction with iodide leads to an equilibrium with $K_{eq} = 0.018$ (measured by NMR), $k_f = 0.0034\ \text{M}^{-1}\text{s}^{-1}$ and $k_r = 0.25\ \text{M}^{-1}\text{s}^{-1}$ (77°C, mixed $CDCl_3$/CD_3CN solvent). The activation energies observed for demethylation of $PdI_2(o\text{—}CH_3SC_6H_4PPh_2)$ and S-adenosylmethionine are similar, indicating that coordination of thioether in an uncharged palladium(II) complex generates a methyl group of electrophilicity comparable to one in a sulphonium ion. This observation is consistent with the previously noted generalization that it is the *number* of groups bonded to sulphur, rather than the *nature* of these groups, that primarily determines the chemistry of the sulphur centre.

E. Intramolecular reactions

Several examples are known wherein sulphur-containing ligands participate in intramolecular processes. These processes range from simple ligand isomerizations (e.g. conversion of M—SCN to M—NCS) to complicated, multi-step, intraligand condensations which exemplify the effect of coordination upon reactions that are more usually associated with organic chemistry. This section briefly describes some of these examples, many of which are treated in more detail in other areas of the review.

The chemistry of thiocyanate and isothiocyanate complexes has been extensively reviewed,[204] and there have been several mechanistic investigations of the M—SCN to M—NCS intramolecular isomerization process. These mechanistic studies have involved "hard" chromium(III) and cobalt(III) centres wherein the N-bonded isomer is thermodynamically more stable. The spontaneous aquation and isomerization reactions of $(H_2O)_5CrSCN^{2+}$ appear to proceed through the same intimate ion-pair intermediate[205]:

$$(H_2O)_5CrSCN^{2+} \rightleftharpoons [(H_2O)_5Cr, SCN]^{2+} \xrightarrow{H_2O} \begin{array}{l} (H_2O)_6Cr^{3+} + SCN^- \\ (H_2O)_5CrNCS^{2+} \end{array}$$

Scheme II

This mechanism is suggested both by observed activation entropies (which reflect considerable charge separation in the transition state) and by previous observations on the anation of $(NH_3)_5CrOH_2^{3+}$ by SCN^-.[206,207a] The aquation and isomerization reaction of $(H_2O)_5CrSCN^{2+}$ proceeds through acid-independent and inverse-acid paths; since the ratio of isomerization to aquation products is pH-independent, it appears that both paths lead to the same ion-pair intermediate. The mercury(II)-assisted aquation and isomerization of $(H_2O)_5CrSCN^{2+}$ presumably proceeds through a $(H_2O)_5Cr—S(Hg)CN^{4+}$ intermediate which either aquates or rearranges to $(H_2O)_5CrNCS—Hg^{4+}$; the percentage of aquation product is greater than that observed for the unassisted reaction.

The ion-pair intermediate depicted in Scheme II presumably involves a dissociatively generated five-coordinate complex in loose association with a thiocyanate anion. To further characterize this type of intermediate, the aquation-isomerization reaction of $trans$-(en)$_2$Co(NH$_3$)(SCN)$^{2+}$ was investigated.[207] Both aquation and isomerization reactions lead to mixtures of cis and $trans$ isomers, supporting the participation of a dissociatively activated intermediate. In addition, isomerization occurs with very little incorporation of free $N^{14}CS^-$ from the bulk solution; this observation demands that the ion-pair be very tight (i.e. the thiocyanate ligand does not have time to exchange with thiocyanate in bulk solution). The limit of a "tight" ion pair would be one in which the thiocyanate ligand "slid" along π orbitals while proceeding from S-coordination to N-coordination; in this limit the thiocyanate would always retain some degree of bonding to the "five-coordinate" metal centre. Analysis of the *trans*-$(en)_2Co(NH_3)(SCN)^{2+}$ kinetic data leads to the conclusions that the sulphur atom of SCN^- has a four-fold greater affinity for the five-coordinate intermediate than does the nitrogen atom, and that S-bonded SCN^- is about as good a leaving group as is chloride.

The isomerization reactions of ammine sulphito–cobalt(III) complexes have recently been investigated in some detail by Harris and co-workers.[105,208,209] In all cases reaction of the aquo–cobalt(III) complex with SO_2 leads to the O-bonded sulphito complex by nucleophilic attack of a coordinated hydroxo group on coordinatively unsaturated SO_2. The fate of this initial O-bonded isomer then appears to be dependent on both the nature of the ancillary ammine ligands and the pH of the reaction medium. For $(NH_3)_5CoOSO_2^+$, and the *cis*- and *trans*-isomers of $(en)_2Co(OH_2)(OSO_2)^+$, decomposition occurs solely by intramolecular electron transfer (IET) to yield Co_{aq}^{2+} and ultimately SO_4^{2-}; no S-bonded isomers are observed. This is a somewhat surprising result given the successful synthesis of S-bonded $(NH_3)_5CoSO_3^+$ aquopentaammine-cobalt(III) and sodium sulphite in aqueous media,[11,256] but may result from differences in reaction conditions between the kinetic and synthetic studies. For $Co(tren)(OH_2)(OSO_2)^+$ (tren = 2,2′,2″-triaminotriethylamine) IET occurs only within a narrow pH range, the dominant reaction above pH 7·2 being addition of a second sulphito ligand.[208] This is similar to the reaction of sulphite with S-bonded *trans*-$(en)_2Co(OH_2)(SO_3)^+$ to yield an O-bonded species which subsequently rearranges to the S-bonded complex *trans*-$(en)_2Co(SO_3)_2^-$ with no detectable competition from IET.[210] Finally, for $(tetren)Co(OSO_2)^+$ (tetren = tetraethylenepentaammine) the only detectable reaction is rearrangement to the S-bonded isomer which is stable to IET decomposition.[209] Thus, the intramolecular reactions involving sulphite can include isomerization from O-bonded to S-bonded forms, intramolecular electron transfer to cobalt(III) from O-bonded sulphite and from S-bonded sulphite,[104] and labilization of the *trans*-situated ligand by S-bonded sulphite.[11] In general, if the S-bonded isomer can form before the O-bonded isomer undergoes IET or loses SO_2 by S–O bond fission, the resulting Co–S bond is very stable and generates a marked labilizing effect on the resulting complex. The factors which govern the relative rates of these competing processes have not yet been completely delineated. Comparisons with other systems do not clarify the situation. While syn-thetically $(NH_3)_5CoOH_2^{3+}$ reacts with SO_3^{2-} to yield only the S-bonded isomer, reaction with SeO_3^{2-} yields only the O-bonded isomer $(NH_3)_5CoOSeO_2^+$.[211,212] Also, only the O-bonded isomer is obtained upon reaction of SO_3^{2-} with $(H_2O)_6Cr^{3+}$.[213]

Intramolecular isomerizations of coordinated sulphoxides[214] and sulphinates[215] are important to the chemistries of these species, but have not been subject to detailed kinetic analyses. The photolytically generated O-bonded sulphinato complex $(en)_2Co(OS(O)CH_2CH_2NH_2)^{2+}$ slowly $(k = 10^{-7}\ s^{-1}$ at 25°C) reverts to the more stable S-bonded isomer.[216]

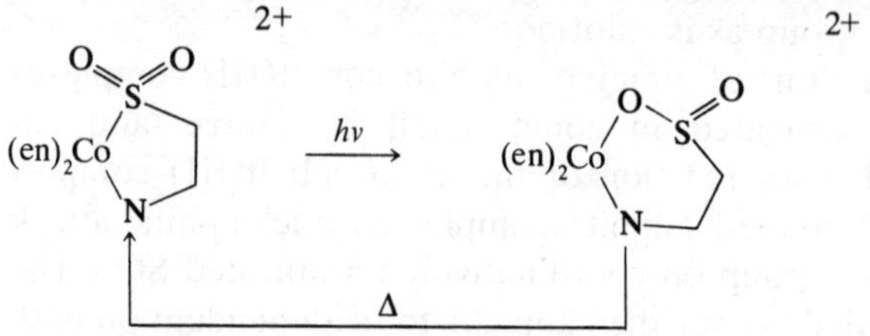

Contrariwise, the S-bonded sulphoxide complex $(en)_2Co(S(O)(CH_3)CH_2CH_2NH_2)^{3+}$, generated by methylation of the sulphenato complex $(en)_2Co(S(O)CH_2CH_2NH_2)^{2+}$, rearranges to the more stable O-bonded isomer:[217]

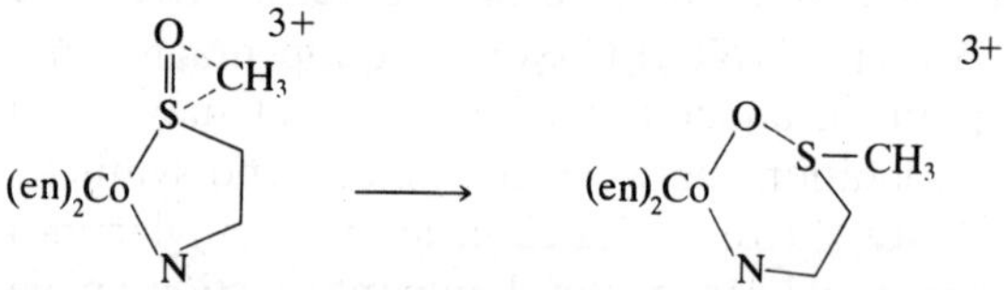

The position of the methyl group in the S-bonded species has not been determined. This reaction is reminiscent of the rearrangement of the S-bonded sulphoxide complex $Cl_2Hg—S(O)R_2$, generated by H_2O_2 oxidation of $Cl_2Hg—SR_2$, to the O-bonded isomer:[214]

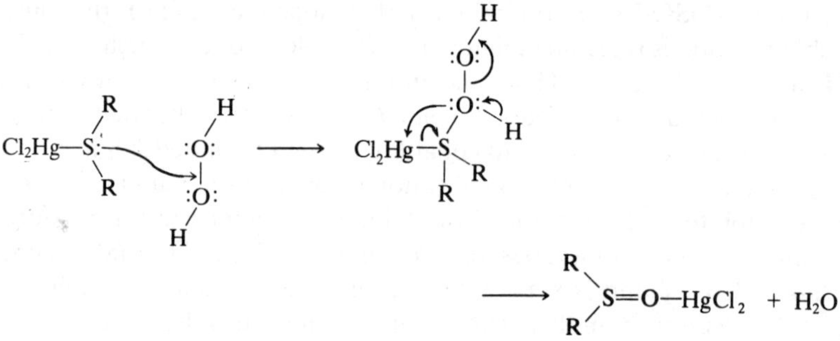

$$\longrightarrow \quad {R \atop R}{\Large\diagup}S{=}O{-}HgCl_2 + H_2O$$

Some of the more intricate intramolecular reactions that can occur with organo-sulphur ligands are illustrated in Section II.B.2. Initial oxidation of $(en)_2Co(cysteine—N,S)^{2+}$ leads to C–S bond fission; Co–O bond formation and S–N bond formation to yield an unusual sulphenamide complex.[78] Subsequent reactions of this sulphenamide complex[96,97] illustrate the diverse character of the reactions of coordinated organo-sulphur ligands (Section II.B.2).

F. Insertion reactions

Reactions wherein a small molecule or atom is inserted into a metal–carbon bond have been much studied because of their applicability to industrially important processes. The literature concerned with the insertion of S and SO_2 has been reviewed[215] and the mechanism of SO_2 insertion into $CpFe(CO)_2R$ complexes discussed in some detail. Reaction of these complexes in liquid SO_2 leads to rapid insertion to yield the S-bonded sulphinato complex $CpFe(CO)_2SO_2R$. Pertinent kinetic and stoichiometric observations on this system are as follows:

(1) The rate of insertion varies with R; $CH_3 \gg CH_2C(CH_3)_3$ and $CH_2CH(CH_3)_2 > CH_2C(CH_3)_3$.

(2) The stereochemistry at the M–R bond of $CpFe(CO)_2CHDCHDC(CH_3)_3$ shows inversion of configuration upon SO_2 insertion.

(3) The rate of insertion increases as the base strength of the ancillary ligands increases.

(4) When R = aryl, the Hammett substituent parameter ρ is $-4 \cdot 3$ indicating increased charge in the transition state.

(5) The rate of insertion increases as the polarity of the solvent increases, though this result is complicated by the high concentrations of SO_2 required to have the reactions proceed at a measurable rate.

(6) Rate data in organic solvents indicate that the reaction is first-order in complex and first-order in SO_2.

(7) In many reactions an O-bonded suphinato intermediate can be detected before it rearranges to the stable S-bonded form.

(8) The reaction is characterized by large negative activation entropies and small positive activation enthalpies.

These results imply an S_E2 mechanism with "backside attack" of the SO_2 on the coordinated carbon atom, and subsequent rearrangement of the resulting intimate ion-pair to either the S- or O-bonded sulphinato complex. The O-bonded form can then rapidly isomerize to the S-bonded form. Recent work[218, 219] confirms that SO_2 insertion leads to inversion of configuration at the carbon atom and retention of configuration at the metal, in accordance with this mechanism. However, as Wojcicki notes,[215] not all results are compatible with this mechanism, and certainly the mechanism is not applicable to square planar complexes which (as noted previously for methylation reactions) can proceed through a five-coordinate intermediate. One interesting complication arises during the SO_2 insertion into $CpFe(CO)_2CH_2C(R) = CR'R''$; this reaction yields the two products (**I** and **II**):

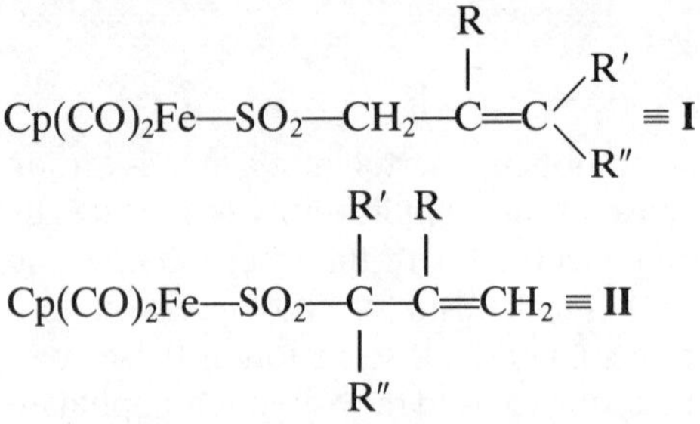

$$Cp(CO)_2Fe-SO_2-CH_2-\underset{\underset{R}{|}}{C}=C\underset{R''}{\overset{R'}{<}} \equiv I$$

$$Cp(CO)_2Fe-SO_2-\underset{\underset{R''}{|}}{\overset{\overset{R'\ R}{|\ \ |}}{C}}-C=CH_2 \equiv II$$

The first product results from normal insertion into the Fe–C bond while the second product derives from attack of SO_2 on the outermost carbon atom and subsequent rearrangement to the S-bonded form through a π-bonded intermediate. Recent work[220] has shown that the ordering of rates of insertion of SO_2 into cis-$Fe(R)(I)(CO)_4$ in DMF is $R = CF_3 < C_2F_5 < C_6F_{13}$, although both the stoichiometry and mechanism of this reaction are unclear.

Very little kinetic data are available on the reverse of the insertion reaction, i.e. disinsertion. the only reaction studied in any detail is

$$RSO_2Ir(PPh_3)_2Cl_2 \longrightarrow trans\text{-}IrCl_2(PPh_3)_2(R)(SO_2)$$

When R = aryl the presence of electron-withdrawing groups on the aryl moiety increases the rate of reaction; the reaction is slower when R = alkyl than when R = aryl; the reaction rate is decreased as more branching groups are added to the alkyl moiety. These data imply a mechanism wherein the R–SO_2 bond is stretched in the transition state to yield a transient cis isomer which rapidly rearranges to the more stable $trans$ form.[215]

Insertion of elemental sulphur into metal–nonmetal bonds has recently been briefly reviewed.[16,221] Mass spectral evidence shows that photochemical insertion of S into complexes of the general structure **A** (M = Zn, Ni) occurs between the carbon and sulphur atoms and *not* between the metal and sulphur atoms.[222] The related reverse reaction, i.e. abstraction of the sulphur atom by triphenylphosphine, is first-order in both phosphine and complex, the sulphur atom extracted being that which was inserted.[223,224] It also appears that when M = Zn the ^{34}S-labelled sulphur atom "scrambles" and the resultant complex contains ^{34}S at all possible positions.

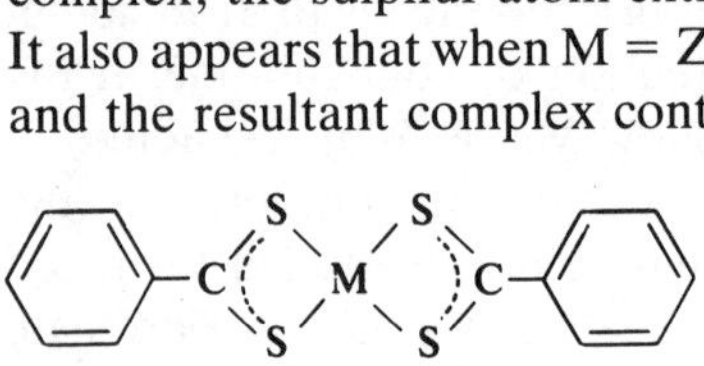

A

G. *Trans* effects

Trans effects, especially as detected in square-planar complexes, have been the subject of many review articles[225,226] and have been included in a large number of reviews and books dedicated to reaction mechanisms of transition metal complexes. Most relevant to this section are reviews on *cis* and *trans* effects in cobalt(III) complexes,[227] *trans* activation in cobalt(III) complexes,[228] and the measurement and significance of *trans* effects.[225] In this section the "*trans* influence" versus "*trans* effect" nomenclature proposed by Appleton, Clark and Manzer[225] is not used since this terminology is unnecessarily restrictive and confusing. Instead the more descriptive and pragmatic nomenclature advocated by Pratt and Thorp is adopted. A *trans* effect is defined as the change in some property of a ligand A (or of the M–A bond) which occurs on changing the group *trans* to A from X to Y, all other factors remaining constant; the structural *trans* effect (STE), therefore refers to the change in the M–A bond length, a purely ground state phenomenon; the kinetic *trans* effect (KTE) refers to the change in the rate of substitution of A by another ligand, a phenomenon involving both the ground state and transition state. Within this nomenclature there are also thermodynamic *trans* effects, NMR *trans* effects, etc., which will not be discussed here. The various *trans* effects are obviously related to one another, and indeed it has recently been shown that for ammine–cobalt(III) complexes which exhibit sulphur-induced *trans* effects, log (KTE) depends linearly on STE.[229]

1. Square-planar complexes

Substitution reactions of square-planar complexes have been extensively studied and reviewed.[225,226] Analysis of the KTE in these reactions is complicated by the associative nature of the process.[230,231] Thus, the rate of substitution is determined to a large extent by the ability of the metal centre to adopt a five-coordinate geometry, both π-accepting and σ-donating ligands stabilizing the proposed trigonal pyramidal transition state. While not always readily interpretable, considerable data have been obtained on *trans*-labilized substitution reactions of platinum(II) centres and a consistent KTE series has been constructed.[230] This series appears to hold for reactions at Ni(II), Pd(II), Rh(I), Ir(I) and Au(III) centres, although data are relatively scarce for these metals. For sulphur-containing ligands the KTE series is $NH_3 \simeq (CH_3)_2S < (CH_3CH_2)_2S < (CH_3)_2S = 0$[232,233] and the KTE of thiourea is about the same as that of CH_3^-.[230]

2. Octahedral complexes

Interpretation of the KTE in octahedral complexes is simplified relative to square planar complexes since substitutions on octahedral complexes proceed predominantly through dissociatively activated transition states and thus the nature of the incoming ligand has less effect on the observed rate. Also, most of the octahedral complexes studied to date contain either ammine or aquo leaving ligands, and since these species do not have low-lying π orbitals they bond to the metal centre through essentially pure σ interactions. Using these advantages, a systematic effort has been made to understand the nature of the sulphur-induced KTE in cobalt(III) complexes.[11,229,234,235]

Essentially all *trans*-labilized substitutions on octahedral complexes follow the general rate law

$$k_{obsd} = \frac{A + BC[L]}{1 + C[L]} \tag{9}$$

where L represents the incoming ligand and the leaving ligand is a solvent molecule. Thus, as the concentration of the incoming ligand is increased, the observed ligation rate becomes less than first-order in L and eventually zero-order in L at sufficiently high concentrations of L ($k_{obsd} = B$). More often observed is the situation where at low concentrations of L the denominator term is not detectable and thus $k_{obsd} = A + BC[L]$. As previously noted for the reactions of the *trans*-bis(dimethylglyoximato)-cobalt(III) and *trans*-bis(ethylenediamine)cobalt(III) complexes T–Co–S (T = *trans*-labilizing group, S = solvent) this rate law is consistent with both a limiting S_N1 mechanism and a prior association mechanism.[234,236]

Limiting S_N1 mechanism

$$T\!-\!Co\!-\!S \underset{k_2}{\overset{k_1}{\rightleftarrows}} T\!-\!Co + S \qquad L + T\!-\!Co \underset{k_4}{\overset{k_3}{\rightleftarrows}} T\!-\!Co\!-\!L$$

$$k_{obsd} = \frac{k_4 + \dfrac{k_1 k_3}{k_2'}[L]}{1 + \dfrac{k_3}{k_2'}[L]} \qquad k_2' = k_2[S] \tag{10}$$

$$A = k_4 \qquad B = k_1 \qquad C = \frac{k_3}{k_2'} = \frac{k_3}{k_2[S]}$$

Within this mechanism the observed rate parameter B represents the specific rate of formation of the five-coordinate intermediate by Co–S bond fission, A represents the specific rate of formation of this intermediate by Co–L bond fission, and C represents the competition ratio for reaction of the steady state intermediate with L and S.

Prior association mechanism

$$L + T\!-\!Co\!-\!S \overset{K}{=\!=} T\!-\!Co\!-\!S, L \qquad T\!-\!Co\!-\!S, L \underset{k_6}{\overset{k_5}{\rightleftarrows}} T\!-\!Co\!-\!L + S$$

$$k_{obsd} = \frac{k_6' + (k_5 + k_6')K[L]}{1 + K[L]} \qquad k_6' = k_6[S] \tag{11}$$

$$A = k_6' \qquad B = k_5 + k_6' \qquad C = K$$

Within this mechanism the observed rate parameter C represents the equilibrium constant controlling association of the entering ligand with the complex, A represents the specific rate of attack of S on the Co–L bond, while B represents a sum of specific rates.

Most mechanistic discussions concerning the KTE in octahedral complexes centre around distinguishing between the limiting S_N1 and the prior association mechanisms, although this issue is often confused by the use of various nomenclatures to identify these two mechanisms. Probably the most useful nomenclature is that of Langford and Gray[231] in which the limiting S_N1 mechanism is referred to as D (representing dissociative) and the prior association mechanism is referred to as I_d (representing dissociative interchange). This nomenclature is advantageous since it focuses on the dissociative nature of these *trans*-labilization processes and highlights the fact that there is a continuum of transition states ranging from that of the D process through that of the I_d process. It is reasonably anticipated that strongly *trans*-labilizing ligands such as *S*-bonded sulphite will operate more on the D end of this continuum, while weaker *trans*-labilizing ligands such as S-bonded thiosulphate will operate on the I_d end, and this does appear to be the situation for ammine–cobalt(III) complexes.[11,229]

The parameter most useful in distinguishing between the limiting S_N1 and prior association mechanisms is B, the value of the limiting rate at high concentrations of L. Within the limiting S_N1 mechanism, B should be independent of the nature of L since it represents the specific rate of Co–S bond cleavage; but within the prior association mechanism B is very likely to be dependent on the nature of L since it represents in part the rate of Co–L bond cleavage. Thus it is very important in these studies to determine limiting rates for a wide variety of entering groups; unfortunately, excessively high concentrations of L are often required to observe deviations from first-order behaviour. If the limiting rate B *does* depend on the nature of L, and if the experimental conditions necessary to observe the limiting rate do not introduce any artifacts, then it can be safely concluded that the prior association mechanism is operative. If B *does not* depend on the nature of L then it is very probable that the S_N1 mechanism is operative, but this conclusion is not absolutely definitive since similar B values could arise by happenstance. Positive evidence for the operation of the prior association mechanism can also be obtained by adding a relatively unreactive ligand, L', to the reaction solution. This should have no effect in the limiting S_N1 mechanism, but within the prior association mechanism it will retard the formation of T—Co—L by tying up T—Co—S as unproductive T—Co—S,L' and thus reducing the concentration of productive T—Co—S,L.[209,229] Also, within the prior association scheme, derived values of C should agree with values of outer-sphere association constants (K_{os}) either observed experimentally[238,239] or calculated theoretically;[240,241] for +1 charged complexes, K_{os} values are expected to be in the range $0\cdot1-0\cdot2\ \text{M}^{-1}$ for uncharged ligands, $0\cdot3-1\cdot0\ \text{M}^{-1}$ for −1 charged ligands, and $10-20\ \text{M}^{-1}$ for −2 charged ligands. Unfortunately, attempts to distinguish between the S_N1 limiting and prior association mechanisms are often made on the basis of very indirect arguments (e.g. values of activation parameters) and without the availability of the crucial limiting rates. It should be especially noted that the easily accessible second-order rate parameters for *trans*-labilization correspond to the term BC in Equation (9) and therefore are not necessarily independent of the nature of L within either of the two mechanisms. However, within the S_N1 limiting mechanism, if the five-coordinate intermediate is very reactive, then the competition ratio C will be ~1 and BC will approximately be equal to B, and thus the second-order rate parameter *can* be independent of the nature of L. The difficulties inherent in distinguishing between the S_N1 limiting and prior association mechanisms on the basis of limited data are amply illustrated by two recent studies on the *trans*-labilized ligation reactions of *trans*-$(en)_2Co(SO_3)(OH_2)^+$. Studying exactly the same reaction, one group of researchers[242] assigned an S_N1 limiting mechanism on the basis of second-order rate parameters, while a second group[236] assigned a prior association mechanism on the basis of limiting rate data. This second group has also re-analysed the original data obtained for *trans*-labilized substitutions onto $(NH_3)_5CoSO_3^+$.[243] While these data were initially interpreted as indicating the limiting S_N1 mechanism, re-analysis shows that they are equivalently well described within the prior association mechanism.[236]

(a) *Ammine–cobalt(III) complexes.* Until recently the only sulphur-containing ammine–cobalt(III) complexes available for mechanistic investigation were those containing S-bonded sulphite. Dating from the early observations of Halpern and co-workers[243] it has been known that S-bonded sulphite generates a strong *trans* labilizing effect on the cobalt(III) centre—ligands situated *trans* to SO_3^{2-} undergo substitution 10^6–10^8 times faster than when they are situated *trans* to NH_3.[236] This effect is specific for the *trans* site, *cis* labilization being so slight as to be undetectable. Early considerations of this phenomenon[244] were concerned with whether it resulted from a ground state effect or a transition state effect. This is a difficult point to decide when only *S*-bonded sulphito systems are available, but even using data restricted to sulphite systems recent work[236] has shown to be improbable an early, strained, explanation of the *trans* labilizing ability of SO_3^{2-} as resulting from a special transition state bonding arrangement.[244] More recent results on other *S*-bonded ligands has totally debunked this original explanation.[11,234]

Recently there have become available sulphur-containing ammine–cobalt(III) complexes suitable for mechanistic investigation that contain *S*-bonded sulphinato (RSO_2^-) and thiosulphato ($S_2O_3^{2-}$) ligands.[11,229] Combined kinetic and structural studies of SO_3^{2-}, RSO_2^- and $S_2O_3^{2-}$ complexes make it clear that the sulphur-induced kinetic *trans* effect (KTE) arises either totally or in great part from a ground state phenomenon.[229] Structural studies on the *S*-bonded complexes (NH_3)$_5$Co—SO_3^+, (NH_3)$_5$Co—SO_2R^{2+} [11] and (NH_3)$_5$Co—$S_2O_3^+$ [59] show that the structural *trans* effect (STE) induced by the coordinated sulphur atom decreases along the series $SO_3^{2-} > RSO_2^- > S_2O_3^{2-}$. Kinetic studies on the *S*-bonded complexes (NH_3)$_5$Co—SO_3^+, (NH_3)$_5$Co—SO_2R^{2+},[11] *trans*-(en)$_2$Co(SO_3)(OH_2)$^+$,[236] and *trans*-(en)$_2$Co(S_2O_3)(OH_2)$^+$ [229] show that the KTE decreases along the same series. This correlation is to be expected on the simple basis that a longer metal–ligand bond is a weaker bond which should be more readily cleaved no matter what the detailed mechanism.

A quantitative treatment of the above STE–KTE correlation is not straightforward for a variety of reasons, most especially the imprecision inherent in the STE determinations and the lack of basic understanding as to the electronic origins of *trans* effects. However, a nascent model for the quantitative analysis of STE–KTE interrelationships has been presented.[11] This model assumes (1) a simple harmonic oscillator description for stretching the *trans* Co–L bond, and (2) that the different ΔH^* values governing the KTE arise from the different energies necessary to stretch the *trans* Co–L bonds from their ground state distances to some *common* transition state distance R*. Using this model R* is calculated to be 3·2 Å, in excellent agreement with the 3·0–3·2 Å distance obtained[245] from volume of activation measurements. Moreover, assuming that relative ΔH^* values can be approximated by relative ΔG^* values (i.e. that ΔS^* remains constant, or varies linearly with ΔH^*, throughout the series), the model predicts that log(KTE) should be linearly dependent on STE. Figure 2 shows a plot of log(KTE) against STE and within the relatively large experimental uncertainties on STE this plot is indeed linear. Thus, it is clear that at least a large portion of the decrease in activation energy governing labilized *trans* ligand substitution (KTE) arises from the ground state weakening of the *trans* metal–ligand bond (STE); i.e., for sulphur-containing cobalt(III) complexes, *trans* labilization results from a ground state phenomenon.

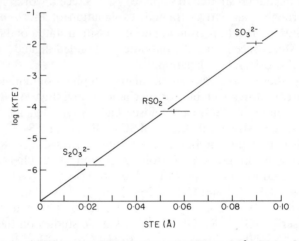

Fig. 2. Log(KTE) against STE for *S*-bonded ligands SO_3^{2-}, RSO_2^-, $S_2O_3^{2-}$.

From these results on the KTE and STE in ammine–cobalt(III) complexes, and other KTE observations on bis(dimethylglyoximato)cobalt(III) complexes,[235] it appears likely that sulphur-induced *trans* effects result from donation of sigma electron density into the *trans* Co–L bond. This is the classic "sigma *trans* effect" first described for platinum(II) complexes.[231] Certainly for the *trans* ligands NH_3 and H_2O, metal–ligand π bonding is insignificant and these ligands must experience *trans* effects solely through the σ bonding system. Thus, the greater the tendency of a sulphur-bonded ligand to donate electron density into the sigma orbital that it shares with the *trans* situated ligand, the greater the resulting STE and KTE. Sigma donation by a sulphur ligand can be increased by increasing the formal negative charge on the coordinated sulphur atom, and, possibly, by synergistic π back-bonding from the cobalt centre to the coordinated sulphur atom. Consistent with this "sigma *trans* effect" view, for cobalt(III) complexes the extent of the sulphur-induced STE is directly correlated with the formal negative charge on the coordinated sulphur atom: $SO_3^{2-} > RSO_2^-$, RSO^-, RS^-, $RC(O)S^- > R_2S$, RSSR, $S_2O_3^{2-}$.[90] Also consistent with this view, the presence of the STE is correlated with the length of the Co–S bond, a shorter, stronger Co–S bond inducing a longer, weaker *trans* Co–L bond. These STE correlations predict that ammine–cobalt(III) complexes containing neutral sulphur ligands (or coordinated sulphur atoms that bear a zero formal negative charge) will not exhibit a marked KTE; this is indeed the situation in both $(NH_3)_5CoS_2O_3^+$ [59] and the thioether complex **A**

$(1,8\text{-diamino-3,6-dithiaoctane})CoX_2^+$

which does not exhibit a KTE for either spontaneous or Hg(II)-catalysed chloride aquation.[246]

Some additional miscellaneous observations on sulphite-induced substitution in ammine–cobalt(III) complexes warrant brief comment. Isotope labelling experiments show conclusively that in $(NH_3)_5CoSO_3^+$ it is *only* the *trans*-NH$_3$ that is labilized.[294] The reaction of SO_3^{2-} with *trans*-$(en)_2Co(SO_3)(OH_2)^+$ leads to the O-bonded intermediate *trans*-$(en)_2Co(SO_3)(OSO_2)^-$ which then rapidly ($t_{1/2} \sim 10$ msec) rearranges to the *S*-bonded product *trans*-$(en)_2Co(SO_3)_2^-$.[210] The rate of this isomerization process is $\sim 10^5$ times faster than the comparable isomerization of $(tetren)CoOSO_3^+$ to $(tetren)CoSO_3^+$,[209] reflecting *trans* labilization by *S*-bonded sulphite in an intramolecular process. The trimethylenediammine complex *trans*-$(tn)Co(SO_3)(OH_2)^+$ undergoes sulphite-labilized substitution 10–25 times faster than the analogous ethylenediamine complex *trans*-$(en)_2Co(SO_3)(OH)^+$, presumably because in the *ground state* the five-membered en rings are more stable than the six-membered tn rings.[242] This explanation is in harmony with the arguments presented above ascribing the KTE to predominantly ground state phemonena. Substitution onto the labilized *trans*-$(en)_2(Co(SO_3)(OH_2)^+$ centre allows the facile synthesis of binuclear species such as $(CN)_5FeCNCo(en)_2(SO_3)^{3-}$.[247]

(b) Bis(dimethylglyoximato)cobalt(III) complexes. Two detailed studies[234,235] on ligation reactions of the *S*-bonded complexes *trans*-SO_3—$Co(DH)_2$—$MeOH^-$ and *trans*-RSO_2—$Co(DH)_2$—MeOH in methanol provide data and arguments that strongly indicate operation of the S_N1 limiting mechanism. These data and arguments discounting the prior

association mechanism are much more compelling in the dimethylglyoximato system than in the ammine–cobalt(III) systems for two reasons. First, *trans* labilization in the SO_3^{2-} and RSO_2^- complexes can be placed in a larger framework by comparison with other $T—Co(DH)_2—MeOH$ complexes where T is a *trans* labilizing group that does not contain sulphur, e.g. CH_3^-. Such related complexes are not available in the ammine–cobalt(III) systems. Second, the electrostatic driving forces for prior association of the entering ligand with the cobalt complex can be minimized by the use of neutral dimethylglyoximato complexes and neutral entering ligands. Prior association is much more favoured for the water-soluble, cationic, ammine–cobalt(III) complexes.

The arguments supporting assignment of the S_N1 limiting mechanism rather than the prior association mechanism can be summarized as follows:

(1) Using the neutral $RSO_2—Co(DH)_2—MeOH$ complex and the neutral entering ligands thiourea and *p*-toluidine, the observed limiting rate is independent of the entering ligand.[234] Limiting rates observed for the anionic sulphito complex and the neutral methyl complex are also independent of the nature of the entering ligand.[235]

(2) For systems in which limiting rates cannot be obtained, observed second-order rate parameters are relatively independent of the entering ligand, implying a reactive five-coordinate intermediate (*vide supra*).

(3) Derived values of C are much too large to be ascribed to outersphere association between the complex and the neutral entering ligands. For the anionic complex $SO_3—Co(DH)_2—MeOH^-$, K_{os} is calculated to be $\sim 0.5 \, M^{-1}$, whereas the observed value of C is $4.7 \, M^{-1}$.[235]

(4) The observed rate parameter B is independent of ionic strength, a result which is entirely consistent with the limiting S_N1 mechanism ($B = k_1$, the specific rate of dissociative cobalt–methanol bond fission, is expected to be independent of ionic strength) but which is difficult to rationalize within the prior association mechanism ($B = k_5 + k_6'$, the rates of exchange between the inner and outer coordination spheres, should be strongly dependent on ionic strength).

In addition, the observation of relatively invariant C values ($\sim 1 \, M^{-1}$) has been presented in support of the S_N1 limiting mechanism being operative in the ligation of $RSO_2—Co(DH)_2—X$ and $(C_6H_5)_3CS—Co(DH)_2—X$ (X = a variety of neutral ligands).[248] However, the pitfalls associated with this type of argument are well known.[234,249]

Figure 3 shows that for the series of complexes $T—Co(DH)_2—MeOH$ with $T = CH_3^-$, $C_6H_5^-$, SO_3^{2-}, $(CH_3O)_2P(O)^-$ and *p*-$CH_3C_6H_4SO_2^-$, log(KTE) is linearly dependent on the Hammett substituent parameter σ_p of the group T (KTE = $B_T/B_{p\text{-}CH_3C_6H_5SO_2^-}$ where $B = k_1$ = specific rate of Co–MeOH bond fission). This shows directly that it is the ability of the *trans* labilizing ligand T to donate sigma electron density to the cobalt centre that is the predominant factor in effecting the KTE. A similar analysis of the rates of Co–thiourea bond fission shows that the relative *trans* labilizing ability of the T group is independent of the nature of the leaving group. These results are entirely consistent with the "σ *trans* effect" description developed above for the ammine–cobalt(III) system.

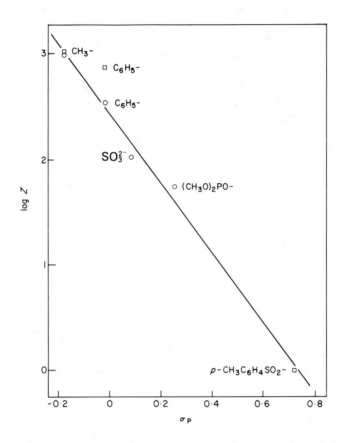

Fig. 3. Log Z against σ_p for R ligand in R—Co(DH)$_2$HOCH$_3$, where Z = KTE.

This correlation of the KTE with Hammett σ_p parameters has been challenged by Marzilli,[250] but the challenge is based on the results of a totally inappropriate system. Marzilli has shown that the rate of bromide-induced C–O bond fission in a coordinated phosphite is highly correlated with the ^{13}C NMR chemical shift of the phosphite carbon atom:

$$Br^- + (CH_3O)_3P-Co(DH)_2-X$$
$$\longrightarrow CH_3Br + (CH_3O)_2P(O)-Co(DH)_2X$$

However, this is no surprise since it has been known for some time that the rate of ester hydrolysis correlates very well with the ^{13}C NMR chemical shift of the carbon atom being attacked. The chemical shift data monitor the electron density at the carbon atom, and of course the electron density at the carbon atom directly affects the rate of nucleophilic attack. This correlation is true whether or not the ester is coordinated to a metal centre, and thus Marzilli's observed correlation is in no way determined by the *trans* effect of X.

Two other studies on bis(dimethylglyoximato)cobalt(III) complexes warrant mention. In a brief report on thiourea and thiosulphato complexes it was noted that thiourea is as efficient as SO_3^{2-} in labilizing the *trans*-situated ligand.[182] The *trans* effect of various ligands was gauged by the ratio of S/N-bonded thiocyanate in $X-Co(DH)_2-(CNS)$ complexes.[251]

(c) Comparison of cobalt(III) systems. A final, persuasive, argument in favour of sulphur-induced *trans* labilization proceeding through the S_N1 limiting mechanism can be made by comparing results from the dimethylglyoximato–cobalt(III) and ammine–cobalt(III) systems. Specifically, the relative *trans* labilizing ability of SO_3^{2-} and RSO_2^- are the same in both systems. Using limiting rate, for cleavage of the $TCo(DH)_2-MeOH$ bond in MeOH $k_{SO_3}/k_{p-CH_3C_6H_4SO_2} = 111 \pm 7$,[235] and for cleavage of the $T(NH_3)_4Co-NH_3$ bond in aqueous media $k_{SO_3}/k_{p-CH_3C_6H_4SO_2} = 120 \pm 4$.[11] Thus the relative abilities of SO_3^{2-} and RSO_2^- to promote *trans*-labilization in cobalt(III) are independent of the nature of the leaving ligand, entering ligand, *cis* ligands, solvent, formal charges, etc. This result is readily explicable within the limiting S_N1 formalism, i.e. the relative rates of dissociative bond cleavage are primarily dependent on the nature of the *trans* ligand. However, the rationalization of this result within the prior association mechanism would require an unrealistically fortuitous cancellation of several factors.

(d) Chromium(III) complexes. The coordinated sulphur atom of $(H_2O)_5CrSR^{n+}$ complexes[24] and of $(H_2O)_5CrSH^{2+}$[184] labilizes the *trans* coordination site towards substitution by a variety of ligands. However, incorporation of a ligand into the *trans* site in turn labilizes Cr–S bond fission and the final reaction products are $(H_2O)_5CrL^{n+}$ and RSH. The mechanism of this complicated process appears to involve a modified Moore–Basolo–Pearson scheme:[24,252]

$$L + (H_2O)_5CrSR \stackrel{K_{os}}{\rightleftharpoons} (H_2O)CrSR,L$$

$$(H_2O)_5CrSR,L \underset{k_2}{\stackrel{k_1}{\rightleftharpoons}} \textit{trans}\text{-}(H_2O)_4Cr(SR)(L) + H_2O$$

$$H_3O^+ + \textit{trans}\text{-}(H_2O)_4Cr(SR)(L) \stackrel{k_3}{\longrightarrow} (H_2O)_5CrL + HSR$$

Detailed kinetic analysis of this complicated system shows that, relative to H_2O, RS^- or H_2S enhance the rate of ligation of chromium(III) by factors of 10^3–10^4. Contrary to the cobalt(III) systems, substitution of L on to the site *trans* to sulphur appears to have considerable associative character,[24] as expected for a chromium(III) centre.[253]

(e) Ruthenium(II) complexes. In the pentaammineruthenium(II) system, coordinated sulphur(IV) produces a marked *trans* labilization and a small *cis* delabilization.[254,255] Thus, the rate of Ru–NH$_3$ bond fission *trans* to SO_3^{2-} is 6000 time faster than when *trans* to NH$_3$, and the rate of Ru–OH$_2$ bond breaking is 250–300 times faster than when *trans* to NH$_3$. These labilizations are much smaller than those observed in the cobalt(III) systems, but are similar in magnitude to those observed in chromium(III). Among the various forms of coordinated sulphur(IV), *trans* labilizing ability decreases $SO_3^{2-} > HSO_3^- > SO_2$ in parallel with decreasing sigma donating ability. This result is quite in harmony with the above discussions of the "σ trans effect" in cobalt(III) complexes, but it must be noted that no evidence is available as to whether the labilized ruthenium(II) substitutions proceed through a dissociatively activated intermediate. In the related complexes $(NH_3)_5RuE(CH_3)_2^{2+}$ with E = S, Se, Te the *trans*-NH$_3$ is also labilized, the rate of substitution decreasing along the series $Te(CH_3)_2 > Se(CH_3)_2 > S(CH_3)_2$.[7,102] Interestingly, whereas reaction of 4-cyanopyridine with the thioether complex $(NH_3)_5RuS(CH_3)_2^{2+}$ leads to *trans*-(CN-py)(NH$_3$)$_4$RuS(CH$_3$)$_2^{2+}$, reaction of this ligand with the thiolato complex $(NH_3)_5RuS(H)C_2H_5^{2+}$ leads to Ru–S bond breaking,[13] presumably via the Moore–Basolo–Pearson scheme outlined above for chromium(III) complexes.[24,252]

IV. AFFINITIES

The affinities of sulphur-containing ligands for metal ions are intimately intertwined with the reactions of metal–sulphur species. Often the driving force for bonding of a sulphur species determines whether or not a reaction

TABLE 14

Rate parameters for substitution reactions at position *trans* to sulphur ligands in octahedral complexes[a]

Complex[b]	X[c]	Solvent	L[b]	A (s^{-1})	B (s^{-1})	BC ($M^{-1}\,s^{-1}$)	C (M^{-1})	ΔH^* (kcal mol⁻¹)	ΔS^* (eu)	Conditions[n]	Ref.
Sulphite Complexes											
tr-[Co(DH)₂(X)SO₃]⁻	CH₃OH	CH₃OH	S=C(NH₂)₂	—	24·7	—	2·8	—	—	I = 0·1 M	[235]
	CH₃OH	CH₃OH		—	24·6	—	4·7	—	—	I ≅ 0	[235]
	CH₃OH	CH₃OH	p-CH₃C₆H₄NH₂	—	34·6	—	0·75	—	—	I ≅ 0	[235]
	CH₃OH	CH₃OH	S=C(NH₂)₂	—	—	65·2	—	—	—	I ≅ 0	[235]
	CH₃OH	CH₃OH		—	—	36·6	—	—	—	I = 0·1 M	[235]
tr-[Co(en)₂(X)(SO₃)]ⁿ⁺	H₂O	H₂O	S=C(NH₂)₂	—	—	8·34	—	—	—		[293]
	H₂O	H₂O	N₃⁻	—	—	7·30	—	—	—		[293]
	H₂O	H₂O	HSO₃⁻	—	—	6·06	—	—	—		[293]
	H₂O	H₂O	I⁻	—	—	5·50	—	—	—	I = 1·0 M (NaClO₄)	[293]
	H₂O	H₂O	pyridine	—	—	5·00	—	—	—		[293]
	H₂O	H₂O	S₂O₃²⁻	—	—	1·45	—	—	—		[293]
	H₂O	H₂O	SO₃²⁻	0·56	—	—	—	—	—		[293]
	H₂O	H₂O	Fe(CN)₆³⁻	0·0034	—	1725	—	14·6	5·1		[247]
	H₂O	H₂O	Fe(CN)₆⁴⁻	0·0026	—	7450	—	13·6	4·7		[247]
	H₂O	H₂O	Fe(CN)₅NO₃³⁻	0·0011	—	700	—	14·2	2·5		[247]
	H₂O	H₂O	SO₃²⁻ᵈ⁻ᵉ	—	20	—	30	—	—		[210]
	OSO₂²⁻	H₂O	SCN⁻	—	59	294	—	—	—		[210]
	OH⁻	H₂O	SO₃²⁻	0·111	≥3	0·044[f]	≥50	21[f]	24[f]	I = 1·0 M (Na/LiClO₄)	[244]
	H₂O	H₂O	SO₃²⁻	—	13·0	—	<10³	15·9[f]	0[f]		[244]
tr-[Co(en)₂(X)SO₃]ⁿ⁺	OH⁻	H₂O	N₃⁻	0·556	—	0·0362[f]	—	—	—		[242]
	OH⁻	H₂O	NO₂⁻	8·21 × 10⁻²	—	0·0134[f]	—	—	—		[242]
	OH⁻	H₂O	NCS⁻	4·00 × 10⁻²	—	0·0253[f]	—	—	—		[242]
	OH⁻	H₂O	CN⁻	2·41 × 10⁻⁵	—	0·0133[f]	—	—	—		[242]
	OH⁻	H₂O	N₃⁻	6·75	—	0·455[f]	—	—	—	I = 1·0 M (NaClO₄)	[242]
	OH⁻	H₂O	NO₂⁻	0·810	—	0·251[f]	—	—	—		[242]
	OH⁻	H₂O	NCS⁻	1·00	—	0·289[f]	—	—	—		[242]
	OH⁻	H₂O	CN⁻	3·6 × 10⁻³	—	0·448[f]	—	—	—		[242]
tr-[Co(en)₂(X)SO₃]ⁿ⁺	OH⁻	H₂O	SO₃²⁻	1·41	—	0·331[f]	—	16·7	−2		[242]
	H₂O	H₂O	S₂O₃²⁻	9·0	—	1270	—	10·8	—		[236]
	H₂O	H₂O	SCN⁻	0·11	—	275	—	—	—		[236]
	H₂O	H₂O	NO₂⁻	0·20	—	206	—	—	—		[236]
	H₂O	H₂O	N₃⁻	0·8	—	235	—	—	—	I = 1·0 M (NaClO₄)	[236]
	H₂O	H₂O	imidazole	0·02	—	5·2	—	—	—		[236]
	H₂O	H₂O	NH₃	0·02	—	6·7	—	—	—		[236]
	H₂O	H₂O	OH⁻	≤10⁻²	—	—	—	—	—		[236]
	H₂O	H₂O	Cl⁻	>10³	—	—	—	—	—		[236]
	H₂O	H₂O	HN₃	—	—	14·3	—	—	—		[236]

Complex	L	Solvent	Entering group						Conditions	Ref.
$(NH_3)_5CoSO_3^+$	NH_3	H_2O	OH^-	—	—	—	—	—	⎫	[243]
	NH_3	H_2O	CN^-	0.12[g]	—	—	—	—	⎬ $I = 0.46$ M $(NaClO_4)$	[243]
	NH_3	H_2O	NO_3^-		—	—	—	—		[243]
	NH_3	H_2O	SCN^-		—	—	—	—	⎭	[243]
$tr\text{-}[(NH_3)_4Co(OH)SO_3]$	OH^-	H_2O	CN^-	—	3.8×10^{-2}	—	—	—		[11]
$(NH_3)_5CoSO_3^+$	NH_3	H_2O	SCN^-	0.065	0.0103	—	0.53	—	$I = 1.05$ M $(NaClO_4)$	[294]
$cis\text{-}[(NH_3)_4Co(SO_3)]^-$	NH_3	H_2O	CN^-, SO_3^{2-}, SCN^-	0.15	—	—	35.2	—	$I = 1.0$ M $(NaClO_4)$	[295]
$tr\text{-}[Co(CN)_4(X)SO_3]^{n-}$	H_2O	H_2O	CN^-	4.5×10^{-3}[h]	1.73	13.5[h]	16.3[i]	0.8[i]	⎫	[254]
$tr\text{-}[Ru(NH_3)_4(X)SO_3]$	H_2O	H_2O	pyrazine	—	—	—	25.8	17.4[i]	⎬	[254]
$tr\text{-}[Ru(NH_3)_4(X)HSO_3]^{n+}$	H_2O	H_2O	isonicotinamide	6×10^{-3}[h]	—	24[h]	—	—	$I = 0.1$ M $(NaHCO_3)$	[254]
$tr\text{-}[Ru(NH_3)_4(X)SO_2]^{m+}$	H_2O	H_2O	pyrazine	8×10^{-4}	—	0.20[h]	—	—		[254]
$(NH_3)_5RuSO_3$	NH_3	H_2O	pyrazine	4.5×10^{-3}[h]	9.2×10^{-3}	0.033[h]	—	—	⎭	[254]
$cis\text{-}[Ru(NH_3)_4(H_2O)SO_3]$	H_2O	H_2O	pyrazine	1×10^{-2}	—	—	—	—		[254]
Sulphides, hydrosulphides (H_2S, HS^-, S^{2-})										
$(H_2O)_5CrSH^{2+}$	H_2O	H_2O	SCN^-	—	—	8.6×10^{-4}[k]	—	—		[184]
$(H_2O)_5CrSH_2^{3+}$	H_2O	H_2O	SCN^-	—	—	$\geqslant 1.6 \times 10^{-3}$[k]	—	—		[184]
$[(NH_3)_5RuSH_2]^{2+}$	NH_3	H_2O	4-cyanopyridine	—	$\leqslant 6.7 \times 10^{-5}$	—	—	—	$I = 0.1$ M (trifluoroacetic acid)	[102]
Thiosulphate and thiourea										
$tr\text{-}[Co(DH)_2(OH)S{=}C(NH_2)_2]$	H_2O	H_2O	$S_2O_3^{2-}$	—	3.4	—	—	—	⎫ $45°C, I = 4.04$ M	[182]
	H_2O	H_2O	$S{=}C(NH_2)_2$	—	10.3	—	—	—	⎬ $(NaClO_4)$	[182]
$tr\text{-}[Co(DH)_2(OH)S_2O_3]^{2-}$	H_2O	H_2O	$S_2O_3^{2-}$	—	1.7×10^{-3}	—	—	—	$26.4°C$	[182]
$tr\text{-}[Co(DH)_2(OH)S_2O_3]^{2-}$	H_2O	H_2O	$S_2O_3^{2-}$	—	6.5×10^{-3}	—	—	—	$26.4°C$	[182]
$tr\text{-}[Co(en)_2(OH_2)S_2O_3]^+$	H_2O	H_2O	SCN^-	—	4.0×10^{-2}	—	—	—		[229]
	H_2O	H_2O	NO_2^-	—	4.6×10^{-2}	—	—	—		[229]
Thiols, thiolates and thioethers										
$[(H_2O)_5CrSR]^{3+}$ $R = CH_2CH_2NH_3$	H_2O	H_2O	H_2O	—	3.2×10^{-6}	—	—	3.9[l]		[24]
	H_2O	H_2O	Cl^-	1.84×10^{-3}	6.0×10^{-4}	0.324	22.4[l]	3.9[l]		[24]
	H_2O	H_2O	Br^-	—	6.0×10^{-5}	$\ll 1$	—	—		[24]
	H_2O	H_2O	HF	—	3.05×10^{-4}	$\ll 1$	—	11.7[l]	⎫	[24]
$R = C_6H_4NH_3$	H_2O	H_2O	CH_3CO_2H	—	2.83×10^{-4}	—	—	—	⎬ $I = 2.00$ M $(NaClO_4)$	[24]
	H_2O	H_2O	H_2O	—	2.7×10^{-7}	—	—	—		[24]
	H_2O	H_2O	Cl^-	2.31×10^{-4}	1.12×10^{-4}	0.486	25.9[l]	—		[24]
	H_2O	H_2O	HF	—	1.30×10^{-3}	—	—	—	⎭	[24]
	H_2O	H_2O	CH_3CO_2H	—	3.80×10^{-5}	—	—	—		[24]
$tr\text{-}[(NH_3)_4Ru(S(CH_3)_2)X]^{2+}$	NH_3	H_2O	4-cyanopyridine	4.2×10^{-6}	—	—	—	—	⎫	[102]
	isonicotinamide	H_2O	H_2O	9×10^6	—	—	—	—	⎬ $I = 0.1$ M (trifluoroacetic acid)	[102]
$tr\text{-}[(NH_3)_4Ru(S(H)CH_2CH_3)X]^{2+}$	NH_3	H_2O	4-cyanopyridine	$\leqslant 3 \times 10^{-5}$	—	—	—	—		[102]
$tr\text{-}[(NH_3)_4Ru(S(H)CH_2CH_3)X]^{2+}$	isonicotinamide	H_2O	H_2O	$< 1 \times 10^{-3}$	—	—	—	—	⎭	[102]
$tr\text{-}[Co(DH)_2(S(C_6H_5)_3)X]$	$(C_6H_5)_3P$	CH_2Cl_2	$(CH_3O)_3P$	—	7.4	1.41	—	—	$I = 0$	[248]

TABLE 14 (cont.)

Complex[b]	X[c]	Solvent	L[p]	A (s^{-1})	B (s^{-1})	BC (M^{-1} s^{-1})	C (M^{-1})	ΔH^* (kcal mol^{-1})	ΔS^* (eu)	Conditions[n]	Ref.
Sulphinates											
tr-[Co(DH)$_2$(X)SO$_2$C$_6$H$_4$CH$_3$]	CH$_3$OH	CH$_3$OH	S=C(NH$_2$)$_2$	—	0.222	—	0.564	—	—	$I = 0$	[235]
	CH$_3$OH	CH$_3$OH	p-CH$_3$C$_6$H$_4$NH$_2$	—	0.209	—	0.400	—	—	$I = 0$	[235]
	4-cyano-pyridine	CH$_2$Cl$_2$	(CH$_3$O)$_3$P	—	2.0×10^{-4}	—	0.84	—	—	$I = 0$	[248]
tr-[Co(DH)$_2$(X)SO$_2$CH$_3$]	CH$_3$OH	CH$_3$OH	S=C(NH$_2$)$_2$	—	—	0.140	—	—	—		[234]
	CH$_3$OH	CH$_3$OH	p-CH$_3$C$_6$H$_4$NH$_2$	—	—	6.67×10^{-2}	—	—	—		[234]
	CH$_3$OH	CH$_3$OH	pyridine	—	—	3.56×10^{-2}	—	20.0^m	2^m		[234]
	CH$_3$OH	CH$_3$OH	P(C$_6$H$_5$)$_3$	—	—	3.72×10^{-2}	—	20.7^m	4^m		[234]
	CH$_3$OH	CH$_3$OH	As(C$_6$H$_5$)$_3$	9.6×10^{-4}	—	3.72×10^{-2}	—	20.2^m	3^m		[234]
	CH$_3$OH	CH$_3$OH	Sb(C$_6$H$_5$)$_3$	1.87×10^{-3}	—	4.28×10^{-2}	—	20.7^m	8^m		[234]
tr-[Co(DH)$_2$(X)SO$_2$C$_6$H$_4$NH$_3$]	CH$_3$OH	CH$_3$OH	S=C(NH$_2$)$_2$	—	—	0.182	—	—	—		[234]
	CH$_3$OH	CH$_3$OH	p-CH$_3$C$_6$H$_4$NH$_2$	—	—	8.68×10^{-2}	—	18.8^m	-1^m	$I = 0$, 24.8°C	[234]
	CH$_3$OH	CH$_3$OH	pyridine	—	—	4.79×10^{-2}	—	—	—		[234]
	CH$_3$OH	CH$_3$OH	P(C$_6$H$_5$)$_3$	—	—	5.22×10^{-2}	—	21.4^m	8^m		[234]
	CH$_3$OH	CH$_3$OH	As(C$_6$H$_5$)$_3$	8.6×10^{-4}	—	5.12×10^{-2}	—	24.3^m	17^m		[234]
	CH$_3$OH	CH$_3$OH	Sb(C$_6$H$_5$)$_3$	1.43×10^{-3}	—	8.67×10^{-2}	—	25.5^m	22^m		[234]
	CH$_3$OH	CH$_3$OH	(CH$_3$CH$_2$CH$_2$)$_2$S	1.7×10^{-3}	—	5.25×10^{-2}	—	—	—		[234]
	H$_2$O	H$_2$O	pyridine	7.4×10^{-5}	—	4.16×10^{-3}	—	—	—		[234]
	H$_2$O		pyridine^f	6.6×10^{-5}	—	8.60×10^{-3}	—	—	—		[234]
	CH$_3$CH$_2$OH	CH$_3$CH$_2$OH		5.5×10^{-3}	—	1.21×10^{-1}	—	—	—	$I = 1.0$ M (LiClO$_4$), 25°C	[234]
(NH$_3$)$_5$CoSO$_2$C$_6$H$_5^{2+}$	H$_2$O	H$_2$O	Br$^-$	2.4×10^{-4}	—	1.46×10^{-3}	0.30	27.2^l	14^l	$I = 0$	[11]
(NH$_3$)$_5$CoSO$_2$C$_6$H$_4$CH$_3^{2+}$	NH$_3$	H$_2$O	SCN$^-$	5.9×10^{-4}	—	6.6×10^{-3}	0.84	—	—	$I = 1.0$ M (KNO$_3$)	[11]
	NH$_3$	H$_2$O	SCN	—	—	8.8×10^{-5}	—	—	—		[11]

^{a} Data fit to rate law, $k_{obs} = \dfrac{A + BC[L]}{1 + C[L]}$, unless otherwise specified. See Ref. [234] for interpretation of this rate law within S_N1(lim) and prior association mechanisms.

^{b} DH = dimethylglyoxime monoanion, en = ethylenediamine, tn = trimethylenediamine.

^{c} Leaving group.

^{d} For formation of O-bonded sulphite, k_2 (O → S isomerization) = 59 s^{-1} (vide infra).

^{e} O → S isomerization of sulphite ligand via an ion-paired intermediate.

^{f} Units are s^{-1} due to competition rate law: $k_{obs} = (k_f[SO_3^{2-}]/[OH^-]) + k_f$.

^{g} Limiting value of NH$_3$ dissociation.

^{h} Values used are $k_{-1} \equiv A$ and $k_1 \equiv BC$.

^{i} Values for pyrazine substitution onto tr-[Ru(NH$_3$)$_4$(SO$_3$)H$_2$O].

^{j} Values for aquation of tr-[Ru(NH$_3$)$_4$(SO$_3$)(pyz)] where pyz = pyrazine.

^{k} Anation rate constants (k_f) for the reaction $(H_2O)_5CrSH^{2+}$ (or $(H_2O)_5CrSH_3^+ + NCS^- \underset{k_r}{\overset{k_f}{\rightleftharpoons}} tr-[(H_2O)_4Cr(SH)SCN]^+$ (or tr-[(H$_2$O)$_4$Cr(SH$_2$)SCN]$^{2+}$.

^{l} Corresponding to activation energy for parameter B. For additional activation parameters see individual references.

^{m} Corresponding to activation energy for parameter BC. For activation parameters of A term see Ref. [234].

^{n} $T = 25$°C, $I = 1.0$ M (LiClO$_4$) unless otherwise specified.

^{p} Entering group.

proceeds measurably in a given direction, and often kinetic analysis is the sole source of thermodynamic information about equilibrium processes. Moreover, many of the model sulphur–metal complexes synthesized to explicate mechanistic phenomena are in fact thermodynamically unstable (either towards M–S bond cleavage or towards internal redox decomposition) and this fact always influences, and often determines, the reactivities of these complexes. Unfortunately, because of (1) the tendency of ligands such as HS^- and RS^- to form polymeric complexes which are often not well defined, and (2) the very low affinities of ligands such as R_2S, $RSSR$, and R_2SO for most metal centres, affinity data for metal–sulphur systems are scarce. Most available data have recently been reviewed,[13,14] and thus this section presents only recently reported data and briefly highlights some old and new points of mechanistic relevance.

A. Thioethers

The affinity of weakly bonding, monodentate thioethers for several metals has been measured by determining the position of the equilibrium:[257]

$$M^{n+} + Cu—SR_2^{2+} = M—SR_2^{n+} + Cu^{2+}$$

Table 15 lists some of the resulting data which show that in general the affinities are very low and that the potentially chelating thioether $(HOCH_2CH_2)_2S$ exhibits higher binding constants than does $(CH_2)_4S$. The affinities of a number of macrocyclic polythioethers for Cu(II) and, through redox measurements, Cu(I) have been reported.[178,258] As expected, the "softer" Cu(I) centre has greater affinity for the thioether ligands than does Cu(II), macrocyclic ligands have higher binding constants than do open chain ligands, and the size of the ring affects the magnitude of the binding constant. In other studies the affinities for metal ions of carboxylate ligands with and without thioether functionalities were determined.[259,260] As expected, the thioether functionality can complete a chelate ring and thus enhance the affinity of a carboxylate-containing ligand.

B. Thiols

Thiols have considerably higher affinity for Cu(I) than do thioethers.[13] The affinity constants for monodentate thioethers are estimated to be in the range 10–100, while monodentate thiols exhibit affinity constants of the order 10^{12}; chelating thiols such as cysteine bind Cu(I) with affinity constants as large as 10^{18}.[260] Recently the apparent formation constant for

TABLE 15

Selected affinities of metals for sulphur-containing ligands

Ligands	Metal complex	Calculated affinity ($\log K$)	Ref.
Sulphides			
H_2S	$(NH_3)_5Ru(OH_2)^{2+}$	3·18	[13]
HS^-	$(NH_3)_5Ru(OH_2)^{3+}$	−3·62	
	$(NH_3)_5Ru(OH_2)^{2+}$	6·18	
	$(NH_3)_5Ru(OH_2)^{3+}$	13·4	
	Ag^+	13·3	
	CH_3Hg^+	21	
	Tl^+	2·27	
	Cd^{2+}	7·6	
	Hg^{2+}	37·7[a]	
	MoO_4H^-	11·8	[171]
	$MoO_2S_2^{2-}$	13·6	
	$MoOS_3^{2-}$	<12	
Thiols			
$HSCH_2CO_2^-$	$(H_2O)_4Cr^{3+}$	1·01[b]	[175]
CH_3CH_2SH	$(NH_3)_5Ru(OH_2)^{2+}$	≥3·48	[13]
$HSCH_2CH_2SO_3^-$	$Cu(OH_2)_4^+$	12·5[c]	[260]
$HSCH_2CH_2N(CH_3)_3^+$	$Cu(OH_2)_4^+$	11·7[c]	
$HSCH_2CH(COO)NH_3$	$Cu(OH_2)_4^+$	18·3[c]	
$HSC(CH_3)_2CH(COO)NH_3$	$Cu(OH_2)_4^+$	18·6[c]	

Ligand	Species		Ref.
CH₃CH₂CH₂SH	Co(cap)ᵍ	<−1	[262]
	Co(T-p—OCH₃PP)ʰ	−0.35	
	Co(cap)ᵍ	3.0	
	Fe(cap)ᵍ	4.2	
	Co(T-p—OCH₃)PP	3.4	
	Fe (protoporphyrin dimethyl ester)	4.4	
CH₃CH₂CH₂S⁻ ⁱ			[257]

Thioethers

Ligand	Species		Ref.
(CH₃CH₂)₂S (HOCH₂CH₂)₂S	Cu²⁺	−0.47	
	Cu²⁺	0.18	
	Ca²⁺	−0.09	
	Mn²⁺	−0.22	
	Ni²⁺	−0.16	
	Zn²⁺	−0.18	
	Cd²⁺	−0.32	
	Ag⁺	3.8	
	Hg²⁺	>3.85	
(CH₂)₄S	Cu²⁺	0.02	
	Ca²⁺	−0.30	
	Mn²⁺	−0.31	
	Ni²⁺	−0.16	
	Zn²⁺	−0.21	
	Cd²⁺	—	
	Ag⁺	—	
	Hg²⁺	—	
(CH₃)₂S	(NH₃)₅Ru(OH₂)²⁺	>3.6	[102]
	(NH₃)₅Ru(OH₂)³⁺	>5	[102]
	Ca²⁺	>−1.80	[266]
	Cd²⁺	−1.6	
		−0.3	
	Ag⁺	3.7	

TABLE 15 (*cont.*)

Ligands	Metal complex	Calculated affinity (log K)	Ref.
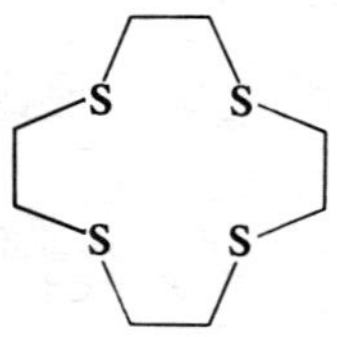	Cu^{2+}	2·44 (80% $CH_3OH/H_2O)^d$ 3·39 (H_2O)	[178]
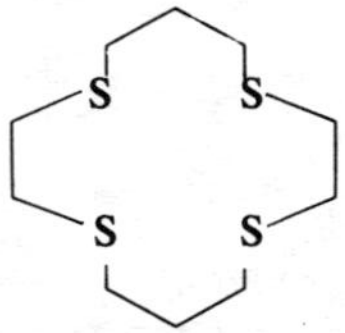	Cu^{2+}	3·48^d 4·34 (H_2O)	[178]
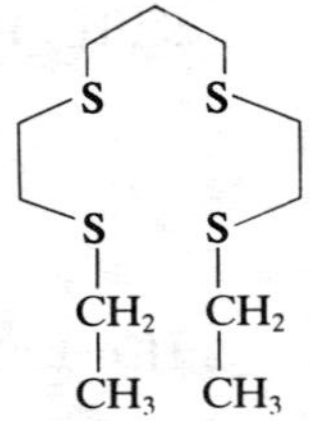	Cu^{2+}	1·10^d 2·18 (H_2O)	[178]

C₆H₅SCH₃	Co(cap)^g	0·52	[262]
	Co(T(O—OCH₃)PP)^h	−0·35	[262]
CH₃SSCH₃	Co(mesoporphyrin IX dimethylester)	1·35	[262]
	Co(cap)^g	1·00 ± 0·05	[262]

Disulphides

CH₃SSCH₃	Zn²⁺, Ca²⁺, Cd²⁺	−1·4	[266]
	Cu²⁺	0·49	
	Ag⁺	2·01	

Other ligands

S₂O₃²⁻	Ru^{II}(edta)OH³⁻	0·70	[296]
(en)₂Co(SCH₂CH₂NH₂)²⁺	Ag⁺	4·6	[111]
	CH₃Hg⁺	4·7	
2Ni(SCH₂CH₂NH₂)₂	Ni²⁺	≅7^e	[191, 192]
	Pd²⁺	⩾7^e	

^{a} Value for log K_1K_2.

^{b} Ring closure of (H₂O)₅Cr(OCOCH₂SH)²⁺.

^{c} Calculated from data adjusting for complexation of Cu⁺ by 2CH₃CH (log R_2 = 4·34).

^{d} Data assumed to be for complete ring closure around Cu²⁺.

^{e} Actually K_1K_2.

^{f} See individual references for conditions at which affinities were determined.

^{g} 5,10-15,20[pyromellitoyl(tetrakis-o-oxyethoxyphenyl)]porphyrin.

^{h} tetrapara-methoxy meso-tetraphenylporphine.

^{i} As the dibenzo-18-crown-6-potassium salt.

the reaction

$$Au(cysteine)^- + cysteine^{2-} = Au(cysteine)_2^{3-}$$

has been determined to be $4 \cdot 4 \times 10^4 \, M^{-1}$ [261] which seems surprisingly low in view of the high affinities of thiols for Cu(I), and the expected enhanced affinity of Au(I) over Cu(I) for "soft" thiol ligands. Affinity constants governing the coordination of thiols and thioethers to cobalt(II) and iron(II) porphyrins have been measured[262] although the results are complicated by formation of sulphur bridges between metal centres.

C. Disulphides

Certain disulphide–metal complexes have been synthesized and well characterized in the solid state, but in general these are thermodynamically unstable materials that have been kinetically trapped.[90,187,263] In other systems the existence of disulphide–metal complexes has been inferred from indirect evidence; e.g. the CH_3Hg^+ catalysis of dimethyldisulphide cleavage by triethylphosphine,[264] and the enhanced binding of nickel(II) by ammine ligands containing a disulphide linkage.[265] The only available quantitative affinity data concern the binding of a variety of metals by dimethyldisulphide and the cyclic disulphide I:[266]

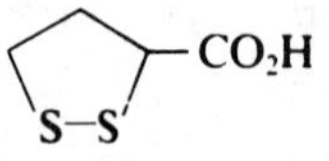

I

From ^1H NMR studies it is concluded that the affinities for dimethyldisulphide decrease in the order $Ag^+ \gg Cu^{2+} \gg Ca^{2+}$, Mn^{2+}, Zn^{2+}, Cd^{2+}, and that the disulphide linkage of I does contribute to the binding of this ligand.

In general, thioethers and disulphides are both much poorer ligands than are thiols and have significant affinities only for softer metals such as Ag(I) and Cu(II). As expected, for a given ligand the affinities increase Cu(II) < Ag(I) and Zn(II) < Cd(II) < Hg(II) reflecting the "softer" character of the heavier metals. It has been noted[13] that the binding for thioethers increases in the order Cd(II) $\ll$ Pd(II) $\cong$ Ru(II), and this phenomenon has been discussed in terms of π backbonding from Ru(II) to the coordinated sulphur atom.

V. PHOTOCHEMISTRY

While the photochemistry of transition metal complexes has generated a good deal of interest during the last decade, only a few studies have been reported on sulphur-containing complexes. This situation is largely due to the lack of stable, well defined, complexes available for such investigations. However, the few existing reports do indicate that complexes containing Co–S bonds have a rich photochemistry, several examples of photoinduced redox, aquation and isomerization reactions having already been noted. From the few data available it appears that cobalt(III) complexes undergo photo-induced reduction if the sulphur-containing ligand is a good reductant (e.g. thiol), but undergo photo-induced aquation and/or isomerization reactions if the sulphur-containing ligand is a poor reductant (e.g. thioether).

Much of classical inorganic photochemistry has been concerned with ammine complexes of chromium(III) and cobalt(III). The photosubstitution reactions of these complexes have led to much discussion and have been used as the basis for defining reaction patterns.[267] Among these complexes, those containing SCN^- are prominent since until recently they have provided the only examples of materials with Co–S and Cr–S bonds. The photolysis of $(NH_3)_5CoSCN^{2+}$ [268,269] leads predominantly to Co^{2+}_{aq} but also to smaller amounts of the photoaquation product $(NH_3)_5CoOH_2^{3+}$ and the photoisomerization product $(NH_3)_5CoNCS^{2+}$. Both the redox and non-redox pathways are presumed to proceed through the same charge transfer state, forming a $Co(NH_3)_5^{2+}$—·SCN ion–radical pair. In this system decay of the ion–radical pair follows competitive paths; the components either separate to yield Co^{2+}_{aq} and ·SCN (which then goes on to thiocyanogen and subsequent hydrolysis products), or the ion–radical pair collapses by reverse internal electron transfer to form the thermodynamically more stable N-bonded isomer $(NH_3)_5CoNCS^{2+}$. In most other Co–S systems, one or the other of the paths is predominant and a mixture of products is not observed. Photolysis of the linkage isomer $(NH_3)_5CoNCS^{2+}$ has also been studied.[270,271]

Photolysis of the thiolato and selenolato cobalt(III) complexes $(en)_2Co(ECH_2CH_2NH_2)^{2+}$ (E = S, Se) and $(en)_2Co(SeCH_2COO)^+$ leads solely to cobalt(II), presumably because of the thermodynamic reducing power of coordinated thiols and selenols.[272] Contrariwise, photolysis of the thioether complex $(en)_2Co(S(CH_3)CH_2CH_2NH_2)^{3+}$ leads to photo-aquation and *not* photoreduction, presumably because thioether ligands are relatively poor reductants. Consistent with this theme, photolysis of the S-bonded sulphinato complex $(en)_2Co(S(O)_2CH_2CH_2NH_2)^{2+}$ also does *not* lead to photoreduction·since sulphinato ligands are poor reductants.[216]

Interestingly, photolysis of this complex leads to linkage isomerization, forming in high yield the thermodynamically unfavored six-membered ring:

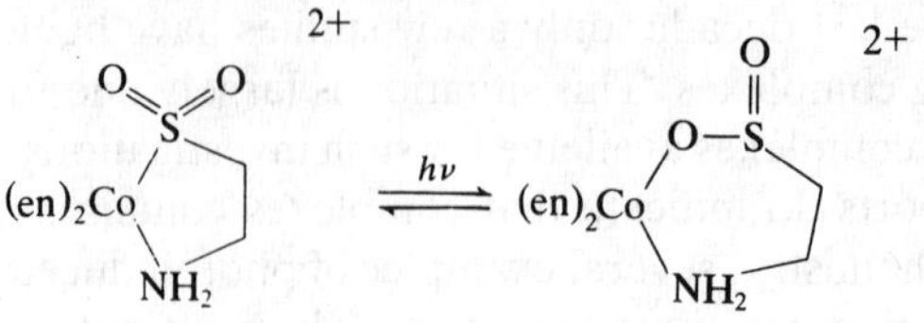

more stable

On standing, the O,N-isomer thermally isomerizes back to the more stable S,N-isomer containing a five-membered chelate ring. This system is controlled by a balance between ring size effects (the five-membered ring being more stable than the six-membered ring) and ligand effects (O-coordination to cobalt(III) being more favoured than S-coordination). That these effects are closely balanced can be seen by comparison with the related equilibrium

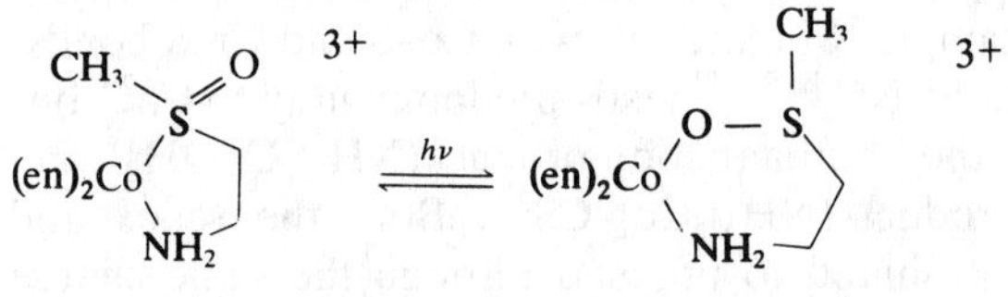

more stable

wherein the six-membered, O,N-chelate ring is more stable.[217] Another example of a photoisomerization reaction involves the solid state photolysis of $Ru(NH_3)_4(Cl)(SO_2)^+$ wherein the S-bonded SO_2 ligand rearranges to the η^2—SO_2 isomer in which both a sulphur atom and an oxygen atom are bonded to the metal centre.[273] In addition, the aerobic photolysis of thiolato–indium(III) porphyrinato complexes, to yield the corresponding sulphinato and sulphonato complexes, presumably involves linkage isomerization steps.[274] Photolytic oxygenation of the dithioether complex $RuBr_3(NO)(Et_2S)_2$ yields a product containing O-bonded sulphoxide, and again this process presumably involves an intramolecular isomerization step.[275]

The photo-induced oxidation of thiocyanate by UO_2^{2+} has been reported to yield the $(SCN)_2^-$ radical based on an observed transient absorption.[276] In a related system, excited state $Ru(bpy)_3^{2+*}$ generated by photolysis of $Ru(bpy)_3^{2+}$, oxidizes 1,1-dithio compounds to the corresponding disulphides; the $Ru(bpy)_3^+$ generated by this process subsequently reduces the newly formed disulphides (or the presumed disulphide radical intermediate in the absence of other electron acceptors).[277]

VI. X-RAY STRUCTURE DETERMINATIONS

Discussion of x-ray structure analyses in a review dedicated to kinetics and mechanisms may at first seem incongruous. However, as is apparent from many of the preceding sections, the definitive information provided by structural analyses has been crucial to our understanding of the chemistry and reactivity of a variety of metal–sulphur systems. This is especially true in systems wherein a coordinated sulphur atom is modified by oxidation or substitution. For many such systems the only clues to the mechanism of the reaction are the structures of the initial complex and the product complex, and these structures are often only definitively assigned by x-ray techniques. In addition, coordination to cobalt(III) stabilizes many reactive sulphur-containing species to the extent that they can be structurally characterized; such characterizations provide the only accessible structural information on these reactive species which are often proposed as transient intermediates in organic and biochemical reaction schemes. Finally, x-ray structural analysis of sulphur-containing cobalt(III) complexes has led to delineation of the structural *trans* effect (STE), which has been shown to be highly correlated with the kinetic *trans* effect (KTE). For these reasons, this section briefly surveys those x-ray structures relevant to our understanding of the reactivities of metal–sulphur systems.

Oxidation of the coordinated thiolate functionality in $(en)_2Co(SCH_2CH_2NH_2)^{2+}$ by H_2O_2 leads successively to the coordinated sulphenate[12] and sulphinate[10] derivatives. Both products of this stepwise

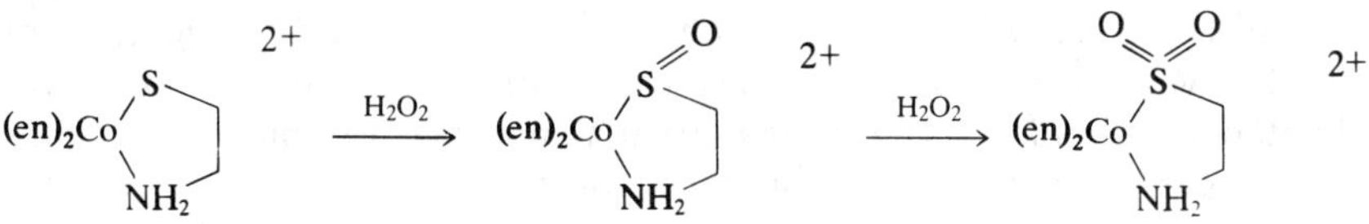

oxidation reaction have been structurally characterized, as has an analogous sulphenato complex.[81] Noncoordinated sulphenic acids have been proposed as reactive intermediates in a variety of organic and biochemical reactions.[278]

Oxidation of the coordinated thiolate functionality in $(en)_2Co(SCH_2CH_2NH_2)^{2+}$ by I_2 leads to a product wherein I^+ bridges two thiolato–cobalt(III) complexes; this material can be equivalently formulated as a sulphenyl iodide derivative:[91]

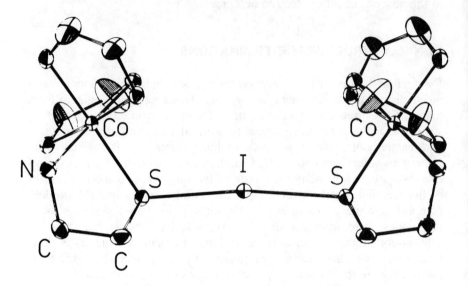

Fig. 4. ORTEP drawing of $[(en)_2Co(NH_2CH_2CH_2S)_2]^{5+}$.

Noncoordinted sulphenyl iodides are reactive intermediates in a variety of organic reactions.[93]

Oxidation of coordinated thiolates by one-equivalent agents such as Np(VI) and Co_{aq}^{3+} leads to a product that was originally proposed to be a coordinated disulphide on the basis of indirect evidence.[9,72] This tentative assignment was central to the proposed oxidation mechanism. Recently, coordinated disulphides have been prepared by *N*-ethylthiophthalimide oxidation of $(en)_2Co(SCH_2CH_2NH_2)^{2+}$ [90] and by Co_{aq}^{3+} oxidation of $(en)Co(SC(CH_3)_2COO)^+$.[217a] Structural characterization of these coordinated disulphides confirms the original product assignment and thus supports the proposed oxidation mechanism.

$$
\underset{(en)_2Co(SCH_2CH_2NH_2)}{\overset{\overset{\displaystyle SCH_2CH_3 \quad 3+}{|}}{}}
\qquad
\underset{(en)_2Co(SC(CH_3)_2COO)}{\overset{\overset{\displaystyle SC(CH_3)_2COOH \quad 2+}{|}}{}}
$$

The product resulting from oxidation of $(en)_2Co(cysteine-N,S)^{2+}$ with acetic anhydride/dimethyl sulphoxide is an unusual sulphenamide complex which was identified by x-ray analysis (Figure 5).[78]

Oxidation of this sulphenamide product leads to the sulphinamide and sulphonamide analogues, the sulphinamide having been structurally char-

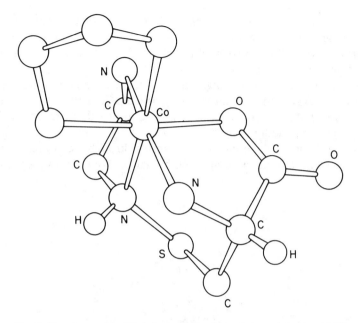

Fig. 5. Structure of (en)Co(ethylenediaminecysteinesulphenamide)$^{2+}$.

acterized.[95] Noncoordinated sulphenamides and sulphinamides are rather uncommon species. Reduction of the sulphenamide complex generates the (en)$_2$Co(cysteine-N,O)$^{2+}$ complex which features a pendant thiol functionality which can undergo further chemistry. Reaction of this complex with the original sulphenamide complex yields the (en)$_2$Co(μ-cystine-N,N',O,O')Co(en)$_2^{4+}$ dimer, also identified by structural analysis (Figure 6).[96]

X-ray analysis shows that oxidation of the thiolato complex (en)$_2$Co(SCH$_2$COO)$^+$ by a variety of one- and two-equivalent agents leads

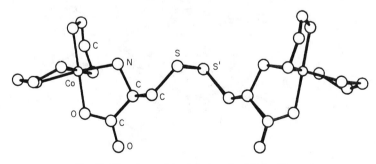

Fig. 6. Structure of (en)$_2$Co(cystine)Co(en)$_2^{4+}$.

to the *S,O*-monothiooxalato complex $(en)_2Co(SC(O)COO)^+$.[77,279] These processes are unique among oxidations of coordinated thiols in that it is the carbon atom adjacent to sulphur, rather than the sulphur atom itself, that suffers net oxidation.

Soft metal centres have high affinity for coordinated thiolates.[111] Addition of Ag(I) to a solution of $(en)_2Co(SCH_2COO)^+$ generates a Ag(I)-bridged dimer which has been structurally characterized (Figure 7).[188] While this adduct could be viewed as a model for the precursor complex in the inner-sphere electron transfer through a coordinated thiolate, it does not exhibit the bond length changes which are thought to be

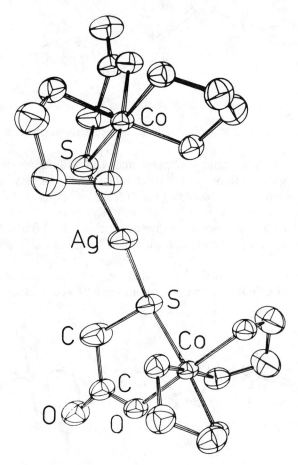

Fig. 7. ORTEP drawing of $[(en)_2Co(OOCCH_2S)_2Ag^{3+}$.

required to attain the transition state geometry for electron transfer. An adduct which does exhibit these changes is the tetranuclear cluster formed by adding Cu(I) to a solution of $(en)_2Co(SCH_2CH_2NH_2)^{2+}$ (Figure 8).[189]

Structural data show that the Co–S bond in the Cu_2Co_2 tetramer (2·273 Å) is longer than that in the Co_2Ag trimer (2·247 Å) and longer than those in $(en)_2Co(SCH_2COO)^+$ (2·243 Å) and $(en)_2Co(SCH_2CH_2NH_2)^{2+}$ (2·226 Å).[21] Lengthening of the Co–S bond is, of course, expected in the inner-sphere electron transfer transition state.

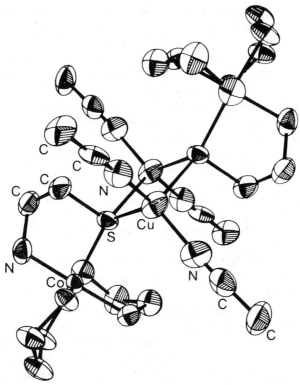

Fig. 8. ORTEP drawing of $[(en)_2Co(NH_2CH_2CH_2S)—Cu(NCCH_3)_2]_2^{6+}$.

Sulphur-induced structural *trans* effects (STE) have been determined in a variety of ammine–cobalt(III) complexes, and for sulphito, thiosulphato and sulphinato ligands the STE is linearly correlated with the kinetic *trans* effect (KTE).[229] The STE has also been implicated as a factor in determining relative rates of inner-sphere electron transfer.[11,19,25,28]

The oxidation states of both sulphur and ruthenium in $(NH_3)_5RuSSRu(NH_3)_5NH_5^{4+}$ are uncertain.[101] The dimer can be formulated as (1) two Ru(II) centres bridged by S_2^0, (2) two Ru(III) centres bridged by persulphide, S_2^{2-}, or (3) a Ru(II)–Ru(III) mixed-valence ion bridged by supersulphide, S_2^-. Structural, and other, evidence indicates the last configuration to be the most important.[103]

VII. INVERSION OF COORDINATED SULPHUR

Coordinated sulphur atoms which also contain a non-bonding pair of electrons can undergo pyramidal inversion; such sulphur atoms are present in coordinated thioethers (M—S(R)R′), disulphides (M—S(SR)—R′) and sulphenates (M—S(O)—R). The process is most conveniently monitored by NMR techniques, and considerable data have been obtained since the first observation of coordinated thioether inversion.[280] Most data are available for thioethers coordinated to square planar metal centres, and these systems have recently been reviewed in detail.[14] The salient conclusions of this review are as follows:

(1) The mechanism of inversion does not involve M–S bond cleavage, but rather most probably proceeds through a planar intermediate in which two electron pairs of the sulphur atom are associated with the metal centre. In this view the metal centre smoothly "slides" from one sulphur electron pair to the next. Any factors which stabilize the planar intermediate will lower the activation barrier for inversion and lead to a lower NMR coalescence temperature.

(2) The ligand situated *trans* to the coordinated thioether effects the rate of inversion by affecting the strength of the M–S bond. Thus, the greater the *trans* effect of the *trans*-situated ligand, the greater the rate of inversion.

(3) Inversion of chelating dithioethers involves individual site inversions rather than synchronous inversions.

(4) The rate of inversion appears to be related to the extent of p_π–d_π overlap between the sulphur atom and the metal centre, greater overlap leading to faster rates by stabilization of the planar intermediate.

Several studies on the inversion of thioethers and disulphides coordinated to Pt(IV) and Re(I) have recently been reported.[281–286] From this work it can be concluded that the activation barrier for inversion of a monodentate thioether is lower than the barrier for inversion of a chelating thioether, presumably because of less strain in the planar transition state for the monodentate ligand. Also, sulphur inversion is more difficult on Pt(IV) than on Pt(II).

Only two reports on the inversion of sulphur coordinated to cobalt(III) have appeared.[81,287] In both the *S*-bonded sulphenato complex $(en)_2Co(S(O)CH_2CH(COOH)NH_2)^{2+}$ and the thioether complex

$(tren)Co(S(CH_3)CH_2CH_2NH_2)^{3+}$, inversion is slow on the NMR time scale. Since the sulphenato complex can be resolved, inversion of the coordinated sulphenato sulphur atom must be very slow. Since the thioether complex cannot be resolved, the specific rate for sulphur atom inversion must lie in the range $0.1-10 \, s^{-1}$ at 25°C.

Acknowledgment

Preparation of this review was supported by the National Science Foundation, Grant No. CHE 79-26497.

REFERENCES

[1] Livingstone, S.E. *Quart. Rev. (London)* **1965**, *19*, 386–425.
[2] Lane, R.H.; Bennett, L.E. *J. Am. Chem. Soc.* **1970**, *92*, 1089–1090.
[3] Asher, L.E.; Deutsch, E. *Inorg. Chem.* **1972**, *11*, 2927–2933.
[4] Asher, L.E.; Deutsch, E. *Inorg. Chem.* **1973**, *12*, 1774–1778.
[5] Asher, L.E.; Deutsch, E. *Inorg. Chem.* **1975**, *14*, 2799–2804.
[6] Koch, S.; Tang, S.C.; Holm, R.H.; Frankel, R.B. *J. Am. Chem. Soc.* **1975**, *97*, 914–916.
[7] Stein, C.A.; Taube, H. *Inorg. Chem.* **1979**, *18*, 1168–70.
[8] Stein, C.A.; Taube, H. *Inorg. Chem.* **1979**, *18*, 2212–2216.
[9] Woods, M.; Karbwang, J.; Sullivan, J.C.; Deutsch, E. *Inorg. Chem.* **1976**, *15*, 1678–1682.
[10] Lange, B.A.; Libson, K.; Deutsch, E.; Elder, R.C. *Inorg. Chem.* **1976**, *15*, 2985–2989.
[11] Elder, R.C.; Heeg, M.J.; Payne, M.D.; Trkula, M.; Deutsch, E. *Inorg. Chem.* **1978**, *17*, 431–440.
[12] Adzamli, I.K.; Libson, K.; Lydon, J.D.; Elder, R.C.; Deutsch, E. *Inorg. Chem.* **1979**, *18*, 303–311.
[13] Kuehn, C.; Isied, S.S. *Prog. Inorg. Chem.* **1979**, *27*, 153–221.
[14] Murray, S.G.; Hartley, F.R. *Chem. Rev.* **1981**, *81*, 365–414.
[14a] Murray, R.S.; Stranks, D.R.; Yandell, J.K. *Chem. Commun.* **1969**, 604–605.
[15] Coe, J.S. In *"Reaction Mechanisms in Inorganic Chemistry"*. Tobe, M.L., Ed.; University Park Press: Baltimore, 1974; Vol. IX, pp. 45–62.
[16] Coucouvanis, D. *Prog. Inorg. Chem.* **1979**, *26*, 301–482.
[17] Burns, R.P.; McAuliffe, C.A. *Advances in Inorg. Chem. Radiochem.* **1979**, *22*, 303–348.
[18] Balahura, R.J.; Lewis, N.A. *Inorg. Chem.* **1977**, *16*, 2213–2221.
[19] Lane, R.H.; Sedor, F.A.; Gilroy, M.J.; Eisenhardt, P.F.; Bennett, J.P.; Ewall, R.X.; Bennett, L.E. *Inorg. Chem.* **1977**, *16*, 93–101.
[20] Farr, J.K.; Lane, R.H. *J. Chem. Soc.*, Chem. Commun. **1977**, 153–154.
[21] Elder, R.C.; Florian, L.R.; Lake, R.E.; Yacynych, A.M. *Inorg. Chem.* **1973**, *17*, 2691–2699.
[22] Deutsch, E.; Asher, L.E. *J. Inorg. Nucl. Chem. Lett.* **1977**, *13*, 91–94.
[23] Ramasami, T.; Taylor, R.S.; Sykes, A.G. *Chem. Commun.* **1976**, 383–384.

[24] Asher, L.E.; Deutsch, E. *Inorg. Chem.* **1976**, *15*, 1531–1537.
[25] Weschler, C.J.; Deutsch, E. *Inorg. Chem.* **1976**, *15*, 139–145.
[26] Lane, R.H.; Sedor, F.A.; Gilroy, M.J.; Bennett, L.E. *Inorg. Chem.* **1977**, *16*, 102–108.
[27] Gilroy, M.; Sedor, F.A.; Bennett, L.E. *Chem. Commun.* **1972**, 181–182.
[28] Kennard, G.J.; Deutsch, E. *Inorg. Chem.* **1978**, *17*, 2225–2232.
[29] Stein, C.A.; Taube, H. *J. Am. Chem. Soc.* **1978**, *100*, 336–337.
[30] Toppen, D.L.; Linck, R.G. *Inorg. Chem.* **1971**, *10*, 2635–2636.
[31] Taube, H. *J. Amer. Chem. Soc.* **1955**, *77*, 4481–4484.
[32] Linck, R.G. In "Reaction Mechanisms in Inorganic Chemistry"; MTP International Review of Science, Inorganic Chemistry Series One; Tobe, M.L., Ed.; Butterworths: London, 1972; Vol. 9, pp. 303–352.
[33] Candlin, J.P.; Halpern, J.; Trimm, D.L. **1964**, *86*, 1019–1022.
[34] Espenson, J.H. *Inorg. Chem.* **1965**, *4*, 121–123.
[35] Haim, A. *J. Am. Chem. Soc.* **1963**, *85*, 1016–1017.
[36] Adegite, A.; Kuku, T.A. *J. Chem. Soc. Dalton Trans.* **1976**, 158–161.
[37] Birk, J.P. *Inorg. Chem.* **1975**, *14*, 1724–1726.
[38] Ball, D.L.; King, E.L. *J. Am. Chem. Soc.* **1958**, *80*, 1091–1094.
[39] Snellgrove, R.; King E.L. *Inorg. Chem.* **1964**, *3*, 288–289.
[40] Candlin, J.P.; Halpern, J.; Nakamura, S. *J. Am. Chem. Soc.* **1963**, *85*, 2517–2518.
[41] Fay, D.P.; Sutin, N. *Inorg. Chem.* **1970**, *9*, 1291–1293.
[42] Shea, C.; Haim, A. *J. Am. Chem. Soc.* **1971**, *93*, 3055–3056.
[43] Adegite, A.; Ojo, J.F. *Inorg. Chem.* **1977**, *16*, 477–479.
[44] Haim, A.; Sutin, N.; *J. Am. Chem. Soc.* **1965**, *87*, 4210–4211.
[45] Orhanovic, M.; Po, H.N.; Sutin, N. *J. Am. Chem. Soc.* **1968**, *90*, 7224–7229.
[46] Shea, C.; Haim, A. *Inorg. Chem.* **1973**, *12*, 3013–3015.
[47] Davies, K.M.; Espenson, J.H. *J. Am. Chem. Soc.* **1969**, *91*, 3093–3094.
[48] Conocchioli, T.J.; Sutin, N. *J. Am. Chem. Soc.* **1967**, *89*, 282–286.
[49] Haim, A.; Sutin, N. *J. Am. Chem. Soc.* **1966**, *88*, 434–440.
[50] Lee, R.A.; Earley, J.E. *Inorg. Chem.* **1981**, *20*, 1739–1742.
[51] Adegite, A.; Dosumu, M.; Ojo, J.F. *J. Chem. Soc. Dalton Trans.* **1977**, 630–634.
[52] Pasternack, R.F. *Inorg. Chem.* **1976**, *15*, 643–646.
[53] Baker, B.R.; Orhanovic, M.; Sutin, N. *J. Am. Chem. Soc.* **1967**, *89*, 722–723.
[54] Fraser, R.T.M. *Inorg. Chem.* **1963**, *2*, 954–957.
[55] Peters, D.E.; Fraser, R.T.M.; *J. Am. Chem. Soc.* **1965**, *87*, 2758–2759.
[56] Green, M.; Taylor, R.S.; Sykes, A.G. *J. Chem. Soc. A* **1971**, 509–512.
[57] Thompson, G.A.K.; Sykes, A.G. *Inorg. Chem.* **1976**, *15*, 638–642.
[58] Taylor, R.S.; Green, M.; Sykes, A.G. *J. Chem. Soc. A* **1971**, 277–282.
[59] Restivo, R.J.; Ferguson, G.; Balahura, R.J. *Inorg. Chem.* **1977**, *16*, 167–172.
[60] Gould, E.S. *J. Am. Chem. Soc.* **1965**, *87*, 4730–4740.
[61] Gould, E.S. *J. Am. Chem. Soc.* **1966**, *88*, 2983–2994.
[62] Benson, P.; Haim, A. *J. Am. Chem. Soc.* **1965**, *87*, 3826–3835.
[63] Worrell, J.H.; Jackman, T.A. *J. Am. Chem. Soc.* **1971**, *93*, 1044–1046.
[64] Goddard, R.A.; Worrell, J.H. *Inorg. Chem.* **1977**, *16*, 1249–1251.
[65] Worrell, J.H.; Goddard, R.A.; Gupton, E.M.; Jackman, T.A. *Inorg. Chem.* **1972**, *11*, 2734–2737.

[66] Worrell, J.H.; Goddard, R.A.; Blanco, R. *Inorg. Chem.* **1978**, *17*, 3308–3310.

[67] Worrell, J.H.; Goddard, R.A.; Jackman, T.A. *Inorg. Chim. Acta* **1979**, *32*, L71–L79.

[68] Weschler, C.J.; Sullivan, J.C.; Deutsch, E. *J. Am. Chem. Soc.* **1973**, *95*, 2720–2722.

[69] Adams, G.E.; McNaughton, G.S.; Michael, B.D. *In* "The Chemistry of Ionization and Excitation"; Johnson, G.R.A.; Scholes, G., Eds.; Taylor and Francis: London, 1967, pp. 281–283.

[70] Hoffman,, M.Z.; Hayan, E. *J. Am. Chem. Soc.* **1972**, *94*, 7950–7957.

[71] Hoffman, M.Z.; Hayon, E. *J. Phys. Chem.* **1973**, *77*, 990–996.

[72] Woods, M.; Sullivan, J.C.; Deutsch, E. *Chem. Commun.* **1975**, 749.

[73] Weschler, C.J.; Sullivan, J.C.; Deutsch, E. *Inorg. Chem.* **1974**, *13*, 2360–2366.

[74] Stein, C.; Bouma, S.; Carlson, J.; Cornelius, C.; Maeda, J.; Weschler, C.; Deutsch, E.; Hodgson, K.O. *Inorg. Chem.* **1976**, *15*, 1183–1186.

[75] Shelly, R.S.; Lane, R.H. ACS/CSJ Chemical Congress, Honolulu, HI, Abstract INOR. 498, 1979.

[76] Ramasami, T.; Taylor, R.S.; Sykes, A.G. *Inorg. Chem.* **1977**, *16*, 1931–1935.

[77] Lydon, J.D.; Mulligan, K.J.; Elder, R.C.; Deutsch, E. *Inorg. Chem.* **1980**, *19*, 2083–2087.

[78] Gainsford, G.J.; Jackson, W.G.; Sargeson, A.M. *J. Am. Chem. Soc.* **1977**, *99*, 2383–2384.

[79] Sullivan, J.C.; Deutsch, E.; Adams, G.E.; Gordon, S.; Mulak, W.A.; Schmidt, K.H. *Inorg. Chem.* **1976**, *15*, 2864–2868.

[80] Sloan, C.P.; Krueger, J.H. *Inorg. Chem.* **1975**, *14*, 1481–1485.

[81] Jackson, W.G.; Sargeson, A.M.; Whimp, P.O. *Chem. Commun.* **1976**, 943–946.

[82] Herting, D.L.; Sloan, C.P.; Cabral, A.W.; Krueger, J.H. *Inorg. Chem.* **1978**, *17*, 1649–1654.

[83] Adzamli, I.K.; Deutsch, E. *Inorg. Chem.* **1980**, *19*, 1366–1373.

[84] Dickman, M.H.; Doedens, R.J.; Deutsch, E. *Inorg. Chem.* **1980**, *19*, 945–950.

[85] Weschler, C.J.; Deutsch, E. *Inorg. Chem.* **1973**, *12*, 2582–2590.

[86] Edwards, J.O. "Inorganic Reaction Mechanisms"; Benjamin: New York, 1963; ch. 5.

[87] Schug, K.; Gilmore, M.D.; Olson, L.A. *Inorg. Chem.* **1967**, *6*, 2180–2185.

[88] Caldwell, S.M.; Norris, A.R. *Inorg. Chem.* **1968**, *7*, 1667–1669.

[89] Schug, K.; Miniatas, M.; Sadowski, A.J.; Yano, T.; Ueno, K. *Inorg. Chem.* **1968**, *7*, 1669–1670.

[90] Nosco, D.L.; Elder, R.C.; Deutsch, E. *Inorg. Chem.* **1980**, *19*, 2545–2551.

[91] Nosco, D.L.; Heeg, M.J.; Glick, M.D.; Elder, R.C.; Deutsch, E. *J. Am. Chem. Soc.* **1980**, *102*, 7784–7786.

[92] Lin, G.H.-Y.; Hope, H. *Acta Cryst.* **1972**, *B28*, 643–646.

[93] Danehy, J.P. *Int. J. Sulfur Chem.* **1971**, *C 6*, 159–166.

[94] Mittleman, J.P.; Cooper, J.N.; Deutsch, E. *J. Chem. Soc. Chem. Commun.* **1980**, 733–734.

[95] Gainsford, G.J.; Jackson, W.G.; Sargeson, A.M. *Chem. Commun.* **1981**, 875–877.

[96] Jackson, W.G.; Sargeson, A.M.; Tucker, P.A. *Chem. Commun.* **1977**, 199–200.
[97] Gainsford, G.J.; Jackson, W.G.; Sargeson, A.M. *J. Am. Chem. Soc.* **1979**, *101*, 3966–3967.
[98] Brown, G.M.; Sutton, J.E.; Taube, H. *J. Am. Chem. Soc.* **1978**, *100*, 2767–2774.
[99] Isied, S.S.; Taube, H. *J. Am. Chem. Soc.* **1973**, *95*, 8198–8200.
[100] Halpern, J.; Taube, H. *J. Am. Chem. Soc.* **1952**, *74*, 380–382.
[101] Brulet, C.R.; Isied, S.S.; Taube, H. *J. Am. Chem. Soc.* **1973**, *95*, 4758–4759.
[102] Kuehn, C.G.; Taube, H. *J. Am. Chem. Soc.* **1976**, *98*, 689–702.
[103] Elder, R.C.; Trkula, M. *Inorg. Chem.* **1977**, *16*, 1048–1051.
[104] Thacker, M.A.; Scott, K.L.; Simpson, M.E.; Murray, R.S.; Higginson, W.C.E. *J. Chem. Soc. Dalton Trans.* **1974**, 647–651.
[105] van Eldik, R.; Harris, G.M. *Inorg. Chem.* **1980**, *19*, 880–886.
[106] James, A.D.; Murray, R.S. *Dalton Trans.* **1977**, 319–321.
[107] Murray, R.S.; Stranks, D.R. *Inorg. Chem.* **1970**, *9*, 1472–1475.
[108] Reynolds, J.G.; Holm, R.H. *Inorg. Chem.* **1981**, *20*, 1873–1878.
[109] Root, M.J.; Deutsch, E. *Inorg. Chem.* **1981**, *20*, 4376–4301.
[111] Heeg, M.J.; Elder, R.C.; Deutsch, E. *Inorg. Chem.* **1979**, *18*, 2036–2039.
[112] Ellis, K.J.; Lappin, A.G.; McAuley, A. *J. Chem. Soc. Dalton Trans.* **1975**, 1930–1934.
[113] Root, M.J.; Adzamli, I. K.; Deutsch, E. *Inorg. Chem.* **1981**, *20*, 4017–4019.
[114] Lavallee, D.K.; Sullivan, J.C.; Deutsch, E. *Inorg. Chem.* **1973**, *12*, 1440–1442.
[115] Bohning, J.J.; Weis, K. *J. Am. Chem. Soc.* **1960**, *82*, 4724–4728.
[116] Kolthoff, I.M.; Meehan, E.J.; Tsao, M.S.; Choi, O.W. *J. Phys. Chem.* **1962**, *66*, 1233–1237.
[117] Meehan, E.J.; Kolthoff, I.M.; Kakiuchi, H. *J. Phys. Chem.* **1962**, *66*, 1238–1241.
[118] Wiberg, K.B.; Maltz, H.; Okano, M. *Inorg. Chem.* **1968**, *7*, 830–831.
[119] Kapoor, R.C.; Kachawaha, O.P.; Sinha, B.P. *J. Phys. Chem.* **1969**, *73*, 1627–1631.
[120] Hill, J.; McAuley, A. *J. Chem. Soc. A* **1968**, 156–159.
[120a] Hill, J.; McAuley, A. *J. Chem. Soc. A* **1968**, 1169–1173.
[121] Amjad, Z.; McAuley, A. *J. Chem. Soc. Dalton Trans.* **1974**, 2521–2526.
[122] Hill, J.; McAuley, A. *J. Chem. Soc. A* **1968**, 2405–2408.
[123] Birker, P.J.M.W.L.; Freeman, H.C. *J. Am. Chem. Soc.* **1977**, *99*, 6890–6899.
[124] Lappin, A.G.; McAuley, A. *J. Chem. Soc. Dalton Trans.* **1978**, 1606–1609.
[125] Pickering, W.F.; McAuley, A. *J. Chem. Soc. A* **1968**, 1173–1176.
[126] McCann, J.P.; McAuley, A. *J. Chem. Soc. Dalton Trans.* **1975**, 783–796.
[127] Martin, J.F.; Spence, J.T. *J. Phys. Chem.* **1970**, *74*, 2863–2867.
[128] Ng, F.T.T.; Henry, P.M. *Can. J. Chem.* **1975**, *53*, 3319–3326.
[129] Nord, G.; Petersen, B; Fary, O. *Inorg. Chem.* **1978**, *17*, 2233–2238.
[130] Stanbury, D.M.; Wilmarth, W.K. Khalaf, S.; Po, H.N.; Byrd, J.E. *Inorg. Chem.* **1980**, *19*, 2715–2722.
[131] Betts, R.H.; Dainton, F.S. *J. Am. Chem. Soc.* **1953**, *75*, 5721–5727.
[132] Kratochvik, B.; Long, R. *Anal. Chem.* **1970**, *42*, 43–46.
[133] Davies, G.; Watkins, K.O. *J. Phys. Chem.* **1970**, *74*, 3388–3392.
[134] Davies, G. *Inorg. Chem.* **1972**, *11*, 2488–2494.
[135] Muirhead, K.A.; Haight, G.P. *Inorg. Chem.* **1973**, *12*, 1116–1120.

[136] Elding, L.I.; Groening, A.-B.; Groening, O. *J. Chem. Soc. Dalton Trans.* **1981**, 1093–1100.

[137] Hambright, P.; Fleischer, E.B. *Inorg. Chem.* **1965**, *4*, 912.

[138] Sutin, N.; Foreman, A. *J. Am. Chem. Soc.* **1971**, *93*, 5274–5275.

[139] Yandell, J.K.; Fay, D.P.; Sutin, N. *J. Am. Chem. Soc.* **1973**, *95*, 1131–1137.

[140] Przystas, T.J.; Sutin, N. *J. Am. Chem. Soc.* **1973**, *95*, 5545–5555.

[141] Pasternack, R.F.; Sutin, N. *Inorg. Chem.* **1974**, *13*, 1956–1960.

[142] Po, H.N.; Eran, H.; Kim, Y.; Byrd, J.E. *Inorg. Chem.* **1979**, *18*, 197–201.

[143] Davies, G. *Inorg. Chim. Acta* **1975**, *14*, L13–L14.

[144] Zatko, D.A.; Kratochvk, B. *Anal. Chem.* **1968**, *40*, 2120–2123.

[145] Kratochvik, B.; Zatko, D.A.; Markuszewski, R. *Anal. Chem.* **1966**, *38*, 770–772.

[146] Hunt, G.W.; Griffith, E.A.H.; Amma, E.L. *Inorg. Chem.* **1976**, *15*, 2993–2997.

[147] Krzewska, S.; Pajdowski, L.; Podsiadly, H. *J. Inorg. Nucl. Chem.* **1980**, *42*, 87–88, 89–94.

[148] Gomwalk, U.D.; McAuley, A. *J. Chem. Soc. A* **1968**, 2948–2951.

[149] Alexander, W.A.; Marsh, C.J.; McAuley, A. *Analyst* **1970**, *95*, 657–660.

[150] McAuley, A.; Gomwalk, U.D.; *J. Chem. Soc. A* **1969**, 977–980.

[151] McAuley, A.; Shanker, R. *J. Chem. Soc. Dalton Trans.* **1973**, 2321–2326.

[152] Olatunji, M.A.; McAuley, A. *J. Chem. Soc. Dalton Trans.* **1975**, 682–688.

[153] Cristiani, F.; Diaz, A. *Inorg. Chim. Acta* **1977**, *24*, L7–L8.

[154] Shaw, C.F. *Inorg. Perspect. Biol. Med.* **1979**, *2*, 287–355.

[155] Shaw, C.F.; Eldridge, J.; Cancro, M.P. *J. Inorg. Biochem.* **1981**, *14*, 267–274.

[156] Natile, G.; Bordignon, E.; Cattalini, L. *Inorg. Chem.* **1975**, *15*, 246–248.

[157] Diamond, S.E.; Tovrog, B.S.; Mares, F. *J. Am. Chem. Soc.* **1980**, *102*, 5909–5910.

[158] Lever, F.M.; Powell, A.R. *J. Chem. Soc A* **1969**, 1477–1482.

[159] Anson, F.C. *Acc. Chem. Res.* **1975**, *8*, 400–407, and references therein.

[160] Tanaka, N.; Kyuna, E.; Sato, G.; Tamamushi, R. *J. Phys. Chem.* **1962**, *66*, 2706–2707.

[161] Barclay, D.J.; Passeron, E.; Anson, F.C. *Inorg. Chem.* **1970**, *9*, 1024–1030.

[162] Armor, J.N.; Haim, A. *J. Am. Chem. Soc.* **1971**, *93*, 867–873.

[163] Frank, S.N.; Anson, F.C. *J. Electroanal. Chem.* **1974**, *54*, 55–74.

[164] Anson, F.C.; Rodgers, R.S. *J. Electroanal. Chem.* **1973**, *47*, 287–309.

[165] Yanaoka, H. *J. Electroanal. Chem.* **1970**, *25*, 381–396.

[166] Weaver, M.J.; Anson, F.C. *J. Electroanal. Chem.* **1975**, *58*, 95–121.

[167] Peerce, P.J.; Gray, H.B.; Anson, F.C. *Inorg. Chem.* **1979**, *18*, 2593–2599.

[168] Peerce, P.J.; Anson, F.C. *J. Electroanal. Chem.* **1979**, *105*, 317–328.

[169] Henney, R.C.; Holtzclaw, H.F.; Larson, R.C. *J. Electroanal. Chem.* **1967**, *14*, 435–445.

[170] Hargens, R.D.; Min, W.; Henney, R.C. *J. Electroanal. Chem.* **1970**, *26*, 285–291.

[171] Harmer, M.A.; Sykes, A.G. *Inorg. Chem.* **1980**, *19*, 2881–2885.

[172] Gilbert, K.; Kustin, K. *J. Am. Chem. Soc.* **1976**, *98*, 5502–5512.

[172a] Holm, R.H. *Acc. Chem. Res.* **1977**, *10*, 427–434.

[172b] Holm, R.H. *In* "Biological Aspects of Inorganic Chemistry"; Addison, A.W.; Cullen, W.R.; Dolphin, D.; James, B.R., Eds.; Wiley-Interscience: New York, 1977, pp. 71–111, and references therein.

[173] Bruice, T.C.; Maskiewicz, R.; Job, R. *Proc. Nat. Acad. Sci. USA* **1975**, *72*, 231–234.
[174] Ardon M.; Taube, H. *J. Am. Chem. Soc.* **1967**, *89*, 3661–3662.
[175] Lane, R.H.; Bennett, L.E. *Chem. Commun.* **1971**, 491–492.
[176] Job, R.; Bruice, T.C. *Proc. Nat. Acad. Sci. USA* **1975**, 72, 2478–2482.
[177] Dukes, G.R.; Holm, R.H. *J. Am. Chem. Soc.* **1975**, *97*, 528–533.
[178] Diadarrio, L.L.; Zimmer, L.; Jones, T.E.; Sokol, L.S.W.L.; Cruz, R.B.; Yee, E.B.; Ochymowycz, L.A.; Rorabacher, D.B. *J. Am. Chem. Soc.* **1979**, *101*, 3511–3520.
[179] Balt, S.; Meuldjik, J. *Z. Naturforsch.* **1979**, *34b*, 843–849.
[180] Palmer, D.A.; van Eldik, R.; Kelm, H. *Z. Inorg. Allg. Chem.* **1980**, *468*, 77–81.
[181] Rosseinsky, D.R.; Jauregui, G.A. *J. Chem. Soc. Dalton Trans.* **1979**, 805–809.
[182] Early, J.E.; Zimmerman, J.G. *Inorg. Nucl. Chem. Lett.* **1972**, *8*, 687–688.
[183] MaCartney, D.H.; McAuley, A. *Inorg. Chem.* **1979**, *18*, 2891–2895.
[184] Ramasami, T.; Sykes, A.G. *Inorg. Chem.* **1976**, *15*, 1010–1014.
[185] Adzamli, I.K.; Nosco, D.L.; Deutsch, E. *J. Inorg. Nucl. Chem.* **1980**, *42*, 1364–1366.
[186] Treichel, P.M.; Rosenhein, L.D. *Inorg. Chem.* **1981**, *20*, 942–944.
[187] Treichel, P.M.; Rosenhein, L.D. *J. Am. Chem. Soc.* **1981**, *103*, 691–692.
[188] Heeg, M.J.; Elder, R.C.; Deutsch, E. *Inorg. Chem.* **1980**, *19*, 554–556.
[189] Lane, R.H.; Pantaleo, N.S.; Farr, J.K.; Coney, W.M.; Newton, M.G. *J. Am. Chem. Soc.* **1978**, *100*, 1610–1611.
[190] Busch, D.H.; Jicha, D.C. *Inorg. Chem.* **1962**, *1*, 884–887.
[191] Jicha, D.C.; Busch, D.H. *Inorg. Chem.* **1962**, *1*, 872–877.
[192] Jicha, D.C.; Busch, D.H. *Inorg. Chem.* **1962**, *1*, 878–883.
[193] Freeh, G.; Cheapman, K.; Blinn, E.L. *Inorg. Nucl. Chem. Lett.* **1977**, *9*, 91–94.
[194] DeSimone, R.; Ontko, T.; Wardman, L.; Blinn, E.L. *Inorg. Chem.* **1975**, *14*, 1313–1316.
[195] Blinn, E.L.; Butler, P.; Chapman, K.M.; Harris, S. *Inorg. Chim. Acta* **1977**, *24*, 139–143.
[196] Busch, D.H.; Burke, J.A.; Jicha, D.C.; Thompson, M.C.; Morris, M.L. *Adv. Chem. Ser.* **1963**, *37*, 125–142.
[197] Lindoy, L.L. Livingstone, S.E. *Inorg. Chem.* **1968**, *12*, 1149–1154.
[198] Blinn, E.L.; Busch, D.H. *J. Am. CHem. Soc.* **1968**, *90*, 4280–4285.
[199] Blinn, E.L.; Busch, D.H. *Inorg. Chem.* **1968**, *7*, 482–485.
[200] Burke, J.A.; Brink, E.C. *Inorg. Chem.* **1969**, *8*, 386–389.
[201] Shoup, J.C.; Burke, J.A. *Inorg. Chem.* **1973**, *2*, 1851–1855.
[202] Chandra, S.; Pandeya, K.B.; Singh, R.P. *Synth. React. Inorg. Met.-Org. Chem.* **1981**, *11*, 53–64.
[202a] Friedman, M. "The Chemistry and Biochemistry of the Sulfhydryl Group in Amino Acids, Peptides and Proteins"; Pergamon Press: Braunschweig; pp. 1–6.
[203] Roundhill, D.M. Roundhill, S.G.N.; Beaulieu, W.B.; Uttrayan, B. *Inorg. Chem.* **1980**, *19*, 3365–3373.
[204] Norbury, A.H. *Adv. Inorg. Chem. Radiochem.* **1975**, *17*, 231–386.
[205] Orhanovic, M.; Sutin, N. *J. Am. Chem. Soc.* **1968**, *90*, 4286–4290.
[206] Duffy, N.V.; Early, J.E. *J. Am. Chem. Soc.* **1967**, *89*, 272–278.

[207] Buckingham, D.A.; Creaser, I.I.; Marty, W.; Sargeson, A.M. *Inorg. Chem.* **1972**, *11*, 2738–2743.
[207a] Holba, V. *Coll. Czech. Chem. Commun.* **1967**, *32*, 2469–2477.
[208] El-Awady, A.A.; Harris, G.M. *Inorg. Chem.* **1981**, *20*, 1660–1666.
[209] Dash, A.C.; El-Awady, A.A.; Harris, G.M. *Inorg. Chem.* **1981**, *20*, 3160–3166.
[210] Farrell, S.M.; Murray, R.S. *J. Chem. Soc. Dalton Trans.* **1977**, 322–325.
[211] Fowless, A.D.; Strunks, D.R. *Inorg. Chem.* **1977**, *16*, 1271–1286.
[212] Elder, R.C.; Ellis, P.E. Jr. *Inorg. Chem.* **1978**, *17*, 870–874.
[213] Carlyle, D.W.; King, E.L. *Inorg. Chem.* **1970**, *9*, 2333–2339.
[214] Davies, J.A. *Advances Inorg. Radiochem.* **1981**, *24*, 116–187.
[215] Wojcicki, A. *Advances Organomet. Chem.* **1974**, *12*, 31–81.
[216] Maecke, H.; Houlding, V.; Adamson, A. *J. Am. Chem. Soc.* **1980**, *102*, 6888–6890.
[217] Lydon, J.D.; Deutsch, E. *Inorg. Chem.* to be published.
[217a] Lydon, S.D.; Elder, R.C.; Deutsch, E. *Inorg. Chem.* **1982** in press.
[218] Dong, D.; Slack, D.A.; Baird, M.C. *J. Organomet. Chem.* **1978**, *153*, 219–228.
[219] Flood, T.C.; Disanti, F.J.; Miles, D.L. *Inorg. Chem.* **1976**, *15*, 1910–1918.
[220] von Werner, K.; Blank, H. *Angew. Chem.* **1980**, *92*, 124–125.
[221] Fackler, J.P. Jr. "Inorganic Reactions and Methods"; Zuckerman, J.J., Ed.; Verlag Chemie, in press.
[222] Fackler, J.P. Jr.; Fetchin, J.A.; Smith, J.A. *J. Am. Chem. Soc.* **1970**, *92*, 2910–2912.
[223] Fackler, J.P. Jr.; Fetchin, T.A. *J. Am. Chem. Soc.* **1970**, *92*, 2912–2913.
[224] Fackler, J.P. Jr.; Fetchin, J.A.; Fries, D.C. *J. Am. Chem. Soc.* **1972**, *94*, 7323–7333.
[225] Appleton, T.G.; Clark, H.C.; Menzer, L.E. *Coord. Chem. Rev.* **1973**, *10*, 355–422.
[226] Hartley, F.R. *Chem. Soc. Rev.* **1973**, *2*, 163–179.
[227] Pratt, J.M.; Thorp, R.G. *Advances Inorg. Chem. Radiochem.* **1969**, *12*, 375–427.
[228] Byrd, J.E.; Wilmarth, W.K. *Inorg. Chim. Acta Rev.* **1971**, *5*, 7–18.
[229] Cooper, J.N.; McCoy, J.D.; Katz, M.G.; Deutsch, E. *Inorg. Chem.* **1980**, *19*, 2265–2271.
[230] Cotton, F.A.; Wilkinson, G. "Advanced Inorganic Chemistry", Fourth Edition; Wiley: New York, 1981.
[231] Langford, C.H.; Gray, H.B. "Ligand Substitution Processes"; Benjamin: New York; 1965; p. 66.
[232] Kennedy, B.P.; Gosling, R.; Tobe, M.L. *Inorg. Chem.* **1977**, *16*, 1744–1749.
[233] Gosling, R.; Tobe, M.L. *Inorg. Chim. Acta* **1980**, *42*, 223–226.
[234] Palmer, J.M.; Deutsch, E. *Inorg. Chem.* **1975**, *14*, 17–25.
[235] Seibles, L.; Deutsch, E. *Inorg. Chem.* **1977**, *16*, 2273–2278.
[236] Yandell, J.K.; Tomlins, L.A. *Aust. J. Chem.* **1978**, *31*, 561–571.
[237] Pearson, R.G. *J. Chem. Ed.* **1968**, *45*, 581–587, 643–648.
[238] Pyartman, A.K.; Sof'in, M.V.; Kolobov, N.P.; Mironov, V.E. *Russian J. Inorg. Chem. (Engl. Trans.)* **1976**, *21*, 571–573.
[239] Larsson, R. *Acta Chem. Scand.* **1960**, *14*, 697–710.
[240] Fouss, R.M. *J. Am. Chem. Soc.* **1958**, *80*, 5059–5061.
[241] Hyde, M.R.; Sykes, A.G. *Chem. Commun.* **1972**, 1340–1341.

[242] Ito, Y.; Terek, A.; Kanaguchi, S. *Bull. Chem. Soc. Japan* **1978**, *51*, 2898–2904.

[243] Halpern, J.; Palmer, R.A.; Blakely, L.M. *J. Am. Chem. Soc.* **1966**, *88*, 2877–2878.

[244] Stranks, D.; Yandell, J. *Inorg. Chem.* **1970**, *9*, 751–757.

[245] Stranks, D.R.; Vanderhoeck, N. *Inorg. Chem.* **1976**, *15*, 2645–2648.

[246] Worrell, J. *Inorg. Chem.* **1975**, *14*, 1699–1705.

[247] Scott, K.L.; Murray, R.S.; Higginson, W.C.E. *J. Chem. Soc. Dalton Trans.* **1973**, 2335–2338; **1975**, 1339–1344.

[248] Stewart R.C.; Marzilli, L.G. *J. Am. Chem. Soc.* **1978**, *100*, 817–822.

[249] Ewen, J.A.; Darensbourg, D.J. *J. Am. Chem. Soc.* **1976**, *98*, 4317–4319.

[249a] Everse, J.; Kujundzic, N. *Biochemistry* **1979**, *18*, 2668–2673.

[250] Toscano, P.J.; Marzilli, L.G. *J. Am. Chem. Soc.* **1979**, *101*, 421–424.

[251] Kaargol, J. A.; Lavin, K.D.; Crecely, R.W.; Burmeister, J.L. *J. Am. Chem. Soc.* **1980**, *101*, 1515–1522.

[252] Moore, P.; Basolo, F.; Pearson, R.G. *Inorg. Chem.* **1966**, *5*, 223–228.

[253] Swaddle, T.W. *Coord. Chem. Rev.* **1974**, *14*, 217.

[254] Isied, S.S.; Taube, H. *Inorg. Chem.* **1974**, *13*, 1545–1551.

[255] Isied, S.S.; Taube, H. *Inorg. Chem.* **1976**, *15*, 3070–3075.

[256] Siebert, V.H.; Wittke, G.Z. *Inorg. Allg. Chem.* **1973**, *399*, 43–51.

[257] Sigel, H.; Rheinberger, V.M.; Fischer, B.E. *Inorg. Chem.* **1979**, *18*, 3334–3339.

[258] Dockal, E.R.; Jones, T.E.; Sokol, W.F.; Engerer, R.J.; Rorabacher, D.B.; Ochrymowycz, L.A. *J. Am. Chem. Soc.* **1976**, *98*, 4322–4324.

[259] Sigel, H.; Griesser, R.; McCormick, D.B. *Inorg. Chim. Acta* **1972**, *6*, 559–563.

[260] Vortisch, V.; Eroneck, P.; Heinmerich, P. *J. Am. Chem. Soc.* **1976**, *98*, 2821–2826.

[261] Shaw, C.F.; Schmitz, G.; Thompson, H.O.; Witkiewicz, P. *J. Inorg. Biochem.* **1979**, *11*, 317–330.

[262] Ellis, P.E. Jr.; Jones, R.D.; Basolo, F. *Proc. Nat. Acad. Sci. USA* **1979**, *76*, 5418–5420.

[263] Otterson, T.; Warner, L.G.; Seff, K. *Inorg. Chem.* **1974**, *13*, 1904–1911.

[264] Bach, R.D.; Rajan, S.J. *J. Am. Chem. Soc.* **1979**, *101*, 3112–3114.

[265] Foye, W.O.; Hu, J.-M. *J. Pharm. Sci.* **1979**, *68*, 202–205.

[266] Sigel, H.; Scheller, K.H.; Rheinberger, V.M.; Fischer, B.E. *J. Chem. Soc. Dalton Trans.* **1980**, 1022–1028.

[267] Zinato, E. In "Concepts of Inorganic Photochemistry"; Adamson, A.W., Fleischauer, P.D., Eds.; Wiley-Interscience; New York, 1975; Ch. 4 and references therein.

[268] Vogler, A.; Kunkely, H. *Inorg. Chim. Acta* **1975**, *14*, 247–250.

[269] Orhanovic, M.; Sutin, N. *Inorg. Chem.* **1977**, *16*, 550–554.

[270] Adamson, A.W.; Waltz, W.L.; Zinato, E.; Watts, D.W.; Fleischauer, P.D.; Lindholm, R.D. *Chem. Rev.* **1968**, *68*, 541–585.

[271] Ferraudi, G.F.; Endicott, J.F.; Barber, J.R. *J. Am. Chem. Soc.* **1975**, *97*, 6406–6415.

[272] Houlding, V.H.; Maecke, H.; Adamson, A.W. *Inorg. Chim. Acta* **1979**, *33*, L175–L176.

[273] Johnson, D.A.; Dew, V.C. *Inorg. Chem.* **1979**, *18*, 3273–3274.

[274] Cocolios, P.; Fournari, P.; Guilard, R.; Lecomte, C.; Protus, J.; Boubel, J.C. *Dalton Trans.* **1980**, 2081–2089.
[275] Fergusson, J.E.; Page, C.T.; Robinson, W.T. *Inorg. Chem.* **1976**, *15*, 2270–2273.
[276] Burrows, H.D.; DeJesus, J.D.P. *J. Photochem.* **1976**, *5*, 265–275.
[277] Deronzier, A.; Meyer, T.J. *Inorg. Chem.* **1980**, *19*, 2912–2917.
[278] Allison, W.S. *Acc. Chem. Res.* **1976**, *9*, 293–299.
[279] Gainsford, G.J.; Jackson, W.G.; Sargeson, A.M. *Aust. J. Chem.* **1980**, *33*, 707–715.
[280] Abel, E.W.; Bush, R.P.; Hopton, F.J.; Jenkins, C.R. *Chem. Commun.* **1966**, 58–59.
[281] Abel, E.W.; Khan, A.R.; Kite, K.; Orrell, K.G.; Sik, V. *J. Chem. Soc. Dalton Trans.* **1980**, 1169–1174.
[282] Abel, E.W.; Khan, A.R.; Kite, K.; Orrell, K.G.; Sik, V. *J. Chem. Soc. Dalton Trans.* **1980**, 1175–1181.
[283] Abel, E.W.; Khan, A.R.; Kite, K.; Orrell, K.G.; Sik, V. *J. Chem. Soc. Dalton Trans.* **1980**, 2208–19.
[284] Abel, E.W.; Khan, A.R.; Kite, K.; Orrell, K.G.; Sik, V. *J. Chem. Soc. Dalton Trans.* **1980**, 2220–2227.
[285] Abel, E.W.; Bhatti, M.M.; Orrell, K.G.; Sik, V. *J. Organomet. Chem.* **1981**, *208*, 195–200.
[286] Gulliver, D.J.; Levason, W.; Smith, K.G.; Selwood, M.J.; Murray, S.G. *J. Chem. Soc. Dalton Trans.* **1980**, 1872–1878.
[287] Jackson, W.G.; Sargeson, A.M. *Inorg. Chem.* **1978**, *17*, 2165–2169.
[288] Deutsch, E.; Taube, H. *Inorg. Chem.* **1968**, *7*, 1532–1544.
[289] Hwang, C.; Haim, A. *Inorg. Chem.* **1970**, *9*, 500–505.
[290] Martin, J.F.; Spence, J.T. *J. Phys. Chem.* **1970**, *74*, 3589–3596.
[291] Amjad, Z.; McAuley, A. *Inorg. Chim. Acta* **1977**, *25*, 127–130.
[292] However, it should be noted that this report[203] presents very limited data, and the conclusions reached must therefore be considered tentative.
[293] Tsaing, H.G.; Wilmarth, W.K. *Inorg. Chem.* **1968**, *7*, 2535–2542.
[294] Richards, L.; Halpern, J. *Inorg. Chem.* **1976**, *15*, 251–252.
[295] Tewari, P.H.; Gaver, R.W.; Wilkos, H.I.; Wilmarth, W.K. *Inorg. Chem.* **1967**, *6*, 611–616.
[296] Yoshino, Y.; Uehiro, T.; Saito, M. *Bull. Chem. Soc. Japan* **1979**, *52*, 1060–1062.

Reexamination of the $Co(NH_3)_6^{3+/2+}$ Self-exchange Rate

D. Geselowitz and H. Taube

Department of Chemistry, Stanford University

I. INTRODUCTION

Cobaltammines have played a central role in the development of the chemistry of coordination compounds. Their study provided much of the descriptive matter which comprises the general structural foundations of the subject. In a later phase of the development, when the major concern was that of trying to understand substitution reactions, studies with cobalt-ammines again dominated the field.[1] Concurrent with these, other studies were directed to a basic understanding of redox reactions of complex ions. Many of the critical experiments in this aspect of the subject have exploited substitution inertia of the cobaltammines. A seminal study in this field was that of Lewis, Coryell and Irvine,[2] the object of which was to measure the self-exchange rates for $Coen_3^{3+/2+}$ and $Co(NH_3)_6^{3+/2+}$. They were successful for the trisethylenediamine case, and k_{ex} at 25°C, $\mu = 0.98$, was found to be 5.2×10^{-5} M^{-1} s^{-1}.

These experiments represent the first successful measurements of the specific rate of self-exchange for a reaction of defined mechanism—the reaction is commonly accepted as proceeding by an outer-sphere path. The study is seminal in another sense: it appears to be the first time that a cobalt(III) ammine was deliberately used as an oxidizing agent. There was this lesson to be learned from the experiments of Lewis *et al.*: since $Coen_3^{2+}$ can reduce $Coen_3^{3+}$, other reducing agents also might be expected to effect the reduction. Few, however, seem to have appreciated the opportunities thus opened up, or to have put them to avail.

The experiments by Lewis *et al.* were done using ^{60}Co as a tracer. The measurements on the $Coen_3^{3+/2+}$ systems were repeated by Dwyer and Sargeson[3] using the racemization method of Dwyer and Gyarfas[4]. For the conditions of the experiments by Lewis *et al.*, Dwyer and Sargeson reported the specific rate of self-exchange as $7 \cdot 7 \times 10^{-5} \, M^{-1} s^{-1}$, in quite good agreement with the earlier results. The measurements by Dwyer and Sargeson extend over a wide temperature range, 25–98°C, and lead to values of E_a and $\Delta S^{\ddagger}$ of $14 \cdot 1 \pm 0 \cdot 2 \, kcal \, mol^{-1}$ and $-32 \, cal \, deg^{-1} \, mol^{-1}$ respectively. The activation parameters obtained in the earlier studies are in good agreement with those obtained by Dwyer and Sargeson.

The history of the determination of the self-exchange rate for $Coen_3^{3+/2+}$ is easily told and, apart from improving accuracy, is complete. That for the closely related system $Co(NH_3)_6^{3+/2+}$ is not so easily dealt with. McCallum and Hoshowsky[5] reported no measurable exchange ($<0 \cdot 03\%$) between $^{60}Co(NH_3)_6^{3+}$ and Co(II) as chlorides in 6 M NH_3 after 24 h at 25°C with [Co(III)] = [Co(II)] = $0 \cdot 011$ M. In a somewhat later study measurable exchange was observed after 17 days and from this experiment a specific rate for self-exchange of $2 \times 10^{-6} \, M^{-1} s^{-1}$ can be calculated.[6] There are a number of effects which can give rise to spurious exchange and, with only a single experiment to rely on, there is no way of knowing how serious these might be. Among them is the possibility that a slow net oxidation by O_2 is taking place. In the experiments done by McCallum *et al.*, the Co(II) was labelled; net oxidation of Co(II) to Co(III) would lower the specific activity of the Co(III) but not the total activity of the Co(III), and the latter was used to monitor the progress of the reaction. Though net oxidation would not vitiate the measurements, catalysis produced by O_2 might. A complication of the measurements by adventitious O_2 was specifically referred to by Lewis *et al.*[2] who describe a single experiment on the $Co(NH_3)_6^{3+/2+}$ system. Their experiment was done at 45·1°C, in chloride medium ($\mu = 0 \cdot 98$) with NH_4Cl present to lower the pH, thus reducing the risk of producing $Co_2O_3 \cdot nH_2O$ which might catalyse the reaction. In following the reaction to 4% of completion, they noted an initial relatively rapid exchange phase followed by a much slower phase, and attributed the earlier rapid phase to catalysis by oxygen. Details on the proof of such catalysis are lacking, though the statement is made that "Early tests showed the necessity of eliminating oxygen as completely as possible to minimize transitory catalysis of the reaction." At any rate, the authors adopted the view that even their slowest exchange rate would lead to an upper limit on the rate of self-exchange, and reported for the specific rate of this process a value of $<0.0023 \, \text{M}^{-1} \, \text{h}^{-1} \equiv <6 \times 10^{-7} \, \text{M}^{-1} \, \text{s}^{-1}$. If the activation energy is assumed to be the same as it is for the $\text{Coen}_3^{3+/2+}$ case, the value of k_{ex} at 25°C becomes $<2 \times 10^{-7} \, \text{M}^{-1} \, \text{s}^{-1}$ ($\mu = 0.98$, 5.7 M NH₃, 0.174 M NH₄Cl).

In the experiment just described, the radioactivity was originally in $\text{Co(NH}_3)_6^{3+}$, and according to our reading of the Lewis, Coryell and Irvine paper the growth of radioactivity in Co(II) was monitored. Under these conditions, net oxidation of Co(II) to Co(III), which would result from admitting O₂, would not lead to apparent exchange, and any effect of O₂ would be catalytic. It seems, therefore, that unless some other factor was not controlled—for example, a continued leakage of oxygen into the system which eventually converted most of the Co(II) to Co(III)—the experiments by Lewis *et al.* do seem to set an upper limit on the rate of self-exchange in the $\text{Co(NH}_3)_6^{3+/2+}$ system. Because, as will be discussed in greater detail later, the literature data on the affinity of NH₃ for Co(II) in the last stage of association appear to be in doubt, even were reproducible data on the rate of exchange in aqueous NH₃ available, there would still be difficulty in converting the observed rates to a specific rate for the $\text{Co(NH}_3)_6^{3+/2+}$ self-exchange reaction. Even when the concentration of ammonia in water is as high as 6 M, the dominant form of Co(II) may be $\text{Co(NH}_3)_5\text{H}_2\text{O}^{2+}$ rather than $\text{Co(NH}_3)_6^{2+}$.

The ambiguity about the state of Co(II) is avoided when the exchange reaction is studied in liquid NH₃. Such measurements were made by Grossman and Garner[7] who reported for the specific rates at 25°C and 45°C the values $6 \times 10^{-5} \, \text{M}^{-1} \, \text{s}^{-1}$ and $7 \times 10^{-4} \, \text{M}^{-1} \, \text{s}^{-1}$ respectively. The values of $\Delta H^{\ddagger}$ and $\Delta S^{\ddagger}$ then are 23 kcal mol⁻¹ and ~ -3 cal mol⁻¹ deg⁻¹ respectively. Each exchange run done by Grossman and Garner was based on data obtained for separate samples and an occasional point was found to be widely divergent from the exchange curve defined by the remainder. Furthermore, in two runs under identical conditions, the exchange half-lives were found to differ by a factor of 14 so that it is clear that at least the more rapid reaction was subjected to catalysis. The specific rates quoted above were selected as the slowest rates at each temperature, and thus as being closest to the intrinsic rates. It is to be noted that internal consistency of the data for each of the runs which led to such a wide divergence in rates is quite good. Whatever the catalyst—perhaps traces of cobaltic oxide formed by photochemical decomposition, or perhaps adventitious base (note that NH₄⁺ was not added)—that caused the rate acceleration, it was apparently present to the same amount in most of the samples comprising a run. The possibility that even the runs having the longest half-life may have been subject to catalysis explains in part why the measurement by Grossman and Garner had so little influence on the speculation which the self-exchange rate for the $Co(NH_3)_6^{3+/2+}$ system has generated. Another contributing factor is alluded to in the introducton to the Grossman and Garner paper, where the problem of relating rates in liquid ammonia to those in water is raised.

The studies on $Co(NH_3)_6^{3+/2+}$ self-exchange which have widely been accepted are those by Stranks *et al.* The major conclusions were first reported by Stranks:[8] these are that the dominant paths for exchange involve the activated complexes $[Co(NH_3)_6^{3+} \cdot Co(NH_3)_n^{2+} \cdot OH^-]$ and $[Co(NH_3)_6^{3+} \cdot Co(NH_3)_n^{2+} \cdot Cl^-]$, and that the upper limit to the specific rate for exchange by way of the simple activated complex $Co(NH_3)_6^{3+} \cdot Co(NH_3)_6^{2+}$ is $<1\cdot6 \times 10^{-10} \ M^{-1} \ s^{-1}$ at 64·5°C and $\mu = 1\cdot0$. If the activation energy for self-exchange in the ammine system is taken to be the same as for $Coen_3^{3+/2+}$, the upper limit for self-exchange in the former is $10^{-11} \ M^{-1} \ s^{-1}$ at 25°C. The observations which where the basis for the conclusions cited above appeared in a later paper by Biradar, Stranks and Vaidya[9] in which results on the rate of exchange as a function of $[Co(NH_3)_6^{3+}]$, $[Co(II)]$, $[NH_3]$, $[NH_4^+]$, the ratio $[NH_3]/[NH_4^+]$ and thus $[OH^-]$, $[Cl^-]$ and temperature were reported. We will return presently to a critical analysis of these results.

The experimental developments which have been outlined in the foregoing have continued to invite speculation and theorizing. It was not difficult early in the 1950s to adjust to the finding that the rate of self-exchange for $Co(NH_3)_6^{3+/2+}$ is much slower than for $Fe_{aq}^{3+/2+}$.[10,11] The change in the Co–N distance, $\Delta d(Co)$, for the cobalt couple was believed to be much greater than $\Delta d(Fe)$ for the $Fe_{aq}^{3+/2+}$ couple.[12] Furthermore, the cobalt couple is unique among those commonly studied because a large spin change at each of the centres accompanies net electron transfer. The measurements, based on X-ray diffraction studies on crystals of $Co(NH_3)_6Cl_2$ [15,16] and $Co(NH_3)_6I_3$,[16] of Co–N bond distances did change the nature of the discourse, in the sense that now that these distances were known it became possible to estimate the inner-coordination sphere barrier to electron transfer. By resorting to the self-exchange data[17] for the $Ru(NH_3)_6^{3+/2+}$, where the inner-sphere reorganization energy is minor,[18] the contributions to the reaction barrier by the outer-sphere reorganization energy and the work of bringing the reactions partners together can be estimated, and thus the effect of spin change in the $Co(NH_3)_6^{3+/2+}$ couple could be assessed. The results reported by Stranks then leave an enormous factor which can be attributed to spin change.[18] The underlying formal theory was developed by Buhks, Bixon, Jortner and Navon,[19] who accepted for their treatment the upper limit to the self-exchange for $Co(NH_3)_6^{3+/2+}$ set by Stranks, and the results[17] on the self-exchange rate for $Ru(NH_3)_6^{3+/2+}$. They concluded that the change in spin accounts for a factor of 10^{-4} in the rate. The treatment, however, does not engage the issue of the apparent large difference in the self-exchange rate for $Coen_3^{3+/2+}$ and $Co(NH_3)_6^{3+/2+}$, which according to results generally accepted is a factor of at least $1 \cdot 5 \times 10^6$ greater for the former system.

Our interest in the issues under discussion was motivated in large part by the important and instructive extension of the experimental results which have been realized by Sargeson and coworkers, who have prepared a number of caged Co(III) complexes. The study of the Co(III)–Co(II) couple for these systems is facilitated because the Co(II) products of the reduction remain intact even in acidic solution for extended periods of time. A remarkable result of these studies is that the self-exchange reaction is found to be rather facile, even though the Co(III) complex is, as is usually the case, low-spin, and the Co(II) complex is high-spin. For the sepulchrate couple, k_{ex} (0·2 M NaCl or NaClO₄, 25°C) is found to be[20] $5 \cdot 1 \, \text{M}^{-1} \, \text{s}^{-1}$ and the activation parameters E_a and $\Delta S^{\ddagger}$ as 10·0 kcal mol⁻¹ and -23 cal mol⁻¹ deg⁻¹. The Co–N distances for the salts of the sepulchrate complexes, chloride for Co(III) and $ZnCl_4^{2-}$ for Co(II), have been reported[21] as 1·99 Å and 2·16 Å, both distances being substantially greater than those reported for the cobaltammines. This led us to an interest in the Co(II)–N distance in $Coen_3^{2+}$, which had not been determined, and that in turn, to an interest in the question of why there is such an enormous difference in the self-exchange rates for $Coen_3^{3+/2+}$ and $Co(NH_3)_6^{3+/2+}$. Our conclusion, based on critical examination of the evidence in the literature, as well as experiments of our own, still in progress, on a redetermination of the self-exchange rates, is that the self-exchange rates for the two systems are much closer than has been supposed, and the difference that does exist poses no particular mystery.

In the following we will consider first the rate data on cross-reactions for $Co(NH_3)_6^{3+}$ acting as an oxidizing agent, in an effort to extract from them a value of the self-exchange rate for $Co(NH_3)_6^{3+/2+}$ by applying the Marcus correlation,[23] then turn to a critical examination of the data by Stranks *et al.*, and finally, we shall consider and discuss some relevant comparisons in self-exchange rates.

II. KINETIC DATA ON THE REDUCTION OF COBALT(III) AMMINES

In this section we will apply the Marcus correlation to the data which have

TABLE 1
Reductions of $Co(NH_3)_6^{3+}$ at 25°C

Reductant	Ref.	Conditions[a]	k (M^{-1} s^{-1})	Comments[b]	k (adjusted)[c] (M^{-1} s^{-1})
V^{2+}	[25]	$\mu = 1\cdot0$, $[H^+] = 0\cdot10$, ClO_4^-	$1\cdot0 \times 10^{-2}$	$k_{Cl} = 2\cdot4 \times 10^{-2}$ M^{-2} s^{-1}	$1\cdot0 \times 10^{-2}$
	[26]	$\mu = 2\cdot6$	$3\cdot7 \times 10^{-3}$	$k_{Cl} = 2\cdot1 \times 10^{-2}$	
	[27]	$\mu = 0\cdot40$, $[H^+] = 0\cdot10$	$4\cdot4 \times 10^{-3}$	$k_{Cl} = 3\cdot5 \times 10^{-2}$	
Cr^{2+}	[25]	$\mu = 1\cdot0$, $[H^+] = 0\cdot10$, ClO_4^-	$1\cdot0 \times 10^{-3}$	$k_{Cl} = 1\cdot1 \times 10^{-3}$	$1\cdot0 \times 10^{-3}$
	[28]	$\mu = 0\cdot40$, $[H^+] = 0\cdot10$	$8\cdot8 \times 10^{-5}$	$k_{Cl} = 1\cdot2 \times 10^{-2}$	
	[26]	$\mu = 2\cdot6$	$7\cdot2 \times 10^{-3}$	$k_{Cl} = 6 \times 10^{-1}$	
U^{3+}	[29]	$\mu = 0\cdot20$	$1\cdot2$		$3\cdot4$
	[30]	$\mu = 0\cdot20$	$1\cdot38$		
	[31]	$\mu = 0\cdot20$, ClO_4^-	$1\cdot32$		
Eu^{2+}	[32]	$\mu = 0\cdot40$ [$Zn(ClO_4)_2$]	$1\cdot7 \times 10^{-3}$	$k_{Cl} = 22$	$2\cdot6 \times 10^{-3}$
$Ru(NH_3)_6^{2+}$	[33]	$0\cdot20$ M NaCl	$1\cdot1 \times 10^{-2}$		$2\cdot3 \times 10^{-2}$
Yb^{2+}	[34]	$\mu = 0\cdot40$, $CF_3SO_3^-$	6×10^{-3}		
	[35]	$\mu = 0\cdot18$, ClO_4^-	$2\cdot2 \times 10^3$	$k_{Cl} = 2\cdot0 \times 10^{-4}$	$6\cdot6 \times 10^3$
$Coen_3^{2+}$	[2]	$\mu = 0\cdot98$, en $= 0\cdot27$, Cl^-	$2\cdot0 \times 10^{-2}$		
$Cosep^{2+}$	[34]	$\mu = 1\cdot0$, en $= 0\cdot20$, $CF_3SO_3^-$	$2\cdot6 \times 10^{-3}$		$8\cdot2 \times 10^{-3}$
	[34]	$\mu = 1\cdot0$, NaCl	~3		~4
$Crbpy_3^{2+}$	[36]	$\mu = 0\cdot40$, $CF_3SO_3^-$	9×10^{-1}		$6\cdot5 \times 10^2$
		$\mu = 0\cdot20$ NaCl	$2\cdot5 \times 10^2$		
$Ruen_3^{2+}$	[34]	$\mu = 0\cdot60$, $CF_3SO_3^-$	$4\cdot4 \times 10^{-4}$		$1\cdot7 \times 10^{-3}$

[a] Ionic strength and medium used to maintain ionic strength.
[b] k_{Cl} is the rate constant for $k_{Cl}[Cl^-][Co(III)][red]$ when such a term was observed in the rate law.
[c] See text.

TABLE 2
Reductions of $Coen_3^{3+}$ at 25°C

Reductant	Ref.	Conditions[a]	k (M^{-1} s^{-1})	Comments[b]	k (adjusted)[c] (M^{-1} s^{-1})
V^{2+}	[25]	$\mu = 1\cdot0$, $[H^+] = 0\cdot10$, ClO_4^-	$7\cdot2 \times 10^{-4}$	$k_{Cl} = 1\cdot9 \times 10^{-3}$ M^{-2} s^{-1}	$7\cdot2 \times 10^{-4}$
	[37]	$\mu = 1\cdot0$, $[H^+] = 0\cdot50$	$\sim 2 \times 10^{-4}$		
Cr^{2+}	[25]	$\mu = 1\cdot0$, $[H^+] = 0\cdot10$, ClO_4^-	$3\cdot4 \times 10^{-4}$	$k_{Cl} = 1\cdot5 \times 10^{-3}$	$3\cdot4 \times 10^{-4}$
	[37]	$\mu = 0\cdot40$, $[H^+] = 0\cdot10$	$\sim 2 \times 10^{-5}$		
U^{3+}	[29]	$\mu = 0\cdot20$	$0\cdot18$		$0\cdot40$
	[30]	$\mu = 0\cdot35$	$0\cdot22$		
	[31]	$\mu = 0\cdot20$	$0\cdot133$		
Eu^{2+}	[37]	$\mu = 1\cdot0$	$\sim 5 \times 10^{-3}$		4×10^{-4}
	[38]	$1\cdot0$ M $HClO_4$	4×10^{-4}		
Yb^{2+}	[35]	$\mu = 0\cdot18$, ClO_4^-	$4\cdot5 \times 10^2$	$k_{Cl} = 5\cdot0 \times 10^3$	$1\cdot4 \times 10^3$
	[36]	$\mu = 0\cdot10$, Cl^-, $pH \sim 4$	37		$1\cdot6 \times 10^2$
$Crbpy_3^{2+}$		$\mu = 0\cdot20$	63		
$Coen_3^{3+}$	[3]	$\mu = 0\cdot98$, Cl^-	$7\cdot7 \times 10^{-5}$	Independent of Cl^- or SO_4^{2-} as counterion	$7\cdot7 \times 10^{-5}$
$Ruen_3^{2+}$	[34]	$\mu = 0\cdot60$, $CF_3SO_3^-$	2×10^{-6}		8×10^{-6}
$Cosep^{2+}$	[34]	$\mu = 0\cdot40$, $CF_3SO_3^-$	$4\cdot7 \times 10^{-2}$		$0\cdot2$

[a] Ionic strength and medium used to maintain ionic strength.
[b] k_{Cl} is the rate constant for $k_{Cl}[Cl^-][Co(III)][red]$ when such a term was observed in the rate law.
[c] See text.

been obtained in studies of the redox reactions of cobaltammine species. The equation which relates the specific rate on a cross-reaction to the self-exchange rate takes the form

$$k_{13} = \sqrt{k_{11}k_{33}K_{13}f} \qquad \ln f = (\ln K_{13})^2/4 \ln(k_{11}k_{33}/Z^2)$$

where k_{11} and k_{33} are the self-exchange rates for the two couples, K_{13} is the equilibrium constant for the reaction and Z is the collision frequency. In the following, the subscript 1 will refer to the hexaammine couple, subscript 2 to the trisethylenediamine couple and subscript 3 to the complementary couple. The specific rates of reduction of hexaamminecobalt(III) and trisethylenediaminecobalt(III) which have been reported are shown in Tables 1 and 2 respectively, together with the selected "best" values, which then have been adjusted to unit ionic strength. Whenever possible, rates observed in ClO_4^- or $CF_3SO_3^-$ media were used. Adjustments to standard conditions, ionic strength $1 \cdot 0$ with ClO_4^- as anion, were made using the ionic strength dependences given in Fig. 1 of Ref. [24], which are for the reaction of $Ru(NH_3)_4bpy^{3+} + Ru(NH_3)_4phen^{2+}$ in ClO_4^- and $CF_3SO_3^-$ media. Reactions done with Cl^- as counter-ion were assumed to behave as with ClO_4^- unless the chloride dependence was given explicitly. In the event of a serious discrepancy between literature rates, the lower rate was taken. The rate of reduction of $Coen_3^{3+}$ by $Ruen_3^{2+}$ could not be determined directly; in this system the rate of the reverse reaction was measured and that of the forward reaction was calculated by making use of the equilibrium quotient.

Since the outer-sphere self-exchange rates of most of the reducing agents are not accurately known, the data are of limited usefulness in leading to an estimate of the value of k_{11}. However, the comparison of the rates of reduction of $Co(NH_3)_6^{3+}$ and $Coen_3^{3+}$ by the same reducing agent is itself informative. According to the Marcus cross-relation

$$\frac{k_{13}}{k_{23}} = \left(\frac{k_{11}}{k_{22}} K_{12} \frac{f_{13}}{f_{23}}\right)^{1/2}$$

The ratios k_{13}/k_{23} (and the calculated self-exchange rates where k_{33} is known), are shown in Table 3.

If the Marcus relation holds, the factor k_{13}/k_{23} is expected to be a constant irrespective of the identity of reactant 3, that is, if the slight variation in f_{13}/f_{23} is neglected (in the most extreme case the f ratio affects the comparison by less than a factor of $1 \cdot 5$). For the hexaaqua couples, and the $Crbpy_3^{2+}$ couple, the ratios k_{13}/k_{23} differ by less than a factor of 4 from the geometric mean. On choosing a value of 10 for this ratio, and using recorded values for k_{22} and K_{12}, k_{11} is calculated as 2×10^{-8} M^{-1} s^{-1}.

We have no explanation for the deviation in k_{13}/k_{23} values which is observed with Ruen_3^{2+}. The value of k_{11}/k_{22} using 200 as the ratio k_{13}/k_{23} would be ~400 times higher than that calculated in the previous paragraph.

In Table 3 also are listed values of k_{11} and k_{22} calculated when k_{33} is known. For Ruen_3^{2+}, k_{22} as calculated from the Marcus cross-relation is found to be 10^3 smaller than the experimental value, while k_{11}, calculated in the same way, is not out of line with the values obtained with other

TABLE 3

Comparison of rate constants for the reduction of hexaammine and tris(ethylenediame) complexes

Reductant	$E°(V)$	k_{13}/k_{23}	k_{33}	$k_{11}(calc)^a$	$k_{22}(calc)^b$
V^{2+}	$-0\cdot255^{[40]}$	$14\cdot0$	$1\cdot0 \times 10^{-2\,[41]}$	$9\cdot1 \times 10^{-8}$	$4\cdot5 \times 10^{-5}$
Cr^{2+}		$2\cdot9$			
U^{3+}		$9\cdot0$			
Eu^{2+}		~7			
Yb^{2+}		$4\cdot7$			
$Crbpy_3^{2+}$	$-0\cdot25^{[42]}$	$4\cdot0$	$\sim10^{9\,[43]}$	$\sim5 \times 10^{-9}$	$\sim2 \times 10^{-5}$
$Coen_3^{2+\,c}$	$-0\cdot259$	~110	$7\cdot7 \times 10^{-5}$	$7\cdot2 \times 10^{-6}$	
$Ruen_3^{2+}$	$0\cdot21^{[17]}$	~200	$4 \times 10^{4\,[44]}$	3×10^{-8}	4×10^{-7}
$Cosep^{2+}$	$-0\cdot30^{[20]}$	~18	$13\cdot0$	3×10^{-6}	6×10^{-4}

^{a} $k_{11}(calc) = \dfrac{k_{13}^2}{K_{13}k_{33}f}$; f and K_{13} calculated assuming $E_1° = 0\cdot057$ V (Ref. [39]) and assuming $k_{11} = 10^{-5}$ M^{-1} s^{-1} (f is rather insensitive to changes in k_{11}), and $Z = 10^{11}$; k_{13} values from Table 1.

^{b} Calculated analogously to (a) using $E_2° = -0\cdot259$, Ref. [39], k_{23} values from Table 2.

^{c} Here k_{23} refers to $Coen_3^{3+/2+}$ self-exchange.

reductants. The specific rates k_{11} calculated using known values of k_{33} span the range 3×10^{-9} to 7×10^{-6}. Note that the values of k_{11} and k_{22} obtained in this way are a sensitive function of the cross-reaction rates, and vary with its square. Departures as large as those recorded, of experimental rates from those calculated by the Marcus cross-relation, due to specific factors affecting the work terms of outer-sphere reorganizational energies, are not beyond the realm of possibility.

If, as we believe, the dominant form of Co(II) even in strongly ammonia-cal solution is $Co(NH_3)_5H_2O^{2+}$ rather than $Co(NH_3)_6^{2+}$, the value of k_{11} as calculated will be a lower limit. The factor that would be affected would be the value of $E°$ for the $Co(NH_3)_6^{3+/2+}$ couple, the recorded value then being too high. The measurements on which the accepted value of the sixth association quotient are based are rather insensitive to its value, and if the quotient were overestimated by a factor of 10, the calculated values of k_{11} would become a factor of 10 greater than those shown in Table 3. At any rate, the data on cross-reactions seem to be rather consistent in pointing to a self-exchange rate for $Co(NH_3)_6^{3+/2+}$ much greater than the upper limit which has commonly been accepted.

III. REEXAMINATION OF DATA FOR THE RATE OF $Co(NH_3)_6^{3+/2+}$ SELF-EXCHANGE

In Ref. [8] are summarized conclusions about the cobaltammine self-exchange rates which are based on experimental work detailed in Ref. [9]. The salient ones are these: at 64·5°C and $\mu = 1·0$, the dominant paths for exchange in media in which $[NH_3]$ covers the range 0·53–6 M, $[NH_4^+]$ the range 0·2–0·7 M and $[Cl^-]$ the range 0–0·75 M are governed by the rate laws $k_{OH}[Co(NH_3)_6^{3+} \cdot OH^-][Co(NH_3)_n^{2+}]$ (1) and $k_{Cl}[Co(NH_3)_6^{3+} \cdot Cl^-]$ $[Co(NH_3)_n^{2+}]$ (2) where k_{OH} and k_{Cl} have the values $5·7 \times 10^{-3} M^{-1} s^{-1}$ and $7·3 \times 10^{-4} M^{-1} s^{-1}$. Further, it is asserted that the specific rate k_{11} for the self-exchange reaction corresponding to the activated complex $Co(NH_3)_6^{3+} \cdot Co(NH_3)_6^{2+}$ is less than $1·7 \times 10^{-10} M^{-1} s^{-1}$. In reporting rate law (1), Biridar et al.[9] made use of value cited by Caton and Prue[45] for the stability of $Co(NH_3)_6^{3+} \cdot OH^-(K_{assoc} = 71)$ as determined at 25°C. No mention is made in Ref. [9] of how this was converted to 64·5°C. In the following, we assume that the K_{assoc} at 25°C was actually used in Ref. [9]. The value of K_{assoc} is high enough so that when $[OH^-]$ is maintained at 0·10 M, the specific rate governing the exchange of $Co(NH_3)_6^{3+}$ and $Co(NH_3)_n^{2+}$ would be $5 \times 10^{-3} M^{-1} s^{-1}$. That is, 0·10 M OH^- would accelerate the exchange between $Co(NH_3)_6^{2+}$ and $Co(NH_3)_n^{2+}$ by a factor of greater than 3×10^7. Such an acceleration by a purely outer-sphere mechanism seems unreasonable, but there is the possibility that an inner-sphere mechanism obtains:

$$Co(NH_3)_6^{3+} + OH^- = Co(NH_3)_5NH_2^{2+} + H_2O$$

$$Co(NH_3)_5NH_2^{2+} + Co^*(NH_3)_5^{2+} \rightarrow Co(NH_3)_5^{2+} + Co^*(NH_3)_5NH_2^{2+}$$

A similar defence of the acceleration of the $Co(NH_3)_6^{3+/2+}$ exchange by Cl^-,however, does not seem possible. The value of k_{Cl} in relation to the upper limit set for k_{11} implies that 1 M Cl^- will enhance the rate of the $Co(NH_3)_6^{3+/2+}$ self-exchange by a factor of $>2 \times 10^6$. An effect of this magnitude is unprecedented for outer-sphere reactions, and, we believe, even when substitution in the inner-coordination sphere of one of the reagents is possible. The acceleration observed by Biradar et al. in replacing

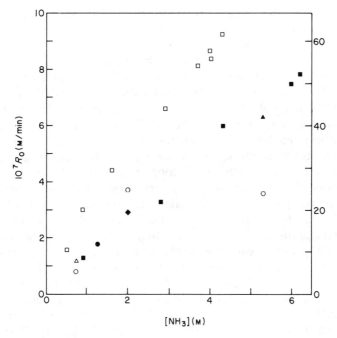

Fig. 1. Data of Ref. [9], Table 1, in a plot of the rate of exchange as a function of $[NH_3]$ (ionic strength = 1·00; $[Co(NH_3)_6^{3+}]$ = 0·022 M; [Co(II)] = 0·0260). Open symbols, data at 65·4°C, scale on left; solids symbols, 80·1°C, scale on right. Squares, $[NH_4^+]$ =0·20 M; triangles, $[NH_4^+]$ =0·40 M; diamond, $[NH_4^+]$ = 0·50 M; circles, $[NH_4^+]$ =0·70 M.

75% of the ClO_4^- at 1 M by Cl^- is a factor of ~1·3. If the rate in the absence of ClO_4^- is assumed to correspond to an activated complex of composition $Co(NH_3)_6^{3+} \cdot Co(NH_3)_n^{2+}$ rather than to $Co(NH_3)_6^{3+} \cdot OH^-Co(NH_3)_6^{2+}$, the effect attributed to Cl^- is in harmony with other observations. It should be noted that the rate of the self-exchange reaction of Co sepulchrate$^{3+/2+}$ has been found[22] to be independent of whether the counter anion is Cl^- or ClO_4^-. Moreover, reference to the data in Table 1 shows that the maximum rate acceleration by Cl^- is observed for U^{3+} as reducing agent. Here the inner-sphere of the reducing agent is open to entry by Cl^-, and the rate acceleration produced by 1 M Cl^- is less than a factor of 17. These observations reinforce the conclusion that the value of k_{11} has been grossly underestimated in Refs. [8] and [9].

The analysis which follows indicates that the rate data published by Biradar *et al.* are not at variance with the suggestion that the path lacking

OH⁻ in the activated complex is important in their system, or at any rate, we feel that the interpretation which we offer is in better agreement with the data of Biradar *et al.* than is their own.

In Fig. 1 the values of R, the rates of the reaction carrying the exchange, at each of the temperatures 64·5°C and 80·1°C are shown plotted against $[NH_3]$. The ionic strength is constant at 1·0 M, and $[Co(III)]$ and $[Co(II)]$ are 0·0122 M and 0·026 M respectively. At each temperature, the concentration of NH_4^+ was varied, and thus $[OH^-]$; the variation is indicated in Fig. 1 by the symbols of different shapes. The data at the higher temperature show that there is no significant change in the rate with the ratio $[NH_3]/[NH_4^+]$ and thus with $[OH^-]$, contrary to the conclusions reached by the authors. The rate is observed to vary linearly with $[NH_3]$, and a rate law of the form $k[Co(NH_3)_6^{3+}][Co(II)][NH_3]$ is clearly indicated by these data. The variation of rate with $[NH_3]$ is indicated also by the data at the lower temperature, but here the relation of the rate to the ratio $[NH_3]/[NH_4^+]$ is less clear. The conclusions reached by Biradar *et al.* rest heavily on two data points with $[NH_4^+] = 0.70$ M , one with $[NH_3] = 2.0$ M, and the other with $[NH_3] = 5.3$ M. One of these at least is suspect. The authors, who relied on measurements of pH rather than the ratio $[NH_3]/[NH_4^+]$ to fix $[OH^-]$, report $[H^+]$ to be 1.1×10^{-9} M and 1.2×10^{-9} M, which is inconsistent with the ratios of $[NH_3]/[NH_4^+]$. The datum with $[NH_4^+] = 0.70$ M , and $[NH_3] = 2.0$ M, in relation to others at lower $[NH_4^+]$ indicates that there is no strong dependence of rate on $[OH^-]$.

All in all, we feel that there is no firm basis for ascribing an important role to the activated complex of composition $[Co(NH_3)_6^{3+} \cdot Co(NH_3)_n^{2+} \cdot OH^-]$. Our own results also suggest that the path involving OH⁻ in the activated complex plays only a minor role. In two experiments at 40°C, $\mu = 2.5$ (maintained with KCl), $[Co(II)] = 0.40$, $[Co(III)] = 0.012$ M, $[NH_3]_{total} = 6.2$ M, and with $[NH_4^+] = 1.2$ M and 0·3 M, the values of k_{obsd} were 2.1×10^{-7} s⁻¹ and 2.0×10^{-7} s⁻¹ respectively.

In interpreting the exchange data, it is important to know what the equilibrium distribution of the Co(III) species is under the conditions of the experiments. For the majority of the experiments, Biradar *et al.* introduced the radioactivity in Co(II) and assayed the total amount of it as it appeared in all the Co(II) forms. For one series of experiments, they report the distribution of radioactivity between $Co(NH_3)_6^{3+}$, $Co(NH_3)_5OH^{2+}$ and $Co(NH_3)_4(OH)_2^+$, but since the time of reaction is not given, it is impossible to calculate the concentrations of the three species at the time of assaying. We have studied the equilibrium constant for the reaction

$$Co(NH_3)_6^{3+} + H_2O = Co(NH_3)_5OH^{2+} + NH_4^+ \tag{1}$$

at 65°C, $\mu = 1.0$, making use of charcoal as a catalyst and find that $K =$

0·10, 0·07 and 0·04 at $[NH_3] = 0.50$ M, 2·5 M and 5·0 M respectively. We detected no $Co(NH_3)_4(OH)_2^+$ and conclude that less than 1% of this species is present at equilibrium under our conditions. The conditions most favouring lower ammine formation in the experiments at 64·5°C shown in Table 1 of Ref. [9] would have been 0·5 M NH_3 and 0·2 M NH_4^+, where at equilibrium $\approx 34\%$ of the Co(III) would be present as $Co(NH_3)_5OH^{2+}$.

There are then two concerns: to what extent was the pentaammine produced in the experiments done by Biradar *et al.*?; to what extent did the formation of $Co(NH_3)_5OH^{2+}$ contribute to the observed rate? The rate of reaction (1) has been studied by Takemoto and Jones [46] and thus the second question can be answered. This suffices for our purposes, even though we cannot answer the first for lack of the necessary data.

According to Takemoto and Jones,[46] reaction (1) conforms to the rate law

$$\text{rate} \simeq \frac{k[Co(NH_3)_6^{3+}]}{[H^+]}$$

where k has the value 1.8×10^{-16} $M^{-1}s^{-1}$ at 61·8°C. Reaction (1) provides a mechanism for exchange between $Co(NH_3)_6^{3+}$ and Co(II) because the reaction

$$Co(NH_3)_5OH^{2+} + Co^*(NH_3)_5^{2+} \rightarrow Co(NH_3)_6^{2+} + Co^*(NH_3)_5OH^{2+} \qquad (2)$$

is relatively rapid,[47,48] and $Co(NH_3)_6^{3+}$ can be reconstituted by the reverse of reaction (1). The measurements by Takemoto and Jones have been checked, with good agreement, and extended.[34] These rates are high enough so that at the relatively low values of [Co(II)] of the experiments by Biradar *et al.*, much of the reported exchange at 65°C will have been carried by the hydrolytic path. It should be noted that in these experiments, though [Co(II)] is rather low, it is high enough so that the hydrolysis of $Co(NH_3)_6^{3+}$ is rate-determining for exchange by this path (see below).

It is apparent that the path involving NH_3 loss can contribute significantly to the exchange, particularly at high ratios of $[NH_3]/[NH_4^+]$ and, because the rate by this path is inverse in $[H^+]$, may account for some of the variation in rate with this ratio which is indicated in Fig. 1. What is puzzling is that no such effect is apparent in the data at the higher temperature. Moreover, in a mechanism for exchange from Co(II) into any form of Co(III) based on

$$Co(NH_3)_6^{3+} + OH^- \underset{k_{-3}}{\overset{k_3}{\rightleftharpoons}} Co(NH_3)_5OH_2^{2+} + NH_3 \qquad (3)$$

followed by reaction (2) the rate law becomes

$$\frac{k_3k_2[Co(NH_3)_6^{3+}][Co(NH_3)_5^{2+}][OH^-]}{k_2[Co(NH_3)_5^{2+}] + k_{-3}[NH_3]}$$

The rate of reaction (2) is high enough[47,48] so that under all conditions of the exchange experiments $k_2[\text{Co(NH}_3)_5^{2+}] > k_{-3}[\text{NH}_3]$ and the rate law reduces to $k_3[\text{Co(NH}_3)_6^{3+}][\text{OH}^-]$ i.e. the rate of exchange by this path is independent of [Co(II)]. It should be noted that a slight contamination of the hexaamminecobalt(III) salt by a pentaammine in the experiments of Lewis *et al.*[2] can explain the rapid initial exchange observed by them.

The activation energy for exchange by the hydrolytic path is much greater than that for the direct path—in our work at 40°C the hydrolytic path makes a negligible contribution to the rate— and under the conditions of the experiments of Ref. [9] at 80°C, the hydrolytic path is expected to dominate. This being so, the rate law of the form implied by the plot in Fig. 1 is difficult to understand. The data at 64·5°C seem to leave room for a direct path of the form

$$k'_{11}[\text{Co(NH}_3)_6^{3+}][\text{Co(II)}][\text{NH}_3]$$

A contribution to the exchange of one-half the total rate at the lower temperature would lead to $k'_{11} = 1 \times 10^{-6}\,\text{M}^{-2}\,\text{s}^{-1}$ at 64·5°C; our own data suggest a value for k'_{11} at 40°C of $\sim 1 \times 10^{-7}\,\text{M}^{-2}\,\text{s}^{-1}$. The variation of rate with [NH$_3$] incorporated into the rate function for the k'_{11} term requires that $\text{Co(NH}_3)_5^{2+}$ rather than $\text{Co(NH}_3)_6^{2+}$ be the dominant form of Co(II) in the system under all conditions. This is consistent with the conclusion which has been reached on the basis of results obtained by applying cyclic voltammetry to the cobaltammine systems.[49] This conclusion is that at 25°C in 6 M NH$_3$ and 1 M NH$_4$Cl less than 15% of the Co(II) is present as $\text{Co(NH}_3)_6^{2+}$. If in 1 M NH$_3$ only 10% of Co(II) is present as $\text{Co(NH}_3)_6^{3+}$, and this appears to be a very safe upper limit, k_{11} at 64·5°C would be about $1 \times 10^{-5}\,\text{M}^{-1}\,\text{s}^{-1}$.

IV. RATE COMPARISONS

The value of comparing the self-exchange rates for $\text{Ru(NH}_3)_6^{3+/2+}$ and for $\text{Co(NH}_3)_6^{3+/2+}$ was referred to in the introduction. The accepted upper limit to the latter specific rate fixed the ratio of the self-exchange rates of $\text{Ru(NH}_3)_6^{3+/2+}$ and $\text{Co(NH}_3)_6^{3+/2+}$ as in excess of 10^{14} and, after allowance was made for the greater inner-sphere reorganization energy in the cobalt system, still left a large factor ascribable to the spin change it undergoes. When the force constants for the metal nitrogen stretching frequencies, 1·27 and 2·45 mdyn Å^{-1} for Co(II) and Co(III) respectively[50] are used in conjunction with the newest value of $\Delta d(\text{Co}) = 2\cdot16^{[51]} - 1\cdot96^{[52]} = 0\cdot20$

Å, the energy expenditure for inner-sphere reorganization is calculated as $\sim 15 \, \text{kcal mol}^{-1}$. This accounts for a factor of 10^{10} between the self-exchange rates in the two systems. A value as large as $1 \times 10^{-5} \, \text{M}^{-1} \, \text{s}^{-1}$ for the $Co(NH_3)_6^{3+/2+}$ system is not excluded by the analyses outlined in the last two sections. In fact the specific rate $6 \times 10^{-5} \, \text{M}^{-1} \, \text{s}^{-1}$ at 25°C reported by Grossman and Garner[7] for liquid ammonia as solvent would close the gap in the self-exchange rates of the two systems. A somewhat greater outer-sphere reorganization is expected for the cobalt than for the ruthenium system and all in all there seems to be no compelling reason now to invoke a large barrier arising from spin change.

This conclusion is reinforced by the comparisons which follow. The self-exchange rate constant for $Ru(bpy)_3^{3+/2+}$ ($k \sim 10^9 \, \text{M}^{-1} \, \text{s}^{-1}$)[53] is a factor of about 10^4 greater than for $Ruen_3^{3+/2+}$ ($k = 4 \times 10^4 \, \text{M}^{-1} \, \text{s}^{-1}$);[44] for $Co(bpy)_3^{3+/2+}$ ($k \sim 10 \, \text{M}^{-1} \, \text{s}^{-1}$)[54] compared to $Coen_3^{3+/2+}$ ($k = 7 \cdot 7 \times 10^{-5}$) the ratio is about 10^5. The unsaturated ligand stabilizes the low-spin state relative to the high-spin ground state, and if there were a substantial barrier which required circumvention either by spin–orbit coupling or by a pre-equilibrium involving the low-spin state of Co(II), a very pronounced effect on the self-exchange rate caused by replacement of bipyridine by ethylenediamine in the cobalt system would be expected. The slightly greater sensitivity of the cobalt couple compared to the ruthenium to the ligand change may reflect a small contribution from a spin barrier, but it may equally well have other explanations. The changes in dimensions for the cobalt system attending substitution are expected to be somewhat greater than in the ruthenium case; moreover, the self-exchange rate for the $Rubpy_3^{3+/2+}$ system is approaching the ceiling imposed by the rate of diffusion.

Our view of the self-exchange rate for the cobaltammine system suggests that the theory as applied to this system may need reexamination and refinement. On the experimental side, a major problem remains: that of determining the composition of aqueous solutions containing Co(II), NH_4^+ and NH_3. Even were definitive data on the rate of exchange in such media available, it would still be impossible with current information to specify the self-exchange rate for $Co(NH_3)_6^{3+/2+}$. Also needed are the rates as a function of temperature, which then necessitate getting the equilibrium data for Co(II)–NH_3–NH_4^+ as a function of temperature. This constitutes a major experimental undertaking, particularly because the equilibrium, not mentioned in the foregoing, involving acid dissociation of $Co(NH_3)_5OH_2^{2+}$, needs also to be taken into account. Much remains to be done and our paper, it should be made clear, is in the nature of an interim, not a final report.

Acknowledgment

We gratefully acknowledge the support by National Science Foundation Grant No. CHE79-08633 of the research of Daniel Geselowitz.

REFERENCES

[1] Basolo, F.; Pearson, R.G. "Mechanism of Inorganic Reactions," 2nd edn.; Wiley: New York, 1967.

[2] Lewis, W.B.; Coryell, C.D.; Irvine, J.W., Jr. *J. Chem. Soc.* **1949**, S386.

[3] Dwyer, F.P.; Sargeson, A.M. *J. Phys. Chem.* **1961**, *65*, 1892.

[4] Dwyer, F.P.; Gyarfas, E.C. *Nature* **1950**, *166*, 481.

[5] McCallum, K.J.; Hoshowsky, S.A. *J. Chem. Phys.* **1948**, *16*, 254.

[6] Hoshowsky, S.A.; Holmes, O.G.; McCallum, K.J. *Can. J. Research* **1949**, *27B*, 258.

[7] Grossman, J.J.; Garner, C.S. *J. Chem. Phys.* **1958**, *28*, 268.

[8] Stranks, D.R. *Faraday Soc. Disc.* **1961**, 73.

[9] Biradar, N.S.; Stranks, D.R.; Vaidya, M.S. *Trans. Faraday Soc.* **1962**, *58*, 2421.

[10] Dodson, R.W. *J. Am. Chem. Soc.* **1950**, *72*, 3315.

[11] Silverman, J.; Dodson, R.W. *J. Phys. Chem.* **1952**, *56*, 846.

[12] $\Delta d(\text{Co}) = 0.6$ Å was cited[13] by H.C. Brown in discussion following a paper by Libby.[14]

[13] Biltz, N. *Z. Anorg. Chem.* **1927**, *164*, 246.

[14] Libby, W.F. *J. Phys. Chem.* **1952**, *56*, 863.

[15] Barnet, M.T.; Craven, B.M.; Freeman, H.C.; Kime, N.E.; Ibers, J.A. *Chem. Comm.* **1966**, 307.

[16] Kime, N.E.; Ibers, J.A. *Acta Cryst.* **1969**, B *25*, 168.

[17] Meyer, T.J.; Taube, H. *Inorg. Chem.* **1968**, *7*, 2369.

[18] Stynes, H.C.; Ibers, J.A. *Inorg. Chem.* **1971**, *10*, 2304.

[19] Buhks, E.; Bixon, M.; Jortner, J.; Navon, G. *Inorg. Chem.* **1979**, *18*, 2014.

[20] Creaser, I.I.; Harrowfield, J. MacB.; Herlt, A.J.; Sargeson, A.M.; Springborg, J.; Geue, R.J.; Snow, M.R. *J. Am. Chem. Soc.* **1977**, *99*, 3181.

[21] Snow, M.R.; Geue, R.J. referred to by Sargeson.[22]

[22] Sargeson, A.M. *Chem. in Britain* **1979**, *15*, 23.

[23] Marcus, R.A. *J. Phys. Chem.* **1963**, *67*, 853.

[24] Brown, G.M.; Sutin, N. *J. Am. Chem. Soc.* **1979**, *10*, 883.

[25] Przystas, T.J.; Sutin, N. *J. Am. Chem. Soc.* **1973**, *95*, 5545.

[26] Manning, P.V.; Jarnagin, R.C. *J. Phys. Chem.* **1963**, *67*, 2884.

[27] Dodel, P.H.; Taube, H. *Z. Phys. Chem.* (Frankfurt am Main) **1965**, *44*, 92.

[28] Zwickel, A.M.; Taube, H. *J. Am. Chem. Soc.* **1961**, *83*, 783.

[29] Espenson, J.H.; Wang, R.T. *J. Chem. Soc. Chem. Comm.* **1970**, 207.

[30] Loar, M.K.; Sens, M.A.; Loar, G.W.; Gould, E.S. *Inorg. Chem.* **1978**, *17*, 330.

[31] Wang, R.T.; Espenson, J.H. *J. Am. Chem. Soc.* **1971**, *93*, 380.

[32] Doyle, J.; Sykes, A.G. *J. Chem. Soc. A* **1968**, 2836.

[33] Endicott, J.; Taube, H. *J. Am. Chem. Soc.* **1964**, *86*, 1686.

[34] Geselowitz, D. Ph.D. Thesis, Stanford University, 1982.

[35] Christenson, J.H.; Espenson, J.H.; Butcher, A.B. *Inorg. Chem.* **1973**, *12*, 564.
[36] Zwickel, A.M.; Taube, H. *Disc. Faraday Soc.* **1960**, *29*, 42.
[37] Candlin, J.P.; Halpern, J.; Trimm, D.L. *J. Am. Chem. Soc.* **1964**, *86*, 1019.
[38] FanChaing, Y.T.; Gould, E.S. *J. Am. Chem. Soc.* **1977**, *99*, 5226.
[39] Bjerrum, J. "Metal Ammine Formation in Aqueous Solution," P. Haase and Son: Copenhagen, 1957.
[40] Latimer, W.M. "Oxidation Potentials," 2nd edn.; Prentice-Hall: Englewood Cliffs, 1952.
[41] Krishnamurty, K.V.; Wahl, A.C. *J. Am. Chem. Soc.* **1958**, *80*, 5921.
[42] Baker, B.R.; Mehta, B.D. *Inorg. Chem.* **1965**, *4*, 848.
[43] Chou, M.; Creutz, C.; Sutin, N. *J. Am. Chem. Soc.* **1977**, *99*, 5615.
[44] Smollenaers, P.; Beattie, J.K., private communication.
[45] Caton, J.A.; Prue, J.E. *J. Chem. Soc.* **1956**, 671.
[46] Takemoto, J.H.; Jones, M.M. *J. Inorg. Nucl. Chem.* **1970**, *32*, 175.
[47] Appelman, E.; Anbar, M.; Taube, H. *J. Phys. Chem.* **1959**, *63*, 126.
[48] Williams, T.J.; Hunt, J.P. *J. Am. Chem. Soc.* **1968**, *90*, 7210.
[49] Weaver, M.J., private communication (based on research done by Stephen Barr at Michigan State University).
[50] Schmidt, K.M.; Muller, A. *Inorg. Chem.* **1975**, *14*, 2183.
[51] Freeman, H.C., private communication.
[52] Herlinger, A.W.; Brown, J.N.; Dwyer, M.A.; Pavkovic, S.F. *Inorg. Chem.* **1981**, *20*, 2366.
[53] Young, R.C.; Keene, F.R.; Meyer, T.J. *J. Am. Chem. Soc.* **1977**, *99*, 2468.
[54] Ellis, P.; Wilkins, R.G.; Williams, M.J.G. *J. Chem. Soc.* **1957**, 4456.

INDEX